JUVENILE DELINQUENCY

Fifth Edition

JUVENILE DELINQUENCY

THE CORE

Larry J. Siegel
University of Massachusetts, Lowell

Brandon C. Welsh
Northeastern University

WADSWORTH
CENGAGE Learning·

Australia • Brazil • Japan • Korea • Mexico • Singapore • Spain • United Kingdom • United States

WADSWORTH
CENGAGE Learning·

Juvenile Delinquency: The Core, **Fifth Edition**
Larry J. Siegel and Brandon Welsh

Publisher: Linda Ganster

Acquisitions Editor: Carolyn Henderson Meier

Developmental Editor: Shelley Murphy

Assistant Editor: Casey Lozier

Media Editor: Ting Jian Yap

Brand Manager: Melissa Larmon

Market Development Manager:
Michelle Williams

Content Project Manager: Michelle Clark

Art Director: Maria Epes

Manufacturing Planner: Judy Inouye

Rights Acquisitions Specialist: Dean Dauphinais

Production Service: Aaron Downey, Matrix
Productions, Inc.

Photo Researcher: Kim Adams

Text Researcher: Karyn Morrison

Copy Editor: Lunaea Weatherstone

Text Designer: Ellen Pettengell

Cover Designer: Riezebos Holzbaur /
Tim Heraldo

Cover Image: Banque d'Images, ADAGP /
Art Resource, NY

Compositor: PreMediaGlobal

For product information and technology assistance, contact us at
Cengage Learning Customer & Sales Support, 1-800-354-9706.

For permission to use material from this text or product,
submit all requests online at **www.cengage.com/permissions**
Further permissions questions can be emailed to
permissionrequest@cengage.com

Library of Congress Control Number: 2012941414

Student Edition:

ISBN-13: 978-1-285-06760-5

ISBN-10: 1-285-06760-6

Loose-leaf Edition:

ISBN-13: 978-1-285-06765-0

ISBN-10: 1-285-06765-7

Wadsworth
20 Davis Drive
Belmont, CA 94002-3098
USA

Cengage Learning is a leading provider of customized learning solutions with office locations around the globe, including Singapore, the United Kingdom, Australia, Mexico, Brazil, and Japan. Locate your local office at **www.cengage.com/global.**

Cengage Learning products are represented in Canada by Nelson Education, Ltd.

To learn more about Wadsworth, visit **www.cengage.com/wadsworth**

Purchase any of our products at your local college store or at our preferred online store **www.cengagebrain.com.**

Printed in the United States of America
2 3 4 5 16 15 14 13

This book is dedicated to my children, Eric, Andrew, Julie, and Rachel, and to my grandchildren, Jack, Kayla, and Brooke. It is also dedicated to Jason Macy (thanks for marrying Rachel) and Therese J. Libby (thanks for marrying me).

—LJS

To my wife, Jennifer, and our son, Ryan.

—BCW

ABOUT THE AUTHORS

The author with his wife

Larry J. Siegel

Larry J. Siegel was born in the Bronx. While living on Jerome Avenue and attending City College of New York in the 1960s, he was swept up in the social and political currents of the time. He became intrigued with the influence contemporary culture had on individual behavior: Did people shape society or did society shape people? He applied his interest in social forces and human behavior to the study of crime and justice. After graduating CCNY, he attended the newly opened program in criminal justice at the State University of New York at Albany, earning both his M.A. and Ph.D. degrees there. After completing his graduate work, Dr. Siegel began his teaching career at Northeastern University, where he was a faculty member for nine years. After leaving Northeastern, he held teaching positions at the University of Nebraska–Omaha and Saint Anselm College in New Hampshire. He is currently a professor at the University of Massachusetts, Lowell. Dr. Siegel has written extensively in the area of crime and justice, including books on juvenile law, delinquency, criminology, criminal justice, corrections, and criminal procedure. He is a court-certified expert on police conduct and has testified in numerous legal cases. The father of four and grandfather of three, Larry Siegel and his wife, Terry, now reside in Bedford, New Hampshire, with their two dogs, Watson and Cody.

Brandon C. Welsh

Brandon C. Welsh received his undergraduate and M.A. degrees at the University of Ottawa in Canada and his Ph.D. from Cambridge University in England. Dr. Welsh is a Professor of Criminology at Northeastern University. He is also Senior Research Fellow at the Netherlands Institute for the Study of Crime and Law Enforcement at Free University in Amsterdam. His research interests focus on the prevention of crime and delinquency and evidence-based crime policy. Dr. Welsh has published extensively in these areas, and is an author or editor of ten books.

ABOUT THE COVER ARTIST

© Julio Donoso/Sygma/Corbis

Jean-Michel Basquiat

Jean-Michel Basquiat was a reigning genius of the pop art movement. He was born on December 22, 1960, in Brooklyn, New York, and by the age of 25 had become an international art celebrity. His style is vibrant and evocative, embodying multiculturalism and employing a devil-may-care energy. He was a study in contrasts: his images were raw and primitive, yet he mingled with the rich and famous, painting with his mentor Andy Warhol and dating Madonna. He was also a poet and musician. He died all too young at age 27. We would like all of our students to become familiar with his work—it is quite brilliant.

BRIEF CONTENTS

CONTENTS

CHAPTER FOURTEEN

Juvenile Corrections: Probation, Community Treatment, and Institutionalization   381

PREFACE

It's a story that has become all too common. Eden Wormer, a 14-year-old eighth grader at Cascade Middle School in Vancouver, Washington, hanged herself on March 8, 2012, after enduring two years of bullying by her classmates. Eden had changed her appearance several times in an effort to fit in, and begged her older sister not to report the bullying because she thought it would only make the problem worse.

Eden left a Facebook page that aptly demonstrated her tween angst: "im super funny and out going i love all my friends n family n that includes all my haterz.! :) n im funn to hang around too. :)." A month before she took her life she wrote: "omg im such a loner i dont have a valentines n the only thing im celebrating valentines day with is my bummble bee pillow pet. like this iff u hhave no valentines too or iff u wanna be my valentine. :)."*

Eden's plight aptly shows the difficult road adolescents must now navigate in a rapidly changing society. They must cope with technology that allows school yard bullies to follow their victim home via the Internet. Unlike their parents' generation, today's youth must be on the lookout for chat room predators who want to lure kids into sexual encounters or involve them in the commercial sex trade itself. The U.S. Department of Justice estimates that as many as 100,000 children are currently involved in prostitution, child pornography, and trafficking, but the true number may be in the millions. In addition, adolescents face a variety of serious social problems, ranging from educational deficiencies to income inequality. They routinely experience family breakup and substance abuse, and many are forced to live in communities where crime and violence are daily occurrences. It is not surprising considering these challenges that some kids fall prey to the lure of juvenile delinquency, getting involved in theft, violence, and substance abuse.

We have written *Juvenile Delinquency: The Core* to help students understand the nature of juvenile delinquency, its cause, and correlates, as well as the current strategies being used in its prevention and control. Our text also reviews the legal rules that have been set down to either protect innocent minors or control adolescent misconduct: Can children be required to submit to drug testing in school? Can teachers search suspicious students or use corporal punishment as a method of discipline? Should children be allowed to testify on closed circuit TV in child abuse cases?

Because the study of juvenile delinquency is a dynamic, ever-changing field of scientific inquiry and because the theories, concepts, and processes of this area of study are constantly evolving, we have revised *Juvenile Delinquency: The Core* to include changes, events, and conditions that have taken place during the past few years. This new edition includes a review of recent legal cases, research studies, and policy initiatives. We analyze and describe the nature and extent of delinquency, the suspected causes of delinquent behavior, and the environmental influences on youthful misbehavior. It also covers what most experts believe are the critical issues in juvenile delinquency and analyzes crucial policy issues, including the use of pretrial detention, waiver to adult court, and restorative justice programs.

* Marissa Taylor, "Bullied Teen Hangs Self After Writing She Loves 'All My Haterz,'" ABC News, March 9, 2012, http://abcnews.go.com/US/bullied-teen-commits-suicide-posting-loves-haterz/story?id=15887174 (accessed August 24, 2012).

GOALS AND OBJECTIVES

Our primary goals in writing this edition remain the same as in the previous editions:

1. To be as objective as possible, presenting the many diverse views and perspectives that characterize the study of juvenile delinquency and reflect its interdisciplinary nature. We take no single position nor espouse a particular viewpoint or philosophy.
2. To maintain a balance of research, theory, law, policy, and practice. It is essential that a text on delinquency not solely be a theory book without presenting the juvenile justice system or contain sections on current policies without examining legal issues and cases.
3. To be as thorough and up-to-date as possible. We have attempted to include the most current data and information available.
4. To make the study of delinquency interesting as well as informative. We want to encourage reader interest in the study of delinquency so that they will pursue it on an undergraduate or graduate level.

We have tried to provide a text that is both scholarly and informative, comprehensive yet interesting, well organized and objective, as well as provocative and thought provoking.

ORGANIZATION OF THE TEXT

The fifth edition of *Juvenile Delinquency: The Core* has 14 chapters:

Chapter 1, Childhood and Delinquency contains extensive material on the history of childhood and the development of the juvenile justice system. We examine the legal concept of delinquency and status offending. This material enables students to understand how the concept of adolescence evolved over time and how that evolution influenced the development of the juvenile court and the special status of delinquency.

Chapter 2, The Nature and Extent of Delinquency covers the measurement of delinquent behavior, trends and patterns in teen crime, and also discusses the correlates of delinquency, including race, gender, class, and age and chronic offending.

Chapter 3, Individual Views of Delinquency: Choice and Trait covers individual level views of the cause of delinquency, which include choice, biological and psychological theories.

Chapter 4, Sociological Views of Delinquency looks at theories that hold that economic, cultural, and environmental influences control delinquent behavior. These include structure, process, reaction, and conflict theories.

Chapter 5, Developmental Views of Delinquency covers developmental theories of delinquency, including such issues as the onset, continuity, and termination of a delinquent career.

Chapter 6, Gender and Delinquency explores the sex-based differences that are thought to account for the gender patterns in the delinquency rate.

Chapter 7, The Family and Delinquency covers the influence of families on children and delinquency. The concept of child abuse is covered in detail and the steps in the child protection system are reviewed.

Chapter 8, Peers and Delinquency: Juvenile Gangs and Groups reviews the effect peers have on delinquency and the topic of teen gangs.

Chapter 9, Schools and Delinquency looks at the influence of schools and the education process as well as delinquency within the school setting.

Chapter 10, Drug Use and Delinquency reviews the influence drugs and substance abuse has on delinquent behavior and what is being done to reduce teenage drug use.

Chapter 11, Delinquency Prevention and Juvenile Justice Today examines the role of prevention programs and juvenile justice in contemporary American society. It overviews key features of delinquency prevention and reviews the effectiveness of delinquency prevention programs for children and adolescents. It also covers the major stages in the juvenile justice process, the differences between the adult and juvenile justice systems, and a comprehensive juvenile justice strategy.

Chapter 12, Police Work with Juveniles discusses the role of police in delinquency prevention. It covers legal issues such as major court decisions on searches and the *Miranda* rights of juveniles. It also contains material on race and gender effects on police discretion as well as efforts by police departments to control delinquent behavior.

Chapter 13, Juvenile Court Process: Pretrial, Trial, and Sentencing contains information on plea bargaining in juvenile court, the use of detention, transfer to adult court. It contains analysis of the critical factors that influence the waiver decision, the juvenile trial, and sentencing.

Chapter 14, Juvenile Corrections: Probation, Community Treatment, and Institutionalization covers material on probation and other community dispositions, including restorative justice and secure treatment. There is an emphasis on legal issues such as the right to treatment, juvenile aftercare, and reentry.

WHAT'S NEW IN THIS EDITION

Chapter 1 updates information on changes in the nations' poverty rate. It covers new data and research on family and educational problems. There is a major new section on problems in cyberspace, including cyberbullying and cyberstalking. We cover sexting and the fact that adolescents now have to worry about far-reaching repercussions from compromising photos they send their boyfriends or girlfriends. We cover new research that shows that the average cost for each chronic delinquent offender is over $1.5 million, and the fact that their cost to society increases as they grow older.

Chapter 2 updates recent trends and patterns in delinquency and juvenile victimization. It contains new information on the victim–offender relationship, the compatibility of juvenile delinquency data sources, and the time and place of delinquency. There is new information on the critical concept of racial profiling and the racial threat hypothesis.

Chapter 3 contains new research findings on such topics as mental illness and delinquency, twin studies, conduct disorders, disruptive behavior disorder, and the genetic basis of delinquency. Research shows that kids "learn from their mistakes" and that a young offender who is caught by police will be more afraid of punishment than another adolescent who has escaped detection. A new section asks the question, "Can Delinquency Be Deterred?" There is also new material on antisocial substance disorder (ASD).

Chapter 4 covers the most recent developments in social theory. We look at research on peer relations and how it influences delinquency. New research shows that kids who are not popular are prone to delinquent behaviors. We cover recent reviews of the research on social learning theory. A new Focus on Delinquency feature entitled "Learning to Be Bad" covers research on how some kids develop a jaundiced, pessimistic, and cynical view of life early in their adolescence. There is a new Prevention/Intervention/Treatment feature on Communities That Care, a comprehensive community-based delinquency prevention program that combines many interventions.

Chapter 5 has been significantly reorganized, with sections covering life course, age-graded, and latent trait/propensity theories, as well as trajectory theory, a new approach that combines elements of latent trait and life course theory. The basic premise is that there is more than one path to crime and more than one class of offender, and each must be studied independently.

Chapter 6 has new data on gender differences in cognition and socialization. We cover new research showing that girls may benefit more from parental attachment than boys. We look at research on the impact of adolescent deviance on marriage. Other studies now covered look at how early victimization—including sexual abuse—affects girls and may help produce a precocious maturity that facilitates a young woman's path into drug use and offending.

Chapter 7 has updated material on the legacy of divorce and parental deviance. The newest data on child abuse and sexual abuse are presented. We cover the Sandusky case that rocked Penn State and the nation. The Prevention/Intervention/Treatment box is on Homebuilders, an in-home, intensive family preservation service (IFPS) and reunification program for families with children (newborn to 17 years old) returning from or at risk of placement into foster care, group or residential treatment, psychiatric hospitals, or juvenile justice facilities. We cover research that shows the damaging influence of observing the abuse of a sibling. There is new research that shows that attachment to parents weakens after kids get involved in delinquency. Yet new research also shows that parents do not give up on their troubled teens and give them support after they have been in trouble with the law.

Chapter 8 covers new research on peers and delinquency. Research now shows that even children born into high-risk families—such as those with single teen mothers—can avoid delinquency if their friends refrain from drug use and criminality. The chapter updates information on the number of gangs and gang members and the extent of the gang problem. There is new material on female gangs and the role of girls in male gangs. A new Prevention/Intervention/Treatment box covers "Strategies to Prevent Gang Delinquency."

Chapter 9 has new material on educational achievement, including data showing that reading scores have not had a significant improvement in the past decade, and racial and ethnic differences in reading and math achievement have proven difficult to erase. There is a new section on economic disadvantage and educational achievement. A Focus on Delinquency box entitled "School Discipline, School Opportunities, and Minority Youth" shows that race-based disciplinary practices may help sustain high minority dropout rates. There are new sections on bullying, both in the school yard and online, and the toll it takes on its targets. Another Focus on Delinquency feature looks at "Race, Ethnicity, Activities, and School Violence," showing that minority students who are involved in academic extracurricular activities are more likely to be selected as targets for violent victimization. We also cover a recent report from the U.S. Department of Education showing that minority students, especially boys, face much harsher discipline in public schools than other students. Another new section, "Speech in Cyberspace," discusses how the courts have dealt with issues that arise when students test the limits of free speech, whether it be through personal websites, Twitter messages, texts, or e-mails.

Chapter 10 updates recent trends and patterns in juvenile drug use based on three national surveys, including the large-scale Monitoring the Future (MTF) survey. We have expanded coverage of the major explanations for why youths take drugs and added new material reviewing the most up-to-date research on what works to reduce juvenile drug use.

Chapter 11 is a brand new chapter on delinquency prevention and juvenile justice today. It begins with an overview of key features of delinquency prevention and reviews the effectiveness of delinquency prevention programs for children and adolescents. A new Focus on Delinquency box highlights public support for delinquency prevention. The juvenile justice process is also covered. A comprehensive juvenile justice strategy, which combines elements of delinquency prevention and intervention and justice approaches, is discussed, along with the latest research findings on teen courts and juvenile drug courts. The chapter concludes with a look at key issues facing the future of delinquency prevention and juvenile justice.

Chapter 12 presents new research on juveniles' attitudes toward the police and the discretionary powers of the police. It updates statistics on the handling of juvenile offenders by the police, which show that two-thirds of all juveniles who are arrested are referred to juvenile court. It brings together the latest findings on what works when it comes to police efforts to prevent juvenile crime, including a new Prevention/Intervention/Treatment feature on "pulling levers" policing. It also presents the latest findings on the national evaluation of the G.R.E.A.T. program.

Chapter 13 includes up-to-date statistics on the juvenile court case flow, from the decision to release or detain, to waivers to adult court, to juvenile court dispositions. It updates the Focus on Delinquency box that examines the effectiveness of transfers to adult court. The chapter also covers a new Supreme Court ruling on life without parole for juvenile offenders that put an end to life sentences without parole for *all* juvenile offenders.

Chapter 14 reports on the latest trends in juvenile probation and incarceration. It updates material on disproportionate minority confinement. The latest research findings on what works in treating juvenile offenders are reviewed, including Multidimensional Treatment Foster Care and other evidence-based programs. It also updates material on juvenile aftercare and reentry services.

LEARNING TOOLS

The text contains the following features designed to help students learn and comprehend the material:

Chapter Outline and Learning Objectives Each chapter begins with an outline and a list of learning objectives.

Success Story ("Real Cases/Real People") Each chapter opens with a vignette describing a real-life situation in which an at-risk youth worked his or her way out of delinquency. These real-life stories are then tied to the material in the chapter with thought-provoking critical thinking boxes ("Looking Back to ____'s Story").

Concept Summary This feature is used throughout the text to help students review material in an organized fashion.

Checkpoints Summaries of key points from preceding sections appear in each chapter and are now linked to the learning objectives set out in the beginning of the chapter.

What Does This Mean to Me? These are short yet provocative discussion designed to provoke student interest, interaction, and analysis.

Focus on Delinquency As in previous editions, these boxed inserts focus attention on topics of special importance and concern. For example, in Chapter 4, a Focus on Delinquency feature entitled "The Code of the Streets" reviews Elijah Anderson's widely cited view of the interrelationship of culture and behavior.

Professional Spotlight These boxes focus on the careers of people working in the field of juvenile delinquency so that students can get a here-and-now glimpse of what professional opportunities are available in the area of delinquency treatment, prevention, and intervention. Featured in Chapter 14, for example, is Kristi Swanson, a teacher in the Idaho prison juvenile unit.

Juvenile Delinquency: Prevention/Intervention/Treatment These boxes discuss major initiatives and programs. For example, the evidence-based program of multisystemic therapy is profiled in Chapter 10.

Weblinks In the margins of every chapter are links to websites that can be used to help students enrich their understanding of important issues and concepts found within the text.

Chapter Summary Each chapter ends with a summary of key concepts from the chapter.

Key Terms Key terms are defined throughout the text when they appear in a chapter.

Questions for Review Each chapter now has review questions that determine whether students have retained key concepts from the chapter and help them prepare for tests

Questions for Discussion Each chapter ends with thought-provoking discussion questions.

Applying What You Have Learned This feature provides students with an intriguing hypothetical dilemma and asks them to write an essay solving the problem or addressing the issue using the knowledge they acquired in the chapter.

Running Glossary A glossary is included which sets out and defines key terms used in the text. The definitions appear in the text margin where the concept is introduced, as well as in the comprehensive glossary at the end of the book.

ANCILLARIES

An extensive package of supplemental aids accompanies this edition of *Juvenile Delinquency: The Core.* They are available to qualified adopters. Please consult your local sales representative for details.

Instructor Resources

Instructor's Resource Manual with Test Bank Fully updated and revised by Deborah Vegh of Edinboro University of Pennsylvania, the manual includes learning objectives, key terms, a detailed chapter outline, a chapter summary, discussion topics, student activities, media tools, and a newly expanded test bank. The learning objectives are correlated with the discussion topics, student activities, and media tools. Each chapter's test bank contains questions in multiple-choice, true/false, completion, and essay formats, with a full answer key. The test bank has almost 60 percent more questions than the prior edition and features new scenario-based questions to test student's critical thinking skills. The test bank is coded to the learning objectives that appear in the main text, and includes the page numbers in the main text where the answers can be found. Finally, each question in the test bank has been carefully reviewed by experienced criminal justice instructors for quality, accuracy, and content coverage. Our Instructor Approved seal, which appears on the front cover, is our assurance that you are working with an assessment and grading resource of the highest caliber. The manual is available for download on the password-protected website and can also be obtained by e-mailing your local Cengage Learning representative.

Lesson Plans Prepared by Wesley Jennings of the University of Southern Florida, the Lesson Plans bring accessible, masterful suggestions to every lesson. This supplement includes a sample syllabus, learning objectives, lecture notes, discussion topics and in-class activities, a detailed lecture outline, assignments, media tools, and "What if . . ." scenarios. The learning objectives are integrated throughout the

Lesson Plans, and current events and real-life examples in the form of articles, websites, and video links are incorporated into the class discussion topics, activities, and assignments. The lecture outlines are correlated with PowerPoint® slides for ease of classroom use. Lesson Plans are available on the PowerLecture resource and the instructor website.

PowerPoint Lecture Slides Prepared by Chau-Pu Chiang of California State University of Stanislaus, the PowerPoint slides help you make your lectures more engaging while effectively reaching your visually oriented students with classroom-ready chapter presentations. The PowerPoint slides are updated to reflect the content and organization of the new edition of the text and feature some additional examples and real world cases for application and discussion. Available for download on the password-protected instructor book companion website, the presentations can also be obtained by e-mailing your local Cengage Learning representative.

ExamView® Computerized Testing The comprehensive Instructor's Resource Manual is backed up by ExamView, a computerized test bank available for PC and Macintosh computers. With ExamView you can create, deliver, and customize tests and study guides (both print and online) in minutes. You can easily edit and import your own questions and graphics, change test layouts, and reorganize questions. And using ExamView's complete word-processing capabilities, you can enter an unlimited number of new questions or edit existing questions.

PowerLecture™ with ExamView The fastest, easiest way to build customized, media-rich lectures, PowerLecture provides a collection of book-specific Microsoft® PowerPoint lecture and class tools to enhance the educational experience. PowerLecture includes lesson plans, lecture outlines linked to the learning objectives for each chapter, art from the text, new videos, animations, and more. The DVD-ROM also contains electronic copies of the Instructor's Resource Manual, test bank, and Lesson Plans, and ExamView testing software, which allows you to create customized tests in minutes using items from the test bank in computerized format.

The Wadsworth Criminal Justice Video Library So many exciting new videos—so many great ways to enrich your lectures and spark discussion of the material in this text. Your Cengage Learning representative will be happy to provide details on our video policy by adoption size. The library includes these selections and many others.

- **ABC® Videos**. ABC videos feature short, high-interest clips from current news events as well as historic raw footage going back 40 years. Perfect for discussion starters or to enrich your lectures and spark interest in the material in the text, these brief videos provide students with a new lens through which to view the past and present, one that will greatly enhance their knowledge and understanding of significant events and open up to them new dimensions in learning. Clips are drawn from such programs as *World News Tonight, Good Morning America, This Week, PrimeTime Live, 20/20*, and *Nightline*, as well as numerous ABC News specials and material from the Associated Press Television News and British Movietone News collections.

- **Cengage Learning's "Introduction Criminal Justice Video Series."** This series features videos supplied by the BBC Motion Gallery. These short, high-interest clips from CBS and BBC news programs—everything from nightly news broadcasts and specials to *CBS News Special Reports, CBS Sunday Morning, 60 Minutes*, and more—are perfect classroom discussion starters.

- **Criminal Justice Media Library.** Cengage Learning's Criminal Justice Media Library includes nearly 300 media assets on the topics you cover in your courses. Available to stream from any Web-enabled computer, the Criminal Justice Media Library's assets include such valuable resources as: Career Profile Videos featuring interviews with criminal justice professionals from a range of roles and locations; simulations that allow students to step into various roles and practice their decision-making skills; video clips on current topics from ABC and other sources; animations that illustrate key concepts; interactive learning modules that help students check their knowledge of important topics; and Reality Check exercises that compare expectations and preconceived notions against the real-life thoughts and experiences of criminal justice professionals. The Criminal Justice Media Library can be uploaded and used within many popular Learning Management Systems, and all video assets include assessment questions that can be delivered straight to the gradebook in your LMS. You can also customize it with your own course material. Please contact your Cengage Learning representative for ordering and pricing information.

- **WebTutor™ on Blackboard® and WebCT®.** Jump-start your course with customizable, rich, text-specific content within your Course Management System. Whether you want to web-enable your class or put an entire course online, WebTutor delivers. WebTutor offers a wide array of resources, including media assets, test bank, practice quizzes linked to chapter learning objectives, and additional study aids. Visit www.cengage.com/webtutor to learn more.

Student Resources

CourseMate. Cengage Learning's Criminal Justice CourseMate brings course concepts to life with interactive learning, study, and exam preparation tools that support the printed textbook. CourseMate includes an integrated e-book, quizzes mapped to chapter learning objectives updated by Venessa Garcia of Kean University, flashcards, videos, and more, and EngagementTracker, a first-of-its-kind tool that monitors student engagement in the course. The accompanying instructor website offers access to password-protected resources such as an electronic version of the instructor's manual and PowerPoint slides.

Careers in Criminal Justice Website. *Can be bundled with this text at no additional charge.* Featuring plenty of self-exploration and profiling activities, the interactive Careers in Criminal Justice website helps students investigate and focus on the criminal justice career choices that are right for them. Includes interest assessment, video testimonials from career professionals, résumé and interview tips, links for reference, and a wealth of information on "soft skills" such as health and fitness, stress management, and effective communication. Ask your rep about the state-specific Careers in Criminal Justice website, which features information that only pertains to an individual state.

CLeBook. Cengage Learning's Criminal Justice e-books allow students to access our textbooks in an easy-to-use online format. Highlight, take notes, bookmark, search your text, and, for most texts, link directly into multimedia. In short, CLeBooks combine the best features of paper books and e-books in one package.

ACKNOWLEDGEMENTS

We gratefully acknowledge the work of our colleagues who reviewed the previous edition and made important suggestions for improvements in this edition:

Michael G. Bisciglia, Southeastern Louisiana University

Kenneth Colburn, Butler University

Jason Hale, County College of Morris

Miriam Lorenzo, Miami Dade College

Riane Miller, University of South Carolina

Anne Strouth, North Central State College

Christine Yalda, Grand Valley State University

The preparation of this text would not have been possible without the aid of Carolyn Henderson Meier, our phenomenal editor extraordinaire. Shelley Murphy is the world's most wonderful developmental editor, that's the least we can say. We would like to give special thanks to our terrific and supportive production manager Michelle Clark and fabulous production editor Aaron Downey, without whom this volume would have never been published. Lunaea Weatherstone, the copy editor, did a thorough job, and it is always a great pleasure to work with her. Kim Adams, our photo editor, to put it bluntly, is as always creative and enthusiastic. Special thanks to Kashif Siddiqi for excellent research assistance.

Larry Siegel

Brandon Welsh

Childhood and Delinquency

© i love images/teenagers/Alamy

LEARNING OBJECTIVES

After reading this chapter you should:

1. Be familiar with the risks faced by youth in American culture.
2. Develop an understanding of the history of childhood.
3. Be able to discuss development of the juvenile justice system.
4. Trace the history and purpose of the juvenile court.
5. Be able to describe the differences between delinquency and status offending.

Aaliyah's Story

Aaliyah Parker ran away from home at the age of 17. She struggled with family issues and felt she could no longer live with her mother, stepfather, and younger siblings in their California home. Arriving in Colorado with no family support, no money, and no place to live, she joined other runaway adolescents, homeless on the streets. Aaliyah began using drugs and was eventually arrested and detained at a juvenile detention center for possession of methamphetamines and providing false information to a police officer.

When Aaliyah entered the juvenile justice system she was a few months from turning 18. Due to issues of jurisdiction, budget concerns, and Aaliyah's age, system administrators encouraged the case worker assigned to Aaliyah to make arrangements for her to return to her family in California. The case worker could see that Aaliyah had a strong desire to get her life back on track. She needed assistance, but the cost of her treatment would be over $3,000 per month, and the county agency's budget was already stretched. She was transported from the juvenile detention center to a 90-day drug and alcohol treatment program where she was able to detoxify her body and engage in intensive counseling. The program also provided family therapy through phone counseling for Aaliyah's mother, allowing the family to reconnect. Despite this renewed contact, returning home was not an option for Aaliyah.

Aaliyah contacted a group home run by a local church that takes runaway adolescents through county placements and provides a variety of services for clients and their families. Aaliyah entered the group home, was able to get her high school diploma, and eventually enrolled in an independent living program that assisted her in finding a job and getting her own apartment. Aaliyah has remained in contact with her juvenile case worker. Although she has struggled with her sobriety on occasion, she has been able to refrain from using methamphetamines. Her case worker continues to encourage Aaliyah and has been an ongoing source of support, despite the fact that the client file was closed several years ago. Aaliyah's success can be credited to the initial advocacy of her case worker, the effective interventions, and to the strong determination demonstrated by this young woman.

There are now 75 million children in the United States under age 17—about 37 percent of the population—many of whom share some of the same problems as Aaliyah.[1] Thousands become runaways and wind up on the streets where their safety is compromised, and they may turn to drugs, alcohol, and crime as street survival strategies. Simply spending time on the streets increases their likelihood for violence.[2]

The present generation of adolescents faces many risks. They have been described as cynical, preoccupied with material acquisitions, and uninterested in creative expression.[3] By age 18, the average American adolescent has spent more time in front of a television set than in the classroom. In the 1950s, teenagers were reading comic books, but today they watch TV shows and movies that rely on graphic scenes of violence as their main theme; each year they may see up to 1,000 rapes, murders, and assaults. When they are not texting and tweeting, teens are listening to rap songs by Gucci Mane, V-Nasty, and Tyga, whose best-selling 2012 song "Rack City" includes these romantic lyrics:

I'mma M—f— star

Look at the paint on the car

Too much rim make the ride too hard

Tell that bitch hop out, walk the boulevard

I need my money pronto

These artists' explicit lyrics routinely describe substance abuse and promiscuity and glorify the gangsta lifestyle. How does exposure to this music affect young listeners? Should we be concerned? Maybe we should. Research has found that kids who listen to music with a sexual content are much more likely to engage in precocious sex than adolescents whose musical tastes run to Adele and Justin Bieber.[4]

THE RISKS AND REWARDS OF ADOLESCENCE

The problems of American society have had a significant effect on our nation's youth. Adolescence is a time of trial and uncertainty, a time when youths experience anxiety, humiliation, and mood swings. During this period, the personality is still developing and is vulnerable to a host of external factors. Adolescents also undergo a period of rapid biological development. During just a few years' time, their height, weight, and sexual characteristics change dramatically. A hundred and fifty years ago girls matured sexually at age 16, but today they do so at 12.5 years of age. Although they may be capable of having children as early as 14, many youngsters remain emotionally immature long after reaching biological maturity. At age 15, a significant number of teenagers are unable to meet the responsibilities of the workplace, the family, and the neighborhood. Many suffer from health problems, are underachievers in school, and are skeptical about their ability to enter the workforce and become productive members of society.

In later adolescence (ages 16 to 18), youths may experience a crisis that psychologist Erik Erikson described as a struggle between ego identity and role diffusion. **Ego identity** is formed when youths develop a firm sense of who they are and what they stand for; **role diffusion** occurs when youths experience uncertainty and place themselves at the mercy of leaders who promise to give them a sense of identity they cannot mold for themselves.[5] Psychologists also find that late adolescence is dominated by a yearning for independence from parental control.[6] Given this mixture of biological change and desire for autonomy, it isn't surprising that the teenage years are a time of conflict with authority at home, at school, and in the community.

Youth at Risk

Problems in the home, the school, and the neighborhood have placed a significant portion of American youths at risk. Youths considered at risk are those who engage in dangerous conduct, such as drug abuse, alcohol use, and precocious sexuality. Although it is impossible to determine precisely the number of **at-risk youths** in the United States, one estimate is that 25 percent of the population under age 17, or about 18 million youths, are in this category. The teen years bring many new risks—including some that are life-threatening. Each year almost 14,000 Americans ages 15 to 19 lose their lives in such unexpected incidents as motor vehicle accidents, homicide, and suicide. It is estimated that three-quarters of teen deaths are due to preventable causes, yet little is being done to reduce the death rate.[7] The most pressing problems facing American youth revolve around five issues: poverty, health and mortality problems, family problems, substandard living conditions, and inadequate education.[8]

Poverty. Poverty in the United States is more prevalent now than in the late 1960s and early 1970s, and has escalated rapidly since 2000. While poverty problems have risen for nearly every age, gender, and race/ethnic group, the increases in poverty have been most severe among the nation's youngest families (adults under 30), especially those with one or more children present in the home. Since 2007, the poverty rate has risen by 8 percent among these families, hitting 37 percent in 2010; in 1967 it stood at only 14 percent. Among young families with children residing in the home, 4 of every 9 were poor or near poor and close to 2 out of 3 were low income.[9]

Working hard and playing by the rules is not enough to lift families out of poverty: even if parents work full-time at the federal minimum wage, the family still lives in poverty. Consequently, about 6 million children live in extreme poverty, which means less than $10,000 for a family of four; the younger the child, the more likely they are to live in extreme poverty.[10]

Which kids live in poverty? Minority kids are much more likely than white, non-Hispanic children to experience poverty, though because of their numerical representation, there are actually a larger number of poor white children in the population. Nonetheless, proportionately, Hispanic and black children are about three

ego identity According to Erik Erikson, ego identity is formed when persons develop a firm sense of who they are and what they stand for.

role diffusion According to Erik Erikson, role diffusion occurs when youths spread themselves too thin, experience personal uncertainty, and place themselves at the mercy of leaders who promise to give them a sense of identity they cannot develop for themselves.

at-risk youths Young people who are extremely vulnerable to the negative consequences of school failure, substance abuse, and early sexuality.

FIGURE 1.1 Percentage of Children Ages 0–17 Living in Poverty by Family Structure

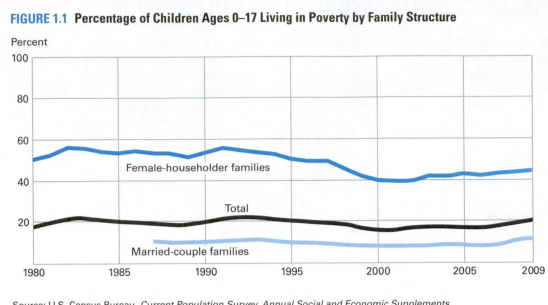

Source: U.S. Census Bureau, *Current Population Survey, Annual Social and Economic Supplements,* www.childstats.gov/americaschildren/surveys2.asp (accessed June 12, 2012).

times as likely to be poor than their white peers.[11] And as Figure 1.1 shows, kids living in a single-parent female-headed household are significantly more likely to suffer poverty than those in two-parent families.

Child poverty can exact a terrible lifelong burden and have long-lasting negative effects on the child's cognitive achievement, educational attainment, nutrition, physical and mental health, and social behavior. Educational achievement scores between

Poverty hits kids especially hard, making it difficult for them to be part of the American Dream. Here Jalinh Vasquez holds her sister Jayshel Barthelemy in the FEMA Diamond trailer park in Port Sulphur, Louisiana, where they still live with five other children and four adults four years after Hurricane Katrina destroyed their home. They are still awaiting money from the federal Road Home program to purchase a new home. Approximately 2,000 families in the New Orleans metropolitan area live in FEMA trailers, and 80 percent of those still in trailers were homeowners who are unable to return to their storm-damaged houses.

children in affluent and low-income families have been widening over the years, and the incomes and wealth of families have become increasingly important determinants of adolescents' high school graduation, college attendance, and college persistence and graduation. The chances of an adolescent from a poor family with weak academic skills obtaining a bachelor's degree by their mid-20s is now close to zero.[12]

Health and Mortality Problems. Receiving adequate health care is another significant concern for American youth. There are some troubling signs. Recent national estimates indicate that only about 18 percent of adolescents meet current physical activity recommendations of one hour of physical activity a day, and only about 22 percent eat five or more servings of fruits and vegetables per day.[13]

Kids with health problems may only be helped if they have insurance. And while most kids now have health care coverage of some sort, about 10 percent or 7.5 million youth do not.[14] As might be expected, children who are not healthy, especially those who live in lower-income families and children from ethnic and minority backgrounds, are subject to illness and early mortality. Recently, the infant mortality rate rose for the first time in more than 40 years, and is now 7 per 1,000 births. The United States currently ranks 25th in the world among industrialized nations in preventing infant mortality, and the percent of children born at low birth weight has increased.[15]

While infant mortality remains a problem, so does violent adolescent death. More than 3,000 children and teens are killed by firearms each year, the equivalent of 120 public school classrooms of 25 students each; more than half of these deaths were of white children and teens. Another 16,000 children and teens suffer non-fatal firearm injuries. Today, more preschoolers are killed by firearms than law enforcement officers killed in the line of duty.[16]

Family Problems. Family dissolution and disruption also plague American youth. Divorce has become an all too common occurrence in the United States; it is estimated that between 40 and 50 percent of first marriages end in divorce. Second and third marriages fare even worse: second marriages fail at a rate of 60 to 67 percent, and third marriages fail at a rate of 73 to 74 percent.[17] In 2010, 69 percent of children under age 17 lived with two parents (66 percent with two married parents—down from 77 percent in 1980—and 3 percent with two biological/adoptive cohabiting parents), 23 percent lived with only their mothers, 3 percent with only their fathers, and 4 percent with neither of their parents.[18]

As families undergo divorce, separation, and breakup, kids are often placed in foster care. Among the 3 million children (4 percent of all children) not living with either parent, 54 percent (1.7 million) lived with grandparents, 21 percent lived with other relatives only, and 24 percent lived with nonrelatives. Of children in nonrelatives' homes, 27 percent (200,000) lived with foster parents.[19] About 130,000 kids in foster care are waiting to be adopted, and 44 percent of them entered care before age 6. Each year, on their 18th birthday, more than 25,000 kids leave foster care without family support; these young adults share an elevated risk of becoming homeless, unemployed, and

Kids are often caught in the crossfire of marital strife and all too often become its innocent victims. Family friend Margaret Fischer holds up a picture of Amanda Peake and her two children in front of the family's home in Red Bank, South Carolina. Peake's estranged boyfriend, Chancey Smith, shot her, then her 9-year-old son Cameron, then her 6-year-old daughter Sarah inside the family's home in the community of Red Bank. Smith then turned the gun on himself.

WHAT DOES THIS MEAN TO ME?

▶ **Older, but Wiser** "When I was a boy of fourteen, my father was so ignorant I could hardly stand to have the old man around. But when I got to be twenty-one, I was astonished at how much he had learned in seven years" (Mark Twain, "Old Times on the Mississippi," *Atlantic Monthly*, 1874).

Do you agree with Mark Twain? When you look back at your adolescence, are you surprised at how much you thought you knew then and how little you know now? Did you do anything that you now consider silly and immature? Of course, as they say, "Hindsight is always 20/20." Maybe there is a benefit to teenage rebellion. For example, would it make you a better parent knowing firsthand about all the trouble your kids get into and why they do?

TEEN RISK TAKING

Teens are risk takers. The Centers for Disease Control and Prevention (CDC) sponsors an annual Youth Risk Behavior Survey (YRBS) that monitors health-risk behaviors among youth and young adults. Among the risky behaviors measured include dangerous driving habits, tobacco, alcohol and other drug use, and sexual behaviors that contribute to unintended pregnancy. The many findings of the most recent survey include the following:

- 10 percent of students rarely or never wore a seat belt when riding in a car driven by someone else.

- Among the 70 percent of students who had ridden a bicycle during the 12 months before the survey, 85 percent had rarely or never worn a bicycle helmet.

- 28 percent of students rode in a car or other vehicle driven by someone who had been drinking alcohol one or more times during the 30 days before the survey.

- 10 percent of students had driven a car or other vehicle one or more times when they had been drinking alcohol during the 30 days before the survey.

- 17 percent of students had carried a weapon (e.g., a gun, knife, or club) on at least one day during the 30 days before the survey.

- 20 percent of students had been bullied on school property during the 12 months before the survey.

- Almost 14 percent of students had seriously considered attempting suicide, and 6 percent of students had attempted suicide one or more times during the 12 months before the survey.

- 19 percent of students smoked cigarettes on at least one day during the 30 days before the survey.

- 72 percent of students had had at least one drink of alcohol on at least one day during their life, and 42 percent of students had had at least one drink of alcohol on at least one day during the 30 days before the survey.

- 46 percent of students had had sexual intercourse.

- 18 percent of students were physically active at least 60 minutes per day on each of the seven days before the survey.

- 23 percent of students did not participate in at least 60 minutes of physical activity on at least one day during the seven days before the survey.

Why do youths take such chances? Research has shown that kids may be too immature to understand how dangerous risk taking can be and are unable to properly assess the chances they are taking. Criminologist Nanette Davis

---

incarcerated. They are also at great risk at developing physical, developmental, and mental health challenges across their lifespan.[20]

Looking Back to Aaliyah's Story

Housing is a major issue for many teens "aging out" of the system. Often, children placed in alternative care settings, such as foster homes or residential treatment centers, are not prepared to live on their own when they turn 18 or are released from juvenile custody.

CRITICAL THINKING Discuss what can be done to help kids in foster care be better prepared for adult life. Make a list of life skills that must be mastered.

Substandard Living Conditions. Many children continue to live in substandard housing—such as high-rise, multiple-family dwellings—which can have a negative influence on their long-term psychological health.[21] Adolescents living in deteriorated urban areas are prevented from having productive and happy lives. Many die from random bullets and drive-by shootings. Some adolescents are homeless and living on the street, where they are at risk of drug addiction and sexually transmitted diseases (STDs), including AIDS.

Inadequate Education. The U.S. educational system seems to be failing many young people. It is now estimated that about 70 percent of fourth graders in our public schools cannot read at grade level.[22] Because reading proficiency is an essential element for educational success, students who are problem readers are at high risk of grade repetition and dropping out of school. Educational problems are likely to hit

suggests there is a potential for risky behavior among youth in all facets of American life. *Risky* describes behavior that is emotionally edgy, dangerous, exciting, hazardous, challenging, volatile, and potentially emotionally, socially, and financially costly—even life threatening. Youths commonly become involved in risky behavior as they negotiate the hurdles of adolescent life, learning to drive, date, drink, work, relate, and live. Davis finds that social developments in the United States have increased the risks of growing up for all children. The social, economic, and political circumstances that increase adolescent risk taking include these:

- *The uncertainty of contemporary social life.* Planning a future is problematic in a society where job elimination and corporate downsizing are accepted business practices, and divorce and family restructuring are epidemic.

- *Lack of legitimate opportunity.* In some elements of society, kids believe they have no future, leaving them to experiment with risky alternatives, such as drug dealing or theft.

- *Emphasis on consumerism.* In high school, peer respect is bought through the accumulation of material goods. For those kids whose families cannot afford to keep up, drug deals and theft may be a shortcut to getting coveted name-brand clothes and athletic shoes.

- *Racial, class, age, and ethnicity inequalities.* These discourage kids from believing in a better future. Children are raised to be skeptical that they can receive social benefits from any institution beyond themselves or their immediate family.

- *The "cult of individualism."* This makes people self-centered and hurts collective and group identities. Children are taught to put their own interests above those of others.

As children mature into adults, the uncertainty of modern society may prolong their risk-taking behavior. Jobs have become unpredictable, and many undereducated and undertrained youths find themselves competing for the same low-paying job as hundreds of other applicants; they are a "surplus product." They may find their only alternative for survival is to return to their childhood bedroom and live off their parents. Under these circumstances, risk taking may be a plausible alternative for fitting in in our consumer-oriented society.

CRITICAL THINKING

1. Davis calls for a major national effort to restore these troubled youths using a holistic, nonpunitive approach that recognizes the special needs of children. How would you convince kids to stop taking risks?

2. Do you agree that elements of contemporary society cause kids to take risks, or is it possible that teens are natural risk takers and their risky behavior is a biological reaction to "raging hormones"?

Writing Assignment Everyone has taken risks in their life and some of us have paid the consequences. Write an essay detailing one of your riskiest behaviors and what you learned from the experience

Sources: Centers for Disease Control and Prevention (CDC), *Youth Risk Behavior Survey (YRBS), 2009,* www.cdc.gov/HealthyYouth/yrbs/pdf/us_overview_yrbs.pdf (accessed June 13, 2012); "Unintentional Strangulation Deaths from the 'Choking Game' Among Youths Aged 6–19 Years, United States, 1995–2007," February 15, 2008, www.cdc.gov/mmwr/preview/mmwrhtml/mm5706a1.htm (accessed June 13, 2012); Patrick Nickoletti and Heather Taussig, "Outcome Expectancies and Risk Behaviors in Maltreated Adolescents," *Journal of Research on Adolescence* 16:217–228 (2006); Nanette Davis, *Youth Crisis: Growing Up in the High-Risk Society* (New York: Praeger/Greenwood, 1998).

minority kids the hardest. According to the nonprofit Children's Defense Fund, African American children are:

- Half as likely to be placed in a gifted and talented class.
- More than one and a half times as likely to be placed in a class for students with emotional disturbances.
- Almost twice as likely to be placed in a class for students with mental retardation.
- Two and a half times as likely to be held back or retained in school.
- Almost three times as likely to be suspended from school.
- More than four times as likely to be expelled.[23]

Why the discrepancy? Poor minority-group children attend the most underfunded schools, receive inadequate educational opportunities, and have the fewest opportunities to achieve conventional success.

The problems faced by kids who do poorly in school do not end in adolescence.[24] Adults 25 years of age and older with less than a high school diploma earn 30 percent less than those who have earned a high school diploma. High school graduation is the single most effective preventive strategy against adult poverty; as Table 1.1 shows, 13 percent of American adults age 25 to 34 are not high school graduates; only 31 percent have a college degree or more.

WAW

Formed in 1985, the **Children's Rights Council (CRC)** is a national nonprofit organization based in Washington, D.C., that works to ensure children meaningful and continuing contact with both their parents and extended family, regardless of the parents' marital status. Find this website by visiting the Criminal Justice CourseMate at CengageBrain.com, then accessing the Web Links for this chapter.

TABLE 1.1 Educational Attainment Among 25- to 34-Year-Olds

United States	%
Not a high school graduate	13%
High school diploma or GED	48%
Associate's degree	8%
Bachelor's degree	22%
Graduate degree	9%

Source: Anna E. Casey Foundation, Kids Count Program, 2010 data, http://datacenter.kidscount.org/data/acrossstates/Rankings.aspx?ind=6294 (accessed June 12, 2012).

Considering that youth are at risk during the most tumultuous time of their lives, it comes as no surprise that, as the Focus on Delinquency box entitled "Teen Risk Taking" suggests, they are willing to engage in risky, destructive behavior.

Problems in Cyberspace

Kids today are forced to deal with problems and issues that their parents could not even dream about. While the Internet and other technological advances have opened a new world of information gathering and sharing, they have brought with them a basketful of new problems ranging from sexting to cyberstalking.

Not only are kids at risk of real-time bullying, but they may be bullied in cyberspace by people they hardly know and whose identity is hard to discover. Here, John Halligan shows the web page devoted to his son. Ryan was bullied for months online. Classmates sent the 13-year-old Essex Junction, Vermont, boy instant messages calling him gay. He was threatened, taunted, and insulted incessantly by cyberbullies. Finally, Ryan killed himself. His father says he couldn't take it anymore.

Cyberbullying. Phoebe Prince, a 15-year-old Massachusetts girl, hanged herself in a stairwell at her home after enduring months of torment by her fellow students at South Hadley High School. Prince, who had immigrated from Ireland, was taunted in the school's hallways and bombarded with vulgar insults by a pack of kids led by the ex-girlfriend of a boy she had briefly dated. As she studied in the library on the last day of her life, she was openly hounded and threatened physically while other students and a teacher looked on and did nothing. In the aftermath of her death, prosecutors accused two boys of statutory rape and four girls of violating Prince's civil rights and criminal harassment. Ironically, most of these students were still in school, and some continued to post nasty remarks on Prince's memorial Facebook page after her death.[25]

Experts define bullying among children as repeated, negative acts committed by one or more children against another.[26] These negative acts may be physical or verbal in nature—for example, hitting or kicking, teasing or taunting—or they may involve indirect actions such as manipulating friendships or purposely excluding other children from activities. While bullying is a problem that remains to be solved, it has now morphed from the physical to the virtual. Because of the creation of cyberspace, physical distance is no longer a barrier to the frequency and depth of harm doled out by a bully to his or her victim.[27] Cyberbullying is the willful and repeated harm inflicted through the medium of electronic text. Like their real-world counterparts, cyberbullies are malicious aggressors who seek implicit or explicit pleasure or profit through the mistreatment of other individuals. Although power in traditional bullying might be physical (stature) or social (competency or popularity), online power may simply stem from Internet proficiency.

It is difficult to get an accurate count of the number of teens who have experienced cyberbullying. Published estimates range from 72 percent all the way down to less than 6 percent; the average found in published articles is about one quarter of all students have been cyberbully victims. A recent study by cyberbullying experts Justin Patchin and Sameer Hinduja found that about 21 percent of youth had been the target of cyberbullying; this means that one out of every five kids has been cyberbullied.[28] As Figure 1.2 shows, adolescent girls are significantly more likely to have experienced cyberbullying in their lifetimes (25.8 percent vs. 16 percent) than boys. Girls are also more likely to report cyberbullying others during their lifetime (21.1 percent vs. 18.3 percent). The type of cyberbullying tends to differ by gender; girls are more likely to spread rumors while boys are more likely to post hurtful pictures.[29]

Cyberbullies who are able to navigate the Net and utilize technology in a way that allows them to harass others are in a position of power relative to a victim. A bully can send harassing e-mails or instant messages; post obscene, insulting, and slanderous messages on social networking sites; develop websites to promote and disseminate defamatory content; or send harassing text messages via cell phone.[30]

Cyberstalking. Cyberstalking refers to the use of the Internet, e-mail, or other electronic communications devices to stalk another person. Some predatory adults pursue minors through online chat rooms, establish a relationship with the child, and later make contact. Today, Internet predators are more likely to develop relationships with at-risk adolescents and beguile underage teenagers, rather than use coercion and violence.[31]

Sexting. Adolescents now have to worry that the compromising photos they send their boyfriends or girlfriends—a practice called sexting—can have terrible repercussions. In 2008, Jesse Logan, an 18-year-old Ohio high school girl, made the mistake of sending nude pictures of herself to her boyfriend. When they broke up, he sent them around to their schoolmates. As soon as the e-photos got into the hands

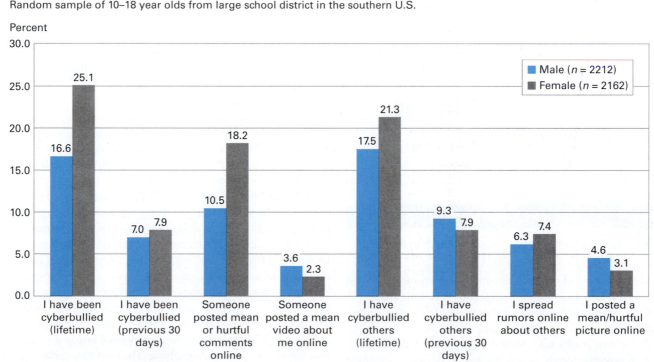

FIGURE 1.2 Cyberbullying by Gender

Random sample of 10–18 year olds from large school district in the southern U.S.

Source: Justin Patchin and Sameer Hinduja, Cyberbullying Research Center, http://cyberbullying.us/research.php (accessed June 12, 2012). Used by permission.

juvenile delinquency Participation in illegal behavior by a minor who falls under a statutory age limit.

of her classmates, they began harassing her, calling her names, and destroying her reputation. Jesse soon became depressed and reclusive, afraid to go to school, and in July 2008 she hanged herself in her bedroom.[32]

While the sexting phenomenon has garnered national attention, there is some question of how often teens actually engage in the distribution of sexually compromising material. One recent survey of 1,560 Internet users ages 10 through 17 found that about 2.5 percent had appeared in or created nude or nearly nude pictures or videos and that 1 percent of these images contained sexually explicit nudity.[33] Of the youth who participated in the survey, 7 percent said they had received nude or nearly nude images of others; few youth distributed these images. It is possible that sexting is not as common as previously believed or that it was a fad that is quickly fading.

Is There Reason for Hope?

These social conditions have a significant impact on kids. Children are being polarized into two distinct economic groups: those in affluent, two-earner, married-couple households and those in poor, single-parent households.[34] Kids whose parents divorce may increase their involvement in delinquency, especially if they have a close bond with the parent who is forced to leave.[35] They may turn to risky behavior instead of traveling down a conventional life path.

Yet despite the many hazards faced by teens, there are some bright spots on the horizon. Teenage birthrates nationwide have declined substantially during the past decade, with the sharpest declines among African American girls. The teen abortion rate has also dropped significantly. These data indicate that more young girls are using birth control and practicing safe sex. Fewer children with health risks are being born today than in 1990. This probably means that fewer women are drinking or smoking during pregnancy and that fewer are receiving late or no prenatal care. In addition, since 1990 the number of children immunized against disease has increased.

Education is still a problem area, but more parents are reading to their children, and math achievement is rising in grades 4 through 12. And more kids are going to college. College enrollment is now about 18 million and is expected to continue setting new records for the next decade.[36] Almost 30 percent of the adult population in the United States now have college degrees.

There are also indications that youngsters may be rejecting hard drugs. Teen smoking and drinking rates remain high, but fewer kids are using heroin and crack cocaine and the numbers of teens who report cigarette use has been in decline since the mid-1990s.[37] Although these are encouraging signs, many problem areas remain, and the improvement of adolescent life continues to be a national goal. **CHECKPOINTS**

JUVENILE DELINQUENCY

The problems of youth in modern society have long been associated with **juvenile delinquency**, or criminal behavior engaged in by minors. The study of juvenile delinquency is important both because of the damage suffered by its victims and the problems faced by its perpetrators. About 1.7 million youths under age 18 are arrested each year for crimes ranging from loitering to murder.[38] Though most juvenile law violations are minor, some young offenders are extremely dangerous and violent. More than 800,000 youths belong to street gangs. Youths involved in multiple serious criminal acts, referred to as *repeat* or *chronic juvenile offenders*, are considered a serious social problem. State juvenile authorities must deal with these offenders while responding to a range of other social problems, including child abuse and neglect, school crime and vandalism, family crises, and drug abuse. The cost to society of these high-rate offenders can be immense. In a series of studies, Mark Cohen, Alex Piquero, and Wesley Jennings examined the costs to society of various groups of juvenile offenders,

> ### CHECKPOINTS
>
> **LO1** Be familiar with the risks faced by youth in American culture.
>
> ✔ The problems of American youth have become a national concern and an important subject of academic study.
>
> ✔ There are more than 75 million youths in the United States, and the number is expected to rise.
>
> ✔ American youth are under a great deal of stress. They face poverty, family problems, urban decay, inadequate education, teen pregnancy, and social conflict.
>
> ✔ Kids take risks that get them in trouble.

including high-rate chronic offenders who kept on committing serious crimes as adults.[39] They found that the average cost for each of these offenders was over $1.5 million, and their cost to society increased as they grew older. The "worst of the worst" of these offenders, ones who committed more than 50 crimes, cost society about $1.7 million by the time they reached their mid-20s. In all, the high-rate offenders in the study had an annual cost to society of over half a billion dollars.

Clearly, there is an urgent need for strategies to combat juvenile delinquency. But formulating effective strategies demands a solid understanding of the causes of delinquency. Is it a function of psychological abnormality? A reaction against destructive social conditions? The product of a disturbed home life? Does serious delinquent behavior occur only in urban areas among lower-class youths? Or is it spread throughout the social structure? What are the effects of family life, substance abuse, school experiences, and peer relations?

The study of delinquency also involves the analysis of the **juvenile justice system**— the law enforcement, court, and correctional agencies designed to treat youthful offenders. How should police deal with minors who violate the law? What are the legal rights of children? What kinds of correctional programs are most effective with delinquent youths? How useful are educational, community, counseling, and vocational development programs? Is it true, as some critics claim, that most efforts to rehabilitate young offenders are doomed to failure? The reaction to juvenile delinquency frequently divides the public. While people favor policies that provide rehabilitation of violent offenders, other Americans are wary of teenage hoodlums and gangs, and believe that young offenders should be treated no differently than mature felons.[40] Should the juvenile justice system be more concerned about the long-term effects of punishment? Can even the most violent teenager one day be rehabilitated?

In summary, the scientific study of delinquency requires understanding the nature, extent, and cause of youthful law violations and the methods devised for their control. We also need to study environmental and social issues, including substance abuse, child abuse and neglect, education, and peer relations. All of these aspects of juvenile delinquency will be discussed in this text. We begin, however, with a look back to the development of the concept of childhood, how children were first identified as a unique group with their own special needs and behaviors, and how a system of justice developed to treat and care for needy, at-risk youth.

THE DEVELOPMENT OF CHILDHOOD

Treating children as a distinct social group with special needs and behavior is a relatively new concept. Only for the past 350 years has any formal mechanism existed to care for even the neediest children. In Europe during the Middle Ages (C.E. 700–1500), the concept of childhood as we know it today did not exist. In the **paternalistic family** of the time, the father exercised complete control over his wife and children.[41] Children who did not obey were subject to severe physical punishment, even death.

Custom and Practice in the Middle Ages

During the Middle Ages, as soon as they were physically capable, children of all classes were expected to take on adult roles. Boys learned farming or a skilled trade such as masonry or metalworking; girls aided in food preparation or household maintenance.[42] Some peasant youths went into domestic or agricultural service on the estates of powerful landowners or became apprenticed in trades or crafts.[43] Children of the landholding classes also assumed adult roles at an early age. At age 7 or 8, boys born to landholding families were either sent to a monastery or cathedral school or were sent to serve as squires, or assistants, to experienced knights.

chronic juvenile offenders (also known as chronic delinquent offenders, chronic delinquents, or chronic recidivists) Youths who have been arrested four or more times during their minority and perpetuate a striking majority of serious criminal acts. This small group, known as the "chronic 6 percent," is believed to engage in a significant portion of all delinquent behavior; these youths do not age out of crime but continue their criminal behavior into adulthood.

juvenile justice system The segment of the justice system, including law enforcement officers, the courts, and correctional agencies, that is designed to treat youthful offenders.

paternalistic family A family style wherein the father is the final authority on all family matters and exercises complete control over his wife and children.

During the Middle Ages, children like those shown in this sixteenth-century woodcut were expected to be obedient and compliant or face the wrath of their parents, who would not hesitate to use corporal punishment.

At age 21, young men of the knightly classes received their own knighthood and returned home to live with their parents. Girls were educated at home and married in their early teens. A few were taught to read, write, and do sufficient mathematics to handle household accounts in addition to typical female duties, such as supervising servants.

Some experts, most notably Philippe Aries, have described the medieval child as a "miniature adult" who began to work and accept adult roles at an early age and was treated with great cruelty.[44] In many families, especially the highborn, newborns were handed over to *wet nurses* who fed and cared for them during the first two years of life; parents had little contact with their children. Discipline was severe. Young children of all classes were subjected to stringent rules and regulations. Children were beaten for any sign of disobedience or ill temper, and many would be considered abused by today's standards. Children were expected to undertake responsibilities early in their lives, sharing in the work of siblings and parents. Those thought to be suffering from disease or retardation were often abandoned to churches, orphanages, or foundling homes.[45]

The Development of Concern for Children

Throughout the seventeenth and eighteenth centuries, a number of developments in England heralded the march toward the recognition of children's rights. Among them were changes in family style and childcare, the English Poor Laws, the apprenticeship movement, and the role of the chancery court.[46]

Changes in Family Structure. Family structure began to change after the Middle Ages. Extended families, which were created over centuries, gave way to the nuclear family structure with which we are familiar today. It became more common for marriage to be based on love rather than parental consent and paternal dominance. This changing concept of marriage from an economic arrangement to an emotional commitment also began to influence the way children were treated. Although parents still rigidly disciplined their children, they formed closer ties and had greater concern for the well-being of their offspring.

Toward the close of the eighteenth century, the work of such philosophers as Voltaire, Rousseau, and Locke launched a new age for childhood and the family.[47] Their vision produced a period known as the Enlightenment, which stressed a humanistic view of life, freedom, family, reason, and law. These new beliefs influenced the family. The father's authority was tempered, discipline became more relaxed, and the expression of affection became more commonplace. Upper- and middle-class families began to devote attention to childrearing, and the status of children was advanced.

As a result of these changes, children began to emerge as a distinct group with independent needs and interests. Serious questions arose over the treatment of children in school. Restrictions were placed on the use of the whip, and in some schools academic assignments or the loss of privileges replaced corporal punishment. Despite such reforms, punishment was still primarily physical, and schools continued to mistreat children.

Poor Laws. As early as 1535, the English passed statutes known as **Poor Laws**.[48] These laws allowed for the appointment of overseers to place destitute or neglected children as servants in the homes of the affluent, where they were trained in agricultural, trade, or domestic services. The Elizabethan Poor Laws of 1601 created a system of church wardens and overseers who, with the consent of justices of the peace, identified vagrant, delinquent, and neglected children and put them to work. Often this meant placing them in poorhouses or workhouses or apprenticing them to masters.

The Apprenticeship Movement. Apprenticeship existed throughout almost the entire history of Great Britain.[49] Under this practice, children were placed in the care of adults who trained them in specific skills, such as being a blacksmith or a farrier (a shoer of horses). *Voluntary apprentices* were bound out by parents or guardians in exchange for a fee. Legal authority over the child was then transferred to the apprentice's master. The system helped parents avoid the costs and responsibilities of childrearing. *Involuntary apprentices* were compelled by the legal authorities to serve a master until they were 21 or older. The master–apprentice relationship was similar to the parent–child relationship in that the master had complete authority over the apprentice and could have agreements enforced by local magistrates.

Chancery Court. Throughout Great Britain in the Middle Ages, **chancery courts** were established to protect property rights and seek equitable solutions to disputes and conflicts. Eventually, their authority was extended to the welfare of children in cases involving the guardianship of orphans. This included safeguarding their property and inheritance rights and appointing a guardian to protect them until they reached the age of majority.

The courts operated on the proposition that children were under the protective control of the king; thus, the Latin phrase ***parens patriae*** was used, which refers to the role of the king as the father of his country. The concept was first used by English kings to establish their right to intervene in the lives of the children of their vassals.[50] As time passed, the monarchy used *parens patriae* more and more to justify its intervention in the lives of families and children.[51]

Childhood in America

While England was using its chancery courts and Poor Laws to care for children in need, the American colonies were developing similar concepts. The colonies were a haven for people looking for opportunities denied them in England and Europe. Along with the adult early settlers, many children came not as citizens, but as indentured servants, apprentices, or agricultural workers. They were recruited from workhouses, orphanages, prisons, and asylums that housed vagrant and delinquent youths.[52]

At the same time, the colonists themselves produced illegitimate, neglected, and delinquent children. The initial response to caring for such children was to adopt court and Poor Law systems similar to those in England. Poor Law legislation

Poor Laws English statutes that allowed the courts to appoint overseers for destitute and neglected children, allowing placement of these children as servants in the homes of the affluent.

chancery courts Court proceedings created in fifteenth-century England to oversee the lives of highborn minors who were orphaned or otherwise could not care for themselves.

parens patriae The power of the state to act on behalf of the child and provide care and protection equivalent to that of a parent.

WWW

For more information on the early history of childhood and the development of education, read **"Factors Influencing the Development of the Idea of Childhood in Europe and America," by Jim Vandergriff.** Find the website by going to the Criminal Justice CourseMate at CengageBrain.com, then accessing the Web Links for this chapter.

requiring poor and dependent children to serve apprenticeships was passed in Virginia in 1646 and in Massachusetts and Connecticut in 1673.[53]

It was also possible, as in England, for parents to voluntarily apprentice their children to a master for care and training. The master in colonial America acted as a surrogate parent, and in certain instances apprentices would actually become part of the family. If they disobeyed their masters, they were punished by local tribunals. If masters abused apprentices, courts would make them pay damages, return the children to the parents, or find new guardians for them. Maryland and Virginia developed an orphans' court that supervised the treatment of youths placed with guardians. These courts did not supervise children living with their natural parents, leaving intact parents' rights to care for their children.[54]

CHECKPOINTS

LO2 Develop an understanding of the history of childhood.

✔ The concept of a separate status of childhood has developed slowly over the centuries.

✔ Early family life was controlled by parents. Punishment was severe and children were expected to take on adult roles early in their lives.

✔ With the start of the seventeenth century came greater recognition of the needs of children. In Great Britain, the chancery court movement, the Poor Laws, and apprenticeship programs greatly affected the lives of children.

✔ In colonial America, many of the characteristics of English family living were adopted.

✔ In the nineteenth century, neglected, delinquent, and dependent or runaway children were treated no differently than criminal defendants. Children were often charged and convicted of crimes.

Controlling Children

In the United States, as in England, moral discipline was rigidly enforced. Stubborn-child laws were passed that required children to obey their parents.[55] It was not uncommon for children to be whipped if they were disobedient or disrespectful to their families. Children were often required to attend public whippings and executions, because these events were thought to be important forms of moral instruction. Parents referred their children to published writings on behavior and expected them to follow their precepts carefully. The early colonists, however, viewed family violence as a sin, and child protection laws were passed as early as 1639 (in New Haven, Connecticut). These laws expressed the community's commitment to God to oppose sin, but offenders usually received lenient sentences.[56] Although most colonies adopted a protectionist stance, few cases of child abuse were actually brought before the courts. **CHECKPOINTS**

DEVELOPING JUVENILE JUSTICE

Though the personal rights of children slowly developed, until the twentieth century little distinction was made between adult and juvenile offenders who were brought before the law. Although judges considered the age of an offender when deciding on punishment, both adults and children were eligible for prison, corporal punishment, and even the death penalty. In fact, children were treated with extreme cruelty at home, at school, and by the law.[57]

Over the years this treatment changed as society became sensitive to the special needs of children. Beginning in the mid-nineteenth century, there was official recognition that children formed a separate group with their own special needs. In New York, Boston, and Chicago, groups known as *child savers* were formed to assist children. They created community programs to service needy children and lobbied for a separate legal status for children, which ultimately led to development of a formal juvenile justice system.

Juvenile Justice in the Nineteenth Century

At the beginning of the nineteenth century, delinquent, neglected, and runaway children in the United States were treated in the same way as adult criminal offenders.[58] Like children in England, when convicted of crimes they received harsh sentences similar to those imposed on adults. The adult criminal code applied to children, and no juvenile court existed.

During the early nineteenth century, various pieces of legislation were introduced to humanize criminal procedures for children. The concept of probation, introduced in Massachusetts in 1841, was geared toward helping young people avoid imprisonment. Many books and reports written during this time heightened public interest in juvenile care.

Despite this interest, no special facilities existed for the care of youths in trouble with the law, nor were there separate laws or courts to control their behavior. Youths who committed petty crimes, such as stealing or vandalism, were viewed as wayward children or victims of neglect and were placed in community asylums or homes. Youths who were involved in more serious crimes were subject to the same punishments as adults—imprisonment, whipping, or death.

Several events led to reforms and nourished the eventual development of the juvenile justice system: urbanization, the child-saving movement and growing interest in the concept of *parens patriae*, and development of institutions for the care of delinquent and neglected children.

Urbanization

Especially during the first half of the nineteenth century, the United States experienced rapid population growth, primarily due to an increased birthrate and expanding immigration. The rural poor and immigrant groups were attracted to urban commercial centers that promised jobs in manufacturing.

Urbanization gave rise to increased numbers of young people at risk, who overwhelmed the existing system of work and training. To accommodate destitute youths, local jurisdictions developed poorhouses (almshouses) and workhouses. The poor, the insane, the diseased, and vagrant and destitute children were all housed there in crowded and unhealthy conditions.

Urbanization and industrialization also generated the belief that certain segments of the population (youths in urban areas, immigrants) were susceptible to the influences of their decaying environment. The children of these classes were considered a group that might be "saved" by a combination of state and community intervention.[59] Intervention in the lives of these so-called dangerous classes became acceptable for wealthy, civic-minded citizens. Such efforts included *settlement houses*, a term used around the turn of the twentieth century to describe shelters, and nonsecure residential facilities for vagrant children.

WWW

To learn more about this era, go to the **Library of Congress** website devoted to American history; visit the Criminal Justice CourseMate at CengageBrain.com, then access the Web Links for this chapter.

The Child-Saving Movement

The problems generated by urban growth sparked interest in the welfare of the "new" Americans, whose arrival fueled this expansion. In 1817, prominent New Yorkers formed the Society for the Prevention of Pauperism. Although they concerned themselves with attacking taverns, brothels, and gambling parlors, they also were concerned that the moral training of children of the dangerous classes was inadequate. Soon other groups concerned with the plight of poor children began to form. Their focus was on extending government control over youthful activities (drinking, vagrancy, and delinquency) that had previously been left to private or family control.

These activists became known as **child savers**. Prominent among them were penologist Enoch Wines; Judge Richard Tuthill; Lucy Flowers, of the Chicago Women's Association; Sara Cooper, of the National Conference of Charities and Corrections; and Sophia Minton, of the New York Committee on Children.[60] Poor children could become a financial burden, and the child savers believed these children presented a threat to the moral fabric of society. Child-saving organizations influenced state legislatures to enact laws giving courts the power to commit children who were runaways or criminal offenders to specialized institutions.

The most prominent of the care facilities developed by child savers was the **House of Refuge**, which opened in New York in 1825.[61] It was founded on the concept of protecting potential criminal youths by taking them off the streets and reforming them in a family-like environment. When the House of Refuge opened, the majority of children admitted were status offenders placed there because of

child savers Nineteenth-century reformers who developed programs for troubled youth and influenced legislation creating the juvenile justice system; today some critics view them as being more concerned with control of the poor than with their welfare.

House of Refuge A care facility developed by the child savers to protect potential criminal youths by taking them off the street and providing a family-like environment.

vagrancy or neglect. Children were placed in the institution by court order, sometimes over their parents' objections. Their length of stay depended on need, age, and skill. Once there, youths were required to do piecework provided by local manufacturers or to work part of the day in the community. The institution was run like a prison, with strict discipline and absolute separation of the sexes. Such a harsh program drove many children to run away, and the House of Refuge was forced to take a more lenient approach.

Despite criticism, the concept enjoyed expanding popularity. In 1826, the Boston City Council founded the House of Reformation for juvenile offenders. Similar institutions were opened elsewhere in Massachusetts and in New York in 1847.[62] The courts committed children found guilty of criminal violations, or found to be beyond the control of their parents, to these schools. Because the child savers considered parents of delinquent children to be as guilty as convicted offenders, they sought to have the reform schools establish control over the children. Refuge managers believed they were preventing poverty and crime by separating destitute and delinquent children from their parents and placing them in an institution.[63]

WWW

To read more about the **child savers**, visit the Criminal Justice CourseMate at CengageBrain .com, then access the Web Links for this chapter.

Were They Really Child Savers?

Debate continues over the true objectives of the early child savers. Some historians conclude that they were what they seemed—concerned citizens motivated by humanitarian ideals.[64] Modern scholars, however, have reappraised the child-saving movement. In *The Child Savers*, Anthony Platt paints a picture of representatives of the ruling class who were galvanized by immigrants and the urban poor to take action to preserve their own way of life.[65]

Contemporary scholars believe that the reformers applied the concept of *parens patriae* for their own purposes, including the continuance of middle- and upper-class values and the furtherance of a child labor system consisting of marginal and lower-class skilled workers.

In the course of "saving children" by turning them over to houses of refuge, the basic legal rights of children were violated: children were simply not granted the same constitutional protections as adults.

Development of Juvenile Institutions

State intervention in the lives of children continued well into the twentieth century. The child savers influenced state and local governments to create institutions, called *reform schools*, devoted to the care of vagrant and delinquent youths. State institutions opened in Westboro, Massachusetts, in 1848, and in Rochester, New York, in 1849.[66] Institutional programs began in Ohio in 1850, and in Maine, Rhode Island, and Michigan in 1906. Children spent their days working in the institution, learning a trade where possible, and receiving some basic education. They were racially and sexually segregated, discipline was harsh, and their physical care was poor. Most of these institutions received state support, unlike the privately funded houses of refuge and settlement houses.

Although some viewed reform schools as humanitarian answers to poorhouses and prisons, many were opposed to such programs. As an alternative, New York philanthropist Charles Loring Brace helped develop the **Children's Aid Society** in 1853.[67] Brace's formula for dealing with delinquent youths was to rescue them from the harsh environment of the city and provide them with temporary shelter.

Deciding there were simply too many needy children to care for in New York City, and believing the urban environment was injurious to children, Brace devised what he called his *placing-out plan* to send these children to western farms where they could be cared for and find a home. They were placed on what became known as **orphan trains**, which made preannounced stops in western farming communities. Families wishing to take in children would meet the train, be briefly introduced to the passengers, and leave with one of the children. Brace's plan was activated in 1854 and very soon copied by other child-care organizations. Though the majority

Children's Aid Society Child-saving organization that took children from the streets of large cities and placed them with farm families on the prairie.

orphan trains A practice of the Children's Aid Society in which urban youths were sent west for adoption with local farm couples.

Here, young boys are shown working in the machine shop of the Indiana Youth Reformatory, circa 1910.

© American Correctional Association

of the children benefited from the plan and did find a new life, others were less successful and some were exploited and harmed by the experience. By 1930, political opposition to Brace's plan, coupled with the negative effects of the Great Depression, spelled the end of the orphan trains, but not before 150,000 children were placed in rural homesteads. **CHECKPOINTS**

WWW

To read more about **Charles Loring Brace**, and the Children's Aid Society, visit the Criminal Justice CourseMate at Cengage Brain.com, then access the Web Links for this chapter.

Society for the Prevention of Cruelty to Children (SPCC)

In 1874, the first Society for the Prevention of Cruelty to Children (SPCC) was established in New York; by 1900, there were 300 such societies in the United States.[68] Leaders of the SPCCs were concerned that abused boys would become lower-class criminals and that mistreated young girls might become sexually promiscuous women. A growing crime rate and concern about a rapidly changing population served to swell SPCC membership. In addition, these organizations protected children who had been subjected to cruelty and neglect at home and at school.

SPCC groups influenced state legislatures to pass statutes protecting children from parents who did not provide them with adequate food and clothing or made them beg or work in places where liquor was sold.[69] Criminal penalties were created for negligent parents, and provisions were established for removing children from the home. In some states, agents of the SPCC could actually arrest abusive parents; in others, they would inform the police about suspected abuse cases and accompany officers when they made an arrest.[70]

CHECKPOINTS

LO3 Be able to discuss development of the juvenile justice system

✔ The movement to treat children in trouble with the law as a separate category began in the nineteenth century.

✔ Urbanization created a growing number of at-risk youth in the nation's cities.

✔ The child savers sought to control children of the lower classes.

✔ The House of Refuge was developed to care for unwanted or abandoned youth.

✔ Some critics now believe the child savers were motivated by self-interest and not benevolence.

✔ Charles Loring Brace created the Children's Aid Society to place urban kids with farm families.

The Illinois Juvenile Court Act and Its Legacy

Although reform groups continued to lobby for government control over children, the committing of children under the doctrine of *parens patriae* without due process of law began to be questioned by members of the child-saving movement. This concern and consequent political activity culminated in passage of the Illinois Juvenile Court Act of 1899. The principles motivating the Illinois reformers were these:

1. Children should not be held as accountable as adult transgressors.
2. The objective of the juvenile justice system is to treat and rehabilitate rather than punish.
3. Disposition should be predicated on analysis of the youth's special circumstances and needs.
4. The system should avoid the trappings of the adult criminal process with all its confusing rules and procedures.

The Illinois Juvenile Court Act was a major event in the juvenile justice movement. Just what were the ramifications of passage of this act? The traditional interpretation is that the reformers were genuinely motivated to pass legislation that would serve the best interests of the child.

Interpretations of its intentions differ, but unquestionably the Illinois Juvenile Court Act established juvenile delinquency as a legal concept. For the first time the distinction was made between children who were neglected and those who were delinquent. Most important, the act established a court and a probation program specifically for children. In addition, the legislation allowed children to be committed to institutions and reform programs under the control of the state. The key provisions of the act were these:

- A separate court was established for delinquent and neglected children.
- Special procedures were developed to govern the adjudication of juvenile matters.
- Children were to be separated from adults in courts and in institutional programs.
- Probation programs were to be developed to assist the court in making decisions in the best interests of the state and the child.

Following passage of the Illinois Juvenile Court Act, similar legislation was enacted throughout the nation; by 1917, juvenile courts had been established in all but three states. Attorneys were not required, and hearsay evidence, inadmissible in criminal trials, was admissible in the adjudication of juvenile offenders. The major functions of the juvenile justice system were to prevent juvenile crime and to rehabilitate juvenile offenders. The roles of the judge and the probation staff were to diagnose the child's condition and prescribe programs to alleviate it. Until 1967, judgments about children's actions and consideration for their constitutional rights were secondary.

By the 1920s, noncriminal behavior, in the form of incorrigibility and truancy from school, was added to the jurisdiction of many juvenile court systems. Of particular interest was the sexual behavior of young girls, and the juvenile court enforced a strict moral code on working-class girls, not hesitating to incarcerate those who were sexually active.[71] Programs of all kinds, including individualized counseling and institutional care, were used to *cure* juvenile criminality.

Great diversity also marked juvenile institutions. Some maintained a lenient orientation, but others relied on harsh punishments, including beatings, straitjacket restraints, immersion in cold water, and solitary confinement with a diet of bread and water.

Reforming the System

Reform of this system was slow in coming. In 1912, the U.S. Children's Bureau was formed as the first federal child welfare agency. By the 1930s, the bureau began to investigate the state of juvenile institutions and tried to expose some of their more repressive aspects.[72]

From its origin, the juvenile court system denied children procedural rights normally available to adult offenders. Due process rights, such as representation by counsel, a jury trial, freedom from self-incrimination, and freedom from unreasonable search and seizure, were not considered essential for the juvenile court system, because its primary purpose was not punishment but rehabilitation. However, the dream of trying to rehabilitate children was not achieved. Individual treatment approaches failed, and delinquency rates soared.

Reform efforts, begun in earnest in the 1960s, changed the face of the juvenile justice system. In 1962, New York passed legislation creating a family court system.[73] The new court assumed responsibility for all matters involving family life, with emphasis on delinquent and neglected children. In addition, the legislation established the PINS classification (person in need of supervision). This category included individuals involved in such actions as truancy and incorrigibility. By using labels like PINS and CHINS (children in need of supervision) to establish jurisdiction over children, juvenile courts expanded their role as social agencies. Because noncriminal children were now involved in the juvenile court system to a greater degree, many juvenile courts had to improve their social services. Efforts were made to personalize the system of justice for children. These reforms were soon followed by a due process revolution, which ushered in an era of procedural rights for court-adjudicated youth.

In the 1960s and 1970s, the U.S. Supreme Court radically altered the juvenile justice system when it issued a series of decisions that established the right of juveniles to receive due process of law.[74] The Court established that juveniles had the same rights as adults in important areas of trial process, including the right to confront witnesses, notice of charges, and the right to counsel.

Federal Commissions. In addition to the legal revolution brought about by the Supreme Court, a series of national commissions sponsored by the federal government helped change the shape of juvenile justice. In 1967, the President's Commission on Law Enforcement and the Administration of Justice, organized by President Lyndon Johnson, suggested that the juvenile justice system must provide underprivileged youths with opportunities for success, including jobs and education. The commission also recognized the need to develop effective law enforcement procedures to control hard-core offenders while also granting them due process. The commission's report acted as a catalyst for passage of the federal Juvenile Delinquency Prevention and Control (JDP) Act of 1968. This law created a Youth Development and Delinquency Prevention Administration, which concentrated on helping states develop new juvenile justice programs, particularly programs involving diversion of youth, decriminalization, and decarceration. In 1968, Congress also passed the Omnibus Safe Streets and Crime Control Act.[75] Title I of this law established the **Law Enforcement Assistance Administration (LEAA)** to provide federal funds for improving the adult and juvenile justice systems. In 1972, Congress amended the JDP to allow the LEAA to focus its funding on juvenile justice and delinquency-prevention programs. State and local governments were required to develop and adopt comprehensive plans to obtain federal assistance.

Because crime continued to receive much publicity, a second effort called the National Advisory Commission on Criminal Justice Standards and Goals was established in 1973 by the Nixon administration.[76] Its report identified such strategies as preventing delinquent behavior, developing diversion activities, establishing dispositional alternatives, providing due process for all juveniles, and controlling violent and chronic delinquents. This commission's recommendations formed the basis for the Juvenile Justice and Delinquency Prevention Act of 1974.[77] This act eliminated the Youth Development and Delinquency Prevention Administration and replaced it with the **Office of Juvenile Justice and Delinquency Prevention (OJJDP)** within the LEAA. In 1980, the LEAA was phased out, and the OJJDP became

Law Enforcement Assistance Administration (LEAA) Unit in the U.S. Department of Justice established by the Omnibus Crime Control and Safe Streets Act of 1968 to administer grants and provide guidance for crime prevention policy and programs.

Office of Juvenile Justice and Delinquency Prevention (OJJDP) Branch of the U.S. Justice Department charged with shaping national juvenile justice policy through disbursement of federal aid and research funds.

CHECKPOINTS

LO4 Trace the history and purpose of the juvenile court

✔ The juvenile court movement spread rapidly around the nation.

✔ Separate courts and correctional systems were created for youths. However, children were not given the same legal rights as adults.

✔ Reformers helped bring due process rights to minors and create specialized family courts.

✔ Federal commissions focused attention on juvenile justice and helped revise the system.

WWW

To read about the **Juvenile Justice and Delinquency Prevention Act of 1974**, visit the Criminal Justice CourseMate at CengageBrain.com, then access the Web Links for this chapter.

an independent agency in the Department of Justice. Throughout the 1970s, its two most important goals were removing juveniles from detention in adult jails, and eliminating the incarceration together of delinquents and status offenders. During this period, the OJJDP stressed the creation of formal diversion and restitution programs.

CHECKPOINTS

Delinquency and *Parens Patriae*

The current treatment of juvenile delinquents is a by-product of this developing national consciousness of children's needs. The designation *delinquent* became popular at the onset of the twentieth century when the first separate juvenile courts were instituted. The child savers believed that treating minors and adults equally violated the humanitarian ideals of American society. Consequently, the emerging juvenile justice system operated under the *parens patriae* philosophy. Minors who engaged in illegal behavior were viewed as victims of improper care at home. Illegal behavior was a sign that the state should step in and take control of the youths before they committed more serious crimes. The state should act in the **best interests of the child**. Children should not be punished for their misdeeds, but instead should be given the care necessary to control wayward behavior. It makes no sense to find children guilty of specific crimes, such as burglary or petty larceny, because that stigmatizes them as thieves or burglars. Instead, the catchall term *juvenile delinquency* should be used, because it indicates that the child needs the care and custody of the state.

The Current Legal Status of Delinquency

The child savers fought hard for a legal status of juvenile delinquent, but the concept that children could be treated differently before the law can actually be traced to the British legal tradition. Early British jurisprudence held that children under the age of 7 were legally incapable of committing crimes. Children between the ages of 7 and 14 were responsible for their actions, but their age might be used to excuse or lighten their punishment. Our legal system still recognizes that many young people are incapable of making mature judgments and that responsibility for their acts should be limited. Children can intentionally steal cars and know that the act is illegal, but they may be incapable of fully understanding the consequences of their behavior. Therefore, the law does not punish a youth as it would an adult, and it sees youthful misconduct as evidence of impaired judgment.

Today, the legal status of *juvenile delinquent* refers to a minor child who has been found to have violated the penal code. Most states define *minor child* as an individual who falls under a statutory age limit, most commonly 17 years of age.

Juveniles are usually kept separate from adults and receive different treatment under the law. Most large police departments employ officers whose sole responsibility is delinquency. Every state has some form of juvenile court with its own judges, probation department, and other facilities. Terminology is also different. Adults are *tried* in court; children are *adjudicated*. Adults can be *punished*; children are *treated*. If treatment is mandated, children can be sent to secure detention facilities, but they cannot normally be committed to adult prisons.

Children also have a unique legal status. A minor apprehended for a criminal act is usually charged with being a juvenile delinquent, regardless of the offense. These charges are confidential, and trial records are kept secret. The purpose of these safeguards is to shield children from the stigma of a criminal conviction and to prevent youthful misdeeds from becoming a lifelong burden.

Each state defines juvenile delinquency differently, setting its own age limits and boundaries. The federal

delinquent Juvenile who has been adjudicated by a judicial officer of a juvenile court as having committed a delinquent act.

best interests of the child A philosophical viewpoint that encourages the state to take control of wayward children and provide care, custody, and treatment to remedy delinquent behavior.

Looking Back to Aaliyah's Story

Teens close to the age of 18 like Aaliyah may be too old for the juvenile justice system, but too young for the adult system.

CRITICAL THINKING What should be done with juveniles who are close to 18 years when they receive a delinquency charge? Come up with a proposal to help them bridge the gap between the juvenile justice system and the adult criminal justice system.

government also has a delinquency category for youngsters who violate federal laws, but typically allows the states to handle delinquency matters.

Legal Responsibility of Youths

In our society the actions of adults are controlled by two types of law: criminal law and civil law. Criminal laws prohibit activities that are injurious to the well-being of society, such as drug use, theft, and rape; criminal legal actions are brought by state authorities against private citizens. In contrast, civil laws control interpersonal or private activities, and legal actions are usually initiated by individual citizens. Contractual relationships and personal conflicts (torts) are subjects of civil law. Also covered under civil law are provisions for the care of people who cannot care for themselves—for example, the mentally ill, the incompetent, and the infirm.

Today juvenile delinquency falls somewhere between criminal and civil law. Under *parens patriae*, delinquent acts are not considered criminal violations. The legal action against them is similar (though not identical) to a civil action that, in an ideal situation, is based on their **need for treatment**. This legal theory recognizes that children who violate the law are in need of the same treatment as are law-abiding citizens who cannot care for themselves.

Delinquent behavior is treated more leniently than adult misbehavior, because the law considers juveniles to be less responsible for their behavior than adults. Compared with adults, adolescents are believed to:

- Have a stronger preference for risk and novelty
- Be less accurate in assessing the potential consequences of risky conduct
- Be more impulsive and more concerned with short-term consequences
- Have a different appreciation of time and self-control
- Be more susceptible to peer pressure[78]

Even though youths have a lesser degree of legal responsibility, like adults they are subject to arrest, trial, and incarceration. Their legal predicament has prompted the courts to grant children many of the same legal protections conferred on adults accused of criminal offenses. These include the right to consult an attorney, to be free from self-incrimination, and to be protected from illegal searches and seizures.

Although most children who break the law are considered salvageable and worthy of community treatment efforts, there are also violent juvenile offenders whose behavior requires a firmer response. Some state authorities have declared that these hard-core offenders cannot be treated as children and must be given more secure treatment that is beyond the resources of the juvenile justice system. This recognition has prompted the policy of **waiver**—also known as **bindover** or **removal**—that is, transferring legal jurisdiction over the most serious juvenile offenders to the adult court for criminal prosecution. And while punishment is no more certain or swift once they are tried as adults, kids transferred to adult courts are often punished more severely than they would have been if treated as the minors they really are.[79] To the chagrin of reformers, waived youth may find themselves serving time in adult prisons.[80] So although the *parens patriae* concept is still applied to children whose law violations are considered not to be serious, the more serious juvenile offenders can be treated in a manner similar to adults.

STATUS OFFENDERS

The Juvenile Court Act recognized a second classification of youthful offender, the wayward minor or **status offender**, a child who is subject to state authority by reason of having committed an act forbidden to youth and illegal solely because the child is underage (e.g., underage drinking, underage smoking, etc.). Exhibit 1.1,

need for treatment The criteria on which juvenile sentencing is based. Ideally, juveniles are treated according to their need for treatment and not for the seriousness of the delinquent act they committed.

waiver (also known as bindover or removal) Transferring legal jurisdiction over the most serious and experienced juvenile offenders to the adult court for criminal prosecution.

status offender A child who is subject to state authority by reason of having committed an act forbidden to youth and illegal solely because the child is underage.

showing the status offense law of Maryland, describes typical status offenses. Eleven states classify these youths using the term *child in need of supervision*, whereas the remainder use terms such as *unruly child*, *incorrigible child*, or *minor in need of supervision*. The court can also exercise control over dependent children who are not being properly cared for by their parents or guardians.

State control over a child's noncriminal behavior supports the *parens patriae* philosophy, because it is assumed to be in the best interests of the child. Usually, a status offender is directed to the juvenile court when it is determined that his parents are unable or unwilling to care for or control him and that the adolescent's behavior is self-destructive or harmful to society. More than 250,000 juveniles are arrested each year for such status-type offenses as running away from home, breaking curfew, and violating liquor laws.[81] About 160,000 of these status offenders are petitioned to juvenile court.[82] Girls are more likely than boys to be petitioned for running away, while a majority of curfew violators are males.

Origins of the Status Offense Concept

A historical basis exists for status offense statutes. It was common practice early in the nation's history to place disobedient or runaway youths in orphan asylums, residential homes, or houses of refuge.[83] When the first juvenile courts were established in Illinois, the Chicago Bar Association described part of their purpose as follows:

> *The whole trend and spirit of the [1889 Juvenile Court Act] is that the State, acting through the Juvenile Court, exercises that tender solicitude and care over its neglected, dependent wards that a wise and loving parent would exercise with reference to his own children under similar circumstances.*[84]

When the juvenile court was first created, status offenders and juvenile delinquents were treated in a similar fashion. Both could be arrested, taken into custody, tried in the same courts and placed in the same institutions. A trend begun about 50 years ago has resulted in the creation of separate status offense categories that vary from state to state: children, minors, persons, youths, or juveniles in need of supervision (CHINS, MINS, PINS, YINS, or JINS). The purpose is to shield noncriminal youths from the stigma attached to the juvenile delinquent label and to signify that they have special needs and problems (see Concept Summary 1.1). But even where there are separate legal categories for delinquents and status offenders, the distinction between them can sometimes become blurred. Some noncriminal conduct may be included in the definition of delinquency, and some less serious criminal offenses occasionally may be labeled as status offenses.[85] In some states the juvenile court judge may substitute a status offense for a delinquency charge.[86] This possibility can be used to encourage youths to admit to the charges against them in return for less punitive treatment.

CONCEPT SUMMARY 1.1 | Treatment of Juveniles

	Juvenile Delinquents	Status Offenders
Act	Burglary, shoplifting, robbery	Truancy, running away, disobedient
Injured party	Crime victim	Themselves, their family
Philosophy	*Parens patriae*	Best interests of the child
Legal status	Can be detained in secure confinement	Must be kept in nonsecure shelter
Is there resulting stigma?	Yes	Yes

The Status Offender in the Juvenile Justice System

Separate status offense categories may avoid some of the stigma associated with the delinquency label, but they have little effect on treatment. Youths in either category can be picked up by the police and brought to a police station. They can be petitioned to the same juvenile court, where they have a hearing before the same judge and come under the supervision of the probation department, the court clinic, and the treatment staff. At a hearing, status offenders may see little difference between the treatment they receive and the treatment of the delinquent offenders sitting across the room. Although status offenders are usually not detained or incarcerated with delinquents, they can be transferred to secure facilities if they are considered uncontrollable. The toll this treatment takes on status offenders can be significant. A recent study by Wesley Jennings found that the effect of formal processing on status offenders' can increase the likelihood that they will get involved in subsequent delinquency. Half of the status offenders he studied in Florida, both males and females, accumulated delinquent arrests in adolescence following their initial referral for a status offense. [87]

Reforming the Treatment of Status Offenders

For more than 30 years, national crime commissions have called for limiting control over status offenders. [88] In 1974, the U.S. Congress passed the Juvenile Justice and Delinquency Prevention Act (JJDPA), which provides the major source of federal funding to improve states' juvenile justice systems. Under the JJDPA and its subsequent reauthorizations, in order to receive federal funds, states were and are required to remove status offenders from secure detention and lockups in order to insulate them from more serious delinquent offenders. The act created the Office of Juvenile Justice and Delinquency Prevention (OJJDP), which was authorized to distribute grants and provide support to those states that developed alternate procedural methods. [89] Title III of the JJDPA, referred to as the Runaway and Homeless Youth Act (RHYA) of 1974, provides funds for nonsecure facilities where status offenders who need protection can receive safe shelter, counseling, and education until an effective family reunion can be realized. [90]

This has been a highly successful policy, and the number of status offenders kept in secure pretrial detention has dropped significantly during the past three decades. The act that created the OJJDP was amended in 1987 to allow status offenders to be detained for violations of valid court orders. [91]

Looking Back to Aaliyah's Story

What should happen with teens who run away from home? This is considered a status offense, but many communities do not charge runaways or require them to be involved in the juvenile justice system.

CRITICAL THINKING Can you propose a program that would effectively help runaways adjust to society?

School programs have been designed to keep kids away from the lure of the streets and status offending. Here, medals are presented to successful students at the Oakland Military Institute, a public school funded by the Pentagon and the National Guard and administered by the California State Board of Education. Its mission is to tame unruly youngsters through discipline and military-style conformity. Parents see the school as a way out of a crumbling public education system that, in Oakland and other urban centers, is woefully underfunded and understaffed.

WWW

To learn more about the efforts to remove status offenders from secure lockups, read **Gwen A. Holden and Robert A. Kapler, "Deinstitutionalizing Status Offenders: A Record of Progress"** by visiting the Criminal Justice CourseMate at Cengage Brain.com, then accessing the Web Links for this chapter.

The Effects of Reform. What has been the effect of this reform effort? It has become routine for treatment dispensing agencies other than juvenile courts to be given responsibility for processing status offense cases. In some communities, for example, family crisis units and social service agencies have assumed this responsibility. When a juvenile charged with a status offense is referred to juvenile court, the court may divert the juvenile away from the formal justice system to other agencies for service rather than include them in the formal juvenile justice process.

A number of states have changed the way they handle status offense cases. Kentucky, for example, has amended its status offense law in order to eliminate vague terms and language. Instead of labeling a child who is "beyond control of school" as a status offender, the state is now required to show that the student has repeatedly violated "lawful regulations for the government of the school," with the petition describing the behaviors "and all intervention strategies attempted by the school."[92] A few states, including Maine, Delaware, and Idaho, have attempted to eliminate status offense laws and treat these youths as neglected or dependent children, giving child protective services the primary responsibility for their care. Addressing the special needs of status offenders, several states now require that they and their families receive precourt diversion services in an effort to prevent them from being placed out-of-home by strengthening family relations and reducing parent–teen conflicts. They also identify which agency must respond to status offenses, how they are to respond, who will pay, and/or who will evaluate the process to assure positive and cost-effective outcomes. In Florida, all status offense cases are handled by a special agency that refers them to precourt prevention services; only if these services fail will court intervention be contemplated. New York's status offense statute prohibits family courts from considering a status offense petition unless the adolescent has already participated in diversion services. New York requires that an agency filing a status offense petition to convene a conference with the individuals involved discuss providing diversion services and attempt to engage the family in targeted community-based services before the juvenile court can become involved. A status offense petition can *only* be filed if the lead agency states it terminated diversion services because there was "no substantial likelihood that youth and his or her family will benefit from further attempts" at getting help.[93] The Juvenile Delinquency Prevention/Intervention/Treatment feature describes one program designed to maintain control over at risk status offenders.

Family Keys Program

In 2003, officials in Orange County, New York, became concerned about the projected impact of the state's increasing number of at-risk kids, and therefore wanted to increase its jurisdiction over status offenders to age 18. After much study, and with the legislature's backing, the community-based Family Keys program was officially launched. Under the program, the county probation department receives inquiries from parents about PINS (persons in need of supervision). If, after a brief screening, the intake officer finds sufficient allegations to support a PINS complaint, the officer refers the case to Family Keys rather than to probation intake. Depending on the severity of the case, Family Keys dispatches counselors to assess the family's situation 2 to 48 hours after receiving a referral. Based on the assessment, the agency develops an appropriate short-term intervention plan for the youth and family and provides links to community-based programs. Family Keys works with the family for up to three weeks to ensure that the family is engaged in the service plan.

The Family Keys intervention takes place in lieu of filing a PINS complaint, provides intensive, short-term crisis intervention to families, and diverts PINS cases from the court system. When these short-term interventions do not suffice, cases are referred to an interagency team operated through the mental health department's Network program. Following a family conferencing model, the Network team performs an in-depth assessment and serves as the gateway to the county's most high-end services, such as multisystemic therapy or family functional therapy. Under Orange County's system, a PINS case is referred to court only as a last resort.

Evaluation of the Family Keys program has been very promising. The time between a parent's first contact with probation and subsequent follow-up has decreased dramatically, from as long as six weeks under the previous system to as low as two hours through the Family Keys process. The number of PINS cases referred to court and the number of PINS placements have also been sharply reduced. The evaluation showed that between April and September 2009, 184 young people and their families were offered services. The program served both males and females ages 10 to 17; the majority of youths were 15 or 16 years old:

- 93 percent of youths were living at home in the community with their parents/guardians. None had been placed in out-of-home care. This is a 7 percent increase from intake to exit of youths living at home and a 3 percent decrease in the number of youths whose living arrangement was categorized as "'runaway."
- There was a 25 percent increase in the number of youths who improved "connectedness" with parents/guardians and a 24 percent increase in the number of youths who improved "connectedness" with a sibling or other family members.
- School attendance remained the same, with 100 percent of the program youths regularly attending school.
- There was an 18 percent increase in the number of youths who improved their health-protecting skills, which includes reducing use of alcohol and drugs.

Since its inception, almost 99 percent of the 2,500 children enrolled in the program have avoided residential, out-of-home placement.

Critical Thinking

How would you answer a critic who argues that all social programs should be cut and that social programs are a waste of time? Does the Orange County success story influence your thinking about intervening with troubled youth?

Sources: Tina Chiu and Sara Mogulescu, *Changing the Status Quo for Status Offenders: New York State's Efforts to Support Troubled Teens* (Vera Foundation, New York, 2004), www.vera.org/content/changing-status-quo-status-offenders-new-york-states-efforts-support-troubled-teens (accessed June 14, 2012); Office of Juvenile Justice and Delinquency Prevention, "Family Keys PINS Diversion Program, 2010," www2.dsgonline.com/dso2/dso_program_detail.aspx?ID=757&title=Family+Keys+PINS+Diversion+Program (accessed June 14, 2012).

The Future of the Status Offense Concept

Changes in the treatment of status offenders reflect the current attitude toward children who violate the law. On the one hand, there appears to be a movement to severely sanction youths who commit serious offenses and transfer them to the adult court. On the other hand, a great effort has been made to remove nonserious cases from the official agencies of justice and place these youths in community-based treatment programs.

WWW

Do curfew laws work in reducing the rate of youth crime? To find out, visit the website of the **Justice Policy Institute** by going to the Criminal Justice Course-Mate at CengageBrain.com, then accessing the Web Links for this chapter.

✔ The separate status of juvenile delinquency is based on the *parens patriae* philosophy, which holds that children have the right to care and custody and that if parents are not capable of providing that care, the state must step in to take control.

✔ Delinquents are given greater legal protection than adult criminals and are shielded from stigma and labels.

✔ More serious juvenile cases may be waived to the adult court.

✔ Juvenile courts also have jurisdiction over noncriminal status offenders.

✔ Status offenses are illegal only because of the minority status of the offender.

This movement is not without its critics. Some juvenile court judges believe that reducing judicial authority over children will limit juvenile court jurisdiction to hard-core offenders and constrain its ability to help youths before they commit serious antisocial acts.[94] Their concerns are fueled by research that shows that many status offenders, especially those who are runaways living on the streets, often have serious emotional problems and engage in self-destructive behaviors ranging from substance abuse to self-mutilation; they have high rates of suicide.[95] There is evidence that kids who engage in status offending are significantly more likely than nonstatus offenders to later engage in delinquent behaviors such as drug abuse.[96] Consequently, some jurisdictions have resisted weakening status offense laws and gone in the opposite direction by mandating that habitual truants and runaways be placed in secure detention facilities, and if found to be in need of supervision, placed in secure treatment facilities. **CHECKPOINTS**

Curfews

One way jurisdictions have attempted to maintain greater control over wayward youth has been the implementation of curfew laws. The thought is that the opportunity to commit crimes will be reduced if troubled kids are given a curfew.

The first curfew law was created in Omaha, Nebraska, in 1880, and today about 500 U.S. cities have curfews for teenage youth. Curfews typically prohibit children under 18 from being on the streets after 11:00 P.M. during the week and after midnight on weekends. About 100 cities also have daytime curfews designed to keep children off the streets and in school.[97]

Each year about 60,000 youths are arrested for curfew violations, and their number is considered responsible for the decade-long increase in the status offender population in juvenile court. As yet there is little conclusive evidence that curfews have a significant impact on youth crime rates. While surveys find that police favor curfews as an effective tool to control vandalism, graffiti, nighttime burglary, and auto theft, empirical studies found that both juvenile arrests and juvenile crime do not seem to decrease significantly during curfew hours.[98] Some research efforts have even found that after curfews were implemented victimizations increased significantly during no curfew hours. This indicates that, rather than suppressing delinquency, curfews merely shift the time of occurrence of the offenses. Some studies have found that strict enforcement of curfew laws actually increases juvenile crime rates.[99] The failure of curfews to control crime coupled with their infringement on civil rights prompted the American Civil Liberties Union to condemn the practice.[100] Other civil libertarians maintain that curfews are an overreaction to juvenile crime, are ineffective, and give the police too much power to control citizens who being punished merely because of their age.[101]

There are a number of ongoing legal challenges to curfew laws, arguing that they are violations of the constitutional right to assembly, and some have been successful. A challenge to the Rochester, New York, law (*Anonymous v. City of Rochester*) found that the ordinance enabled police to arrest and interrogate a disproportionate percentage of minority youth; 94 percent of youths picked up on curfew violations were black or Hispanic. On June 9, 2009, New York's State Court of Appeals invalidated Rochester's curfew, finding that the ordinance gives parents too little flexibility and autonomy in supervising their children, while violating children's rights to freedom of movement, freedom of expression and association, and equal protection under the law. Influencing the court was data showing that young people in Rochester were more likely to be involved in a crime—either as a victim or offender—when the curfew was not in effect.[102] Similarly, the Massachusetts Supreme Judicial Court struck down provisions of a local curfew law that made it a

Philadelphia Mayor Michael Nutter walks with community leaders and several teens in the Center City neighborhood in an effort to combat marauding groups of teenagers and preteens known as "flash mobs." The mayor ordered a curfew requiring anyone under 18 to be off the streets by 9 P.M. on Friday and Saturday nights in problem-plagued areas of the city.

crime for youth under 17 to be on the streets after 11 P.M. unless accompanied by a parent or a guardian. While they left in place civil penalties that allowed individuals convicted of violating the curfew to be fined up to $300, it is no longer permissible to charge curfew violators with a crime.[103]

Disciplining Parents

So what happens if kids repeatedly break curfew and get into trouble and their parents refuse or are incapable of doing anything about it? Since the early twentieth century, there have been laws aimed at disciplining parents for *contributing to the delinquency of a minor.* The first of these was enacted in Colorado in 1903, and today all states have some form of statute requiring parents to take some responsibility for their children's misbehavior.[104] All states make it either mandatory or discretionary for the juvenile court to require a parent or guardian to pay at least part of the support costs for a child who is adjudicated delinquent and placed out of the home. Even when the payment is required, however, payment is based on the parent's financial ability to make such payments. During the past decade, approximately one-half of the states enacted or strengthened existing parental liability statutes that make parents criminally liable for the actions of their delinquent children. These laws can generally fall into one of three categories:

- *Civil liability.* An injured party may bring a case against the parents for property damage or personal injury caused by one of their children.
- *Criminal liability.* The guardian or other adult may be held criminally responsible for contributing to the delinquency of a minor. These laws apply when an adult does some action that encourages delinquent behavior by a child.
- *General involvement.* These statutes are based upon legislative efforts to make parents more involved in the juvenile court process and include such things as requiring the parents to pay for court costs, restitution, and treatment, and to participate in the juvenile's case. Failure to comply with the parental involvement requirements can lead to more punitive sanctions.[105]

Within this general framework there is a great deal of variation in responsibility laws. Some states (Florida, Idaho, Virginia) require parents to reimburse the government for the costs of detention or care of their children. Others (Maryland, Missouri, Oklahoma) demand that parents make restitution payments—for example, paying for damage caused by their children who vandalized a school. All states have incorporated parental liability laws in their statutes, although most recent legislation places limits on recovery; in some states, such as Texas, the upward boundary can be as much as $25,000.

Parents may also be held civilly liable, under the concept of *vicarious liability*, for the damages caused by their child. In some states, parents are responsible for up to $300,000 in damages; in others the liability cap is $3,500 (sometimes homeowner's insurance covers at least some of liability). Parents can also be charged with civil negligence if they should have known of the damage a child was about to inflict but did nothing to stop them—for example, when they give a weapon to an emotionally unstable youth. Juries have levied awards of up to $500,000 in such cases. During the past two decades, parents have been ordered to serve time in jail because their children have been truant from school.

Some critics charge that these laws contravene the right to due process, because they are unfairly used only against lower-class and minority parents. As legal scholar Elena Laskin points out, imposing penalties on these parents may actually be detrimental.[106] Forcing a delinquent's mother to pay a fine removes money from someone who is already among society's poorest people. If a single mother is sent to jail, it leaves her children, including those who are not delinquent, with no parent to raise them; the kids may become depressed, and lose concentration and sleep. Even if punishment encourages the parent to take action, it may be too late, because by the time a parent is charged with violating the statute, the child has already committed a crime, indicating that any damaging socialization by the parent has already occurred. Finally, responsibility laws may not take the age of the child into account,[107] leaving an important question unanswered: are parents of older offenders equally responsible as those whose much younger children violate the law? Does an adolescent's personal share of responsibility increase with age? Despite these problems, surveys indicate that the public favors parental responsibility laws.[108]

SUMMARY

The study of delinquency is concerned with the nature and extent of the criminal behavior of youths, the causes of youthful law violations, the legal rights of juveniles, and prevention and treatment.

The problems of American youths have become an important subject of academic study. Many children live in poverty, have inadequate health care, and suffer family problems. Kids today are also at risk from threats that are on the Internet, ranging from cyberbullying to sexting. Consequently, adolescence is a time of taking risks, which can get kids into trouble with the law.

Our modern concept of a separate status for children is quite different than in the past. In earlier times, relationships between children and parents were remote. Punishment was severe, and children were expected to take on adult roles early in their lives. With the start of the seventeenth century came greater recognition of the needs of children. In Great Britain, the chancery court movement, Poor Laws, and apprenticeship programs helped reinforce the idea of children as a distinct social group. In colonial America, many of the characteristics of English family living were adopted. In the nineteenth century, delinquent and runaway children were treated no differently than criminal defendants. During this time, however, increased support for the *parens patriae* concept resulted in steps to reduce the responsibility of children under the criminal law.

The concept of delinquency was developed in the early twentieth century. Before that time, criminal youths and adults were treated in almost the same fashion. A group of reformers, referred to as child savers, helped create a separate delinquency category to insulate juvenile offenders from the influence of adult criminals. The status of juvenile delinquency is still based on the *parens patriae* philosophy, which holds that children have the right to care and custody and that if parents are not capable of providing that care, the state must step in to take control. Juvenile courts also have jurisdiction over noncriminal status offenders, whose offenses (truancy, running away, sexual misconduct) are illegal only because of their minority status.

Some experts have called for an end to juvenile court control over status offenders, charging that it further stigmatizes already troubled youths. Some research indicates that status offenders are harmed by juvenile court processing. Other research indicates that status offenders and delinquents are quite similar. There has been a successful effort to separate status offenders from delinquents and to maintain separate facilities for those who need to be placed in a shelter care program. Some jurisdictions have implemented curfew and parental laws, but so far there is little evidence that they work as intended. Research indicates that neither attempt at controlling youthful misbehavior works as planned. Consequently, the treatment of juveniles is an ongoing dilemma. Still uncertain is whether young law violators respond better to harsh punishments or to benevolent treatment.

KEY TERMS

ego identity, p. 3
role diffusion, p. 3
at-risk youths, p. 3
juvenile delinquency, p. 10
chronic juvenile offenders, p. 11
juvenile justice system, p. 11
paternalistic family, p. 11
Poor Laws, p. 13

chancery courts, p. 13
parens patriae, p. 13
child savers, p. 15
House of Refuge, p. 15
Children's Aid Society, p. 16
orphan trains, p. 16
Law Enforcement Assistance
  Administration (LEAA), p. 19

Office of Juvenile Justice and
  Delinquency Prevention
  (OJJDP), p. 19
delinquent, p. 20
best interests of the child, p. 20
need for treatment, p. 21
waiver (bindover, removal), p. 21
status offender, p. 21

REVIEW QUESTIONS

1. What are the effects of poverty, family problems, urban decay, inadequate education, teen pregnancy, and social conflict on American youth?

2. Compare early and contemporary family life. What are the differences in such issues as parental controls, punishment, and role taking?

3. What is meant by the term *"parens patriae* philosophy"? How is this manifested in modern society?

4. In what ways are delinquents given greater legal protection than adult criminals, and how they are shielded from stigma and labels?

5. What is meant by the concept of waiver and how is it being used today?

6. What are examples of status offenses?

7. What are the pros and cons of parental responsibility laws?

8. Discuss the trends in juvenile curfews.

QUESTIONS FOR DISCUSSION

1. Is it fair to have a separate legal category for youths? Considering how dangerous young people can be, does it make more sense to group offenders on the basis of what they have done rather than on their age?

2. At what age are juveniles truly capable of understanding the seriousness of their actions? Should juvenile court jurisdiction be raised or lowered?

3. Is it fair to institutionalize a minor simply for being truant or running away from home? Should the jurisdiction of status offenders be removed from juvenile court and placed with the state's department of social services or some other welfare organization?

4. Should delinquency proceedings be secret? Does the public have a right to know who juvenile criminals are?

5. Can a "get tough" policy help control juvenile misbehavior, or should *parens patriae* remain the standard?

6. Should juveniles who commit felonies such as rape or robbery be treated as adults?

APPLYING WHAT YOU HAVE LEARNED

You have just been appointed by the governor as chairperson of a newly formed group charged with overhauling the state's juvenile justice system. One primary concern is the treatment of status offenders—kids who have been picked up and charged with being runaways, sexually active, truant from school, or unmanageable at home. Under existing status offense statutes, these youth can be sent to juvenile court and stand trial for their misbehaviors. If the allegations against them are proven valid, they may be removed from the home and placed in foster care or even in a state or private custodial institution.

Recently, a great deal of media attention has been given to the plight of runaway children who live on the streets, take drugs, and engage in prostitution. At an open hearing, advocates of the current system argue that many families cannot provide the care and control needed to keep kids out of trouble and that the state must maintain control of at-risk youth. They contend that many status offenders have histories of drug and delinquency problems and are little different from kids arrested on criminal charges; control by the juvenile court is necessary if the youths are ever to get needed treatment.

Another vocal group argues that it is a mistake for a system that deals with criminal youth to also handle troubled adolescents, whose problems usually are the result of child abuse and neglect. They believe that the current statute should be amended to give the state's department of social welfare (DSW) jurisdiction over all noncriminal youths who are in need of assistance. These opponents of the current law point out that, even though status offenders and delinquents are held in separate facilities, those who run away or are unmanageable can be transferred to more secure correctional facilities that house criminal youths. Furthermore, the current court-based process, where troubled youths are involved with lawyers, trials, and court proceedings, helps convince them that they are "bad kids" and social outcasts.

Writing Assignment: Write a policy statement setting out the recommendations you would make to the governor. In your statement, address the issues raised by those who believe that status offenders and delinquents have similar issues, and those who maintain they are two separate categories of youth and should be dealt with by different state agencies. Finally, give your assessment of the issue and what course of treatment you would choose.

GROUPWORK

Divide the class into equal number groups and have each group identify an aspect of childhood that is still controlled by the court system and governed by the *parens patriae* philosophy.

Each group should choose a single behavior pattern such as sex, substance use, running away, truancy, and so on. Have them gather laws that govern these activities in the "best interests of the child."

CHAPTER TWO

The Nature and Extent of Delinquency

© Hector Mata/AFP/Getty Images

LEARNING OBJECTIVES

After reading this chapter you should:

1. Be familiar with the various ways to gather data on delinquency.
2. Recognize the trends in the delinquency rate and the factors that influence and shape its direction.
3. List and discuss the social and personal correlates of delinquency.
4. Discuss the concept of the chronic offender.
5. Be familiar with the factors that predict teen victimization.

Members of the Pico Norte 19th Street gang pose flashing their hand signs in El Paso, Texas.

Jamesetta's Story

Jamesetta was born in a poor, urban neighborhood. As her parents struggled with substance abuse, poverty, and unemployment, Jamesetta suffered both physical and sexual abuse before being placed in foster care at the age of 5. By the age of 9, Jamesetta was shoplifting, skipping school, and violating curfew. At age 13, she physically assaulted her foster mother and entered the juvenile justice system with charges of disorderly conduct and being a habitual delinquent. Her foster home placement was terminated, and Jamesetta was sent to live with her aunt, uncle, and six cousins. It wasn't long before her relatives began to have additional concerns that Jamesetta was exhibiting sexualized behavior, "sneaking around" with her 17-year-old boyfriend, staying out all night, and being disrespectful. They felt she was out of control.

Jamesetta had been ordered by the juvenile court to cooperate with her family's household rules, attend school on a regular basis, have no further law violations, complete 25 hours of community service, and pay restitution for the shoplifting, but she refused to cooperate with any of the programs or services, continuing to come and go as she pleased. The family was receiving support from Jamesetta's intensive supervision program counselor, as well as a family therapist, but during the second month of placement with her relatives, at the age of 14, Jamesetta disclosed that she was pregnant and

planning to keep her baby. The program counselor and other professionals involved in Jamesetta's case had to work with her and her family to reevaluate their plan.

Jamesetta was enrolled in a school specifically designed to support teens who were pregnant or already parenting, where in addition to her academic studies to complete high school, she would receive help from parenting classes, independent living courses, and relationship counseling. Even with these additional supports and interventions, Jamesetta continued to have status offenses. She skipped school, didn't come home on time, and would not follow household rules; however, she did not have any further law violations.

After the baby was born, Jamesetta began to understand the consequences of her actions. With continued services and support from her counselors, she started following the rules and expectations of her family. Upon taking responsibility to find the necessary medical and child care for her daughter, Jamesetta found employment, a position in retail, and started planning for her future. Despite being at high risk for dropping out of school, Jamesetta was able to complete her high school education and have a positive view of her future. The team of involved professionals continued to provide needed support and encouraged Jamesetta to make good decisions for herself and her new baby. She still struggles at times, but has remained free of further law violations.

High-risk kids such as Jamesetta get involved in more than 1 million serious illegal acts each year. Who commits delinquent acts, and where are they most likely to occur? Is the juvenile crime rate increasing or decreasing? Are juveniles more likely than adults to become the victims of crime? To understand the causes of delinquent behavior and to devise effective means to reduce its occurrence, we must seek answers to these questions.

Delinquency experts have devised a variety of methods to measure the nature and extent of delinquency. We begin with a description of the most widely used sources of data on crime and delinquency. We also examine the information these resources furnish on juvenile crime rates and trends. These data sources will then be used to provide information on the characteristics of adolescent law violators.

Federal Bureau of Investigation (FBI) Arm of the U.S. Department of Justice that investigates violations of federal law, gathers crime statistics, runs a comprehensive crime laboratory, and helps train local law enforcement officers.

MEASURING DELINQUENCY WITH THE UNIFORM CRIME REPORTS

Each year, the U.S. Justice Department's **Federal Bureau of Investigation (FBI)** compiles information gathered by police departments on the number of criminal acts reported by citizens and the number of persons arrested.[1] This information is published in the annual **Uniform Crime Report (UCR)**, which is the most widely used source of national crime and delinquency statistics.

The UCR is compiled from statistics sent to the FBI from more than 17,000 police departments. It groups offenses into two categories. **Part I offenses** include homicide and non-negligent manslaughter, forcible rape, robbery, aggravated assault, burglary, larceny, arson, and motor vehicle theft. Police record every reported incident of these offenses and report them on a quarterly basis to the FBI. Data are broken down by city, county, metropolitan area, and geographical divisions. In addition, the UCR provides information on individuals who have been arrested for these and all other criminal offenses, including vandalism, liquor law violations, and drug trafficking; these are known as **Part II offenses**. The arrest data are then presented by age, sex, and race.

In addition, each month, law enforcement agencies also report how many crimes were cleared. Crimes are cleared in two ways: (1) when at least one person is arrested, charged, and turned over to the court for prosecution, or (2) by exceptional means, when some element beyond police control precludes the physical arrest of an offender (for example, the offender leaves the country). Data on the number of clearances involving the arrest of only juvenile offenders, data on the value of property stolen and recovered in connection with Part I offenses, and detailed information pertaining to criminal homicide are also reported. Nationwide in 2010, 47 percent of violent crimes and 18 percent of property crimes were cleared by arrest or exceptional means (see Figure 2.1 for a breakdown of crimes cleared by arrest).

Violent crimes are more likely to be solved than property crimes because police devote more resources to these more serious acts, witnesses (including the victim) are frequently available to identify offenders, and in many instances the victim and offender were previously acquainted.

The UCR uses three methods to express crime data. First, the number of crimes reported to the police and arrests made are expressed as raw figures (for example, in 2010, 14,748 murders occurred). Second, crime rates per 100,000 people are computed. In other words, when the UCR indicates that the murder rate was about

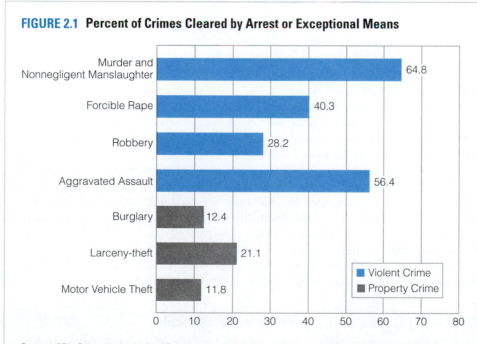

FIGURE 2.1 Percent of Crimes Cleared by Arrest or Exceptional Means

Murder and Nonnegligent Manslaughter — 64.8
Forcible Rape — 40.3
Robbery — 28.2
Aggravated Assault — 56.4
Burglary — 12.4
Larceny-theft — 21.1
Motor Vehicle Theft — 11.8

■ Violent Crime
■ Property Crime

Source: FBI, *Crime in the United States, 2010*, www.fbi.gov/about-us/cjis/ucr/crime-in-the-u.s/2010/crime-in-the-u.s.-2010/clearances (accessed June 25, 2012).

Uniform Crime Report (UCR) Compiled by the FBI, the UCR is the most widely used source of national crime and delinquency statistics.

Part I offenses Offenses including homicide and non-negligent manslaughter, forcible rape, robbery, aggravated assault, burglary, larceny, arson, and motor vehicle theft. Recorded by local law enforcement officers, these crimes are tallied quarterly and sent to the FBI for inclusion in the UCR.

Part II offenses All crimes other than Part I offenses. Recorded by local law enforcement officers, arrests for these crimes are tallied quarterly and sent to the FBI for inclusion in the UCR.

4.8 in 2010, it means that almost 5 people in every 100,000 were murdered between January 1 and December 31, 2010. This is the equation used:

$$\frac{\text{Number of Reported Crimes}}{\text{Total U.S. Population}} \times 100,000 = \text{Rate per } 100,000$$

Third, the FBI computes changes in the number and rate of crimes over time. Even though almost 15,000 murders in a year seems like a lot, the number and rate of murder has declined significantly over the past 20 years: in 1991, there were almost 25,000 murders recorded, a rate of 9.8 per 100,000 citizens.

Validity of the UCR

While it is widely used as a measure of crime rates and trends, the UCR's "official crime data" is not without its critics. Because official UCR data are derived entirely from police records, we can assume that a significant number of crimes are not accounted for in the UCR. There are also concerns that police departments make systematic errors in recording crime data or manipulate the data in order to give the public the impression that they are highly effective crime fighters.[2]

Using official arrest data to measure delinquency rates is particularly problematic for a number of reasons:

- Victim surveys show that less than half of all victims report the crime to police. Teens are unlikely to report crimes to police in which they are most vulnerable: crimes committed by peers that occur on school grounds.[3] They may be more willing to talk to parents than they are to police.

- The arrest data count only adolescents who have been *caught*, and these youths may be different from those who evade capture.

- Victimless crimes, such as drug and alcohol use, are significantly undercounted using this measure. Teens may be the group most likely to use illicit drugs and engage in alcohol violations.

- Arrest decision criteria vary among police agencies. Some police agencies practice full enforcement, arresting all teens who violate the law, whereas others follow a policy of discretion that encourages unofficial handling of juvenile matters through social service agencies. Hence, regional differences in the delinquency rate may reflect police arrest practices and not delinquent activities.

While these issues are troubling, UCR arrest statistics are **disaggregated** (broken down) by suspect's age, so they can be used to estimate adolescent delinquency. However, juvenile arrest data must be interpreted with caution. First, the number of teenagers arrested does not represent the actual number of youths who have committed delinquent acts. Some offenders are never counted, because they are never caught. Others are counted more than once because multiple arrests of the same individual for different crimes are counted separately in the UCR. Consequently, the total number of arrests does not equal the number of people who have been arrested. Put another way, if 2 million arrests of youths under 18 years of age were made in a given year, we could not be sure if 2 million individuals had been arrested once or if 500,000 chronic offenders had been arrested four times each. In addition, when an arrested offender commits multiple crimes, only the most serious one is recorded. Therefore, if 2 million juveniles are arrested, the number of crimes committed is at least 2 million, but it may be much higher.

Despite these limitations, the nature of arrest data remains constant over time so it can provide some indication of trends in juvenile crime.

disaggregated Analyzing the relationship between two or more independent variables (such as murder convictions and death sentence) while controlling for the influence of a dependent variable (such as race).

Measuring Delinquency with Survey Research

Another important method of collecting crime data is through surveys in which people are asked about their attitudes, beliefs, values, and characteristics, as well as their experiences with crime and victimization. Surveys typically involve

sampling, the process of selecting for study a limited number of subjects who are representative of an entire group that has similar characteristics, called the **population**. To understand the social forces that produce crime, a criminologist might interview a sample of 3,000 prison inmates drawn from the population of more than 2 million inmates in the United States; in this case, the sample should represent the entire population of U.S. inmates. It is assumed that the characteristics of people or events in a carefully selected sample will be similar to those of the entire population.

The National Crime Victimization Survey (NCVS)

Because many victims do not report their experiences to the police, the UCR cannot measure all the annual criminal activity. To address the nonreporting issue, the federal government sponsors the National Crime Victimization Survey (NCVS), a comprehensive, nationwide survey of victimization in the United States conducted annually by the U.S. Census Bureau for the Bureau of Justice Statistics (BJS).

In the most recent survey, about 40,000 households and more than 70,000 individuals age 12 or older were interviewed twice for the NCVS.[4] Households stay in the sample for three years. New households are rotated into the sample on an ongoing basis. The NCVS collects information on crimes suffered by individuals and households, whether or not those crimes were reported to law enforcement. It estimates the proportion of each crime type reported to law enforcement, and it summarizes the reasons that victims give for reporting or not reporting. In 1993, the survey was redesigned to provide detailed information on the frequency and nature of the crimes of rape, sexual assault, personal robbery, aggravated and simple assault, household burglary, theft, and motor vehicle theft. In 2006, significant changes were made to the way the NCVS is collected, so victimization estimates are not totally comparable to previous years. The methodological changes included a new sampling method, a change in the method of handling first-time interviews with households, and a change in the method of interviewing. Some selected areas were dropped from the sample while others were added. Finally, computer-assisted personal interviewing (CAPI) replaced paper and pencil interviewing (PAPI). While these issues are critical, there is no substitute available that provides national information on crime and victimization with extensive detail on victims and the social context of the criminal event.

The survey provides information about victims (age, sex, race, ethnicity, marital status, income, and educational level), offenders (sex, race, approximate age, and victim–offender relationship), and crimes (time and place of occurrence, use of weapons, nature of injury, and economic consequences). Questions also cover the experiences of victims with the criminal justice system, self-protective measures used by victims, and possible substance abuse by offenders. Supplements are added periodically to the survey to obtain detailed information on topics such as school crime.

The greatest advantage of the NCVS over official data sources such as the UCR is that it can estimate the total amount of annual crimes, not just those that are reported to police. Nonreporting is a significant issue: fewer than half of all violent victimizations and about a third of all property crimes are routinely reported to the police. As a result, the NCVS provides a more nearly complete picture of the nation's crime problem. Also, because some crimes are significantly underreported, the NCVS is an indispensable measure of their occurrence. Take the crime of rape and sexual assault, of which only about 40 percent of incidents are reported to police. The UCR reports that slightly more than 85,000 rapes or attempted rapes occur each year, compared to about 188,000 uncovered by the NCVS. In addition, the NCVS helps us understand why crimes are not reported to police and whether the type and nature of the criminal event influences whether the police will ever know it occurred. With the crime of rape, research shows that victims are much more likely to report rape if it is accompanied by another crime, such as robbery, than they are if the rape is the only crime that occurred. Official data alone cannot provide that type of information.[5]

sampling Selecting a limited number of people for study as representative of a larger group.
population All people who share a particular characteristic, such as all high school students or all police officers.

Validity of the NCVS. Although its utility and importance are unquestioned, the NCVS may suffer from some methodological problems. As a result, its findings must be interpreted with caution. Among the potential problems are the following:

- Overreporting due to victims' misinterpretation of events. A lost wallet may be reported as stolen or an open door may be viewed as a burglary attempt.

- Underreporting due to the embarrassment of reporting crime to interviewers, fear of getting in trouble, or simply forgetting an incident.

- Inability to record the personal criminal activity of those interviewed, such as drug use or gambling; murder is also not included, for obvious reasons.

- Sampling errors, which produce a group of respondents who do not represent the nation as a whole.

- Inadequate question format that invalidates responses. Some groups, such as adolescents, may be particularly susceptible to error because of question format.[6]

Self-Report Surveys

Another survey tool commonly used to measure the extent of delinquency is the **self-report survey** that asks adolescents to describe, in detail, their recent and lifetime participation in criminal activity. Self-reports are given in groups, and the respondents are promised anonymity in order to ensure the validity and honesty of their responses. Most self-report studies have focused on juvenile delinquency and youth crime.[7] However, self-reports can also be used to examine the offense histories of prison inmates, drug users, and other segments of the criminal population.[8]

Most self-report surveys also contain questions about attitudes, values, and behaviors. There may be questions about a participant's substance abuse history ("How many times have you used marijuana or cocaine?") and the participant's family history ("Did your parents ever strike you with a stick or a belt?"). By correlating the responses, criminologists can analyze the relationship between personal factors and criminal behaviors and explore such issues as whether people who report being abused as children are also more likely to use drugs as adults and whether school failure leads to delinquency.[9]

Validity of Self-Reports. Critics of self-report studies frequently suggest that expecting adolescents to candidly admit illegal acts is unreasonable. This is especially true of those with official records—the very adolescents who may be engaging in the most criminality. Some adolescents may forget some of their criminal activities or be confused about what is being asked. Some surveys contain an overabundance of trivial offenses, such as shoplifting small items or using false identification to obtain alcohol, often lumped together with serious crimes to form a total crime index. Consequently, comparisons between groups can be highly misleading. Responses may also be embellished by some subjects who wish to exaggerate the extent of their deviant activities, and understated by others who want to shield themselves from possible exposure. Research by David Kirk shows that some kids with an official arrest record deny legal involvement, whereas others who remain arrest-free report having an official record. Why would adolescents claim to have engaged in antisocial behaviors, such as getting arrested or using drugs, when in fact they had not? One reason is that they may live in a subculture that requires kids to be tough rule breakers unafraid of conventional authority. Kids may fear that they would be taunted or harassed if anyone found out they were not really "experienced" delinquents.[10] In other cultures, offending is considered unacceptable and kids may underreport their involvement in delinquency. Such culturally related differences in self-reporting can skew data and provide misleading results.[11]

The "missing cases" phenomenon is also a concern. Even if 90 percent of a school population voluntarily participate in a self-report study, researchers can never be sure whether the few who refuse to participate or are absent that day constitute a significant portion of the school's population of persistent high-rate offenders. Research indicates that offenders with the most extensive prior criminality are the

self-report survey A research approach that requires subjects to reveal their own participation in delinquent or criminal acts.

most likely "to be poor historians of their own crime commission rates."[12] It is also unlikely that the most serious chronic offenders in the teenage population are willing to cooperate with criminologists administering self-report tests.[13] Institutionalized youths, who are not generally represented in the self-report surveys, not only are more delinquent than the general youth population but also are considerably more misbehaving than the most delinquent youths identified in the typical self-report survey.[14] Consequently, self-reports may measure only nonserious, occasional delinquents, while ignoring hard-core chronic offenders who may be institutionalized and unavailable for self-reports.

To address these criticisms, various techniques have been used to verify self-report data.[15] The "known group" method compares youths known to be offenders with those who are not, to see whether the former report more delinquency. Research shows that when kids are asked whether they have ever been arrested or sent to court, their responses accurately reflect their true life experiences.[16]

One way to improve the reliability of self-reports is to use them in a consistent fashion with different groups of subjects over time. That makes it possible to measure trends in self-reported crime and drug abuse to see whether changes have occurred. One example is the Monitoring the Future study, which researchers at the University of Michigan Institute for Social Research (ISR) have been conducting annually since 1978. This national survey typically involves thousands of high school students each year and is one of the most important sources of self-report data.[17]

Although these studies are supportive, self-report data must be interpreted with some caution. Asking subjects about their past behavior may capture more serious crimes but miss minor criminal acts; that is, adolescents remember armed robberies and rapes better than they do minor assaults and altercations.[18] In addition, some classes of offenders (for example, substance abusers) may have a tough time accounting for their prior misbehavior.[19]

Evaluating the Primary Data Sources

Each source of crime data has strengths and weaknesses. The FBI survey contains data on the number and characteristics of adolescents arrested, information that

It is often difficult to measure the full extent of delinquency because many acts are not included in the UCR. Here, a young man is escorted past his family after a court appearance on a charge of making a false bomb threat while boarding a flight. Would this act be reported to the FBI's program?

the other data sources lack. Some recent research indicates that for serious crimes, such as drug trafficking, arrest data can provide a meaningful measure of the level of criminal activity in a particular neighborhood environment, which other data sources cannot provide. It is also the source of information on particular crimes such as murder, which no other data source can provide.[20] The UCR remains the standard unit of analysis on which most criminological research is based. However, this survey omits the many crimes that victims choose not to report to police, and it is subject to the reporting caprices of individual police departments.

The NCVS includes unreported crime and important information on the personal characteristics of victims. However, the data consist of estimates made from relatively limited samples of the total U.S. population, so even narrow fluctuations in the rates of some crimes can have a major impact on findings. The NCVS also relies on personal recollections that may be inaccurate. It does not include data on important crime patterns, including murder and drug abuse.

Self-report surveys can provide information on the personal characteristics of offenders (such as their attitudes, values, beliefs, and psychological profiles) that is unavailable from any other source. Yet, at their core, self-reports rely on the honesty of criminal offenders and drug abusers, a population not generally known for accuracy and integrity. Consequently, discrepancies and inaccuracies do occur.[21]

Although their tallies of crimes are certainly not in synch, the crime patterns and trends that all three sources record are often quite similar.[22] For example, they all generally agree about the personal characteristics of serious criminals (such as age and gender) and where and when crime occurs (such as urban areas, nighttime, and summer months). When David Kirk compared self-report and official data, he found that despite significant differences on arrest reporting, the effects of family supervision, parent–child conflict, and neighborhood disadvantage operate similarly across data types.[23] In addition, the problems inherent in each source are consistent over time. Therefore, even if the data sources are incapable of providing a precise and valid count of delinquency at any given time, they are reliable indicators of changes and fluctuations in yearly delinquency rates. Concept Summary 2.1 lists the main characteristics of these sources of delinquency data.

CONCEPT SUMMARY 2.1 | Data Collection Methods

Uniform Crime Report
- Data are collected from records from police departments across the nation, crimes reported to police, and arrests.
- Strengths of the UCR are that it measures homicides and arrests and that it is a consistent, national sample.
- Weaknesses of the UCR are that it omits crimes not reported to police, omits most drug usage, and contains reporting errors.

National Crime Victimization Survey
- Data are collected from a large national survey.
- Strengths of the NCVS are that it includes crimes not reported to the police, uses careful sampling techniques, and is a yearly survey.
- Weaknesses of the NCVS are that it relies on victims' memory and honesty and that it omits substance abuse.

Self-Report Surveys
- Data are collected from local surveys.
- Strengths of self-report surveys are that they include unreported crimes, substance abuse, and offenders' personal information.
- Weaknesses of self-report surveys are that they rely on the honesty of offenders and omit offenders who refuse or are unable, as a consequence of incarceration, to participate (and who therefore may be the most deviant).

In addition to these primary sources of crime data, other data collection methods have been used to measure delinquent behavior. These are discussed in Exhibit 2.1.

Crime Trends in the United States

In general, crime rates increased gradually following the 1930s until the 1960s, when the growth rate became much greater. The homicide rate, which had actually declined from the 1930s to the 1960s, also began a sharp increase that continued through the 1970s; by 1991, police recorded about 15 million crimes. Since then, the number of crimes has been in decline; today, about 10 million crimes occur each year despite the fact that the population increased by about 60 million people since 1991.

In addition to these data, the UCR finds that about 13 million arrests are now being made each year, or about 4,200 per 100,000 population. Of these, more than 2 million were for serious Part I crimes and 11 million for less serious Part II crimes. The number of people arrested has remained about the same during the past decade; arrests for serious violent crime were down about 8 percent while arrests for property crimes actually increased about 16 percent.

Delinquency Trends. Today, juveniles are responsible for about 14 percent of the Part I violent crime arrests and about 23 percent of the property crime arrests

---

EXHIBIT 2.1 Alternative Measures of Delinquent Behavior

Cohort Research Data

Collecting cohort data involves observing over time a group of people who share certain characteristics. If the cohort is carefully drawn, it may be possible to accumulate a complex array of data that can be used to determine which life experiences are associated with criminal careers. Another approach is to take a contemporary cohort, and then look back into their past—a format known as a retrospective cohort study.

Experimental Data

Sometimes criminologists conduct controlled experiments to collect data on the cause of crime. To conduct experimental research, criminologists manipulate, or intervene in, the lives of their subjects to see the outcome or the effect of the intervention. True experiments usually have three elements: (1) random selection of subjects, (2) a control or comparison group, and (3) an experimental condition.

Observational and Interview Research

Sometimes criminologists focus their research on relatively few subjects, interviewing them in depth or observing them as they go about their activities. This research often results in the kind of in-depth data that large-scale surveys do not yield.

Meta-analysis and Systematic Review

Meta-analysis involves gathering data from a number of previous studies. Compatible information and data are extracted and pooled together. When analyzed, the grouped data from several different studies provide a more powerful and valid indicator of relationships than the results provided by a single study. A systematic review involves collecting the findings from previously conducted scientific studies that address a particular problem, appraising and synthesizing the evidence, and using the collective evidence to address a particular scientific question.

Sources: Rod K. Brunson and Jody Miller, "Schools, Neighborhoods, and Adolescent Conflicts: A Situational Examination of Reciprocal Dynamics," *Justice Quarterly* 26:1–28 (2009); William F. Whyte, *Street Corner Society* (Chicago: University of Chicago Press, 1955), p. 38; David Farrington and Brandon Welsh, "Improved Street Lighting and Crime Prevention," *Justice Quarterly* 19:313–343 (2006).

TABLE 2.1 Persons Arrested, by Age

	Under 15	Under 18	Over 18
Serious violent crime	4%	14%	86%
Serious property crime	6%	23%	77%
Total all crimes	3%	13%	87%

Source: FBI, *Crime in the United States, 2010,* Table 38, www.fbi.gov/about-us/cjis/ucr/crime-in-the-u.s/2010/crime-in-the-u.s.-2010/tables/10tbl38.xls (accessed June 25, 2012).

(see Table 2.1). Because kids ages 14 through 17 (who account for almost all underage arrests) constitute only about 6 percent of the population, these data show that teens account for a significantly disproportionate share of all arrests.

An additional 900,000 juvenile arrests are now being made each year for Part II offenses that include less serious acts such as drug abuse violations, prostitution, and vandalism. Part II arrests also include status offenses, including more than 120,000 for disorderly conduct and 70,000 for curfew violations.

While juvenile offenders continue to be overrepresented in the crime rate, the number and rate of juvenile offenses and offenders have been in a decade-long decline. The juvenile arrest rate began to climb in the 1980s, peaked during the mid-1990s, and then began to fall; it has since been in decline. Even the teen murder rate, which had remained stubbornly high, has undergone a decline of more than 20 percent during the past decade. The actual number of minors arrested for murder annually has declined from 1,500 in 1998 to less than 800 today. Similarly, 3,800 juveniles were arrested for rape in 1998, compared to about 2,200 today. In all, during the past decade, the number of juvenile arrests declined more than 23 percent; juvenile property crime arrests declined 25 percent and violent crime arrests declined about 22 percent. **CHECKPOINTS**

Self-Reported Patterns and Trends

Most self-report studies indicate that the number of children who break the law is far greater than official statistics would lead us to believe and that a great deal of juvenile delinquency is unknown to the police; these unrecorded delinquent acts are referred to as the **dark figures of crime**.[24] In fact, when truancy, alcohol consumption, petty theft, and recreational drug use are included in self-report scales, delinquency appears to be almost universal. The most common offenses are truancy, drinking alcohol, using a false ID, shoplifting or larceny under five dollars, fighting, using marijuana, and damaging the property of others. In Chapter 10, self-report data will be used to gauge trends in adolescent drug abuse.

Monitoring the Future, the annual national self-report survey conducted by the Institute for Social Research (ISR) is probably the nation's most important ongoing self-report survey. Each year, a total of approximately 50,000 8th-, 10th-, and 12th-grade students are surveyed (12th-graders since 1975, and 8th- and 10th-graders since 1991).[25] Table 2.2 contains some of the data from the most recent MTF survey.

A surprising number of these *typical* teenagers reported involvement in serious criminal behavior: about 14 percent reported hurting someone badly enough that the victim needed medical care (7 percent said they did it more than once); about 27 percent reported stealing something worth less than $50, and another 11 percent stole something worth more than $50; 27 percent reported shoplifting; 10 percent had damaged school property.

If the MTF data are accurate, the juvenile crime problem is much greater than official statistics would lead us to

dark figures of crime Incidents of crime and delinquency that go undetected by police.

CHECKPOINTS

LO1 Be familiar with the various ways to gather data on delinquency.

✔ The FBI's Uniform Crime Report is an annual tally of crime reported to local police departments; it is the nation's official crime data.

✔ Self-report surveys ask respondents about their criminal activity.

✔ They are useful in measuring crimes such as drug usage that are rarely reported to police.

✔ Self-reports show that a significant number of kids engage in criminal acts, far more than is measured by the arrest data.

✔ The National Crime Victimization Survey collects data from a large national survey in order to make estimates of the annual number of criminal victimizations.

TABLE 2.2 Monitoring the Future Survey of Criminal Activity of High School Seniors—Percentage Engaging in Offenses

Type of Delinquency	Committed at Least Once	Committed More than Once
Set fire on purpose	2%	1%
Damaged school property	5%	5%
Damaged work property	2%	2%
Auto theft	2%	3%
Auto part theft	2%	3%
Break and enter	11%	13%
Theft, less than $50	12%	15%
Theft, more than $50	6%	5%
Shoplift	11%	16%
Gang or group fight	10%	8%
Hurt someone badly enough to require medical care	7%	7%
Used force or a weapon to steal	2%	2%
Hit teacher or supervisor	1%	3%
Participated in serious fight	6%	6%

Source: *Monitoring the Future, 2010* (Ann Arbor, MI: Institute for Social Research, 2012).

While the overall delinquency rate has trended downward, self-report studies show that delinquency has remained more stable. Here, Gabriel Huston, left, and Robert Woodard, members of the Cleveland Peacemakers Alliance, talk with a girl gang member who reported being jumped as school let out at John F. Kennedy High School.

© Gus Chan/*The Plain Dealer*/Landov

believe. There are approximately 40 million youths between the ages of 10 and 18. Extrapolating from the MTF findings, this group accounts for more than 100 percent of all the theft offenses reported in the UCR. About 4 percent of high school students said they had used force to steal (which is the legal definition of a robbery). At this rate, high school students alone commit more than 1.6 million robberies per

SHAPING TEEN CRIME TRENDS

Delinquency rates have risen and fallen during the past few decades. What causes rates to climb, peak, fall, and rise once again? Crime experts have identified a variety of social, economic, personal, and demographic factors that influence delinquency rate trends, and some of the most important influences are discussed below.

Population Makeup

It is sad but true that the general crime rate follows the proportion of young males in the population: teens commit more crime than adults, so more teens means more crime. One reason is that a surge in the teenage population strains both the educational and welfare systems, resulting in fewer services for at-risk kids and increasing the chance that they will engage in antisocial activities. A large teen cohort also reduces the likelihood of employment and admission to college (since admissions and scholarships tend to lag population growth). As a result, illegal activities such as gang membership and drug dealing may become attractive alternatives to conventional methods of achievement. The number of juveniles should be increasing over the next decade, and some crime experts fear this will signal a return to escalating crime rates.

Economy and Jobs

It seems logical that when the economy turns downward, kids who find it hard to get after-school jobs or find employment after they leave school could be motivated to seek other forms of income such as theft and drug dealing. This has been the subject of some controversy because the existing research data show that kids with jobs are actually the most delinquent. The lack of supervision and freedom presented by a job counteracts the economic benefits of employment. In fact, the only unemployed teens who report high crime rates are ones who want to work long hours but are unable to find work.

Another reason the lack of jobs may actually reduce crime rates is that unemployed parents have more time to supervise kids after school and keep them out of trouble. Because there is less money to spend, people have fewer valuables worth stealing and those who do are more likely to carefully guard what they own. It is also unlikely that a law-abiding teen will suddenly join a gang because he or she can't get a summer job.

Social Problems

As the level of social problems increases, so do delinquency rates. For example, delinquency rates tend to rise when the number of unwed teenage mothers in the population increases. The teenage birth rate has trended downward in recent years, and so have delinquency rates. Racial conflict may also increase delinquency rates. Areas undergoing racial change, especially those experiencing a migration of minorities into predominantly European American neighborhoods, seem prone to significant increases in their delinquency rate. Racially motivated crimes actually diminish as neighborhoods become more integrated and power struggles are resolved.

Abortion

John J. Donohue III and Steven D. Levitt found empirical evidence that the drop in the delinquency rate can be attributed to the availability of legalized abortion. It is possible that the link between delinquency rates and abortion is the result of two independent mechanisms: (1) selective abortion on the part of women most at risk to have children who will eventually engage in delinquent activity, (2) improved childrearing or environmental circumstances, because women are having fewer children.

Immigration

Some political figures decry high rates of illegal immigration, suggesting that "illegals" have high delinquency rates and undermine social stability. However, research conducted by highly respected scholars finds that immigrants are

---

year. In comparison, the UCR now tallies about 360,000 robberies for all age groups yearly. Moreover, while official data show that the overall crime rate is in decline, the MTF surveys indicate that, with a few exceptions, self-reported teenage participation in theft, violence, and damage-related crimes seems to be more stable than the trends reported in the UCR arrest data.

What factors account for change in the crime and delinquency rate? This is the topic of the Focus on Delinquency feature entitled "Shaping Teen Crime Trends."

actually less crime prone than the general population and that there is little (if any) association between delinquency rates and the immigrant population.

Guns

The availability of firearms may influence the delinquency rate, especially the proliferation of weapons in the hands of teens. Surveys of high school students indicate that between 6 and 10 percent carry guns at least some of the time. Guns also cause escalation in the seriousness of delinquency. As the number of gun-toting students increases, so does the seriousness of violent delinquency: a schoolyard fight may well turn into murder.

Gangs

According to government sources, there are now more than 800,000 gang members in the United States and 24,000 gangs. Criminal gangs commit as much as 80 percent of the crime in many communities, including armed robbery, assault, auto theft, drug trafficking, extortion, fraud, home invasions, identity theft, murder, and weapons trafficking. Gang members are far more likely to possess guns than non-gang members; criminal activity increases when kids join gangs. Drug-dealing gangs are heavily armed, a condition that persuades non–gang-affiliated kids to arm themselves for self-protection. The result is an arms race that produces an increasing spiral of violence.

Drug Use

Some experts tie increases in the violent delinquency rate between 1980 and 1990 to the crack epidemic, which swept the nation's largest cities, and to drug-trafficking gangs that fought over drug turf. These well-armed gangs did not hesitate to use violence to control territory, intimidate rivals, and increase market share. As the crack epidemic has subsided, so has the violence in New York City and other metropolitan areas where crack use was rampant. A sudden increase in drug use, on the other hand, may be a harbinger of future increases in the delinquency rate.

Media

Some experts argue that violent media can influence the direction of delinquency rates. The introduction of home video players, DVDs, cable TV, computers, and video games coincided with increasing teen violence rates. Perhaps the increased availability of media violence on these platforms produced more aggressive teens? Watching violence on TV may be correlated with aggressive behaviors, especially when viewers have a preexisting tendency toward delinquency and violence. Research shows that the more kids watch TV, the more often they get into violent encounters. While this logic seems persuasive, teen violence rates have declined while availability of violent media has become commonplace.

Juvenile Justice Policy

Some law enforcement experts have suggested that a reduction in delinquency rates may be attributed to adding large numbers of police officers and using them in aggressive police practices aimed at reducing gang membership, gun possession, and substance abuse. It is also possible that tough laws such as waiving juveniles to adult courts or sending them to adult prisons can affect crime rates. The fear of punishment may inhibit some would-be delinquents, and tough laws place a significant number of chronic juvenile offenders behind bars, lowering delinquency rates.

CRITICAL THINKING

Although juvenile delinquency rates have been declining in the United States, they have been increasing in Europe. Is it possible that factors that correlate with delinquency rate changes in the United States have little utility in predicting changes in other cultures? What other factors may increase or reduce delinquency rates?

Writing Assignment This list of factors is not exhaustive. Write an essay that lists and discusses some of the other factors that you believe influence the delinquency rate.

Sources: Jeremy Staff, D. Wayne Osgood, John Schulenberg, Jerald Bachman, and Emily Messersmith, "Explaining the Relationship Between Employment and Juvenile Delinquency," *Criminology* 48:1101–1131 (2010); Tim Wadsworth, "Is Immigration Responsible for the Crime Drop? An Assessment of the Influence of Immigration on Changes in Violent Crime Between 1990 and 2000," *Social Science Quarterly* 91:531–553 (2010); Carter Hay and Michelle M. Evans, "Has *Roe v. Wade* Reduced U.S. Crime Rates? Examining the Link Between Mothers' Pregnancy Intentions and Children's Later Involvement in Law-Violating Behavior," *Journal of Research in Crime and Delinquency* 43:36–66 (2006); Jacob I. Stowell, Steven F. Messner, Kelly McGeever, and Lawrence Raffalovich, "Immigration and the Recent Violent Crime Drop in the United States: A Pooled, Cross-Sectional Time-Series Analysis of Metropolitan Areas," *Criminology* 47:889–928 (2009); Steven Levitt, "Understanding Why Crime Fell in the 1990s: Four Factors that Explain the Decline and Six that Do Not," *Journal of Economic Perspectives* 18:163–190 (2004); *Brad Bushman and Craig Anderson, "Media Violence and the American Public," American Psychologist 56:477–489 (2001);* John J. Donohue III and Steven D. Levitt, "The Impact of Legalized Abortion on Crime," *Quarterly Journal of Economics* 116:379–420 (2001).

What the Future Holds

It is possible that if current population trends persist juvenile crime may soon begin to increase. There are approximately 50 million school-age children in the United States, many younger than 10—more than we have had for decades—and many of them lack stable families and adequate supervision; these are some of the children who will soon enter their prime crime years.

Not all agree with this scenario. Economist Steven Levitt believes that even though teen crime rates may eventually rise, their influence on the nation's total crime rate may be offset by the growing number of relatively crime-free senior citizens.[26] Levitt also believes that punitive policies, such as putting more kids behind bars and adding police, may help control delinquency. Of course, all prognostications, predictions, and forecasts are based on contemporary conditions that can change at any time due to the sudden emergence of war, terrorism, social unrest, economic meltdown, and the like. Although the number of adolescents in the population may shape crime rates under current conditions, serious social and economic conditions can alter the trajectory of delinquency.[27] **CHECKPOINTS**

CHECKPOINTS

LO2 Recognize the trends in the delinquency rate and the factors that influence and shape its direction.

✔ Crime rates peaked in the early 1990s and have been in decline ever since.

✔ During the past decade, the number of youths arrested for delinquent behavior has also declined, including a significant decrease in those arrested for violent offenses.

✔ Even the teen murder rate has undergone a particularly steep decline.

✔ A number of factors influence delinquency trends, including the economy, drug use, availability of guns, and crime control policies.

✔ Two controversial issues are immigration and abortion. Research indicates that both may have helped drive down the delinquency rate.

WWW

To find out more about the **Institute for Social Research**, visit the Criminal Justice CourseMate at CengageBrain.com, then access the Web Links for this chapter.

CORRELATES OF DELINQUENCY

What are the personal traits and social characteristics associated with adolescent misbehavior? This is a key element of delinquency research because it guides the application of treatment and prevention efforts. If, for example, a strong association exists between delinquent behavior and indicators of economic status such as personal and family income, than job creation and vocational training might be effective methods of reducing delinquent behavior and youth crime. If, in contrast, delinquency rates were unrelated to economic indicators, then programs aimed at improving financial position and providing economic opportunities might prove to be a waste of time. The next sections discuss the relationship between delinquency and the characteristics of gender, race, social class, and age.

The Time and Place of Delinquency

Most delinquent acts occur during the warm summer months of July and August. Weather may affect delinquent behavior in a number of ways. During the summer, teenagers are out of school and have greater opportunity to commit crime. Homes are left vacant more often during the summer, making them more vulnerable to property crimes. Weather may also have a direct effect on behavior: as it gets warmer, kids get more violent.[28] However, some experts believe if it gets too hot, over 85 degrees, the frequency of some violent acts such as sexual assault begins to decline.[29]

There are also geographic differences in the incidence of delinquent behaviors. Large urban areas have by far the highest juvenile violence rates; rural areas have the lowest. Typically, the western and southern states have had consistently higher delinquency rates than the Midwest and Northeast, a fact that has been linked to differences in cultural values, population makeup, gun ownership, and economic status.

Gender and Delinquency

With a few exceptions, males are significantly more delinquent than females. The teenage gender ratio for serious violent crime is approximately four to one, and for property crime approximately two to one, male to female. The only exception to this pattern is arrests for being a runaway; girls are more likely than boys to be arrested as runaways. There are two possible explanations for this: girls are actually more likely than boys to run away from home, or police may view the female runaway as the more serious

Looking Back to Jamesetta's Story

Jamesetta received a number of interventions to address her issues, but it still took a long time for her to reduce her delinquent behavior.

CRITICAL THINKING How long should the juvenile justice system give a young person to change? How many chances should a teen get before they are put in detention?

While boys are more violent than girls, violent crimes committed by females are not unknown. Here, Kayla Hassall, 16, center, one of five teenagers accused of beating fellow teen Victoria N. Lindsay, tries to contain her emotions as she sits in court with her parents prior to a plea hearing before Circuit Judge Keith Spoto at the Polk County Courthouse, in Bartow, Florida. Hassall and April Cooper were among the teens accused of attacking the 16-year-old girl, with whom they had a online squabble. The attack was recorded on video and seen around the world via the Internet and TV. Under the terms of her plea, prosecutors agreed to drop felony kidnapping charges. April Cooper pleaded guilty to two counts of misdemeanor battery. Both had to write letters of apology to Lindsay and agree to not talk to the media for profit. One of the girls involved in the incident received a 15-day jail sentence.

problem and therefore more likely to process girls through official justice channels. This may reflect paternalistic attitudes toward girls, who are viewed as likely to "get in trouble" if they are on the street.

Today, there are more similarities than differences between male and female offenders, and the gender gap seems to be closing.[30] During the past decade, a period of rapidly declining delinquency rates, the number of arrests of male delinquents decreased about 27 percent, whereas the number of female delinquents arrested declined by 15 percent. If this trend continues as it has, there will eventually be gender convergence in delinquency. Monitoring the Future data show that while males commit more serious crimes (such as robbery, assault, and burglary) than females, gender ratios are narrowing. More than 25 percent of all boys and girls admit to shoplifting and 22 percent of boys and 15 percent of girls said they were involved in a gang fight. Over the past decade, girls have increased their self-reported delinquency, whereas boys report somewhat less involvement. Because the relationship between gender and delinquency rate is so important, this topic will be discussed further in Chapter 6.

Race and Delinquency

There are approximately 40 million European American and 10 million African American youths ages 5 to 17, a ratio of about four to one. Yet racial minorities are disproportionately represented in the arrest statistics. In 2010, 69 percent of all persons arrested were white, 28 percent were black, and the remaining 3 percent were of other races. African American juveniles account more than half of all juveniles arrested for serious violent crime and about one-third of all arrests for serious property crime.[31]

These official statistics show that minority youths are arrested for serious criminal behavior at a rate that is disproportionate to their representation in the population. How can this overrepresentation be explained? Some delinquency experts blame racial discrimination in the juvenile justice system. In other words, African American youths are more likely to be formally arrested by the police, who, in contrast, will treat European American youths informally. One way to examine this issue is to compare the racial differences in self-reported data with those found in the official delinquency records. Given the disproportionate numbers of African Americans arrested, charges of racial discrimination would be supported if few differences were found between the number of self-reported minority and European American crimes.

Self-report studies such as the MTF survey, for example, generally show similarity in offending differences between African American and European American youths for most crimes, but for some serious offenses, such as stealing more than $50, getting into a gang fight, and using a weapon to steal, African American youth do in fact admit more offending than white youth, a finding that is reflective of the UCR arrest data.[32] How can this disproportionate minority group involvement in serious crime be explained?

Bias Effects. Research shows that minority group members are more likely to be formally stopped, searched, and arrested than European American youths.[33] Police officers are more likely to single out young black men while treating older African Americans with greater deference. For example, police are much more likely to stop young black drivers than they are white or older black men. This creates a cycle of hostility: young black men see their experience with police as unfair or degrading; they approach future encounters with preexisting hostility. Police officers may take this as a sign that young black men pose a special danger; they respond with harsh treatment.[34]

According to the **racial threat theory**, as the size of the African American population increases, the perceived threat to the European American population increases, resulting in a greater amount of social control imposed against African Americans by police.[35] Police will then routinely search, question, and detain all African American males in an area if a violent criminal has been described as "looking or sounding black"; this is called *racial profiling.* African American youth who develop a police record are more likely to be severely punished if they are picked up again and sent back to juvenile court.[36] Consequently, the racial discrimination that is present at the early stages of the justice system ensures that minorities receive greater punishments at its conclusion.[37]

Juvenile court judges may see the offenses committed by African American youths as more serious than those committed by European American offenders. Consequently, they are more likely to keep minority juveniles in detention pending trial in juvenile court than they are European American youth with similar backgrounds.[38] European American juveniles are more likely to receive lenient sentences or have their cases dismissed.[39] As a result, African American youths are more likely to get an official record.

According to this view, then, the disproportionate number of minority youth who are arrested is less a function of their involvement in serious crime and more the result of the race-based decision making that is found in the juvenile justice system.[40] Institutional racism by police and the courts is still an element of daily life in the African American community, a factor that undermines faith in social and political institutions and weakens confidence in the justice system.[41] When politicians use veiled hints of racial threat in their political campaigns, the result is excessive punishment of minority citizens.[42]

racial threat theory As the size of the African American population increases, the amount of social control imposed against African Americans by police grows proportionately.

A special prosecutor in Florida charged George Zimmerman (left) with second-degree murder in the shooting death of unarmed black teenager Trayvon Martin (right), in a racially charged case that riveted the United States.

© Reuters/Landov

Race Matters. An alternative view is that although evidence of racial bias does exist in the justice system, there is enough correspondence between official and self-report data to conclude that racial differences in the crime rate are real.[43] If African American youths are arrested at a disproportionately high rate for crimes, such as robbery and assault, it is a result of actual offending rates rather than bias on the part of the criminal justice system.[44]

According to this view, racial differentials are tied to the social and economic disparity suffered by African American youths. Forced by their impoverished circumstances to live in the nation's poorest areas, many African American youth attend essentially segregated schools that are underfunded and deteriorated.[45] The burden of social and economic marginalization has weakened the African American family structure. When families are weakened or disrupted, their ability to act as social control agents is compromised.[46]

Even during times of economic growth, lower-class African Americans are left out of the economic mainstream, causing a growing sense of frustration and failure.[47] As a result of being shut out of educational and economic opportunities enjoyed by the rest of society, African American kids are vulnerable to the lure of illegitimate gain and criminality. Consequently, racial differences in the delinquency rate would evaporate if African American kids could enjoy the same social, economic, and educational privileges enjoyed by children of the white majority.[48] Economic parity would help strengthen the African American family, which serves as a buffer to the lure of gangs and criminality. Children of all races who live in stable families with reasonable incomes and educational achievement are much less likely to engage in violent behaviors than those lacking family support.[49]

Race differences in family structure, economic status, education achievement, and other social factors persist. Does that mean that racial differences in the delinquency rate will persist, or is convergence possible? It is possible that when economic conditions improve in the minority community, differences in the delinquency rate will eventually disappear.[50] The trend toward residential integration, underway since 1980, may also help reduce crime rate differentials.[51] An important study (2010) by Gary LaFree and his associates tracked race-specific homicide arrest differences in 80 large U.S. cities from 1960 to 2000, and found substantial convergence in black/white homicide arrest rates over time.[52] If America's racial divide can be breached and overcome, so too will racial differences in the crime and delinquency rate.

Social Class and Delinquency

Self-report data do in fact show that kids in all levels of society and in all social classes commit crime.[53] Middle-class kids may commit crime, but it is generally of the less serious nuisance variety, such as selling pot or committing vandalism, rather than serious felony offenses. It is lower-class youth who are responsible for the majority of serious delinquent acts.[54] It is possible, as some research shows, that lower-class kids are simply arrested more often, and punished more harshly than their wealthier peers, creating the illusion that delinquency is a lower-class phenomenon.[55] However, the weight of recent evidence suggest that serious crime is more prevalent in socially disorganized lower-class areas, whereas less serious offenses are spread more evenly throughout the social structure.[56]

What is the connection between poverty and delinquency? Community-level indicators of poverty and disorder—deteriorated neighborhoods, lack of informal social control, income inequality, presence of youth gangs, and resource deprivation—are all associated with the most serious violent crimes, including homicide and assault.[57] The lure of crime, drug dealing, and gang life is irresistible for kids living in a deteriorated neighborhood, with substandard housing and schools, and where the opportunity for legitimate advancement is limited or nonexistent. Family life is disrupted in these low-income areas, and law-violating youth groups thrive in a climate that undermines and neutralizes adult supervision.[58]

What is the connection between class and delinquency? Lower-class kids who live in these areas believe that they can never compete socially or economically with adolescents being raised in more affluent areas. They may turn to criminal behavior for monetary gain and psychological satisfaction.[59] Lower-class kids are more deeply affected by the changes in the economy that have occurred in recent years: women have joined the workforce in large numbers; union influence has shrunk; manufacturing has moved overseas; and computers and the Internet have changed the way that resources are created and distributed. As manufacturing has moved overseas, less-educated, untrained young males have been frozen out of the job market. These workers may find themselves competing in illegal markets: selling drugs may be more profitable than working in a fast food restaurant. Similarly, a young woman may find prostitution or other sex work more lucrative relative to work in the legitimate market. When the economy turns, drug dealers do not suddenly quit the trade and get a job with GE or IBM. As criminologist Shawn Bushway points out, labor markets are the economic engine that shapes the crime rate and creates incentives for teens and adolescents to participate in illegal activities.[60]

In sum, poverty does not cause delinquency per se; many poor kids are not delinquent at all. However, poverty is linked to social problems—family disruption, poor educational opportunities, lack of resources—that are highly associated with youthful misbehaviors.

Age and Delinquency

It is generally believed that age is inversely related to criminality: as people age, the likelihood that they will commit crime declines.[61] Official statistics tell us that young people are arrested at a disproportionate rate to their numbers in the population, and this finding is supported by victim surveys. As you may recall, youths ages 14 through 17 make up about 6 percent of the total U.S. population, but account for about 15 percent for all arrests. In contrast, adults age 50 and older, who make up slightly less than a third of the population, account for only about 6 percent of arrests.

© Ralf-Finn Hestoft/Corbis

A policewoman searches the jacket of a teenage African American boy for drugs and weapons in the graffiti covered Cabrini Green Housing Project, an area long noted for social problems and gang violence. Part of the project has been demolished and the number of residents has declined to fewer than 5,000 from more than 15,000 at its peak. The area is being redeveloped, and new housing is being built on the 70-acre site. It is planned that the development will include 30 percent public housing replacement homes and 20 percent "workforce affordable" housing. Do you suppose redevelopment will reduce area delinquency rates?

Why Age Matters. Why do people commit less crime as they age? One view is that the relationship is constant: regardless of race, sex, social class, intelligence, or any other social variable, people commit less crime as they age.[62] This is referred to as the **aging-out process**, sometimes called *desistance from crime* or *spontaneous remission*. According to some experts, even the most chronic juvenile offenders will commit less crime as they age.[63] Because almost everyone commits less crime as they age, it is difficult to predict or identify the relatively few offenders who will continue to commit crime as they travel through their life course.[64]

Age may impact on delinquency in a number of different ways. Evidence exists, for example, that the **age of onset** of a delinquent career has an important effect on its length. Those who demonstrate antisocial tendencies at a very early age are more likely to commit more crimes for a longer period of time. This is referred to as the *developmental view of delinquency*.

In summary, some criminologists believe youths who get involved with delinquency at a very early age are most likely to become career criminals. These researchers believe age is a key determinant of delinquency.[65] Those opposed to this view find that all people commit less crime as they age and that because the relationship between age and crime is constant, it is irrelevant to the study of delinquency.[66]

Why Does Crime Decline with Age? Although there is certainly disagreement about the nature of the aging-out process, there is no question that people commit less crime as they grow older. Delinquency experts have developed a number of reasons for the aging-out process:

- *Growing older means having to face the future.* Young people, especially the indigent and antisocial, tend to "discount the future."[67] Why should they delay gratification when faced with an uncertain future?

- *With maturity comes the ability to resist the "quick fix" to their problems.*[68] Research shows that some kids may turn to crime as a way to solve the problems of adolescence, loneliness, frustration, and fear of peer rejection. As they mature, conventional means of problem solving become available. Life experience helps former delinquents seek out nondestructive solutions to their personal problems.[69]

- *Maturation coincides with increased levels of responsibility.* Petty crimes are risky and exciting social activities that provide adventure in an otherwise boring world. As youths grow older, they take on new responsibilities that are inconsistent with criminality. Young people who marry, enlist in the armed services, or enroll in vocational training courses are less likely to pursue criminal activities.[70]

- *Personalities can change with age.* As youths mature, rebellious youngsters may develop increased self-control and be able to resist antisocial behavior.[71]

- *Young adults become more aware of the risks that accompany crime.* As adults, they are no longer protected by the relatively kindly arms of the juvenile justice system.[72]

- *Changes in human biology.* Some experts now believe that biology is the key to desistance and aging out is linked to human biology. Biocriminologist Kevin Beaver and his colleagues have found evidence that the neurotransmitters serotonin and dopamine play a role in aggression, the former limiting offensive behavior and the latter facilitating its occurrence. Levels of these neurotransmitters ebb and flow over the life course. During adolescence, dopamine increases while serotonin is reduced; in adulthood, dopamine levels recede while serotonin levels become elevated. If delinquents commit less crime in adulthood, the cause might be the level of hormone activity in the brain.[73]

Of course, not all juvenile criminals desist as they age; some go on to become chronic adult offenders. Yet even they slow down as they age. Crime is too dangerous, physically taxing, and unrewarding, and punishments too harsh and long

W/\W

To get information on the **economic status of America's children**, visit the Criminal Justice CourseMate at Cengage Brain.com, then access the Web Links for this chapter.

aging-out process (also known as **desistance from crime or spontaneous remission**) The tendency for youths to reduce the frequency of their offending behavior as they age. Aging out is thought to occur among all groups of offenders.

age of onset Age at which youths begin their delinquent careers. Early onset is believed to be linked with chronic offending patterns.

✔ Official arrest statistics, victim data, and self-reports indicate that males are significantly more delinquent than females. In recent years, however, the female delinquency rate appears to be increasing faster than that for males.

✔ Although the true association between class and delinquency is still unknown, the official data tell us that delinquency rates are highest in areas with high rates of poverty.

✔ African American youths are arrested for a disproportionate number of delinquent acts, such as robbery and assault, whereas European American youths are arrested for a disproportionate share of arson and alcohol-related violations.

✔ One view is that institutional racism, such as police profiling, accounts for the racial differences in the delinquency rate. A second view is that racial differences in the delinquency rate are a function of living in a racially segregated society.

✔ Kids who engage in the most serious forms of delinquency are more likely to be members of the lower class.

✔ Delinquency rates decline with age. As youthful offenders mature, the likelihood that they will commit offenses declines.

lasting, to become a way of life for most people.[74] There are a number of factors that affect a delinquent career, including family and peer relations, guns, gangs, and the like.

CHRONIC OFFENDING: CAREERS IN DELINQUENCY

Although most adolescents age out of crime, a relatively small number of youths begin to violate the law early in their lives (early onset) and continue at a high rate well into adulthood (persistence).[75] The association between early onset and high-rate persistent offending has been demonstrated in samples drawn from a variety of cultures, time periods, and offender types.[76] These offenders are resistant to change and seem immune to the effects of punishment. Arrest, prosecution, and conviction do little to slow down their offending careers. These chronic offenders are responsible for a significant amount of all delinquent and criminal activity.

Current interest in the delinquent life cycle was prompted in part by the "discovery" in the 1970s of the chronic juvenile (or delinquent) offender. According to this view, a relatively small number of youthful offenders commit a significant percentage of all serious crimes, and many of these same offenders grow up to become chronic adult criminals. A number of research efforts have set out to chronicle the careers of serious delinquent offenders. The next sections describe these initiatives.

Delinquency in a Birth Cohort

The concept of the chronic career offender is most closely associated with the research efforts of Marvin Wolfgang.[77] In 1972, Wolfgang, Robert Figlio, and Thorsten Sellin published a landmark study, *Delinquency in a Birth Cohort*. They followed the delinquent careers of a cohort of 9,945 boys born in Philadelphia from birth until they reached age 18. Data were obtained from police files and school records. Socioeconomic status was determined by locating the residence of each member of the cohort and assigning him the median family income for that area. About one-third of the boys (3,475) had some police contact. The remaining two-thirds (6,470) had none. Those boys who had at least one contact with the police committed a total of 10,214 offenses.

The most significant discovery of Wolfgang and his associates was that of the so-called chronic offender. The data indicated that 54 percent (1,862) of the sample's delinquent youths were repeat offenders. The repeaters could be further categorized as non-chronic recidivists and **chronic recidivists**.

The non-chronic recidivists had been arrested more than once but fewer than five times. In contrast, the 627 boys labeled chronic recidivists had been arrested five times or more. Although these offenders accounted for only 18 percent of the delinquent population (6 percent of the total sample), they were responsible for 52 percent of all offenses. Known today as the "chronic 6 percent," this group perpetrated 71 percent of the homicides, 82 percent of the robberies, and 64 percent of the aggravated assaults (see Figure 2.2).

Arrest and juvenile court experience did little to deter chronic offenders. In fact, the greater the punishment, the more likely they were to engage in repeat delinquent behavior. Strict punishment also increased the probability

chronic recidivist Someone who has been arrested five times or more before age 18.

Looking Back to Jamesetta's Story

Consider what you know of Jamesetta's life.

CRITICAL THINKING What childhood risk factors increase the possibility of becoming a persistent delinquent? Write a short essay spelling out what you think is the best way to reduce chronic offending among at-risk youth.

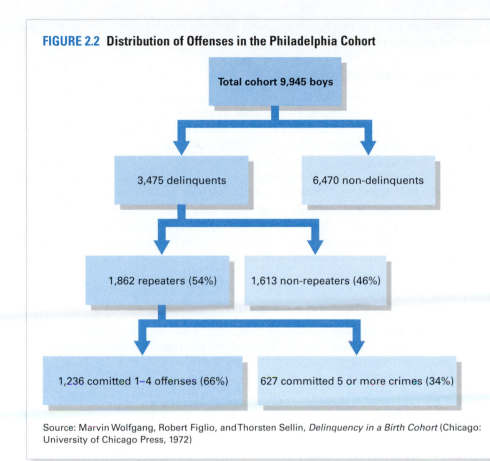

FIGURE 2.2 Distribution of Offenses in the Philadelphia Cohort

Total cohort 9,945 boys

3,475 delinquents

6,470 non-delinquents

1,862 repeaters (54%)

1,613 non-repeaters (46%)

1,236 comitted 1–4 offenses (66%)

627 committed 5 or more crimes (34%)

Source: Marvin Wolfgang, Robert Figlio, and Thorsten Sellin, *Delinquency in a Birth Cohort* (Chicago: University of Chicago Press, 1972)

that further court action would be taken. Two factors stood out as encouraging recidivism: the seriousness of the original offense and the severity of the punishment. The researchers concluded that efforts of the juvenile justice system to eliminate delinquent behavior may be futile.

Wolfgang and his colleagues conducted a second cohort study with children born in 1958 and substantiated the finding that a relatively few chronic offenders are responsible for a significant portion of all delinquent acts.[78] Wolfgang's results have been duplicated in a number of research studies conducted in locales across the United States and in Great Britain.[79] Some have used the records of court-processed youths, and others have employed self-report data.

Stability in Crime: From Delinquent to Criminal

Do chronic juvenile offenders grow up to become chronic adult criminals? One study that followed a 10 percent sample of the original Pennsylvania cohort (974 subjects) to age 30 found that 70 percent of the "persistent" adult offenders had also been chronic juvenile offenders. Chronic juvenile offenders had an 80 percent chance of becoming adult offenders and a 50 percent chance of being arrested four or more times as adults.[80] Paul Tracy and Kimberly Kempf-Leonard conducted a follow-up study of all the subjects in the second 1958 cohort. By age 26, Cohort II subjects were displaying the same behavior patterns as their older peers. Kids who started their delinquent careers early, committed a violent crime, and continued offending throughout adolescence were most likely to persist in criminal behavior as adults. Delinquents who began their offending careers with serious offenses or who quickly increased the severity of their offending early in life were most likely to persist in their criminal behavior into adulthood. Severity of offending rather than frequency of criminal behavior had the greatest impact on later adult criminality.[81]

These studies indicate that chronic juvenile offenders continue their law-violating careers as adults, a concept referred to as the **continuity of crime**. Kids who

continuity of crime The idea that chronic juvenile offenders are likely to continue violating the law as adults.

are disruptive as early as age 5 or 6 are most likely to exhibit disruptive behavior throughout adolescence.[82]

What Causes Chronic Offending?

Research indicates that chronic offenders suffer from a number of personal, environmental, social, and developmental deficits, as shown in Exhibit 2.2. Other research studies have found that involvement in criminal activity (for example, getting arrested before age 15), relatively low intellectual development, and parental drug involvement were key predictive factors for future chronic offending.[83] Measurable problems in learning and motor skills, cognitive abilities, family relations, and other areas also predict chronicity.[84] Youthful offenders who persist are more likely to abuse alcohol, become economically dependent, have lower aspirations, and have a weak employment record.[85] Apprehension and punishment seem to have little effect on their offending behavior. Youths who have long juvenile records will most likely continue their offending careers into adulthood.

Policy Implications

Efforts to chart the life cycle of crime and delinquency will have a major influence on both theory and policy. Rather than simply asking why youths become delinquent or commit antisocial acts, theorists are charting the onset, escalation,

---

EXHIBIT 2.2 Childhood Risk Factors for Persistent Delinquency

Individual Factors
- Early antisocial behavior
- Emotional factors, such as high behavioral activation and low behavioral inhibition
- Poor cognitive development
- Low intelligence
- Hyperactivity

School and Community Factors
- Failure to bond to school
- Poor academic performance
- Low academic aspirations
- Living in a poor family
- Neighborhood disadvantage
- Disorganized neighborhoods
- Concentration of delinquent peer groups
- Access to weapons

Family Factors
- Inconsistent Parenting
- Maltreatment
- Family violence
- Divorce
- Parental psychopathology
- Familial antisocial behaviors
- Teenage parenthood
- Large family size

Peer Factors
- Association with deviant peers
- Peer rejection

Source: Gail Wasserman, Kate Keenan, Richard Tremblay, John Coie, Todd Herrenkohl, Rolf Loeber, and David Petechuk, "Risk and Protective Factors of Child Delinquency," *Child Delinquency Bulletin Series* (Washington, DC: Office of Juvenile Justice and Delinquency Prevention, 2003).

frequency, and cessation of delinquent behavior. Research on delinquent careers has also influenced policy. If relatively few offenders commit a great proportion of all delinquent acts and then persist as adult criminals, it follows that steps should be taken to limit their criminal opportunities.[86] One approach is to identify persistent offenders at the beginning of their offending careers and provide early treatment.[87] This might be facilitated by research aimed at identifying traits (for example, impulsive personalities) that can be used to classify high-risk offenders.[88] Because many of these youths suffer from a variety of problems, treatment must be aimed at a broad range of educational, family, vocational, and psychological problems. Focusing on a single problem, such as lack of employment, may be ineffective.[89] **CHECKPOINTS**

JUVENILE VICTIMIZATION

Juveniles are also victims of crime, and data from victim surveys can help us understand the nature of juvenile **victimization**. As discussed earlier in this chapter, one source of juvenile victimization data is the National Crime Victimization Survey (NCVS), an ongoing cooperative effort of the Bureau of Justice Statistics of the U.S. Department of Justice and the U.S. Census Bureau.[90]

Young Victims

NCVS data indicate that young people are much more likely to be the victims of crime than adults. The chance of victimization declines with age. The difference is particularly striking when we compare teens under age 19 with people over age 65: teens are more than 10 times as likely to become victims than their grandparents. The data also indicate that male teenagers have a significantly higher chance than females of becoming victims of violent crime, and that African American youth have a greater chance of becoming victims of violent crimes than European Americans of the same age. Juveniles are much more likely to become crime victims than adults. They have a more dangerous lifestyle, which places them at risk for crime. They spend a great deal of time in one of the most dangerous areas in the community, the local school, and hang out with the most dangerous people, fellow teenagers!

The Victims and Their Criminals

In general, teens tend to be victimized by their peers. A majority of teens are victimized by other teens. Victims of violent crime report that a disproportionate number of their attackers are young, ranging in age from 16 to 25.

Victimization is intraracial (that is, within a race). European American teenagers tend to be victimized by European American teens, and African American teenagers tend to be victimized by African American teens.

Most teens are victimized by people with whom they are acquainted, and their victimization is more likely to occur during the day. In contrast, adults are more often victimized by strangers and at night. One explanation for this pattern is that youths are at greatest risk from their own family and relatives. Another possibility is that many teenage victimizations occur at school,

victimization The number of people who are victims of criminal acts.

JAYCEE LEE DUGARD AND THE SEXUAL ABDUCTION OF CHILDREN

On August 24, 2009, Phillip Garrido, a long-time sex offender, left a four-page essay at FBI headquarters in San Francisco telling how he had overcome his sexual disorder and how his insights could help others. He also went to the University of California and asked if he could hold a special Christian event on campus. When he made a return trip the next day with two of his daughters, university officials became suspicious of Garrido and contacted his parole officer. He was asked to come in for an interview and arrived with his wife, two children, and a young woman named Alyssa. After being separated from Garrido for a further interview, "Alyssa" told authorities that she was really Jaycee Lee Dugard, and the two young girls were children that she had

borne Garrido, who along with his wife was placed under immediate arrest.

As the nation soon learned, at age 11 Jaycee Lee Dugard had been abducted, on June 10, 1991, at a school bus stop within sight of her home in South Lake Tahoe, California. After being grabbed off the street by Garrido, she had been held captive for 18 years, living in a tent in a walled-off compound on land the Garridos owned in Antioch, California. Raped repeatedly, Dugard bore two daughters, in 1994 and 1998. Law enforcement officers had visited the residence at least twice in recent years, but failed to detect Dugard or her children. Though Dugard helped Garrido in his print shop and over the years had been spotted and spoken to by a number of neighbors

and customers, no one investigated or called the police. On August 28, 2009, Garrido and his wife were indicted on charges including kidnapping, rape, and false imprisonment. After pleading guilty, Garrido was sentenced to 431 years; his wife received 36 years to life. In July 2010, the State of California approved a $20 million settlement with Jaycee Dugard, to compensate her for "various lapses by the Corrections Department [which contributed to] Dugard's continued captivity, ongoing sexual assault and mental and/or physical abuse." Dugard has written a book about her experience in order to help other victims of abuse.

The Jaycee Dugard story shocked the nation and had a chilling effect on the general public. How was it possible,

AP Photo/Charles Sykes

in school buildings, or on school grounds because that is where most predatory delinquents are located. At school, victims may be selected because they are considered suitable targets for school yard bullies. Research shows, for instance, that students who are involved in academic extracurricular activities are more likely to be selected as suitable targets for violent victimization. These students may be viewed as "weak" and vulnerable to victimization by motivated offenders. [91]

Sexual Victimization. As the 2012 trial of Penn State coach Jerry Sandusky showed, teens are also the victim of sexual abuse (more

Thousands of children are the victims of adult sexual predators. One of the most notorious cases involved Jaycee Lee Dugard, who survived being kidnapped, raped, and held captive for 18 years. She is shown here with Oprah Winfrey as she is presented an award for her courage at the United Nations in New York. Dugard plans to live in hiding until her two daughters, who were conceived in rapes by Dugard's kidnapper, are older and can better understand the circumstances in which they were born.

people asked, for a known sex offender to be able to grab a child off the streets and keep her in captivity for 18 years without anyone knowing? But while shocking, the case is not unique. On June 5, 2002, in another highly publicized case, Elizabeth Smart was abducted from her Salt Lake City, Utah, bedroom at the age of 14 and not found again until nine months later, even though she had been held only 18 miles from her home. Elizabeth's captors, Brian David Mitchell and Wanda Ileen Barzee, were both considered mentally incompetent and unfit to stand trial.

While cases such as these, and TV shows such as *To Catch a Predator*, convince the public that thousands of children are taken by sexual predators each year, how true is that perception? A national survey conducted by David Finkelhor and his associates found the following:

- During the study year, there were an estimated 115 *stereotypical kidnappings*, defined as abductions perpetrated by a stranger or slight acquaintance and involving a child who was transported 50 or more miles, detained overnight, held for ransom or with the intent to keep the child permanently, or killed. In 40 percent of stereotypical kidnappings, the child was killed, and in another 4 percent, the child was not recovered.

- There were an estimated 58,200 child victims of *nonfamily abduction*, defined more broadly to include all nonfamily perpetrators (friends and acquaintances as well as strangers) and crimes involving lesser amounts of forced movement or detention in addition to the more serious crimes entailed in stereotypical kidnappings.

- Fifty-seven percent of children abducted by a nonfamily perpetrator were missing from caretakers for at least one hour, and police were contacted to help locate 21 percent of the abducted children.

- Teenagers were by far the most frequent victims of both stereotypical kidnappings and nonfamily abductions.

- Nearly half of all child victims of stereotypical kidnappings and nonfamily abductions were sexually assaulted by the perpetrator.

According to these data, almost 30,000 children are taken and sexually assaulted by strangers each year. So while cases involving long-term abduction and sexual exploitation, such as those of Jaycee Lee Dugard and Elizabeth Smart, are relatively rare, detention and rape of children is all too common.

CRITICAL THINKING

The death penalty can only be used in cases of first-degree murder. Should the law be changed to include someone who kidnaps, rapes, and impregnates a child? Explain your reasoning.

Writing Assignment Write an essay on the proper punishment for someone who kidnaps, rapes, and impregnates a young child. Would the death penalty be justified in such cases? What might be the downside to executing child abductors/rapists?

Source: BBC News, "Jaycee Dugard Kidnap: Victim Rues 'Stolen Life,'" June 2, 2011, www.bbc.co.uk/news/world-us-canada-13631641 (accessed June 25, 2012); David Finkelhor, Heather Hammer, and Andrea J. Sedlak, "Nonfamily Abducted Children: National Estimates and Characteristics," United States Department of Justice, 2002, www.missingkids.com/en_US/documents/nismart2_nonfamily.pdf (accessed June 25, 2012); Sarah Netter and Sabina Ghebremedhin, "Jaycee Dugard Found After 18 Years, Kidnap Suspect Allegedly Fathered Her Kids," ABC News, August 27, 2009, http://abcnews.go.com/US/jaycee-lee-dugard-found-family-missing-girl-located/story?id=8426124 (accessed June 25, 2012).

on the Sandusky case in Chapter 7). It has been estimated that about 2 million adolescents ages 12 to 17 have been sexually assaulted, and 4 million have been severely physically assaulted. Another 2 million have been punished by physical abuse. Not surprisingly, a significant number of these youth suffer post-traumatic stress disorder and are more prone to antisocial behaviors such as substance abuse in adulthood. Approximately 25 percent of physically assaulted or abused adolescents reported lifetime substance abuse or dependence; rates of substance problems among adolescents who were not physically assaulted or abused were roughly 6 percent.[92]

While most sexual abuse occurs in the home, there have also been numerous highly publicized cases involving children who have been abducted and abused by strangers. The accompanying Focus on Delinquency feature covers this frightening event. **CHECKPOINTS**

CHECKPOINTS

LO5 Be familiar with the factors that predict teen victimization.

✔ The National Crime Victimization Survey (NCVS) samples estimate the total number of criminal incidents, including those not reported to police.

✔ Males are more often the victims of delinquency than females.

✔ Younger people are more often targets than older people.

✔ African American rates of violent victimization are much higher than European American rates. Crime victimization tends to be intraracial.

✔ Self-report data show that a significant number of adolescents become crime victims. The NCVS may underreport juvenile victimization.

SUMMARY

There are a variety of ways to measure and record juvenile delinquency. The Federal Bureau of Investigation collects data from local law enforcement agencies and publishes them yearly in their Uniform Crime Report (UCR). The National Crime Victimization Survey (NCVS) is a nationwide survey of victimization in the United States. Self-report surveys ask people to describe, in detail, their recent and lifetime participation in criminal activity.

Many serious crimes are not reported to police and therefore are not counted by the UCR. The NCVS may have problems due to victims' misinterpretation of events and underreporting due to the embarrassment of reporting crime to interviewers, fear of getting in trouble, or simply forgetting an incident. Self-report studies have problems because people may exaggerate their criminal acts, forget some of them, or be confused about what is being asked. These data sources show that crime rates peaked 1991 when police recorded almost 15 million crimes. Since then the number of delinquent acts has been in decline. Teenagers have extremely high crime rates. Crime experts view changes in the population age distribution as having the greatest influence on crime trends. There is general agreement that delinquency rates decline with age.

As a general rule, the crime rate follows the proportion of young males in the population. There is debate over the effect the economy has on crime rates. Drop in the delinquency rate has been linked to a strong economy. Some believe that a poor economy may actually help lower delinquency rates because it limits the opportunity kids have to commit crime. As the level of social problems increases—such as single-parent families, dropout rates, racial conflict, and teen pregnancies—so do delinquency rates. Racial conflict may also increase delinquency rates. Minority youth are overrepresented in the delinquency rate, especially for violent crime.

Some experts believe that adolescent crime is a lower-class phenomenon, whereas others see it throughout the social structure. Some experts believe this phenomenon is universal, whereas others believe a small group of offenders persist in crime at a high rate. The age–crime relationship has spurred research on the nature of delinquency over the life course.

Delinquency data show the existence of a chronic persistent offender who begins his or her offending career early in life and persists as an adult. Marvin Wolfgang and his colleagues identified chronic offenders in a series of cohort studies conducted in Philadelphia. Early involvement in criminal activity, relatively low intellectual development, and parental drug involvement have been linked to later chronic offending. Measurable problems in learning and motor skills, cognitive abilities, family relations, and other areas also predict chronicity. Apprehension and punishment seem to have little effect on offending behavior.

Teenagers are much more likely to become victims of crime than are people in other age groups. A majority of teens have been victimized by other teens, whereas victims age 20 and over identified their attackers as being 21 or older. Teen victimization is intraracial. White teenagers tend to be victimized by white teens, and African American teenagers tend to be victimized by African American teens.

KEY TERMS

Federal Bureau of Investigation (FBI), p. 32

Uniform Crime Report (UCR), p. 33

Part I offenses, p. 33

Part II offenses, p. 33

disaggregated, p. 34

sampling, p. 35

population, p. 35

self-report survey, p. 36

dark figures of crime, p. 40

racial threat theory, p. 46

aging-out process, desistance, spontaneous remission, p. 49

age of onset, p. 49

chronic recidivist, p. 50

continuity of crime, p. 51

victimization, p. 53

QUESTIONS FOR REVIEW

1. List at least five ways to measure delinquent behavior.

2. Describe possible errors in the Uniform Crime Reports.

3. Mention the factors that influence the juvenile delinquency rate.

4. What is the racial threat hypothesis?

5. List the factors that predict chronic offending.

1. What factors contribute to the aging-out process?
2. Why are males more delinquent than females? Is it a matter of lifestyle, culture, or physical properties?
3. Discuss the racial differences found in the crime rate. What factors account for differences in the African American and European American crime rates?
4. Should kids who have been arrested more than three times be given mandatory incarceration sentences?
5. Do you believe that self-reports are an accurate method of gauging the nature and extent of delinquent behavior?

APPLYING WHAT YOU HAVE LEARNED

As a juvenile court judge, you are forced to make a tough decision during a hearing: whether a juvenile should be waived to the adult court. It seems that gang activity has become a way of life for residents living in local public housing projects. The "Bloods" sell crack, and the "Wolfpack" controls the drug market. When the rivalry between the two gangs exploded, 15-year-old Shatiek Johnson, a Wolfpack member, shot and killed a member of the Bloods; in retaliation, the Bloods put out a contract on his life. While in hiding, Shatiek was confronted by two undercover detectives who recognized the young fugitive. Fearing for his life, Shatiek pulled a pistol and began firing, fatally wounding one of the officers. During the hearing, you learn that Shatiek's story is not dissimilar from that of many other children raised in tough housing projects. With an absent father and a single mother who could not control her five sons, Shatiek lived in a world of drugs, gangs, and shootouts long before he was old enough to vote. By age 13, Shatiek had been involved in the gang-beating death of a homeless man in a dispute over $10, for which he was given a one-year sentence at a youth detention center and released after six months. Now charged with a crime that could be considered first-degree murder if committed by an adult, Shatiek could—if waived to the adult court—be sentenced to life in prison.

At the hearing, Shatiek seems like a lost soul. He claims he thought the police officers were killers out to collect the bounty put on his life by the Bloods. He says that killing the rival gang boy was an act of self-defense. The district attorney confirms that the victim was in fact a known gang assassin with numerous criminal convictions. Shatiek's mother begs you to consider the fact that her son is only 15 years old, that he has had a very difficult childhood, and that he is a victim of society's indifference to the poor.

Writing Assignment: Take the role of an assistant district attorney arguing for waiver of Shatiek to the adult court. Then take the role of the defense counsel arguing for his retention in juvenile court. Finally, take the role of a juvenile court judge assigned to hear the case and make a decision in the matter. Explain your reasoning.

GROUPWORK

Divide the class into three groups. Have one choose the UCR, one the NCVS, and one self-reports, and have each group make a pitch to have their "method" be the primary measure of juvenile delinquency.

CHAPTER THREE

Individual Views of Delinquency:
Choice and Trait

© I. Glory/Alamy

LEARNING OBJECTIVES

After reading this chapter you should:

1. Know the principles of choice theory and routine activities theory.

2. Compare the principles of general deterrence, specific deterrence, and situational crime prevention.

3. Trace the history and development of trait theory.

4. Be familiar with the branches and substance of biological trait theory.

5. Know the various psychological theories of delinquency.

Eric's Story

Sixteen-year-old Eric Peterson's parents divorced when he was very young; there had been a history of domestic violence in his Minnesota family. Eric, an only child, was diagnosed with attention deficit hyperactivity disorder (ADHD) at the age of 8, and also was suffering from reading and math deficiencies. Diagnosed with learning disabilities, Eric had challenges at school and was struggling academically.

Eric's mother became extremely concerned about his behavior, both at home and at school. Eric was acting aggressively at school and had been involved in several fights. Although his teachers were understanding, some were openly concerned about his sudden aggressiveness and believed he posed a threat to the safety of the other children; he was on the verge of expulsion. At home, Eric was defiant, refused to obey his mother's rules, and was often verbally abusive. He made verbal threats toward his mother and damaged property in their home. Part of Eric's problem might have been linked to his expanding substance abuse. He had a history of smoking marijuana on a regular basis. Although he had recently completed a drug and alcohol assessment and treatment program, his drug use persisted.

Sensing that a crisis was about to explode, Eric's mother got in contact with Family and Children's Services of Minnesota and requested assistance. After completing their initial assessment, Family and Children's Services provided Eric and his mother with family therapy and individual counseling. Eric participated in individual counseling to address his anger issues. He was referred to the Adolescent Domestic Abuse Program, a unique counseling program for boys ages 13 through 17 who are physically abusive or intimidating to a family member or dating partner. The program involves 10 weeks of group counseling with other young men who have also been involved in this type of violent behavior. The treatment protocol includes a family counseling component to help stop the abuse and help the family heal. Eric made an excellent connection with the group facilitator and worked very hard to address his behavior.

In this instance, the Adolescent Domestic Abuse Program proved to be a successful treatment milieu: Eric was able to stop his abusive behavior and create a better life for himself and his family. He has gone on to help other teens stop the cycle of domestic violence by becoming a regular speaker and volunteer at the Adolescent Domestic Abuse Program and at local schools. Eric has also graduated from high school and has even started college classes. His goal: to work with troubled teens and set them on the path to a better life, just like the one he took himself.

Eric's involvement in antisocial behavior may reflect personal, individual-level problems. Considering stories such as Eric's, some delinquency experts question whether the root cause of juvenile misbehavior can be found among social factors, such as poverty and neighborhood conflict. Are delinquents really a "product of their environment" or are they troubled individuals beset by personal, emotional, and/or physical problems? If social and economic factors alone can determine behavior, how is it that many youths residing in dangerous neighborhoods live law-abiding lives and that many middle- and upper-class kids get involved in drugs, alcohol, and other antisocial behaviors? Though millions of kids now live in poverty, the vast majority do not become delinquents and criminals.

What is it about some kids that makes them delinquent? Why do some kids become delinquents while others remain conventional and law abiding? There are actually two views that focus on the individual delinquent:

- **Choice theory** suggests that juvenile offenders are rational decision makers who *choose* to engage in antisocial activity because they believe their actions will be beneficial. Whether they join a gang, steal cars, or sell drugs, their delinquent acts are motivated by the belief that crime can be a relatively risk-free way to better their situation, make money, and have fun. They have little fear of getting caught or being harshly punished. Some have fantasies of riches, and others may enjoy the excitement produced by criminal acts such as beating up someone or stealing a car. They may be greedy, thoughtless, selfish, and even cruel; they do what they have to do, to get what they want to get.

choice theory Holds that youths will engage in delinquent and criminal behavior after weighing the consequences and benefits of their actions. Delinquent behavior is a rational choice made by a motivated offender who perceives that the chances of gain outweigh any possible punishment or loss.

- **Trait theory** suggests that delinquent acts, such as the behaviors that Eric was getting involved in, are the product of personal problems and conditions. Many forms of delinquency, such as substance abuse and violence, appear more impulsive than rational, and these behaviors may be inspired by aberrant physical or psychological traits. Kids who commit crime are not really rational decision makers, but troubled youths driven by personal problems such as hyperactivity, low intelligence, biochemical imbalance, or genetic defects.

Choice and trait theories are linked, because they both focus on the individual delinquent. Both suggest that each person reacts to environmental and social circumstances in a unique fashion. Faced with the same set of conditions, one person will live a law-abiding life, whereas another will use antisocial or violent behavior to satisfy his or her needs.

Why do some kids "choose" antisocial activities? This important question is discussed in the sections below.

CHOICE THEORY

The first formal explanations of crime held that human behavior was a matter of choice. It was assumed that people had **free will** to choose their behavior and that those who violated the law were motivated by greed, revenge, survival, or hedonism. More than 200 years ago, philosophers Cesare Beccaria and Jeremy Bentham argued that people weigh the consequences of their actions before deciding on a course of behavior.[1] Their writings formed the core of what used to be called **classical criminology** and is now referred to as *rational choice theory* (or more simply *choice theory*).

Choice theory holds that the decision to violate the law comes after a careful weighing of the benefits and costs of criminal behaviors. Most potential law violators would cease their actions if the pain associated with a behavior outweighed the gain; conversely, law-violating behavior seems attractive if the rewards seem greater than the punishment.[2] Delinquents are not the product of a bad environment or difficult life. They choose to commit crime because they find violating the law attractive and not because they are a product of a broken home or troubled family.[3]

According to the choice view, youths who decide to become drug dealers compare the benefits, such as cash to buy cars and other luxury items, with the penalties, such as arrest followed by a long stay in a juvenile facility. Many have learned the drug trade from more experienced adult criminals who show them the ropes—how to avoid detection by camouflaging their activities within the bustle of their daily lives. They sell crack while hanging out in a park or shooting hoops in a playground. They try to act normal, appearing to have a good time, in order to not draw attention to themselves and their business.[4] If they take their "lessons" to heart and become accomplished dealers, they may believe they cannot be caught or even if they are, they can avoid severe punishments. They may know or hear about criminals who make a significant income from their illegal activities and want to follow in their footsteps.[5]

THE RATIONAL DELINQUENT

The view that delinquents *choose* to violate the law remains a popular approach in the study of delinquency. According to this view, delinquency is not merely a function of social ills, such as lack of economic opportunity or family dysfunction. In reality, many youths from affluent families choose to break the law, and most indigent adolescents are law abiding. For example, at first glance drug abuse appears to be a senseless act motivated by grinding poverty and a sense of desperation. However, economic hopelessness cannot be the motivating force behind the substance abuse of millions of middle-class users, many of whom plan to finish high school and go

trait theory Holds that youths engage in delinquent or criminal behavior due to aberrant physical or psychological traits that govern behavioral choices. Delinquent actions are impulsive or instinctual rather than rational choices.

free will The view that youths are in charge of their own destinies and are free to make personal behavior choices unencumbered by environmental factors.

classical criminology Holds that decisions to violate the law are weighed against possible punishments and to deter crime the pain of punishment must outweigh the benefit of illegal gain. Led to graduated punishments based on seriousness of the crime (let the punishment fit the crime).

WWW

To read a selection from **Cesare Beccaria's *On Crime and Punishment***, visit the Criminal Justice CourseMate at CengageBrain.com, then access the Web Links for this chapter.

Is delinquency truly rational? Shane, a Portland, Oregon, youth, left an abusive family and has been homeless since he was 17. He struggles with heroin addiction and is in and out of housing. Portland has the highest population per capita of homeless youth in the United States. An estimated 2,500 youth lack permanent housing and live on the streets, in shelters, or "squats." According to studies, over 90 percent of Portland's street kids are victims of sexual and physical abuse. The epidemic spread of "meth" and some of the cheapest heroin in the nation fuel a high rate of drug addiction. Infection of incurable diseases such as Hepatitis C and HIV are also rampant among homeless youth. The average life expectancy for a homeless youth living on the streets is 26 years of age. Do kids like Shane really "choose" delinquency and drug abuse?

on to college. These kids are more likely to be motivated by the desire for physical gratification, peer group acceptance, and other social benefits. They choose to break the law because—despite the inherent risks—they believe that taking drugs and drinking provide more pleasure than pain. Their entry into substance abuse is facilitated by their perception that valued friends and family members endorse and encourage drug use and abuse substances themselves.[6] Subscribers to the rational choice model believe the decision to commit a specific type of crime is a matter of personal decision making, hence the term *rational choice*.

Choosing Delinquent Acts

According to choice theory, the concepts of delinquent and delinquency must be considered separately. Delinquents are youths who maintain the propensity to commit delinquent acts. Delinquency is an event during which an adolescent chooses to violate the law.[7] Delinquents do not violate the law all the time; like other kids they also go to school, engage in leisure activities, and play sports. But when they choose to, if they want money, possessions, or revenge, they use illegal methods to get what they want.

Delinquent kids can be observed carefully choosing targets, and their behavior seems both systematic and selective. Teen burglars seem to choose targets based on their value, freshness, and resale potential. A piece of electronic gear that retains its high value, such as an iPhone or iPad, may be a prime target.[8]

Delinquents also seem to choose the place of crime. They do not like to travel because familiarity with an area gives kids a ready knowledge of escape routes; this is referred to as their "awareness space."[9] A well-known location allows them to blend in, not look out of place, and not get lost when returning home with their loot.[10]

Rational choice theory holds that delinquency is not spontaneous or random, but a matter of weighing potential gains and losses. Even if youths have a delinquent

WWW

To learn more about the causes of alcoholism, go to the **National Council on Alcoholism and Drug Dependence, Inc. (NCADD)**, visit the Criminal Justice CourseMate at CengageBrain.com, then access the Web Links for this chapter.

LIVE FOR TODAY, TOMORROW WILL TAKE CARE OF ITSELF

We know that teens are risk takers. Many habitually drink, take drugs, drive fast, and some do all these things at once. Hard-core offenders, seemingly fearless in the face of the dangers they face, routinely carry guns, join gangs, and engage in violence. Over the course of their short lives they have experienced stabbings, shootings, and life-threatening injuries and yet remain undeterred from a risky and criminal lifestyle. Timothy Brezina, Erdal Tekin, and Volkan Topalli have conducted research to determine whether risk-taking kids believe they will have a relatively short life and whether perceptions of early mortality translate into a "live for today" mentality.

The first part of their research consisted of analysis of a survey administered to a large sample of adolescents. The data showed that respondents who perceive their high-risk lifestyle will bring an early death are much more willing to engage in risky, antisocial behaviors than those who have a longer life view. For example, among those who perceive that the chances of being killed by age 21 is greater than 50 percent, the probability of offending behavior increases by 3.3 percentage points (property damage) to 7.3 percentage points (pulling a knife or gun).

The researchers also interviewed risk-taking young offenders to determine what caused their fatalistic attitudes and how they affected their behavior and lifestyle. What emerged from the discussions was the conclusion that such fatalism emanated from their day-to-day exposure to violence. As one youth said:

I grew up with shootin' and fightin' all over. You grew up with books

propensity and are motivated to commit crimes, they may not do so if the opportunity is restricted or absent. They may want to break into a home, but are frightened off by a security system, guard dog, or gun-toting owner. They may be restricted in their opportunity to commit crime because they are supervised. In contrast, an adolescent may turn to crime if the rewards are very attractive, the chance of apprehension small, and the punishment tolerable. Why a child has the propensity to commit delinquent acts is an issue quite distinct from the reasons a delinquent decides to break into a particular house one day or to sell narcotics the next.

Delinquent Motivations

What personal factors are linked to the decision to choose delinquency? What motivates a potential delinquent to act on his or her antisocial propensities?

Economic Need/Opportunity. Some kids are motivated by economic need. Drug users, for example, may increase their delinquent activities to pay for the spiraling cost of their habit. As the cost of their drug habit increases, the need to make greater illegal profits becomes overwhelmingly attractive.[11] Kids choose delinquency when they believe they have little chance of becoming financially successful in the conventional world. They view drug dealing and car thefts as more attractive alternatives than working for minimum wage in a fast-food restaurant.

Problem Solving. Kids may choose crime as a means to solve personal problems and show their competence. Delinquent acts are an ideal mechanism for displaying

and s...t. Where I'm from you never know if you gonna live one minute to the next. It's like a war out there. People die every day. You can go to sleep and hear gunshots all night, man, all night. Bullets be lying on the street in the morning. Ambulances and police cars steady riding through my neighborhood, man. (Deathrow, age 19)

In some interviews, offenders told the researchers that their bleak outlooks were reinforced by family members and friends, either as a way of informally indoctrinating them into the violent culture they were a part of or as an attempt to scare them into abandoning their lifestyles. Ironically, attempts to scare these young men away from crime by highlighting their prospects for an early death may have backfired. When asked about how he had thought about his future, Cris Cris responded as follows:

I swore that I wasn't gonna see 19. I swear. The way I was goin', I didn't think I was ever gonna see 19. I swear. My aunties used to always say, "Man, you gonna be dead." My aunties, my whole family. . . . Made me wanna go do some more stuff. Made me wanna go do some more bad stuff.

So instead of scaring them off, the possibility of a shortened lifespan encouraged them to focus on the here and now. The threat of an early death caused these at-risk youth to embrace a macho attitude: never give in; be ready to die; never be afraid.

Brezina, Tekin, and Topalli conclude that their findings fit well within a rational choice framework: the delay of present gratification for future rewards will make little sense to individuals who do not perceive they have much of a future. If kids do choose crime, it makes sense that the choice will be shaped by reflecting upon their futures. While some young people may respond to such threats with noncriminal adaptations, many others seem prone to adopting a reckless "live for today and tomorrow will take care of itself" attitude and lifestyle. The result: increased involvement in delinquent activities.

CRITICAL THINKING

Is it possible that religion might help kids believe they have a future? While most programs for teens focus on improving their future prospects through legitimate means, such as getting a job or finishing their education, should spiritual beliefs be emphasized since they often focus on such qualities as hope and redemption?

Writing Assignment Write an essay discussing what can be done, if anything, to help kids living in violence-prone areas to believe they really do have a future. Can you list at least five principles that can be used to guide their lives and behaviors?

Source: Timothy Brezina, Erdal Tekin, and Volkan Topalli, "Might Not Be a Tomorrow: A Multimethods Approach to Anticipated Early Death and Youth Crime," *Criminology* 47:101–138 (2009).

courage and fearlessness. What could be a better way for kids to show their peers how tough they are than being able to get into a gang fight? Rather than creating overwhelming social problems, a delinquent way of life may help kids overcome the problems and stresses they face in their daily lives. Some turn to substance abuse to increase their sense of personal power, to become more assertive, and to reduce tension and anxiety. Some kids embrace deviant lifestyles, such as joining a gang, in order to compensate for their feelings of social powerlessness. Engaging in risky behavior helps them feel alive and competent.[12] The accompanying Focus on Delinquency feature explores another element of this.

False Expectations. Some delinquent youth have the false belief that "crime pays." They may admire older criminals who have made "big scores" and seem to be quite successful at crime. They get the false impression that crime is an easy way to make a buck.[13] In reality, the rewards of crime are often quite meager. When Steven Levitt and Sudhir Alladi Venkatesh studied the financial rewards of being in a drug gang, they found that despite enormous risks to their health, life, and freedom, average gang members earned slightly more than what they could in the legitimate labor market (about $6 to $11 per hour).[14] Why then did they stay in the gang? Members believed that there was a strong potential for future riches if they achieved a "management" position (that is, gang leaders earned a lot more than mere members). In this case, the rational choice to commit crime is structured by the adolescent's perception that they can make a lot of money by being a gang boy as opposed to the limited opportunities available in the legitimate world.[15]

Opportunity. Choosing delinquency may be directly associated with the opportunity to commit crime. Kids who are granted a lot of time socializing with peers are more likely to engage in deviant behaviors, especially if their parents are not around to supervise or control their behavior.[16] Teenage boys may have higher crime rates because they generally have more freedom than girls to engage in unsupervised socialization.[17] Girls who are physically mature and have more freedom without parental supervision are the ones most likely to have the opportunity to engage in antisocial acts.[18] In contrast, kids who are well supervised by parents and whose unsupervised activities are limited simply have less opportunity to commit crime.[19]

If lifestyle influences choice, can providing kids with "character-building" activities—such as a part-time job after school—reduce their involvement in delinquency? Research shows that adolescent work experience may actually increase antisocial activity rather than limit its occurrence. Kids who get jobs may be looking for an easy opportunity to acquire cash to buy drugs and alcohol; after-school jobs may attract teens who are more impulsive than ambitious.[20] At work, the opportunity to socialize with deviant peers combined with lack of parental supervision increases criminal motivation.[21] Although some adults may think that providing teens with a job will reduce their criminal activity ("idle hands are the devil's workshop"), many qualities of the work experience—autonomy, increased social status among peers, and increased income—may neutralize the positive effects of working. If providing jobs is to have any positive influence on kids, the jobs must in turn provide a learning experience and support academic achievement.[22]

Routine Activities Theory

If the motivation to commit delinquent acts is a constant, why do delinquency rates rise and fall? Why are some areas more delinquency ridden than others? To answer these questions, some choice theorists believe that attention must be paid to the opportunity to commit delinquent acts.[23]

AP Photo/Antonio Sierra, File

The motivation for delinquency can reflect both cultural factors and personal decision making. Here, Mexican soldiers present Edgar "El Ponchis" Jimenez Lugo to the media in the city of Cuernavaca, Mexico. A Mexican judge sentenced the 14-year-old U.S. citizen to three years in prison for organized crime, homicide, kidnapping, and drug and weapons possession. Authorities say the teenager confessed to working for the Beltran Leyva brothers' cartel and to killing four people whose beheaded bodies were hung from a bridge in the tourist town of Cuernavaca. As a child, Lugo lived a turbulent life of poverty and distant or absent parents and guardians, and fell into the drug underworld in small-town Jiutepec, near Cuernavaca.

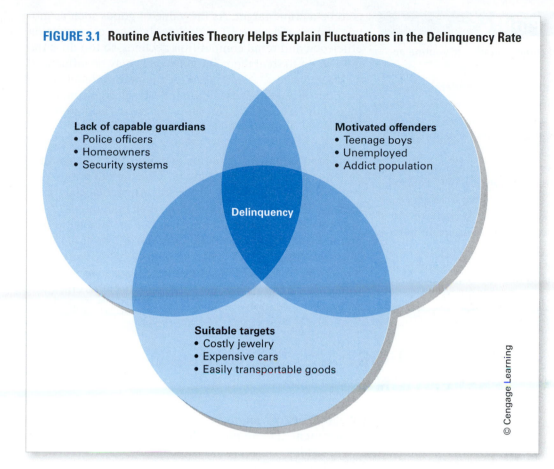

FIGURE 3.1 Routine Activities Theory Helps Explain Fluctuations in the Delinquency Rate

Lack of capable guardians
• Police officers
• Homeowners
• Security systems

Motivated offenders
• Teenage boys
• Unemployed
• Addict population

Delinquency

Suitable targets
• Costly jewelry
• Expensive cars
• Easily transportable goods

© Cengage Learning

According to **routine activities theory**, developed by Lawrence Cohen and Marcus Felson, the volume and distribution of **predatory crimes** (violent crimes against persons, and crimes in which an offender attempts to steal an object directly from its holder) in a particular area and at a particular time are influenced by the interaction of three variables: the availability of *suitable targets* (such as homes containing easily saleable goods), the absence of *capable guardians* (such as homeowners, police, and security guards), and the presence of *motivated offenders* (such as unemployed teenagers)[24] (see Figure 3.1).

This approach gives equal weight to opportunity and propensity: the decision to violate the law is influenced by opportunity, and the greater the opportunity, the greater the likelihood of delinquency.[25]

Lack of Capable Guardians. Kids will commit crimes when they believe their actions will go undetected by guardians, such as police, security guards, neighbors, teachers, or homeowners. They choose what they consider safe places to commit crimes and to buy and sell drugs.[26]

Research does show that crime levels are relatively low in neighborhoods where residents keep a watchful eye on their neighbors' property.[27] Delinquency rates trend upward as the number of adult caretakers (guardians) who are at home during the day decreases. With mothers at work and children in day care, homes are left unguarded, becoming vulnerable targets. In our highly transient society, the traditional neighborhood, in which streets are monitored by familiar guardians, such as family members, neighbors, and friends, has been vanishing and replaced by anonymous housing developments.[28] Potential thieves look for these unguarded neighborhoods in order to plan their break-ins and burglaries.[29]

Suitable Targets. The availability of suitable targets, such as DVD players, smartphones, digital cameras, jewelry, and cash, will increase crime rates. Research has generally supported the fact that the more wealth a home contains, the more likely it

routine activities theory The view that crime is a normal function of the routine activities of modern living. Offenses can be expected if there is a motivated offender and a suitable target that is not protected by capable guardians.

predatory crimes Violent crimes against persons and crimes in which an offender attempts to steal an object directly from its holder.

LO1 Know the principles of choice theory and routine activities theory.

✔ Choice theory suggests that young offenders choose to engage in antisocial activity because they believe their actions will be beneficial and profitable.

✔ Choice theory assumes that people have free will to choose their behavior.

✔ Kids who violate the law are motivated by personal needs such as greed, revenge, survival, and hedonism.

✔ The decision to violate the law comes after a careful weighing of the benefits and costs of criminal behaviors. Punishment should be only severe enough to deter a particular offense.

✔ Routine activities theory suggests that delinquent acts are a function of motivated offenders, lack of capable guardians, and availability of suitable targets.

is to be a crime target. As the value of goods such as mobile phones and camcorders declines because of production efficiency, and retail competition declines, so too does the motivation to steal them; burglary rates may be influenced by resale values.[30] And even if they contain valuable commodities, private homes and/or public businesses containing them may be considered off-limits if they are well protected by capable guardians and efficient security systems.[31]

Motivated Offenders. Routine activities theory also links delinquency rates to the number of kids in the population who are highly motivated to commit crime. If social forces increase the motivated population, then delinquency rates may rise. For example, if the number of teenagers in a given population exceeds the number of available part-time and after-school jobs, the supply of motivated offenders may increase.[32] As the crack epidemic of the 1980s waned, the delinquency rate dropped, because crack addicts are highly motivated offenders. **CHECKPOINTS**

CHOICE THEORY AND DELINQUENCY PREVENTION

If delinquency is a rational choice and a routine activity, then delinquency prevention is a matter of convincing potential delinquents that they will be punished for committing delinquent acts, punishing them so severely that they never again commit crimes, or making it so difficult to commit crimes that the potential gain is not worth the risk. The first of these strategies is called *general deterrence,* the second *specific deterrence,* and the third *situational crime prevention.* Let's look at each of these strategies in more detail.

General Deterrence

The **general deterrence** concept holds that the choice to commit delinquent acts can be controlled by the threat of punishment. The concept is simple: People will commit crime if they believe they will be successful in their criminal endeavor.[33] In contrast, if people believe illegal behavior will result in severe sanctions, they will choose not to commit crimes.[34] If kids believed that their delinquencies would result in apprehension and punishment, then only the truly irrational would commit crime.[35]

A guiding principle of deterrence theory is that the more severe, certain, and swift the punishment, the greater the deterrent effect.[36] Even if a particular delinquent act carries a very severe punishment, there will be relatively little deterrent effect if most adolescents do not believe they will be caught. Conversely, even a mild sanction may deter crime if kids believe punishment is certain.[37] So if the juvenile justice system can convince would-be delinquents that they will be caught, these youths may decide that delinquency simply does not pay.[38]

Deterrence and Delinquency. Traditionally, juvenile justice authorities have been reluctant to incorporate deterrence-based punishments on the ground that they interfere with the *parens patriae* philosophy. Children are punished less severely than adults, limiting the power of the law to deter juvenile crime. However, during the 1990s the increase in teenage violence, gang activity, and drug abuse prompted a reevaluation of deterrence strategies. Some juvenile courts shifted from an emphasis on treatment to an emphasis on public safety.[39] Police began to focus on particular problems in their jurisdiction rather than to react after a crime occurred.[40] They began to use aggressive tactics to deter membership in drug-trafficking gangs.[41] Some

general deterrence Crime control policies that depend on the fear of criminal penalties, such as long prison sentences for violent crimes. The aim is to convince law violators that the pain outweighs the benefit of criminal activity.

police officers were sent into high schools undercover to identify and arrest student drug dealers.[42] Proactive, aggressive law enforcement officers who quickly got to the scene of the crime were found to help deter delinquent activities.[43]

Another deterrent effort was to toughen juvenile sentencing codes and make it easier to waive juveniles to the adult court. In addition, legislators have passed more restrictive juvenile codes, and the number of incarcerated juveniles continues to increase. To those who advocate a get-tough approach to juvenile crime, these efforts have had a beneficial effect: the overall delinquency rate declined as the threat of punishment increased. Even the most committed juvenile offenders, gang boys, may now fear legal punishments, helping to explain the downward trend in juvenile crime. [44] There is evidence that adolescents who perceive they will be arrested and punished for their misdeeds are also the ones to forego delinquent behavior.[45]

Specific Deterrence

It stands to reason that if delinquents truly are rational and commit crimes because they see them as beneficial, they will stop offending if they are caught and severely punished. What rational person would recidivate after being exposed to an arrest, court appearance, and incarceration in an unpleasant detention facility, with the promise of more to come? According to the concept of **specific deterrence**, if young offenders are punished severely, the experience will convince them not to repeat their illegal acts. Juveniles are punished by state authorities with the understanding that their ordeal will deter future misbehavior.[46]

There is some evidence that kids learn from their mistakes. Research now shows that if a young offender commits a crime and is arrested for it, his or her risk perception of punishment will be higher than that of another adolescent who has escaped detection.[47] However, this effect may have limits: the more seasoned, experienced offender is less likely to be influenced by a current arrest than the novice delinquent. The deterrent effect of an arrest becomes attenuated or, in some cases, lost altogether, as the number of arrests continues to mount. For some reason, the more kids are arrested, the less likely they are to fear arrest!

In some instances, experiencing punishment may actually increase the likelihood that offenders will commit new crimes (recidivate).[48] In fact, a history of prior arrests, convictions, and punishments has proven to be the best predictor of rearrest among young offenders released from correctional institutions.[49] Kids who are placed in a juvenile justice facility are just as likely to become adult criminals as those treated with greater leniency, such as a community sentence.[50] And as sentence length increases, so too does the chance of recidivism.[51]

Why doesn't specific deterrence and strict punishment work with juveniles? There are a number of possible reasons:

- Punishment may breed defiance rather than deterrence. Kids who are harshly treated may want to show that they cannot be broken by the system.

- The stigma of harsh treatment labels adolescents and helps lock offenders into a criminal career instead of convincing them to avoid one.

- Kids who are punished may also believe that the likelihood of getting caught twice for the same type of crime is remote: "Lightning never strikes twice in the same spot," they may reason; no one is that unlucky.[52]

- Experiencing harsh punishment may cause severe psychological problems.[53]

- In neighborhoods where everyone has a criminal record, the effect of punishment erodes and juvenile offenders may begin to feel they have been victimized rather than fairly treated for their crimes.[54]

- Harsh punishments will mix novice offenders with experienced violent juveniles who will serve as mentors and role models, further involving them in a criminal way of life.

- Incarcerating youths cuts them off from prosocial supports in the community, making them more reliant on deviant peers. For example, incarceration may

specific deterrence Sending convicted offenders to secure incarceration facilities so that punishment is severe enough to convince them not to repeat their criminal activity.

diminish chances for successful employment, reducing access to legitimate opportunities and increasing the lure of a delinquent way of life.

Can Delinquency Be Deterred? The evidence on deterring juveniles is a mixed bag. Delinquency rates have undergone a two-decade decline during a period when there are more police on the street than ever before, and the nation has embraced a get-tough policy on crime and delinquency. However, these facts alone do not prove that deterrence actually works as expected. Research indicates that even the harshest punishment, such as a sentence to a secure juvenile correctional facility, does little to "correct" delinquent behavior. Incarcerated youth are often released back into the same disorganized communities that produced their original delinquencies; they often find it is easy to slip back into their old antisocial habits. Despite being severely sanctioned, a large percentage of serious juvenile offenders continue to commit crimes and reappear in the juvenile justice system. Research indicates that over 80 percent of youth under the age of 18 are rearrested after being released from custody, compared to less than half of adults 45 and older.[55]

Why does a deterrence strategy fail to get the desired result? There are a number of problems with relying on a strict punishment/deterrence strategy to control delinquency:

- Deterrence strategies are based on the idea of a "rational" offender, and therefore may not be effective when applied to young people. Minors tend to be less capable of making mature judgments, and many younger offenders are unaware of the content of juvenile legal codes. A deterrence policy will have little effect on delinquency rates of kids who are not even aware these statutes exist.[56] Teens seem more fearful of being punished by their parents or of being the target of disapproval from their friends than they are of the police.[57]

- Experienced offenders do not fear the legal consequences of their behavior. Research has found that getting arrested has little deterrent effect on youth and that kids who are experienced offenders are the ones most likely to continue committing crime after suffering an arrest. Crime-prone youth, ones who have a long history of criminality, know that crimes provide immediate gratification, whereas the threat of punishment is far in the future.[58]

- High-risk offenders—teens living in economically depressed neighborhoods—may not have internalized the norms that hold that getting arrested is wrong. They have less to lose if arrested; they have a limited stake in society and are not worried about their future. They also may not connect their illegal behavior with punishment, because they see many people committing crimes and not getting caught or being punished.

- Many juvenile offenders are under the influence of drugs or alcohol, a condition that might impair their decision-making ability.[59]

- Juveniles often commit crimes in groups, a process called **co-offending**, and peer pressure may outweigh the deterrent effect of the law.

- The most serious delinquents may neither fully comprehend the seriousness of their acts nor appreciate their consequences. As you may recall, many adolescents are risk takers who discount future consequences. According to deterrence theory, the *perception* that punishment will be forthcoming has a powerful influence on the decision to violate the law; people who perceive that they will be punished for crimes in the future will be the ones to avoid crime in the present.[60] The threat of punishment has little effect on kids who are risk takers who can't believe they will ever be caught and suffer punishment for their misdeeds.[61]

- Punishment may produce defiance rather than deterrence. Kids who believe they have been unfairly punished and stigmatized may reoffend, especially if they do not feel ashamed about what they have done.[62] Kids who have weak bonds to parents and others are especially prone to be defiant compared to those who have strong social bonds and can understand why they were being punished.[63]

co-offending Committing criminal acts in groups.

In sum, while there is some evidence that deterrent measures can work with novice offenders who commit minor or petty offenses, more experienced and serious delinquents are harder to discourage.[64] It is also possible that some delinquent acts are more "deterrable" than others, and future research should be directed at identifying and targeting these preventable offenses.[65] And while delinquency rates have dropped during a period when deterrence strategies have been in vogue, it is possible that social factors in play during the same period may have explained the drop in the delinquency rate, including lower rates of drug abuse or reduced teen pregnancy. In addition, changing public opinion may alter punishment/deterrence-based strategies: as delinquency rates have declined and state budgets are in crisis, the public may demand low-cost alternatives to the "lock 'em up" policies that have been predominant for the past few decades.[66]

Situational Crime Prevention

According to the concept of **situational crime prevention**, in order to reduce delinquent activity, crime control efforts must recognize the characteristics of sites and situations that are at risk to crime; the things that draw or push kids toward these sites and situations; what equips potential delinquents to take advantage of illegal opportunities offered by these sites and situations; and what constitutes the immediate triggers for delinquent actions.[67] Delinquency can be neutralized if (1) potential targets are carefully guarded, (2) the means to commit crime are controlled, and (3) potential offenders are carefully monitored. Some desperate kids may contemplate crime, but only the truly irrational will attack a well-defended, inaccessible target and risk strict punishment.

Situational crime prevention strategies are designed to make it so difficult to commit delinquent acts that would-be offenders will be convinced the risks are greater than the rewards.[68] Rather than deterring or punishing individuals, these strategies aim to reduce opportunities to commit delinquent acts. This can be accomplished by:

- Increasing the effort to commit delinquent acts
- Increasing the risks of delinquent activity
- Reducing the rewards attached to delinquent acts
- Increasing the shame of committing a delinquent act
- Reducing provocations that produce delinquent acts
- Removing excuses for committing a delinquent act

Increasing the effort of delinquency might involve *target-hardening techniques*, such as placing unbreakable glass on storefronts. Some successful target-hardening efforts include installing a locking device on cars that prevents drunken drivers from starting the vehicle (the breath-analyzed ignition interlock device).[69] Access can be controlled by locking gates and fencing yards.[70] Facilitators of crime can be controlled by banning the sale of spray paint to adolescents in an effort to cut down on graffiti, or putting ID photos on credit cards to limit their use if stolen.

Increasing the risks of delinquency might involve improving lighting, creating neighborhood watch programs, controlling building exits, installing security systems, or increasing the number of security officers and police patrols. The installation of street lights may convince would-be burglars that their entries will be seen and reported.[71] Closed-circuit TV cameras have been shown to reduce the amount

situational crime prevention A crime prevention method that relies on reducing the opportunity to commit criminal acts by making them more difficult to perform, reducing their reward, and increasing their risks.

AP Photo/Jamie-Andrea Yanak

By controlling the means to commit delinquent acts, motivated offenders may be deterred from attempting to commit crimes. A student is patted down after passing through a newly installed metal detector at Success Tech Academy in Cleveland. The school reopened for the first time since a student went on a shooting rampage inside the school and then committed suicide. Can such measures prevent a determined person from committing similar crimes?

hot spot A particular location or address that is the site of repeated and frequent criminal activity.

crackdown A law enforcement operation that is designed to reduce or eliminate a particular criminal activity through the application of aggressive police tactics, usually involving a larger than usual contingent of police officers.

of car theft from parking lots, also reducing the need for higher-cost security personnel.[72] Cameras on school buses might reduce the incidence of violence, currently captured on cell phone cameras and quickly posted on the Internet.

Reducing the rewards of delinquency could include strategies such as making car stereos removable so they can be kept in the home at night, marking property so it is more difficult to sell when stolen, and having gender-neutral phone listings to discourage obscene phone calls. Tracking systems help police locate and return stolen vehicles. Increasing shame might include efforts to publish the names of some offenders in the local papers.

It might also be possible to reduce delinquency rates by creating programs that reduce conflict. Posting guards outside schools at closing time might prevent childish taunts from escalating into full-blown brawls. Anti-bullying programs that have been implemented in schools are another method of reducing provocation.

Some delinquents neutralize their responsibility for their acts by learning to excuse their behavior by saying things like "I didn't know that was illegal" or "I had no choice." It might be possible to reduce delinquency by eliminating excuses. For example, vandalism may be reduced by setting up brightly colored litter receptacles that help eliminate the excuse, "I just didn't know where to throw my trash." Reducing or eliminating excuses in this way also makes it physically easy for people to comply with laws and regulations, thereby reducing the likelihood they will choose crime.

Hot Spots and Crackdowns. One type of situational crime prevention effort targets locales that are known to be the scene of repeated delinquent activity. By focusing on a **hot spot**—for example, a shopping mall, public park, or housing project—law enforcement efforts can be used to crack down on persistent youth crime. A police task force might target gang members who are street-level drug dealers by using undercover agents and surveillance cameras in known drug-dealing locales. Unfortunately, these efforts have not often proven to be successful mechanisms for lowering crime and delinquency rates.[73] **Crackdowns** seem to be an effective short-term strategy, but their effect begins to decay once the initial shock effect wears off.[74] Crackdowns also may displace illegal activity to areas where there are fewer police.

Although these results are discouraging, delinquency rates seem to be reduced when police officers combine the use of aggressive problem solving with community improvement techniques (increased lighting, cleaned vacant lots) to fight particular crimes in selected places.[75] For example, an initiative by the Dallas Police Department to aggressively pursue truancy and curfew enforcement resulted in lower rates of gang violence.[76]

Concept Summary 3.1 summarizes these three methods of delinquency prevention and control.

Do Delinquents Choose Crime?

Although the logic of choice theory seems plausible, before we can accept its propositions several important questions need to be addressed. First, why do some poor and desperate kids choose to break the law, whereas others who live in the same neighborhoods manage to live law-abiding lives? Conversely, why do affluent suburban youths choose to break the law when they have everything to lose and little to gain?

Police prepare to arrest subjects during a crackdown on alleged gang members in Newburgh, New York. Crackdowns have an immediate impact that may erode over time since police cannot keep up a constant vigil.

CONCEPT SUMMARY 3.1 | Delinquency Prevention Methods

Method	Central Premise	Technique
General deterrence	Kids will avoid delinquency if they fear punishment.	Make punishment swift, severe, and certain.
Specific deterrence	Delinquents who are punished severely will not repeat their detention.	Use harsh punishments, such as a stay in secure offenses.
Situational crime prevention	Make delinquency more difficult and less profitable.	Harden targets, use prevention surveillance, street lighting.

Choice theorists also have difficulty explaining seemingly irrational crimes, such as vandalism, arson, and even drug abuse. To say a teenager painted swastikas on a synagogue after making a "rational choice" seems inadequate. Is it possible that violent adolescents—such as Dylan Klebold and Eric Harris, who killed 13 and wounded 21 classmates at Columbine High School in 1999—were rational decision makers? Or was their behavior the product of twisted minds? To assume they made a rational choice to kill their classmates seems ill advised.

In summary, choice theory helps us understand criminal events and victim patterns. However, the question remains, why are some adolescents motivated to commit crime whereas others in similar circumstances remain law abiding? Why do some kids choose crime over legal activities? The remaining sections of this chapter present some possible explanations. **CHECKPOINTS**

WWW

To get detailed information on the **Columbine tragedy**, visit the Criminal Justice CourseMate at CengageBrain.com, then access the Web Links for this chapter.

CHECKPOINTS

LO2 Compare the principles of general deterrence, specific deterrence, and situational crime prevention.

✔ General deterrence models are based on the fear of punishment. If punishments are severe, swift, and certain, then would-be delinquents would choose not to risk breaking the law.

✔ Specific deterrence aims at reducing crime through the application of severe punishments. Once offenders experience these punishments, they will be unwilling to repeat their delinquent activities.

✔ Situational crime prevention efforts are designed to reduce or redirect crime by making it more difficult to profit from illegal acts.

Eric was acting aggressively at school and had been involved in several fights.

CRITICAL THINKING If you were the assigned juvenile probation officer, what would you recommend to the judge regarding rules of supervision and services for Eric? Make a list of the goals you would like him to accomplish.

TRAIT THEORIES: BIOSOCIAL AND PSYCHOLOGICAL VIEWS

Choice theorists would have us believe that young people select crime after weighing the benefits of delinquent over legal behavior. Teens may decide to commit a robbery if they believe they will make a good profit, have a good chance of getting away, and even if caught, stand little chance of being severely punished. Conversely, they will forgo criminal activities if they see a lot of cops around and come to the conclusion they will get caught and punished. Their choice is both rational and logical.

However, not all social scientists agree with this scenario; there are those who do not believe that people are in control of their own fate. According to psychologist Bernard Rimland, antisocial behaviors are more correctly linked to genetically determined physical or mental traits and/or the effects of a toxic environment than they are to personal choice. In his book *Dyslogic Syndrome*, Rimland observes:

> . . . most "bad" children . . . suffer from toxic physical environments, often coupled with genetic vulnerability, rather than toxic family environments. . . . America's children are not their parents, but rather the poor-quality food substitutes they eat, the pollutants in the air they breathe, the chemically contaminated water they drink, and other less well-known physical insults that cause malfunctioning brains and bodies.[77]

Most trait theorists recognize that the child's environment and social world play important roles in shaping their behaviors; personal traits are not enough to control behaviors. For example, when Kevin Beaver and his associates examined teens who carried a gene pathology affecting the neurotransmitter dopamine, they found that they were more likely than noncarriers to join a delinquent crowd. However, kids from close-knit families were not influenced by their genetic makeup. It is possible that kids with more nurturing parents are able to mitigate the effects of the gene anomaly.[78] This study supports an interactive association between genetic influences and environment that is a feature of most contemporary trait theories.

So some scholars question whether adolescents choose crime after careful thought and consideration and instead maintain that delinquency and adolescent antisocial behavior are closely linked to an individual's mental and physical makeup. Youths who choose to engage in antisocial behavior manifest mental and physical traits that influence their choices and shape their behavior.

The *source* of behavioral control, therefore, is one of the main differences between trait and choice theories. Although both views focus on the individual, the choice theorist views delinquents as rational and self-serving decision makers. The trait theorist views their "decisions" as by-products of personal traits or experiences. To a choice theorist, reducing the benefits of crime by increasing the likelihood of punishment will lower the crime rate. Because trait theorists question whether delinquents are rational decision makers, they focus more on the treatment of mental and physical conditions as a method of delinquency reduction. In the next sections, the primary components of trait theory are reviewed.

The Origins of Trait Theory

The first attempts to discover why criminal tendencies develop focused on biological traits present at birth. This school of thought is generally believed to have originated with the Italian physician Cesare Lombroso (1835–1909).[79] Known as the father of criminology, Lombroso developed the theory of **criminal atavism**.[80] He found that delinquents manifest physical anomalies that make

criminal atavism The idea that delinquents manifest physical anomalies that make them biologically and physiologically similar to our primitive ancestors, savage throwbacks to an earlier stage of human evolution.

them similar to our primitive ancestors. These individuals are throwbacks to an earlier stage of human evolution. Because of this link, the "born criminal" has such traits as enormous jaws, strong canines, a flattened nose, and supernumerary teeth (double rows, as in snakes). Lombroso made statements such as: "[I]t was easy to understand why the span of the arms in criminals so often exceeds the height, for this is a characteristic of apes, whose forelimbs are used in walking and climbing."[81]

Contemporaries of Lombroso refined the notion of a physical basis of crime. Raffaele Garofalo (1851–1934) shared Lombroso's belief that certain physical characteristics indicate a criminal nature.[82] Enrico Ferri (1856–1929), a student of Lombroso, accepted the biological approach to explaining criminal activity, but he attempted to interweave social factors into his explanation.[83] The English criminologist Charles Goring (1870–1919) challenged the validity of Lombroso's research and claimed instead that delinquent behaviors bore a significant relationship to "defective intelligence."[84] Consequently, he advocated that criminality could best be controlled by regulating the reproduction of families exhibiting abnormal traits, such as "feeblemindedness."[85]

The early views that portrayed delinquent behavior as a function of a single biological trait had a significant impact on American criminology; biocriminologists helped develop a science of "criminal anthropology."[86] Eventually, these views evoked criticism for their unsound methodology and shoddy experimental designs (i.e., they failed to use control groups).[87] By the middle of the twentieth century, biological theories had fallen out of favor.

Contemporary Trait Theory

For most of the twentieth century, most delinquency research focused on social factors, such as poverty and family life. However, a small group of researchers kept alive the biological approach.[88] Some embraced *sociobiology*, a perspective suggesting that behavior will adapt to the environment in which it evolved.[89] Creatures of all species are influenced by their innate need to survive and dominate others. Sociobiology revived interest in a biological basis for crime. If biological (genetic) and psychological (mental) makeup controls all human behavior, it follows that a person's genes should determine whether he or she chooses law-violating or conventional behavior.[90]

Trait theorists argue that a combination of personal traits and environmental influences produce individual behavior patterns.[91] This risk may be elevated by environmental stresses, such as poor family life, educational failure, and exposure to delinquent peers. The reverse may also apply: a supportive environment may counteract adverse biological and psychological traits.[92]

Individual deficits by themselves do not cause delinquency. However, possessing suspect individual traits may make a child more susceptible to the delinquency-producing factors in the environment. For example, Ronald Simons and his associates recently found that adolescents who possess a particular genetic makeup are more susceptible to the effect of community and family adversity than others. Their genetic codes cause them to adopt a street code that relies on aggressive responses to provocation. They find that a substantial proportion of the population is genetically predisposed to be more responsive to their social environment than those with other genotypes.[93]

Today trait theory can be divided into two separate branches: the first, most often called biosocial theory, assumes that the cause of delinquency can be found in a child's physical or biological makeup, and the second points the finger at psychological traits and characteristics.

CHECKPOINTS

WAW

For a complete list of the **crime-producing physical traits identified by Lombroso**, visit the Criminal Justice CourseMate at CengageBrain.com, then access the Web Links for this chapter.

CHECKPOINTS

LO3 Trace the history and development of trait theory.

✔ The first attempts to discover why delinquent tendencies develop focused on the physical makeup of offenders.

✔ Biological traits present at birth were thought to predetermine whether people would live a life of crime.

✔ The origin of this school of thought is generally credited to the Italian physician Cesare Lombroso.

✔ These early views portrayed delinquent behavior as a function of a single factor or trait, such as body build or defective intelligence.

BIOSOCIAL THEORIES OF DELINQUENCY

The first branch of trait theory—**biosocial theory**—focuses on the association between biological makeup, environmental conditions, and antisocial behaviors. As a group, these theories suggest that kids who exhibit abnormal biological traits also have difficulty adjusting to the social environment. Their adjustment problems make normal social relations challenging. Because their biological inadequacy makes them socially dysfunctional, they are vulnerable to crime-producing stimulus in the environment. Three areas of biological functioning are suspect: biochemical makeup, neurological function, and genetic history.

Biochemical Factors

One area of concern is the suspected relationship between antisocial behavior and biochemical makeup.[94] Biochemical problems can begin at conception when mothers ingest harmful substances during pregnancy.[95] Maternal alcohol abuse during gestation has long been linked to prenatal damage and subsequent antisocial behavior in adolescence.[96]

Environmental contamination has been linked to adverse behavior changes as well. Children exposed to high levels of air pollution show evidence of cognitive impairment and inflammation in the prefrontal lobes of the brain, factors correlated with antisocial behavior in adolescence.[97] Early exposure to the environmental contaminant PCB (polychlorinated biphenyls) has been associated with lower IQ and greater distractibility in adolescence, conditions that have been linked to antisocial behaviors.[98] However, the primary focus is exposure to the metal lead, which can also begin at the prenatal stage due to the mother's consumption of foods that are high in lead content, such as seafood.[99] A number of research studies have confirmed that lead ingestion may be a direct cause of antisocial behaviors.[100]

Diet and Delinquency. There is evidence that a child's diet may influence his or her behavior through its impact on body chemistry. Either eliminating harmful substances or introducing beneficial ones into the diet can reduce the threat of antisocial behaviors.[101] Research conducted over the past decade shows that an over- or undersupply of certain chemicals and minerals in the adolescent diet, including sodium, mercury, potassium, calcium, amino acids, and/or iron, can lead to depression, hyperactivity, cognitive problems, intelligence deficits, memory loss, or abnormal sexual activity; these conditions have been associated with crime and delinquency.[102] It is also possible that a poor diet is indirectly related to antisocial activity. For example, attention deficit hyperactive disorder (ADHD) has been linked to delinquency, and its cause may be diet driven. Substances linked to a higher rate of ADHD include fast foods, processed meats, red meat, high-fat dairy products, and candy.[103]

A survey of existing research found that the combination of nutrients most commonly associated with good mental health and well-being is as follows:[104]

- Polyunsaturated fatty acids (particularly the omega-3 types found in oily fish and some plants)
- Minerals, such as zinc (in whole grains, legumes, meat, and milk), magnesium (in green leafy vegetables, nuts, and whole grains), and iron (in red meat, green leafy vegetables, eggs, and some fruit)
- Vitamins, such as folate (in green leafy vegetables and fortified cereals), a range of B vitamins (in whole grain products, yeast, and dairy products), and antioxidant vitamins, such as C and E (in a wide range of fruits and vegetables)

People eating diets that lack any of this combination of polyunsaturated fats, minerals, and vitamins, and/or contain too much saturated fat (or other elements,

biosocial theory The view that both thought and behavior have biological and social bases.

including sugar and a range of food and agricultural chemicals) seem to be at higher risk of developing the following conditions:

- Attention deficit hyperactivity disorder (ADHD)
- Depressive conditions
- Schizophrenia
- Dementia, including Alzheimer's disease

The survey found that we are eating too much saturated fat, sugar, and salt and not enough vitamins and minerals. This type of diet not only fuels obesity, cardiovascular disease, diabetes, and some cancers, but may also be contributing to rising rates of mental ill-health and antisocial behavior.

A number of research studies have found a link between diet and aggressive behavior patterns. In some cases, the relationship is direct; in others, a poor diet may compromise individual functioning, which in turn produces aggressive behavior responses. For example, a poor diet may inhibit school performance, and children who fail at school are at risk for delinquent behavior and criminality. Student misbehavior levels have been reduced in controlled experiments in which school-age subjects were provided with improved diets and provided with nutritional supplements.[105]

Hormonal Levels. Antisocial behavior allegedly peaks in the teenage years because hormonal activity is then at its greatest level. It is possible that increased levels of testosterone are responsible for excessive violence among teenage boys. Adolescents who experience more intense moods, anxiety, and restlessness also have the highest crime rates.[106] Hormonal sensitivity may begin very early in life if the fetus is exposed to abnormally high levels of testosterone. This may trigger a heightened response to the release of testosterone at puberty. Although testosterone levels may appear normal, the young male is at risk for overly aggressive behavior.[107] Females may be biologically protected from deviant behavior in the same way they are immune from some diseases that strike males.[108] Girls who have high levels of testosterone or are exposed to testosterone in utero may become more aggressive in adolescence.[109] Chapter 6 further discusses hormonal activity as an explanation of gender differences in delinquency.

Neurological Dysfunction

Another focus of biosocial theory is the neurological—brain and nervous system—structure of offenders. It has been suggested that children who manifest behavioral disturbances may have neurological deficits, such as damage to the hemispheres of the brain; this is sometimes referred to as **minimal brain dysfunction (MBD)**.[110] Such damage can lead to reduction in executive functioning (EF), a condition that refers to impairment of the cognitive processes that facilitate the planning and regulation of goal-oriented behavior. Impairments in EF have been implicated in a range of developmental disorders, including attention deficit hyperactivity disorder (ADHD), conduct disorder (CD), autism, and Tourette syndrome. EF impairments also have been implicated in a range of neuropsychiatric and medical disorders, including schizophrenia, major depression, alcoholism, structural brain disease, diabetes mellitus, and normal aging.[111]

Impairment in brain functioning may be present at birth, produced by factors such as low birth weight, brain injury during pregnancy, birth complications, and inherited abnormalities. Brain injuries can also occur later in life as a result of brutal beatings or child abuse by a parent. Emotional trauma can actually cause adverse physical changes in the brain, and these deformities can lead to depression, anxiety, and other serious emotional conditions.[112] The association between crime and neurological impairment is quite striking: about 20 percent of known offenders report some type of traumatic brain injury and suffer from a number of antisocial traits throughout their life course.[113]

minimal brain dysfunction (MBD) Damage to the brain itself that causes antisocial behavior injurious to the individual's lifestyle and social adjustment.

There is a suspected link between brain dysfunction and antisocial behaviors ranging from lying to murder.[114] Conduct disorder (CD), considered a precursor of long-term chronic offending, has been linked to neurological deficits. Children with CD lie, steal, bully other children, frequently get into fights, and break schools' and parents' rules; many are callous and lack empathy and/or guilt.[115] Adolescent boys with antisocial substance disorder (ASD) repeatedly engage in risky antisocial and drug-using behaviors. Research has linked this behavior with misfiring in particular areas of the brain and suppressed neural activity.[116] Similarly, an extensive meta-analysis conducted by James Ogilvie and his associates that analyzed existing research studies measuring the association between EF and antisocial behavior found that antisocial groups performed significantly worse on measures of EF compared with controls, and this association held across studies with varied subject classes and methodological approaches.[117]

Teenage Brains. Is there something about teenage brains that make their owners crime prone? There is evidence that aggressive teen behavior may be linked to the amygdala, an area of the brain that processes information regarding threats and fear, and to a lessening of activity in the frontal lobe, a brain region associated with decision making and impulse control. Research indicates that reactively aggressive adolescents—most commonly boys—frequently misinterpret their surroundings, feel threatened, and act inappropriately aggressive. They tend to strike back when being teased, blame others when getting into a fight, and overreact to accidents. Their behavior is emotionally "hot," defensive, and impulsive. Brain scans of impulsive teenagers exhibit greater activity in the amygdala than the brains of nonimpulsive teenagers.[118]

ADHD: Attention Deficit Hyperactivity Disorder. One neurological condition that has been linked to antisocial behavior patterns, attention deficit hyperactivity disorder (ADHD), is a condition in which a child shows a developmentally inappropriate distractibility, impulsivity, hyperactivity, and lack of attention.[119] Kids suffering from ADHD have a tough time paying attention, are easily distracted, and frequently act without thinking. They constantly run around and climb on things, cannot sit still, and have difficulty regulating their emotions.

No one is really sure how ADHD develops, but some psychologists believe it is tied to brain dysfunction or neurological damage to the frontal lobes of the brain. Whatever the cause, ADHD may result in poor school performance, including a high dropout rate, bullying, stubbornness, mental disorder, and a lack of response to discipline; these conditions are highly correlated with delinquent behavior. Children with ADHD are more likely to use illicit drugs, alcohol, and cigarettes in adolescence and are more likely to be arrested, to be charged with a felony, and to have multiple arrests than non-ADHD youths. There is also evidence that ADHD youths who also exhibit early signs of MBD and conduct disorder (e.g., fighting) are the most at risk for persistent antisocial behaviors continuing into adulthood. ADHD children are most often treated by giving them doses of stimulants, most commonly Ritalin and Dexedrine (or dextroamphetamine), which, ironically, help these children control their emotional and behavioral outbursts. The antimanic, anticonvulsant drug Tegretol has also been used effectively. New treatment techniques featuring behavior modification and drug therapies are constantly being developed to help children who have attention or hyperactivity problems.

Learning Disabilities. The relationship between **learning disabilities (LD)** and delinquency has been highlighted by studies showing that arrested and incarcerated children have a far higher LD rate than do children in the general population. Although approximately 10 percent of all youths have some form of learning disorder, LD among adjudicated delinquents is much higher.[120] There

learning disabilities (LD) Neurological dysfunctions that prevent an individual from learning to his or her potential.

Looking Back to Eric's Story

Eric, an only child, was diagnosed with attention deficit hyperactivity disorder (ADHD) at the age of 8, and also was suffering from reading and math deficiencies.

CRITICAL THINKING Could Eric's aggressive behavior have a biological basis? If so, write up a treatment plan that would be effective for helping him control his behavior.

There are a number of programs designed to help kids who suffer from ADHD. Here, students eat while camping out at the Center for Attention and Related Disorders (CARD) camp at the Great Hollow Wilderness School in New Fairfield, Connecticut. The four-week camp boasts one instructor for every two campers and provides the structure, discipline, and social order necessary for children who suffer from attention deficit hyperactivity disorder and similar disorders. The CARD program has only 39 students, and while the cost is out of reach for many, it is supplemented by scholarships, grants, and private donations.

are two possible explanations for the link between learning disabilities and delinquency.[121] One view, known as the *susceptibility rationale,* argues that the link is caused by side effects of learning disabilities, such as impulsiveness and inability to take social cues. In contrast, the *school failure rationale* assumes that the frustration caused by poor school performance will lead to a negative self-image and acting-out behavior.

Psychologist Terrie Moffitt has evaluated the literature on the connection between LD and delinquency and concludes that it is a significant correlate of persistent antisocial behavior (or conduct disorders).[122] She finds that LD correlates highly with early onset of deviance, hyperactivity, and aggressiveness.[123] And there is new evidence that the factors that cause learning disabilities are also highly related to substance abuse, which may help explain the learning disability–juvenile delinquency connection. The National Center on Addiction and Substance Abuse at Columbia University released findings that show how learning disabilities are linked to substance abuse:

- Risk factors for adolescent substance abuse are very similar to the behavioral effects of learning disabilities—reduced self-esteem, academic difficulty, loneliness, depression, and the desire for social acceptance. Thus, learning disabilities may indirectly lead to substance abuse by generating the types of behavior that typically lead adolescents to abuse drugs.

- A child with a learning disability is twice as likely to suffer ADHD as a member of the general population, and there is a high incidence of ADHD among individuals who abuse alcohol and drugs. It is known that as many as half of those suffering ADHD self-medicate with drugs and alcohol.

- Children who are exposed to alcohol, tobacco, and drugs in the womb are at higher risk for various developmental disorders, including learning disabilities. Furthermore, a mother who uses drugs while pregnant may be a predictor that the child will grow up in a home with a parent who is a substance abuser. This too will increase the risk that the child will abuse drugs or alcohol himself.[124]

Despite this evidence, the learning disability–juvenile delinquency link has always been controversial. It is possible that the LD child may not be more susceptible to delinquent behavior than the non-LD child and that the link may be an artifact of bias in the way LD children are treated at school or by the police. LD youths are more likely to be arrested, and if petitioned to juvenile court, they bring with them a record of school problems that may increase the likelihood of their being sent to juvenile court.

Arousal Theory. It has long been suspected that adolescents may engage in crimes such as shoplifting and vandalism, because they offer the thrill of "getting away with it."[125] Is it possible that thrill seekers have some form of abnormal brain functioning? Arousal theorists believe that some people's brains function differently in response to environmental stimuli. We all seek to maintain an optimal level of arousal: too much stimulation leaves us anxious, and too little makes us feel bored. However, there is variation in the way children's brains process sensory input. Some nearly always feel comfortable with little stimulation, whereas others require a high degree of environmental input to feel comfortable. The latter become "sensation seekers," who seek out stimulating activities that may include aggressive behavior.[126] The factors that determine a person's level of arousal are not fully understood. Suspected sources include brain chemistry and brain structure. Another view is that adolescents with low heart rates are more likely to commit crimes, because they seek out stimulation to increase their arousal to normal levels.[127]

Genetic Influences

It has been hypothesized that some youths inherit a genetic configuration that predisposes them to aggression.[128] Biosocial theorists believe antisocial behavior characteristics and mental disorders may be passed down in the same way that people inherit genes that control height and eye color. One connection may be direct: (1) antisocial behavior is inherited, (2) the genetic makeup of parents is passed on to children, and (3) genetic abnormality is directly linked to a variety of antisocial behaviors.[129] It is also possible that the association is indirect: genes are related to some intervening factor that predisposes kids toward delinquency. For example, genetic makeup may shape our friendship patterns and orient people toward associating with conventional or antisocial friends. Those who maintain deviant peers are more likely to become crime prone.[130] Similarly, attachment to parents may be influenced by a genetic component; adolescents whose attachment to their parents is weak and attenuated may be more likely to engage in delinquent acts.[131]

How has the gene–delinquency association been tested? The approaches include the following.

Parental Deviance. If criminal tendencies are inherited, then the children of criminal parents should be more likely to become law violators than the offspring of conventional parents. A number of studies have found that parental criminality and deviance do, in fact, powerfully influence delinquent behavior.[132] Some of the most important data on parental deviance were gathered by Donald J. West and David P. Farrington as part of the long-term Cambridge Youth Survey. These cohort data indicate that a significant number of delinquent youths have criminal fathers.[133] Whereas 8 percent of the sons of noncriminal fathers eventually became chronic offenders, about 37 percent of boys with criminal fathers were multiple offenders.[134] Farrington has continued to examine intergenerational factors in delinquency. In one of his most important analysis, Farrington found that one type of parental deviance—schoolyard aggression or bullying—may be both inter- and intragenerational. Bullies have children who bully others, and these second-generation bullies grow up to father children who are also bullies, in a never-ending cycle.[135]

Farrington's findings are supported by some data from the Rochester Youth Development Study (RYDS), a longitudinal analysis that has been monitoring the

According to **arousal theory**, all of us seek to maintain a preferred or optimal level of arousal: Too much stimulation leaves us anxious and stressed out; too little makes us feel bored and weary. Some of us, such as singer Katy Perry shown here crowd surfing as Rihanna and Calvin Harris perform "We Found Love" during the 2012 Coachella Valley Music and Arts Festival in Indio, California, can channel our needs in productive ways. Others may get involved in dangerous or even violent behaviors.

behavior of 1,000 area youths since 1988. RYDS researchers have also found an intergenerational continuity in antisocial behavior: criminal fathers produce delinquent sons who grow up to have delinquent children themselves.[136]

In sum, there is growing evidence that crime is intergenerational: criminal fathers produce criminal sons who then produce criminal grandchildren. It is possible that at least part of the association is genetic.[137]

Twin Studies. One method of studying the genetic basis of delinquency is to compare twins to non-twin siblings. If crime is an inherited trait, identical twins should be quite similar in their behavior because they share a common genetic makeup. Because twins are usually brought up in the same household, however, any similarity in their delinquent behavior might be a function of environmental influences and not genetics. To guard against this, biosocial theorists have compared the behavior of identical, monozygotic (MZ) twins with fraternal, dizygotic (DZ) twins; the former have an identical genetic makeup, whereas the latter share only about 50 percent of their genes. Studies conducted on twin behavior detected a significant relationship between the criminal activities of MZ twins and a much lower association between those of DZ twins.[138] About 60 percent of MZ twins share criminal behavior patterns (if one twin was criminal, so was the other), whereas only 30 percent of DZ twins are similarly related.[139] If one twin joins a gang, the other is sure to follow.[140]

Among relevant findings:

- There is a significantly higher risk for suicidal behavior among monozygotic twin pairs than dizygotic twin pairs.[141]
- Differences in concordance between MZ and DZ twins have been found in tests measuring psychological dysfunctions, such as conduct disorders, impulsivity, and antisocial behavior.[142]

W/W

To learn more about twin research, go to the **Minnesota Twin Family Study, "What's Special About Twins to Science?"** by visiting the Criminal Justice CourseMate at Cengage Brain.com and accessing the Web Links for this chapter.

- MZ twins are closer than DZ twins in such crime relevant measures as level of aggression and verbal skills.[143]
- Both members of MZ twin pairs who suffer child abuse are more likely to engage in later antisocial activity more often than DZ pairs.[144]

Although this seems to support a connection between genetic makeup and delinquency, it is also true that MZ twins are more likely to look alike and to share physical traits than DZ twins, and they are more likely to be treated similarly. Shared behavior patterns may therefore be a function of socialization and not heredity.

One famous study of twin behavior still under way is the Minnesota Study of Twins Reared Apart, which is part of the Minnesota Twin Family Study. This research compares the behavior of MZ and DZ twin pairs who were raised together with others who were separated at birth and in some cases did not even know of the other's existence. The study shows some striking similarities in behavior and ability for twin pairs raised apart. The conclusion:

> We have found that an identical twin reared away from his or her co-twin seems to have about an equal chance of being similar to the co-twin in terms of personality, interests, and attitudes as one who has been reared with his or her co-twin. This finding leads us to believe that the similarities between twins are due to genes, not environment. Given that the differences between twins reared apart must be due totally to the environment, and given that these twins are just as similar as twins reared together, we can conclude that the environment, rather than making twins alike, makes them different.[145]

According to these findings, similarities between twins are due to genes, not to the environment.[146]

Adoption Studies. Another way to determine whether delinquency is an inherited trait is to compare the behavior of adopted children with that of their biological parents. If the criminal behavior of children is more like that of their biological parents (whom they have never met) than that of their adoptive parents (who brought them up), it would indicate that the tendency toward delinquency is inherited.

Studies of this kind have generally supported the hypothesis that there is a link between genetics and behavior.[147] Adoptees share many of the behavioral and intellectual characteristics of their biological parents despite the conditions found in their adoptive homes. Genetic makeup is sufficient to counteract even extreme conditions, such as malnutrition and abuse.[148]

In sum, twin studies and adoption studies provide some evidence that delinquent-producing traits may be inherited. Concept Summary 3.2 reviews the biological basis of delinquency. **CHECKPOINTS**

CONCEPT SUMMARY 3.2 | Biological Views of Delinquency

Theory	Major Premise	Focus
Biochemical	Delinquency, especially violence, is a function of diet, vitamin intake, hormonal imbalance, or food allergies.	Explains irrational violence. Shows how the environment interacts with personal traits to influence behavior.
Neurological	Delinquents often suffer brain impairment, as measured by the EEG. ADHD and minimal brain dysfunction are related to antisocial behavior.	Explains the relationship between child abuse and delinquency. May be used to clarify the link between school problems and delinquency.
Genetic	Criminal traits and predispositions are inherited. The criminality of parents can predict the delinquency of children.	Explains why only a small percentage of youth in a high-crime area become chronic offenders.

PSYCHOLOGICAL THEORIES OF DELINQUENCY

Some experts view the cause of delinquency as psychological.[149] After all, most behaviors labeled delinquent seem to be symptomatic of some psychological problem. Psychologists point out that many delinquent youths have poor home lives, conflicts with authority figures, and destructive relationships with neighbors, friends, and teachers. These relationships seem to indicate a disturbed personality. Furthermore, studies of incarcerated youths indicate that their personalities are marked by antisocial characteristics. One recent study of incarcerated youth found that at least 88 percent of males and 92 percent of females had a psychiatric disorder of some kind and that for some disorders, such as anxiety disorder, females (55 percent) were more likely to manifest symptoms than males (26 percent).[150] Because delinquent behavior occurs among youths in every racial, ethnic, and socioeconomic group, psychologists view it as a function of mental disturbance, rather than of social factors such as racism and poverty. Many delinquents do not manifest significant psychological problems, but enough do to give clinicians a powerful influence on delinquency theory.

Because psychology is a complex discipline, more than one psychological perspective on crime exists. Three prominent psychological perspectives on delinquency are psychodynamic theory, behavioral theory, and cognitive theory.[151] Figure 3.2 outlines these perspectives.

Psychodynamic Theory

According to the **psychodynamic theory**, which originated with the Austrian physician Sigmund Freud (1856–1939), law violations are a product of an abnormal personality formed early in life.[152] The theory argues that the personality contains three major components. The *id* is the unrestrained, pleasure-seeking component with which each child is born. The *ego* develops through the reality of living in the world and helps restrain the id's need for immediate gratification. The *superego* develops through interactions with parents and others and represents the conscience and the moral rules that are shared by most adults.

All three segments of the personality operate simultaneously. The id dictates needs and desires, the superego counteracts the id by fostering feelings of morality, and the ego evaluates the reality of a position between these two extremes. If these components are balanced, the individual can lead a normal life. If one aspect of the personality becomes dominant at the expense of the others, however, the individual exhibits abnormal personality traits. Furthermore, the theory suggests that an imbalance in personality traits caused by a traumatic early childhood can result in long-term psychological difficulties. For example, if parents fail to help the child develop his or her superego adequately, the child's id may become dominant. The absence of a strong

psychodynamic theory Branch of psychology that holds that the human personality is controlled by unconscious mental processes developed early in childhood.

FIGURE 3.2 **Psychological Perspectives of Delinquency**

Theory	Cause
Psychodynamic (psychoanalytic)	**Intrapsychic processes** • Unconscious conflicts • Childhood traumas • Family abuse • Neurosis • Psychosis
Behavioral	**Learning processes** • Past experiences • Stimuli • Rewards and punishments
Cognitive	**Information processing** • Thinking • Problem solving • Script • Moral development

© Cengage Learning

AP Photo/Kelley McCall, Pool, File

Alyssa Bustamante, 15, listens during a brief hearing where her attorney entered not-guilty pleas on her behalf to charges of armed criminal action and first-degree murder in Cole County Circuit Court in Jefferson City, Missouri. Bustamante admitted stabbing, strangling, and slitting the throat of a young neighbor girl, writing in her journal on the night of the killing that it was an "ahmazing" and "pretty enjoyable" experience—then headed off to church with a laugh. The words written by Bustamante were read aloud in court as part of a sentencing hearing to determine whether she should get life in prison or something less for the murder of her neighbor, 9-year-old Elizabeth Olten, in a small town west of Jefferson City. Bustamente received a life sentence but will one day be eligible for parole. Can someone like this be considered truly normal or were her actions the product of a mental defect or illness?

superego results in an inability to distinguish clearly between right and wrong. Later, the youth may demand immediate gratification, lack sensitivity for the needs of others, act aggressively and impulsively, or demonstrate psychotic symptoms. Antisocial behavior may result from conflict or trauma occurring early in a child's development, and delinquent activity may become an outlet for these feelings.

Disorders and Delinquency. According to Freud's version of psychodynamic theory, people who experience anxiety and fear they are losing control are suffering from a form of *neurosis* and are referred to as *neurotics*. People who have lost control and are dominated by their id are known as *psychotics*; their behavior may be marked by hallucinations and inappropriate responses.

Psychosis takes many forms, the most common being *schizophrenia*, a condition marked by illogical thought processes, distorted perceptions, and abnormal emotional expression. According to the classical psychoanalytic view, the most serious types of antisocial behavior might be motivated by psychosis, whereas neurotic feelings would be responsible for less serious delinquent acts and status offenses.[153]

Contemporary psychologists no longer use the term *neuroses* to describe all forms of unconscious conflict, and it is now more common to refer to specific types of disorders, including anxiety disorder, mood disorder, sleep disorder, and **bipolar disorder**, in which moods alternate between periods of wild elation and deep depression.[154]

Attachment and Delinquency. According to psychologist John Bowlby's **attachment theory**, the ability to have an emotional bond to another person has important lasting psychological implications that follow people across the lifespan.[155] Attachments are formed soon after birth, when infants bond with their mothers. Babies will become frantic, crying and clinging, to prevent separation or to reestablish contact with a missing parent. Attachment figures, especially the mother, must provide support and care, and without attachment an infant would be helpless and could not survive.

Failure to develop proper attachment may cause kids to fall prey to a number of psychological disorders, some which resemble attention deficit hyperactivity disorder (ADHD). They may be impulsive and have difficulty concentrating, and consequently experience difficulty in school. As adults, they often have difficulty initiating and sustaining relationships with others and find it difficult to sustain romantic relationships. Criminologists have linked people having detachment problems with a variety of antisocial behaviors including sexual assault and child abuse.[156] It has been suggested that boys disproportionately experience disrupted attachment and that these disruptions are causally related to disproportionate rates of male offending.[157]

bipolar disorder A psychological condition producing mood swings between wild elation and deep depression.

attachment theory Bowlby's view that the ability to have an emotional bond to another person has important lasting psychological implications for normal development from childhood into adulthood.

identity crisis Psychological state, identified by Erikson, in which youths face inner turmoil and uncertainty about life roles.

The Psychodynamic Tradition and Delinquency. How do psychodynamic theorists explain delinquency? Erik Erikson speculated that many adolescents experience a life crisis in which they feel emotional, impulsive, and uncertain of their role and purpose.[158] He coined the phrase **identity crisis** to denote this period of inner turmoil. Erikson's approach might characterize the behavior of youthful drug abusers as an expression of confusion over their place in society, inability to direct their behavior toward useful outlets, and perhaps dependence on others to offer solutions to their problems.

According to this vision, some kids (especially those who have been abused or mistreated) may experience unconscious feelings of fear and hatred toward their parents. Unresolved feelings of anger also occur when parents are inconsistent caregivers, sometimes being overindulgent and weak, and other times inconsiderate and self-indulgent. Inconsistent parenting places the child in an unpredictable and forbidding world in which they feel alone and helpless. While they are justifiably angry, they also instinctively know that parents are needed for survival. Faced with this dilemma, and because "good" kids are supposed to love their parents, the abused/neglected child represses anger toward the parents and turns their frustrations inward, creating a sense of self-anger or self-hatred. Wanting to be loved, they outwardly strive for perfection, while inwardly feel weak and unacceptable. This dissonance makes them prone to depression and mood disorders.[159]

The psychodynamic view is supported by research that shows that juvenile offenders suffer from a disproportionate amount of mental health problems and personality disturbance.[160] Violent youths have been clinically diagnosed as overtly hostile, explosive or volatile, anxious, and depressed.[161] Research efforts have found that juvenile offenders who engage in serious violent crimes often suffer from some sort of mental disturbance, such as depression.[162]

Mental Disorders and Crime. Some forms of delinquency have been linked to mental disorders that prevent youths from appreciating the feelings of victims or controlling their need for gratification.[163] Some delinquents exhibit indications of such psychological abnormalities as schizophrenia, paranoia, and obsessive thoughts and behaviors.[164] Offenders may suffer from a wide variety of mood and/or behavior disorders rendering them histrionic, depressed, antisocial, or narcissistic.[165] What are some of the specific disorders that have been linked to antisocial youth?

- *Oppositional defiant disorder (ODD).* Victims of this disease experience an ongoing pattern of uncooperative, defiant, and hostile behavior toward authority figures that seriously interferes with day-to-day functioning. Symptoms of ODD may include frequent loss of temper; constant arguing with adults; defying adults or refusing adult requests or rules; deliberately annoying others; blaming others for mistakes or misbehavior; being angry and resentful; being spiteful or vindictive; swearing or using obscene language; or having a low opinion of themselves.[166]

- *Conduct disorder (CD).* Kids suffering from conduct disorder have great difficulty following rules and behaving in a socially acceptable way.[167] They are often viewed by other children, adults, and social agencies as severely antisocial. They are frequently involved in such activities as bullying, fighting, committing sexual assaults, and behaving cruelly toward animals. Adolescents with elevated levels of conduct disorder in childhood and adolescence have been found to be at risk for engaging in a pattern of delinquency that persists from adolescence into adulthood. [168]

- *Clinical depression.* This psychiatric disorder is characterized by an inability to concentrate, insomnia, loss of appetite, and feelings of extreme sadness, guilt, helplessness, and hopelessness; there may be thoughts of death. Research shows that kids who are clinically depressed are more likely to engage in a wide variety of delinquent acts.[169]

- *Alexithymia.* Another disorder linked to delinquency is alexithymia, a deficit in emotional cognition that prevents people from being aware of their feelings or being able to understand or talk about their thoughts and emotions.[170]

- *Eating disorders.* Kids with eating disorders may take illegal drugs to lose weight or to keep from gaining weight.[171]

Although this evidence is persuasive, the association between mental disturbance and delinquency is unresolved. It is possible that any link is caused by some intervening variable or factor:

- Psychologically troubled youth do poorly in school and school failure leads to delinquency.[172]

- Psychologically troubled youth have conflict-ridden social relationships that make them prone to commit delinquent acts.[173]

- Kids who suffer child abuse are more likely to have mental anguish and commit violent acts; child abuse is the actual cause of both problems.[174]

- Living in a stress-filled urban environment may produce symptoms of both mental illness and crime.[175]

- The police may be more likely to arrest the mentally ill, giving the illusion that they are crime prone.[176]

© Julie Medlin

Julie Medlin, Ph.D.

Juvenile Psychologist, Director, Medlin Treatment Center

Julie Medlin is a licensed psychologist who currently serves as director of the Georgia-based Medlin Treatment Center, an outpatient counseling center specializing in the evaluation and treatment of sexual abuse and sexual deviancy. Medlin became interested in working with juvenile sex offenders after she conducted research with inmates in prison. When interviewing the inmates, she noticed that the sex offenders in particular appeared to be normal on the surface. She wondered how someone who appeared so normal could have molested a child or raped a woman.

After working in the field for many years, she still finds it fascinating to talk to sex offenders and try to understand their motivations.

Medlin finds her job to be rewarding because she believes that by treating sex offenders, she is helping reduce the number of children who will be sexually abused in the future. She also helps children who have already been sexually abused by seeing them for evaluations and therapy, and sometimes testifying on their behalf in court. She finds it gratifying to share her expertise with the judge and jury so they can make the best decision in each case. Medlin finds that treating sex offenders is an emotionally difficult job; the offenders tend to be in denial and often do not want to stop offending. Her job is to help them find the desire to change their abusive patterns and then teach them the tools they can use to prevent relapse.

In addition, in some instances delinquent behavior may actually produce positive psychological outcomes: it helps some youths feel independent, provides excitement and the chance to develop skills and imagination, provides the promise of monetary gain, allows kids to blame others (e.g., the police) for their predicament, and provides some youths with a chance to rationalize their sense of failure ("If I hadn't gotten into trouble, I could have been a success").[177] So while psychological disturbance has been linked to delinquency, antisocial behaviors may also create some psychological rewards!

The Professional Spotlight focuses on the career of Dr. Julie Medlin, a psychologist who works with adolescents who suffer from psychological disorders.

Behavioral Theory

Not all psychologists agree that behavior is controlled by unconscious mental processes determined by relationships early in childhood. Behavioral psychologists argue that personality is learned throughout life during interaction with others. Based primarily on the work of the American psychologist John B. Watson (1878–1958), and popularized by Harvard professor B. F. Skinner (1904–1990), **behaviorism** concerns itself with measurable events rather than unobservable psychic phenomena.

Behaviorists suggest that individuals learn by observing how people react to their behavior. Behavior is triggered initially by a stimulus or change in the environment. If a particular behavior is reinforced by some positive reaction or event, that behavior will be continued and eventually learned. However, behaviors that are not reinforced or are punished will be extinguished. For example, if children are given a reward (dessert) for eating their entire dinner, eventually they will learn to eat successfully. Conversely, if children are punished for some misbehavior, they will associate disapproval with that act and avoid that behavior.

Social Learning Theory. Some behaviorists hold that learning and social experiences, coupled with values and expectations, determine behavior. This is known as **social learning theory**. The most widely read social learning theorists are Albert Bandura,

behaviorism Branch of psychology concerned with the study of observable behavior rather than unconscious processes; focuses on particular stimuli and responses to them.

social learning theory The view that behavior is modeled through observation, either directly through intimate contact with others or indirectly through media. Interactions that are rewarded are copied, whereas those that are punished are avoided.

Walter Mischel, and Richard Walters.[178] They hold that children will model their behavior according to the reactions they receive from others; the behavior of adults, especially parents; and the behavior they view on television and in movies (see Focus on Delinquency, "Violent TV, Violent Kids?"). If children observe aggression and see that it is approved or rewarded, they will likely react violently during a similar incident. Eventually, they will master the techniques of aggression and become more confident that their behavior will bring tangible rewards.[179]

Social learning suggests that children who grow up in homes where violence is a way of life may learn to believe that such behavior is acceptable. Even if parents tell children not to be violent and punish them if they are, the children will model their behavior on the observed violence. Thus, children are more likely to heed what parents *do* than what they *say*. By middle childhood, some children have already acquired an association between their use of aggression against others and the physical punishment they receive at home. Often their aggressive responses are directed at other family members. The family may serve as a training ground for violence, because the child perceives physical punishment as the norm during conflict situations.[180]

Adolescent aggression is a result of disrupted dependency relations with parents. This refers to the frustration a child feels when parents provide poor role models and hold back affection. Children who lack close ties to their parents may have little opportunity or desire to model themselves after them or to internalize their standards.

In the absence of such internalized controls, the child's frustration is likely to be expressed in a socially unacceptable fashion, such as aggression.

Cognitive Theory

A third area of psychology that has received increasing recognition in recent years is **cognitive theory**. Psychologists with a cognitive perspective focus on mental processes. The pioneers of this school were Wilhelm Wundt (1832–1920), Edward Titchener (1867–1927), and William James (1842–1920). This perspective contains several subgroups. Perhaps the most important of these for delinquency theory is the one that is concerned with how people morally represent and reason about the world.

Jean Piaget (1896–1980), founder of this approach, hypothesized that reasoning processes develop in an orderly fashion, beginning at birth and continuing until age 12 and older.[181] At first, during the *sensorimotor stage*, children respond to the environment in a simple manner, seeking interesting objects and developing their reflexes. By the fourth and final stage, the *formal operations stage*, they have developed into mature adults who can use logic and abstract thought.

Lawrence Kohlberg applied this concept to issues in delinquency.[182] He suggested that there are stages of moral development during which the basis for moral decisions changes. It is possible that serious offenders have a moral orientation that differs from that of law-abiding citizens. Kohlberg classified people according to the stage at which their moral development has ceased to grow. In his studies, the majority of delinquents were revealed as having a lack of respect for the law and a personality marked by self-interest; in contrast, nonoffenders viewed the law as something that benefits all of society and were willing to honor the rights of others.[183]

Subsequent research has found that a significant number of nondelinquent youths displayed higher stages of moral reasoning than delinquents and that engaging in delinquent activities leads to reduced levels of moral reasoning, which in turn produces more delinquency in a never-ending loop.[184] For example, one recent study of juvenile sex offenders found that they suffered from impaired moral reasoning, especially if they themselves had earlier been the victim of sex offenses.[185]

cognitive theory The branch of psychology that studies the perception of reality and the mental processes required to understand the world we live in.

VIOLENT TV, VIOLENT KIDS?

One aspect of social learning theory that has received a great deal of attention is the belief that children will model their behavior after characters they observe on TV or see in movies. Many parents are concerned about the effects of their children's exposure to violence in the mass media. Often the violence is of a sexual nature, and some experts fear there is a link between sexual violence and viewing pornography.

Children are particularly susceptible to TV imagery. It is believed that many children consider television images to be real, especially if the images are authoritatively presented by an adult (as in a commercial). Some children, especially those considered emotionally disturbed, may be unable to distinguish between fantasy and reality when watching TV shows. Children begin frequent TV viewing at 2.5 years of age and continue at a high level during the preschool and early school years. But what do they watch? Marketing research indicates that adolescents ages 11 to 14 rent violent horror movies at a higher rate than any other age group; adolescents also use older peers and siblings or apathetic parents to gain access to R-rated films. Even children's programming is saturated with violence. It is estimated that the average child views 8,000 TV murders before finishing elementary school

MEDIA-VIOLENCE LINKAGE

A number of hypotheses have been formulated to explain the media–violence linkage:

- Media violence influences specific areas of the brain, including the precuneus, posterior cingulate, amygdala, inferior parietal, and prefrontal and premotor cortex of the right hemisphere region. These areas of the brain are involved in the regulation of emotion, arousal and attention, episodic memory encoding and retrieval, and motor programming. Extensive viewing may result in a large number of aggressive scripts stored in long-term memory in the posterior cingulate, which can then be used as a guide for social behavior.

- Observing media violence promotes negative attitudes, such as suspiciousness and the expectation that the viewer will become involved in violence. Those who watch television frequently view aggression and violence as common, socially acceptable behavior.

Information Processing. Cognitive theorists who study information processing try to explain antisocial behavior in terms of perception and analysis of data. When people make decisions, they engage in a sequence of thought processes. First, they encode information so it can be interpreted. Then they search for a proper response and decide on the most appropriate action. Finally, they act on their decision.[186] Law violators may lack the ability to perform cognitive functions in a normal and orderly fashion.[187] Some may be sensation seekers who are constantly looking for novel experiences, whereas others lack deliberation and rarely think through problems. Some may give up easily, whereas others act without thinking when they get upset.[188]

Adolescents who use information properly and can make reasoned decisions when facing emotion-laden events are best able to avoid antisocial behavior.[189] In contrast, delinquency-prone adolescents may have cognitive deficits and use information incorrectly when they make decisions.[190] They have a distorted view of the world that shapes their thinking and colors their judgments. These youths view crime as an appropriate means to satisfy their immediate personal needs, which take precedence over more distant social needs, such as obedience to the law.[191] They have difficulty making the right decision while under stress. As a result of their faulty calculations, they pursue behaviors that they perceive as beneficial and satisfying, but that turn out to be harmful and detrimental.[192] They may take aggressive

- Media violence allows aggressive youths to justify their behavior. Rather than causing violence, television may help violent youths rationalize their behavior as socially acceptable.

- Extensive and repeated exposure to media violence desensitizes kids to real-world violence, thereby increasing aggression by removing normal inhibitions against aggression.

- Media violence may disinhibit aggressive behavior, which is normally controlled by other learning processes. Disinhibition takes place when adults are viewed as being rewarded for violence and when violence is seen as socially acceptable. This contradicts previous learning experiences in which violent behavior was viewed as wrong.

Empirical research has supported the violence–media link. L. Rowell Huesmann and his associates found that children ages 6 to 9 who watched more violent television displayed more aggressive behavior than their peers. Recently Robert Morris and Matthew Johnson found a strong association between kids who spend a lot of time watching media and deviant behaviors and concluded that these sedentary activities might be even more important than having deviant peers in the production of delinquent behaviors.

Though this evidence is persuasive, the relationship between TV viewing and violence is still uncertain. Children may have an immediate reaction to viewing violence on TV, but aggression is extinguished once the viewing ends. Although experiments do show that children act aggressively in a laboratory setting after watching violent TV shows, that does not mean they will actually later go on to commit rape and assault. Despite the inconclusive evidence, efforts are ongoing to reduce TV violence and the ability of children to access violent programming.

CRITICAL THINKING

1. Should TV shows with a violent theme be prohibited from being aired on commercial TV before 9:00 P.M.? If you say yes, would you also prohibit news programs?

2. Even if a violence–TV link could be established, is it not possible that aggressive, antisocial youths may simply enjoy watching TV shows that support their personal behavioral orientation, in the same way that science fiction fans flock to *Star Wars* and *Star Trek* films?

Writing Assignment Write an essay entitled "The Myth of Violent Media: Why Violent Media Has NO Effect on People." Make sure to discuss both macro and micro issues. For example, if violent media has an effect, violence rates should have been lower in the centuries before media was available. Is that the case?

Sources: Robert Morris and Matthew Johnson, "Sedentary Activities, Peer Behavior, and Delinquency Among American Youth," *Crime and Delinquency*, published online November 4, 2010; Ingrid Möller, Barbara Krahé, Robert Busching, and Christina Krause, "Efficacy of an Intervention to Reduce the Use of Media Violence and Aggression: An Experimental Evaluation with Adolescents in Germany," *Journal of Youth and Adolescence* 41:105–120 (2012); L. Rowell Huesmann, Jessica Moise-Titus, Cheryl-Lynn Podolski, and Leonard Eron, "Longitudinal Relations Between Children's Exposure to TV Violence and Their Aggressive and Violent Behavior in Young Adulthood: 1977–1992," *Developmental Psychology* 39:201–221 (2003).

---

action because they wrongly believe that a situation demands forceful responses when it actually does not. They find it difficult to understand or sympathize with other people's feelings and emotions, which leads them to blame their victims for their problems.[193] Thus, the sexual offender believes their target either "led them on" or secretly wanted the encounter to occur.[194]

One reason for this may be that they are relying on mental scripts learned in early childhood that tell them how to interpret events, what to expect, how they should react, and what the outcome of the interaction should be.[195] Hostile children may have learned improper scripts by observing how others react to events; their own parents' aggressive, inappropriate behavior would have considerable impact. Some may have had early, prolonged exposure to violence (such as child abuse), which increases their sensitivity to slights and maltreatment.[196] Oversensitivity to rejection by their peers is a continuation of sensitivity to rejection by their parents.[197] Violence becomes a stable behavior, because the scripts that emphasize aggressive responses are repeatedly rehearsed as the child matures. When they attack victims, they may believe they are defending themselves, even though they are misreading the situation.[198] They may have a poor sense of time, leaving them incapable of dealing with social problems in an effective manner.[199]

Cognitive Treatment. Treatment based on information processing acknowledges that people are more likely to respond aggressively to a provocation when thoughts stir feelings of anger. Cognitive therapists attempt to teach people to control aggressive impulses by experiencing provocations as problems demanding a solution rather than as insults requiring retaliation. Programs teach problem-solving skills that may include self-disclosure, listening, following instructions, and using self-control.[200] Areas for improvement include (a) coping and problem-solving skills, (b) relationships with peers, parents, and other adults, (c) conflict resolution and communication skills, (d) decision-making abilities, (e) prosocial behaviors, including cooperation with others and respecting others, and (f) awareness of feelings of others (empathy).[201]

Personality and Delinquency

Personality can be defined as the stable patterns of behavior, including thoughts and emotions, that distinguish one person from another.[202] Personality reflects characteristic ways of adapting to life's demands. The way we behave is a function of how our personality enables us to interpret events and make appropriate choices. More than 50 years ago, Sheldon and Eleanor Glueck identified a number of personality traits that characterize delinquents, including self-assertiveness, extraversion, defiance, ambivalence, and impulsiveness.[203]

Following the Glueck effort, researchers have continued to examine the personality traits of delinquents, finding that many are impulsive individuals with short attention spans.[204] Among the most well-known efforts was psychologist Hans Eysenck's identification of two traits he closely associates with antisocial behavior: **extraversion** and **neuroticism**.[205] Extraverts are impulsive individuals who lack the ability to examine their own motives; those high in neuroticism are anxious and emotionally unstable.[206] Youths who are both neurotic and extraverted often lack insight and are highly impulsive. They act self-destructively, for example, by abusing drugs, and are the type of offender who will repeat their criminal activity over and over.[207]

The Antisocial Personality. It has also been suggested that delinquency may result from a syndrome interchangeably referred to as the **antisocial**, **psychopathic**, or **sociopathic personality**.[208]

Antisocial youths exhibit low levels of guilt and anxiety and persistently violate the rights of others. Although they may exhibit charm and be highly intelligent, these traits mask a disturbed personality that makes them incapable of forming enduring relationships.[209] Frequently involved in such deviant behaviors as truancy, lying, and substance abuse, antisocial people lack the ability to empathize with others. From an early age, the antisocial person's home life was filled with frustration and quarreling. Consequently, throughout life the antisocial youth is unreliable, unstable, and demanding.

Youths diagnosed as being clinically antisocial are believed to be thrill seekers who engage in destructive behavior. Some may become almost addicted to thrill seeking, resulting in repeated and dangerous risky behaviors.[210] Some become gang members and participate in violent sexual escapades to compensate for a fear of responsibility and an inability to maintain relationships.[211] Delinquents have been described as sensation seekers who desire an extraverted lifestyle, including partying, drinking, and having a variety of sexual partners.[212]

The Origins of Antisocial Personality. A number of factors contribute to the development of antisocial personalities. One source may be family dysfunction and include having an emotionally disturbed parent, parental rejection during childhood, and inconsistent or overly abusive discipline.[213] Callous, unemotional traits in very young children can be a warning sign for future psychopathy and antisocial behavior.[214]

extraversion Impulsive behavior without the ability to examine motives and behavior.

neuroticism A personality trait marked by unfounded anxiety, tension, and emotional instability.

psychopathic personality (also known as sociopathic or antisocial personality) A person lacking in warmth, exhibiting inappropriate behavior responses, and unable to learn from experience. The condition is defined by persistent violations of social norms, including lying, stealing, truancy, inconsistent work behavior, and traffic arrests.

Another possibility is that psychopaths may have brain-related physical anomalies that cause them to process emotional input differently than non-psychopaths.[215] Another view is that antisocial youths suffer from lower levels of arousal than the general population. Consequently, they may need greater-than-average stimulation to bring them up to comfortable levels.[216] Psychologists have attempted to treat antisocial youths by giving them adrenaline, which increases their arousal levels.

Intelligence and Delinquency

Early criminologists thought that if they could determine which individuals were less intelligent, they might be able to identify potential delinquents before they committed socially harmful acts.[217] Psychologists began to measure the correlation between IQ and crime by testing adjudicated juvenile delinquents. Delinquent juveniles were believed to be substandard in intelligence and thus inclined to commit more crimes than more intelligent persons. Thus, juvenile delinquents were used as a test group around which numerous theories about intelligence were built.

Nature Theory. When IQ tests were administered to inmates of prisons and juvenile training schools early in the twentieth century, a large proportion of the inmates scored low on the tests. Henry Goddard found in 1920 that many institutionalized persons were "feebleminded" and concluded that at least half of all juvenile delinquents were mental defectives.[218] In 1926, William Healy and Augusta Bronner tested a group of delinquents in Chicago and Boston and found that 37 percent were subnormal in intelligence.[219] They concluded that delinquents were 5 to 10 times more likely to be mentally deficient than nondelinquent boys. These and other early studies were embraced as proof that a correlation existed between innate low intelligence and deviant behavior. IQ tests were believed to measure genetic makeup, and many psychologists accepted the predisposition of substandard individuals toward delinquency. This view is referred to as the **nature theory** of intelligence.

Nurture Theory. In the 1930s, more culturally sensitive explanations of behavior led to the **nurture theory**. Nurture theory argues that intelligence is not inherited and that low-IQ parents do not necessarily produce low-IQ children.[220] This view holds that intelligence must be viewed as partly biological and primarily sociological. Nurture theorists discredit the notion that people commit crimes because they have low IQs. Instead, they postulate that environmental stimulation from parents, schools, peer groups, and others create a child's IQ level, and that low IQs result from an environment that also encourages delinquent behavior.[221] For example, if educational environments could be improved, the result might be both an elevation in IQ scores and a decrease in delinquency.[222]

Rethinking IQ and Delinquency. The relationship between IQ and delinquency is controversial, because it implies that a condition is present at birth that accounts for delinquent behavior throughout the life cycle and that this condition is not easily changed. Research shows that measurements of intelligence taken in infancy are good predictors of later IQ.[223] By implication, if delinquency is not spread evenly through the social structure, neither is intelligence.

Some social scientists actively dispute that any association actually exists. As early as 1931, Edwin Sutherland evaluated IQ studies of criminals and delinquents and found evidence disputing the association between intelligence and criminality.[224] His findings did much to discredit the notion that a strong relationship exists between IQ and criminality, and for many years the IQ–delinquency link was ignored. Sutherland's research has been substantiated by a number of contemporary studies that find that IQ has a negligible influence on behavior.[225]

nature theory The view that intelligence is inherited and is a function of genetic makeup.
nurture theory The view that intelligence is determined by environmental stimulation and socialization.

✔ According to psychodynamic theory, unconscious motivations developed early in childhood propel some people into destructive or illegal behavior.

✔ Behaviorists view aggression as a learned behavior.

✔ Some learning is direct and experiential while other types are observational, such as watching TV and movies. A link between media and violence has not been proven, but there is some evidence linking observing violent media with aggressive behavior.

✔ Cognitive theory stresses knowing and perception. Some adolescents have a warped view of the world.

✔ There is evidence that kids with abnormal or antisocial personalities are delinquency prone.

✔ Although some experts find a link between intelligence and delinquency, others dispute any linkage between IQ level and law-violating behaviors.

Even those experts who believe that IQ influences delinquent behavior are split on the structure of the associations. Some believe IQ has an *indirect influence* on delinquency. For example, Travis Hirschi and Michael Hindelang, after conducting a statistical analysis of IQ and delinquency data, found that "the weight of evidence is that IQ is more important than race and social class" for predicting delinquency.[226] They concluded that the link was indirect: children with low IQs are more likely to engage in delinquent behavior because low IQ leads to school failure, and educational underachievement is associated with delinquency.

In contrast, some experts believe IQ may have a *direct influence* on delinquency. The key linkage is the ability to manipulate abstract concepts. Low intelligence limits adolescents' ability to "foresee the consequences of their offending and to appreciate the feelings of victims."[227] Therefore, youths with limited intelligence are more likely to misinterpret events, take risks, and engage in harmful behavior.

Concept Summary 3.3 reviews the psychological basis of delinquency. **CHECKPOINTS**

Trait Theory and Delinquency Prevention

Trait theory perspectives on delinquency suggest that prevention efforts should be directed at strengthening a youth's home life and relationships. If parents cannot supply proper nurturing, discipline, nutrition, and so on, the child cannot develop properly. Whether we believe that delinquency has a biosocial basis, a psychological basis, or a combination of both, it is evident that prevention efforts should be oriented to reach children early in their development.

County welfare agencies and private treatment centers offer counseling and other mental health services to families referred by schools, welfare agents, and court authorities. In some instances, intervention is focused on a particular family problem that has the potential for producing delinquent behavior—for example, alcohol and drug problems, child abuse, or sexual abuse. In other situations, intervention is oriented toward developing the self-image of parents and children or improving discipline in the family. The accompanying box "Early Prevention Pays Off" describes one such program.

CONCEPT SUMMARY 3.3	**Psychological Views of Delinquency**	
Theory	**Major Premise**	**Focus**
Psychodynamic	The development of the unconscious personality early in childhood influences behavior for the rest of a person's life. Criminals have weak egos and damaged personalities.	Explains the onset of delinquency and why crime and drug abuse cut across class lines.
Behavioral	People commit crime when they model their behavior after others they see being rewarded for the same acts. Behavior is reinforced by rewards and extinguished by punishment.	Explains the role of significant others in the delinquency process. Shows how family life and media can influence crime and violence.
Cognitive	Individual reasoning processes influence behavior. Reasoning is influenced by the way people perceive their environment.	Shows why criminal behavior patterns change over time as people mature and develop their reasoning powers. May explain the aging-out process.

Early Prevention Pays Off

Helping a young person prior to engagement in a delinquent act can pay big dividends. In some instances, early prevention means helping kids develop defenses to resist the crime-promoting elements in their immediate environment. These early prevention programs focus on improving the general well-being of individual children. They are aimed at positively influencing the early risk factors or "root causes" of delinquency. Early risk factors may include structural factors such as poverty and residency in a lower-class neighborhood, socialization issues such as inadequate parental supervision and harsh or inconsistent discipline, and individual or trait issues such as a high level of hyperactivity or impulsiveness. Consequently, early prevention efforts are often multidimensional, targeting more than one risk factor at a time.

Children's Health and Well-Being

Because a supportive and loving home is so important for the successful development of a child, prevention programs are often aimed at improving family well-being. These programs are designed to help parents care for their children's health and general well-being, instill in their children positive values such as honesty and respect for others, and nurture prosocial behaviors.

One of the most important types of family-based programs to prevent juvenile delinquency involves the provision of home visitation by experienced and trained human resource personnel. One of the best-known home visitation programs is the Prenatal/Early Infancy Project (PEIP), which was started in Elmira, New York. This program has three broad objectives:

- To improve the outcomes of pregnancy

- To improve the quality of care that parents provide to their children (and their children's subsequent health and development)

- To improve the women's own personal life-course development (completing their education, finding work, and planning future pregnancies)

The program provides nurse home-visiting services to teenage, Medicaid-eligible, and first-time mothers. Prenatal and postpartum home visiting are available for the mother and for the child. Home visiting for routine health guidance is available to the child for two years after birth.

Prenatal and postpartum home visiting services are made by County Health Department Maternal Child Health (MCH) nurses upon referral from physicians, hospitals, local departments of social services, and other service providers. The MCH program provides prenatal, postpartum, and health guidance assessment to high-risk clients. MCH nurses also are able to provide skilled services to ill pediatric clients through the Certified Home Health Agency. There are no restrictive criteria for entry into the program.

The program targets first-time mothers-to-be who are under 19 years of age, unmarried, or poor. These mothers-to-be receive home visits from nurses during pregnancy and then during the first two years of their child's life. Each home visit lasts about one and a quarter hours, and the mothers are visited on average every two weeks. The home visitors give advice to the young women about child care, infant development, and the importance of eating properly and avoiding smoking and drinking during pregnancy.

Several cost/benefit analyses show that the benefits of this program outweigh its costs for the higher-risk mothers. Peter Greenwood and his colleagues measured benefits to the government or taxpayer (welfare, education, employment, and criminal justice), whereas Steven Aos and his colleagues measured a somewhat different range of benefits to the government (education, public assistance, substance abuse, teen pregnancy, child abuse and neglect, and criminal justice), as well as tangible benefits to crime victims. Both reported that for every dollar spent on the program, benefits were about three to four times greater: $4.06 according to Greenwood and his colleagues, and $2.88 according to Aos and his colleagues.

Critical Thinking

Is there a danger that early prevention will label or stigmatize kids as potential delinquents? Can trying to do good result in something that creates long-term harm?

Sources: Rand Corporation, "Early Childhood Interventions Benefits, Costs, and Savings," 2008, www.rand.org/pubs/research_briefs/RB5014/index1.html (accessed July 21, 2012); Peter Greenwood, Lynn Karoly, Susan Everingham, Jill Houbé, M. Rebecca Kilburn, C. Peter Rydell, Matthew Sanders, and James Chiesa, "Estimating the Costs and Benefits of Early Childhood Interventions: Nurse Home Visits and the Perry Preschool," in Costs and Benefits of Preventing Crime, ed. Brandon C. Welsh, David P. Farrington, and Lawrence W. Sherman (Boulder, CO: Westview Press, 2001); Steve Aos, Roxanne Lieb, Jim Mayfield, Marna Miller, and Annie Pennucci, Benefits and Costs of Prevention and Early Intervention Programs for Youth (Olympia, WA: Washington State Institute for Public Policy, 2004).

Some programs utilize treatment regimens based on specific theories (such as behavioral modification therapies). For example, the Decisions to Actions program in Kincheloe, Michigan, is organized around cognitive-behavioral restructuring of children's personalities. Its main focus is changing attitudes and beliefs associated with improper feelings and behaviors. Youths are taught to identify poor decision making and to explore the thinking behind bad decisions. They also are taught relapse prevention techniques that enable them to better manage their emotions and behavior. The 10-week program includes an assessment, meetings between the youths and mentors, victim empathy sessions where convicted felons speak with the youths, and team-building exercises.[228]

In addition, individual approaches have been used to prevent adjudicated youths from engaging in further criminal activities. Incarcerated and court-adjudicated youths are now almost universally given some form of mental and physical evaluation before they begin their correctional treatment. Such rehabilitation methods as psychological counseling and psychotropic medication (drugs like Ritalin) are often prescribed. In some instances, rehabilitation programs are provided through drop-in centers that service youths who are able to remain in their homes; more intensive programs require residential care. The creation of such programs illustrates that agents of the juvenile justice system believe that many delinquent youths and status offenders have psychological or physical problems and that their treatment can help reduce repeat criminal behavior. Faith in this approach suggests widespread agreement that delinquency can be traced to individual pathology.

The influence of psychological theory on delinquency prevention has been extensive, and programs based on biosocial theory have been dormant for some time. However, institutions are beginning to sponsor projects designed to study the influence of diet on crime and to determine whether regulating metabolism can affect behavior. Such efforts are relatively new and untested. Similarly, schools are making an effort to help youths with learning disabilities and other developmental problems. Delinquency prevention efforts based on biocriminological theory are still in their infancy.

SUMMARY

Choice theory suggests that young offenders choose to engage in antisocial activity because they believe their actions will be beneficial and profitable. Trait theory suggests that youthful misbehavior is driven by biological or psychological abnormalities, such as hyperactivity, low intelligence, biochemical imbalance, or genetic defects. Both views suggest that delinquency is an individual problem, not a social problem. Choice theory assumes that people have free will to choose their behavior. Kids who violate the law were motivated by personal needs such as greed, revenge, survival, and hedonism. The decision to violate the law comes after a careful weighing of the benefits and costs of criminal behaviors.

Routine activities theory holds that delinquency is produced by the lack of capable guardians, the availability of suitable targets, and the presence of motivated offenders (such as unemployed teenagers).

The general deterrence concept holds that the choice to commit delinquent acts is structured by the threat of punishment. One of the guiding principles of deterrence theory is that the more severe, certain, and swift the punishment, the greater its deterrent effect will be. Deterrence strategies are based on the idea of a rational, calculating offender. The theory of specific deterrence holds that if offenders are punished severely, the experience will convince them not to repeat their illegal acts. Some research studies show that arrest and conviction may under some circumstances lower the frequency of reoffending. Imprisoning established offenders may open new opportunities for competitors. An incapacitation strategy is also terribly expensive. Even if incarceration can have a short-term effect, almost all delinquents eventually return to society. In addition, incarceration exposes younger offenders to higher-risk, more experienced inmates who can influence their lifestyle and help shape their attitudes.

According to the concept of situational crime prevention, delinquency can be neutralized if (a) potential targets are carefully guarded, (b) the means to commit crime are controlled, and (c) potential offenders are carefully monitored. Situational crime prevention strategies aim to reduce the opportunities people have to commit particular crimes.

The first attempts to discover why delinquent tendencies develop focused on the physical makeup of offenders. Biological traits present at birth were thought to predetermine whether people would live a life of crime. The origin of this school of thought is generally credited to the Italian physician Cesare Lombroso. These early views portrayed delinquent behavior as a function of a single factor or trait, such as body build or defective intelligence.

There is a suspected relationship between antisocial behavior and biochemical makeup. One view is that body chemistry can govern behavior and personality, including levels of aggression and depression. Overexposure to particular environmental contaminants puts kids at risk for antisocial behavior. There is also evidence that diet may influence behavior through its impact on body chemistry. Hormonal levels are another area of biochemical research. Another focus of biosocial theory is the neurological—or brain and nervous system—structure of offenders. Biosocial theorists also study the genetic makeup of delinquents.

Some experts view the cause of delinquency as essentially psychological. According to psychodynamic theory, law violations are a product of an abnormal personality structure formed early in life and which thereafter controls human behavior choices. Behaviorists suggest that individuals learn by observing how people react to their behavior. Behavior is triggered initially by a stimulus or change in the environment. Cognitive theorists who study information processing try to explain antisocial behavior in terms of perception and analysis of data. A common theme is that delinquents are hyperactive, impulsive individuals with short attention spans (attention deficit hyperactivity disorder), who frequently manifest conduct disorders, anxiety disorders, and depression.

KEY TERMS

choice theory, p. 59

trait theory, p. 60

free will, p. 60

classical criminology, p. 60

routine activities theory, p. 65

predatory crimes, p. 65

general deterrence, p. 66

specific deterrence, p. 67

co-offending, p. 68

situational crime prevention, p. 69

hot spot, p. 70

crackdown, p. 70

criminal atavism, p. 72

biosocial theory, p. 74

minimal brain dysfunction (MBD), p. 75

learning disabilities (LD), p. 76

psychodynamic theory, p. 81

bipolar disorder, p. 82

attachment theory, p. 82

identity crisis, p. 82

behaviorism, p. 84

social learning theory, p. 84

cognitive theory, p. 85

extraversion, p. 88

neuroticism, p. 88

psychopathic personality (sociopathic or antisocial personality), p. 88

nature theory, p. 89

nurture theory, p. 89

QUESTIONS FOR REVIEW

1. Compare and contrast nature versus nurture theory of IQ.
2. List three mood disorders.
3. Distinguish between general and specific deterrence.
4. List three ways scientists link violent media to violent crime.
5. Name the three routine activities that produce crime and enhance the chances of victimization.
6. Define situational crime prevention.

QUESTIONS FOR DISCUSSION

1. Are all delinquent acts psychologically abnormal? Can there be "normal" crimes?
2. How would you apply psychodynamic theory to delinquent acts such as shoplifting or breaking and entering a house?
3. Can delinquent behavior be deterred by the threat of punishment? If not, how can it be controlled?
4. Do you think that watching violence on TV and in films encourages youths to be aggressive and antisocial?
5. Do beer advertisements that feature attractive, scantily dressed young men and women encourage drinking? If they do not encourage people to drink, why bother advertising? If suggestive advertising works in getting people to buy beer, then why shouldn't suggestive violence encourage kids to be violent?
6. Discuss the characteristics of psychopaths. Do you know anyone who fits the description?

You are a state legislator who is a member of the subcommittee on juvenile justice. Your committee has been asked to redesign the state's juvenile code, because of public outrage over serious juvenile crime.

At an open hearing, a professor from the local university testifies that she has devised a surefire test to predict violence-prone delinquents. The procedure involves brain scans, DNA testing, and blood analysis. Used with samples of incarcerated adolescents, her procedure has been able to distinguish with 90 percent accuracy between youths with a history of violence and those who are exclusively property offenders. The professor testifies that, if each juvenile offender were tested with her techniques, the violence-prone career offender could easily be identified and given special treatment. Their scores could be kept in a registry and law enforcement agencies notified of the offenders' whereabouts.

Opponents argue that this type of testing is unconstitutional, because it violates the Fifth Amendment protection against self-incrimination and can unjustly label nonviolent offenders. Any attempt to base policy on biosocial makeup seems inherently wrong and unfair. Those who favor the professor's approach maintain that it is not uncommon to single out the insane or mentally incompetent for special treatment and that these conditions often have a biological basis. It is better that a few delinquents be unfairly labeled than to ignore seriously violent offenders until it is too late.

Writing Assignment: Write a memo to your subcommittee addressing this issue. Make sure you cover your view on whether some kids are born to be delinquents or if they purposely choose crime. Make a recommendation: Should kids be tested to see if they have traits related to crime even if they have never committed a single offense? And if so, should special laws be created to deal with the potentially dangerous offender?

GROUPWORK

Divide the class into a number of small groups. Have each schedule an interview with someone who works directly with adolescents in either the social service or juvenile justice system personnel and discover their viewpoint on free will vs. determinism. Do they see the kids they work with as "damaged goods" or clear-headed, rational decision makers?

CHAPTER FOUR

Sociological Views of Delinquency

© Bushnell/Soifer/Getty Images

LEARNING OBJECTIVES

After reading this chapter you should:

1. Be familiar with the association between social conditions and crime.
2. Describe the principles of social disorganization theory.
3. Define the concepts of anomie and strain and how they are applied to the study of delinquency.
4. Be familiar with the concepts of social process and socialization and the theories that hold they are the key to understanding delinquent behavior.
5. Explain how the labeling process is related to delinquent careers.

CHAPTER OUTLINE

Jay's Story

Jay Simmons, the youngest of six children, was living with his family in an impoverished community when he entered the juvenile justice system. Around the age of 11, his problems were becoming more evident at home and school. He was absent from school on a regular basis, often stayed out all night with friends, and was eventually arrested on retail theft charges. Jay's parents were struggling to find permanent housing and faced being homeless, so Jay was voluntarily placed in foster care.

Jay was an engaging person and a talented athlete who excelled in school sports. Many adults could see great potential in him, but Jay's criminal activity continued. His foster parents became increasingly concerned that they could not provide the care and treatment Jay needed. In a short period of time, Jay was arrested on two more violations for disorderly conduct and battery while becoming involved in fights at school. He was at risk for being placed in a more secure living environment. Jay was sentenced to community supervision and probation.

Although his foster parents had established clear rules for him, Jay felt torn between his old way of life and the new possibilities. Jay struggled with the new rules and expectations. He missed some of his initial appointments with his probation officer and continued to skip school. There were also concerns that Jay was drinking alcohol and becoming involved in gang activities.

Jay's probation officer, family, and foster parents encouraged him to follow the court-ordered recommendations and understand the consequences of his behavior. He developed a strong relationship with his foster parents, who were direct and honest with Jay. The Substitute Care Unit at the local human services agency provided valuable support to Jay, his family, and foster parents. The team of professionals, coaches, and parents remained in close contact regarding Jay's behavior, as well as his academic progress. He began to see his own potential and the need to make changes in his life.

Accountability was a key ingredient of Jay's success. He attended a retail theft group to address his criminal behavior and to encourage him to take responsibility for his actions. With fellow group members, Jay could discuss the nature of his crimes, why they were wrong, the impact on victims, and how to prevent future delinquent acts by making better choices. Jay was also held accountable by being required to complete 15 hours of community service. He worked with the Youth Restitution Program and was assigned a counselor who helped him locate volunteer opportunities and verified his participation.

Jay's involvement with a variety of programs and the many caring adults in his life made a significant difference. Although Jay never returned to his parental home, with the support of his foster parents, he did remain in close contact with his family and they regularly attended activities together. Jay started thinking seriously about going to college. He successfully completed his court-ordered programs and stayed out of trouble, eventually graduating from high school and receiving a full athletic scholarship to attend college.

Jay's story is not atypical; however, unlike Jay, many troubled youths are not able to turn their lives around. Delinquents often live in tough urban environments in families torn apart and in stress. Although there may be some factors related to delinquent behavior at the individual level, some delinquency experts believe that the key to understanding delinquent behavior lies in the social environment. Most delinquents are indigent and desperate, not calculating or evil. Most grew up in deteriorated parts of town and lack the social support and economic resources familiar to more affluent members of society. Explanations of delinquency as an individual-level phenomenon fail to account for the consistent social patterns in the delinquency rate. Understanding delinquent behavior, then, may require identifying the destructive social forces in the environment and understanding the process in which they impact on human behavior.

SOCIAL FACTORS AND DELINQUENCY

What are the critical social factors believed to cause or affect delinquent behaviors?

Interpersonal Interactions

Social relationships with families, peers, schools, jobs, criminal justice agencies, and the like may play an important role in shaping behavioral choices. Inappropriate and disrupted social relations have been linked to crime and delinquency.[1]

Community Ecological Conditions

Social scientists have noted that the harm caused by residence in a deteriorated inner-city area, beset by poverty, decay, fear, and despair, extends from an increase in poor health to higher risk of criminal victimization.[2] Not surprisingly, these areas are the home of delinquent gangs and groups. Because these areas often have high violence rates, neighborhood kids are exposed to a constant stream of antisocial behaviors, which makes them susceptible to associating with violent peers and becoming the victim of violent crimes.[3] Even when neighborhood disadvantage and poverty are taken into account, the more often children are exposed to violence within their residential community the more likely they are to become violent themselves.[4]

Social Change

Political unrest and mistrust, economic stress, and family disintegration are social changes that have been found to precede sharp increases in crime rates. Conversely, stabilization of traditional social institutions typically precedes crime rate declines.[5]

Socioeconomic Status

The government estimates that there are now 46 million Americans living in poverty, defined as a family of four earning about $23,000 per year, who have scant, if any, resources, and suffer socially and economically as a result; this number has been increasing during the past decade.[6] In the United States, income inequality has become a national concern. The top 1 percent of households (the upper class) now own more than 35 percent of all privately held wealth, and the next 20 percent (managers, professionals, and small business owners) have 50 percent, which means that just 20 percent of the people possess 85 percent of all wealth, leaving only 15 percent for the bottom 80 percent (wage and salary workers). In terms of financial wealth (total net worth minus the value of one's home), the top 1 percent of households had an even greater share: 43 percent.[7]

It seems logical that people on the lowest rung of the economic ladder will have the greatest incentive to commit crime. They may be enraged by their lack of economic success or simply financially desperate and disillusioned. In either instance, delinquency, despite its inherent dangers, may seem an appealing alternative to a life of indigence. Economic influences may be heightened by the rapid advance in technology; kids who lack the requisite social and educational training have found the road to success almost impassable. A lack of opportunity for upward mobility may make drug dealing and other crimes an attractive solution for socially deprived, but economically enterprising people.[8] Because social institutions are frayed or absent, law-violating youth groups and gangs form and are free to recruit neighborhood youth. Both boys and girls who feel detached and alienated from their social world are at risk to become gang members.[9]

Racial Disparity

The consequences of racial disparity take a toll on youth. According the Census Bureau report, the average African American family median income was $32,068 in comparison to $54,620 for non-Hispanic white families. About 27 percent of African Americans in comparison to 10 percent of non-Hispanic whites were living at the poverty level. The current unemployment rate for blacks was twice that

In Candelaria, Texas (population 55), a remote town on the border of Texas and Mexico, necessities such as water are hard to come by. Poverty rates among minority groups are still double that of whites. How does growing up in conditions of limited socioeconomic resources affect behavior?

for non-Hispanic whites (16 percent and 7.5 percent, respectively). This pattern is consistent for both men and women.[10] The share of young black men without jobs has climbed relentlessly, with only a slight pause during the economic peak of the late 1990s. At last tally, the unemployment rates for whites is half that for blacks and 30 percent lower than that of Hispanics.[11] There are also race-based differences in high school completion; white rates are higher than those of minorities.[12]

Not only does race influence economic well-being, it also seems to determine how adolescents are treated if they become involved in the juvenile or adult justice systems. Because the juvenile justice system routinely provides less favorable outcomes for minority youth, it increases the chances they will develop an official criminal record at an early age. Consequently, any subsequent encounter with the law will result in more punitive treatment.[13] It is not surprising, considering this treatment disparity, that while for white males 1 in 30 men between the ages of 20 and 34 is behind bars, for black males in that age group the figure is 1 in 9; 1 in 100 black women in their mid- to late 30s is incarcerated compared to 1 in 355 European American women.[14]

All of these social problems and conditions take a toll on American youth and may help turn them toward anti-social behaviors. In this chapter, we will review the most prominent social theories of delinquency that are based on the effects of social problems and social relations. They are divided into three main groups: (1) *social structure theories* hold that delinquency is a function of a person's place in the economic structure, (2) *social process theories* view delinquency as the result of a person's interaction with critical elements of socialization, and (3) *critical theories* consider delinquent behavior to be a result of economic deprivation caused by the inequities of the capitalist system of production. **CHECKPOINTS**

CHECKPOINTS

LO1 Be familiar with the association between social conditions and crime.

✔ Poor kids are more likely to commit crimes, because they are unable to achieve monetary or social success in any other way.

✔ Some kids lack the social support and economic resources familiar to more affluent members of society.

✔ Harm caused by residence in a deteriorated inner-city area, wracked by poverty, decay, fear, and despair, extends from an increase in poor health to higher risk of criminal victimization.

✔ Children are hit especially hard by poverty.

✔ The burdens of underclass life are often felt most acutely by minority group members.

✔ Latino and African American children are more likely to be poor than Asian and white children.

SOCIAL STRUCTURE THEORIES

In 1966, sociologist Oscar Lewis coined the phrase **culture of poverty** to describe the crushing burden faced by the urban poor.[15] According to Lewis, the culture of poverty is marked by apathy, cynicism, helplessness, and mistrust of institutions, such as police and government. Mistrust of authority prevents the impoverished from taking advantage of the few conventional opportunities available to them. The result is a permanent **underclass** whose members have little chance of upward mobility or improvement. This extreme level of economic and social hardship has been related to psychological maladjustment: people who live in poverty are more likely to suffer low self-esteem, depression, and loneliness.

Nowhere are urban problems more pressing than in the inner-city neighborhoods that experience constant population turnover as their more affluent residents move to stable communities or suburbs. Social conditions have actually worsened in some urban areas during the past decade.[16] As a city becomes *hollowed out*, with a deteriorated inner core surrounded by less devastated communities, delinquency rates spiral upward.[17] Those remaining are forced to live in communities with poorly organized social networks, alienated populations, and high crime. Members of the urban underclass, typically minority group members, are referred to by sociologist William Julius Wilson as the **truly disadvantaged**.[18]

The impoverished are deprived of a standard of living enjoyed by most other citizens, and their children suffer from much more than financial hardship. They attend poor schools, live in substandard housing, and lack good health care. More than half of families in poverty are fatherless and husbandless; many are supported entirely by government aid. Instead of increasing government aid to the needy, states have limited the eligibility for public assistance.

Neighborhoods that provide few employment opportunities are the most vulnerable to predatory crime. Unemployment destabilizes households, and unstable families are more likely to produce children who choose aggression as a means of dealing with limited opportunity. Lack of employment opportunity also limits the authority of parents, reducing their ability to influence children. The cycle of poverty can lead to a variety of adverse outcomes, including life- and health-endangering conditions. Providing adequate care to children under these circumstances can be an immense undertaking.

Because adults cannot serve as role models, and social institutions are frayed or absent, law-violating youth groups and gangs form and are free to recruit neighborhood youths. Both boys and girls who feel detached and alienated from their social world are at risk to become gang members.[19] While most teen gangs engage in a variety of illegal activities, including drug dealing and crime, their true purpose is to provide a platform for members to confront poverty, racism, and conflict. They have their own culture language (i.e., gangsta rap), and members espouse a philosophy of survival by any means necessary.[20] (Gangs will be covered further and in more detail in Chapter 8.) As gang membership flourishes, predatory crime increases to levels that cannot easily be controlled by police. Higher crime rates cause the few remaining middle-class residents to flee the area, causing a further breakdown in the ability of the community to control crime.

This view of delinquency is both *structural* and *cultural*. It holds that delinquency is a consequence of (a) the inequalities built into the social structure and (b) the cultural values that form in inner-city poverty areas. Even youths who receive the loving support of family members are at risk of delinquency if they suffer from social disadvantage and are forced to live in disorganized areas.

The **social structure theories** tie delinquency rates to both socioeconomic structural conditions (e.g., poverty, chronic unemployment, neighborhood deterioration)

Looking Back to Jay's Story

Jay's parents had a tough time finding permanent housing, and because of this Jay was placed in foster care.

CRITICAL THINKING Considering Jay's rough beginnings, does his life show how poverty and homelessness are related to delinquent behavior? Respond to this statement: A supportive caretaker can overcome the effects of a destructive environment.

WWW

To read the transcript of an interview with **Dr. William Julius Wilson,** visit the Criminal Justice CourseMate at CengageBrain.com, then access the Web Links for this chapter.

---

culture of poverty The view that lower-class people form a separate culture with their own values and norms, which are sometimes in conflict with conventional society.

underclass Group of urban poor whose members have little chance of upward mobility or improvement.

truly disadvantaged According to William Julius Wilson, those people who are left out of the economic mainstream and reduced to living in the most deteriorated inner-city areas.

social structure theories Those theories that suggest that social and economic forces operating in deteriorated lower-class areas, including disorganization, stress, and cultural deviance, push residents into criminal behavior patterns.

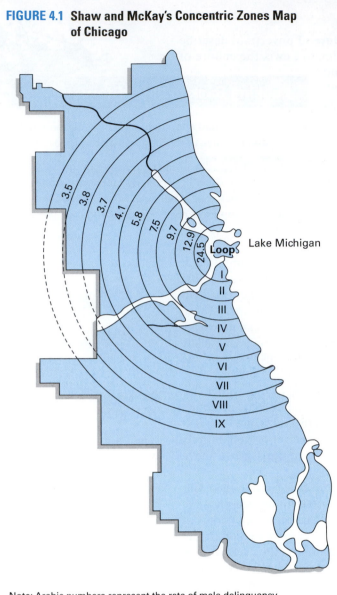

FIGURE 4.1 Shaw and McKay's Concentric Zones Map of Chicago

Lake Michigan

Loop

3.5 3.8 3.7 4.1 5.8 7.5 9.7 12.9 24.5

I
II
III
IV
V
VI
VII
VIII
IX

Note: Arabic numbers represent the rate of male delinquency.

Source: Clifford R. Shaw, *Delinquency Areas* (Chicago: University of Chicago Press, 1929), p. 99.

and cultural values (e.g., gang culture). Areas that experience high levels of poverty and social disorganization and also maintain deviant cultural values will also have high delinquency rates. Residents of such areas view conventional social values, such as hard work and getting an education, skeptically. They believe that they can never be part of the American Dream.

All social structure theorists are linked in their belief that social conditions control behavior choices. However, there are different interpretations of the nature of the interaction between social structure and individual behavior choices. Three prominent views stand out: social disorganization, anomie/strain, and cultural deviance.

Social Disorganization

The concept of **social disorganization** was first recognized early in the twentieth century by sociologists Clifford Shaw and Henry McKay. These Chicago-based scholars found that delinquency rates were high in what they called **transitional neighborhoods**—areas that had changed from affluence to decay. Here, factories and commercial establishments were interspersed with private residences. In such environments, teenage gangs developed as a means of survival, defense, and friendship. Gang leaders recruited younger members, passing on delinquent traditions and ensuring survival of the gang from one generation to the next, a process referred to as **cultural transmission**. While mapping delinquency rates in Chicago, Shaw and McKay noted that distinct ecological areas had developed what could be visualized as a series of concentric zones, each with a stable delinquency rate (see Figure 4.1).[21] The areas of heaviest delinquency concentration appeared to be the poverty-stricken, transitional, inner-city zones. The zones farthest from the city's center were the least prone to delinquency. Analysis of these data indicated a stable pattern of delinquent activity in the ecological zones over a 65-year period.[22]

social disorganization Neighborhood or area marked by culture conflict, lack of cohesiveness, a transient population, and insufficient social organizations. These problems are reflected in the problems at schools in these areas.

transitional neighborhood Area undergoing a shift in population and structure, usually from middle-class residential to lower-class mixed use.

cultural transmission The process of passing on deviant traditions and delinquent values from one generation to the next.

According to the social disorganization view, a healthy, organized community has the ability to regulate itself so that common goals (such as living in a crime-free area) can be achieved; this is referred to as **social control**.[23] Those neighborhoods that become disorganized are incapable of social control, because they are undermined by deterioration and economic failure; they are most at risk for delinquency.[24] Social control can come in variety of forms, including formal (e.g., police, courts, government agencies) and informal (e.g., parents, neighbors) sources. In areas where social control remains high, children are less likely to become involved with deviant peers and engage in problem behaviors.[25] Social institutions such as schools and churches can work effectively in maintaining order. Neighbors work together to control problem kids and keep police in the community.

In contrast, children who reside in disorganized neighborhoods live in an environment absent of social control. Their involvement with conventional social institutions, such as schools and after-school programs, is either absent or blocked, which puts them at risk for recruitment into gangs.[26] Because informal and formal avenues of social control have become frayed, kids are given a free hand to mix with deviant peers.[27] As a result, poor kids are more likely to engage in drug use and violence than the affluent. A recent federal survey found that kids who live at or near the poverty level are much more likely to engage in violent behavior than those whose families earn above the poverty line (see Figure 4.2).[28]

These problems are stubborn and difficult to overcome. Even when an attempt is made to revitalize a disorganized neighborhood by creating institutional support programs such as community centers and better schools, the effort may be countered by the ongoing drain of deep-rooted economic and social deprivation.[29] Even in relatively crime-free rural areas, areas that are disorganized as a result of residential instability, family disruption, and changing ethnic composition have relatively high rates of delinquent behavior and youth violence.[30]

A number of concepts define contemporary social disorganization theory.

Relative Deprivation. According to the concept of **relative deprivation**, in communities where the poor and the wealthy live relatively close to one another, kids who feel they are less well off than others begin to form negative self-feelings and hostility, a condition that motivates them to engage in delinquent and antisocial behaviors.[31] This feeling of relative deprivation fuels the frustration that eventually produces high delinquency rates.

Community Change. Some impoverished areas are being rehabilitated or **gentrified**, going from poor, commercial, or transient to stable, residential, and affluent. Other formerly affluent communities are becoming rundown. As the manufacturing economy is sent overseas, formerly affluent areas may experience job loss and a permanent change in their socioeconomic climate. Minority neighborhoods are especially hard hit by the loss of relatively high-paid manufacturing jobs and their replacement with a relatively low-paid service economy. Such change may foreshadow increases in substance abuse and drug-related arrests.[32]

Communities on the downswing are likely to experience increases in the number of single-parent families, changes in housing from owner- to renter-occupied units, a loss of semiskilled and unskilled jobs, and the growth in the numbers of discouraged, unemployed workers who are no longer seeking jobs. These communities also

WWW

The Northwestern University/ University of Chicago Joint Center for Poverty Research examines what it means to be poor and live in America. To find this website, visit the Criminal Justice CourseMate at CengageBrain.com, then access the Web Links for this chapter.

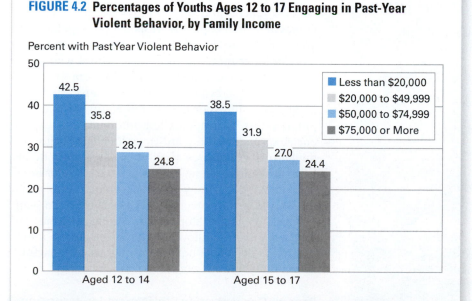

FIGURE 4.2 **Percentages of Youths Ages 12 to 17 Engaging in Past-Year Violent Behavior, by Family Income**

Percent with Past Year Violent Behavior

Legend:
- Less than $20,000
- $20,000 to $49,999
- $50,000 to $74,999
- $75,000 or More

Aged 12 to 14: 42.5, 35.8, 28.7, 24.8
Aged 15 to 17: 38.5, 31.9, 27.0, 24.4

Source: National Survey on Drug Use and Health (NSDUH), *Violent Behaviors and Family Income Among Adolescents*, August 19, 2010, www.samhsa.gov/data/2k10/189ViolentBehaviors/violentbehaviors.htm (accessed August 9, 2012).

social control Ability of social institutions to influence human behavior. The justice system is the primary agency of formal social control.

relative deprivation Condition that exists when people of wealth and poverty live in close proximity to one another. The relatively deprived are apt to have feelings of anger and hostility, which may produce criminal behavior.

gentrified The process of transforming a lower-class area into a middle-class enclave through property rehabilitation.

tend to develop mixed-use areas in which commercial and residential properties stand by side, an ecological development that increases the opportunity to commit crime.[33] Poverty becomes highly concentrated as people become despondent and employment opportunities nonexistent.[34] Urban areas marked by concentrated poverty become isolated and insulated from the social mainstream and more prone to gangs and juvenile.[35]

As communities deteriorate, those who can do so move to more affluent neighborhoods to improve their lifestyles.[36] Because of racial differences in economic well-being, those "left behind" are all too often minority citizens.[37] The remaining European American population may feel threatened as the percentage of minorities in the community increases and they are forced to compete with them for jobs and political power.[38] As racial prejudice increases, the call for "law and order" aimed at controlling the minority population grows louder.[39] Police become more aggressive, and young minority men believe they are the targets of unwarranted and unfair police harassment and discrimination.[40] See Figure 4.3.

Neighborhood change can produce conflict and increased violence in any neighborhood, regardless of racial/ethnic makeup. When John Hipp and his associates studied violence patterns in the South Bureau Policing Area of the Los Angeles Police Department, they found that the area had experienced dramatic demographic change as it transitioned from a predominately African American area to a predominately Latino area. Racial/ethnic transition led to greater levels of intergroup violence by both groups as well as more intragroup violence by Latinos.[41]

Community Fear. Disorganized neighborhoods suffer social incivility—trash and litter, graffiti, burned-out buildings, drunks, vagabonds, loiterers, prostitutes, noise, congestion, angry words. Having parks and playgrounds where teens hang out and loiter may contribute to fear.[42] As fear increases, quality of life deteriorates.[43] Residents become convinced that their neighborhood is dangerous and in decline.[44] They become fearful and wary and try not to leave their homes at night. People lose respect for the police: they are supposed to "serve and protect" the community but cannot seem to do their job.[45] Those who doubt that the agencies of justice can help them develop a degree of "legal cynicism"—they perceive the law as illegitimate, unresponsive, and ill equipped to ensure public safety.[46] Residents tell others of their experiences, spreading the word that the neighborhood is dangerous. Businesses avoid these areas, and neighbors try to move out and relocate to other, safer areas.

Ironically, fear may convince young people that the only way to protect themselves is to join a gang. While gang membership may be a dangerous pastime, increasing the likelihood of victimization and injury, gang boys do report being less anxious and fearful.[47] Community fear may breed gang membership.

Poverty Concentration. In fear-ridden transitional neighborhoods where residents are trying to get out as fast as possible, social institutions cannot mount an

FIGURE 4.3 The Cycle of Social Disorganization

Poverty
- Development of isolated lower-class areas
- Lack of conventional social opportunities
- Racial and ethnic discrimination

▼

Social disorganization
- Breakdown of social institutions and organizations such as school and family
- Lack of informal and formal social control

▼

Erosion of traditional values
- Development of gangs, groups
- Peer group replaces family and social institutions

▼

Limited collective efficacy
- Absence of informal social control
- Weakened institutional social control

▼

Development of criminal areas
- Neighborhood becomes crime-prone
- Stable pockets of crime develop
- Lack of external support and investment

▼

Cultural transmission
Adults pass norms (focal concerns) to younger generation, creating stable lower-class culture

▼

Criminal careers
Most youths age out of delinquency, marry, and raise families, but some remain in life of crime

© Cengage Learning

When fear grips a neighborhood, some residents flee while others fight. These neighbors in Austin, Texas, protest against crime and incivility in front of a local "adult bookstore," demanding changes in their community. This action may be considered an element of collective efficacy.

effective social control effort.[48] People who can get out do, and relocate to more stable, suburban areas. There they find that their exposure to crime and violence is significantly decreased; adolescents avoid gangs and involvement in criminal activities.[49] For those who are left behind, the future is not so rosy. Area poverty becomes concentrated as the more fortunate families flee to suburbia.[50] As the working and middle classes move out to the suburbs, they take with them their financial and institutional resources and support, undermining informal social control and reducing the inner city's ability to regulate itself.[51] The people left behind have even a tougher time managing with urban decay and conflict or controlling youth gangs and groups; after all, the most successful people in the community have left for greener pastures. Kids living in these disadvantaged areas are prone to conduct problems, and their misbehavior helps to unsettle the neighborhood even further.[52]

Because the population is transient, interpersonal relationships tend to be superficial. Neighbors don't know each other and can't help each other out. Social institutions such as schools and religious groups cannot work effectively in a climate of mistrust. Social control efforts are weak and attenuated.[53] Eventually the effect of concentrated poverty undermines community functions.[54]

Collective Efficacy. In contrast to disorganized areas, cohesive communities have high levels of social control and social integration; people know one another and develop interpersonal ties.[55] They experience relatively low crime rates and have the strength to restrict substance abuse and criminal activity.[56] Residents of these areas develop a sense of **collective efficacy**: mutual trust and a willingness to intervene in the supervision of children and help maintain public order.[57] Communities that are able to maintain collective efficacy can utilize their local institutions—businesses, stores, schools, churches, and social service and volunteer organizations—to control juvenile crime.[58] Parents in these areas are able to call on neighborhood resources to help control their children; single mothers do not have to face the burden of providing adequate supervision alone.[59] In neighborhoods with high levels of collective efficacy, parents are better able to function and effectively supervise their children. Confident and authoritative parents are able to prevent kids from joining gangs and getting involved in delinquent behavior.[60] This benefit of collective efficacy cuts across ethnic and racial lines.[61]

collective efficacy A process in which mutual trust and a willingness to intervene in the supervision of children and help maintain public order create a sense of well-being in a neighborhood and help control antisocial activities.

✔ The social structure view is that position in the socioeconomic structure influences the chances of becoming a delinquent.

✔ Poor kids are more likely to commit crimes, because they are unable to achieve monetary or social success in any other way.

✔ Kids who live in socially disorganized areas commit crime because the forces of social control have broken down.

✔ Social disorganization theory focuses on the conditions within the urban environment that affect delinquency rates, such as socioeconomic conditions.

✔ Delinquency rates are sensitive to the destructive social forces operating in lower-class urban neighborhoods.

✔ Poverty undermines the basic stabilizing forces of the community—family, school, peers, and neighbors—rendering them weakened, attenuated, and ineffective.

✔ The ability of the community to control its inhabitants—to assert informal social control—is damaged and frayed.

✔ Contemporary social disorganization theorists have found an association between delinquency rates and community deterioration: disorder, poverty, alienation, disassociation, and fear of delinquency.

When neighborhood kids see that people care in the community, the presence of informal social controls helps shape their behavior. It provides them with expectations on how they should behave even when adults are not around to monitor their activities.[62] Perceptions of collective efficacy are effective in helping kids avoid gang membership, thereby lowering neighborhood crime rates.[63] **CHECKPOINTS**

Anomie/Strain

Inhabitants of a disorganized inner-city area feel isolated, frustrated, ostracized from the economic mainstream, hopeless, and eventually angry. These are all signs of what sociologists call **strain**. How do these feelings affect criminal activities? To relieve strain, indigent people may achieve their goals through deviant methods, such as theft or drug trafficking, or they may reject socially accepted goals and substitute more deviant goals, such as being tough and aggressive.

It was Robert Merton (1910–2003), one of America's preeminent sociologists, who adopted the concept of strain to explain crime and delinquency. Merton argued that although most people share common values and goals, the means for legitimate economic and social success are stratified by socioeconomic class. Upper-class kids have ready access to good education and prestigious jobs; kids in the lower class rarely have such opportunities. Without acceptable means for obtaining success, individuals feel social and psychological strain; Merton called this condition **anomie**. Consequently, these youths may either (a) use deviant methods to achieve their goals (for example, stealing money) or (b) reject socially accepted goals and substitute deviant ones (for example, becoming drug users or alcoholics). Feelings of anomie or strain are not typically found in middle- and upper-class communities, in which education and prestigious occupations are readily obtainable. In lower-class areas, however, strain occurs because legitimate avenues for success are closed. Considering the economic stratification of U.S. society, anomie predicts that crime will prevail in lower-class culture, which it does.[64]

General Strain Theory. Merton's view focuses on the strain that builds up when lower-class kids become frustrated because they lack the means for achieving their personal goals. In his **general strain theory**, sociologist Robert Agnew argues that there are actually more sources of strain than Merton realized (see Figure 4.4).[65]

- *Strain caused by failure to achieve positively valued goals.* This type of strain will occur when youths aspire to wealth and fame, but assume that such goals are impossible to achieve. Also falling within this category is the strain that occurs when individuals compare themselves with peers who seem to be doing a lot better, or when youths believe they are not being treated fairly by a parent or a teacher. Such perceptions may result in reactions ranging from running away from the source of the problem to lowering the benefits of others through physical attacks or vandalism of their property. The student who believes he is being picked on unfairly by a teacher slashes the tires on the teacher's car for revenge.

- *Strain as the removal of positively valued stimuli.* Strain may occur because of the loss of a positively valued stimulus.[66] The loss of a girlfriend or boyfriend can produce strain, as can the death of a loved one, moving to a new neighborhood, or the divorce or separation of parents.[67] Loss of positive stimuli may lead to delinquency as the adolescent tries to prevent the loss, retrieve what has been lost, obtain substitutes, or seek revenge against those responsible for the loss. A child who

strain A condition caused by the failure to achieve one's social goals.

anomie Normlessness produced by rapidly shifting moral values; according to Merton, anomie occurs when personal goals cannot be achieved using available means.

general strain theory Links delinquency to the strain of being locked out of the economic mainstream, which creates the anger and frustration that lead to delinquent acts.

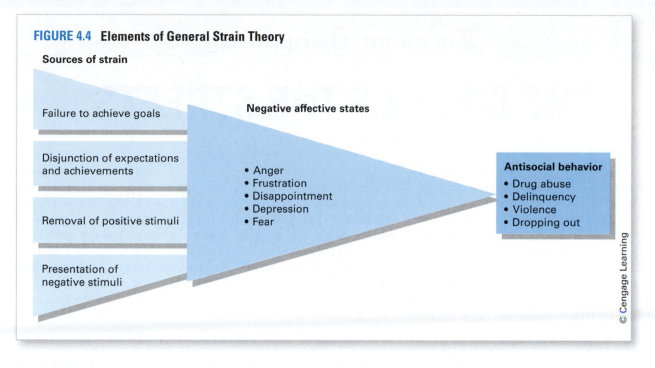

FIGURE 4.4 Elements of General Strain Theory

Sources of strain

- Failure to achieve goals
- Disjunction of expectations and achievements
- Removal of positive stimuli
- Presentation of negative stimuli

Negative affective states

- Anger
- Frustration
- Disappointment
- Depression
- Fear

Antisocial behavior

- Drug abuse
- Delinquency
- Violence
- Dropping out

© Cengage Learning

experiences parental separation or divorce early in his life may seek out deviant peers to help fill his emotional needs and in so doing increase his chances of delinquency.[68]

- *Strain as the presentation of negative stimuli.* Strain may also be caused by negative stimuli. Included in this category are such pain-inducing social interactions as child abuse, criminal victimization, school failure, and stressful events ranging from verbal threats to air pollution. Children who are abused at home may take their rage out on younger children at school or become involved in violent delinquency.[69]

According to Agnew, adolescents engage in delinquency as a result of **negative affective states**—the anger, frustration, fear, and other adverse emotions that derive from strain. The greater the intensity and frequency of strain experienced, the greater their impact and the more likely they are to cause delinquency. Even though some kids are better able to cope with strain, other kids are more likely to feel its effect, especially those with an explosive temperament, low tolerance for adversity, poor problem-solving skills, and who are overly sensitive or emotional.[70] As their perception of strain increases, so too does their involvement in antisocial behaviors.[71]

A number of research efforts have found support for many of Agnew's claims: kids who report feelings of stress and anger are more likely to interact with delinquent peers and engage in criminal behaviors[72]; kids who fail to meet success goals are more likely to engage in illegal activities.[73]

Agnew himself has found evidence that experiencing violent victimization and anticipating future victimization are associated with antisocial behavior.[74] This finding indicates not only that strain is produced by actual experiences, but that it may result from anticipated ones.

Cultural Deviance Theory

The third structural theory, **cultural deviance theory**, holds that delinquency is a result of youths' desire to conform to lower-class neighborhood cultural values that conflict with those of the larger society. In a socially disorganized neighborhood, conventional values, such as honesty, obedience, and hard work, exist but are hard to achieve. They exist side by side with lower-class values that stress being tough,

negative affective states Anger, depression, disappointment, fear, and other adverse emotions that derive from strain.

cultural deviance theory Links delinquent acts to the formation of independent subcultures with a unique set of values that clash with the mainstream culture.

Looking Back to Jay's Story

Initially, Jay struggled with rules and expectations. His team worked with him to help him establish and accomplish his goals.

CRITICAL THINKING Write an essay that covers the topic of motivation. How would you try to motivate a teen in trouble with the law?

THE CODE OF THE STREETS

A widely cited view of the interrelationship of culture and behavior is Elijah Anderson's concept of the code of the streets. He sees that life circumstances are tough for the "ghetto poor"—lack of jobs that pay a living wage, stigma of race, fallout from rampant drug use and drug trafficking, and alienation and lack of hope for the future. Living in such an environment places young people at special risk of crime and deviant behavior.

There are two cultural forces running through the neighborhood that shape their reactions. *Decent values* are taught by families committed to middle-class values and representing mainstream goals and standards of behavior. Although they may be better off financially than some of their street-oriented neighbors, they are generally "working poor." They value hard work and self-reliance and are willing to sacrifice for their children; they harbor hopes that their sons and daughters will achieve a better future. Most go to church and take a strong interest in education. Some see their difficult situation as a test from God and derive great support from their faith and from the church community.

In opposition, *street values* are born in the despair of inner-city life and are in opposition to those of mainstream society. The street culture has developed what Anderson calls a code of the streets, informal rules setting down both proper attitudes and ways to respond if challenged. If the rules are violated, there are penalties and sometimes violent retribution.

At the heart of the code is the issue of respect—loosely defined as being treated "right." The code demands that disrespect be punished or else hard-won respect will be lost. With the right amount of respect, a person can avoid

CHECKPOINTS

LO3 Define the concepts of anomie and strain and how they are applied to the study of delinquency.

✔ Anomie describes a society in which rules of behavior have broken down during periods of rapid social change or social crisis.

✔ Strain occurs when kids feel frustrated about their place in the social structure.

✔ Strain can also be produced by negative life events.

✔ Sociologist Robert Agnew's general strain theory explains why individuals who feel stress and strain are more likely to engage in delinquent acts.

✔ Delinquency is the direct result of negative affective states—the anger, frustration, and adverse emotions that kids feel in the wake of negative and destructive social relationships.

✔ Cultural deviance theories hold that a unique value system develops in lower-class areas; lower-class kids approve of behaviors such as being tough and having street smarts.

culture conflict When the values of a subculture clash with those of the dominant culture.

using your wits, not showing fear, and defying authority. Those adolescents who share lower-class values and admire criminals, drug dealers, and pimps may find it difficult to conform to the middle-class values that impress authority figures such as teachers or employers. They experience a form of **culture conflict** and are rendered incapable of achieving success in a legitimate fashion; as a result, they join together in gangs and engage in behavior that is malicious and negativistic.[75] Sociologist Elijah Anderson has studied this dilemma in his research on the "code of the streets." This concept is explored in the accompanying Focus on Delinquency feature.

Both legitimate and illegitimate opportunities are closed to youths in the most disorganized inner-city areas.[76] Consequently, they may join violent gangs to defend their turf, displaying their bravery and fighting prowess.[77] Instead of aspiring to be "preppies," they want to be considered tough and street-smart.

Youths living in disorganized areas consider themselves part of an urban underclass whose members must use their wits to survive or they will succumb to poverty, alcoholism, and drug addiction.[78] By joining gangs and committing crimes, lower-class youths are rejecting the culture that has already rejected them; they may be failures in conventional society, but they are the kings and queens of the neighborhood. CHECKPOINTS

"being bothered" in public. If he is bothered, not only may he be in physical danger, but he has been disgraced or "dissed" (disrespected). Some forms of dissing, such as maintaining eye contact for too long, may seem pretty mild. But to street kids who live by the code, these actions become serious indications of the other person's intentions and a warning of imminent physical confrontation.

These two orientations—decent and street—socially organize the community. Their coexistence means that kids who are brought up in decent homes must be able to successfully navigate the demands of the street culture. Even in decent families, parents recognize that the code must be obeyed or at the very least negotiated; it cannot simply be ignored.

The Respect Game

Young men in poor inner-city neighborhoods build their self-image on the foundation of respect. Having "juice" (as respect is sometimes called on the street) means they can take care of themselves even if it means resorting to violence. For street youth, losing respect on the street can be damaging and dangerous. Once they have demonstrated that they can be insulted, beaten up, or stolen from, they become an easy target. Kids from decent families may be able to keep their self-respect by getting good grades or a scholarship. Street kids do not have that luxury. With nothing to fall back on, they cannot walk away from an insult. They must retaliate with violence.

One method of preventing attacks is to go on the offensive. Aggressive, violence-prone people are not seen as easy prey. Robbers do not get robbed, and street fighters are not the favorite targets of bullies. A youth who communicates an image of not being afraid to die and not being afraid to kill gives himself a sense of power on the street.

CRITICAL THINKING

1. Does the code of the street, as described by Anderson, apply in the neighborhood in which you were raised? That is, is it universal?

2. Is there a form of "respect game" being played out on college campuses? If so, what is the substitute for violence?

Writing Assignment Write an essay discussing decent and street values. Focus on such issues as where street values come from and what reinforces them in contemporary society—for example, link street values to the media.

Source: Elijah Anderson, *Code of the Street: Decency, Violence, and the Moral Life of the Inner City* (New York: Norton, 2000).

SOCIAL PROCESS THEORIES: SOCIALIZATION AND DELINQUENCY

Not all sociologists believe that merely living in an impoverished, deteriorated, lower-class area is determinant of a delinquent career. Instead, they argue that the root cause of delinquency may be traced to learning delinquent attitudes from peers, becoming detached from school, or experiencing conflict in the home. Although social position is important, **socialization** is considered to be the key determinant of behavior. If the socialization process is incomplete or negatively focused, it can produce an adolescent with a poor self-image who is alienated from conventional social institutions.

Socialization is the process of guiding people into acceptable behavior patterns through information, approval, rewards, and punishments. It involves learning the systems needed to function in society. Socialization is a developmental process that is influenced by family and peers, neighbors, teachers, and other authority figures.

Early socialization experiences have a lifelong influence on self-image, values, and behavior. Even children living in the most deteriorated inner-city environments will not get involved in delinquency if their socialization experiences are positive.[79] After all, most inner-city youths do not commit serious crimes, and relatively few of those who do become career criminals. More than 14 million youths live in poverty, but the majority do not become chronic offenders. Simply living in a violent neighborhood does not produce violent children; research shows that family, peer, and individual characteristics play a large role in predicting violence in childhood.[80] Only those who experience improper socialization are at risk for crime.

What are the major influences on a child's socialization?

socialization The process of learning the values and norms of the society or the subculture to which the individual belongs.

In the Jenkins family, their nightly dinner is a happy time. It's the only time when the family sits and talks with everybody at once, without the ubiquitous game or computer in hand. The parents like to give the kids words of wisdom over the dinner table. Delinquency experts believe that parental efficacy can reduce the likelihood that kids will get involved in crime.

Family Relations

Research consistently shows a relationship between the elements of socialization and delinquency. The primary influence is the family. When parenting is inadequate, a child's maturational processes will be interrupted and damaged. Children who grow up in homes where parents use severe discipline, yet lack warmth and involvement in their lives, are prone to antisocial behavior.[81] Marital distress and conflict are significantly related to harsh and hostile negative parenting styles. Adolescents who live in this type of environment develop poor emotional well-being, externalizing problems, and antisocial behavior.[82]

The effects of family dysfunction are felt well beyond childhood. Kids who experience high levels of family conflict grow up to lead stressful adult lives, punctuated by periods of depression.[83] Children whose parents are harsh, angry, and irritable are likely to behave in same way toward their own children, putting their own offspring at risk.[84] Children who experience abuse, neglect, or sexual abuse are believed to be more crime prone and suffer from other social problems, such as depression, suicide attempts, and self-injurious behaviors.[85] Thus the seeds of adult dysfunction are planted early in childhood. In contrast, parents who are supportive and effectively control their children in a noncoercive fashion are more likely to raise children who refrain from delinquency; this is referred to as **parental efficacy**.[86] Delinquency will be reduced if parents provide the type of structure that integrates children into the family, while giving them the ability to assert their individuality and regulate their own behavior.[87] The family–crime relationship is significant across racial, ethnic, and gender lines and is one of the most replicated findings in the criminological literature.[88]

parental efficacy Parents are said to have parental efficacy when they are supportive and effectively control their children in a noncoercive fashion.

School

The literature linking delinquency to poor school performance and inadequate educational facilities is extensive. Youths who feel that teachers do not care, who consider themselves failures, and who drop out of school are more likely to become involved in a delinquent way of life than adolescents who are educationally successful. Many drop out and once they do are forced to enter the adult world.

Looking Back to Jay's Story

When juveniles are involved in the justice system, the issue of placement is always of concern. In this case, Jay was placed in foster care due to his parental situation. Jay developed an excellent relationship with his foster family, but there were some very difficult times.

CRITICAL THINKING Write an essay that discusses the positive and negative aspects of the foster care system. Make sure you include some suggestions on how the system could be improved.

Peers

Psychologists have long recognized that the peer group has a powerful effect on human conduct and can have a dramatic influence on decision making and behavior choices.[89] Peer influence on delinquent and criminal behavior has been recorded in different cultures and may be a universal norm.[90]

Youths who become involved with peers who engage in antisocial behavior and hold antisocial attitudes may be deeply influenced by negative peer pressure.[91] Kids who feel alienated and alone may become involved with similarly disaffected youth.[92] Being a social outcast causes them to hook up with friends who are dangerous and get them into trouble.[93]

Peer relations can be a double-edged sword. Popular kids who hang out with their friends without parental supervision are at risk for delinquent behaviors mainly because they have more opportunity to get into trouble.[94] Less-popular kids, who are routinely rejected by their peers, are more likely to display aggressive behavior and to disrupt group activities through bickering, bullying, or other antisocial behavior.[95] Those who report inadequate or strained peer relations, and who also say they are not popular with the opposite sex, are prone to delinquent behaviors.[96]

Once acquired, deviant peers may sustain or amplify antisocial behavior trends and delinquent careers.[97] Loyalty to delinquent peers is a powerful force that may neutralize other elements of social control, such as the fear of punishment.[98] In contrast, having prosocial friends who are committed to conventional success may help shield

Schools are a key ingredient in helping communities control delinquency. Here, a group of students demonstrates for equal access to education for low-income students from minority groups in south central Los Angeles. The demonstration was called during the 50th anniversary of the landmark Supreme Court decision *Brown v. Board of Education,* which banned segregation in public schools. The organizers, South Central Youth Empowered through Action (SCYEA), claimed that the ban has not done enough and more efforts are needed to grant access to college to students from low-income families. SCYEA launched a campaign to redefine student achievement by creating school policies that prepare students for graduation and post-secondary education. The Equal Access to A-G Classes campaign has helped more than 3,000 students to attend universities.

Social Process Theories: Socialization and Delinquency **109**

kids from crime-producing inducements in their environment.[99] Kids want to be like their best friends and may moderate their antisocial behavior in order to be in balance with their friends' behaviors.[100]

While social process theorists agree that these elements of socialization affect delinquency, they may interpret the association in different ways:

- *Learning.* Delinquency may be learned through interaction with other people. By interacting with deviant peers, parents, neighbors, and relatives, kids may learn both the techniques of crime and the attitudes necessary to support delinquency. According to this view, because they learn to commit crimes, children who are born good learn to be bad from others.

- *Control.* Delinquency may result when life circumstances weaken the attachment a child has to family, peers, school, and society. Because their bonds to these institutions are severed, some adolescents feel free to exercise antisocial behavior. This view assumes that people are born bad and then must be taught to control themselves through the efforts of parents and teachers.

- *Labeling.* Some kids are considered to be winners; they are admired and envied. Others are labeled as troublemakers, losers, or punks. They are stigmatized and find themselves locked out of conventional society and into a deviant or delinquent way of life. This view holds that kids are born neither bad nor good, but become what they are through the reactions of others.

Each of these views is discussed in the following sections.

Social Learning Theories

Social learning theories hold that children living in even the most deteriorated areas can resist inducements to crime if they have learned proper values and behaviors. Delinquency, by contrast, develops by learning the values and behaviors associated with criminal activity. Kids can learn deviant values from their parents, relatives, or peers. Social learning can involve the techniques of crime (how to hot-wire a car) as well as the psychological aspects (how to deal with guilt). The former are needed to commit crimes, whereas the latter are required to cope with the emotional turmoil that follows.

The best-known social learning theory is Edwin Sutherland's **differential association theory**.[101] Sutherland believed that as children are socialized, they are exposed to and learn prosocial and antisocial attitudes and behavior from friends, relatives, parents, and so on. A prodelinquency definition might be "don't get mad, get even" or "only suckers work for a living" (see Figure 4.5). Simply put, if the prodelinquency definitions they have learned outweigh the conventional ones, an adolescent will engage in antisocial behaviors.[102] The prodelinquency definitions will be particularly influential if they come from significant others, such as parents or peers, and are frequent and intense. Some kids may meet and associate with criminal "mentors," who teach them how to be successful criminals and gain the greatest benefits from their criminal activities.[103] In contrast, if a child is constantly told by her parents to be honest and never harm others, and is brought up in environment in which people "practice what they preach," then she will have learned the necessary attitudes and behaviors to allow her to avoid environmental inducements to delinquency.

While it is difficult to test the principles of differential association, there are indications that the

social learning theories Posit that delinquency is learned through close relationships with others; children are born good and learn to be bad from others.

differential association theory Asserts that criminal behavior is learned primarily in interpersonal groups and that youths will become delinquent if definitions they learn in those groups that are favorable to violating the law exceed definitions favorable to obeying the law.

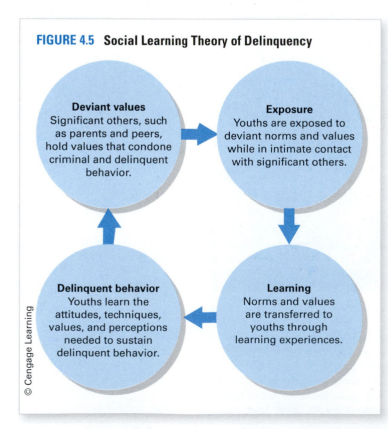

FIGURE 4.5 **Social Learning Theory of Delinquency**

Deviant values
Significant others, such as parents and peers, hold values that condone criminal and delinquent behavior.

Exposure
Youths are exposed to deviant norms and values while in intimate contact with significant others.

Learning
Norms and values are transferred to youths through learning experiences.

Delinquent behavior
Youths learn the attitudes, techniques, values, and perceptions needed to sustain delinquent behavior.

© Cengage Learning

theory has validity. For example, criminal careers appear to be intergenerational: kids whose parents are deviant and criminal are more likely to become criminals themselves and eventually to produce criminal children. The more time kids are exposed to, learn from, and are involved with criminal parents, the more likely they are to commit crime themselves.[104] Kids are more likely to engage in antisocial or deviant behavior when the attitudes that support it are reinforced by significant others such as parents or best friends.[105] Adolescents also seem to learn a lot from their boyfriends or girlfriends. Kids who go out with someone who is involved in antisocial behavior are more delinquent than those youths who have more law-abiding romantic partners.[106]

There is also an element of peer group pressure in social learning theory. If a valued friend drinks and smokes, it makes it a lot easier for a kid to engage in those behaviors himself; if his best friend does it, can it be so bad?[107]

Learning deviant values may also involve a cognitive shift: exposure to delinquency-reinforcing cues in the environment may make kids rethink their attitudes and values, perhaps developing a more cynical and detached view of life. This theme is explored in the Focus on Delinquency feature, which describes how kids "learn to be bad."

Recent reviews of the research on social learning theory have been positive, showing that kids who are exposed to antisocial values will eventually incorporate them into personal attitudes and behaviors.[108] Due to this continuing empirical support, social learning theory remains a pillar of delinquency theory.

Looking Back to Jay's Story

Jay was helped by supportive service agencies who worked closely with him and his foster parents.

CRITICAL THINKING Design a community service program that would help someone like Jay adjust to more conventional behavior patterns.

Social Control Theories

Social control theories, the second main branch of the social process approach, suggest that the cause of delinquency resides in the strength of the relationships a child forms with conventional individuals and groups. Those who are socialized to have close relationships with their parents, friends, and teachers will develop a positive self-image and the ability to resist the lure of deviant behaviors. They develop a strong commitment to conformity that enables them to resist pressures to violate the law. If, however, their bonds to society become fractured or broken, youths will feel free to violate the law because they are not worried about jeopardizing their social relationships (see Figure 4.6).

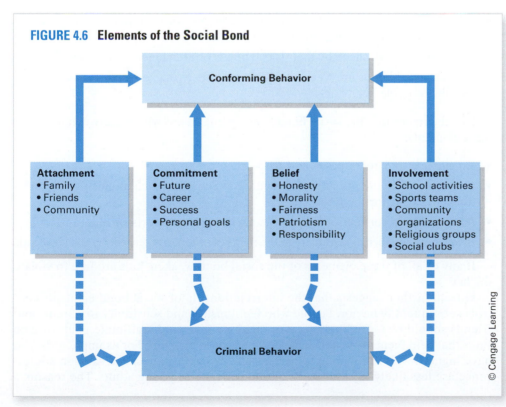

FIGURE 4.6 Elements of the Social Bond

social control theories Posit that delinquency results from a weakened commitment to the major social institutions (family, peers, and school); lack of such commitment allows youths to exercise antisocial behavioral choices.

LEARNING TO BE BAD

Some kids develop a jaundiced, pessimistic, and cynical view of life early in their adolescence. They learn to trust no one, take a dim view of their future, and figure out that the only way to get ahead in life is to break social rules. They see drug dealing rather than higher education as a roadway to success. Criminologists Ronald Simons and Callie Harbin Burt have suggested that the path to delinquency involves learning to accept a unique cognitive framework that shapes not only the way kids look at the world, but also their behavioral choice. As they try to cope with their environment, they incorporate a set of attitudes that Simon and Burt call "social schemas" into their personality that become the core of their world view. The three schemas are:

- *Hostile view of relationships.* Individuals who possess an optimistic, trusting model of relationships engage in warm, cooperative interactions with other people, whereas those who hold a hostile, distrusting model approach others with suspicion and aggression. They begin to believe such things as "When people are friendly, they usually want something from you" and "Some people oppose you for no good reason." A hostile view of relationships would be expected to promote situational definitions leading to aggression, intimidation, and exploitation of others

- *Immediate gratification (discounting the future).* This view represents a person's propensity to discount the future in choosing courses of action. They want everything right away and are willing to take risks to get what they want. Exposure to information suggesting the world is unjust may enhance a person's preferences for immediate versus larger, delayed rewards.

The most prominent control theory is the one developed by sociologist Travis Hirschi.[109] In his classic book *Causes of Delinquency*, Hirschi set out the following arguments:

- All people have the potential to commit crimes—for example, underage drinking—because they are pleasurable.
- People are kept in check by their social bonds or attachments to society.
- If these social bonds are weakened, kids are able to engage in antisocial but personally desirable behaviors.

Hirschi argues that the **social bond** a person maintains with society contains four main elements:

- *Attachment* to parents, peers, and schools
- *Commitment* to the pursuit of conventional activities, such as getting an education and saving for the future
- *Involvement* in conventional activities, such as school, sports, or religion
- *Belief* in values, such as sensitivity to the rights of others and respect for the legal code

If any or all of these elements of the social bond weaken, kids are free to violate the law.

Hirschi further suggests that the interrelationship of social bond elements controls subsequent behavior. People who feel kinship and sensitivity to parents and friends should be more likely to adopt and work toward legitimate goals or gain skills that help them avoid antisocial or dangerous behaviors. For example, girls who have higher levels of bonding to parents and develop good social skills in adolescence are less likely to experience dating violence as young adults. The reason: a

social bond Ties a person to the institutions and processes of society; elements of the bond include attachment, commitment, involvement, and belief.

- *Low commitment to social conventions.* Some individuals consider social norms prohibiting sexual promiscuity, fighting, substance use, cheating on tests, and so on to be legitimate, morally compelling standards of behavior, whereas others possess a cynical, contemptuous view of these social rules. A disparaging view of conventional norms increases the probability of engaging in criminal behavior.

According to Simons and Burt, persistent exposure to antagonistic social circumstances and lack of exposure to positive conditions increase the chances of someone developing social schemas involving a hostile view of relationships, a focus on immediate rewards, and cynicism regarding conventional conduct norms. Conversely, embracing these schemas fosters situational definitions that lead to actions that are aggressive, opportunistic, and sometimes criminal.

To test their views they drew on data from Family and Community Health Study (FACHS), a multisite (Georgia and Iowa) investigation of neighborhood and family processes that contribute to the development of African American children in families living in a wide variety of community settings. The data showed that social-environmental factors predicted changes in the three schemas: community crime, deviant peers, and perceptions of discrimination increased acceptance of the crime-producing schemas; collective efficacy and supportive parenting decreased belief in the schemas. Taken together the three schemas represent a criminogenic knowledge structure. The more people learned to embrace them, the more they committed crime. While environmental factors appeared to produce crime, it was actually their influence on a person's learned attitude that was responsible. In fact, gender differences in the delinquency rate were a result of males being more committed to a hostile view of relationships and less committed to social conventions than females.

In sum, according to Simon and Burt, learning to distrust the world and the people in it, to embrace a here-and-now orientation, and to discount prohibitions against deviance is what drives kids into a delinquent way of life.

CRITICAL THINKING

Can you think of some incidents in your own life where you had to "learn to be bad"? What would have happened you if you refused to adopt a "bad" attitude and viewpoint?

Writing Assignment Write an essay entitled "Learning to Be Bad: Culture or Personality—or Both?"

Source: Ronald L. Simons and Callie Harbin Burt, "Learning to Be Bad: Adverse Social Conditions, Social Schemas, and Crime," *Criminology* 49:553–598 (2011).

---

close bond to parents reduces early adolescent alcohol use, a factor that shields girls from victimization.[110]

A boy who is not attached to his parents may also lack commitment to his future. It is unlikely that he will be involved in conventional activities, such as sports, school, or church. It is also likely that he will not believe in conventional values, such as honesty, hard work, and discipline. Because he does not have to worry what his parents or teachers think about him or about how his behavior will affect his future, he is free to engage in unconventional activities, such as shoplifting, substance abuse, and precocious sex. It really doesn't matter if he gets caught—he has little to lose.

A significant amount of research evidence has been accumulated that supports Hirschi's ideas:

- Positive social attachments help control delinquency.[111]
- Kids who are detached from the educational experience are at risk of criminality.[112]
- Kids who do well and are committed to school are less likely to engage in delinquent acts.[113] In contrast, youths who are detached and alienated from the educational experience are at significant risk of criminality.[114]
- Kids who are attached to their families are less likely to get involved in a deviant peer group and consequently less likely to engage in criminal activities.[115] Attachment is significant regardless of gender or family structure.[116]
- Youths who are involved in conventional leisure activities, such as supervised social activities and noncompetitive sports, are less likely to engage in delinquency than those who are involved in unconventional leisure activities and unsupervised, peer-oriented social pursuits.[117]

✔ Some experts believe that delinquency is a function of socialization.

✔ Socialization involves the interactions people have with various organizations, institutions, and social processes of society.

✔ People from all walks of life have the potential to become delinquents if they maintain destructive social relationships with families, schools, peers, and neighbors.

✔ Social learning theory stresses that kids learn both how to commit crimes and the attitudes needed to support the behavior.

✔ People learn criminal behaviors just as they learn conventional behaviors. Social learning theories suggest that delinquency is learned in a process that is similar to learning any other human behavior.

✔ Social control theories analyze the failure of society to control antisocial tendencies.

✔ All youths have the potential to become delinquents, but their bonds to conventional society prevent them from violating the law.

✔ Travis Hirschi links the onset of delinquency to the weakening of the ties that bind people to society.

While this evidence is persuasive, some important questions have been raised about Hirschi's views. He argues that commitment to future success, such as an exciting career, reduces delinquent involvement. What about the adolescent who wants to be a success, but fails to achieve what he desires? Would the resulting strain make him crime prone? Questions have also been raised about the social relations of delinquents. Hirschi portrays them as "lone wolves," detached from family and friends, whereas some critics believe that delinquents do maintain close peer group ties.[118] Hirschi would counter that what appears to be a close friendship is really a relationship of convenience—"birds of a feather flock together." Recently, Lisa Stolzenberg and Stewart D'Alessio found evidence to back Hirschi's views: most juvenile offenses are committed by individuals acting alone rather than in groups. Delinquents may indeed be lone wolves.[119]

Despite these questions, Hirschi's vision of social control has remained one of the most influential models of delinquency for the past 40 years. **CHECKPOINTS**

Social Reaction/Labeling Theories

Another group of delinquency experts believes that the way *society* reacts to individuals and the way *individuals* react to society determines individual behavior. Becoming **stigmatized**, or labeled, by agents of social control, including official institutions (such as the police and the courts) and unofficial institutions (such as parents and neighbors), creates and sustains delinquent careers.

According to this view, also known as **labeling theory**, kids may violate the law for a variety of reasons, including poor family relationships, peer pressure, psychological abnormality, and so on. Regardless of the original cause, if their deviant behavior is detected and punished, the result is a negative label that can follow them throughout life. These labels include "juvenile delinquent," "mentally ill," "junkie," and many more. Although the original cause of the misbehavior is important, it is the labeling process that transforms the youngsters' identity. Without the label and stigma, they might be able to return to a conventional lifestyle; with it, they are locked forever into a delinquent way of life.

stigmatized People who have been negatively labeled as a result of their participation, or alleged participation, in deviant or outlawed behaviors.

labeling theory Posits that society creates deviance through a system of social control agencies that designate (or label) certain individuals as delinquent, thereby stigmatizing them and encouraging them to accept this negative personal identity.

Labeling Effects. The degree to which youngsters are perceived as deviant may affect their treatment at home and at school. Parents may consider them a bad influence on younger brothers and sisters. Neighbors may tell their children to avoid the "troublemakers." Teachers may place them in classes reserved for students with behavior problems, minimizing their chances of obtaining higher education.

Beyond these results, and depending on the visibility of the label and the manner in which it is applied, youths will have an increasing commitment to delinquent careers. They may seek out others who are similarly labeled, for example, joining delinquent gangs and groups. Involvement with these new-found delinquent peers increases their involvement in delinquent activities and helps further enmesh them in criminality.[120]

As labeled teens get further involved in their new deviant peer group and increase the frequency of their deviant activities, they face renewed condemnation from law enforcement officers, teachers, and other authority figures. This new round of labeling strengthens their commitment to antisocial behavior. The labeled teens may begin to view themselves as outcasts, abandoned by society. They may actually join others beginning to see themselves as troublemakers and "screw-ups." Thus, through a process of identification and sanctioning, re-identification, and even greater penalties, the young offender is transformed. They are no longer children in trouble; they are delinquents, and they accept that label as a personal identity—a process called **self-labeling** (see Figure 4.6).[121]

Degradation Ceremonies. Labels are often applied in what sociologist Harold Garfinkel described as "degradation ceremonies" that are designed to impress their target with the gravity and seriousness of his or her offenses. Sanctioning ceremonies, such as school disciplinary hearings, are not only aimed at punishing transgressions, but also serve as rituals to impress the mischief maker both with the seriousness of their behavior and the community's outrage over their misconduct.[122] They ought to be ashamed of what they did! The effect of this process is a durable negative label and an accompanying loss of status. The labeled deviant becomes a social outcast who should be prevented from enjoying higher education, well-paying jobs, and other societal benefits. Because this label is "official," few question the accuracy of the assessment. People who may have been merely suspicious now feel justified in their assessments: "I always knew he was a bad kid."

A good example of the labeling ceremony occurs in juvenile courts. Here offenders find (perhaps for the first time) that authority figures consider them incorrigible outcasts who must be separated from the right-thinking members of society. To reach that decision, the judge relies on the testimony of witnesses—parents, teachers, police officers, social workers, and psychologists—who may testify that the offender is unfit to be part of conventional society. As the label "juvenile delinquent" is conferred on offenders, their identities may be transformed from kids who have done something bad to "bad kids."[123] Kids who perceive that they have been negatively labeled by significant others, such as peers and teachers, are also more likely to self-report delinquent behavior and adopt a deviant self-concept.[124] The labeling process helps create a **self-fulfilling prophecy**.[125] If children continually receive negative feedback from parents, teachers, and others whose opinion they take to heart, they will interpret this rejection as accurate. Their behavior will begin to conform to the negative expectations; they will become the person that others perceive them to be ("Teachers already think I'm stupid, so why should I bother to study?"). The self-fulfilling prophecy leads to a damaged self-image and an increase in antisocial behaviors.[126]

The labeling perspective can offer important insights:

- It identifies the role played by social control agents in the process of delinquency causation. Delinquent behavior cannot be fully understood if the agencies empowered to control it are ignored.

- It recognizes that delinquency is not a pathological behavior. It focuses on the social interactions that shape behavior.

- It distinguishes between delinquent acts and delinquent careers, and shows that they must be treated differently.[127]

Labeling theory, then, may help explain the onset and continuation of a delinquent career. It clarifies why some youths continue down the path of antisocial behavior (they are self-labeled), whereas most are able to desist from crime (they are stigma-free). **CHECKPOINTS**

self-labeling The process by which a person who has been negatively labeled accepts the label as a personal role or identity.

self-fulfilling prophecy Deviant behavior patterns that are a response to an earlier labeling experience; youths act out these social roles even if they were falsely bestowed.

CHECKPOINTS

LO5 Explain how the labeling process is related to delinquent careers.

✔ Labeling theory (also known as social reaction theory) maintains that negative labels produce delinquent careers.

✔ Labels create expectations that the labeled person will act in a certain way; labeled people are always watched and suspected.

✔ Becoming stigmatized, or labeled, by agents of social control creates and sustains delinquent careers.

✔ Kids whose deviant behavior is detected and punished will develop negative labels that can follow them throughout life.

✔ The labeling process transforms the youngsters' identity.

✔ Labels and stigma lock offenders forever into a delinquent way of life.

CRITICAL THEORY

According to **critical theory**, society is in a constant state of internal conflict, and different groups strive to impose their will on others. Those with money and power succeed in shaping the law to meet their needs and to maintain their interests. Those adolescents whose behavior cannot conform to the needs of the power elite are defined as delinquents and criminals.

Those in power use the justice system to maintain their status while keeping others subservient: men use their economic power to subjugate women; members of the majority want to stave off the economic advancement of minorities; capitalists want to reduce the power of workers to ensure they are willing to accept low wages. Critical thinkers are deeply concerned about the current state of the American political system and the creation of what they consider to be an American empire abroad. Their concern stems from recent events ranging from the war in Iraq to the efforts to penalize immigrants and close the borders.[128] The conservative agenda, they believe, calls for the dismantling of welfare and health programs, lowering of labor costs through union busting, tax cuts that favor the wealthy, ending affirmative action, and reducing environmental control and regulation. Racism still pervades the American system and manifests itself in a wide variety of social practices ranging from the administration of criminal justice to hiring practices.[129] Critical theory thus centers around a view of society in which an elite class uses the law as a means of meeting threats to its status. The ruling class is a self-interested collective whose primary interest is self-gain.

Law and Justice

Critical theorists view the law and the justice system as vehicles for controlling the have-not members of society; legal institutions help the powerful and rich impose their standards of good behavior on the entire society. The law helps control the behavior of those who might otherwise threaten the status quo or prevent wealthy businesspeople from making huge profits.[130]

According to critical theory, the poor may or may not commit more crimes than the rich, but they certainly are arrested more often. Police may act more forcefully in areas where class conflict creates the perception that extreme forms of social control are needed to maintain order. It is not surprising to critical theorists that complaints of police brutality are highest in minority neighborhoods.[131] Police misbehavior, which is routine in such neighborhoods, would never be tolerated in affluent European American areas. All too often these unwarranted stops lead to equally unfair arrests. In 2011, the team of Tammy Rinehart Kochel, David Wilson, and Stephen Mastrofski thoroughly reviewed the existing literature on police arrest practices, screening more than 4,500 published and unpublished research studies. Their meta-analysis found that minority suspects stopped by police are significantly more likely to be arrested than are white suspects. The chances of a white being arrested was 0.20, whereas the average probability for a nonwhite was calculated at 0.26. These findings may be used by critical criminologists as clear evidence of the racial bias they suspect is present in American policing.[132] Consequently, a deep-seated hostility is generated among members of the lower class toward a social order they may neither shape nor share in.[133]

The Cause of Delinquency

Critical theorists view delinquency as a normal response to the conditions created by capitalism.[134] In fact, the creation of the legal category *delinquency* is a function of the class consciousness that occurred around the turn of the twentieth century.[135] In *The Child Savers*, Anthony Platt documented the creation of the delinquency concept and the role played by wealthy child savers in forming the philosophy of the juvenile court. Platt believed that the child-saving movement's real goal was to maintain order and control while preserving the existing class system.[136] He and others have concluded that the child savers were powerful citizens who aimed to control the behavior of disenfranchised youths.[137]

critical theory The view that intergroup conflict, born out of the unequal distribution of wealth and power, is the root cause of delinquency.

Critical theorists still view delinquent behavior as a function of the capitalist system's inherent inequity. They argue that capitalism accelerates the trend toward replacing human labor with machines so that youths are removed from the labor force.[138] From early childhood, the values of capitalism are reinforced. Social control agencies such as schools prepare youths for placement in the capitalist system by presenting them with behavior models that will help them conform to later job expectations. For example, rewards for good schoolwork correspond to the rewards a manager uses with employees. In fact, most schools are set up to reward youths who show promise in self-discipline and motivation and are therefore judged likely to perform well in the capitalist system. Youths who are judged inferior as potential job prospects wind up in delinquent roles. Their economic rank and position become a master status that subjects them to lives filled with suffering. If social policies could be embraced that reduce the tremendous class differences in society, such as universal health care, the prevalence of economic suffering in contemporary society would diminish and so too would delinquency rates.[139]

Concept Summary 4.1 summarizes the various sociological theories of delinquency.

CONCEPT SUMMARY 4.1 | Social Theory

Theory	Core Premise	Strengths
Social disorganization	Crime is a product of transitional neighborhoods that manifest social disorganization and value conflict. The conflicts and problems of urban social life and communities, including fear, unemployment, deterioration, and siege mentality, influence crime rates.	Identifies why crime rates are highest in lower-class areas. Points out the factors that produce the delinquency.
Strain	People who adopt the goals of society but lack the means to attain them seek alternatives, such as crime.	Points out how competition for success creates conflict and crime. Suggests that social conditions and not personality can account for crime. Can explain middle- and upper-class crime.
Cultural deviance	Obedience to the norms of their lower-class culture puts people in conflict with the norms of the dominant culture.	Identifies the aspects of lower-class life that produce street crime. Creates the concept of culture conflict.
Social learning	People learn to commit delinquent acts through exposure to others who hold deviant values and engage in deviant behaviors.	Explains why some at-risk kids do not become delinquents. Accounts for the effects of parental deviance on kids.
Social control	A person's bond to society prevents him or her from violating social rules. If the bond weakens, the person is free to commit delinquent acts.	Explains the onset of delinquency; can apply to both middle- and lower-class crime. Explains its theoretical constructs adequately so they can be measured. Has been empirically tested.
Social reaction	People enter into law-violating careers when they are labeled for their acts and organize their personalities around the labels.	Explains the role of society in creating deviance. Explains why some juvenile offenders do not become adult criminals. Develops concepts of criminal careers.
Critical theory	Crime is a function of class conflict. The law is defined by people who hold social and political power. The capitalist system produces delinquency.	Accounts for class differentials in the delinquency rate. Shows how class conflict influences behavior.

THEORY AND DELINQUENCY PREVENTION

Each of the various branches of social theory has had an impact on delinquency prevention activities and programs. The following sections describe a few of these efforts.

Social Structure Theory and Delinquency Prevention

If social factors produce delinquency, it is no wonder that social programs have been designed to reduce or eliminate its occurrence. Some are based on social structure theory, attempting to remake society in order to provide alternatives to crime. One current effort is Operation Weed and Seed, a multilevel action plan for revitalizing communities.[140] The concept of this program is that no single approach can reduce crime rates and that social service and law enforcement agencies must cooperate to be effective. There are four basic elements in this plan: law enforcement; community policing; prevention, intervention, and treatment; and neighborhood restoration. The last element, neighborhood restoration, is the one most closely attached to social structure theory because it is designed to revitalize distressed neighborhoods and improve the quality of life in the target communities. The neighborhood restoration element focuses on economic development activities, such as economic opportunities for residents, improved housing conditions, enhanced social services, and improved public services in the target area. Programs are being developed that will improve living conditions; enhance home security; allow for low-cost physical improvements; develop long-term efforts to renovate and maintain housing; and provide educational, economic, social, recreational, and other vital opportunities. A key feature is the fostering of self-worth and individual responsibility among community members.

The accompanying Prevention/Intervention/Treatment feature focuses on one such comprehensive community-based effort.

© James Estrin/New York Times/Redux

According to the social structure approach, a community that can support its residents reduces the lure of delinquency. Here, kids are preparing to row at the Peter Jay Sharp Boathouse on the Harlem River. The idea for a recreational community boathouse first came from singer Bette Midler, who saw local college and university rowing teams practicing on the river. Not long after, she also learned that many academic and athletic scholarships being made available to Upper Manhattan high school students who participated in rowing programs were being unused due to the lack of such local programs. As a result, Midler's New York Restoration Project engaged celebrated architect Robert A.M. Stern to design the first community boathouse of its kind on the river in over 100 years.

Communities That Care

Comprehensive community-based delinquency prevention programs typically involve a diverse group of community and government agencies that are concerned with the problem of juvenile delinquency, such as the YMCA/YWCA, Boys and Girls Clubs of America, social services, and health organizations.

One contemporary example of a comprehensive community-based delinquency prevention program is the Communities That Care (CTC) program, which emphasizes the reduction of risk factors for delinquency and the enhancement of protective factors against delinquency for different developmental stages from birth through adolescence. CTC follows a rigorous, multilevel planning process that includes drawing upon treatments that have previously demonstrated success and tailoring them to the needs of the community.

The CTC relies on a systematic planning model to develop prevention modalities. This includes analysis of the delinquency problem, identification of available resources in the community, development of priority delinquency problems, and identification of successful programs in other communities and tailoring them to local conditions and needs. Not all comprehensive community-based prevention programs follow this model, but there is evidence to suggest that this approach will produce the greatest reductions in juvenile delinquency.

One example of the CTC approach is Project COPE, which serves the Lynn, Massachusetts area. Established in 2004, COPE works collaboratively with multiple local agencies, including Girls Incorporated of Lynn, the city's health department, police department, public schools, and other agencies whose goals include reducing risk factors for youth and promoting healthy family and neighborhood development. The coalition includes a large and active youth subcommittee. Originally focused on substance abuse prevention in youth, the coalition expanded its initiatives to include the prevention of fatal and nonfatal opiate overdoses, teen suicide, teen pregnancy, bullying and violence, and obesity.

In 2009, data from a comprehensive effort to evaluate the CTC program were released. Researchers had studied a group of 4,407 fifth-graders from 24 communities in Colorado, Illinois, Kansas, Maine, Oregon, Utah, and Washington. Twelve communities were randomly assigned to undergo CTC training and implementation, and 12 served as the control communities that did not implement CTC. In the CTC communities,

participants (including educators, business and public leaders, health workers, religious leaders, social workers, and other community volunteers) received six training sessions over a year to help them identify the dominant risk and protective factors for substance use in their areas. The groups of treatment providers then chose and implemented from two to five evidence-based prevention programs tailored to their risk factors, from a menu of tested and effective prevention strategies. The strategies focused on a variety of topics depending on community need, including alcohol and drugs, violence prevention, reducing family conflict, life skills training, HIV/AIDS prevention, dating safety, tobacco, and anger management. The youth were surveyed annually for four years concerning their risky behaviors to determine the impact of delivering programs through the CTC system.

By the eighth grade, students in the CTC communities were 32 percent less likely to begin using alcohol, 33 percent less likely to begin smoking, and 33 percent less likely to begin using smokeless tobacco than their peers in the control communities. Students from CTC communities were also 25 percent less likely to initiate delinquent behavior, itself a risk factor for future substance use and an important target for prevention.

Critical Thinking

1. To many juvenile justice officials, policy makers, and politicians, community-based prevention is tantamount to being soft on crime, and delinquency prevention programs are often referred to as "pork barrel," or wasteful, spending. Do you agree? If so, what alternative would you suggest?
2. There is concern about the labeling and stigmatization associated with programs that target high-risk populations. Children and families receiving support may be called hurtful names or looked down upon by fellow community members. What can be done to avoid negative labels?

Sources: Project Cope, 2012, www.projectcope.com/communitiesthatcare.html (accessed July 22, 2012); National Institute of Health, "Innovative Community-Based Prevention System Reduces Risky Behavior in 10–14 Year Olds: Communities That Care System Lowers Rates of Substance Abuse and Delinquent Behavior in Seven States," September 7, 2009, www.nih.gov/news/health/sep2009/nida-07.htm (accessed July 22, 2012).

Social Process Theories and Delinquency Prevention

Social process theories suggest that delinquency can be prevented by strengthening the socialization process. Some theories are aimed at improving self-image, an outcome that may help kids develop revamped identities and desist from crime. With proper treatment, former offenders are able to cast off their damaged identities and develop new ones. As a result, they develop an improved self-concept that reflects the positive reinforcement they receive while in treatment.[141] One approach has been to help social institutions improve their outreach. Educational programs have been improved by expanding preschool programs, developing curricula relevant to students' lives, and stressing teacher development. Counseling and remedial services have been aimed at troubled youth.

After-school programs have also been employed. More than two-thirds of all married couples with school-age children (ages 6 to 17) have both parents working outside the home, and the proportion of single parents with school-age children working outside the home is even higher.[142] This leaves many unsupervised young people in communities during the after-school hours (2:00 P.M. to 6:00 P.M.), which is believed to be the main reason for the elevated rates of delinquency during this period of time.[143] After-school programs have become a popular response to this problem in recent years. After-school options include child-care centers, tutoring programs at school, dance groups, basketball leagues, and drop-in clubs. State and federal budgets for education, public safety, delinquency prevention, and child care provide some funding for after-school programs.

Some of the most successful after-school programs are provided by Boys and Girls Clubs of America. Founded in 1902, Boys and Girls Clubs of America is a nonprofit organization with a membership of nearly 4 million boys and girls nationwide. Boys and Girls Clubs (BGC) provide programs in six main areas: cultural enrichment, health and physical education, social recreation, personal and educational development, citizenship and leadership development, and environmental education.[144] Evaluations of the BGC programs show that they are mostly successful and produce reductions in substance abuse, drug trafficking, and other drug-related delinquency activity.[145]

In a large-scale study of after-school programs in the state of Maryland, Denise Gottfredson and her colleagues found that participation in the programs reduced delinquent behavior among children in middle school, but not elementary school. The researchers found that increasing intentions not to use drugs as well as positive peer associations were the key reasons for the favorable effects on delinquency among the older children. Interestingly, decreasing the time spent unsupervised or increasing the involvement in constructive activities was found to play no significant role.[146]

Although the evidence shows that after-school programs can be successful, there is a need for further evaluation.[147] The fact that some (but not all) types of delinquency are elevated during the after-school hours underscores the importance of high-quality after-school programs.[148]

Prevention programs have also been aimed at strengthening families in crisis. Because attachment to parents is a cornerstone of all social process theories, developing good family relations is an essential element of delinquency prevention. Programs have been developed that encourage families to help children develop the positive self-image necessary to resist the forces promoting delinquency.[149]

Prevention programs have also focused on providing services for youngsters who have been identified as delinquents or predelinquents. Such services usually include counseling, job placement, legal assistance, and more. Their aim is to reach out to troubled youths and provide them with the skills necessary to function in their environment before they get into trouble with the law.

Looking Back to Jay's Story

Jay's family struggled with poverty, homelessness, and unemployment issues. Jay was skipping school, using alcohol, committing crimes, and was possibly involved with gang activity.

CRITICAL THINKING Design a delinquency prevention program to assist youth dealing with these types of concerns. Make sure you address these issues: expectations for the involved clients, goals of your program, and how you would measure success.

© Darren McCollester/ Copyright 2009 NBAE via Getty Images

After-school programs can help reduce the opportunity of delinquency while reinforcing social bonds. Here, Boston Celtics stars Paul Pierce and Glen "Big Baby" Davis play Christmas Bingo with Niyah Winspeare and fellow classmates from the Marshall Elementary School at the Ames Hotel in Boston. Members of the Celtics read and played games with the school children as part of the Read to Achieve and GRASP afterschool programs.

In addition to these local efforts, the federal government has sponsored several delinquency prevention efforts using the principles of social process theory. These include educational enrichment programs, such as Head Start for preschoolers, which will be discussed in a later chapter. One such program is described in the accompanying Prevention/Intervention/Treatment feature.

Reducing Stigma and Labeling. Some prevention programs have attempted to limit the interface of youths with the juvenile justice system in order to reduce the effects of labeling and stigma. One approach has been to divert youths from official processing at the time of their initial contact with police. The usual practice is to have police refer children to treatment facilities rather than to the juvenile court. In a similar vein, children who are petitioned to juvenile court may be eligible for alternative programs rather than traditional juvenile justice processing. For example, restitution programs allow children to pay back the victims of their crimes for the damage (or inconvenience) they have caused instead of receiving an official delinquency label.

If a youth is found delinquent, efforts are being made to reduce stigma by using alternative programs, such as boot camp or intensive probation monitoring. Alternative community-based sanctions are substituted for state training schools, a policy known as **deinstitutionalization**. Whenever possible, anything producing stigma is to be avoided, a philosophy referred to as *nonintervention*.

The federal government has been a prime mover in the effort to divert children from the justice system. The Office of Juvenile Justice and Delinquency Prevention has sponsored numerous diversion and restitution programs. In addition, it made one of its priorities the removal of juveniles from adult jails and the discontinuance of housing status offenders and juvenile delinquents together. These programs were designed to limit juveniles' interaction with the justice system, reduce stigma, and make use of informal treatment modalities. (Chapter 14 covers diversion and deinstitutionalization in detail.)[150]

deinstitutionalization Removing juveniles from adult jails and placing them in community-based programs to avoid the stigma attached to these facilities.

Homeboy Industries

Many kids who want to leave gangs and join conventional society lack the means to do so. One program designed to ease the way is known as Homeboy Industries, located in Los Angeles, California. The program was founded in 1992 by Father Gregory Boyle, a Jesuit priest, whose guiding principle was that when people are employed, they're much more likely to lead happy lives, because they can be productive and constructive. Homeboy's many programs reflect this viewpoint. Youths in the program not only receive access to numerous free services—counseling, job referrals, tattoo removal, and life-skills training—but are able to work (with pay) in the program's several businesses, which include silk-screening, maintenance, and food service (a Mexican-food café and bakery).

AP Photo/Philip Scott Andrews

Workers print T-shirts at the Homeboy Industries shop in the Boyle Heights area of Los Angeles. This successful organization provides everything from work training to parenting classes to drivers' education and high school equivalency services to 8,000 gang members a year from all over Los Angeles County, plus a couple thousand others seeking help and hope.

For many of the former gang members in the program, this is their first real job. Receiving a paycheck and developing meaningful skills count as tangible benefits of the program. But the participants also benefit from intangibles—altered perspectives and fresh hopes—that truly change their lives. Some of the many services included in the program are discussed below.

Employment Services

Homeboy assists at-risk, disadvantaged, and gang-involved youth to find employment. They employ three full-time job developers to assist in job placement.

Because many of their clients are not obvious choices for employers, these job developers go out into the community and foster relationships with local businesses, search out employers who would be willing to work with parolees or former gang members, and take the time to overcome possible fears and reservations. Because of this extra effort, they are better able to create a positive work environment

Work Is Noble

Through collaboration with the Cathedral of Our Lady of the Angels, Homeboy offers a special program for young people called Work Is Noble (WIN). Participants are assigned to work in a local business in an area in which they have expressed interest, and Homeboy covers their salary. The young men and women are given the opportunity to work in a field that interests them while developing concrete skills that will help them continue to work in that field. Participating businesses are able to make use of extra help at no extra cost. This program not only teaches the young men and women that there are constructive alternatives to life on the streets, but also gives them real work experience, preferably in a company that may hire them after the program is completed. In the work environment, young people are surrounded by adults who are living examples of a commitment to earning an honest day's wage and who can serve as mentors.

Counseling

Many of Homeboy's clients face severe challenges adjusting to life outside the gangs. Many are struggling to overcome abusive or dysfunctional home situations, or are trying to transition to life outside prison or detention camps. Youth on probation are now court-mandated to have mental health counseling. Both male and female counselors are available to offer much-needed counseling services to Homeboy clients, free of charge.

Homeboy's services are open to the community, and have become a welcome resource for clients who wish to successfully overcome the pressures of the workplace, or who want to establish a more stable home life. Additionally, as leaving a gang and/or adjusting to life off the streets is an ongoing process, and not a simple, one-time decision, having a staff of full-time counselors has proved to be a significant benefit for kids who want to leave the gang life. Recently Homeboy launched a new volunteer therapist program involving licensed psychologists, social workers, and marriage and family therapists who are willing to donate their time. The Homeboy Heals Program asks providers within a 10-mile radius of their facility to counsel one Homeboy client weekly—at no charge—in his or her private office. Those whose offices are further away are asked to schedule a three- to four-hour block of time each week at Homeboy's First Street location.

Like many other social service programs, Homeboy has been hit hard by the economic downturn and has been forced to lay off employees. Facing bankruptcy, they have launched a snack food business to raise funds and the effort may be working. Homeboy Industries' tortilla chips and salsa have been hot items in local supermarkets and profits may help prop up this innovative anti-gang agency.

Sources: Homeboy Industries. www.homeboy-industries.org (accessed July 21, 2012); Betty Hallock, "Homeboy Industries Pins Hopes on Chips and Salsa," *Los Angeles Times*, February 17, 2011, http://articles.latimes.com/2011/feb/17/food/la-fo-homeboy-chips-20110217 (accessed July 22, 2012).

Critical Theories and Delinquency Prevention

If conflict is the source of delinquency, then conflict resolution may be the key to its demise. This is the aim of **restorative justice**, an approach that relies on nonpunitive strategies for delinquency control.[151] The restorative justice movement has a number of origins. Negotiation, mediation, and peacemaking have been part of the dispute resolution process in European and Asian communities for centuries.[152] Native American and Native Canadian people have long used participation of community members in the adjudication process (sentencing circles, panels of elders).[153] Members of the U.S. peacemaking movement have also championed the use of nonpunitive alternatives to justice.

Restoration involves turning the justice system into a healing process rather than a distributor of retribution. Most people involved in offender–victim relationships actually know one another or are related. Restorative justice attempts to address the issues that produced conflict between these people rather than to treat one as a victim deserving sympathy and the other as a delinquent deserving punishment. Rather than choose whom to punish, society should try to reconcile the parties.[154]

Gordon Bazemore and his associates have suggested policies that center on the principle of *balanced and restorative justice* (BARJ).[155] BARJ attempts to link community protection and victims' rights. Offenders must take responsibility for their actions, a process that can increase self-esteem and decrease recidivism.[156]

restorative justice Nonpunitive strategies for dealing with juvenile offenders that make the justice system a healing process rather than a punishment process.

In contrast, over-reliance on punishment can be counterproductive.[157] According to BARJ, the juvenile justice system should give equal weight to:

- *Holding offenders accountable to victims.* Offender accountability refers specifically to the requirement that offenders make amends for the harm resulting from their crimes by repaying or restoring losses to victims and the community.

- *Providing competency development.* Competency development, the rehabilitative goal for intervention, requires that people who enter the justice system should exit the system more capable of being productive and responsible in the community.

- *Ensuring community safety.* The community protection goal explicitly acknowledges and endorses a long-time public expectation—a safe and secure community.

The BARJ approach means that juvenile justice policies and priorities should seek to address each of the three goals in each case and that system balance should be pursued. The goal of achieving balance suggests that no single objective can take precedence over any other without creating a system that is "out of balance," and implies that efforts to achieve one goal (e.g., offender accountability) should not hinder efforts to achieve other goals. BARJ is founded on the belief that justice is best served when the victim, community, and offender are viewed as equal clients of the justice system who will receive fair and balanced attention, be actively involved in the justice process, and gain tangible benefits from their interactions with the justice system.

To counteract the negative effects of punishment, restorative justice programs for juveniles typically involve diversion from the court process, reconciliation between offenders and victims, victim advocacy, mediation programs, and sentencing circles, in which crime victims and their families are brought together with offenders and their families in an effort to formulate a sanction that addresses the needs of each party. Restorative justice programs will be discussed further in Chapter 14.

SUMMARY

We know that most serious delinquents grow up in deteriorated parts of town and lack the social support and economic resources familiar to more affluent members of society. Latino and African American children are more than twice as likely to be poor as Asian and white children. It is also apparent that social relationships with families, peers, schools, jobs, criminal justice agencies, and the like may play an important role in shaping behavioral choices. As a result, many delinquency theorists believe that elements of social life are responsible for kids getting involved in antisocial behaviors. Social disorganization theory focuses on the conditions within the urban environment that affect delinquency rates, such as socioeconomic conditions. Poverty undermines the basic stabilizing forces of the community—family, school, peers, and neighbors—rendering them weakened, attenuated, and ineffective. As a result, the ability of the community to control its inhabitants—to assert informal social control—is damaged and frayed.

Gangs flourish in deteriorated neighborhoods with high levels of poverty, lack of investment, high unemployment rates, and population turnover. In contrast, cohesive communities develop collective efficacy: mutual trust, a willingness to intervene in the supervision of children, and the maintenance of public order.

Another approach rests on the work of French sociologist Émile Durkheim who coined the term *anomie* to describe a society in which rules of behavior have broken down during periods of rapid social change or social crisis. From this origin strain theory emerged. Sociologist Robert Agnew's general strain theory explains why individuals who feel stress and strain are more likely to engage in delinquent acts.

Delinquency is the direct result of negative affective states—the anger, frustration, and adverse emotions that kids feel in the wake of negative and destructive social relationships.

Because their lifestyle is draining, frustrating, and dispiriting, members of the lower class create an independent subculture with its own set of rules and values. Because social conditions make them incapable of achieving success legitimately, lower-class youths experience a form of culture conflict.

Some social theorists believe that delinquency is a function of socialization, the interactions people have with various organizations, institutions, and processes of society. If these relationships are positive and supportive, kids can succeed within the rules of society; if these relationships are dysfunctional and destructive, conventional success may be impossible, and delinquent solutions may become a feasible alternative.

Social learning theories suggest that delinquency is learned in a process that is similar to learning any other human behavior. One of the most prominent social learning theories is Edwin H. Sutherland's differential association theory, which asserts that criminal behavior is learned primarily within interpersonal groups and that youths will become delinquent if definitions they have learned favorable to violating the law exceed definitions favorable to obeying the law within that group. In contrast, social control theories maintain that all people have the potential to violate the law and that modern society presents many opportunities for illegal activity. Travis Hirschi links the onset of delinquency to the weakening of the ties that bind people to society.

Other experts focus on how becoming stigmatized, or labeled, by agents of social control creates and sustains delinquent careers. Kids whose deviant behavior is detected and punished will develop negative labels that can follow them throughout life. The labeling process transforms the youngsters' identity. Labels and stigma lock offenders forever into a delinquent way of life.

Another social view considers the effect of the capitalist economic system on behavior. Society is set up to favor a few wealthy people over the great majority who have little hope of advancement. Delinquency is a result of the inequities built into contemporary society.

KEY TERMS

culture of poverty, p. 99

underclass, p. 99

truly disadvantaged, p. 99

social structure theories, p. 99

social disorganization, p. 100

transitional neighborhood, p. 100

cultural transmission, p. 100

social control, p. 101

relative deprivation, p. 101

gentrified, p. 101

collective efficacy, p. 103

strain, p. 104

anomie, p. 104

general strain theory, p. 104

negative affective states, p. 105

cultural deviance theory, p. 105

culture conflict, p. 106

socialization, p. 107

parental efficacy, p. 108

social learning theories, p. 110

differential association theory, p. 110

social control theories, p. 111

social bond, p. 112

stigmatized, p. 114

labeling theory, p. 114

self-labeling, p. 115

self-fulfilling prophecy, p. 115

critical theory, p. 116

deinstitutionalization, p. 121

restorative justice, p. 123

QUESTIONS FOR REVIEW

1. List the elements present in the culture of poverty.
2. To what does the term *truly disadvantaged* refer?
3. Describe a community that is socially disorganized.
4. Distinguish between the three types of collective efficacy.
5. Discuss the life experiences that produce strain according to Robert Agnew's general strain theory.
6. What are differential associations and how do they produce delinquency?
7. Give an example of a self-fulfilling prophecy .
8. Describe how restorative justice differs from traditional justice.

QUESTIONS FOR DISCUSSION

1. Is there a transitional neighborhood in your town or city?
2. Is it possible that a distinct lower-class culture exists?
3. Have you ever perceived anomie? What causes anomie? Is there more than one cause of strain?
4. How does poverty cause delinquency?
5. Do middle-class youths become delinquent for the same reasons as lower-class youths?
6. Does relative deprivation produce delinquency?

APPLYING WHAT YOU HAVE LEARNED

You have just been appointed as a presidential adviser on urban problems. The president informs you that he wants to initiate a demonstration project in a major city aimed at showing that the government can do something to reduce poverty, crime, and drug abuse. The area he has chosen for development is a large inner-city neighborhood with more than 100,000 residents. The neighborhood suffers from disorganized community structure, poverty, and hopelessness. Predatory delinquent gangs run free and terrorize local merchants and citizens. The school system has failed to provide opportunities and education experiences sufficient to dampen enthusiasm for gang recruitment. Stores, homes, and public buildings are deteriorated and decayed. Commercial enterprise has fled the area, and civil servants are reluctant to enter the neighborhood. There is an uneasy truce among the various ethnic and racial groups that populate the area. Residents feel that little can be done to bring the neighborhood back to life.

You are faced with suggesting an urban redevelopment program that can revitalize the area and eventually bring down the crime rate. You can bring any element of the public and private sector to bear on this rather overwhelming problem—including the military! You can also ask private industry to help in the struggle, promising them tax breaks for their participation.

Writing Assignment: Write a policy statement to the president suggesting the strategies you feel could break the cycle of urban poverty. What role do you see for the family in your proposed delinquency reduction plan?

GROUPWORK

There are a number of TV shows and films that illustrate the crushing burden of living in a disorganized area. Films like *South Central* and TV shows such as *The Wire* come to mind.

Have the group watch a suitable film or show, and then discuss the elements that correspond to the theories discussed in this chapter.

CHAPTER FIVE

Developmental Views of Delinquency:
Life Course, Latent Trait, and Trajectory

© Ingram Publishing/Alamy

LEARNING OBJECTIVES

After reading this chapter you should:

1. Trace the history of and influences on developmental theory.
2. Know the principles of the life course approach to developmental theory.
3. Articulate the principles of Sampson and Laub's age-graded life course theory.
4. Be able to define the concept of the latent trait and assumptions of the general theory of crime.
5. Know the principles of trajectory theory.

Kia's Story

Kia was born in Vietnam and moved to the United States when he was 11. He had problems at school, and when he was 14 years old the teachers at his middle school referred him to the family court crisis intervention program. The program was established to provide a one-time intervention for young people on the verge of getting a more serious referral to the juvenile justice system. The philosophy of the program was to provide short-term assessment and intervention, and any further necessary services were referred out to other community resources and supports. Many of the referrals to this program were for adolescents involved with issues of truancy, running away, and family relationship concerns. Although in the eyes of the community Kia's behaviors did not rise to the level of "delinquent," the adults in his life were very concerned for him. He was verbally aggressive toward both his female peers and teachers— abusive, disrespectful, and threatening. School interventions were attempted to address these concerns, but to no avail. Kia was at risk for school disciplinary action and possible involvement in the juvenile justice system.

During a counseling session it was revealed that Kia's parents had moved to the United States several years before Kia, and that his grandmother had raised Kia in Vietnam until the family could afford to bring their six children to America. This separation had created a significant disruption for the family, but no one had ever talked with the children about why his parents left him behind when they had to leave for the United States. Kia's parents explained that they had worked hard for many years to be able to have the children join them and that they missed their children a great deal, but felt they had no other choice. They wanted to provide a safe home for their children with a multitude of opportunities that they believed were available in the United States, in the hope that the children would transition easily, feel appreciative, and be academically successful. His mother cried and expressed her sadness at leaving the children and being separated for so many years. Kia's parents expressed their love for him and their desire for him to feel important in their lives.

Things soon began to change for Kia and his family. They began to see that Kia had felt rejected and abandoned by his parents, and that he was also having struggles assimilating to the new country. Because his parents had never explained to him their reasons for the separation, Kia had believed his parents did not care about him. The one-time intervention offered by the crisis intervention program was very beneficial to Kia and his family. Kia's disruptive behaviors at school completely vanished.

---

developmental theory The view that criminality is a dynamic process, influenced by social experiences as well as individual characteristics.

life course theory A developmental theory that focuses on changes in behavior as people travel along the path of life and how these changes affect crime and delinquency.

latent trait theory The view that delinquent behavior is controlled by a "master trait," present at birth or soon after, that remains stable and unchanging throughout a person's lifetime.

propensity A natural inclination or personal trait that exists at birth or soon after and remains constant over the life course.

Kia's story jibes with those delinquency experts who believe that the roots of adolescent misbehavior can be traced to a time much earlier in childhood, and that delinquency is the culmination of a long history of improper development. They have produced a variety of **developmental theories** of crime and delinquency, which focus on the onset, continuity, and termination of a delinquent career. These developmental theorists seek answers to such questions as: Why is it that some kids become delinquents and then abandon the delinquent way of life as they mature, whereas others persist in criminality into their adulthood? Why do some offenders escalate their delinquent activities, whereas others decrease or limit their law violations? Why do some offenders specialize in a particular delinquency, whereas others become generalists? Why do some criminals reduce delinquent activity and then resume it once again? Research now shows that some offenders begin their delinquent careers at a very early age, whereas others begin later. How can early- and late-onset criminality be explained?

There are actually three independent yet interrelated developmental views. The first, referred to as the **life course theory**, suggests that delinquent behavior is a dynamic process, influenced by individual characteristics as well as social experiences, and that the factors that cause antisocial behaviors change dramatically over a person's lifespan.

The second vision referred to here as **latent trait theory** suggests that human development is controlled by a "master" trait that remains stable and unchanging throughout a person's lifetime. As people travel through their life course this **propensity** is always there, directing their behavior. Because this master latent trait is enduring, the ebb and flow of delinquent behavior is shaped less by personal change and more by the impact of external forces such as delinquent opportunity. Delinquency may increase when an adolescent joins a gang, which provides him with more opportunities to steal, take drugs, and attack others. In other words, the propensity to commit delinquent acts is constant, but the opportunity to commit them is constantly fluctuating.

A third view suggests there are multiple trajectories in a delinquent career. According to this approach, there are subgroups within a population that follow distinctively different developmental trajectories toward and away from a delinquent career. Some kids may begin early in antisocial activities and demonstrate a propensity for crime, while others begin later and are influenced by life circumstances. **Trajectory theory** suggests that there are different types and classes of offenders.[1]

The main points, similarities, and differences of these positions are set out in Concept Summary 5.1. **CHECKPOINTS**

THE LIFE COURSE VIEW

According to the life course view, even as toddlers people begin relationships and behaviors that will determine their entire life course. As children they must learn to conform to social rules and function effectively in society. Later they are expected to begin thinking about careers, complete their schooling, leave their parents' home, enter the workforce, find permanent relationships, and eventually marry and begin their own families.[2] These transitions are expected to take place in an orderly fashion. Disruptions in life's major transitions can be destructive and ultimately promote criminality. Those who are already at risk because of socioeconomic problems or family dysfunction are the most susceptible during these awkward transitions. The cumulative impact of these disruptions sustains criminality from childhood into adulthood.

WWW

Interested in the **concept of human development**? Access the United Nations' website by going to the Criminal Justice CourseMate at CengageBrain .com, then accessing the Web Links for this chapter.

CHECKPOINTS

LO1 Distinguish among life course, latent trait, and trajectory theories.

✔ Life course theorists view criminality as a dynamic process influenced by a multitude of individual characteristics, traits, and social experiences.

✔ Life course theories look at such issues as the onset of crime, the escalation of offenses, the persistence of crime, and desistance from crime.

✔ Latent trait theorists believe that human development is controlled by a "master trait" that guides human development and gives some people an increased propensity to commit crime.

✔ Trajectory theory holds that there are multiple pathways to crime.

CONCEPT SUMMARY 5.1 | Three Developmental Theories

Latent Trait Theory
- People do not change, delinquent opportunities change; maturity brings fewer opportunities.
- People have a master trait: personality, intelligence, genetic makeup.
- Early social control and proper parenting can reduce delinquent propensity.

Life Course Theory
- People have multiple traits: social, psychological, economic.
- People change over the life course.
- Family, job, peers influence behavior.

Trajectory Theory
- There is more than one path to a delinquent career.
- There are different types of offenders and offending.

Similarities
- All focus on delinquent careers.
- Delinquency must be viewed as a path rather than an event.
- Delinquent careers are a passage.
- All integrate multiple factors.

Differences
- Latent trait: The unchanging propensity to crime controls antisocial behavior.
- Life course: People are constantly evolving.
- Trajectory: There is more than one path to crime.

trajectory theory The view that there are multiple independent paths to a delinquent career and that there are different types and classes of offenders.

In some cases, transitions can occur too early—for example, when adolescents engage in precocious sex. In other cases, transitions may occur too late, as when a student fails to graduate on time because of bad grades or too many incompletes. Sometimes disruption of one trajectory can harm another: having a baby while still a teenager is likely to disrupt educational and career development. These negative life experiences can become cumulative: as kids acquire more personal deficits, the chances of acquiring additional ones increase.[3]

So the boy who experiences significant amounts of anger in early adolescence is the one who is more likely to become involved in antisocial behavior as a teen and to mature into a depressed adult who abuses alcohol.[4] While most adolescents age out of crime and become responsible adults, those growing up in a criminogenic environment and engaging in antisocial behavior as adolescents are the ones who are most likely to engage in antisocial behavior as adults.[5]

The Developmental Process

Because a transition from one stage of life to another can be a bumpy ride, the propensity to commit delinquent acts is neither stable nor constant; it is a *developmental process*. A positive life experience may help some kids desist from delinquency for a while, whereas a negative one may cause them to resume their activities. Delinquent careers are also said to be *interactional*, because people are influenced by the behavior of those around them, and in turn, they influence the behavior of others. For example, a girl who is constantly in trouble may be rejected by her friends, which causes her to (a) seek antisocial friends and (b) increase her involvement in antisocial behavior, which causes even more rejection. Life course theories also recognize that as people mature, the factors that influence their behavior change. At first, family relations may be most influential; in later adolescence, school and peer relations predominate; in adulthood, vocational achievement and marital relations may be the most critical influences. For example, some antisocial children who are in trouble throughout their adolescence may manage to find stable work and maintain intact marriages as adults; these life events help them desist from delinquency. In contrast, the less fortunate adolescents who develop arrest records and get involved with the wrong crowd may find themselves limited to menial jobs and continue to be at risk for delinquent careers.

The Glueck Research

One of the cornerstones of recent life course theories has been renewed interest in the research efforts of Sheldon and Eleanor Glueck. While at Harvard University in the 1930s, the Gluecks popularized research on the life cycle of delinquent careers. In a series of longitudinal research studies, they followed the careers of known delinquents to determine the factors that predicted persistent offending.[6] The Gluecks made extensive use of interviews and records in their elaborate comparisons of delinquents and nondelinquents.[7]

The Gluecks' research focused on early onset of delinquency as a harbinger of a delinquent career: "The deeper the roots of childhood maladjustment, the smaller the chance of adult adjustment."[8] They also noted the stability of offending careers: children who are antisocial early in life are the most likely to continue their offending careers into adulthood.

The Gluecks identified a number of personal and social factors related to persistent offending. The most important of these factors was family relations, considered in terms

Looking Back to Kia's Story

Kia immigrated to the United States when he was 11 and had trouble adjusting to the American way of life.

CRITICAL THINKING What are the special problems of immigrant kids and how might they contribute to negative life experiences? Conduct research on the problems of immigrants in the United States and what is being done to help them to successfully transition.

Looking Back to Kia's Story

Kia's parents had immigrated from Vietnam, leaving their family behind to start a new life.

CRITICAL THINKING Would it have been important for the counselor to ask this family about their culture, background, and decision-making processes? Write an essay on how these factors impact an adolescent's development.

of quality of discipline and emotional ties with parents. The adolescent who was raised in a large, single-parent family of limited economic means and educational achievement was the most vulnerable to delinquency.

The Gluecks did not restrict their analysis to social variables. When they measured such biological and psychological traits as body type, intelligence, and personality, they found that physical and mental factors also played a role in determining behavior. Children with low intelligence, a background of mental disease, and a powerful (mesomorph) physique were the most likely to become persistent offenders.

LIFE COURSE CONCEPTS

A number of key concepts help define the life course view. We describe a few of the most critical concepts in this section.[9]

Age of Onset

We know that most young criminals desist and do not become adult offenders.[10] But some do go on to have a long career as a chronic offender. The seeds of a delinquent career are planted early in life (preschool); **early onset** of deviance strongly predicts more frequent, varied, and sustained criminality later in life.[11] What causes some kids to begin offending at an early age? Among the suspected root causes are inadequate emotional support, distant peer relationships, and psychological issues and problems.[12] Research shows that poor parental discipline and monitoring seem to be a key to the early onset of criminality and that these influences may follow kids into their adulthood. The psychic scars of childhood are hard to erase.[13]

Most of these early onset delinquents begin their careers with disruptive behavior, truancy, cruelty to animals, lying, and theft.[14] They also appear to be more violent than their less precocious peers.[15] The earlier the onset, the more likely an adolescent will engage in serious delinquency and for a longer period of time. Studies of the juvenile justice system show that many incarcerated youths began their offending careers very early in life and that a significant number had engaged in heavy drinking and drug abuse by age 10 or younger.[16]

early onset The view that kids who begin engaging in antisocial behaviors at a very early age are the ones most at risk for a delinquency career.

problem behavior syndrome (PBS) A cluster of antisocial behaviors that may include family dysfunction, substance abuse, smoking, precocious sexuality and early pregnancy, educational underachievement, suicide attempts, sensation seeking, and unemployment, as well as delinquency.

Problem Behavior Syndrome

The life course view is that delinquency is but one of many social problems faced by at-risk youth. Referred to collectively as **problem behavior syndrome (PBS)**, these behaviors include family dysfunction, substance abuse, smoking, precocious sexuality and early pregnancy, educational underachievement, suicide attempts, sensation seeking, and unemployment).[17] People who suffer from one of these conditions typically exhibit many symptoms of the others.[18] Research has found the following problem behaviors cluster together:

- Youths who drink in the late elementary school years, who are aggressive, and who have attention problems are more likely to be offenders during adolescence.

- Youths who are less attached to their parents and school and have antisocial friends are more likely to be offenders.

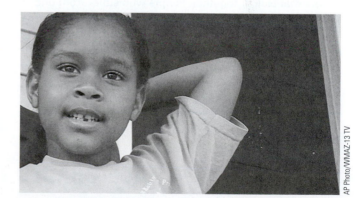

AP Photo/WMAZ-13 TV

How early is too early for the onset of delinquency? Here, Salecia Johnson, age 6, is shown at her home near Milledgeville, Georgia, on April 16, 2012. Police in Georgia handcuffed the kindergartner after the girl threw a tantrum, and the police chief is making no apologies. Salecia was accused of tearing items off the walls and throwing furniture at school. The police report says she knocked over a shelf that injured the principal. How does being handcuffed lock a young girl like Salecia into a delinquent way of life? Might there not be another solution?

WWW

To read highlights of the **Pittsburgh Youth Study** directed by Rolf Loeber, visit the Criminal Justice CourseMate at CengageBrain.com, then access the Web Links for this chapter.

WWW

The Program of Research on the Causes and Correlates of Delinquency, sponsored by the federal government, coordinates longitudinal projects that are often referred to in this text. To find this website, visit the Criminal Justice CourseMate at CengageBrain.com, then access the Web Links for this chapter.

- Youths from neighborhoods where drugs are easily available are more likely to be offenders during adolescence.[19]
- Juvenile delinquents with conduct disorder who have experienced and observed violence, who have been traumatized, and who suffer from a wide spectrum of psychopathology also have high rates of suicidal thoughts and attempts.[20]
- Delinquents exhibit a complex combination of externalizing behaviors, including conduct disorder, attention deficit hyperactivity disorder (ADHD), drug abuse, familial and interpersonal difficulties (such as conflict with parents), and low intelligence.[21]

All varieties of delinquent behavior, including violence, theft, and drug offenses, may be part of a generalized PBS, indicating that all forms of antisocial behavior have similar developmental patterns.[22]

Continuity of Crime and Delinquency

Another aspect of life course theory is *continuity of crime and delinquency*: the best predictor of future criminality is past criminality. Children who are repeatedly in trouble during early adolescence will generally still be antisocial in their middle teens; kids who are delinquent in their mid-teens are the ones most likely to commit crime as adults.[23] Research shows that kids who persist engage in more aggressive acts and are continually involved in theft offenses and aggression. As they emerge into adulthood, persisters report less emotional support, lower job satisfaction, distant peer relationships, and more psychiatric problems than those who desist.[24]

Early delinquent activity is likely to be sustained, because these offenders seem to lack the social survival skills necessary to find work or to develop the interpersonal relationships they need to allow them to drop out of delinquency. Delinquency may be *contagious*: kids at risk for delinquency may be located in families and neighborhoods in which they are constantly exposed to deviant behavior. Having brothers, fathers, neighbors, and friends who engage in and support their activities reinforces their deviance.[25]

As they mature, delinquents may continue to be involved in antisocial behavior. But even if they aren't, they are still at risk for a large variety of adult social behavior problems. There are gender differences in the effect. For males, the path runs from delinquency to problems at work and substance abuse. For females, antisocial behavior in youth leads to relationship problems, depression, a tendency to commit suicide, and poor health in adulthood.[26]

CHECKPOINTS

CHECKPOINTS

LO2 Know the principles of the life course approach to developmental theory.

✔ At an early age, people begin relationships and behaviors that will determine their adult life course.

✔ Some individuals are incapable of maturing in a reasonable and timely fashion.

✔ A positive life experience may help some criminals desist from crime for a while, but a negative experience may cause them to resume their criminal activities.

✔ As people mature, the factors that influence their behavior change. The social, physical, and environmental influences on their behavior are transformed.

✔ Crime is one of a group of interrelated antisocial behaviors that cluster together. People who suffer from one of these conditions typically exhibit many symptoms of the rest.

✔ Early onset of antisocial behavior predicts later and more serious criminality. Adolescent offenders whose criminal behavior persists into adulthood are likely to have begun their deviant careers at a very early (preschool) age.

AGE-GRADED THEORY

Criminologists have formulated a number of systematic theories that account for onset, continuance, and desistance from delinquency. One of the most prominent of these is age-graded theory, which has emerged as a principle life course model. Exhibit 5.1 summarizes two other prominent attempts at creating a systematic life course theory.

Age-graded theory was first articulated in an important 1993 work, *Crime in the Making*, in which Robert Sampson and John Laub identified the fact there are

EXHIBIT 5.1 Examples of Life Course Theory

The Social Development Model (SDM)

J. David Hawkins and Richard Catalano's social development model seeks to explain the interaction between community and individual factors and their influence on antisocial behavior:

- Community-level risk factors make some people susceptible to antisocial behaviors.
- Preexisting risk factors are either reinforced or neutralized by socialization.
- To control the risk of antisocial behavior, a child must maintain prosocial bonds. Over the life course, involvement in prosocial or antisocial behavior determines the quality of attachments.
- Commitment and attachment to conventional institutions, activities, and beliefs insulate youths from the criminogenic influences in their environment.
- The prosocial path inhibits deviance by strengthening bonds to prosocial others and activities. Without the proper level of bonding, adolescents can succumb to the influence of deviant others.

Interactional Theory

Terence Thornberry and his colleagues Marvin Krohn, Alan Lizotte, and Margaret Farnworth have developed the interactional theory, which attempts to show how delinquency is an interactive process:

- The onset of crime can be traced to a deterioration of the social bond during adolescence, marked by weakening of attachment to parents, commitment to school, and belief in conventional values.
- The cause of crime and delinquency is bidirectional: weak bonds lead kids to develop friendships with deviant peers and get involved in delinquency.
- Frequent delinquency involvement further weakens bonds and makes it difficult to reestablish conventional ones. Delinquency-promoting factors tend to reinforce one another and sustain a chronic criminal career.
- Kids who go through stressful life events, such as a family financial crisis, are more likely to get involved later in antisocial behaviors and vice versa. Criminality is a developmental process that takes on different meaning and form as a person matures. During early adolescence, attachment to the family is critical. By mid-adolescence, the influence of the family is replaced by friends, school, and youth culture. By adulthood, a person's behavioral choices are shaped by his or her place in conventional society and his or her own nuclear family.
- Although crime is influenced by these social forces, it also influences these processes and associations. Therefore, crime and social processes are interactional.

Sources: Terence Thornberry, "Toward an Interactional Theory of Delinquency," *Criminology* 25:863–891 (1987); Richard Catalano and J. David Hawkins, "The Social Development Model: A Theory of Antisocial Behavior," in *Delinquency and Crime: Current Theories*, ed. J. David Hawkins (New York: Cambridge University Press, 1996), pp. 149–197.

important events, which they called **turning points**, in a delinquent career that either help kids knife off from a life of crime or solidify and amplify their criminality.[27] Reanalyzing the original Glueck data, they found that the stability of delinquent behavior can be affected by events that occur later in life, even after a chronic delinquent career has been established. They also believe that formal and informal social controls restrict criminality, and that delinquency begins early in life and continues over the life course.

turning points Critical life events, such as career and marriage, which may enable adult offenders to desist from delinquency.

Turning Points in the Life Course

Sampson and Laub's most important contribution is identifying the life events that produce informal social control and enable people to desist from delinquency as they mature and enter their adulthood. Two critical turning points are career and marriage:

- *Adolescents who are at risk for delinquency can live conventional lives if they can find good jobs or achieve successful careers.* Their success may hinge on a lucky break. Even those who have been in trouble with the law may turn from delinquency if employers are willing to give them a chance despite their records. Serving in the military also helps kids achieve success and leave deviant pathways.

- *Adolescents who have had significant problems with the law are also able to desist from delinquency if, as adults, they become attached to a spouse who supports and sustains them, regardless of their past.*[28] Spending time in marital and family activities reduces exposure to deviant peers, which reduces the opportunity to become involved in delinquent activities.[29] People who cannot sustain secure marital relations are less likely to desist from delinquency.

Developing Social Capital

A cornerstone of age-graded theory is the influence of **social capital** on behavior. Social scientists recognize that people build social capital—positive relations with individuals and institutions that are life sustaining. Social capital, which includes the resources accessed through interpersonal connections and relationships, is as critical to individuals (and to social groups, organizations, and communities) in obtaining their objectives as is human capital, what a person (or organization) actually possesses.[30]

Although building financial capital improves the chances for economic success, building social capital also produces elements of informal social control that produce and support conventional behavior and inhibit deviant behavior (see Figure 5.1).[31] As they travel the life course, kids who accumulate social capital can knife off from a deviant path. If they can find love, enter into a successful marriage, and enter a rewarding career, they accumulate social capital that will enhance their stature, create feelings of self-worth, and encourage others to trust them. Social capital inhibits delinquency by creating a stake in conformity: Why risk a successful relationship? Why commit delinquency when you are doing well at your job? The relationship is reciprocal. If people are chosen to be employees, they return the favor by doing the best job possible; if they are chosen as spouses, they blossom into devoted partners.

In contrast, losing or wasting social capital increases both personal deficits and the likelihood of getting involved in delinquency. For example, moving to a new city reduces social capital by closing people off from long-term relationships.[32] Losing social capital has a cumulative effect, and as kids develop more and more disadvantages the likelihood of their entering a delinquent and criminal career increases.[33]

Testing Age-Graded Theory

Several indicators support the validity of age-graded theory.[34] Research shows that children who are raised in two-parent families are more likely to grow up to have happier marriages than children whose parents were divorced or never married.[35] This finding suggests that the marriage–delinquency association may be intergenerational: if people with marital problems are more delinquency prone, their children will also suffer a greater long-term risk of marital failure and antisocial activity.

Evidence now shows that, once begun, delinquent career trajectories can be reversed if life conditions improve, an outcome predicted by age-graded theory.[36] Youths who accumulate social capital in childhood (for example, by doing well in school or having a tightly knit family) are also the most likely to maintain steady work as adults. In addition, people who are unemployed or underemployed report

social capital Positive relations with individuals and institutions, as in a successful marriage or a successful career, that support conventional behavior and inhibit deviant behavior.

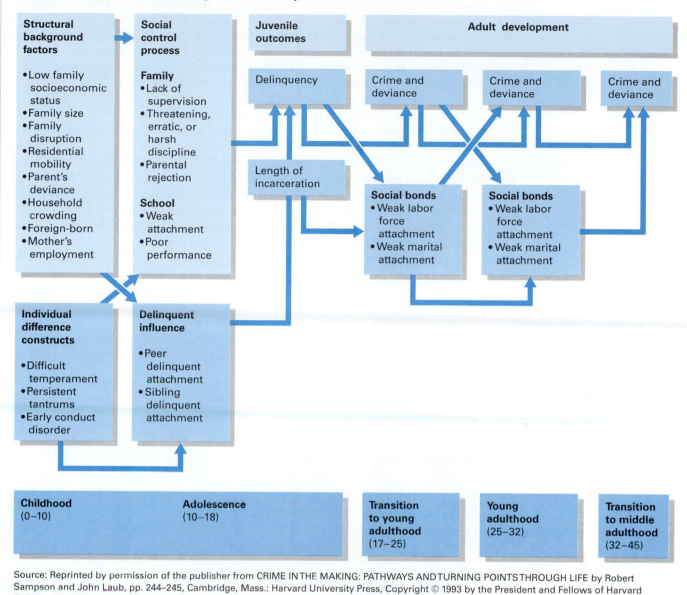

FIGURE 5.1 Sampson and Laub's Age-Graded Theory

Source: Reprinted by permission of the publisher from CRIME IN THE MAKING: PATHWAYS AND TURNING POINTS THROUGH LIFE by Robert Sampson and John Laub, pp. 244–245, Cambridge, Mass.: Harvard University Press, Copyright © 1993 by the President and Fellows of Harvard College. All rights reserved."

higher delinquent participation rates than employed men.[37] As predicted by age-graded theory, delinquent youth who enter the military, serve overseas, and receive veterans' benefits enhance their occupational status (social capital) while reducing delinquent involvement.[38] In contrast, people who are self-centered and present-oriented are less likely to accumulate social capital and more prone to committing delinquent acts.[39]

Several areas still need to be explored. For example, does a military career actually help reduce future criminality? Recent research by John Paul Wright and his colleagues found that Vietnam veterans significantly increased their involvement in substance abuse once they returned home. Considering the strong association between drug abuse and crime, their research sheds some doubt on whether all types of military service can be beneficial as Laub and Sampson suggest. Future research may want to focus on individual experiences in the military and their effect on subsequent civilian behavior.[40]

Love and Delinquency

Age-graded theory places a lot of emphasis on the stability brought about by romantic relationships leading eventually to a good marriage. Kids headed toward a life of crime can knife off that path if they meet the right mate; love is a primary conduit of informal social control. This important element of age-graded theory has found support in recent research conducted by sociologists Bill McCarthy and Teresa Casey.[41] They examined the associations between love, sex, and delinquency among a sample of teens, and found that adolescent romantic love can help fill the emotional void that occurs between the time they break free of parental bonds until they learn to accept adult responsibilities. But only meaningful relationships seem to work: love, not sex, is the key to success. Kids who get involved in sexual activity without the promise of love actually increase their involvement in crime and delinquency; only true love reduces the likelihood of offending. Loveless sexual relations produce feelings of strain, which are correlated with antisocial activity. It is possible that kids who engage in sex without love or romance are willing to partake in other risky and/or self-indulgent behaviors, including delinquency and drug usage. In contrast, romantic love discourages offending by strengthening the social bond.

Of course, there are different kinds of love, not all of which are romantic. Recently, Derek Kreager and his associates found that young women who become mothers are the ones most likely to desist from delinquency. The love of a child may be a more important factor in desistance than love or marriage.[42]

The question then remains: what prompts some kids to engage in loving relationships that lead to marriage, while others are doomed to fall in and out of love without finding lasting happiness? Sociologist Rand Conger and his colleagues have

One of the most important issues separating the branches of developmental theory is whether people can truly change. Take the case of boxing champ Bernard Hopkins, who rose from a tough childhood to athletic fame and fortune. His parents drank, smoked, and did drugs. His mother, Shirley, developed high blood pressure. By age 11, Hopkins smoked marijuana and drank malt liquor, whiskey, and wine. By 13, he had robbed. By 14, he had been stabbed with an ice pick. By 17, he was convicted of armed robbery and assault. Hopkins spent 56 months in prison and turned his life around. Not surprisingly, Hopkins hated the food in prison, all the powdered eggs, yeast, and starch. He learned how to work around the worst meals, smuggling leftovers to his cell or drinking water to fill his stomach. He traded cartons of cigarettes and cases of noodle cups for more desirable food. He could subsist on meals, sometimes for days, of peanut butter and bread. When he got out, he gave up drugs for health foods and was able to knife off from a life of crime. At age 46, Hopkins became the oldest fighter ever to win a world title.

discovered that the seeds of marital success are planted early in childhood: kids who grow up with warm, nurturing parents are the ones most likely to have positive romantic relationships and later intact marriages. Well-nurtured kids develop into warm and supportive romantic partners who have relationships that are likely to endure.[43] It is the quality of parenting, not the observation of adult romantic relations, that socializes a young person to engage in behaviors likely to promote successful and lasting romantic unions as an adult.

Do love and other prosocial life experiences work to help kids avoid antisocial behavior over the long haul? To find out, Laub and Sampson conducted an important follow-up to their original research. They found and interviewed survivors from the original Glueck research, the oldest subject being 70 years old and the youngest 62. The results of their research are examined in the accompanying Focus on Delinquency feature. **CHECKPOINTS**

THE LATENT TRAIT/PROPENSITY VIEW

In a popular 1985 book, *Crime and Human Nature*, two prominent social scientists, James Q. Wilson and Richard Herrnstein, argued that personal traits, such as genetic makeup, intelligence, and body build, operate in tandem with social variables that include poverty and family function. Together these factors influence people to "choose delinquency" over nondelinquent behavioral alternatives.[44]

Following their lead, David Rowe, D. Wayne Osgood, and W. Alan Nicewander proposed the concept of latent traits. Their model assumes that a number of people in the population have a personal attribute or propensity that controls their inclination or to commit delinquent acts.[45] This disposition, or latent trait, is either present at birth or established early in life, and it remains stable over time. Suspected latent traits include defective intelligence, impulsive personality, genetic abnormalities, the physical-chemical functioning of the brain, and environmental influences on brain function, such as drugs, chemicals, and injuries.[46] Those who carry one of these latent traits are in danger of becoming career criminals; those who lack the propensity to commit have a much lower risk.[47]

According to this view, the *propensity* to commit delinquency is stable, but the *opportunity* to commit delinquency fluctuates over time. People age out of delinquency, because, as they mature, there are simply fewer opportunities to commit such acts and greater inducements to remain "straight." They may marry, have children, and obtain jobs. The former delinquents' newfound adult responsibilities leave them little time to hang with their friends, abuse substances, and get into scrapes with the law.

Assume, for example, that a stable latent trait such as low IQ causes some people to commit delinquent acts. Teenagers have more opportunity to do so than adults, so at every level of intelligence, adolescent delinquency rates will be higher. As they mature, however, teens with both high and low IQs will commit less delinquency, because their adult responsibilities provide them with fewer opportunities to do so. Thus, latent trait/propensity theory integrates concepts

WHAT DOES THIS MEAN TO ME?

▶ **Family Ties** When Bill McCarthy, John Hagan, and Monica Martin studied street kids, they found that more than half joined a "street family" for support and emotional connections that their other relationships lacked. One child told the researchers:

My street family gave me more support on the streets and stuff: people loving and caring for you. You know, being there for you. It feels better, you know, than just being, you know, alone when you don't know what to do.

1. Have you ever been involved in a non-family group that provided social capital that could not be gained in any other manner? How did it help?
2. Do you believe that it is instinctual for humans to seek out others for support? Would joining a fraternity or sorority fit the model?

Source: Bill McCarthy, John Hagan, and Monica Martin, "In and Out of Harm's Way: Violent Victimization and the Social Capital of Fictive Street Families," *Criminology* 40:831–836 (2002).

SHARED BEGINNINGS, DIVERGENT LIVES

Why are some delinquents destined to become persistent criminals as adults? To find out, John Laub and Robert Sampson located the survivors of the delinquent sample first collected by Sheldon and Eleanor Glueck. At the time of the follow-up study, the oldest was 70 years old and the youngest was 62. The study involved three sources of new data collection—criminal record checks (both local and national), death record checks (local and national), and personal interviews with a sample of 52 of the original Glueck men, stratified to ensure variability in patterns of persistence and desistance in crime.

They found that explanations of desistance from crime and also for persistent offending in crime are two sides of the same coin. Desistance is a process rather than an event, and it must be continually renewed. The processes of desistance operate simultaneously at different levels (individual, situational, and community) and across different contextual environments (especially family, work, and military service). The process of desistance is more than mere aging and more than individual predisposition.

The interviews showed that delinquency and other forms of antisocial conduct in childhood are strongly related to adult delinquency and drug and alcohol abuse. Former delinquents also suffer consequences in other areas of social life, such as school, work, and family life. They are far less likely to finish high school than are nondelinquents and subsequently are more likely to be unemployed, receive welfare, and experience separation or divorce as adults.

Laub and Sampson also addressed a key question posed by life course theories: is it possible for former delinquents to turn their lives around as adults? The researchers found that most antisocial children do not remain antisocial as adults. Former delinquents who desisted from crime were rooted in structural routines and had strong social ties to family and community. They found that one important element for going straight is the knifing off of individuals from their immediate environment, offering the men a new script for the future. Joining the military can provide this knifing-off effect, as can marriage or changing one's residence. One former delinquent (age 69) told them:

usually associated with trait theories (such as personality and temperament) and concepts associated with rational choice theories (such as delinquent opportunity and suitable targets).

General Theory of Crime

Michael Gottfredson and Travis Hirschi's **general theory of crime (GTC)** modifies and redefines some of the principles articulated in Hirschi's social control theory (see Chapter 4) by integrating the concepts of control with those of biosocial, psychological, routine activities, and rational choice theories.[48]

The Act and the Offender. In their general theory of crime, Gottfredson and Hirschi consider the delinquent offender and the delinquent act as separate concepts.

- Delinquent acts, such as robberies or burglaries, are illegal events or deeds that people engage in when they perceive them to be advantageous. For example, burglaries are typically committed by young males looking for cash, liquor, and entertainment; the delinquency provides "easy, short-term gratification."[49]

- Delinquency is rational and predictable. Kids break the law when it promises rewards with minimal threat of pain. Therefore, the threat of punishment can

general theory of crime (GTC) A developmental theory that modifies social control theory by integrating concepts from biosocial, psychological, routine activities, and rational choice theories.

I'd say the turning point was, number one, the Army. You get into an outfit, you had a sense of belonging, you made your friends. I think I became a pretty good judge of character. In the Army, you met some good ones, you met some foul balls. Then I met the wife. I'd say probably that would be the turning point. Got married, then naturally, kids come. So now you got to get a better job, you got to make more money. And that's how I got to the Navy Yard and tried to improve myself.

Former delinquents who went straight were able to put structure into their lives. Structure often led the men to disassociate from delinquent peers, reducing the opportunity to get into trouble. Getting married, for example, may limit the number of nights available to "hang with the guys." As one wife of a former delinquent said, "It is not how many beers you have, it's who you drink with." Even multiple offenders who did time in prison were able to desist with the help of a stabilizing marriage. So love does in fact conquer all!

Former delinquents who can turn their life around, who have acquired a degree of maturity by taking on family and work responsibilities, and who have forged new commitments are most likely to make a fresh start and find new direction and meaning in life. It seems that men who desisted changed their identity as well, and this, in turn, affected their outlook and sense of maturity and responsibility. The ability to change did not reflect any delinquency "specialty": violent offenders followed the same path as property offenders.

Although many former delinquents desisted from delinquency, others did not and continued a life of crime late into adulthood. These persisters experienced considerable residential instability, marital instability, job instability, failure in school and in the military, and relatively long periods of incarceration. Many were "social nomads," without permanent addresses, steady jobs, spouses, or children. As a consequence of chaotic and unstructured routines, the persisters had increased contact with those individuals who were similarly situated—in this case, similarly unattached and free from nurturing and informal social control. And they paid the price for their unstructured lives: frequent involvement in delinquency during adolescence and alcohol abuse were the strongest predictors of an early and untimely death. So, while many troubled youths are able to reform, their early excesses may haunt them across their lifespan.

CRITICAL THINKING

1. Do you believe that the factors that influenced the men in the original Glueck sample are still relevant for change—for example, a military career?

2. Would it be possible for men such as these to join the military today?

3. Do you believe that some sort of universal service program might be beneficial and help people turn their lives around?

Writing Assignment Write an essay entitled "Turning Points," in which you discuss the various turning points in your life that enabled you to knife off from one path to another. Does any one incident stand out?

Sources: John Laub and Robert Sampson, *Shared Beginnings, Divergent Lives: Delinquent Boys to Age 70* (Cambridge, MA: Harvard University Press, 2003); John Laub and Robert Sampson, "Understanding Desistance from Delinquency," in *Delinquency and Justice: An Annual Review of Research*, vol. 28, ed. Michael Tonry, (Chicago: University of Chicago Press, 2001), pp. 1–71.

---

deter delinquency: if targets are well guarded, and guardians are present, delinquency rates will diminish.

- Delinquent offenders are predisposed to commit crimes. However, they are not robots who commit crimes without restraint; their days are also filled with conventional behaviors, such as going to school, parties, concerts, and church. But given the same set of delinquent opportunities, such as having a lot of free time for mischief and living in a neighborhood with unguarded homes containing valuable merchandise, delinquency-prone kids have a much higher probability of violating the law than do nondelinquents. The propensity to commit delinquent acts remains stable throughout a person's life; change in the frequency of delinquent activity is purely a function of change in opportunity.[50]

By recognizing that there are stable differences in people's propensity to commit delinquent acts, the GTC adds a biosocial element to the concept of social control. The biological and psychological factors that make people impulsive and delinquency prone may be inherited or may develop through incompetent or absent parenting. Once present, they do not change. So unlike life course theory which suggests that experience changes people, the GTC suggests that these observed changes are illusory: a person's core makeup is actually stable and unyielding.

What Makes People Delinquency Prone?

What causes people to become excessively delinquency prone? Gottfredson and Hirschi attribute the tendency to commit delinquent acts to a person's level of **self-control**. Low self-control develops early in life and remains stable into and through adulthood.[51] People with limited self-control tend to be **impulsive**; they are insensitive to other people's feelings, physical (rather than mental), risk takers, shortsighted, and nonverbal. They have a "here and now" orientation and refuse to work for distant goals; they lack diligence, tenacity, and persistence. Impulsive people tend to be adventuresome, active, physical, and self-centered. As they mature, they often have unstable marriages, jobs, and friendships.[52] People lacking self-control are less likely to feel shame if they engage in deviant acts and more likely to find them pleasurable. They are also more likely to engage in dangerous behaviors that are associated with criminality.

Because those with low self-control enjoy risky, exciting, or thrilling behaviors with immediate gratification, they are more likely to enjoy delinquent acts, which require stealth, agility, speed, and power, than conventional acts, which demand long-term study and cognitive and verbal skills. And because they enjoy taking risks, they are more likely to get involved in accidents and suffer injuries than people who maintain self-control.[53] As Gottfredson and Hirschi put it, they derive satisfaction from "money without work, sex without courtship, revenge without court delays."[54] Many of these individuals who have a propensity for committing delinquent acts also engage in risky albeit non-criminal behaviors such as smoking, drinking, gambling, reckless driving, and illicit sexuality, that provide immediate, short-term gratification.[55] Gottfredson and Hirschi claim that self-control theory can explain all varieties of delinquent behavior and all the social and behavioral correlates of delinquency. That is, such widely disparate delinquent acts as burglary, robbery, embezzlement, drug dealing, murder,

self-control Refers to a person's ability to exercise restraint and control over his or her feelings, emotions, reactions, and behaviors.

impulsive Lacking in thought or deliberation in decision making. An impulsive person lacks close attention to details, has organizational problems, is distracted and forgetful.

AP Images/*Beaver County Times*/Sylvester Washington Jr.

According to latent trait theories, delinquency propensity varies among people. Here, Walter Stawarz IV (center) is escorted to the courtroom in Beaver, Pennsylvania. Stawarz, 16, was charged as an adult with attempted homicide, reckless endangerment, and aggravated assault for allegedly beating 15-year-old Jeremy Delon along the Ohio River in Hopewell Township. Police accused Stawarz of beating Delon around the time the teenagers attempted to buy some marijuana. According to Hirschi and Gottfredson, people like Stawarz are impulsive and lack self-control, conditions they either developed at birth or very early in childhood.

rape, and running away from home all stem from a deficiency in self-control. Likewise, gender, racial, and ecological differences in delinquency rates can be explained by discrepancies in self-control: if male delinquency rates are higher than female delinquency rates, it is the result of males having lower levels of self-control than females.

What Causes Low Self-Control? Gottfredson and Hirschi trace the root cause of poor self-control to inadequate child-rearing practices. Even in disadvantaged communities, children whose parents provide adequate and supportive discipline are the ones most like to develop self-control.[56] Parents who are unwilling or unable to monitor a child's behavior, to recognize deviant behavior when it occurs, and to punish that behavior will produce children who lack self-control. Children who are not attached to their parents, who are poorly supervised, and whose parents are delinquent or deviant themselves are the most likely to develop poor self-control. In a sense, lack of self-control occurs naturally when steps are not taken to stop its development.[57]

There may also be a genetic/biosocial component to the development of impulsivity. Brian Boutwell and Kevin Beaver found that children of impulsive parents are the ones most likely to exhibit a lack of self-control.[58] Research by David Farrington shows that antisocial behavior runs in families and that having delinquent relatives is a significant predictor of future misbehaviors.[59] While these studies are not definitive, they raise the possibility that the intergenerational transfer of impulsivity has a biological basis.

Testing the General Theory of Crime

Following the publication of *A General Theory of Crime*, dozens of research efforts tested the validity of Gottfredson and Hirschi's theoretical views. One approach involves identifying indicators of impulsiveness and self-control to determine whether scales measuring these factors correlate with measures of delinquent activity. A number of studies conducted both in the United States and abroad have shown that delinquent kids score much higher on scales measuring impulsivity than nondelinquent youth.[60] When Alexander Vazsonyi and his associates analyzed self-control and deviant behavior with samples drawn from a number of different countries (Hungary, Switzerland, the Netherlands, the United States, and Japan), they found that low self-control is significantly related to antisocial behavior and that the association can be seen regardless of culture or national setting.[61]

There is also research showing that the patterns of antisocial behavior found in groups of youth offenders mimic those predicted by Gottfredson and Hirschi.[62] One such effort found that those delinquents who begin their offending career at an early age and become life course persistent offenders are also the ones who are lacking in self-control.[63] Another study found that victims have lower self-control than nonvictims. Impulsivity predicts both the likelihood that a person will engage in criminal behavior and the likelihood that the person will become a victim of crime. These patterns are all predicted by the GTC.[64]

By integrating the concepts of socialization and criminality, Gottfredson and Hirschi help explain why some people who lack self-control can escape criminality, and conversely, why some people who have self-control might not escape criminality. People who are at risk because they have impulsive personalities may forgo delinquent careers because there are no opportunities to commit delinquent acts; instead, they may find other outlets for their impulsive personalities. In contrast, if the opportunity is strong enough, even people with relatively strong self-control may be tempted to violate the law; the incentives to commit delinquent acts may overwhelm their self-control.

The General Theory of Crime suggests that people do not change. Here, Baltimore Ravens offensive lineman Michael Oher sits on the bench during an NFL football game against the New England Patriots at Gillette Stadium in Foxborough, Massachusetts, on October 4, 2009. Oher was the subject of the popular movie *The Blind Side* (adapted from the best-selling book by Michael Lewis), which told how he was homeless and abandoned and then adopted into a middle-class family who supported his athletic ambitions. It is unlikely Oher would be where he is today without this support. Does his story indicate that people's lives are influenced by social events and that change is possible?

Criticisms and Questions. Although the GTC seems persuasive, several questions and criticisms remain to be answered. Among the most important are the following:

- *Circular reasoning.* Some critics argue that the theory involves circular reasoning. How do we know when people are impulsive? Is it when they commit crime? Are all criminals impulsive? Of course, or else they would not have broken the law![65]

- *Personality disorder.* It is possible that a lack of self-control is merely a symptom of some broader, underlying personality disorder, such as an antisocial personality, that produces delinquency. Other personality traits such as low self-direction (the tendency not to act in one's long-term benefit) may be a better predictor of criminality than impulsivity or lack of self-control.[66]

- *Racial and gender differences.* Although distinct gender differences in the delinquency rate exist, there is little evidence that males are more impulsive than females.[67] Some research efforts have found gender differences in the association between self-control and crime; the theory predicts no such difference should occur.[68] Girls seem more deeply influenced by their delinquent boyfriends than boys are by their delinquent girlfriends.[69] Differences in impulsivity and self-control alone may not be able to explain differences in male and female offending rates.[70] Similarly, Gottfredson and Hirschi explain racial differences in the delinquency rate as a failure of childrearing practices in the African American community.[71] In so doing, they overlook issues of institutional racism, poverty, and relative deprivation, which have been shown to have a significant impact on delinquency rate differentials.

- *People change and so does their level of self-control.* The general theory of crime assumes that delinquent propensity does not change; opportunities change. However, social scientists recognize that behavior-shaping factors that are dominant in early adolescence, such as peer groups, may fade in adulthood and be replaced by others, such as the nuclear family.[72] Personality also undergoes change and so does its impact on antisocial behavior.[73] It is not surprising that research efforts show that the stability in self-control predicted by Gottfredson and Hirschi may be an illusion.[74] As kids mature, the focus of their lives likewise changes and they may be better able to control their impulsive behavior.[75] One recent analysis by Callie Burt and her associates found that kids whose parents improved their parenting skills over time experienced (a) an increase in self-control and (b) a subsequent decrease in the level of their delinquent activities. Also helping to reduce low self-control was developing positive relationships with teachers and reducing exposure to deviant peers. The Burt research is a direct rebuttal of Hirschi and Gottfredson's core premise that once acquired, low self-control is hard to shake.[76]

Environment and Impulsivity. Gottfredson and Hirschi discount the influence of environmental factors: low self-control produces delinquency notwithstanding the characteristics of the adolescent's social world. This issue has become a center of some contention. Some research indicates that an adolescent's social world does mediate the influence of self-control on crime. Social cultural factors have been found to make an independent contribution to criminal offending patterns, but the direction of this influence is still being debated. The prevailing wisdom is that kids who lack self-control and who live in high-crime areas may be more inclined to antisocial activities than youths with similar levels of self-control who reside in areas that work to maintain collective efficacy and that are relatively crime free.[77]

Recently, criminologist Gregory Zimmerman examined how environment and personality interact and reached a somewhat different conclusion. In high-crime neighborhoods, impulsive people are no more criminal than their non-impulsive neighbors. In contrast, in safe, low-crime areas, impulsive residents are much more likely to commit crime than their fellow citizens. How can this surprising finding be explained? In disadvantaged neighborhoods, most people tend to possess a feeling of fatalism and adopt an "I have nothing to lose" attitude. These factors cause both non-impulsive and impulsive individuals to take advantage of criminal opportunities. In these disorganized neighborhoods, nearly everyone commits crime, so that having self-control means relatively little. In low-crime areas, most people conform and it's only the most impulsive who risk engaging in crime. Why bother taking a risk when legitimate opportunities abound? In these higher-income neighborhoods, only those totally lacking in self-control are foolish enough to commit crime.[78]

Not only does this association hold for delinquency, but it also seems to influence juvenile victimization as well. Chris Gibson recently found that self-control's influence on victimization is conditioned by neighborhood type: low self-control had a statistically important influence on victimization for those who live in the least disadvantaged neighborhoods, while it did not affect adolescents living in the most disadvantaged neighborhoods. He agrees with the view that individual differences between people will have less impact on their behavior in disadvantaged neighborhoods because the environment overrides individual risk.[79]

Although questions remain, the strength of the general theory of crime lies in its scope and breadth. By integrating concepts of delinquent choice, delinquent opportunity, socialization, and personality, Gottfredson and Hirschi make a plausible argument that all deviant behaviors may originate from the same source. Continued efforts are needed to test the GTC and establish the validity of its core concepts. It remains one of the key developments of modern criminological theory. **CHECKPOINTS**

TRAJECTORY THEORY

Trajectory theory is a third developmental approach that combines elements of propensity and life course theory. The basic premise is that there is more than one path to crime and more than one class of offender; there are different **trajectories** in a delinquent career. Since all people are different it is unlikely that one model can hope to describe every person's journey through life. According to this view, not all persistent offenders begin at an early age nor do they take the same path to crime. Some are precocious, beginning their delinquent careers early and persisting into adulthood.[80] Others stay out of trouble in adolescence and do not violate the law until their teenage years; they are late bloomers. Some offenders may peak at an early age and quickly desist, whereas others persist into adulthood. Some are high-rate offenders, whereas others offend at relatively low rates.[81] Similarly, offenders who manifest unique behavioral problems, such as conduct disorders or oppositional defiant disorders, may have different career paths. Nor are social patterns the same: some offenders are quite social and have a large peer group while others are loners who make decisions on their own.[82] Males and females also have different offending trajectories, and factors that predict adult offending in males may have little influence on females.[83]

Take for instance the view on *early onset*. Both life course and propensity theory maintain that persistent offenders are early starters, beginning their delinquent

trajectories Differing paths, progressions, or lines of development.

careers in their adolescence and persisting into adulthood. In contrast, trajectory theories recognize that some kids are *late bloomers* who stay out of trouble until relatively late in adolescence.[84] These late bloomers are actually the teens most likely to get involved in serious adult offending.[85] So while these late starters may show little evidence of pathology in early adolescence, they eventually catch up in their late teens.[86]

Because latent trait theories disregard social influences during the lifespan, and life course theories maintain that social events seem to affect all people equally, they both miss out on the fact that there are different classes and types of juvenile offenders, something that trajectory theory can help understand.

Violent Delinquents

Delinquents who commit violent crimes may be different from nonviolent property and drug offenders and maintain a unique set of personality traits and problem behaviors.[87] But even among these violent offenders there may be distinct delinquent paths. Some offenders are of course nonviolent, while others are violent kids who eventually desist, while a third group are escalators whose severity of violence increases over time. Escalators are more likely to live in racially mixed communities, experience racism, and have less parental involvement than kids who avoid or decrease their violent behaviors.[88] A study by Georgia Zara and David Farrington identified another group of violent kids: a late-onset escalator group. These youths began their violent careers relatively late in their adolescence but suffered a variety of psychological and social conditions earlier in childhood, including high anxiety, low IQ, having delinquent friends, and precocious sexuality. Zara and Farrington indicate that childhood risk factors may predict this late-onset group of violent young adults.[89]

Police lead twins Peter McGuane, left, and Daniel McGuane, both 21, of Ayer, Massachusetts, out of Ayer District Court after they were arraigned on manslaughter charges. Police say the twins beat Kelly Proctor, 19, to death after a confrontation while Proctor and his girlfriend were walking home from a Fourth of July fireworks display. The two had a reputation in town for escalating violence and traveling down a path toward more serious crime. The McGuanes were convicted of involuntary manslaughter and received a five-year prison sentence.

Chronic Offending Trajectories

The reality is that there may be different paths or trajectories to a delinquent career. Adolescents offend at a different pace, commit different kinds of crimes, and are influenced by different external forces.[90] There even may be different classes of chronic delinquents. As you may recall from Chapter 2, when Wolfgang first identified the concept of chronicity, he did not distinguish within that grouping. Now research shows that some are very high-rate offenders, whereas others offend at relatively low frequencies but are persistent in their criminal activities, never really stopping.[91] In one recent study, Alex Piquero and his associates examined data from the Cambridge Study in Delinquent Development (CSDD), a longitudinal survey of 411 South London males, mostly born in 1953. They found that the group could be subdivided into five classes based on their offending histories: nonoffenders (62 percent), low-adolescence peak offenders (19 percent), very low-rate chronic offenders (11 percent), high adolescence peak offender (5 percent), and high-rate chronic offenders (3 percent). Following them over time, until they reached their 40s, Piquero found that boys in each of these offending trajectories faced a different degree of social and personal problems, such as living in poor housing, having a troubled romantic life, suffering mental illness, and drug involvement. Not surprisingly, those youth classified as high-rate chronic offenders were more likely to experience life failure into their late 40s than kids placed in the other groups. The research shows that different people who fall into different offender trajectories have different outcomes reaching into midlife.[92]

Pathways to Delinquency

Trajectory theorists recognize that career delinquents may travel more than a single road. Some may specialize in violence and extortion; some may be involved in theft and fraud; others may engage in a variety of delinquent acts.[93] Some of the most important research on delinquent paths or trajectories has been conducted by Rolf Loeber and his associates. Using data from a longitudinal study of Pittsburgh youth, Loeber has identified three distinct paths to a delinquent career (Figure 5.2):[94]

- The **authority conflict pathway** begins at an early age with stubborn behavior. This leads to defiance (doing things one's own way, disobedience) and then to authority avoidance (staying out late, truancy, running away).

- The **covert pathway** begins with minor, underhanded behavior (lying, shoplifting) that leads to property damage (setting nuisance fires, damaging property). This behavior eventually escalates to more serious forms of delinquency, ranging from joyriding, pocket picking, larceny, and fencing to passing bad checks, using stolen credit cards, stealing cars, dealing drugs, and breaking and entering.

- The **overt pathway** escalates to aggressive acts beginning with annoying others or bullying, leading to physical (and gang) fighting, and then to violence (attacking someone, forced theft).

The Loeber research indicates that each of these paths may lead to a sustained deviant career. Some people enter two and even three paths simultaneously: they are stubborn, lie to teachers and parents, are bullies, and commit petty thefts. These adolescents are the most likely to become persistent offenders as they mature.

The path kids take to delinquency is further discussed in the Focus on Delinquency feature.

Adolescent Limited and Life Course Persistent Offenders

According to psychologist Terrie Moffitt, most young offenders follow one of two paths: **adolescent-limited offenders** may be considered "typical teenagers" who get into minor scrapes and engage in what might be considered rebellious teenage behavior with their friends.[95] As they reach their mid-teens, adolescent-limited delinquents begin to mimic the antisocial behavior of more troubled teens, only to reduce the frequency of their offending as they mature to around age 18.[96]

The second path is the one taken by a small group of **life course persisters** who begin their offending career at a very early age and continue to offend well into adulthood.[97] Moffitt finds that life course persisters combine family dysfunction with severe neurological problems that predispose them to antisocial behavior patterns.

authority conflict pathway Pathway to delinquent deviance that begins at an early age with stubborn behavior and leads to defiance and then to authority avoidance.

covert pathway Pathway to a delinquent career that begins with minor underhanded behavior, leads to property damage, and eventually escalates to more serious forms of theft and fraud.

overt pathway Pathway to a delinquent career that begins with minor aggression, leads to physical fighting, and eventually escalates to violent delinquency.

adolescent-limited offenders Kids who get into minor scrapes as youth but whose misbehavior ends when they enter adulthood.

life course persisters Delinquents who begin their offending career at a very early age and continue to offend well into adulthood.

FIGURE 5.2 The General Theory of Crime

Delinquent Offender

Impulsive personality
- Physical
- Insensitive
- Risk-taking
- Short-sighted
- Nonverbal

Low self-control
- Poor parenting
- Deviant parents
- Lack of supervision
- Active
- Self-centered

Weakening of social bonds
- Attachment
- Involvement
- Commitment
- Belief

Delinquent Opportunity
- Presence of gangs
- Lack of supervision
- Lack of guardianship
- Suitable targets

Delinquent Act
- Delinquency
- Smoking
- Drinking
- Underage sex
- Crime

© Cengage Learning

THE PATH TO DELINQUENCY

One of the most important longitudinal studies tracking persistent offenders is the Cambridge Study in Delinquent Development, which has followed the offending careers of 411 London boys born in 1953. This cohort study, directed since 1982 by David Farrington, is one of the most serious attempts to isolate the factors that predict lifelong continuity of delinquent behavior. The study uses self-report data as well as in-depth interviews and psychological testing. The boys have been interviewed eight times over 24 years, beginning at age 8 and continuing to age 32.

The results of the Cambridge study show that many of the same patterns found in the United States are repeated in a cross-national sample: the existence of chronic offenders, the continuity of offending, and early onset of delinquent activity. Each of these patterns leads to persistent delinquency.

Farrington found that the traits present in persistent offenders can be observed as early as age 8. The chronic delinquent begins as a property offender, is born into a large low-income family headed by parents who have delinquent records, and has delinquent older siblings. The future criminal receives poor parental supervision, including the use of harsh or erratic punishment and childrearing techniques; the parents are likely to divorce or separate. The chronic offender tends to associate with friends who are also future criminals. By age 8, the child exhibits antisocial behavior, including dishonesty and aggressiveness; at school the chronic offender tends to have low educational achievement and is restless, troublesome, hyperactive, impulsive, and often truant. After leaving school at age 18, the persistent criminal tends to take a relatively well paid but low-status job and is likely to have an erratic work history and periods of unemployment.

Farrington found that deviant behavior tends to be versatile rather than specialized. That is, the typical offender not only commits property offenses, such as theft and burglary, but also engages in violence, vandalism, drug use, excessive drinking, drunk driving, smoking, reckless driving, and sexual promiscuity—evidence of a generalized problem behavior syndrome. Chronic offenders are more likely to live away from home and have conflicts with their parents. They get tattoos, go out most evenings, and enjoy hanging out with groups of their friends. They are much more likely than nonoffenders to get involved in fights, to carry weapons, and to use them in violent encounters. The frequency of offending reaches a peak in the teenage years (about 17 or 18) and then declines in the 20s, when offenders marry or live with a significant other.

By the 30s, the former delinquent is likely to be separated or divorced and be an absent parent. His employment record remains spotty, and he moves often between rental units. His life is still characterized by evenings out, heavy drinking, substance abuse, and more violent behavior than his contemporaries.

Because the typical offender provides the same kind of deprived and disrupted family life for his own children that he experienced, the social experiences and conditions that produce delinquency are carried on from one generation to the next. The following list summarizes the specific risk factors that Farrington associates with forming a delinquent career:

- *Prenatal and perinatal.* Early childbearing increases the risk of such undesirable outcomes for children as low school attainment, antisocial behavior, substance use, and early sexual activity. An increased risk of offending among children of teenage mothers is associated with low income, poor housing, absent fathers, and poor childrearing methods.

- *Personality.* Impulsiveness, hyperactivity, restlessness, and limited ability to concentrate are associated with low attainment in school and a poor ability to foresee the consequences of offending.

- *Intelligence and attainment.* Low intelligence and poor performance in school, although important statistical predictors of offending, are difficult to disentangle from each other. One plausible explanation of the link between low intelligence and delinquency is its association with a poor ability to manipulate abstract concepts and to appreciate the feelings of victims.

- *Parental supervision and discipline.* Harsh or erratic parental discipline and cold or rejecting parental attitudes have been linked to delinquency and are associated with children's lack of internal inhibitions against offending. Physical abuse by parents has been associated with an increased risk of the children themselves becoming violent offenders in later life.

- *Parental conflict and separation.* Living in a home affected by separation or divorce is more strongly related to delinquency than when the disruption has been caused by the death of one parent. However, it may not be a "broken home" that creates an increased risk of offending so much as the parental conflict that leads to the separation.

- *Socioeconomic status.* Social and economic deprivation are important predictors of antisocial behavior and crime, but low family income and poor housing are better measurements than the prestige of parents' occupations.

- *Delinquent friends.* Delinquents tend to have delinquent friends. But it is not certain whether membership in a delinquent peer group leads to offending or whether delinquents simply gravitate toward each other's company (or both). Breaking up with delinquent friends often coincides with desisting from crime.

- *School influences.* The prevalence of offending by pupils varies widely between secondary schools. But it is not clear how far schools themselves have an effect on delinquency (for example, by paying insufficient attention to bullying or providing too much punishment and too little praise), or whether it is simply that troublesome children tend to go to high-delinquency-rate schools.

- *Community influences.* The risks of becoming criminally involved are higher for young people raised in disorganized inner-city areas, characterized by physical deterioration, overcrowded households, publicly subsidized renting, and high residential mobility. It is not clear, however, whether this is due to a direct influence on children, or whether environmental stress causes family adversities, which in turn cause delinquency.

WHAT CAUSED OFFENDERS TO DESIST?

Holding a relatively good job helped reduce delinquent activity. Conversely, unemployment seemed to be related to the escalation of theft offenses; violence and substance abuse were unaffected by unemployment. In a similar vein, getting married also helped diminish delinquent activity. However, finding a spouse who was also involved in delinquent activity and had a delinquent record increased delinquent involvement.

Physical relocation also helped some offenders desist because they were forced to sever ties with co-offenders. For this reason, leaving the city for a rural or suburban area was linked to reduced delinquent activity. Although employment, marriage, and relocation helped potential offenders desist, not all desisters found success. At-risk youths who managed to avoid delinquent convictions were unlikely to avoid other social problems. Rather than becoming prosperous homeowners with flourishing careers, they tended to live in unkempt homes and have large debts and low-paying jobs. They were also more likely to remain single and live alone. Youths who experienced social isolation at age 8 were also found to experience it at age 32.

CRITICAL THINKING

Farrington finds that the traits present in persistent offenders can be observed as early as age 8. Should such young children be observed and monitored, even though they have not actually committed crimes? Would such monitoring create a self-fulfilling prophecy?

Writing Assignment Farrington suggests that life experiences shape the direction and flow of behavior choices. He finds that while there may be continuity in offending, the factors that predict delinquency at one point in the life course may not be the ones that predict delinquency at another. Although most adult delinquents begin their careers in childhood, life events may help some children forgo delinquency as they mature. Write an essay spelling out the life events that help people turn their lives around. If possible, draw upon the experiences of someone you know or with whom you are acquainted.

Sources: David Farrington, "Key Results from the First Forty Years of the Cambridge Study in Delinquent Development," in *Taking Stock of Delinquency: An Overview of Findings from Contemporary Longitudinal Studies*, ed. Terence Thornberry and Marvin Krohn (New York: Kluwer, 2002), pp. 137–185; David Farrington, "The Development of Offending and Anti-Social Behavior from Childhood: Key Findings from the Cambridge Study of Delinquent Development," *Journal of Child Psychology and Psychiatry* 36:2–36 (1995); David Farrington, *Understanding and Preventing Youth Crime* (London: Joseph Rowntree Foundation, 1996).

According to Terrie Moffitt, adolescent-limited offenders are "typical teenagers" who get into minor scrapes and engage in what might be considered rebellious teenage behavior with their friends, such as recreational drug use. In contrast, life course persistent offenders begin their off ending careers early and remain high-rate offenders into young adulthood

These afflictions can be the result of maternal drug abuse, poor nutrition, or exposure to toxic agents such as lead. It is not surprising then that life course persisters display social and personal dysfunctions, including lower than average verbal ability, reasoning skills, learning ability, and school achievement.

Research shows that the persistence patterns predicted by Moffitt are valid and accurate.[98] Life course persisters offend more frequently and engage in a greater variety of antisocial acts than other offenders; they also manifest significantly more mental health problems, including psychiatric pathologies, than adolescent-limited offenders.[99] Many have deviant friends who support their behavior choices.[100]

Life course persisters are more likely to manifest traits such as low verbal ability and hyperactivity; they display a negative or impulsive personality and seem particularly impaired on spatial and memory functions.[101] Individual traits rather than environment seem to have the greatest influence on life course persistence.[102]

There is also evidence that that there may be other classes of offenders. For example, some people begin their offending career late in their adolescence, but persist into adulthood.[103] These late starters are more likely to be involved in nonviolent crimes such as theft.[104] Research by Daniel Nagin and Richard Tremblay shows that late-onset physical aggression is the exception, not the rule, and that the peak frequency of physical aggression occurs during early childhood and generally declines thereafter.[105]

Abstainers

Despite the fact that self-report studies tell us that most kids engage in a garden variety of antisocial activities and that teen drug use, theft, and general mischief are normative, there are those kids who never break the law; **abstainers**' conventional behavior makes them deviant in the teenage world where offending is the norm! Why do these nonstarters refrain from delinquency of any sort? According to social psychologist Terrie Moffitt, abstainers are social introverts as teens, whose unpopularity shields them from group pressure to commit delinquent acts.[106] David Farrington finds that kids may be able to remain nonoffenders if they also maintain a unique set of personal traits that shield them from antisocial activity: shy personality,

abstainers Kids who are never involved in typical adolescent misbehaviors such as drinking, smoking, sex, or petty crimes.

having few friends (at age 8), having non-deviant families, and being highly regarded by their mothers.[107] Shy children with few friends avoid damaging relationships with other adolescents (members of a high-risk group) and are therefore able to avoid delinquency.

Abstention may be more related to close parental monitoring and involvement with prosocial peer groups than it is to being unpopular.[108] Still another explanation may be biological: abstainers maintain a genetic code that insulates them from delinquency-producing factors in the environment.[109]

Recent research by Xiaojin Chen and Michele Adams puts a different spin on the abstention phenomenon.[110] They found that rather than being shy loners, as Moffitt suggests, abstainers generally appear to have stronger social bonds with parents, schools and peer networks; they also maintain high self-esteem. Abstainers have prosocial friends who themselves are good students and less likely to participate in deviant activities. Delinquency abstention is more the result of careful parental monitoring and adolescents' own strong moral beliefs than social isolation. Considering these roots it's not surprising that Jennifer Gatewood Owens and Lee Ann Slocum's research shows abstainers are more likely than other youth to become successful, well-adjusted adults.[111] **CHECKPOINTS**

CHECKPOINTS

LO5 Know the principles of trajectory theory.

✔ There are different pathways to crime and different types of criminals.

✔ Some career criminals may specialize in violence and extortion; some may be involved in theft and fraud; some may engage in a variety of criminal acts.

✔ Some offenders may begin their careers early in life, whereas others are late bloomers who begin committing crime at about the time when most people desist.

✔ Adolescent-limited offenders begin offending late and age out of delinquency.

✔ Life course persistent offenders exhibit early onset of delinquency that persists into adulthood.

EVALUATING THE DEVELOPMENTAL VIEW

The developmental view is that a delinquent career must be understood as a passage along which people travel, that it has a beginning and an end, and that events and life circumstances influence the journey. The factors that affect a delinquent career may include structural factors, such as income and status; socialization factors, such as family and peer relations; biological factors, such as size and strength; psychological factors, including intelligence and personality; and opportunity factors, such as free time, inadequate police protection, and a supply of easily stolen merchandise. Life course theories emphasize the influence of changing interpersonal and structural factors—that is, people change along with the world they live in. Latent trait theories assume that an individual's behavior is linked less to personal change than to changes in the surrounding world. Trajectory theory recognizes that there is more than one path to a delinquent career.

These perspectives differ in their view of human development. Do people constantly change, as life course theories suggest, or are they more stable, constant, and changeless, as the latent trait view indicates? Are the factors that produce criminality different at each stage of life, as the life course view suggests, or does a master trait—for example, impulsivity or self-control—steer the course of human behavior? Are there different classes of delinquents whose behavior must be understood independently and who have a different developmental history, as trajectory theory states?

It is also possible that these positions are not mutually exclusive, and each may make a notable contribution to understanding the onset and continuity of a delinquent career. For example, research by Bradley Entner Wright and his associates found evidence supporting both latent trait and life course theories.[112] Their research, conducted with subjects in New Zealand, indicated that low self-control in childhood predicts disrupted social bonds and delinquent offending later in life, a finding that supports latent trait theory. They also found that maintaining positive social bonds helps reduce criminality and that such bonds could even counteract the effect of low self-control. Latent traits are an important influence on delinquency, but Wright's findings indicate that social relationships that form later in life appear to influence delinquent behavior "above and beyond" individuals' preexisting characteristics.[113] This finding may reflect the fact that there are two classes of criminals: a less serious group who are influenced by life events and a more chronic group whose latent traits insulate them from any positive prosocial relationships, a finding that supports the trajectory approach.[114]

Developmental Theory and Delinquency Prevention

There have been a number of policy-based initiatives based on premises of developmental theory. One approach involves intervening with children and young people who are viewed as being at high risk for becoming juvenile offenders in order to help them divert from a path toward delinquency. This may mean giving their parents the skills to help kids in a more effective manner. Another approach is to aid kids who have entered a delinquent way of life to knife off into more conventional lines of behavior.

Improving Parenting Skills. Some programs aim to prevent delinquency in the long run by helping parents improve their parenting skills. This is another form of family support that has shown some success in preventing juvenile delinquency. Although the main focus of parent training programs is on the parents, many of these programs also involve children in an effort to improve the parent–child bond. One of the most famous parenting skills programs, the Oregon Social Learning Center (OSLC), is based on the assumption that many parents do not know how to deal effectively with their children, sometimes ignoring their behavior and at other times reacting with explosive rage. Some parents discipline their children for reasons that have little to do with the children's behavior, instead reflecting their own frustrations. The OSLC program uses behavior modification techniques to help parents acquire proper disciplinary methods. Parents are asked to select several behaviors for change and to count the frequency of their occurrence. OSLC personnel teach social skills to reinforce positive behaviors and constructive disciplinary methods to discourage negative ones. Incentive programs are initiated in which a child can earn points for desirable behaviors. Points can be exchanged for allowance, prizes, or privileges. Parents are also taught disciplinary techniques that stress firmness and consistency, rather than "nattering" (low-intensity behaviors, such as scowling or scolding) or explosive discipline, such as hitting or screaming. One important technique is the "time-out," in which the child is removed for brief isolation in a quiet room. Parents are taught the importance of setting rules and sticking to them. A number of evaluation studies show that improving parenting skills can lead to reductions in juvenile delinquency.[115] A Rand study found that parent training costs about one-twentieth what a home visit program costs and is more effective in preventing serious crimes.[116]

Another effort, Guiding Good Choices (GGC), formerly known as "Preparing for the Drug Free Years" (PDFY), is designed to aid parents on many fronts, including teaching them about the risk and protective factors for substance abuse. GGC is a multimedia substance abuse prevention program that gives parents of children in grades 4 through 8 (ages 9 to 14) the knowledge and skills needed to guide their children through early adolescence. The program intends to help parents:

- Provide preteens and teens with appropriate opportunities for involvement in the family
- Recognize competencies and skills
- Teach their children how to keep friends and popularity while using drug-refusal skills
- Set and communicate healthy beliefs and clear standards for their children's behavior

Evaluations show that kids going through the program experienced a significantly slower rate of increase in delinquency and substance use compared to the control group:

- Reduced alcohol and marijuana use by up to 40.6 percent
- Reduced progression to more serious drug abuse by 54 percent
- Increased the likelihood that nonusers will remain drug-free by 26 percent[117]

Multisystemic Programs. Some programs provide a mixture of services ranging from heath care to parenting skill improvement. These typically feature multisystemic treatment efforts designed to provide at-risk kids with personal, social, educational, and family services. For example, one program found that an intervention that promotes academic success, social competence, and educational enhancement during the elementary grades can reduce risky sexual practices and their accompanying health consequences in early adulthood.[118]

Other programs are now employing multidimensional strategies and are aimed at targeting children in preschool through the early elementary grades in order to alter the direction of their life course. Many of the most successful programs are aimed at strengthening children's social-emotional competence and positive coping skills and suppressing the development of antisocial, aggressive behavior.[119] Research evaluations indicate that the most promising multicomponent crime and substance abuse prevention programs for youths, especially those at high risk, are aimed at improving their developmental skills. They may include a school component, an after-school component, and a parent-involvement component. All of these components have the common goal of increasing protective factors and decreasing risk factors in the areas of the family, the community, the school, and the individual.[120] The Boys and Girls Clubs and School Collaborations' Substance Abuse Prevention Program includes a school component called SMART (Skills Mastery and Resistance Training) Teachers, an after-school component called SMART Kids, and a parent-involvement component called SMART Parents. Each component is designed to reduce specific risk factors in the children's school, family, community, and personal environments.[121]

The CODAC Family Health Promotion (FHP) program is a primary prevention program that offers a variety of interventions for children ages 3 through 8 and their families. The program offers children developmentally appropriate activities in childcare, school, and recreation to help develop resiliency skills. Parents are encouraged to become involved in activities that enable them to increase protective factors. Participants requiring treatment services will receive them onsite. The central feature of the FHP is the family services team that serves as the integrating force of the program. Specific program activities include the following:

- Parent advisory council meetings
- The S.T.E.P. Curriculum workshop series
- Support groups
- Family weekend activities
- Training of school personnel in the Building Me program curricula and cultural competence
- Implementation of the Building Me curriculum
- Transportation to the program
- Art therapy sessions

Training in resiliency and protective factors is also provided to parents through home visitation. These visits occur once a month during the first year, twice a month during the second year, and as needed during the third year.

The target population for FHP is predominantly Hispanic/Latino. The risk group is mixed and includes latchkey children, children who live in poverty, children who have substance-abusing parents, and children who have been physically, sexually, or psychologically abused.[122] Across Ages, a well-received prevention program, is described in detail in the Prevention/Intervention/Treatment feature.

JUVENILE DELINQUENCY

Across Ages

Across Ages is a drug intervention program for youth ages 9 to 13. The program's goal is to strengthen the bonds between adults and children to provide opportunities for positive community involvement. It is unique and highly effective in its pairing of older adult mentors (age 55 and above) with young adolescents, mainly those entering middle school.

Designed as a school- and community-based demonstration research project, Across Ages was founded in 1991 by the Substance Abuse and Mental Health Services Administration's Center for Substance Abuse Prevention and was replicated in Philadelphia and West Springfield, Massachusetts. Today, there are more than 30 replication sites in 17 states. Specifically, the program aims to:

- Increase knowledge of health and substance abuse and foster healthy attitudes, intentions, and behavior toward drug use among targeted youth
- Improve school bonding, academic performance, school attendance, and behavior and attitudes toward school
- Strengthen relationships with adults and peers
- Enhance problem-solving and decision-making skills

How It Works

Program materials are offered in English or Spanish so they can be used cross-culturally. A child is matched up with an older adult and participates in activities and interventions that include:

- Mentoring for a minimum of two hours each week in one-on-one contact
- Community service for one to two hours per week
- Social competence training, which involves the "Social Problem-Solving Module," composed of 26 weekly lessons at 45 minutes each
- Activities for the youth and family members and mentors

Participating youth learn positive coping skills and have an opportunity to be of service to their community. The program aims to increase prosocial interactions and protective factors and decrease negative ones.

Critical Thinking

1. Should such issues as early onset and problem behavior syndrome be considered when choosing participants for prevention programs like Across Ages?
2. Could participation in such programs label or stigmatize participants and thereafter lock them into a deviant role?

Source: Across Ages: An Intergenerational Mentoring Approach to Prevention, www.acrossages.org (accessed August 9, 2012).

SUMMARY

The developmental theory of delinquency looks at the onset, continuity, and termination of a delinquent career. The foundation of developmental theory can be traced to the pioneering work of Sheldon and Eleanor Glueck. The Gluecks identified a number of personal and social factors related to persistent offending.

Life course theory suggests that delinquent behavior is a dynamic process, influenced by individual characteristics as well as social experiences, and that the factors that cause antisocial behaviors change dramatically over a person's lifespan. According to the life course view, even as toddlers people begin relationships and behaviors that will determine their adult life course. Some individuals are incapable of maturing in a reasonable and timely fashion because of family, environmental, or personal problems.

Because a transition from one stage of life to another can be a bumpy ride, the propensity to commit crimes is neither stable nor constant. It is a developmental process. Disruptions in life's major transitions can be destructive and ultimately can promote delinquency. As people make important life transitions—from child to adolescent, from adolescent to adult, from single to married—the nature of social interactions changes. One element of life course theory is that delinquency may best be understood as one of many social problems faced by at-risk youth. Problem behavior syndrome (PBS) typically involves family dysfunction, sexual and physical abuse, substance abuse, smoking, precocious sexuality and early pregnancy, educational underachievement, suicide attempts, sensation seeking, and unemployment.

Positive life experiences and relationships can help people become reattached to society and allow them to knife off from a delinquent career path. Two critical turning points are marriage and career.

Latent trait theory suggests that a stable feature, characteristic, property, or condition, such as defective intelligence or impulsive personality, makes some people delinquency prone over the life course. Suspected latent traits include defective intelligence, damaged or impulsive personality, genetic abnormalities, the physical-chemical functioning of the brain, and environmental influences on brain function such as drugs, chemicals, and injuries. These traits are associated with antisocial behaviors.

In *A General Theory of Crime*, Michael Gottfredson and Travis Hirschi argue that the propensity to commit antisocial acts is tied directly to a person's level of self-control. By integrating the concepts of socialization and delinquency, Gottfredson and Hirschi help explain why some people who lack self-control can escape delinquency, and, conversely, why some people who have self-control might not escape delinquency.

Trajectory theorists recognize that career delinquents may travel more than a single road. Some may specialize in violence and extortion; some may be involved in theft and fraud; others may engage in a variety of delinquent acts. Some offenders may begin their careers early in life, whereas others are late bloomers who begin committing delinquency when most people desist. Some are frequent offenders, while others travel a more moderate path or are even abstainers. Experiences in young adulthood and beyond can redirect delinquent trajectories or paths. In some cases people can be turned in a positive direction, while in others negative life experiences can be harmful and injurious.

KEY TERMS

developmental theory, p. 128

life course theory, p. 128

latent trait theory, p. 128

propensity, p. 128

trajectory theory, p. 129

early onset, p. 131

problem behavior syndrome (PBS), p. 131

turning points, p. 133

social capital, p. 134

general theory of crime (GTC), p. 138

self-control, p. 140

impulsive, p. 140

trajectories, p. 143

authority conflict pathway, p. 145

covert pathway, p. 145

overt pathway, p. 145

adolescent-limited offenders, p. 145

life course persisters, p. 145

abstainers, p. 148

QUESTIONS FOR REVIEW

1. Who are the pioneers of the developmental approach to understanding delinquency?

2. List five principles of the life course theory.

3. List three elements of Sampson and Laub's age-graded life course theory.

4. Define what is meant by a latent trait.

5. What is the key personality trait identified by the general theory

of crime as a cause of adolescent misbehavior?

6. Distinguish between the life course persistent and adolescent limited offender.

QUESTIONS FOR DISCUSSION

1. Do you consider yourself a holder of "social capital"? If so, what form does it take?

2. A person gets a 1600 on the SAT. Without knowing this person, what personal, family, and social characteristics would you assume he or she has? Another person becomes a serial killer. Without knowing this person, what personal, family, and social characteristics would you assume he or she has? If bad behavior is explained by multiple problems, is good behavior explained by multiple strengths?

3. Do you believe there is a latent trait that makes a person delinquency prone, or is delinquency a function of environment and socialization?

4. Do you agree with Loeber's multiple pathways model? Do you know people who have traveled down those paths?

5. Do you think that marriage is different than merely being in love? The McCarthy and Casey research discussed earlier indicates that having a romantic relationship may help reduce crime; if so, what happens when kids break up? Does that increase the likelihood of delinquent involvement?

APPLYING WHAT YOU HAVE LEARNED

Luis Francisco is the leader of the Almighty Latin Kings and Queens Nation. He was convicted of murder in 1998 and sentenced to life imprisonment plus 45 years. Luis Francisco's life has been filled with displacement, poverty, and chronic predatory delinquency. The son of a prostitute in Havana, at the age of 9 he was sent to prison for robbery. He had trouble in school, and teachers described him as having attention problems; he dropped out in the seventh grade. In 1980, on his 19th birthday, he emigrated to the United States and soon became a gang member in Chicago, joining the Latin Kings. After moving to the Bronx, he shot and killed his girlfriend in 1981. He fled to Chicago and was not apprehended until 1984. Sentenced to nine years for second-degree manslaughter, Luis Francisco ended up in a New York prison, where he started a prison chapter of the Latin Kings. As King Blood, Inka, First Supreme Crown, Francisco ruled the 2,000 Latin Kings both in and out of prison. Disciplinary troubles erupted when some Kings were found stealing from the organization. Infuriated, King Blood wrote to his street lieutenants and ordered the thieves' termination. Federal authorities, who had been monitoring Francisco's mail, arrested 35 Latin Kings. The other 34 pleaded guilty; only Francisco insisted on a trial, where he was found guilty of conspiracy to commit murder.

Writing Assignment: Write an essay explaining Luis's behavior patterns from a developmental perspective. How would a latent trait theorist explain his escalating delinquent activities? A life course theorist? A trajectory theorist?

GROUPWORK

Divide the class into three separate groups. Have each choose one of the three branches of developmental theory as their own. Take a famous case that has gained notoriety such as the Beltway Sniper Case or the shooting of Trayvon Martin. Have each group analyze all aspects of the case from their perspective and determine whether the facts of the case and the background of the offender match up with the life course, latent trait, or trajectory view of delinquent careers.

CHAPTER SIX

Gender and Delinquency

LEARNING OBJECTIVES

After reading this chapter you should:

1. Be familiar with the gender differences in development.
2. Be familiar with trait explanations of female delinquency.
3. Discuss the association between socialization and female delinquency.
4. Understand feminist views of female delinquency, including power-control theory.
5. Critique the differential treatment of girls in the juvenile justice system.

Rain's Story

Rain is a 15-year-old female attending her sophomore year of high school. Rain attends school on a regular basis and is a member of the school band. Her mother has recently spilt from her long-term partner and has a new girlfriend. Rain is an only child and has sporadic contact with her biological father, who lives out of state. Recently, Rain has reported feeling depressed and somewhat isolated. She has also begun talking with her school social worker on a regular basis to address a decline in her grades and troubles at school. Rain was recently caught purchasing prescription drugs in a school bathroom. She was refereed to a first offenders program and ordered to attend counseling.

Before services could be set up for Rain, the police and rescue workers were called to the family home. Rain had overdosed on a pain medication that her mother had in the medicine cabinet. She was rushed to a local hospital where she received medical care and spent the night. Rain reported to the hospital psychiatrist that she was not currently suicidal, and hospital social workers assisted in creating a community plan for her to be discharged home.

Upon her arrival home, the school social worker and a therapist in the community met with Rain and her mother. They arranged for Rain to meet with the school social worker on a daily basis to check in and for Rain to attend therapy two or three times per week. The therapist specialized in working with adolescents and had a small office at the local community center that was a block from Rain's home. This proximity allowed for frequent contact with providers as well as the ongoing support she needed. It also reduced issues related to a lack of transportation and barriers that often impact compliance. The social worker and therapist initially suspected that Rain was having significant issues with her mother's sexuality. What they learned rather quickly was that Rain had no concerns regarding this issue. Rain reported feeling her mother was a healthy and happy person and that she supported her mother. The main challenges for Rain were the loss of the relationship with her mother's long-term partner and the fact that her mother was spending large portions of time with her new girlfriend. Rain reported feeling lonely, sad, and depressed. She wanted to visit with her mother's ex-partner and also to have more time alone with her mother. Rain longed for the days when she and her mother went bike riding and did other family activities together.

With the assistance of the therapist and school social worker, Rain was able to better understand her deep feelings of sadness and her suicide attempt. They also began to participate in family therapy, which allowed Rain to talk with her mother about her need to spend time with her mother's ex-partner, as well as with her mother. The family was able to arrange for these visits, and Rain and her mother began doing more planned activities together. Rain continued receiving the support at school and within the community center from the therapist and others. She successfully completed the requirements for the first offenders program and did not receive any additional delinquency referrals.

In an earlier time, experts viewed female delinquency as an emotional or family-related matter, and the few "true" female delinquents were sexual oddities whose criminal activity was a function of having masculine traits and characteristics; this was referred to as the **masculinity hypothesis**.[1] Female delinquents were an aberration who engaged in crimes that usually had a sexual connotation—prostitution, running away (which presumably leads to sexual misadventure), premarital sex, and crimes of sexual passion (killing a boyfriend or a husband).[2]

This vision has changed. Contemporary interest in female delinquency has surged, fueled by observations that although adolescent girls still commit less crime than boys, the patterns and types of delinquent acts that young women engage in today seem quite similar to those of young men. There is evidence that girls are getting more heavily involved in gangs and gang violence.[3] Gone are the days when delinquency experts portrayed female delinquents as "fallen women" who were exploited by men and involved in illicit sexual activities. The result has been an increased effort to conduct research that would adequately explain differences and similarities in male and female offending patterns.

masculinity hypothesis View that women who commit crimes have biological and psychological traits similar to those of men.

This chapter provides an overview of gender factors in delinquency. We first discuss some of the gender differences in development and how they may relate to the gender differences in offending rates. Then we turn to some explanations for these differences: (a) the trait view, (b) the socialization view, (c) the liberal feminist view, and (d) the critical feminist view.

WWW

To find information on the state of **adolescent girls and the risks they face**, go to the website of the Commonwealth Fund by visiting the Criminal Justice CourseMate at CengageBrain.com, then accessing the Web Links for this chapter.

GENDER DIFFERENCES IN DEVELOPMENT

Do gender differences in development, including socialization, cognition, and personality, pave the way for future differences in misbehaving?[4] It is possible that gender-based traits that shape antisocial behavior choices may exist as early as infancy—baby girls show greater control over their emotions, whereas boys are more easily angered and depend more on input from their mothers.[5]

Socialization Differences

Psychologists believe that differences in the way females and males are socialized affect their development. Girls may be closer to their parents, especially their mothers, which shields them from antisocial behavior. Since parental attachment is linked to levels of self-control and children who are closer to their parents develop stronger levels of self-control, girls may benefit from both conditions more than boys.[6]

Males learn to value independence, whereas females are taught that their self-worth depends on their ability to sustain relationships. Girls, therefore, run the risk of losing themselves in their relationships with others, whereas boys may experience a chronic sense of alienation. Because so many relationships go sour, females also run the risk of feeling alienated, because of the failure to achieve relational success.[7] Risks have increased in the Internet age: girls are going online in chat rooms and some begin risky online communication behaviors with strangers, posting personal information and meeting offline with online strangers. Some of these risk takers then suffer physical and sexual assaults.[8]

Although there are few gender differences in aggression during the first few years of life, girls are socialized to be less aggressive than boys and are supervised more closely. Differences in aggression become noticeable between ages 3 and 6, when children are socialized into organized groups, such as the daycare center. Males are more likely to display physical aggression, whereas females display relational aggression—for example, by excluding disliked peers from play groups.[9]

As they mature, girls learn to respond to provocation by feeling anxious, unlike boys, who are encouraged to retaliate.[10] It is not surprising that fathers are more likely to teach boys about using and maintaining weapons. Self-report studies show that boys are three times more likely to report hunting or shooting with a family member than girls.[11]

Overall, women are much more likely to feel distressed than men.[12] Although females get angry as often as males, many have been taught to blame themselves for such feelings. Females are, therefore, much more likely than males to respond to anger with feelings of depression, anxiety, and shame. Females are socialized to fear that anger will harm relationships; males are encouraged to react with "moral outrage," blaming others for their discomfort.[13]

Cognitive Differences

There are also cognitive differences between males and females starting in childhood. The more replicated findings about gender difference in cognitive performance suggest female superiority on visual/motor speed and language ability and male superiority on mechanical and

Looking Back at Rain's Story

After they broke up, Rain was disturbed by the loss of her mother's long-term partner and the fact that her mother was spending a lot of time with her new girlfriend.

CRITICAL THINKING Did Rain's home life and socialization lead to her problems? Do you believe a more traditional home produces more traditional offspring?

visual/spatial tasks.[14] Put another way, males excel in tasks that assess the ability to manipulate visual images in working memory, whereas females do better in tasks that require retrieval from long-term memory and the acquisition and use of verbal information.[15] Gender group strengths found in the early school years become more established at adolescence and remain stable through adulthood.[16]

Girls learn to speak earlier and faster, and with better pronunciation, most likely because parents talk more to their infant daughters than to their infant sons. A girl's verbal proficiency enables her to develop a skill that may later help her deal with conflict without resorting to violence.[17] When faced with conflict, women might be more likely to attempt to negotiate, rather than to respond passively or resist physically, especially when they perceive increased threat of harm or death.[18]

When girls are aggressive, they are more likely than boys to hide their behavior from adults; girls who bully others are less likely than boys to admit their behavior.[19] Girls are shielded by their moral sense, which directs them to avoid harming others. Their moral sensitivity may counterbalance the effects of family problems.[20] Females display more self-control than males, a factor that has been related to criminality.[21]

Personality Differences

Girls are often stereotyped as talkative, but research shows that in many situations boys spend more time talking than girls do. Females are more willing to reveal their feelings and more likely to express concern for others. Females are more concerned about finding the "meaning of life" and less interested in competing for material success.[22] Males are more likely to introduce new topics and to interrupt conversations.

Adolescent females use different knowledge than males and have different ways of interpreting their interactions with others. These gender differences may have an impact on self-esteem and self-concept. Research shows that, as adolescents develop, male self-esteem and self-concept rise, whereas female self-confidence is lowered.[23] One reason is that girls are more likely to stress about their weight and be more dissatisfied with the size and shape of their bodies.[24] Young girls are regularly confronted with unrealistically high standards of slimness that make them extremely unhappy with their own bodies; it is not surprising that the incidence of eating disorders such as anorexia and bulimia have increased markedly in recent years. Psychologist Carol Gilligan uncovered an alternative explanation for this decline in female self-esteem: as girls move into adolescence, they become aware of the conflict between the positive way they see themselves and the negative way society views females. Many girls respond by "losing their voices"—that is, submerging their own feelings and accepting the negative view of women conveyed by adult authorities.[25]

Concept Summary 6.1 discusses these various gender differences.

CONCEPT SUMMARY 6.1	Gender Differences	
	Females	**Males**
Socialization	Sustain relationships Are less aggressive Blame self	Are independent Are aggressive Externalize anger
Cognitive	Have superior verbal ability Speak earlier Have better pronunciation Read better	Have superior visual/spatial ability Are better at math
Personality	Have lower self-esteem Are self-aware Have better attention span	Have high self-esteem Are materialistic Have low attention span

What Causes Gender Differences?

Why do these gender differences occur? Some experts suggest that gender differences may have a biological origin: males and females are essentially different. They have somewhat different brain organizations; females are more left brain–oriented and males more right brain–oriented. (The left brain is believed to control language; the right, spatial relations.)[26] Others point to the hormonal differences between the sexes as the key to understanding their behavior.

Another view is that gender differences are a result of the interaction of socialization, learning, and enculturation.[27] Boys and girls may behave differently because they have been exposed to different styles of socialization, learned different values, and had different cultural experiences. It follows, then, that if members of both sexes were equally exposed to the factors that produce delinquency, their delinquency rates would be equivalent.[28] According to psychologist Sandra Bem's **gender-schema theory**, our culture polarizes males and females by forcing them to obey mutually exclusive gender roles, or "scripts." Girls are expected to be "feminine," exhibiting sympathetic and gentle traits. In contrast, boys are expected to be "masculine," exhibiting assertiveness and dominance. Children internalize these scripts and accept gender polarization as normal. Children's self-esteem becomes wrapped up in how closely their behavior conforms to the proper sex role stereotype. When children begin to perceive themselves as either boys or girls (which occurs at about age 3), they search for information to help them define their role; they begin to learn what behavior is appropriate for their sex.[29] Girls are expected to behave according to the appropriate script and to seek approval of their behavior: Are they acting as girls should at that age? Masculine behavior is to be avoided. In contrast, males look for cues from their peers to define their masculinity; aggressive behavior may be rewarded with peer approval, whereas sensitivity is viewed as not masculine.[30]

© Shana Sureck/New York Times/Redux

Game time for Molly Kaissar and friends at the Girls Leadership Institute camp. The goal is to help girls develop esteem and confidence and become survivors in a tough world. Program creator Rachel Simmons believes that because girls fear rocking their all-consuming relationships, they are notoriously inept at addressing everyday conflicts. More aggressive girls fight dirty and mean, bullying, taking command of the lunch table, and spreading rumors about their targets. Their devastated, demoralized victims, furious themselves, feel emotionally paralyzed. Much of the subtle savagery, the clique infighting, flourishes below adult radar.

gender-schema theory A theory of development that holds that children internalize gender scripts that reflect the gender-related social practices of the culture. Once internalized, these gender scripts predispose the kids to construct a self-identity that is consistent with them.

Not So Different After All. Not every social scientist agrees that there are significant differences between the genders. In an important meta-analysis of studies examining gender differences in such traits as personality, cognition, communication skills, and leadership ability, psychologist Janet Shibley Hyde found that men and women are basically more alike than different on these critical psychological variables; she refers to her finding as the *gender similarities hypothesis*. Hyde found that gender differences had either no or a very small effect on most of the psychological variables examined, with only a few exceptions: compared with women, men were more physically aggressive and approved of sex without commitment. Hyde also found that gender differences fluctuate with age, growing smaller or larger at different times in the lifespan. One significant myth she claims to have debunked: boys do better at math. According to her findings, boys and girls perform equally well in math until high school, at which point boys do become more proficient. It is possible that girls avoid advanced classes, believing erroneously that they are doomed to failure, thereby creating a self-fulfilling prophecy.[31]

Hyde's work is not without its critics.[32] Yet she may be addressing an important contemporary phenomenon: even if gender differences existed before, they may now be eroding. If so, this phenomenon may be impacting gender differences in delinquency.

GENDER DIFFERENCES AND DELINQUENCY

Research conducted in the United States and abroad has found that the factors that direct the trajectories of male delinquency are quite different from those that influence female delinquency. In fact, recent research by Shari Miller and her associates concluded that other than base rate differences, developmental patterns and outcomes for girls mimic those previously found for boys.[33]

Among males, early offending is highly correlated with later misbehavior, whereas females take on a more haphazard criminal career path. Females are more likely to be influenced by current levels of social support than they are by their early history of antisocial behavior.[34] Males seem more aggressive and less likely to form attachments to others, which are factors that might help them maintain their crime rates over their lifespan. Males view aggression as an appropriate means to gain status. Boys are also more likely than girls to socialize with deviant peers, and when they do, they display personality traits that make them more susceptible to delinquency.

This pattern fits within the two-cultures view that suggests that girls and boys differ in their social behavior largely because their sex-segregated peer groups demand behaviors (such as aggression) that may not be characteristic of them in other social situations.[35] What is typically assumed to be an inherent difference in antisocial behavior tendencies may actually be a function of peer socialization differences. The fact that young boys perceive their roles as being more dominant than young girls may be a function of peer pressure. Male perceptions of power, their ability to have freedom and hang with their friends, help explain gender differences in personality.[36]

Gender Patterns in Delinquency

As we noted in Chapter 2, both the juvenile and adult crime rates, for both males and females, have been in a decade-long decline. Males (both adults and juveniles) are still being arrested far more often than females, especially for serious violent crimes such as robbery and murder. Only 66 girls age 18 and under were arrested on murder charges in 2010 compared to more than 560 boys.[37]

While males still commit more delinquency than females, and are more likely to be involved in violent crimes, there are indications that the gender gap in crime and delinquency arrests is narrowing. In 1995, the male:female delinquency arrest ratio for all crimes was 3:1; today it's closer to 2:1; the ratio for serious violent crimes has dropped from 8:1 to 4:1. Similarly, self-report studies indicate that the rank-ordering of male and female delinquent behaviors is more similar than ever. As Table 6.1 shows,

TABLE 6.1 Percentage of High School Seniors Admitting to at Least One Offense During the Past 12 Months, by Gender

Delinquent Acts	Males	Females
Serious fight	15	10
Gang fight	22	5
Hurt someone badly	21	4
Used a weapon to steal	5	2
Theft, more than $50	14	7
Theft, less than $50	33	22
Shoplift	31	23
Breaking and entering	30	19
Arson	4	2
Damaged school property	15	5

Source: *Monitoring the Future, 2010* (Ann Arbor, MI: Institute for Social Research, 2012).

the illegal acts most common for boys—petty larceny, shoplifting, breaking in—are also the ones most frequently committed by girls.[38]

Police and the Gender Gap. How can the narrowing of the gender gap in delinquency be explained? One possibility is that police are changing the manner in which they handle cases involving adolescent females, showing them less favoritism, resulting in a greater likelihood of girls getting arrested. Research using self-report data shows that there has been little actual increase in girls' violence or drug use over the past decade.[39] Therefore, any gender convergence in the delinquency arrest rate may be due to changing police procedures and not actual change in delinquent activity. The Girls Study Group, a group of experts sponsored by the Office of Juvenile Justice and Delinquency Prevention (OJJDP), carefully evaluated existing data, and concluded that increases in female violent crime arrests are more likely to have been caused by police arrest procedures and policies than any radical change in female behavior.

The study group found that heightened sensitivity to domestic violence has led many states and localities to implement mandatory arrest policies in response to domestic disturbances, including those between parents and children. Behaviors once considered "ungovernable" (a status offense) may, in a domestic situation, result instead in an arrest for simple assault. Policies of mandatory arrest for domestic violence, initially adopted to protect victims from further attacks, also provide parents with a method for attempting to control their "unruly" daughters. Girls fight with family members or siblings more frequently than boys, who more often fight with friends or strangers. This dynamic makes them more vulnerable to arrest under changing domestic violence laws and therefore increases their presence in the arrest statistics.[40]

What causes female delinquency? Are the factors that produce girls' misbehavior the same that are associated with that of boys? This issue is explored in the following sections. **CHECKPOINTS**

WWW

A number of institutes at major universities are devoted to the **study of women's issues**. To visit the site of the one at the University of Michigan, visit the Criminal Justice CourseMate at CengageBrain.com, then access the Web Links for this chapter.

CHECKPOINTS

LO1 Be familiar with the gender differences in development.

✔ Female delinquency was considered unimportant by early delinquency experts because girls rarely committed crime, and when they did it was typically sexual in nature.

✔ Interest in female delinquency has risen because the female crime rate has been increasing, whereas the male rate is in decline.

✔ There are distinct gender patterns in development that may explain crime rate differences.

✔ Girls are socialized to be less aggressive than boys.

✔ Girls read better and have better verbal skills than boys.

✔ Gender differences may have both biological and social origins.

✔ Though males still are arrested more often than females, the intergender patterns of delinquency are remarkably similar.

TRAIT VIEWS

There is a long tradition of tracing gender differences in delinquency to traits that are uniquely male or female. The argument that biological and psychological differences between males and females can explain differences in crime rates is not a new one. The earliest criminologists focused on physical characteristics believed to be precursors of crime.

Early Biological Explanations

With the publication in 1895 of *The Female Offender*, Cesare Lombroso (with William Ferrero) extended his work on criminality to females.[41] Lombroso maintained that women were lower on the evolutionary scale than men, more childlike, and less intelligent.[42] Women who committed crimes could be distinguished from "normal" women by physical characteristics—excessive body hair, wrinkles, and an abnormal cranium, for example.[43] In appearance, delinquent females appeared closer to men than to other women. The masculinity hypothesis suggested that delinquent girls had excessive male characteristics.[44]

Lombrosian thought had a significant influence for much of the twentieth century. Delinquency rate differentials were explained in terms of gender-based differences. For example, in 1925, Cyril Burt linked female delinquency to menstruation.[45] Similarly, William Healy and Augusta Bronner suggested that males' physical superiority enhanced their criminality. Their research showed that about 70 percent of the delinquent girls they studied had abnormal weight and size, a finding that supported the masculinity hypothesis.[46]

So-called experts suggested that female delinquency goes unrecorded, because the female is the instigator rather than the perpetrator.[47] Females first use their sexual charms to instigate crime and then beguile males in the justice system to obtain deferential treatment. This observation, referred to as the **chivalry hypothesis**, holds that gender differences in the delinquency rate can be explained by the fact that female criminality is overlooked or forgiven by male agents of the justice system. Those who believe in the chivalry hypothesis point to data showing that even though women make up about 20 percent of arrestees, they account for less than 5 percent of inmates. Police and other justice system personnel may be less willing to penalize female offenders than male offenders.[48]

Early Psychological Explanations

Psychologists also viewed the physical differences between males and females as a basis for their behavior differentials. Sigmund Freud maintained that girls interpret their lack of a penis as a sign that they have been punished. Boys fear that they can be punished by having their penis cut off, and thus learn to fear women. From this conflict comes *penis envy*, which often produces an inferiority complex in girls, forcing them to make an effort to compensate for their "defect." One way to compensate is to identify with their mothers and accept a maternal role. Also, girls may attempt to compensate for their lack of a penis by dressing well and beautifying themselves.[49] Freud also claimed that "if a little girl persists in her first wish—to grow into a boy—in extreme cases she will end as a manifest homosexual, and otherwise she will exhibit markedly masculine traits in the conduct of her later life, will choose a masculine vocation, and so on."[50]

At mid-century, psychodynamic theorists suggested that girls are socialized to be passive, which helps explain their low crime rate. However, this condition also makes some females susceptible to being manipulated by men; hence, their participation in sex-related crimes, such as prostitution. A girl's wayward behavior, psychoanalysts suggested, was restricted to neurotic theft (kleptomania) and overt sexual acts, which were symptoms of personality maladaption.[51]

According to these early versions of the psychoanalytic approach, gender differences in the delinquency rate can be traced to differences in psychological

WWW

To read more about the **chivalry hypothesis** and how it relates to gang delinquency, visit the Criminal Justice CourseMate at CengageBrain.com, then access the Web Links for this chapter.

chivalry hypothesis The view that low female crime and delinquency rates are a reflection of the leniency with which police treat female offenders.

orientation. Male delinquency reflects aggressive traits, whereas female delinquency is a function of repressed sexuality, gender conflict, and abnormal socialization.

Contemporary Trait Views

Contemporary biosocial and psychological theorists have continued the tradition of attributing gender differences in delinquency to physical and emotional traits. These theorists recognize that it is the interaction of biological and psychological traits with the social environment that produces delinquency.

Early Puberty/Precocious Sexuality. Early theorists linked female delinquency to early puberty and **precocious sexuality**. According to this view, girls who experience an early onset of physical maturity are most likely to engage in antisocial behavior.[52] Female delinquents were believed to be promiscuous and more sophisticated than male delinquents.[53] Linking female delinquency to sexuality was responsible, in part, for the view that female delinquency is symptomatic of maladjustment.[54]

Equating female delinquency purely with sexual activity is no longer taken seriously, but early sexual maturity has been linked to other problems, such as a higher risk of teen pregnancy and sexually transmitted diseases.[55] Empirical evidence suggests that girls who reach puberty at an early age are at the highest risk for delinquency.[56] One reason is that "early bloomers" may be more attractive to older adolescent boys, and increased contact with this high-risk group places the girls in jeopardy for antisocial behavior. Research shows that young girls who date boys three or more years older are more likely to engage in precocious sex, feel pressured into having sex, and engage in sex while under the influence of drugs and/or alcohol than girls who date more age-appropriate boys.[57]

Girls who are more sexually developed relative to their peers are more likely to socialize at an early age and to get involved in deviant behaviors, especially "party deviance," such as drinking, smoking, and substance abuse.[58] Early puberty is most likely to encourage delinquent activities that occur in the context of socializing with peers and having romantic relationships with boys.[59]

Biological and social factors seem to interact to postpone or accelerate female delinquent activity. The association between early puberty and delinquency is also conditioned by such social factors as the quality of parenting, the nature of the school experience and neighborhood conditions; each of these factors that may exacerbate or ameliorate outcomes.[60] For example, the onset of puberty is associated with increased conflict between parents and teens. During this stage, it is not unusual to see intrafamily conflicts brewing up around issues such as dating, selecting friends, and changing behavioral expectations; conflict breeds delinquency. However, proper parenting can help moderate the association between early puberty and acting out behavior. Parents who use harsh and inconsistent discipline are more likely to be raising children with behavior problems than parents with more positive parenting styles.

Schools can also have a moderating influence on the association between early puberty and delinquency. Early-maturing girls in mixed-gender school settings were at greater risk for delinquency than early-maturing girls in same-gender school settings where exposure to delinquent boys would be limited. Similarly, neighborhood context can exert crucial influences as well. Research shows that girls who experience early-onset puberty and live in highly disadvantaged/ disorganized neighborhoods are at significantly greater risk for exhibiting violent behaviors than those who live in less disadvantaged neighborhoods.

In sum, early puberty, especially when coupled with family conflict, involvement with young men, and residence in a disadvantaged neighborhood, is a key factor in girls' delinquency.

Early Puberty and Victimization. If reaching puberty at an early age increases the likelihood of delinquent behavior, does it also increase victimization risk? Recent research finds that both boys and girls who reached puberty at an early age also increase their chances of victimization. The association was gendered: boys were

precocious sexuality Sexual experimentation in early adolescence.

less likely to become victims if their friendship network contained girls; in contrast, girls' victimization was not moderated by the sexual makeup of their peer group.[61]

Why does peer group makeup influence boys' victimization more than girls? It is possible that females are much less likely to be involved in serious, violent delinquency, and therefore having a higher concentration of them in a male's peer network reduces their exposure to more violent boys. In contrast, boys who associate mostly with male peers may feel compelled to engage in risky behaviors; for example, in order to keep up with their friends they have to drink, drive fast, and get involved in brawls. Girls may feel less peer pressure to engage in risky behavior; their male friends may protect them rather than put them in danger.

Hormonal Effects. As you may recall from Chapter 3, some biosocial theorists link antisocial behavior to hormonal influences.[62] One view is that hormonal imbalance may influence aggressive behavior. For example, changes in the level of the hormone cortisol, which is secreted by the adrenal glands in response to any kind of physical or psychological stress, has been linked to conduct problems in young girls.[63] Another view is that excessive amounts of male hormones (androgens) are related to delinquency. The androgen most often related to antisocial behavior is testosterone.[64] In general, females who test higher for testosterone are more likely to engage in stereotypical male behaviors.[65] Females who have low androgen levels are less aggressive than males, whereas those who have elevated levels will take on characteristically male traits, including aggression.[66]

Some females who are overexposed to male hormones in utero may become "constitutionally masculinized." They may develop abnormal hair growth, large musculature, low voice, irregular menstrual cycle, and are more likely to engage in aggressive behavior later in life.[67]

Premenstrual Syndrome. Early biotheorists suspected that premenstrual syndrome (PMS) was a direct cause of the relatively rare instances of female violence: "For several days prior to and during menstruation, the stereotype has been that 'raging hormones' doom women to irritability and poor judgment—two facets of premenstrual syndrome."[68] The link between PMS and delinquency was popularized by Katharina Dalton, whose studies of English women led her to conclude that females are more likely to commit suicide and be aggressive and otherwise antisocial before or during menstruation.[69]

This issue is far from settled. While it is possible that the stress associated with menstruation produces crime, it is also possible that the stress of antisocial behavior produces early menstruation.[70]

Aggression. According to some biosocial theorists, gender differences in the delinquency rate can be explained by inborn differences in aggression.[71] Some psychologists believe that males are inherently more aggressive—a condition that appears very early in life, before socialization can influence behavior.

Gender-based differences in aggression have been developing for millions of years and reflect the dissimilarities in the male and female reproductive systems. Males are more aggressive because they wish to possess as many sex partners as possible to increase their chances of producing offspring. Females have learned to control their aggressive impulses because having multiple mates does not increase their chances of conception. Instead, females concentrate on acquiring things that will help them rear their offspring, such as a reliable mate who will supply material resources.[72]

Contemporary Psychological Views

Because girls are socialized to be less aggressive than boys, it is possible that the young women who do get involved in antisocial and violent behavior are suffering from some form of mental anguish or abnormality. Girls are also more likely than boys to be involved in status offenses, such as running away and truancy, behaviors that suggest underlying psychological distress.

Research indicates that antisocial adolescent girls do suffer a wide variety of psychiatric problems and have dysfunctional and violent relationships.[73] Girls are more likely than boys to suffer mental health problems linked to life stressors and experiences of victimization, such as depression, anxiety, and posttraumatic stress disorder. Although these disorders are also associated with delinquency among boys, the relationship appears to be much stronger for girls.[74]

Incarcerated adolescent female offenders have more acute mental health symptoms and psychological disturbances than male offenders.[75] Female delinquents score high on psychological tests measuring such traits as psychopathic deviation, schizophrenia, paranoia, and psychasthenia (a psychological disorder characterized by phobias, obsessions, compulsions, or excessive anxiety).[76] Clinical interviews indicate that female delinquents are significantly more likely than males to suffer from mood disorders, including any disruptive disorder, major depressive disorder, and separation anxiety disorder.[77] For example, serious female delinquents have been found to have a relatively high incidence of callous-unemotional (CU) traits, an affective disorder described by a lack of remorse or shame, poor judgment, failure to learn by experience, and chronic lying.[78] In sum, there are some experts who believe that female delinquents suffer from psychological deficits ranging from lack of self-control to serious impairments.[79] **CHECKPOINTS**

CHECKPOINTS

LO2 Be familiar with trait explanations of female delinquency.

✔ Empirical evidence suggests that girls who reach puberty at an early age are at the highest risk for delinquency.

✔ One view is that hormonal imbalance may influence aggressive behavior in young girls.

✔ Another view is that excessive amounts of male hormones (androgens) are related to delinquency.

✔ Clinical interviews indicate that female delinquents are significantly more likely than males to suffer from mood disorders.

SOCIALIZATION VIEWS

Socialization views are based on the idea that a child's social development may be the key to understanding delinquent behavior. If a child experiences impairment, family disruption, and so on, the child will be more susceptible to delinquent associations and criminality.

Linking crime rate variations to gender differences in socialization is not a recent phenomenon. In a 1928 work, *The Unadjusted Girl*, W. I. Thomas suggested that some girls who have not been socialized under middle-class family controls can become impulsive thrill seekers. According to Thomas, female delinquency is linked to the "wish" for luxury and excitement.[80] Inequities in social class condemn poor girls from demoralized families to using sex as a means to gain amusement, pretty clothes, and other luxuries. Precocious sexuality makes these girls vulnerable to older men, who lead them down the path to decadence.[81]

Socialization and Delinquency

Girls are supervised more closely than boys, and if they behave in a socially disapproved fashion, their parents may be more likely to notice. Adults may be more tolerant of deviant behavior in boys and expect boys to act tough and take risks. Closer supervision restricts the opportunity for crime and the time available to mingle with delinquent peers. Girls who are supervised closely may be less likely to engage in deviant behavior in adolescence and later go on to live more conventional adult lifestyles (i.e., marry and raise a family).[82] It follows, then, that the adolescent girl who is growing up in a troubled home and lacks supervision may be more prone to delinquency.

Focus on Socialization. In the 1950s, a number of researchers began to focus on gender-specific socialization patterns. They made three assumptions about gender differences in socialization: families exert a more powerful influence on girls than on boys; girls do not form close same-sex friendships, but compete with their peers; and female criminals are primarily sexual offenders. First, parents are stricter with girls because they perceive them as needing control. In some families, adolescent girls rebel against strict controls. In others, where parents are absent or unavailable, girls may turn to the streets for companionship. Second, girls rarely form close relationships with female peers, because they view them as rivals for males who would make eligible marriage partners.[83] Instead, girls enter into affairs with older men who exploit them, involve them in sexual deviance, and father their illegitimate children.[84] The result is prostitution, drug abuse, and marginal lives. Their daughters repeat this pattern in a never-ending cycle of exploitation.

Broken Homes/Fallen Women. While in the past there was general agreement that dysfunctional family relations were a primary influence on female delinquency, the view of the female delinquent was sharply different than it is today. Fifty years ago, male delinquents were portrayed as rebels who esteemed toughness, excitement, and other lower-class values. Males succumbed to the lure of delinquency when they perceived few legitimate opportunities. In contrast, female delinquents were portrayed as troubled adolescents who suffered inadequate home lives, and more often than not, were victims of sexual and physical abuse. Ruth Morris described delinquent girls as unattractive youths who reside in homes marked by family tensions.[85] In *The Delinquent Girl* (1970), Clyde Vedder and Dora Somerville suggested that female delinquency is usually a problem of adjustment to family pressure; an estimated 75 percent of institutionalized girls have family problems.[86] They also suggested that girls have serious problems in a male-dominated culture with rigid and sometimes unfair social practices.

Other early efforts linked "rebellious" behavior to sexual conflicts in the home.[87] Broken or disrupted homes were found to predict female delinquency.[88] Females petitioned to juvenile court were more likely than males to be charged with ungovernable behavior and sex offenses. They also were more likely to reside in single-parent homes.[89] Studies of incarcerated juveniles found that most of the male delinquents were incarcerated for burglary and other theft-related offenses, but female delinquents tended to be involved in incorrigibility and sex offenses. The conclusion: boys became delinquent to demonstrate their masculinity; girls were delinquent as a result of hostility toward parents and a consequent need to obtain attention from others.[90]

Contemporary Socialization Views

Contemporary investigators continue to support the view that female delinquents have more dysfunctional home lives than male offenders.[91] One focus is the effects of abuse on behavior. Girls seem to be more deeply affected than boys by child abuse, and the link between abuse and female delinquency seems stronger than it is for male delinquency.[92] These experiences take a toll on their behavior choices: research shows that girls who are the victims of childhood sexual abuse and physical abuse are the ones most likely to later engage in criminal behavior.[93] Those with exposure to significant levels of violence are also the ones most likely to become crime victims, and the target of relationship violence.[94]

Girls may be forced into a life of sexual promiscuity because their sexual desirability makes them a valuable commodity for families living on the edge. There are cases of young girls being "lent out" to drug dealers so their parents or partners can get high. Girls on the streets are encouraged to sell their bodies, because they have little else of value to trade.[95] Many of these girls may find themselves pregnant at a very young age. Physical and sexual abuse and the toll they take on young girls is not unique to any one culture.

Running Away. Many young girls bear a heavy load of emotional problems that lead them to run away from home and enter into a delinquent way of life on the streets. Studies of girls who are chronic runaways document significant

Looking Back to Rain's Story

Rain is feeling depressed and isolated. While she has begun talking with her school social worker, she was also caught purchasing prescription drugs.

CRITICAL THINKING Rain and her counselor visited with each other often, and they seem to have had a supportive interaction. Conduct research on the influence of therapists on patient development.

A young, homeless runaway girl receives a handout while panhandling on the street in Seattle, Washington. Many children across the United States face dangers such as suicide, terrorism, drive-by shootings, and abductions—dangers that were unknown to previous generations.

levels of sexual and physical victimization. Although their offense behavior may not appear to be very serious, these girls may be fleeing from serious problems and victimization, some involving illegal behavior by adults, which in turn makes them vulnerable to subsequent victimization and engaging in other behaviors that violate the law such as prostitution, survival sex, and drug use.[96] Using data from a large sample of 10,000 youths petitioned to juvenile court, Pernilla Johansson and Kimberly Kempf-Leonard found that for girls with at least one prior runaway offense, the risk of chronic offending (as compared to occasional offending) was five times higher than the risk for females without a prior runaway; the effect of running way was greater on girls than on boys. Girls in the sample were also much more likely to have been subject to abuse than boys: nearly 25 percent of females but only 7 percent of males had been subject to suspected sexual, physical, or emotional abuse or maltreatment, and had child protective services involvement. Not surprisingly, 30 percent of the females and 15 percent of the males had some form of mental health problems.[97]

Family Breakdown. Some girls suffer family breakdown, a condition with long-term consequences. Some are placed outside the home early in childhood, and institutionalization does little to help matters. Those sent away are much more likely to develop criminal records as adults than similarly troubled girls who manage to stay with their families throughout their childhood.[98] Dominique Eve Roe-Sepowitz discovered this pattern when she examined a sample of 136 male and female juveniles charged with homicide or attempted homicide. Roe-Sepowitz found that, when compared to males, female juvenile homicide offenders had higher rates of reported childhood abuse, more serious substance abuse, and mental health problems, including suicidal ideations, depression, anxiety, anger, and irritability. Even though male juvenile homicide offenders reported higher rates of substance use than their female counterparts, females had more serious substance abuse problems. Female juveniles were found to more often kill a person known to them, and male homicide offenders were found to more often kill a stranger. These findings suggest strongly that the home life of females has an extremely strong impact on their mental health and law violating behaviors.[99]

Trauma, Victimization, and Delinquent Paths. The prevailing research then shows that young girls are more likely to be the target of victimization and abuse than

RESILIENT GIRLS CAN AVOID A LIFE OF CRIME

Why are some at-risk girls able to avoid involvement with a delinquent way of life while others fall victim to drugs and antisocial behaviors? A recent study by Stephanie Hawkins, Phillip Graham, Jason Williams, and Margaret Zahn focused on the effects of support from four sources: the presence of a caring adult, school connectedness, school success, and religiosity.

Hawkins and her colleagues found that the most consistent protective effect was the extent to which a girl felt she had caring adults in her life. However, there were limitations on this protective effect. Physically assaulted girls were protected when they believed they had a caring adult in their lives during mid-adolescence but not in young adulthood; they reported engaging in more aggravated assault than non-assaulted girls as they moved into young adulthood. It is possible that girls who were physically assaulted and have moved into early adulthood may have decided that the adults in their

any other group. Recently, Kristin Carbone-Lopez and Jody Miller found that early victimization—including sexual abuse—may help produce a precocious maturity that facilitates a young women's path into drug use and offending.[100] Their research, involving in-depth interviews with methamphetamine users, also found that the onset of deviance is likely to occur when young women are prematurely thrust into adult roles and responsibilities. The women described their troubled childhoods: more than one-third reported childhood sexual abuse; three-quarters described other family dysfunction, including domestic violence, substance abuse, neglect, and mental illness; and one in six came from homes deeply embedded in methamphetamine markets. All of them described precocious movements into adult roles and responsibilities, whether early independent living, differential association with older, deviant peers and romantic partners, responsibilities for sibling care, early motherhood, or—most often—some combination of these early transitions.

This research illustrates the path from early adversity, to precocious adult role taking, to adult criminality. Girls who are raised in troubled homes, who may be the victim of sexual and physical abuse, are the ones who grow up too fast, accumulate social deficits, and find themselves enmeshed in a delinquent way of life.

The issue of adolescent socialization, the risks it presents, and its effect on female delinquency is the subject of the accompanying Focus on Delinquency feature.

Socialization and Gangs. There is a significant body of literature linking abusive home lives to gang participation and crime. Joan Moore's analysis of gang girls in east Los Angeles found that many came from troubled homes. Sixty-eight percent of the girls she interviewed were afraid of their fathers, and 55 percent reported fear of their mothers.[101] Many of the girls reported that their parents were overly strict and controlling, despite the fact that they engaged in criminality themselves. Moore also details accounts of sexual abuse; about 30 percent of the girls reported that family members had made sexual advances.[102] Emily Gaarder and Joanne

lives have failed them. They may have found support from other adults who were not good role models for prosocial behavior, and being connected to an antisocial adult serves to get them in trouble.

When physically assaulted girls felt connected to their schools, they were less likely to report committing aggressive or antisocial acts. School may provide a refuge from an unsafe home environment. Because the majority of a youth's day is spent at school, becoming connected with this institution and the resources available therein seems to serve as a protection against delinquency for physically assaulted girls.

Religiosity also helped protect girls at high risk for delinquency from violent behavior. Girls from disadvantaged neighborhoods and those who had been sexually abused were less likely to engage in violent forms of delinquency when they were religious.

In sum, Hawkins and her colleagues find that among high-risk girls, the presence of a caring adult, school success, school connectedness, and religiosity may protect against some forms of delinquent behavior for some girls, but this protective effect is subject to complex interactions with risk factors and age.

CRITICAL THINKING

Understanding the role protective factors play in the lives of girls has important implications for creating programs to prevent delinquency. It seems important to consider the life histories and stressors that are present when developing interventions for girls at high risk for delinquency. Considering the factors that produce resiliency, what kind of interventions do you think might benefit at-risk girls the most?

Writing Assignment Write an essay addressing why practicing religion helps sexually abused girls avoid violent delinquency. Make sure to consider whether religion helps protect young women or whether those who have decided to forego antisocial behaviors turn to religion.

Source: Stephanie R. Hawkins, Phillip W. Graham, Jason Williams, and Margaret A. Zahn, *Resilient Girls—Factors that Protect Against Delinquency* (Washington, DC: Office of Juvenile Justice and Delinquency Prevention, 2009), www.ncjrs.gov/pdf-files1/ojjdp/220124.pdf (accessed August 10, 2012).

© Monica Almeida/*New York Times*/Redux

Nicole Clark's story is all too familiar. She ran away from her group home in Medford, Oregon, and spent weeks sleeping in parks and under bridges. Finally, the 14-year-old grew so desperate that she accepted a young man's offer of a place to stay. One day he threatened to kick her out if she did not have sex with several of his friends in exchange for money. She agreed, fearing she had no choice. That first exchange of money for sex led to a downward spiral of prostitution that lasted for 14 months, until she escaped from a pimp who she said often locked her in his garage apartment for months. Now 17, she is on the road back to reclaiming her life.

Belknap's interviews with young women sent to adult prisons indicated that most had endured prolonged sexual abuse and violence. One of their subjects—Lisa, a young European American woman—was serving time for attempted murder. Lisa had used drugs and alcohol, and joined gangs to escape the pain and troubles of her home life. Her mother was an alcoholic, and her father a convicted rapist. She had been sexually and physically abused by her stepfather from the ages of 9 to 11. Soon after, Lisa began skipping school, started using alcohol, and took LSD. She joined a gang when she was 12. "They were like a family to me," she told Gaarder and Belknap. "But I became involved in a lot of stuff. . . . I got high a lot, I robbed people, burglarized homes, stabbed people, and was involved in drive-bys." At age 15, Lisa stabbed a woman in a fight and was sentenced to 7 to 15 years for the crime. She made this statement:

> *I had just gotten out of this group home. The lady I stabbed had been messing with my sister's fiancé. This woman [had] a bunch of my sister's stuff, like her stereo and VCR, so me, my sister, her fiancé, and my boyfriend went over to pick up the stuff. We were all getting high beforehand. When we got to the house, my sister and I went in. . . . They [her sister and the victim] started fighting over him, and I started stabbing her with a knife. I always carried a knife with me because I was in a gang.*[103]

In summary, the socialization approach holds that family interaction is the key to understanding female delinquency. If a girl grows up in an atmosphere of sexual tension, where hostility exists between her parents, or where her parents are absent, she is likely to turn to outside sources for support. In contrast, a strong bond to parents may help insulate girls from social forces that produce delinquency.[104]

Girls are expected to follow narrowly defined behavioral patterns. In contrast, it is not unusual for boys to stay out late, drive around with friends, or get involved in other unstructured behaviors linked to delinquency. If in reaction to loneliness and parental hostility, girls engage in the same "routine activities" as boys (staying out late, partying, and riding around with friends), they run the risk of engaging in similar types of delinquent behavior.[105] **CHECKPOINTS**

Helping Girls Through the Life Course

The socialization approach holds that a poor home life is likely to have an even more damaging effect on females than on males. Girls may become sexually involved with boys to receive support from them, a practice that tends to magnify their problems. In order to help girls through this often painful transition, a number of community programs have focused on socialization. For example, the Friendly PEERsuasion program for girls ages 11 to 14 targets the years during which girls begin to face damaging peer pressure. Friendly PEERsuasion builds knowledge and skills for resisting negative peer pressure by empowering girls to use a process of identifying specifically what they are being pressured to do and the consequences. Participants then determine healthy alternatives and invite peers to join them in acting on their smarter choice. This process is fortified by enhancing girls' communication skills and ability to recognize stress and by providing them with practice in responding to stress in healthy ways. Participants learn about various legal and illicit substances, adopt guidelines for responsible use of readily available prescription and over-the-counter medications and supplements, and analyze media messages that glamorize substance use.[106]

The Prevention/Intervention/Treatment feature shows how helping girls overcome age-related problems can also enable them to avoid involvement in the juvenile justice system.

CHECKPOINTS

LO3 Discuss the association between socialization and female delinquency.

✔ Some experts believe that girls have been socialized to be less violent.

✔ Female delinquents may be the product of a destructive home life, rebelling against abusive parents.

✔ Girls may be supervised more closely than boys. If girls behave in a socially disapproved fashion, their parents may be more likely to notice.

✔ Parents are stricter with girls because they perceive them as needing control. In some families, adolescent girls rebel against strict controls.

✔ Girls seem to be more deeply affected than boys by child abuse, and the link between abuse and female delinquency seems stronger than it is for male delinquency.

Practical Academic Cultural Educational (PACE) Center

Established in 1985, the Practical Academic Cultural Educational (PACE) Center for Girls introduced a gender-responsive, school-based program as an alternative to incarceration or institutionalization for at-risk adolescent girls in Jacksonville, Florida. The success of the Jacksonville program led to replication in other Florida cities. PACE currently operates 17 direct care centers, 1 outreach program, and 2 preteen centers, and provides social and educational services to 2,000 Florida girls and their families each year. The PACE mission is to provide girls and young women an opportunity for a better future through education, counseling, training, and advocacy.

PACE's direct care and outreach programs serve girls ages 11 to 18 who have been identified as dependent (i.e., in need of protective services), truant, runaway, ungovernable, delinquent, pregnant, or in need of academic skills. Girls may be referred by a variety of sources, including the juvenile justice system, the Florida Department of Children and Family Services, school personnel, community service agencies, and parents. PACE aims to decrease risk factors in four domains: school, family, behavior, and substance abuse. A fundamental emphasis of the program is intervention in and prevention of school withdrawal, juvenile delinquency, teen pregnancy, substance abuse, and welfare dependency. Specific program components include academic education, individualized attention, gender-specific life management skills enhancement (through PACE's SPIRITED GIRLS!® curriculum), case management, parental involvement, community volunteer services, and career enhancement and awareness, and transition services. Girls attend PACE daily to meet with their social services staff member and work toward their individualized educational and social goals. Participants are also supported by a teacher/adviser, who provides academic case management, and a social services staff member who oversees all other case management needs, including social, emotional, and physical needs. Once a girl completes the goals on her Individualized Treatment Plan, she transitions from the day program into transitional services. PACE provides 3 years of transitional services to all girls who are enrolled for 30 days or longer and 3 months of transitional services to girls who are enrolled for fewer than 30 days. Throughout the transitional service period, case management, counseling, support, and follow-up are provided to each girl and her family work toward their individualized educational and social goals. Participants are also supported by a teacher/adviser, who provides academic case management, and a social services staff member who oversees all other case management needs, including social, emotional, and physical needs. Once a girl completes the goals on her individualized treatment plan, she transitions from the day program into transitional services. PACE provides three years of transitional services to all girls who are enrolled for 30 days or longer and three months of transitional services to girls who are enrolled for fewer than 30 days. Throughout the transitional service period, case management, counseling, support, and follow-up are provided to each girl and her family.

Critical Thinking

What theoretical perspectives would support the Pace approach? In other words, which theories of delinquency are at work here?

Source: Office of Juvenile Justice and Delinquency Prevention, Practical Academic Cultural Educational (PACE) Center for Girls, Inc., www.pacecenter.org (accessed August 10, 2012).

FEMINIST VIEWS

The feminist movement has, from its origins, fought to help women break away from their traditional roles and gain economic, educational, and social advancement. There is little question that the women's movement has revised the way women perceive their roles in society, and it has altered the relationships of women to many social institutions. Typically, feminist visions of female can be broken down into two broad categories, liberal feminism and critical feminism.

Liberal Feminism

According to **liberal feminism**, females are less delinquent than males because their social roles provide fewer opportunities to commit crime. As the roles of women become more similar to those of men, so will their crime patterns. Female criminality is motivated by the same influences as male criminality. According to Freda Adler's *Sisters in Crime* (1975), by striving for independence women have begun to alter the institutions that had protected males in their traditional positions of power.[107] Adler argued that female delinquency would be affected by the changing role of women. As females entered new occupations and participated in sports, politics, and other traditionally male endeavors, they would also become involved in crimes that had heretofore been male-oriented; delinquency rates would then converge. She noted that girls were becoming increasingly involved in traditionally masculine crimes such as gang activity and fighting.

Adler predicted that the women's movement would produce steeper increases in the rate of female delinquency, because it created an environment in which the roles of girls and boys converge. She predicted that the changing female role would produce female criminals who are similar to their male counterparts.[108]

Support for Liberal Feminism. A number of studies support the feminist view of gender differences in delinquency.[109] More than 40 years ago, Rita James Simon explained how the increase in female criminality is a function of the changing role of women. She claimed that as women were empowered economically and socially, they would be less likely to feel dependent and oppressed. Consequently, they would be less likely to attack their traditional targets: their husbands, their lovers, or even their own children.[110] Instead, their new role as breadwinner might encourage women to engage in traditional male crimes, such as larceny and car theft.

Simon's view has been supported in part by research showing a significant correlation between the women's rights movement and the female crime rate.[111] If 1966 is used as a jumping-off point (because the National Organization for Women was founded in that year), there are indications that patterns of serious female crime (robbery and auto theft) correlate with indicators of female emancipation (the divorce rate and participation in the labor force). Although this research does not prove that female crime is related to social change, it identifies behavior patterns that support that hypothesis.

In addition to these efforts, self-report studies support the liberal feminist view by showing that gender differences in delinquency are fading—that is, the delinquent acts committed most and least often by girls are nearly identical to those reported most and least often by boys.[112] The pattern of female delinquency, if not the extent, is now similar to that of male delinquency, and with few exceptions the factors that seem to motivate both male and female criminality seem similar.[113]

As the sex roles of males and females have become less distinct, their offending patterns have become more similar. Girls may be committing crimes to gain economic advancement and not because they lack parental support. Both of these patterns were predicted by liberal feminists.

Critical Feminist Views

A number of writers take a more critical view of gender differences in crime. **Critical feminism** posits that gender inequality stems from the unequal power of men and women in society and the exploitation of females by fathers and husbands; in a patriarchal society women are a "commodity" like land or money.[114] Female delinquency originates with the onset of male supremacy (patriarchy),

---

liberal feminism Asserts that females are less delinquent than males, because their social roles provide them with fewer opportunities to commit crimes; as the roles of girls and women become more similar to those of boys and men, so too will their crime patterns.

critical feminism Holds that gender inequality stems from the unequal power of men and women and the subsequent exploitation of women by men; the cause of female delinquency originates with the onset of male supremacy and the efforts of males to control females' sexuality.

Looking Back at Rain's Story

At first, Rain's social worker and therapist suspected that she was having significant issues with her mother's sexuality. However, they changed their minds when Rain reported feeling her mother was a healthy and happy person.

CRITICAL THINKING Rain's story reflects changing social values and family dynamics. How do these changes mesh with the core values of liberal feminism?

---

the subordination of women, male aggression, and the efforts of men to control females sexually.[115] Women's victimization rates decline as they are empowered socially, economically, and legally.[116]

Critical feminists focus on the social forces that shape girls' lives. They attempt to show how the sexual victimization of girls is often a function of male socialization and that young males learn to be exploitive of women. James Messerschmidt, an influential feminist scholar, has formulated a theoretical model to show how misguided concepts of masculinity flow from the inequities built into "patriarchal capitalism." Men dominate business in capitalist societies, and males who cannot function well within its parameters are at risk for crime. Women are inherently powerless in such a society, and their crimes reflect their limited access to both legitimate and illegitimate opportunity.[117] It is not surprising that research surveys have found that 90 percent of adolescent girls are sexually harassed in school, with almost 30 percent reporting having been psychologically pressured to "do something sexual," and 10 percent physically forced into sexual behaviors.[118]

The critical view is substantiated by Jody Miller in her landmark study *Getting Played*.[119] Miller found that African American girls in the urban environment were regularly harassed and sexually abused by adolescent boys wanting to demonstrate their manhood. Harassment may have begun in the street but spilled over into the school setting, where it was a routine fixture in the educational experience of young urban girls. Girls were called names and had to endure being touched, groped, and grabbed. Those who fought back found little comfort. They were continually mistreated and turned into outcasts, suffering peer rejection. If, on the other hand, they chose to ignore the mistreatment, it was assumed they liked the sexual attention and they were soon labeled "hood rat." Rather than finding support, they were subject to rejection from their female peers and continued attacks by the boys; it was a no-win situation. Adding to the girls' frustration was the belief that they were being ignored by school personnel who were indifferent to the sexual harassment. The lack of official support forced the young girls Miller interviewed to fend off attacks by themselves. The trouble they encountered in the school then spilled back into the neighborhood. Girls who could not take care of themselves in school would be further victimized once they left school grounds. School harassment was almost a test to see if the girls would be able to take care of themselves at home or whether they could be easily victimized.

What happens to these abused girls? According to the critical feminist view, male exploitation acts as a trigger for female delinquent behavior. Female delinquents recount being so severely harassed at school that they were forced to carry knives. Some reported that boyfriends—men sometimes in their 30s, who "knew how to treat a girl"—would draw them into criminal activity, such as drug trafficking, which eventually entangled them in the justice system.[120]

When female adolescents run away and use drugs, they may be reacting to abuse at home or at school. Their attempts at survival are then labeled delinquent.[121] Research shows that a significant number of girls who are victims of sexual and other forms of abuse will later engage in delinquency.[122] All too often, school officials ignore complaints made by female students. Young girls therefore may feel trapped and desperate.

See the What Does This Mean to Me? feature for an interesting perspective on the issue of sexual harassment.

WHAT DOES THIS MEAN TO ME?

▶ **Sexual Harassment** Research now shows that males and females both generally agree that sexual coercion and sexual propositions constitute sexual harassment. Yet males do not think that sex-stereotyped jokes are a form of harassment, whereas females do; females think that repeated requests for dates after a refusal constitute harassment, whereas males think there is nothing wrong with asking girls out again and again. It is not surprising to discover that females perceive that sexual harassment has occurred in situations where males find no wrongdoing.

1. Do you think that these different perceptions are biologically related or a matter of socialization?
2. (For women): Have you ever been in a situation where you felt yourself being sexually harassed by a male who thought he was doing nothing wrong?
3. (For men): Have you ever been accused of sexual harassment by a woman even though you personally felt you did nothing wrong?

Every year, thousands of young girls become the victim of sex traffickers. Brianna, who was rescued from sex traffickers, attends a press conference with her father Gordy, left. The event was held by former Congresswoman Linda Smith and Shared Hope International at Marshall Park in Vancouver, Washington, to celebrate a new law that increases criminal penalties for pimps and johns.

Power-Control Theory

John Hagan and his associates have speculated that gender differences in delinquency are a function of class differences that influence family life. Hagan, who calls his view **power-control theory**, suggests that class influences delinquency by controlling the quality of family life.[123] In paternalistic families, fathers assume the role of breadwinner and mothers have menial jobs or remain at home. Mothers are expected to control the behavior of their daughters while granting greater freedom to sons. The parent–daughter relationship can be viewed as a preparation for the "cult of domesticity," which makes daughters' involvement in delinquency unlikely. Hence, males exhibit a higher degree of delinquent behavior than their sisters.

In **egalitarian families**—in which the husband and wife share similar positions of power at home and in the workplace—daughters gain a kind of freedom that reflects reduced parental control. These families produce daughters whose law-violating behaviors mirror those of their brothers. Ironically, these kinds of relationships also occur in households with absent fathers. Similarly, Hagan and his associates found that when both fathers and mothers hold equally valued managerial positions, the similarity between the rates of their daughters' and sons' delinquency is greatest. Therefore, middle-class girls are most likely to violate the law, because they are less closely controlled than lower-class girls.

Research conducted by Hagan and his colleagues has tended to support the core relationship between family structure and gender differences in delinquency.[124] However, some of the basic premises of power-control theory, such as the relationship between social class and delinquency, have been challenged. For example, some critics have questioned the assumption that upper-class youths may engage in more petty delinquency than lower-class youths, because they are brought up to be "risk takers" who do not fear the consequences of their misdeeds.[125]

Power-control theory encourages a new approach to the study of delinquency, one that addresses gender differences, class position, and family structure. It also

WAW

For more than 20 years, the **Center for Research on Women** has been at the forefront of research in which the central questions are shaped by the experiences and perspectives of women. Visit the Criminal Justice CourseMate at CengageBrain.com, then access the Web Links for this chapter.

power-control theory Holds that gender differences in the delinquency rate are a function of class differences and economic conditions that influence the structure of family life.

egalitarian families Husband and wife share power at home; daughters gain a kind of freedom similar to that of sons, and their law-violating behaviors mirror those of their brothers.

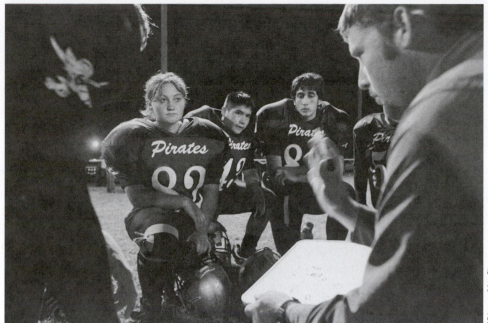

According to power-control theory, as more families become egalitarian, with both parents sharing equal roles and having equal authority, children's roles will become more homogenous. Because sons and daughters are treated equally, their behavior will take on similar patterns. Some like Alice Blair (front left), shown here listening to coach Russ Wilson during a huddle, October 22, 2005, in Paint Creek, Texas, will take on what has been considered a traditional male role. Blair plays defense on the school's six-person football team.

helps explain the relative increase in female delinquency by stressing the significance of changing feminine roles. With the increase in single-parent homes, the patterns Hagan has identified may change. The decline of the patriarchal family may produce looser family ties on girls, changing sex roles, and increased delinquency. Ironically, this raises an interesting dilemma: the daughters of successful and powerful mothers are more at risk for delinquency than the daughters of stay-at-home moms! However, as sociologist Christopher Uggen points out, there may be a bright side to this dilemma: the daughters of independent working mothers may not only be more likely to commit delinquent acts but also be encouraged to take prosocial risks, such as engaging in athletic competition and breaking into traditionally male-dominated occupations, such as policing and the military.[126]

Hagan and his colleagues have conducted research whose findings support the core relationship predicted by power-control theory.[127] Other social scientists have produced similar results. When Brenda Sims Blackwell and Mark Reed measured the gap between brother–sister delinquency, they found that it is greatest in patriarchal families and least in egalitarian families, a finding consistent with the core premise of power-control theory.[128]

Sex Abuse and Sex Trafficking

Critical feminists view **sex trafficking** as the personification of the exploitation of women for financial gain. It is a sad but well-known fact that thousands of young girls are being trafficked from country to country every year, and kept as virtual slaves for men in power.[129] Trafficking activities include recruiting individuals, transporting and transferring them from their home country or region to other transshipment points and to destination countries, receiving such trafficked persons and keeping them in custody or housing them. Many forms of trafficking exist. Young

sex trafficking The recruitment and transportation of people for commercial sex through the use of force, fraud, or coercion.

girls and women are common targets of commercial sexual exploitation. They may be forced into prostitution and other sexual activities such as the production of pornography. There are accounts of women being forced to service 30 men a day and of children trapped in pornography rings. Others become human containers in the transportation of drugs through forced ingestion of condoms filled with cocaine or other illegal substances. Labor servitude can be found in nearly every area of industry. Young girls have been forced to work in sweatshops, factories, agricultural fields, and fisheries. Victims may work long hours in unpleasant, unsanitary, or dangerous conditions for low wages, sometimes unable to take breaks or leave the facility. In some instances, debts may be passed on to other family members or even entire villages from generation to generation, creating a constant supply of indentured servants for traffickers.

How common is sex trafficking? While data are unreliable, estimates of the number of people trafficked internationally each year range from 600,000 men, women, and children to 1.2 million children alone. The United States is not immune: the CIA estimates that 45,000 to 50,000 individuals are trafficked into the United States annually. Despite the differences in these numbers, it is undeniable that a huge amount of trafficking in humans occurs around the globe.

Controlling human trafficking has proven to be difficult. Some countries have recently written laws to prevent their citizens from engaging in sexual activities with minors while traveling outside of their own country. These laws try to deter sex tourism, making travelers reconsider their actions as a result of the consequences. However, enforcement of these laws may prove challenging due to jurisdiction and proof, so that the practice continues unabated in many parts of the world. The United States passed the *Trafficking Victims Protection Act* of 2000 and then strengthened it with a 2005 revision.[130] Included in the bills' $360 million funding package was an expansion of the Operation Innocence Lost program, a nationwide initiative that helps law enforcement agents pursue sex traffickers and child prostitution rings. The federal laws defined several new crimes, including human trafficking, sex trafficking, forced labor, and document servitude, which involves the withholding or destruction of identity or travel documents as a means of controlling victims of the sex trade. The government has also outlawed psychological manipulation, which means that traffickers can be prosecuted if they cause victims to believe they will be harmed if they resist.[131] Whether or not these measures will prove sufficient to reduce the sexual exploitation of children remains to be seen. **CHECKPOINTS**

GENDER AND THE JUVENILE JUSTICE SYSTEM

Gender differences not only have an effect on crime patterns, but also may have a significant impact on the way children are treated by the juvenile justice system. Several feminist scholars argue that girls are not only the victims of injustice at home, but also risk being victimized by agents of the justice system. For the past few decades there has been an increase in delinquency cases being handled by juvenile courts, and females represent a growing proportion of the court caseload. A higher percentage of females' cases were petitioned for formal processing and ultimately adjudicated; females are also handled more punitively than males.[132]

For more than 30 years, delinquency expert Meda Chesney-Lind has conducted well-regarded research to determine whether girls are still "victims" in the juvenile justice system. Among her findings: police are more likely to arrest female adolescents for sexual activity and to ignore the same behavior among male delinquents.[133] Girls, more than boys, are still disadvantaged if their behavior is viewed as morally incorrect by government officials or if they are considered beyond parental control.[134]

Chesney-Lind finds that girls may also be feeling the brunt of the more punitive policies now being used in the juvenile justice system. Tougher juvenile justice standards mean that more cases are being handled formally.[135] While girls are actually committing fewer violent crimes, they are more likely to become enmeshed in the grasp of the juvenile justice system and demonized by policies that punish all young women who do not live up to society's so-called moral standards. Girls are particularly vulnerable to the conservative "zero-tolerance" policy shifts that are designed to punish youthful misbehaviors.[136] Once in the system, girls may receive fewer benefits and services than their male counterparts.

Paul E. Tracy, Kimberly Kempf-Leonard, and Stephanie Abramoske-James used national data to determine whether girls have received harsher treatment than boys in the juvenile justice system during the past two decades.[137] Their findings certainly support Chesney-Lind's views. They found that females were handled more punitively than males at almost every stage of the juvenile justice system:

- Female delinquents were substantially more likely to have been detained for status offenses before final juvenile court disposition or afterward.

- Not only did females represent a higher percentage of juvenile court cases, but they also represented an increasing percentage of cases that were petitioned for formal processing and ultimately adjudicated.

- Females were much more likely than boys to receive the harshest sanction available in a juvenile court—namely, commitment to a juvenile prison—for status offenses and even for technical violations of probation.

- Females were committed to a correctional facility at much younger ages than males.

- Females have achieved parity with males concerning the length of time served in confinement for delinquent conduct; females and males exhibit similar cumulative percentages for each sentence length.

Clearly, these results suggest the possibility of a bias toward paternalism—if not an overreaction—by the juvenile system where girls are concerned.

Why do these differences persist? Girls may still be subject to harsh punishments if they are considered dangerously immoral.[138] Even though girls are still less likely to be arrested than boys, those who fail to measure up to stereotypes of proper female behavior are more likely to be sanctioned than male offenders.[139] Recent research by Tia Stevens and her associates found that over the past decades, regardless of racial/ethnic group, the girls who are involved in assaultive behavior are now much more likely to be formally charged and involved in the juvenile justice system; the increase in justice system involvement has been magnified for black girls. It may be, they conclude, that when girls are more violent, tolerance for their behavior significantly decreases. When girls violate gender norms, the punishment can sometimes be very harsh.[140]

Officials and policy makers still show a lack of concern about girls' victimization and instead are more concerned with controlling their behavior than addressing the factors that brought them to the attention of the juvenile justice system in the first place.[141] **CHECKPOINTS**

CHECKPOINTS

LO5 Critique the differential treatment of girls in the juvenile justice system.

✔ Some critics believe that girls, more than boys, are still disadvantaged if their behavior is viewed as morally incorrect by government officials.

✔ Some are punished because they are considered beyond parental control.

✔ Female status offenders are treated more harshly than male status offenders.

SUMMARY

Early delinquency experts often ignored female offenders, assuming that girls rarely violated the law, or if they did, that their illegal acts were status offenses. Contemporary interest in the association between gender and delinquency has surged, because girls are now getting involved in serious delinquent acts that are quite similar to those of young men. Gender differences in the delinquency rates have narrowed. Boys still account for most of the total number of arrests and especially serious violent crime arrests. Gender patterns in delinquency have become similar.

Some experts suggest that gender differences may have a biological origin: males and females are essentially different. A second view is that gender differences are developed over the life course and reflect different treatment of males and females.

Socialization is also linked to gender differences in delinquency. Girls may be supervised more closely than boys.

If girls behave in a socially disapproved fashion, their parents may be more likely to notice. Girls seem to be more deeply affected than boys by child abuse, and the link between abuse and female delinquency seems stronger than it is for male delinquency.

According to liberal feminists, females are less delinquent than males because their social roles provide fewer opportunities to commit crime. Critical feminists hold that gender inequality stems from the unequal power of men and women and the subsequent exploitation of women by men.

Some critics believe that girls, more than boys, are still disadvantaged if their behavior is viewed as morally incorrect by government officials or if they are considered beyond parental control. Girls may still be subject to harsh punishments if they are considered dangerously immoral.

KEY TERMS

masculinity hypothesis, p. 156

gender-schema theory, p. 159

chivalry hypothesis, p. 162

precocious sexuality, p. 163

liberal feminism, p. 172

critical feminism, p. 172

power-control theory, p. 174

egalitarian families, p. 174

sex trafficking, p. 175

QUESTIONS FOR REVIEW

1. Compare and contrast the chivalry and masculinity hypotheses.

2. Discuss the elements of gender-schema theory.

3. According to liberal feminists, what are the factors that cause females to be less delinquent than males?

4. List five factors that trait theorists believe prevent girls from engaging in stereotypical male behaviors.

5. Address the issue of PMS and delinquency. What was Katharina Dalton's position on this issue?

6. List the elements of power-control theory.

7. Explain the difference between an egalitarian and a paternalistic family structure.

8. List three cognitive differences between males and females.

9. Define human trafficking and discuss its current extent.

10. What evidence suggests that girls are treated more harshly by the juvenile justice system than boys?

QUESTIONS FOR DISCUSSION

1. Are girls delinquent for different reasons than boys? Do girls have a unique set of problems?

2. As sex roles become more homogenous, do you believe female delinquency will become identical to male delinquency in rate and type?

3. Does the sexual double standard still exist?

4. Are lower-class girls more strictly supervised than upper- and middle-class girls? Is control stratified across class lines?

5. Are girls the victims of unfairness at the hands of the justice system or do they benefit from chivalry?

APPLYING WHAT YOU HAVE LEARNED

As the principal of a northeastern junior high school, you get a call from a parent who is disturbed because he has heard a rumor that the student literary digest plans to publish a story with a sexual theme. The work is written by a junior high school girl who became pregnant during the year and underwent an abortion. You ask for and receive a copy of the narrative.

The girl's story is actually a cautionary tale of young love that results in an unwanted pregnancy. The author details the abusive home life that led her to engage in an intimate relationship with another student, her pregnancy, her conflict with her parents, her decision to abort, and the emotional turmoil that the incident created. She tells students to use contraception if they are sexually active and recommends appropriate types of birth control. There is nothing provocative or sexually explicit in the work.

Some teachers argue that girls should not be allowed to read this material, because it has sexual content from which they must be protected, and that in a sense it advocates defiance of parents. Also, some parents may object to a story about precocious sexuality because they fear it may encourage their children to experiment. Such behavior is linked to delinquency and drug abuse. Those who advocate publication believe that girls have a right to read about such important issues and decide on their own course of action.

Writing Assignment: Write a memo back to the complaining parent outlining your decision on whether you will allow the article to be published. Be sure to address legal and social issues. Do you believe that young people should be protected from such material? Is there any evidence that it would cause them damage?

GROUPWORK

Divide the class into two groups, one male, the other female. Ask each group to list areas in which there exists gender inequality and what form that inequality takes. Compare the answers. Is there gender equality in the perceptions of gender inequality?

CHAPTER SEVEN

The Family and Delinquency

© Ghislain & Marie David de Lossy/Getty Images

LEARNING OBJECTIVES

After reading this chapter you should:

1. Be familiar with the link between family relationships and juvenile delinquency.
2. Understand the complex association between family conflict and delinquent behavior.
3. Discuss the nature and extent of child abuse.
4. Be familiar with the child protection system and the stages in the child protection process.
5. Know the various positions in the delinquency–child maltreatment debate.

CHAPTER OUTLINE

Ayden's Story

Ayden is a 15-year-old male referred to the county juvenile justice system for disorderly conduct in the family home and possession of marijuana. Ayden and his family had been evicted from their apartment after the last of many police calls and the family was staying at a local homeless shelter. There was a history of domestic violence in the home as well as other contacts with law enforcement, generally related to family discord.

Ayden's father and mother both had histories of significant alcohol abuse, and Ayden had spent part of his childhood in and out of foster homes due to chronic neglect issues. The local child protection agency had assessed the home on a number of occasions, and records indicated that the living conditions of the home were often found to be deplorable. Ayden and his siblings would be removed from the home while it was being cleaned up, but would then return home again. Ayden's school records indicated that teachers had been concerned about his hygiene as well as a lack of regular attendance. Ayden's grades were poor overall, and he appeared unmotivated academically. Ayden's teachers reported that he was pleasant in the classroom and did not demonstrate any behavioral concerns at school.

Ayden's parents reported to the juvenile justice social worker that Ayden was defiant and belligerent toward them. They described him as "angry all the time" and "unwilling to follow any rules." Although the family was staying at the local homeless shelter, the parents reported that Ayden's whereabouts were unknown to them. They suspected that he was staying with friends but were not really sure. They stated that Ayden was "almost an adult" and "at this point he can do what he wants." They both denied their long-term problem was alcohol and appeared to have very little insight regarding the family system and issues.

Ayden was indeed staying with friends as well as continuing to attend school. The social worker made contact with Ayden at school and began to help him open up about his personal and family situation. Upon further discussion, Ayden disclosed a history of physical abuse by both his parents as well as the neglect. Ayden acknowledged his frustration toward his parents and indicated willingness for treatment related to his anger management and drug use concerns. Due to the new child maltreatment reports as well as the delinquency petition, Ayden was placed in a treatment foster home where he received a number of needed services and interventions. The treatment foster parents chosen for Ayden had successfully worked with many young men with similar backgrounds and delinquent behavior. The foster parents and Ayden also received additional weekly supports in the home, which included addressing behavioral issues, school concerns, family relationships, substance abuse, and anger management.

Within six months of placement, Ayden's grades were improving and he was doing well in his outpatient treatment programs for anger management and substance use. He reported feeling more stable and less focused on his parent's chronic alcohol issues. He also reported feeling relieved that he lived in a home with significantly less chaos. To date, Ayden has not had any further referrals for delinquent behavior. Ayden's parents were repeatedly offered a number of services but have refused to engage with Ayden's treatment or participate in their own.

Many experts believe that family dysfunction is a key ingredient in the development of the emotional deficits that eventually lead to long-term social problems.[1] Interactions between parents and children, and among siblings, provide opportunities for children to acquire or inhibit antisocial behavior patterns.[2] Even kids who are predisposed toward delinquency, because of personality traits such as low self-control and impulsive personality, may find their life circumstances improved and their involvement with antisocial behavior diminished if they are exposed to positive and effective parenting.[3] Others born into troubled, dysfunctional families, such as Ayden's, find that their life path is blocked before they ever begin their life's journey. When Peggy Giordano studied the lives of kids whose parents did time in jail, she found that family problems such as unstable housing, personal stress, and performing poorly in school were actually present before the parents' time in jail, and continued once they were released from incarceration. Economically disadvantaged women partnered up with highly antisocial men, and were locked into a pattern of continued drug use and antisocial behaviors. They created a family climate of extreme unpredictability and stress for their children; family problems were inter-generational. Over time, many of these kids growing up in dysfunctional families find themselves in trouble with the law and are doomed to produce another generation of children who face the same sort and level of social problems.[4]

In contrast, good parenting lowers the risk of delinquency for children living in high-crime areas. Children are able to resist the temptation of the streets if they receive fair discipline and support from parents who provide them with positive role models.[5] Even children in affluent families may be at risk to delinquency if they are being raised in a household characterized by abuse and conflict.[6] Ayden may be one of the lucky ones because his foster parents are supportive and caring, but not all kids with dysfunctional families are so lucky.

The assumed relationship between delinquency and family life is critical today, because the American family is undergoing change. Extended families containing aunts, uncles, cousins, and grandparents living in close contact—once common-place—are now for the most part anachronisms. In their place is the **nuclear family**, described as a "dangerous hothouse of emotions," because of the close contact between parents and children; in these families, problems are unrelieved by contact with other kin living nearby.[7]

And now the nuclear family is showing signs of breakdown. About half of all marriages may one day end in divorce, leading to remarriage and blended families that may be even more unstable.[8] Much of the responsibility for child rearing is delegated to television and day care providers. Despite these changes, some families are able to continue functioning as healthy units, producing well-adjusted children. Others have crumbled under the stress, severely damaging their children.[9] This is particularly true when child abuse and neglect become part of family life.

Because these issues are critical for understanding delinquency, this chapter is devoted to an analysis of the family's role in producing or inhibiting delinquency. We first cover the changing face of the American family. We will review the way family structure and function influence delinquent behavior. The relationships between child abuse, neglect, and delinquency are covered in some depth.

THE CHANGING AMERICAN FAMILY

The so-called traditional family—with a male breadwinner and a female who cares for the home—is a thing of the past. Changing sex roles have created a family where women play a much greater role in the economic process; this has created a more egalitarian family structure. More than three-quarters of all mothers of school-age children are employed, up from 50 percent in 1970 and 40 percent in 1960.[10] The changing economic structure may be reflected in shifting sex roles. Fathers are now spending more time with their children on workdays than they did 20 years ago, and mothers are spending somewhat less time.[11]

Family Makeup

After a decades-long decline, only two-thirds of underage minors now live in two-parent families:

- Of the 75 million children younger than 18, most (69 percent) live with two parents, while another 27 percent live with one parent and 4 percent with no parents. Of those children who live with two parents, 92 percent live with two biological or two adoptive parents.
- Among the children who live with one parent, 87 percent live with their mother.
- Of the children living with no parents present, 57 percent live with at least one grandparent.

nuclear family A family unit composed of parents and their children. This smaller family structure is subject to great stress due to the intense, close contact between parents and children.

- Today, 23 percent of married couple family groups with children younger than age 15 had a stay-at-home mother. This proportion decreased in the last few years during the recession. In 2007—before the recession began—the corresponding figure was 24 percent.[12]

Significant racial differences in family makeup still exist: the percentage of children living with two parents varies by race and ethnic origin. At last count, 75 percent of white non-Hispanic, 61 percent of Hispanic, and 35 percent of black children lived with two married parents. The proportion of Hispanic children living with two married parents decreased from 75 percent in 1980 to 61 percent in 2010.

As Figure 7.1 shows, the number of two-parent households has been in decline for more than three decades.

Teen Moms/Single Moms. Today, more than 90 percent of teens who give birth are unmarried, compared with 62 percent in 1980.[13] Living in a single-parent home, especially one headed by an unmarried teenage mother, has long been associated with difficulties for both the mother and her child. As you may recall (Chapter 1), kids born into single-parent homes are more likely to live in poverty and to experience long-term physical and social difficulties.[14] Very often these conditions are interactive: teen moms suffer social problems, which in turn have a negative effect on their children. Research shows that by age 14, when compared to the children of older moms, the offspring of teen mothers were more likely to have disturbed psychological behavior, poorer school performance, poorer reading ability, were involved with the criminal justice system, and were more likely to smoke and drink on a regular basis. However, the connection between teen moms and troubled children flows through their economic circumstances—those without economic means were much more likely to produce troubled kids than those who enjoyed support, financial and otherwise, from their families.[15]

While teenage moms still experience difficulties, there are significantly fewer of them in the population than there were 20 years ago. Availability of birth control and the legalization of abortion has helped reduce the number of pregnant teens. However, there remains substantial racial and ethnic disparities among the birth rates for adolescents ages 15 to 17. Today, the teen birth rate per 1,000 ranges from 7.0 for Asians to 41.0 for Hispanics. While this disparity is troubling, the birth rates for black, non-Hispanic, white non-Hispanic, and Asian or Pacific Islander females ages 15 to 17 dropped by about half or more since 1991; the decline has been experienced by girls in all racial and ethnic groups.

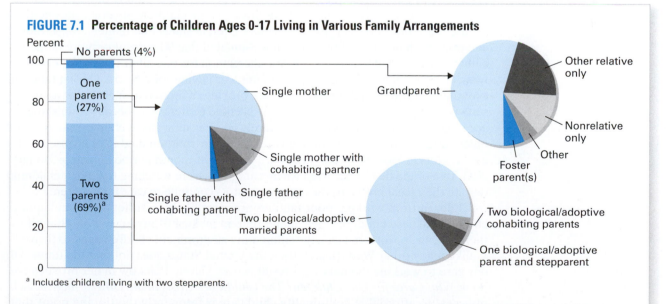

FIGURE 7.1 **Percentage of Children Ages 0–17 Living in Various Family Arrangements**

a Includes children living with two stepparents.

Source: *America's Children: Key National Indicators of Well-Being, 2011*, www.childstats.gov/pdf/ac2011/ac_11.pdf (accessed August 1, 2012).

DO POOR FAMILIES CREATE BAD KIDS?

Rand Conger is one of the nation's leading experts on family life. For the past two decades, he has been involved with four major community studies that have examined the influence of economic stress on families, children, and adolescents; in sum, these studies involve almost 1,500 families and over 4,000 individual family members, who represent a diverse cross-section of society. The extensive information that has been collected on all of these families over time includes reports by family members, videotaped discussions in the home, and data from schools and other community agencies.

One thing that Conger and his associates have learned is that in all of these different types of families, economic stress appears to have a harmful effect on parents and children. According to his "Family Stress Model" of economic hardship, such factors as low income and income loss increase parents' sadness, pessimism about the future, anger, despair, and withdrawal from other family members. Economic stress has this impact on parents' social-emotional functioning through the daily pressures it

Child Care

Today about 48 percent of children ages 0 to 4 with employed mothers are primarily cared for by a relative—their father, grandparent, sibling, or other relative—while she is at work. Twenty-four percent spend the most amount of time in a center-based arrangement (day care, nursery school, preschool, or Head Start). Fourteen percent are primarily cared for by a nonrelative in a home-based environment, such as a family day care provider, nanny, babysitter, or au pair.[16]

Charged with caring for many of these children is a day care system whose workers are often paid minimum wage. Of special concern are "family day care homes," in which a single provider takes care of three to nine children. Several states neither license nor monitor these private providers. Even in states that mandate registration and inspection of day care providers, it is estimated that 90 percent or more of the facilities operate "underground." It is not uncommon for one adult to care for eight infants, an impossible task regardless of training or feelings of concern. During times of economic downturn, unlicensed child care provides a more reasonable alternative to state regulated and therefore more costly licensed centers. And because punishments are typically a small fine, prosecutors rarely go after unlicensed child care operators unless tragedy strikes. Such was the case when four children died in unlicensed child care centers in Jackson County, Missouri, in an eight-month period ending in January 2011. Two of the deaths occurred where caregivers were watching too many children; despite their legal problems the center operators continue to care for children.[17]

Children from working poor families are most likely to suffer from inadequate child care. These children often spend time in makeshift arrangements that allow their parents to work, but lack the stimulating environment children need to thrive.[18] Unlike many other Western countries, the United States does not provide universal day care to working mothers. As a result, writes Valerie Polakow in her provocative book *Who Cares for Our Children? The Child Care Crisis in the Other America*, lack of access to affordable high-quality child care is frequently the tipping point that catapults a family into poverty, joblessness, and homelessness—a constant threat to the well-being of lower-class women and children.[19]

creates for them, such as being unable to pay bills or acquire basic necessities (adequate food, housing, clothing, and medical care). As parents become more emotionally distressed, they tend to interact with one another and their children in a more irritable and less supportive fashion. These patterns of behavior increase instability in the marriage and also disrupt effective parenting practices, such as monitoring children's activities and using consistent and appropriate disciplinary strategies. Marital instability and disrupted parenting, in turn, increase children's risk of suffering developmental problems, such as depression, substance abuse, and engaging in delinquent behaviors. These economic stress processes also decrease children's ability to function in a competent manner in school and with peers.

The findings also show, however, that parents who remain supportive of one another, and who demonstrate effective problem-solving skills in spite of hardship, can disrupt this negative process and shield their children and themselves from these adverse consequences of economic stress. These parenting skills can be taught and used by human service professionals to assist families experiencing economic pressure or similar stresses in their lives.

Writing Assignment Write an essay on the subject, "What are the most important parenting skills and what is the best way to teach them to young parents?"

CRITICAL THINKING

To help deal with these problems, Conger advocates support for social policies that adequately aid families during stressful times as they recover from downturns in the economy. He also advocates educating parents about effective strategies for managing the economic, emotional, and family relationship challenges they will face when hardship occurs. What would you add to the mix to improve family functioning in America?

Sources: Rand D. Conger and Katherine Jewsbury Conger, "Understanding the Processes Through Which Economic Hardship Influences Families and Children," in *Handbook of Families and Poverty*, ed. D. Russell Crane and Tim B. Heaton (Thousand Oaks, CA: Sage Publications, 2008), pp. 64–81; Iowa State University, Institute for Social and Behavioral Research, Rand Conger, www.isbr.iastate.edu/staff/Personals/rdconger/ (accessed August 1, 2012).

Economic Stress

The family is also undergoing economic stress. As you may recall (Chapter 1), about 6 million American youth live in poverty. The majority live in substandard housing without adequate health care, nutrition, or child care. Those whose incomes place them above the poverty line are deprived of government assistance. Recent political trends suggest that the social "safety net" is under attack and that poor families can expect less government aid in the coming years.

Will this economic pressure be reduced in the future? In addition to recent economic upheaval and high unemployment rates, the family will remain under stress because of changes in the population makeup. Lifespans are lengthening, and as a result the number of senior citizens is on the rise. There are currently about 6 million people over 85 in the United States, a number that will rise to 20 million by 2050.[20] As people retire, there will be fewer workers to cover the costs of Social Security, medical care, and nursing-home care. Because the elderly will require a greater percentage of the nation's income for their care, there will be less money available to care for needy children. These costs will put greater economic stress on families. Voter sentiment has an impact on the allocation of public funds, and there is concern that an older generation, worried about health care costs, may be reluctant to spend tax dollars on at-risk kids. The effect of economic stress on families is the topic of the accompanying Focus on Delinquency feature.

THE FAMILY'S INFLUENCE ON DELINQUENCY

The family is the primary unit in which children learn the values and attitudes that guide their actions throughout their lives. Family stress, disruption, or change can have a long-lasting affect. In contrast, effective parenting can help neutralize the effect of both individual (e.g., emotional problems) and social (e.g., delinquent peers) forces, which promote delinquent behaviors.[21]

Four categories of family dysfunction seem to promote delinquent behavior: families disrupted by spousal conflict or breakup (family breakup), families involved in interpersonal conflict (family conflict), ineffective parents who lack proper parenting skills (family effectiveness), and families that contain deviant parents who may transmit their behavior to their children (family deviance) (see Figure 7.2).[22] These factors may also interact: parents involved in crime and deviance may be more likely to experience family conflict, child neglect, and marital breakup. We now turn to the specific types of family problems that have been linked to delinquent behavior. **CHECKPOINTS**

Family Breakup

Research indicates that parents whose marriage is secure produce children who are secure and independent.[23] In contrast, research conducted in both in the United States and abroad shows that children raised in homes with one or both parents absent may be prone to antisocial behavior.[24] The connection seems self-evident, because a child is first socialized at home. Any disjunction in an orderly family structure could be expected to have a negative impact on the child.

The **broken home**–delinquency relationship is important because, if current trends continue, less than half of all children born today will live continuously with their own mother and father throughout childhood. And because stepfamilies, or so-called **blended families**, are less stable than families consisting of two biological parents, an increasing number of children will experience family breakup two or even three times during childhood.[25]

Children who have experienced family breakup are more likely to demonstrate behavior problems and hyperactivity than children in intact families.[26] Family breakup is often associated with conflict, hostility, and aggression; children of divorce are suspected of having lax supervision, weakened attachment, and greater susceptibility to peer pressure.[27] One study of more than 4,000 youths in Denver, Pittsburgh, and Rochester found that the more often children are forced to go through family transitions, the more likely they are to engage in delinquent activity.[28]

broken home Home in which one or both parents are absent due to divorce or separation. Children in such an environment may be prone to antisocial behavior.

blended families Nuclear families that are the product of divorce and remarriage, blending one parent from each of two families and their combined children into one family unit.

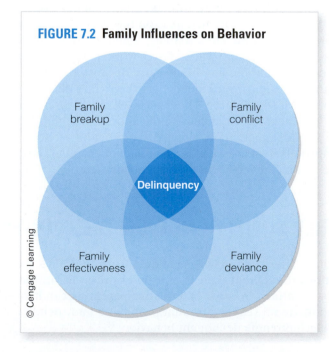

FIGURE 7.2 Family Influences on Behavior

Family breakup

Family conflict

Delinquency

Family effectiveness

Family deviance

© Cengage Learning

The Effects of Divorce. In her study of the effects of parental absence on children, sociologist Sara McLanahan found that children who grow up apart from their biological fathers typically do less well than children who grow up with both biological parents. They are less likely to finish high school and attend college, less likely to find and keep a steady job, and more likely to become teen mothers. Although most children who grow up with a single parent do quite well, differences between children in one- and two-parent families are significant, and there is fairly good evidence that father absence per se is responsible for some social problems.[29]

The McLanahan research has been supported by other studies showing that divorce is in fact related to delinquency and status offending, especially if a child had a close relationship with the parent who is forced to leave the home.[30] Among the research findings on the association between divorce and delinquency are the following:

- Children growing up in families disrupted by parental death are better adjusted than children of divorce. Parental absence is not per se a cause of antisocial behavior.

- Remarriage does not lessen the effects of divorce on youth: children living with a stepparent exhibit (a) as many problems as youths in divorce situations and (b) considerably more problems than do children living with both biological parents.

- Continued contact with the noncustodial parent has little effect on a child's well-being.

- Evidence that the behavior of children of divorce improves over time is inconclusive.

- Post-divorce conflict between parents is related to child maladjustment.

- Parental divorce raises the likelihood of teenage marriage.[31]

The effects of divorce also seem gender-, race- and ethnicity-specific:

- Boys seem to be more affected by the post-divorce absence of the father. In post-divorce situations, fathers seem less likely to be around to solve problems, to discuss standards of conduct, or to enforce discipline. A divorced father who remains actively involved in his child's life reduces his son's chances of delinquency.

- Girls are more affected by both the quality of the mother's parenting and post-divorce parental conflict. It is possible that extreme levels of parental conflict may serve as a model to young girls coping with the aftermath of their parents' separation.[32]

- There are distinct racial and ethnic differences in the impact of divorce/separation on youth. Some groups (i.e., Hispanics, Asians) have been raised in cultures where divorce is rare, and parents have less experience in developing childrearing practices that buffer the effects of family breakup on adolescent problem behavior.[33]

Of course, divorce does not always produce delinquency, and many single moms and dads raise perfectly fine children. In some cases, divorce reduces stress and insulates kids from exposure to harmful parents. When Sara Jaffee and her associates studied the quality of marriage, they found that in general the less time fathers lived with their children, the more conduct problems their children experienced. However, when fathers themselves engaged in high levels of antisocial behavior, having contact with their children produced negative outcomes; their kids displayed more conduct problems than the norm. Staying married, Jaffee concludes, may not be the answer to the problems faced by children unless parents can refrain from deviant behaviors and become reliable sources of emotional and economic support.[34]

Family Conflict

Not all unhappy marriages end in divorce; some continue in an atmosphere of conflict. Intrafamily conflict is a common experience in many American families.[35] The link between parental conflict and delinquency was established more than

Family stress and breakup have been linked to substance abuse and delinquency. Here, Tera Burbank talks to a friend on the phone after an argument with her oldest daughter in Las Vegas. Burbank and her husband, John Clark, epitomize the dreadful economic situation these days in Nevada, where a once-mighty construction boom has given way to a historic recession and a record 15 percent unemployment rate. Burbank and Clark are construction workers who have been out of work for more than a year. They live off unemployment and student loans. Bills go unpaid and minor spats escalate into tense threats of divorce. Their daughters are performing poorly at school, and guidance counselors and teachers blame stress.

50 years ago when F. Ivan Nye found that a child's perception of his or her parents' marital happiness was a significant predictor of delinquency.[36] Contemporary studies also find that children who grow up in maladapted homes and witness discord or violence later exhibit emotional disturbance and behavior problems.[37] There seems to be little difference between the behavior of children who merely *witness* **intrafamily violence** and those who are its *victims*.[38] In fact, some research efforts show that observing the abuse of a family member may be more significant determinant of delinquency than being the actual target of child abuse.[39] In one recent study, family expert Lynette Renner found that children who experienced any form of family violence were more likely to act out than those who avoided relational conflict. However, Renner found that children who experienced indirect types of family violence, such as exposure to the physical abuse of a sibling, were more likely to externalize behavior scores than children who experienced direct maltreatment and child physical abuse.[40]

Research efforts have consistently supported the relationship between family conflict, hostility, and delinquency.[41] Adolescents who are incarcerated report having grown up in dysfunctional homes.[42] Parents of beyond-control youngsters have been found to be inconsistent rule-setters, to be less likely to show interest in their children, and to display high levels of hostile detachment.[43]

Although damaged parent–child relationships are associated with delinquency, it is difficult to assess this relationship. It is often assumed that preexisting family problems cause delinquency, but it may also be true that children who act out put enormous stress on a family. Kids who are conflict prone may actually help to destabilize households. To avoid escalation of their child's aggression, parents may give in to his or her demands. The child learns that aggression pays off.[44] Parents may feel overwhelmed and shut their child out of their lives. Adolescent misbehavior may be a precursor of family conflict; strife leads to more adolescent misconduct, producing an endless cycle of family stress and delinquency.[45]

intrafamily violence An environment of discord and conflict within the family. Children who grow up in dysfunctional homes often exhibit delinquent behaviors, having learned at a young age that aggression pays off.

Which is worse, growing up in a home marked by conflict or growing up in a broken home? Research shows that children in both broken homes and high-conflict intact homes were worse off than children in low-conflict, intact families.[46] However, even when parents are divorced, kids who maintain attachments to their parents are less likely to engage in delinquency than those who are alienated and detached.[47]

Bad Parents or Bad Kids? Which comes first, bad parents or bad kids? Does parental conflict cause delinquency, or do delinquents create family conflict? David Huh and colleagues surveyed nearly 500 adolescent girls from eight different schools to determine their perceived parental support and control and whether they engaged in problem behaviors such as lying, stealing, running away, or substance abuse.[48] Huh and his colleagues found little evidence that poor parenting is a direct cause of children's misbehavior problems or that it escalates misbehavior. Rather, their results suggest that children's problem behaviors undermine parenting effectiveness. Increases in adolescent behavior problems, such as substance abuse, resulted in decreases in parental control and support. Low parental control played a small role in escalating behavior problems. Huh suggests it is possible that the parents of adolescents who consistently misbehave may become more tolerant of their behavior and give up on attempts at control. As their kids' behaviors become increasingly threatening, parents may detach and reject adolescents exhibiting problem behavior.

Huh is not alone in these findings. Recent research by Martha Gault-Sherman shows that attachment to parents weakens after kids get involved in delinquency.[49] But even then, parents may not abandon their delinquent kids: Sonja Siennick found that young adult offenders receive more parental financial assistance than do their non-offending peers and even their own non-offending siblings. Offenders' life circumstances trigger parental assistance even though they have been involved in crime. Siennick's research shows that parents do not give up on their troubled teens.[50]

Genetics and Environment. In her provocative book *The Nurture Assumption*, psychologist Judith Rich Harris questions the cherished belief that parents play an important role in a child's upbringing.[51] Instead of family influence, Harris claims that genetics and environment determine to a large extent how a child turns out. Children's own temperament and peer relations shape their behavior and modify the characteristics they were born with; their interpersonal relations determine the kind of people they will be when they mature.

Harris posits that parenting skills may be irrelevant to children's future success. Most parents don't have a single childrearing style, and they may treat each child in the family differently. They are more permissive with their mild-mannered kids and more strict and punitive with those who are temperamental or defiant. Even if every child were treated the same in a family, this would not explain why siblings raised in the same family under relatively similar conditions turn out so different. Children sent to day care are quite similar to those who remain at home; having working parents seems to have little long-term effect. Family structure also does not seem to matter: adults who grew up in one-parent homes are as likely to be successful as those who were raised in two-parent households.

In addition to genetics, the child's total social environment is the other key influence that shapes behavior. Kids who act one way at home may be totally different at school or with their peers. Some who are mild mannered around the house are hell raisers in the school yard, whereas others who bully their siblings are docile with friends. Children may conform to parental expectations at home, but leave those expectations behind in their own social environment. Children develop their own culture with unique traditions, words, rules, and activities, which often conflict with parental and adult values.

Family Effectiveness

Children raised by parents who lack proper parenting skills are more at risk for delinquency than those whose parents who are supportive and effectively control their children in a noncoercive fashion.[52] Some parents are authoritative, both demanding and controlling, but also warm, receptive to their children's needs and willing to communicate, to explain their rules and listen to their children's opinions about those rules; their children tend to be self-reliant, self-controlled, and content. Others are authoritarian who tend to be demanding and highly controlling, while at the same time detached and unreceptive to their children's needs; they create arbitrary rules and expect them to be obeyed without complaint or question; their children are discontented, withdrawn, and distrustful. Some parents are permissive, warm, and receptive to their children's needs, but place few boundaries and establish few rules; their kids are needy and lack self-control. Parents who are overly authoritarian may lose legitimacy with their offspring and despite their controlling efforts raise delinquent kids. In contrast, those who are authoritative are more highly respected; their kids are less delinquent than average.[53]

Delinquency will be reduced if parents provide the type of structure that integrates children into families while giving them the ability to assert their individuality and regulate their own behavior, a phenomenon referred to as **parental efficacy**.[54] In some cultures, emotional support from the mother is critical, whereas in others the father's support remains the key factor.[55] What are the elements that distinguish effective and ineffective families?

WHAT DOES THIS MEAN TO ME?

▶ **Do Teens Really Listen?** President Harry S. Truman once said, "I have found the best way to give advice to your children is to find out what they want and then advise them to do it."

Do you agree with President Truman? Are teens only willing to listen to what they want to hear? And does that explain why they become risk takers and why punishment does not seem to work?

Harsh Discipline. While most professionals have come out in protest against corporal punishment of children both in school and at home, about 94 percent of parents still continue to support the use of corporal punishment in disciplining children.[56] A recent national survey by Stephanie Hicks-Pass found that parents who advocate physical punishment believe it is a necessary aspect of disciplining practices that produces well-behaved children. Opponents state that physical discipline harms children psychologically and interferes with their development.

While the debate continues, there is growing evidence of a "violence begetting violence" cycle. Children who are subject to even minimal amounts of physical punishment may be more likely to use violence themselves.[57]

Opponents of physical punishment believe that it weakens the bond between parents and children, lowers the children's self-esteem, and undermines their faith in justice. It is possible that physical punishment encourages children to become more secretive and dishonest.[58] Overly strict discipline may have an even more insidious link to antisocial behaviors: abused children have a higher risk of neurological dysfunction than those who are not abused, and brain abnormalities have been linked to violent crime.[59]

Inconsistent Supervision. Evidence also exists that inconsistent supervision can promote delinquency. Early research by F. Ivan Nye found that mothers who threatened discipline but failed to carry it out were more likely to have delinquent children than those who were consistent in their discipline.[60]

Nye's early efforts have been supported by research showing a strong association between ineffective or negligent supervision and a child's involvement in delinquency.[61] The data show that youths who believe their parents care little about their activities are more likely to engage in criminal acts than those who believe their actions will be closely monitored.[62] Kids who are not closely supervised spend more time out in the community with their friends and are more likely to get into trouble. Poorly supervised kids may be more prone to acting impulsively and are therefore less able to employ self-control to restrain their activities.[63]

Poor Communications. Poor child–parent communications have been related to dysfunctional activities such as running away, and in all too many instances these children enter the ranks of homeless street youths who get involved in theft and prostitution to survive.[64] In contrast, even children who appear to be at risk are better able to resist involvement in delinquent activity when they report that they can communicate with

parental efficacy Families in which parents are able to integrate their children into the household unit while at the same time helping them assert their individuality and regulate their own behavior.

their parents.[65] Holding a "my way or the highway" orientation and telling kids that "as long as you live in my house you will obey my rules" does little to improve communications and may instead produce kids who are rebellious and crime prone.[66]

Mother's Employment. Parents who closely supervise their children and have close ties with them help reduce the likelihood of adolescent delinquent behavior.[67] Some critics have suggested that even in intact homes, a working mother who is unable to adequately supervise her children provides the opportunity for delinquency.[68]

The association between mother's employment and delinquency is far from certain. There is some evidence that the children of working moms are more prone to delinquency.[69] Other research efforts have found that a mother's employment may have little effect on youthful misbehavior, especially when the children are adequately supervised.[70]

Resource Dilution. The more children in a family, the greater the chance of youthful misbehavior. Large families find that their resources are spread too thin (**resource dilution**). There is less money to go around and greater economic stress. Parents have less time to help kids with their schoolwork; resource dilution has been linked to educational underachievement, long considered a correlate of delinquency.[71]

Middle children may suffer the most from resource dilution because by definition they are most likely to live in larger families (after all, you need at least two siblings to be a middle child).[72] Larger families are more likely to produce delinquents than smaller ones, and middle children are more likely to engage in delinquent acts than first- or last-born children.

Family Deviance

A number of studies have found that parental deviance has a powerful influence on delinquent behavior.[73] The effects can be long-term and intergenerational: the children of deviant parents produce delinquent children themselves.[74] Fathers with a long history of criminality produce sons who are also likely to get arrested for crimes.[75] The effect can be enhanced if deviant parents are arrested, convicted, and incarcerated. Adolescents whose parents are imprisoned are more likely to later become involved in theft offenses.[76] Kids whose fathers were incarcerated are more likely to suffer an arrest by age 25 than the offspring of conventional, law-abiding parents.[77]

Some of the most important results on the influence of parental deviance were gathered by British criminologist David Farrington, whose research involves longitudinal data he and his colleagues have obtained from a number of ongoing projects, including the Cambridge Youth Survey and the Cambridge Study in Delinquent Development (CSDD). These include:

- A significant number of delinquent youths have criminal fathers. About 8 percent of the sons of noncriminal fathers became chronic offenders, compared to 37 percent of youths with criminal fathers.[78]

- School yard bullying may be both inter- and intragenerational. Bullies have children who bully others, and these "second-generation bullies" grow up to become the fathers of children who are also bullies (see Chapter 9 for more on bullying in the school yard).[79] Thus, one family may have a grandfather, father, and son who are or were school yard bullies.[80]

- Kids whose parents go to prison are much more likely to be at risk of delinquency then children of nonincarcerated parents.

The cause of intergenerational deviance is uncertain. A number of factors may play a role:

- *Genetic factors.* The link between parental deviance and child misbehavior may be genetic.[81] Parents of delinquent youth have been found to suffer neurological conditions linked to antisocial behaviors and these conditions may be inherited genetically.[82]

resource dilution A condition that occurs when parents have such large families that their resources, such as time and money, are spread too thin, causing lack of familial support and control.

There is a strong association between parental and children's deviance. In this photo from surveillance videotape in a Bedford, New Hampshire, store, a woman with her daughter (behind the counter) and her son (at left) are shown in the process of stealing more than $2,000 worth of jewelry. The woman turned herself in after Bedford police made the video public.

WWW

Helping clients deal with issues of teen pregnancy and other family concerns, **Planned Parenthood** is the world's largest and oldest voluntary family planning organization. To find their website, visit the Criminal Justice CourseMate at CengageBrain.com, then access the Web Links for this chapter.

- *Substance abuse.* Children of drug-abusing parents are more likely to get involved in drug abuse and delinquency than the children of nonabusers.[83] This link might have a biological basis: parental substance abuse can produce children with neurological impairments that are related to delinquency.[84]

- *Reduced parenting skills.* Deviant parents are the ones least likely to have close relationships with their offspring. They exhibit lower levels of effective parenting skills. One reason: parents involved in deviant and/or criminal behavior are more likely to have substance abuse problems.[85]

- *Parental absence.* Children may suffer the affects of parental absence when their criminal parents are incarcerated. Absence due to incarceration has a greater effect on kids than parental separation due to illness, death, or divorce.[86]

- *Stigma.* The association between parental deviance and children's delinquency may be related to labeling and stigma. Social control agents may be quick to fix a delinquent label on the children of known law violators, increasing the likelihood that they will pick up an "official" delinquent label.[87] The resulting stigma increases the chances that they may fall into a delinquent career.[88]

Sibling Influences. Research shows that if one sibling is a delinquent, there is a significant likelihood that his or her siblings will engage in delinquent behaviors.[89] For example, if an adolescent takes drugs and engages in delinquent behavior, so too will his brother or sister.[90] A number of interpretations of these data are possible:

- Siblings who live in the same environment are influenced by similar social and economic factors.

- Deviance is genetically determined, and the traits that cause one sibling to engage in delinquency are shared by his or her brother or sister.

- Deviant siblings grow closer because of shared interests. It is possible that the relationship is due to personal interactions: older siblings are imitated by younger siblings. **CHECKPOINTS**

Looking Back to Ayden's Story

Ayden's father and mother both had histories of significant alcohol abuse, and Ayden had spent part of his childhood in and out of foster homes due to chronic neglect issues.

CRITICAL THINKING Considering the family influences on delinquency, which do you think had the greatest impact on Ayden's misbehaviors? Is it possible to single out one factor or do they all contribute?

CHILD ABUSE AND NEGLECT

Concern about the quality of family life has increased because of reports that many children are physically abused or neglected by their parents and that this treatment has serious consequences for their behavior over the life course. Because of this topic's importance, the remainder of this chapter is devoted to the issue of child abuse and neglect and its relationship with delinquent behavior.

Historical Foundation

Child abuse and neglect are not a modern phenomenon. Maltreatment of children has occurred throughout history. Some concern for the negative effects of such maltreatment was voiced in the eighteenth century in the United States, but concerted efforts to deal with the problem did not begin until 1874.

In that year, residents of a New York City apartment building reported to public health nurse Etta Wheeler that a child in one of the apartments was being abused by her stepmother. The nurse found a young child named Mary Ellen Wilson who had been repeatedly beaten and was malnourished from a diet of bread and water. Even though the child was seriously ill, the police agreed that the law entitled the parents to raise Mary Ellen as they saw fit. The New York City Department of Charities claimed it had no custody rights over Mary Ellen.

According to legend, Mary Ellen's removal from her parents had to be arranged through the Society for the Prevention of Cruelty to Animals (SPCA) on the ground that she was a member of the animal kingdom. The truth, however, is less sensational: Mary Ellen's case was heard by a judge. Because the child needed protection, she was placed in an orphanage.[91] The SPCA was actually founded the following year.[92]

Little research into the problems of maltreated children occurred before that of C. Henry Kempe, of the University of Colorado. In 1962, Kempe reported the results of a survey of medical and law enforcement agencies that indicated the child abuse rate was much higher than had been thought. He coined a term, **battered child syndrome**, which he applied to cases of nonaccidental injury of children by their parents or guardians.[93]

Defining Abuse and Neglect

Kempe's pioneering work has been expanded in a more generic expression of child abuse that includes neglect as well as physical abuse. Specifically, it describes any physical or emotional trauma to a child for which no reasonable explanation, such as an accident, can be found. Child abuse is generally seen as a pattern of behavior rather than a single act. The effects of a pattern of behavior are cumulative—that is, the longer the abuse continues, the more severe the effect will be.[94]

Although the terms *child abuse* and *neglect* are sometimes used interchangeably, they represent different forms of maltreatment. **Neglect** refers to deprivations children suffer at the hands of their parents (lack of food, shelter, health care, love). **Child abuse** is a more overt form of aggression against the child, one that often requires medical attention. The distinction between the terms is often unclear because, in many cases, both abuse and neglect occur simultaneously. What are the forms that abuse and neglect may take?

battered child syndrome Nonaccidental physical injury of children by their parents or guardians.

neglect Passive neglect by a parent or guardian, depriving children of food, shelter, health care, or love.

child abuse Any physical, emotional, or sexual trauma to a child, including neglecting to give proper care and attention, for which no reasonable explanation can be found.

While many accusations of abuse go unfounded, others reveal terrible mistreatment of young children. This October 7, 2009, photo shows Katelyn Pendleton leaning against her stepbrother Colby Wells in their Fort Walton Beach, Florida, home. In the spring of 2008, the young girl was at the center of an investigation of one of the worst child abuse cases Okaloosa County lawmen had ever seen. Now, she's the happily adopted daughter of Christie and Jeff Pendleton. Katelyn was born Jamie Leighanna Brooks on February 6, 1997, to Velma Hare, a woman with a long history of prostitution and drug use; her father is a registered sex offender. Hare gave the 9-year-old to a friend, Kizza Monika Lopez, who beat, starved, and tortured the girl until an anonymous tip alerted authorities to her plight.

abandonment Parents physically leave their children with the intention of completely severing the parent–child relationship.

Looking Back to Ayden's Story

Ayden's parents reported to the juvenile justice social worker that Ayden was defiant and belligerent toward them. They described him as "angry all the time" and "unwilling to follow any rules."

CRITICAL THINKING What should be done in situations where juveniles are unwilling to follow rules? Is it appropriate for the state to intervene?

- *Physical abuse* includes throwing, shooting, stabbing, burning, drowning, suffocating, biting, or deliberately disfiguring a child. Included within this category is shaken-baby syndrome (SBS), a form of child abuse affecting between 1,200 and 1,600 children every year. SBS is a collection of signs and symptoms resulting from violently shaking an infant or child.[95]

- *Physical neglect* results from parents' failure to provide adequate food, shelter, or medical care for their children, as well as failure to protect them from physical danger.

- *Emotional abuse* is manifested by constant criticism and rejection of the child.[96] Those who suffer emotional abuse have significantly lower self-esteem as adults.[97]

- *Emotional neglect* includes inadequate nurturing, inattention to a child's emotional development, and lack of concern about maladaptive behavior.

- *Abandonment* refers to the situation in which parents leave their children with the intention of severing the parent–child relationship.[98]

- *Sexual abuse* refers to the exploitation of children through rape, incest, or molestation by parents, family members, friends, or legal guardians. Sexual abuse can vary from rewarding children for sexual behavior that is inappropriate for their level of development to using force or the threat of force for the purposes of sex. It can involve children who are aware of the sexual content of their actions and others too young to have any idea what their actions mean.

The Effects of Abuse

Regardless of how it is defined, the effects of abuse can be devastating. Mental health and delinquency experts have found that abused kids experience mental and social problems across their lifespan, ranging from substance abuse to possession of a damaged personality.[99] Children who have experienced some form of maltreatment possess mental representations characterized by a devalued sense of self, mistrust of others, a tendency to perceive hostility in others in situations where the others' intentions are ambiguous, and a tendency to generate antagonistic solutions to social conflicts. Victims of abuse are prone to suffer mental illness, such as dissociative identity disorder (DID), sometimes known as multiple personality disorder. Research shows that child abuse is present in the histories of the vast majority of DID subjects.[100] Children who experience maltreatment are at increased risk for adverse health effects and behaviors across the life course, including smoking, alcoholism, drug abuse, eating disorders, severe obesity, depression, suicide, sexual promiscuity, and certain chronic diseases.[101] Maltreatment during infancy or early childhood can cause brain impairment, leading to physical, mental, and emotional problems such as sleep disturbances, panic disorder, and attention deficit hyperactivity disorder. Brain dysfunction is particularly common among victims of shaken baby syndrome (SBS). About 25 to 30 percent of infant victims with SBS die from their injuries; nonfatal consequences of SBS include varying degrees of visual impairment, motor impairment (e.g., cerebral palsy), and cognitive impairments.[102]

Psychologists suggest that maltreatment encourages children to use aggression as a means of solving problems and prevents them from feeling empathy for others. It diminishes their ability to cope with stress and makes them vulnerable to the violence in the culture. Abused children have fewer positive interactions with peers, are less well liked, and are more likely to have disturbed social interactions.[103] Not surprisingly, recent research has found that juvenile female prostitutes more often than not came from homes in which abuse, both physical and substance, was present.[104]

Sexual Abuse. In a case that made headlines, in 2011, Gerald Arthur "Jerry" Sandusky, a football coach with a 30-year career at Penn State University, was indicted and convicted on charges that he was a serial child molester. Sandusky used his position of power and trust (he was Assistant Coach of the Year in 1986 and 1999) to found the Second Mile, a nonprofit charity serving underprivileged and at-risk youth in Pennsylvania. Sandusky met his victims through the Second Mile and had forced sexual relations with them on the Penn State campus even after he had retired from coaching. When officials at Penn State found out about the abuse, they did not alert law enforcement officials, fearing the publicity would embarrass the program. On June 22, 2012, Sandusky was found guilty on 45 of the 48 charges and faces a minimum sentence of 60 years in prison.[105]

The Sandusky case and others like it are particularly serious because adolescent victims of sexual abuse are especially at risk for stress and anxiety.[106] Kids who have undergone traumatic sexual experiences have been later found to suffer psychological deficits.[107] Many run away to escape their environment, which puts them at risk for juvenile arrest and involvement with the justice system.[108] Others suffer post-traumatic mental problems, including acute stress disorders, depression, eating disorders, nightmares, anxiety, suicidal ideation, and other psychological problems.[109] This stress does not end in childhood. Children who are psychologically, sexually, or physically abused are more likely to suffer low self-esteem and be more suicidal as adults.[110] They are also placed at greater risk to be abused as adults than those who escaped childhood victimization.[111] The re-abused carry higher risks for psychological and physical problems, ranging from sexual promiscuity to increased HIV infection rates.[112] Abuse as a child may lead to despair, depression, and even homelessness as adults. One study of homeless women found that they were much more likely than other women to report childhood physical abuse, childhood sexual abuse, adult physical assault, previous sexual assault in adulthood, and a history of mental health problems.[113]

The Extent of Child Abuse

It is almost impossible to estimate the extent of child abuse. Many victims are so young that they have not learned to communicate. Some are too embarrassed or afraid to do so. Many incidents occur behind closed doors, and even when another adult witnesses inappropriate or criminal behavior, the adult may not want to get involved in a "family matter." Some indications of the severity of the problem came from a groundbreaking 1979 survey conducted by sociologists Richard Gelles and Murray Straus, who estimated that between 1.4 and 1.9 million children in the United States were subject to physical abuse from their parents.[114]

The Gelles and Straus survey was a milestone in identifying child abuse as a national phenomenon. A subsequent survey they conducted in 1988 found that the incidence of severe violence toward children had declined.[115] One reason was that parental approval of corporal punishment, which stood at 94 percent in 1968, had decreased to less than 65 percent 20 years later.[116] Recognition of the problem may have helped moderate cultural values and awakened parents to the dangers of physically disciplining children. Nonetheless, more than 1 million children were still being subjected to severe violence annually. If the definition of "severe abuse" used in the survey had included hitting with objects such as a stick or a belt, the number of child victims would have been closer to 7 million per year.

Monitoring Abuse. The Department of Health and Human Services (DHHS) has been monitoring the extent of child maltreatment through its annual survey of child protective services (CPS).[117] The DHHS survey counts victim in two ways:

- The duplicate count of child victims counts a child each time he or she was found to be a victim.
- The unique count of child victims counts a child only once regardless of the number of times he or she was found to be a victim during the reporting year.

The last data available (2010) find that using a duplicate count, 3.6 million children received a CPS investigation, or 48 children per 1,000 children in the population. Using a unique count, nearly 3 million children received a CPS response, at a rate of 40 children per 1,000 children in the population. Typically, about 20 percent of the unique investigations discover that child has been victimized in some fashion. This means that today about 700,000 are the victim of child abuse; of these, more than 50,000 are the victim of multiple (duplicate) offenses in a single year.

Though these figures seem staggering, the number and rate of abuse have actually been in decline. Fifteen years ago more than 1 million children were identified as victims of abuse or neglect nationwide, and the rate of victimization of children was approximately 15 per 1,000 children; today the 600,000 substantiated cases of child neglect/abuse amount to a rate of about 10 per 1,000 children under 18. While these results are encouraging, trends in reported child maltreatment may be more reflective of the effect budgetary cutbacks have on CPS's ability to monitor, record, and investigate reports of abuse than an actual decline in child abuse rates.

Who Are the Victims of Abuse? There is a direct association between age and abuse: victimization rates are higher for younger children than their older brothers and sisters. The youngest children are the most vulnerable to maltreatment. More than one-third of victims are under 4 years old; about two-thirds of all abuse victims are under 7 years old. In general, the rate and percentage of victimization decreases with age.

While boys and girls have an almost equal chance of being victimized, there are racial differences in the abuse rate: African American children, Pacific Islander children, and American Indian or Alaska Native children suffer child abuse rates (per 1,000 children) far higher than European American children, Hispanic children, and Asian children.

Who Are the Perpetrators of Abuse? Four-fifths of victims were maltreated by a parent either acting alone or with someone else. Nearly two-fifths of victims were maltreated by their mother acting alone, one-fifth were maltreated by their father acting alone, and one-fifth were maltreated by both parents. About 13 percent of victims were maltreated by a perpetrator who was not a parent of the child.

What Forms Does Child Abuse Take? As Figure 7.3 shows, the most common form of maltreatment is neglect, followed by physical abuse. About 10 percent of the child victims fall into the "other" category, which consists of such conditions as "abandonment," "threats of harm to the child," or "congenital drug addiction."

An additional 9 percent of maltreated children are subject to sexual abuse. Research shows that perhaps one in ten boys and one in three girls have been the victims of some form of sexual exploitation during their lifetime, including sexual abuse, prostitution, use in pornography, and molestation by adults. Many of these kids are runaways, whereas others have fled mental hospitals and foster homes; more than 50,000 are thrown out of their home by a parent or guardian and may be forced into abusive relationships as survival mechanisms.[118]

How Many Children Die from Abuse or Neglect? Child fatalities are the most tragic consequence of maltreatment. At last count, it is estimated that 1,560 children died from abuse and neglect in a single year (2010) or about 2 deaths per 100,000 children;

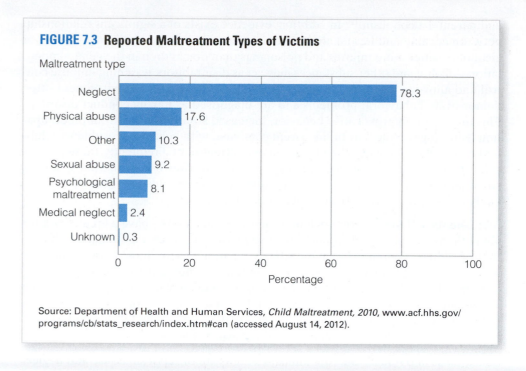

FIGURE 7.3 Reported Maltreatment Types of Victims

Maltreatment type

Type	Percentage
Neglect	78.3
Physical abuse	17.6
Other	10.3
Sexual abuse	9.2
Psychological maltreatment	8.1
Medical neglect	2.4
Unknown	0.3

Percentage

Source: Department of Health and Human Services, *Child Maltreatment, 2010*, www.acf.hhs.gov/programs/cb/stats_research/index.htm#can (accessed August 14, 2012).

nearly 80 percent of all child fatalities were younger than 4 years old. More than 30 percent of child fatalities were attributed exclusively to neglect, and more than 40 percent were caused by multiple maltreatment types.

Causes of Child Abuse and Neglect

Maltreatment of children is a complex problem with neither a single cause nor a single solution. It cuts across racial, ethnic, religious, and socioeconomic lines. Abusive parents cannot be categorized by sex, age, or educational level.

Of all factors associated with child abuse, three are discussed most often: (1) parents who themselves suffered abuse tend to abuse their own children; (2) the presence of an unrelated adult increases the risk of abuse; and (3) isolated and alienated families tend to become abusive. A cyclical pattern of violence seems to be perpetuated from one generation to another. Evidence indicates that a large number of abused and neglected children grow into adulthood with a tendency to engage in violent behavior. The behavior of abusive parents can often be traced to negative experiences in their own childhood—physical abuse, emotional neglect, and incest. These parents become unable to separate their own childhood traumas from their relationships with their children. Abusive parents often have unrealistic perceptions of normal development. When their children are unable to act appropriately—when they cry or strike their parents—the parents may react in an abusive manner.[119] Parents may also become abusive if they are isolated from friends, neighbors, or relatives.

Many abusive parents describe themselves as alienated from their extended families, and they lack close relationships with persons who could provide help in stressful situations. The relationship between alienation and abuse may be particularly acute in homes where there has been divorce or separation, or in which parents have never actually married; abusive punishment in single-parent homes has been found to be twice that of two-parent families. Parents who are unable to cope with stressful events—divorce, financial stress, recurring mental illness, drug addiction—are most at risk.

Substance Abuse and Child Abuse. Abusive families suffer from severe stress, and it is therefore not surprising that they frequently harbor members who turn to drugs and alcohol. Studies have found a strong association between child abuse and parental alcoholism.[120] In addition, evidence exists of a significant relationship between cocaine and heroin abuse and neglect and abuse of children. Children of alcoholics suffer more injuries and poisonings than do children in the general population. Alcohol and other substances may act as disinhibitors, lessening impulse control and allowing parents to behave abusively. Children in this environment often demonstrate behavioral problems and are diagnosed as having conduct disorders. This may result in provocative behavior. Increased stress resulting from preoccupation with drugs on the part of the parent combined with behavioral problems exhibited by the child increases the likelihood of maltreatment. Frequently, these parents suffer from depression, anxiety, and low self-esteem. They live in an atmosphere of stress and family conflict. Children raised in such households are themselves more likely to have problems with alcohol and other drugs.

Stepparents and Abuse. Research indicates that stepchildren have a greater risk for abuse than do biological offspring.[121] Stepparents may have less emotional attachment to the children of another. Often the biological parent has to choose between the new mate and the child, sometimes even becoming an accomplice in the abuse.[122]

Stepchildren are overrepresented in cases of **familicide**, mass murders in which a spouse and one or more children are slain. It is also more common for fathers who kill their biological children to commit suicide than those who kill stepchildren, an indication that the latter act is motivated by hostility and not despair.[123]

Social Class and Abuse. Surveys indicate a high rate of reported abuse and neglect among people in lower economic classes. Children from families with a household income of less than $15,000 per year experience more abuse than children living in more affluent homes. Child care workers indicate that most of their clients either live in poverty or face increased financial stress because of unemployment and economic recession. These findings suggest that parental maltreatment of children is predominantly a lower-class problem. Is this conclusion valid?

One view is that low-income families, especially those headed by a single parent, are often subject to greater environmental stress and have fewer resources to deal with such stress than families with higher incomes.[124] A relationship seems to exist between the burdens of raising a child without adequate resources and the use of excessive force. Self-report surveys do show that indigent parents are more likely than affluent parents to hold attitudes that condone physical chastisement of children.[125]

Higher rates of maltreatment in low-income families reflect the stress caused by the limited resources that lower-class parents have to help them raise their children. In contrast, middle-class parents devote a smaller percentage of their total resources to raising a family.[126]

This burden becomes especially onerous in families with emotionally and physically handicapped children. Stressed-out parents may consider special-needs children a drain on the family's finances with little potential for future respite or success. Research finds that children with disabilities are maltreated at a rate almost double that of other children.[127] CHECKPOINTS

CHECKPOINTS

LO3 Discuss the nature and extent of child abuse.

✔ Although the maltreatment of juveniles has occurred throughout history, the concept of child abuse is relatively recent.

✔ C. Henry Kempe first recognized battered child syndrome.

✔ We now recognize sexual, physical, and emotional abuse, as well as neglect.

✔ Millions of allegations of child abuse and neglect are made each year.

✔ More than 1 million confirmed cases of abuse occur each year.

✔ There are a number of suspected causes of child abuse, including parental substance abuse, isolation, and a history of physical and emotional abuse.

✔ Adolescent victims of sexual abuse are particularly at risk for stress and anxiety.

The Child Protection System: Philosophy and Practice

For most of our nation's history, courts have assumed that parents have the right to bring up their children as they see fit. In the 2000 case *Troxel v. Granville*, the U.S. Supreme Court ruled that the due process clause of the Constitution protects against government interference with certain fundamental rights and liberty interests, including parents' fundamental right to make decisions concerning the care, custody, and control of their children.[128] If the care a child receives falls below reasonable standards, the state may take action to remove a child from the home and

familicide Mass murders in which a spouse and one or more children are slain.

place her or him in a less threatening environment. In these extreme circumstances, the rights of both parents and children are constitutionally protected. In the cases of *Lassiter v. Department of Social Services* and *Santosky v. Kramer*, the Supreme Court recognized the child's right to be free from parental abuse and set down guidelines for a termination-of-custody hearing, including the right to legal representation.[129] States provide a **guardian *ad litem*** (a lawyer appointed by the court to look after the interests of those who do not have the capacity to assert their own rights). States also ensure confidentiality of reporting.[130]

Although child protection agencies have been dealing with abuse and neglect since the late nineteenth century, recent awareness of the problem has prompted judicial authorities to take increasingly bold steps to ensure the safety of children.[131] The assumption that the parent–child relationship is inviolate has been challenged. In 1974, Congress passed the Child Abuse Prevention and Treatment Act (CAPTA), which provides funds to states to bolster their services for maltreated children and their parents.[132] The act provides federal funding to states in support of prevention, investigation, and treatment. It also provides grants to public agencies and nonprofit organizations for demonstration programs.

CAPTA has been the impetus for states to improve the legal frameworks of their child protection systems. Abusive parents are subject to prosecution under statutes against assault, battery, and homicide.

Investigating and Reporting Abuse. Maltreatment of children can easily be hidden from public view. Although state laws require doctors, teachers, and others who work with children to report suspected cases to child protection agencies, many maltreated children are out of the law's reach because they are too young for school or because their parents do not take them to a doctor or a hospital. Parents abuse their children in private, and even when confronted, often accuse their children of lying or blame the children's medical problems on accidents. Social service agencies must find more effective ways to locate abused children and handle such cases once found.

All states have statutes requiring that persons suspected of abuse and neglect be reported. Many have made failure to report child abuse a criminal offense. Though such statutes are rarely enforced, teachers and medical personnel have been criminally charged for failing to report abuse or neglect cases.[133]

Once reported to a child protection agency, the case is screened by an intake worker and then turned over to an investigative caseworker. In some jurisdictions, if CPS substantiates a report, the case will likely be referred to a law enforcement agency that will have the responsibility of investigating the case, collecting evidence that can later be used in court proceedings. If the caseworker determines that the

guardian *ad litem* A lawyer appointed by the court to look after the interests of those who do not have the capacity to assert their own rights.

© Reuters/Brian Snyder/Landov

Hundreds of thousands of children are abused each year. One overlooked influence may be the economy. Here Dr. Alice Newton, medical director at Massachusetts General Hospital's Child Protection Team, looks at the x-rays of a child. Boston hospitals report a spike in child abuse during a recession that has driven some families to the brink and overwhelmed cash-strapped child-protection agencies.

child is in imminent danger of severe harm, the caseworker may immediately re-move the child from the home. A court hearing must be held shortly after to approve custody. Stories abound of children erroneously taken from their homes, but it is much more likely that these "gatekeepers" will consider cases unfounded and take no action. Among the most common reasons for screening out cases is that the reporting party is involved in a child custody case despite the research showing that the risk of abuse increases significantly in the aftermath of divorce.[134]

Even when there is compelling evidence of abuse, most social service agencies will try to involve the family in voluntary treatment. Case managers will do periodic follow-ups to determine if treatment plans are being followed. If parents are unco-operative, or if the danger to the child is so great that he or she must be removed from the home, a complaint will be filed in the criminal, family, or juvenile court system. To protect the child, the court could then issue temporary orders placing the child in shelter and/or foster care during investigation, order additional services, or order suspected abusers to have no contact with the child.

The Process of State Intervention. Although procedures vary from state to state, most follow a similar legal process once a social service agency files a court petition alleging abuse or neglect.[135] Figure 7.4 diagrams this process.

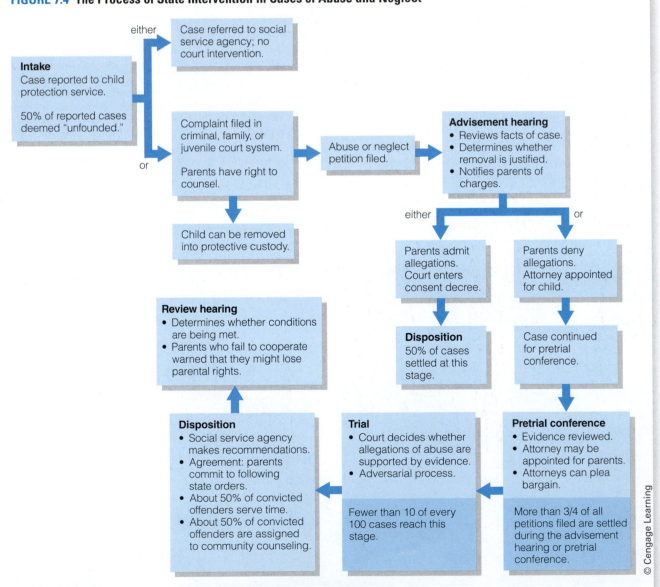

FIGURE 7.4 The Process of State Intervention in Cases of Abuse and Neglect

Intake
Case reported to child protection service.

50% of reported cases deemed "unfounded."

either → Case referred to social service agency; no court intervention.

or → Complaint filed in criminal, family, or juvenile court system.

Parents have right to counsel.

→ Child can be removed into protective custody.

Abuse or neglect petition filed. →

Advisement hearing
• Reviews facts of case.
• Determines whether removal is justified.
• Notifies parents of charges.

either → Parents admit allegations. Court enters consent decree.

or → Parents deny allegations. Attorney appointed for child.

Disposition
50% of cases settled at this stage.

Case continued for pretrial conference.

Pretrial conference
• Evidence reviewed.
• Attorney may be appointed for parents.
• Attorneys can plea bargain.

More than 3/4 of all petitions filed are settled during the advisement hearing or pretrial conference.

Trial
• Court decides whether allegations of abuse are supported by evidence.
• Adversarial process.

Fewer than 10 of every 100 cases reach this stage.

Disposition
• Social service agency makes recommendations.
• Agreement: parents commit to following state orders.
• About 50% of convicted offenders serve time.
• About 50% of convicted offenders are assigned to community counseling.

Review hearing
• Determines whether conditions are being met.
• Parents who fail to cooperate warned that they might lose parental rights.

© Cengage Learning

If the allegation of abuse is confirmed, the child may be placed in protective custody. Most state statutes require that the court be notified "promptly" or "immediately" if the child is removed; some states, including Arkansas, North Carolina, and Pennsylvania, have gone as far as requiring that no more than 12 hours elapse before official action is taken. If the child has not been removed from the home, state authorities are given more time to notify the court of suspected abuse. Some states set a limit of 30 days to take action, whereas others mandate that state action take no more than 20 days once the case has been investigated.

When an abuse or neglect petition is prosecuted, an **advisement hearing** (also called a *preliminary protective hearing* or *emergency custody hearing*) is held. The court will review the facts of the case, determine whether permanent removal of the child is justified, and notify the parents of the charges against them. Parents have the right to counsel in all cases of abuse and neglect, and many states require the court to appoint an attorney for the child as well. If the parents admit the allegations, the court enters a consent decree, and the case is continued for disposition. Approximately one-half of all cases are settled by admission at the advisement hearing. If the parents deny the petition, an attorney is appointed for the child and the case is continued for a **pretrial conference**.

At the pretrial conference, the attorney for the social service agency presents an overview of the case and the evidence. Such matters as admissibility of photos and written reports are settled. At this point, the attorneys can negotiate a settlement of the case, in which the parents accept a treatment plan detailing:

- The types of services that the child and the child's family will receive, such as parenting classes, mental health or substance abuse treatment, and family counseling
- Reunification goals, including visitation schedules and a target date for a child's return home
- Concurrent plans for alternative permanent placement options should reunification goals not be met

About three-fourths of the cases that go to pretrial conference are settled by a consent decree. About 85 out of every 100 petitions filed are settled at either the advisement hearing or the pretrial conference.

Trial and Disposition

Of the 15 remaining cases, 5 are generally settled before trial. Usually no more than 10 cases out of every 100 actually reach the trial stage of the process, an adversarial hearing designed to prove the state's allegations.

If the state's case is proven, the parents may be found guilty of criminal charges of child abuse and face probation or a prison sentence. Often, the most crucial part of an abuse or neglect proceeding is the **disposition hearing**. Here, the social service agency presents its case plan, which includes recommendations such as conditions for returning the child to the parents, or a visitation plan if the child is to be taken permanently from the parents. An agreement is reached by which the parents commit themselves to following the state orders. Between one-half and two-thirds of all convicted parents will be required to serve time in incarceration; almost half will be assigned to a form of treatment. As far as the children are concerned, some may be placed in temporary care; in other cases, parental rights are terminated and the child is placed in the custody of the child protective service. Legal custody can then be assigned to a relative or some other person.

There is considerable controversy over what forms of intervention are helpful in abuse and neglect cases. Today, social service agents avoid removing children from the home whenever possible and instead try to employ techniques to control abusive relationships. In serious cases, the state may remove children from their parents and place them in shelter care or foster homes. Placement of children in foster care is intended to be temporary, but it is not uncommon for children to remain in foster care for three years or more.

Ultimately, the court has the power to terminate the rights of parents over their children, but because the effects of destroying the family unit are far reaching, the

advisement hearing A preliminary protective or temporary custody hearing in which the court will review the facts and determine whether removal of the child is justified and notify parents of the charges against them.

pretrial conference The attorney for the social services agency presents an overview of the case, and a plea bargain or negotiated settlement can be agreed to in a consent decree.

disposition hearing The social service agency presents its case plan and recommendations for care of the child and treatment of the parents, including incarceration and counseling or other treatment.

court does so only in the most severe cases. Jurisdictions have expedited case processing, instituted procedures designed not to frighten child witnesses, coordinated investigations between social service and law enforcement agencies, and assigned an advocate or guardian *ad litem* to children in need of protection.

In making their decisions, courts are guided by three interests: the role of the parents, protection for the child, and the responsibility of the state. Frequently, these interests conflict with each other. In fact, at times even the interests of the two parents are not in harmony. The state attempts to balance the parents' natural right to control their child's upbringing with the child's right to grow into adulthood free from harm. This is referred to as the **balancing-of-the-interests approach**.

Periodically, **review hearings** are held to determine if the conditions of the case plan are being met. Parents who fail to cooperate are warned that they may lose their parental rights. Most abuse and neglect cases are concluded within a year. Either the parents lose their rights and the child is given a permanent placement, or the child is returned to the parents and the court's jurisdiction ends.

The Abused Child in Court

One of the most significant problems associated with abuse cases is the trauma a child must go through in a court hearing. Children get confused and frightened and may change their testimony. Much controversy has arisen over the accuracy of children's reports of physical and sexual abuse, resulting in hung juries. Prosecutors and experts have been accused of misleading children or eliciting incriminating testimony. In probably what is the most well-known case, the McMartin Day Care case in California, children told not only of being sexually abused but also of being forced to participate in bizarre satanic rituals during which the McMartins mutilated animals and forced the children to touch corpses in hidden underground passageways. Prosecutors decided not to press forward after two trials ended in deadlock. Some jurors, when interviewed after the verdict, said that while they believed that children had been abused, the interviewing techniques used by prosecutors had been so suggestive that they had not been able to discern what really happened.[136]

State jurisdictions have instituted procedures to minimize trauma to the child. Most have enacted legislation allowing videotaped statements, or interviews with child witnesses taken at a preliminary hearing or at a formal deposition, to be admissible in court. Videotaped testimony spares child witnesses the trauma of testifying in open court. States that allow videotaped testimony usually put some restrictions on its use. Some prohibit the government from calling the child to testify at trial if the videotape is used; some states require a finding that the child is "medically unavailable," because of the trauma of the case before videotaping can be used; some require that the defendant be present during the videotaping; a few specify that the child not be able to see or hear the defendant.[137]

Most of the states now allow a child's testimony to be given on closed-circuit television (CCTV). The child is able to view the judge and attorneys, and the courtroom participants are able to observe the child. The standards for CCTV testimony vary widely. Some states, such as New Hampshire, assume that any child witness under age 12 would benefit from not having to appear in court. Others require an independent examination by a mental health professional to determine whether there is a "compelling need" for CCTV testimony.

In addition to innovative methods of testimony, children in sexual abuse cases have been allowed to use anatomically correct dolls to demonstrate happenings that

balancing-of-the-interests approach Efforts of the courts to balance the parents' natural right to raise a child with the child's right to grow into adulthood free from physical abuse or emotional harm.

review hearings Periodic meetings to determine whether the conditions of the case plan for an abused child are being met by the parents or guardians of the child.

they cannot describe verbally. The Victims of Child Abuse Act of 1990 allows children to use these dolls when testifying in federal courts; at least eight states have passed similar legislation.[138] Similarly, states have relaxed their laws of evidence to allow out-of-court statements by the child to a social worker, teacher, or police officer to be used as evidence (such statements would otherwise be considered **hearsay**). Typically, corroboration is required to support these statements if the child does not also testify.

The prevalence of sexual abuse cases has created new problems for the justice system. Often accusations are made in conjunction with marital disputes. The fear is growing that children may become pawns in custody battles; the mere suggestion of sexual abuse is enough to affect the outcome of a divorce action. The justice system must develop techniques that can get at the truth without creating a lifelong scar on the child's psyche.

Legal Issues. A number of cases have been brought before the Supreme Court testing the right of children to present evidence at trial using nontraditional methods. Two issues stand out. One is the ability of physicians and mental health professionals to testify about statements made to them by children, especially when the children are incapable of testifying. The second concerns the way children testify in court.

In a 1992 case, *White v. Illinois*, the Supreme Court ruled that the state's attorney is required neither to produce young victims at trial nor to demonstrate the reason why they were unavailable to serve as witnesses.[139] *White* involved statements given by the child to the child's babysitter and mother, a doctor, a nurse, and a police officer concerning the alleged assailant in a sexual assault case. The prosecutor twice tried to call the child to testify, but both times the 4-year-old experienced emotional difficulty and could not appear in court. The outcome hinged solely on the testimony of the five witnesses.

By allowing others to testify as to what the child said, *White* removed the requirement that prosecutors produce child victims in court. This facilitates the prosecution of child abusers in cases where a court appearance by a victim would prove too disturbing or where the victim is too young to understand the court process.[140] The Court noted that statements made to doctors during medical examinations or those

WWW

The American Bar Association maintains a website with information on **legal rights of children in abuse cases**. For more information, visit the Criminal Justice CourseMate at CengageBrain.com, then access the Web Links for this chapter.

The courts have granted leeway in the testimony of child abuse victims. Here, a social worker is shown using a doll to determine the sexual abuse of a young boy. Dolls such as this can be used during trial if they help victims tell their story.

© Charles Gupton/Stone/Getty Images

hearsay Out-of-court statements made by one person and recounted in court by another. Such statements are generally not allowed as evidence except in child abuse cases wherein a child's statements to social workers, teachers, or police may be admissible.

made when a victim is upset carry more weight than ones made after careful reflection. The Court ruled that such statements can be repeated during trial, because the circumstances in which they were made could not be duplicated simply by having the child testify to them in court.

In-Court Statements. Children who are victims of sexual or physical abuse often make poor witnesses. Yet their testimony may be crucial. In a 1988 case, *Coy v. Iowa*, the Supreme Court placed limitations on efforts to protect child witnesses in court. During a sexual assault case, a one-way glass screen was set up so that the child victims would not be able to view the defendant (the defendant, however, could view the witnesses).[141] The Iowa statute that allowed the protective screen assumed that children would be traumatized by their courtroom experience. The court ruled that unless there is a finding that the child witness needs special protection, the Sixth Amendment of the Constitution grants defendants "face-to-face" confrontation with their accusers. In her dissenting opinion, Justice Sandra Day O'Connor suggested that if courts found it necessary, it would be appropriate to allow children to testify via CCTV or videotape.

Justice O'Connor's views became law in *Maryland v. Craig*.[142] In this case, a day care operator was convicted of sexually abusing a six-year-old child; one-way CCTV testimony was used during the trial. The decision was overturned in the Maryland Court of Appeals on the grounds that the procedures used were insufficient to show that the child could only testify in this manner because a trial appearance would be too traumatic. On appeal, the court ruled that the Maryland statute that allows CCTV testimony is sufficient because it requires a determination that the child will suffer distress if forced to testify. The court noted that CCTV could serve as the equivalent of in-court testimony and would not interfere with the defendant's right to confront witnesses. **CHECKPOINTS**

CHECKPOINTS

LO4 Be familiar with the child protection system and the stages in the child protection process.

✔ A child protection system has been created to identify and try abuse cases.

✔ Once reported to a child protection agency, the case is screened by an intake worker and then turned over to an investigative caseworker.

✔ Even when there is compelling evidence of abuse, most social service agencies will try to involve the family in voluntary treatment.

✔ Post-investigation services are offered on a voluntary basis by child welfare agencies to ensure the safety of children.

✔ If the allegation of abuse is confirmed, the child may be placed in protective custody.

✔ State jurisdictions have instituted procedures to minimize trauma to the child.

✔ The courts have made it easier for children to testify in abuse cases, by using CCTV, for example.

ABUSE, NEGLECT, AND DELINQUENCY

There is little question that child abuse creates long-term problems for its victims, including heightened involvement with delinquency and substance abuse (see Exhibit 7.1).

A significant amount of literature suggests that being the target of abuse is associated with subsequent episodes of delinquency and violence.[143] The more often a child is physically disciplined and the harsher the discipline, the more likely they will engage in antisocial behaviors.[144] The effects of abuse appear to be long term: exposure to abuse in early life provides a foundation for violent and antisocial behavior in late adolescence and adulthood.[145] Kids who are abused are likely to grow up to be abusers themselves.[146]

The Cycle of Violence

Cathy Spatz Widom and Michael Maxfield have conducted longitudinal cohort studies with victims of child abuse. Their most important research effort followed the offending careers of 908 youths, reported as abused from 1967 to 1971, for almost 25 years. They then compared the

Looking Back to Ayden's Story

Ayden was placed in a treatment foster home where he received a number of needed services and interventions. Within six months of placement, Ayden's grades were improving and he was doing well in his outpatient treatment programs for anger management and substance use.

CRITICAL THINKING Does Ayden's success indicate that the foster family system can work? Or does it ignore certain realities that cannot be overcome?

> **EXHIBIT 7.1 Consequences of Child Abuse and Neglect**
>
> - A report of child abuse is made every 10 seconds.
> - More than five children die every day as a result of child abuse.
> - Approximately 80 percent of children who die from abuse are under the age of 4.
> - It is estimated that between 50 and 60 percent of child fatalities due to maltreatment are not recorded as such on death certificates.
> - More than 90 percent of juvenile sexual abuse victims know their perpetrator in some way.
> - Child abuse occurs at every socioeconomic level, across ethnic and cultural lines, within all religions, and at all levels of education.
> - About 30 percent of abused and neglected children will later abuse their own children, continuing the horrible cycle of abuse.
> - About 80 percent of 21-year-olds who were abused as children met criteria for at least one psychological disorder.
> - The estimated annual cost of child abuse and neglect in the United States is $124 billion.
>
> Source: Childhelp, *National Child Abuse Statistics*, www.childhelp.org/pages/statistics (accessed August 14, 2012)

offending history of this sample with that of a control group of 667 nonabused youths. Among their findings:

- Being abused or neglected as a child increased the likelihood of arrest as a juvenile by 59 percent, as an adult by 28 percent, and for a violent crime by 30 percent.
- Maltreated children were younger at the time of their first arrest, committed nearly twice as many offenses, and were arrested more frequently.
- Physically abused and neglected (versus sexually abused) children were the most likely to be arrested later for a violent crime.
- Abused and neglected females were also at increased risk of arrest for violence as juveniles and adults.
- There are racial differences in the long-term affect of abuse on violence. White abused and neglected children were no more likely to be arrested for a violent crime than their nonabused and non-neglected white counterparts. In contrast, black abused and neglected children showed significantly increased rates of violent arrests compared with black children who were not maltreated.
- An out-of-home placement was not related to the number of arrests among those who were removed from their homes due only to abuse and neglect.[147]

In sum, the victims of childhood violence are significantly more likely to become violent adults than the nonabused; child abuse then creates a **cycle of violence**.

The Abuse–Delinquency Link

Many questions remain to be answered about the abuse–delinquency link. Even though an association has been found, it does not necessarily mean that most abused children become delinquent. Many do not, and many delinquent youths come from what appear to be model homes.

It is also possible that the abuse–delinquency link is spurious, and the two factors are connected because of some external factor. For example, kids who are abused may want to escape punishment by running away and living on the streets. Runaways have a greater chance of getting involved in delinquency and drug abuse.[148] What appears to be the effect of abuse is actually the effect of running away from home.

cycle of violence The process by which abused kids become abusers themselves.

Research also shows that the timing and extent of abuse may shape its impact. Kids who are maltreated solely during early childhood may be less likely to engage in chronic delinquency than those whose abuse was lasting and persisted into later adolescence. Timothy Ireland speculates that adolescents who have experienced persistent and long-term maltreatment are more likely to have families suffering an array of other social deficits, including poverty, parental mental illness, and domestic violence, which may make children more likely to engage in antisocial behavior. Persistent maltreatment also gives the victims little opportunity to cope or deal with their ongoing victimization.[149]

Finally, abuse may impact on some groups of adolescents more than it does others. For example, there are distinct racial differences in the way the girls react to abuse experiences. For European American girls, there are strong link between a history of abuse and indicators of poor mental health (e.g., suicide attempts and self-injurious behaviors); African American girls who suffered abuse were more likely to externalize their anger and violence. Why this racial divide? African American girls may be socialized to be self-reliant and independent, and therefore more likely to act in a stronger, more assertive manner. European American girls are raised to be dependent and accepting of feminine gender roles; when they experience abuse they tend to internalize their problems—a reaction that produces lower self-esteem and more mental health issues.[150]

The abuse–delinquency link is critical for those concerned with the welfare of children, especially since abused children who commit delinquent acts may be subject to harsh dispositions in the juvenile court. While people are generally sympathetic to abused children, youths get little credit for their background when sentencing decisions are being made. Factors associated with abuse—chaotic family environment, mental health problems, behavioral problems, and school problems— may actually trigger tough punishments.[151]

In summary, the research on delinquency and family relationships offers ample evidence that family life can be a potent force on a child's development. Because inadequate family life may produce delinquent children, it might be possible to prevent delinquency by offering a substitute. One way of helping to prevent delinquency is to mentor kids who are at risk for delinquency. Mentoring programs usually involve nonprofessional volunteers spending time with young people who have been targeted as having the potential for dropping out of school, school failure, and other social problems. They mentor in a supportive, nonjudgmental manner while also acting as role models. In recent years, there has been a large increase in the number of mentoring programs, many of them aimed at preventing delinquency. One of the most successful is the Homebuilders program, discussed in the Prevention/Intervention/Treatment feature. **CHECKPOINTS**

Looking Back to Ayden's Story

Ayden received weekly support in the home, which included addressing behavioral issues, school concerns, family relationships, substance abuse, and anger management.

CRITICAL THINKING Create a prevention program to help abused children avoid criminal behavior in the future. Discuss the necessary elements and describe the services could be provided to affect these children's future in a positive manner.

CHECKPOINTS

LO5 Know the various positions in the delinquency–child maltreatment debate.

✔ The link between maltreatment and delinquency is supported by a number of criminological theories.

✔ Studies of juvenile offenders have confirmed that between 70 and 80 percent may have had abusive backgrounds.

✔ Physically abused and neglected children are the most likely to be arrested later for a violent crime.

✔ Some experts question the link between abuse and delinquency, suggesting some other factor such as poverty or substance abuse may account for both conditions.

Homebuilders

Homebuilders is an in-home, intensive family preservation service (IFPS) and reunification program for families with children (newborn to 17 years old) returning from or at risk of placement into foster care, group or residential treatment, psychiatric hospitals, or juvenile justice facilities. The Homebuilders model is designed to improve parental skills, parental capabilities, family interactions, children's behavior, and family safety. The goals are to prevent the unnecessary out-of-home placement of children through an intensive, on-site intervention and to teach families new problem-solving skills to improve family functioning.

Homebuilders therapists work with youths and families involved in the child welfare, juvenile justice, and mental health system. For high-risk families involved with the child protective services system, the goal of the program is to remove the risk of harm to the child instead of removing the child. Therapists work with families to teach them new behaviors and help them make better choices for their children, while ensuring child safety. Homebuilders also works with youths and their families to address issues that lead to delinquency, while allowing youths to remain in the community. Program staff ensure that kids attend classes regularly, adhere to curfews, comply with the courts, and learn anger management and conflict-resolution skills to avoid getting into more trouble. Youths are helped to avoid the trauma and stigma of psychiatric hospitalization or residential treatment for mental health–related issues by providing crisis intervention and skill building, involving the families in the youths' treatment, and broadening the continuum of care.

The primary intervention components of the Homebuilders model are engaging and motivating family members; conducting holistic, behavioral assessments of strengths and problems; developing outcome-based goals; using evidence-based cognitive–behavioral interventions; teaching skills to facilitate behavior change; and developing and enhancing ongoing supports and resources.

The core program strategies are:

- *Intervention at crisis point.* Homebuilders therapists work with families when they are in crisis. Families are seen within 24 hours of referral to the program.

- *Accessibility.* Services are provided in the family's home and community (e.g., school) at times convenient to families, including evenings, weekends, and holidays. Therapists are available 24 hours a day, 7 days a week, for crisis intervention. This accessibility allows close monitoring of potentially dangerous situations.

- *Flexibility.* Intervention strategies and methods are tailored to meet the needs, values, and lifestyles of each family. Services are provided when and where the families wish. Therapists also provide a wide range of services, such as helping families meet the basic needs of food, clothing, and shelter; using public transportation; budgeting; and, when necessary, dealing with the social services system.

- *Time limited and low caseload.* Families receive 4 to 6 weeks of intensive intervention, with up to two "booster sessions." Therapists typically serve two families at a time and provide 80 to 100 hours of service, with an average of 45 hours of face-to-face contact with the family.

- *Strengths based.* Therapists help clients identify and prioritize goals, strengths, and values, and help them use and enhance strengths and resources to achieve their goals.

- *Ecological/holistic assessment and individualized treatment planning.* Assessments of family strengths, problems, and barriers to service/treatment and outcome-based goals and treatment plans are completed collaboratively with each family.

- *Research-based treatment practices.* Therapists use evidence-based treatment practices, including motivational interviewing, behavioral parent training, cognitive–behavior therapy strategies, and relapse prevention. Therapists teach family members a variety of skills, including child behavior management, effective discipline, positive behavioral support, communication skills, problem-solving skills, resisting peer pressure, mood management skills, safety planning, and establishing daily routines.

- *Support and resource building.* Therapists help families assess their formal and informal support systems and develop and enhance ongoing supports and resources for maintaining and facilitating changes.

Systematic research shows the program can be a cost effective intervention method. A cost benefit analysis found that for each dollar invested in the Homebuilders program, the total benefit-to-cost ratio per participant was $2.54. The total benefits minus the costs amounted to $4,775, a positive result indicating that money is saved by investing in the program.

Critical Thinking

Is it possible for a program like Homebuilders to work in the nation's most disorganized areas? Can an intervention program such as this overcome the effects of neighborhood dysfunction? Is this a Band-Aid approach to social problems?

Source: Office of Juvenile Justice and Delinquency Prevention, Homebuilders, www.ojjdp.gov/mpg/HOMEBUILDERS-MPGProgramDetail-341.aspx (accessed August 1, 2012).

SUMMARY

There is little question that family dysfunction can lead to long-term social problems. Interactions between parents and children provide opportunities for children to acquire or inhibit antisocial behavior patterns. Good parenting lowers the risk of delinquency for children living in high-crime areas.

While critical to child development, the nuclear family is now showing signs of breakdown. Research indicates that parents whose marriage is secure produce children who are secure and independent. Children who have experienced family breakup are more likely to demonstrate behavior problems and delinquency than children in intact families. Remarriage does not lessen the effects of divorce on youth.

Children who grow up in dysfunctional homes often exhibit delinquent behaviors, having learned at a young age that aggression pays off. Kids who are conflict prone may actually help to destabilize households. Delinquency will be reduced if at least one parent can provide great parenting skills, known as parental efficacy. Unfortunately, this is not always the case: studies show that the parents of delinquent youths tend to be inconsistent disciplinarians, either overly harsh or extremely lenient. Parents who closely supervise their children and have close ties with them help reduce the likelihood of adolescent delinquent behavior.

A number of studies have found that parental deviance has a powerful influence on delinquent behavior. Kids whose parents go to prison are much more likely to be at risk for delinquency than children of non-incarcerated parents. The link between parental deviance and child misbehavior may be genetic, experiential, or even related to labeling and stigma.

Many children are physically abused or neglected by their parents. Adolescent victims of sexual abuse are particularly at risk for stress and anxiety. Millions of allegations of child abuse and neglect are made each year, and about 700,000 kids are the victims of abuse each year. Abusive families suffer from severe stress. Research indicates that stepchildren share a greater risk for abuse than do biological offspring.

If the care a child receives falls below reasonable standards, the state may take action to remove the child from the home and place her or him in a less threatening environment. Once reported to a child protection agency, the case is screened by an intake worker and then turned over to an investigative caseworker. Even when there is compelling evidence of abuse, most social service agencies will try to involve the family in voluntary treatment. Post-investigation services are offered on a voluntary basis by child welfare agencies to ensure the safety of children. If the allegation of abuse is confirmed, the child may be placed in protective custody.

State jurisdictions have instituted procedures to minimize trauma to the child during legal proceedings. Most states now allow a child's testimony to be given on closed-circuit television (CCTV). Children in sexual abuse cases have been allowed to use anatomically correct dolls to demonstrate happenings that they cannot describe verbally.

The link between maltreatment and delinquency is supported by a number of criminological theories. Studies of juvenile offenders have confirmed that between 70 and 80 percent may have had abusive backgrounds. It is difficult to assess the temporal order of the linkage: Does early abuse lead to later delinquency? Or conversely, are antisocial kids subject to overly harsh parental discipline and abuse?

KEY TERMS

nuclear family, p. 182

broken home, p. 186

blended families, p. 186

intrafamily violence, p. 188

parental efficacy, p. 190

resource dilution, p. 191

battered child syndrome, p. 193

neglect, p. 193

child abuse, p. 193

abandonment, p. 194

familicide, p. 198

guardian *ad litem*, p. 199

advisement hearing, p. 201

pretrial conference, p. 201

disposition hearing, p. 201

balancing-of-the-interests approach, p. 202

review hearings, p. 202

hearsay, p. 203

cycle of violence, p. 205

QUESTIONS FOR REVIEW

1. What are the changes in the makeup of the contemporary family and how they can affect delinquency?

2. Family courts are guided by what factors in making their decisions in abuse cases?

3. What are the qualities that make up parental efficacy?

4. What effect does inconsistent and ineffective adult supervision have on delinquency?

5. Explain the intergenerational transmission of deviance.

6. What were the findings in *Maryland v. Craig* and *Coy v. Iowa*?

7. What are the various forms that child abuse and neglect may take?

8. What is the cycle of violence and how does it affect delinquent behavior?

9. List the steps in the process of family intervention and tell what happens at each step.

10. What are possible reasons for the high correlation between abuse and delinquency?

QUESTIONS FOR DISCUSSION

1. What are the meanings of the terms *child abuse* and *child neglect*?

2. Give two different explanations for the relationship between abuse and antisocial behavior.

3. What causes parents to abuse their children?

4. What is meant by the child protection system? Do courts act in the best interest of the child when they allow an abused child to remain with the family?

5. Should children be allowed to testify in court via CCTV? Does this approach prevent defendants in child abuse cases from confronting their accusers?

6. Is corporal punishment ever permissible as a disciplinary method?

APPLYING WHAT YOU HAVE LEARNED

You are an investigator with the county bureau of social services. A case has been referred to you by a middle school's head guidance counselor. It seems that a young girl, Emily, has been showing up to school in a dazed and listless condition. She has had a hard time concentrating in class and seems withdrawn and uncommunicative. The 13-year-old has missed more than her normal share of school days and has often been late to class. Last week, she seemed so lethargic that her homeroom teacher sent her to the school nurse. A physical examination revealed that she was malnourished and in poor physical health. She also had evidence of bruising that could only come from a severe beating. Emily told the nurse that she had been punished by her parents for doing poorly at school and failing to do her chores at home.

When her parents were called to school to meet with the principal and guidance counselor, they claimed to be members of a religious order that believes children should be punished severely for their misdeeds. Emily had been placed on a restricted diet as well as beaten with a belt to correct her misbehavior. When the guidance counselor asked them if they would be willing to go into family therapy, they were furious and told her to mind her own business. It's a sad day, they said, when "God-fearing American citizens cannot bring up their children according to their religious beliefs." The girl was in no immediate danger because her punishment had not been life threatening.

The case is then referred to your office. When you go to see the parents at home, they refuse to make any change in their behavior, claiming that they are in the right and you represent all that is wrong with society. The "lax" discipline you suggest leads to drugs, sex, and other teenage problems.

Writing Assignment: Write up your report in the case. What steps would you suggest the court take? Would you recommend removing Emily from her home and requiring the parents to go into counseling?

GROUPWORK

Have the class contact representatives from the child protection services and ask them about the process of state intervention in abuse cases. Determine whether the model and process set out in the book represents a true and accurate picture of what is going on at present and determine whether there are any significant differences.

CHAPTER EIGHT

Peers and Delinquency:
Juvenile Gangs and Groups

© Design Pics Inc./Alamy

LEARNING OBJECTIVES

After reading this chapter you should:

1. Be familiar with the influence of peers on delinquency.
2. Know the definition and historical development of gangs.
3. Describe the makeup of gangs.
4. Compare the various theories of gang formation.
5. Describe the various forms of gang-control efforts that are in use today.

CHAPTER OUTLINE

Luis's Story

Gang-involved Luis was a 16-year-old Latino male charged with substantial battery and resisting arrest, due to a fight with a rival at a party. Luis already had a history of truancy and a police record for several thefts, vandalism, truancy, underage drinking, and curfew violations. He was smoking marijuana on a daily basis, not attending school, and had experienced little success in the educational environment outside of sports. Luis also exhibited significant anger management concerns and was viewed as a threat to the community.

Luis's mother was very involved in his life and was doing her best to raise her four children without any assistance or involvement from their father. Luis had felt like "the man of the family" from an early age and felt responsible for caring for his mother and younger siblings. Despite numerous concerns expressed by his family and the juvenile court, Luis was allowed to return home.

While the next court hearing was pending, Luis participated in an alcohol and drug assessment, and it was recommended that he enter a residential treatment facility for his drug and alcohol issues, anger management problems, and gang involvement. He was also referred to an alternative school program where his chances for success would be better.

At the dispositional hearing, his defense attorney argued that Luis needed alcohol and drug treatment, as well as other services, and that he should be sent to an inpatient treatment facility that had already agreed to take him. The judge ordered Luis to the juvenile correctional facility, but "stayed" the order, permitting Luis to enter treatment. Luis entered the voluntary 90-day alcohol and drug treatment program and began to work on his sobriety, anger issues, gang involvement, and criminal attitude. The team of professionals, along with Luis and his mother, created an aftercare plan that initially included ongoing drug counseling and support, individual counseling, intensive supervision and monitoring, group support, and placement in an alternative educational setting. Through the alternative school, Luis got involved in a program that offered troubled youth the experience of building homes for underprivileged families. Luis was able to gain valuable work skills, as well as time to focus on positive activities. Luis remained living at home with his mother and siblings and was eventually released from the juvenile court–ordered services. The "stayed" correctional order was in place until the juvenile court closed the case upon Luis's 18th birthday.

Kids like Luis often find themselves trapped in a gang culture. Few issues in the study of delinquency are more important today than the problems presented by law-violating gangs and groups.[1] Although some gangs are made up of only a few loosely organized neighborhood youths, others have thousands of members who cooperate in complex illegal enterprises. A significant portion of all drug distribution in the nation's inner cities is believed to be gang controlled; gang violence accounts for more than 1,000 homicides each year. There has been an outcry from politicians to increase punishment for the "little monsters" and to save the "fallen angels," or the victimized youths who are innocent.[2] Nor is the gang problem unique to the United States. John Hagedorn, a noted gang expert, finds that a global criminal economy, especially the illegal distribution of drugs, involves gangs as both major and bit players. Numerous gangs operate in distressed areas, such as the townships of South Africa, where they rule politically and control the underground economy. Chinese criminal organizations known as triads operate all across the globe, but are especially active in South Asia and the United States. In Eastern Europe, the turmoil caused by the move to a market economy and the loss of social safety nets has strengthened gangs and drug organizations. In Albania, for example, one-quarter of all young males are involved in the drug economy.[3]

The problem of gang control is a difficult one. Many gangs flourish in inner-city areas that offer lower-class youths few conventional opportunities, and members are resistant to offers of help that cannot deliver legitimate economic hope. Although gang members may be subject to arrest, prosecution, and incarceration, a new crop of young recruits is always ready to take the place of their fallen comrades. Those sent to prison find that, upon release, their former gangs are only too willing to have them return to action.

We begin this chapter with a discussion of peer relations, showing how they influence delinquent behavior. Then we explore the definition, nature, and structure of delinquent gangs. Finally, the chapter presents theories of gang formation, the extent of gang activity, and gang-control efforts.

ADOLESCENT PEER RELATIONS

Although parents are the primary source of influence and attention in children's early years, children between ages 8 and 14 seek out a stable peer group, and both the number and the variety of friendships increase as children go through adolescence. Friends soon begin to have a greater influence over decision making than parents.

Peer influence is not gender specific. Young girls who engage in aggressive behavior with peers later grow up to have more conflict-ridden relationships with their romantic partners.[4] Boys who are highly aggressive and are therefore rejected by their peers in childhood are also more likely to engage in criminality and delinquency from adolescence into young adulthood.[5]

Peer relations, then, are a significant aspect of maturation. Peer influence may be more important than parental nurturance in the development of long-term behavior.[6] Peers guide each other and help each other learn to share and cooperate, to cope with aggressive impulses, and to discuss feelings they would not dare bring up at home. Youths can compare their own experiences with peers and learn that others have similar concerns and problems.[7] In fact, there is evidence that peers may actually outweigh the influence of parents in producing a delinquent way of life. Even children born into high-risk families—such as those with single teen mothers—can avoid delinquency if their friends refrain from drug use and criminality.[8]

Peers in the Life Course

As they go through adolescence, children form **cliques**, small groups of friends who share activities and confidences. They also belong to **crowds**, loosely organized groups of children who share interests and activities, such as sports, religion, or hobbies. Intimate friends play an important role in social development, but adolescents are also deeply influenced by this wider circle of friends. Adolescent self-image is in part formed by perceptions of one's place in the social world.[9]

In later adolescence, acceptance by peers has a major impact on socialization. By their early teens, children report that their friends give them emotional support when they are feeling bad and that they can confide intimate feelings to peers without worrying about their confidences being betrayed.[10] Poor peer relations, such as negative interactions with best friends, has been found to be related to high social anxiety, whereas, in contrast, close affiliation with a high-status peer crowd seems to afford protection against depression and other negative adolescent psychological symptoms.[11]

Types of Friends. Popular youths do well in school and are socially astute. In contrast, children who are rejected by their peers are more likely to display aggressive behavior and to disrupt group activities by bickering or behaving antisocially. Kids choose friends who are similar in behavior and values and the resemblance increases as the friendship develops; resemblance declines when friendship dissolves. In stable friendships, the more accepted popular partner exerts greater influence over the less accepted partner. If the more popular friend engages in delinquency and alcohol use, the less popular "follower" will be soon to follow.[12]

Another group, **controversial status youth**, are aggressive kids who are either highly liked or intensely disliked by their peers. These controversial youths are the

cliques Small groups of friends who share intimate knowledge and confidences.

crowds Loosely organized groups who share interests and activities.

controversial status youth Aggressive kids who are either highly liked or intensely disliked by their peers and who are the ones most likely to become engaged in antisocial behavior.

ones most likely to become engaged in antisocial behavior. When they find themselves in leadership positions among their peers, they get them involved in delinquent and problem behaviors.[13] In stable friendships, the more socially accepted popular partner is typically able to exert greater influence over the less popular, less accepted partner. As time goes on kids tend to emulate the behavior of their more popular friends and will get involved in drug use and delinquency to maintain the relationship. Kids who have lots of friends and a variety of peer group networks tend to be less delinquent than their less popular mates.[14] While the influence of a "best friend" is important, so too is the influence of a large peer network.[15]

Peer Relations and Delinquency

Research shows that peer group relationships are closely tied to delinquent behaviors: delinquent acts tend to be committed in small groups rather than alone, a process referred to as *co-offending*.[16] Adolescents who maintain delinquent friends are more likely to engage in antisocial behavior and drug abuse themselves.[17]

Boys who mature early are more likely to later engage in a variety of antisocial behavior. The association between early maturation and delinquency may be explained by changes in physical prowess.[18] However, another view is that early maturers are more likely to develop strong attachments to older, more delinquent friends and to be influenced by peer pressure radiating from these experienced offenders.[19] Girls who mature early are also prone to hang out with an older crowd of teenage males, an activity that puts them in close contact with a group who are prone to antisocial behavior choices.[20]

The Direction of Peer Influence. Does having antisocial peers cause delinquency or are delinquents antisocial youths who seek out like-minded companions because they can be useful in committing crimes? There are actually a number of different viewpoints on this question.

- According to social control theory (Chapter 4), delinquents are as detached from their peers as they are from other elements of society.[21] Although they appear to have close friends, delinquents actually lack the social skills to make their peer relations rewarding or fulfilling.[22] Antisocial adolescents seek out like-minded

Peer relations, in all cultures, have been linked to adolescent behavior choices, including substance abuse and delinquency.

peers for criminal associations and to conduct criminal transactions. If delinquency is committed in groups, it is because "birds of a feather flock together."

- According to labeling theory, deviant kids are forced to choose deviant peers.[23] After being labeled deviant, these kids have no choice but to flock to antisocial friends who then help them maintain delinquent careers and obstruct the aging-out process.[24] The social baggage they cart around prevents them from developing associations with conventional peers.[25] Deviant peers do not cause straight kids to go bad, but they amplify the likelihood of a troubled kid getting further involved in antisocial behaviors.[26]

- According to social learning theory, delinquent friends cause law-abiding youth to get in trouble. Kids who fall in with a bad crowd learn bad habits, attitudes and behavior from their more deviant friends. Youths who maintain friendships with antisocial peers are more likely to become delinquent regardless of their own personality or the type of supervision they receive at home.[27] Antisocial peers transmit prodelinquency attitudes that shape an adolescent's life views and increase their involvement with delinquency.[28]

- According to routine activities theory, kids who engage in unstructured socializing with like-minded peers, without parental controls, will have greater opportunities to get involved in delinquent behaviors than those who receive adult monitoring and control.[29]

Is There a Peer–Delinquency Linkage? While these theoretical models suggest that membership in a law-violating peer group is a key to the onset of a delinquent career, others dispute the influence of peers on delinquency. They point to research showing that kids may overestimate their friends' deviant behavior and that it's this perception rather than actual peer behavior that influences delinquent choices.[30]

Similarly, there is evidence that the friendship patterns of delinquents are not dissimilar from those of nondelinquents.[31] Delinquent youths report that their peer relations contain elements of caring and trust and that they can be open and intimate with their friends.[32]

Even if an association exists, it may be nonlinear and may depend on individual and environmental circumstances. Peers seem to have more influence on occasional or one-time delinquents and less on chronic offenders.[33] Peers can influence the onset of delinquency but may have less of an affect after an adolescent enters a delinquent way of life. In neighborhoods with fewer opportunities for crime, peer influence may play a greater role than in communities where criminal opportunities are more commonplace.[34]

There is also some question whether kids choose their friends based on prior delinquent involvement. It seems that many crime-involved youth choose friends who are not delinquent themselves, raising the question of whether birds of a feather really do flock together. And even when antisocial kids congregate together, there is evidence that this shared delinquency may increase rather than diminish social standing; having delinquent friends may turn out to have benefits. Membership in law-violating groups may actually help kids increase their social standing and popularity within their age cohort. For example, by ninth grade kids who belong to the "party crowd," a group that engages in underage drinking, gain rather than lose social capital. Drinking is a normative activity practiced by advantaged students who are at the center of ninth-grade peer culture. Participation in the party subculture has short-term costs (such as lower grades or detachment from school), but in the long term provides gains in the form of social capital and popularity.[35]

Though the association may be more complicated than previously thought, the weight of the empirical evidence clearly indicates that delinquent peers do have some influence on behavior. Kids who hang out with delinquent friends, who spend time socializing with them without parental supervision, and who admire and want to emulate them are the ones most likely to increase involvement in antisocial behaviors.[36] Youths who are loyal to delinquent friends, belong to gangs, and have bad companions are most likely to commit crimes and engage in violence.[37] **CHECKPOINTS**

YOUTH GANGS

As youths move through adolescence, they gravitate toward cliques that provide them with support, assurance, protection, and direction. In some instances, the peer group provides the social and emotional basis for antisocial activity. When this happens, the clique is transformed into a **gang**.

Today, such a powerful mystique has grown up around gangs that mere mention of the word evokes images of black-jacketed youths roaming the streets in groups bearing such names as the MS-13, Latin Kings, Crips, and Bloods. Films (*American History X*, *Boyz n the Hood*), television shows (*The Wire*; *Sons of Anarchy*), novels (*Clockers*, by Richard Price), and even Broadway musicals (*West Side Story* and *Grease*) have popularized the youth gang.[38]

Considering the suspected role gangs play in violent crime and drug activity, it is not surprising that gangs have been the target of a great deal of research interest.[39] Important attempts have been made to gauge their size, location, makeup, and activities.

What Are Gangs?

Delinquency experts are often at odds over the precise definition of a gang. The term is sometimes used broadly to describe any congregation of youths who have joined together to engage in delinquent acts. However, police departments often use it only to refer to cohesive groups that hold and defend territory or turf.[40]

Academic experts have also created a variety of definitions. Gang expert Malcolm Klein argues that two factors stand out in all definitions:

- Members have self-recognition of their gang status and use special vocabulary, clothing, signs, colors, graffiti, and names. Members set themselves apart from the community and are viewed as a separate entity by others. Once they get the label of gang, members eventually accept and take pride in their status.

- There is a commitment to criminal activity, although even the most criminal gang members spend the bulk of their time in noncriminal activities.[41]

The National Gang Center uses this definition:

- The group has three or more members, generally ages 12 to 24.
- Members share an identity, typically linked to a name and often other symbols.
- Members view themselves as a gang, and they are recognized by others as a gang.
- The group has some permanence and a degree of organization.
- The group is involved in an elevated level of criminal activity.[42]

gang Group of youths who collectively engage in delinquent behaviors.

How Did Gangs Develop?

The youth gang is sometimes viewed as uniquely American, but gangs have also been reported in several other nations.[43] Nor are gangs a recent phenomenon. In the 1600s, London was terrorized by organized gangs that called themselves Hectors, Bugles, Dead Boys, and other colorful names. In the seventeenth

The 28,000 youth gangs in the United States contain members such as Carlos (right), with his homeboys from the 19th Street Gang in Los Angeles.

© Joseph Rodriguez/Redux

and eighteenth centuries, English gang members wore distinctive belts and pins marked with serpents, animals, stars, and the like.[44] The first mention of youth gangs in America occurred in the late 1780s, when prison reformers noted the presence of *gangs* of young people hanging out on Philadelphia's street corners. By the 1820s, New York's Bowery and Five Points districts, Boston's North End and Fort Hill, and the outlying Southwark and Moyamensing sections of Philadelphia were the locales of youth gangs with colorful names like the Roach Guards, Chichesters, the Plug Uglies, and the Dead Rabbits.[45]

In the 1920s, Frederick Thrasher initiated the study of the modern gang in his analysis of more than 1,300 youth groups in Chicago.[46] He found that the social, economic, and ecological processes that affect the structure of cities create cracks in the normal fabric of society—weak family controls, poverty, and social disorganization. Thrasher referred to this as an **interstitial area**—one falling within the cracks and crevices of society. According to Thrasher, groups of youths develop to meet such needs as play, fun, and adventure, activities that sometimes lead to delinquent acts. Impoverished areas present many opportunities for conflict between groups of youths and adult authority. If this conflict continues, the groups become more solidified and their activities become primarily illegal, and the groups develop into gangs.

According to Thrasher, adult society does not meet the needs of lower-class youths, and the gang solves the problem by offering excitement, fun, and opportunity. The gang is not a haven for disturbed youths, but an alternative lifestyle for normal boys.

Gangs in the 1950s and 1960s. In the 1950s and early 1960s, the threat of gangs and gang violence swept the public consciousness. Newspapers featured stories on the violent behavior of fighting gangs, such as the Vice Lords and the Fordham Baldies. Gangs were involved in major brawls over territory and turf.

By the mid-1960s, the gang menace seemed to have disappeared. Some experts attribute the decline of gang activity to successful community-based programs.[47] Others believe gangs were eliminated because police gang-control units infiltrated gangs, arrested leaders, and constantly harassed members.[48] Some gangs shifted their emphasis from criminal behavior to get involved in social or political activities. In Chicago, the Vice Lords ran alternative schools and started businesses, and the Blackstone Rangers ran a job training program with educational components. In addition, many gang members were drafted into the army. Others were imprisoned after police crackdowns.

Gangs Reemerge. Interest in gang activity began anew in the early 1970s. Bearing such names as Savage Skulls and Black Assassins, gangs began to form in New York's South Bronx neighborhoods in the spring of 1971 and quickly spread to other parts of the city. By 1975, there were 275 police-verified gangs with 11,000 members.[49]

Gang activity also reemerged in other major cities, such as Chicago and Los Angeles. The Crips gang was created in Los Angeles in 1969 by teens Raymond Washington and Stanley "Tookie" Williams. Initially called the Baby Avenues, they evolved to Avenue Cribs, and then Cribs. According to legend, the gang name evolved into Crips because some of its members used canes to attack victims; it is also possible it was a simple spelling mistake in newspaper articles about the gang. As the Crips rose in power, other rival gangs formed an alliance that morphed into their most significant rival gang, the Bloods. Eventually both these gangs sent representatives to organize chapters in distant areas or to take over existing gangs.

Why Did Gangs Reemerge? One reason for the increase in gang activity may be involvement in the sale of illegal drugs.[50] Early gangs relied on group loyalty to encourage membership, but modern gang members are lured by

To view current examples of **gang graffiti**, visit the Criminal Justice CourseMate at CengageBrain.com, then access the Web Links for this chapter.

interstitial area An area of the city that forms when there is a crack in the social fabric and in which deviant groups, cliques and gangs form.

Looking Back at Luis's Story

Luis eventually decided to change much of his negative behavior.

CRITICAL THINKING How do you think Luis's family culture and structure played a role in his positive decision making?

the quest for drug profits. In some areas, gangs replaced organized crime families as the dominant suppliers of cocaine and crack. The traditional weapons of gangs—chains, knives, and homemade guns—were replaced by automatic weapons.

Gang formation may also have been the natural consequence of the economic and social dislocation that occurred when the economy shifted from a relatively high-paying manufacturing to low-wage service economy.[51] Some U.S. cities that required a large population base for their manufacturing plants now faced economic stress as these plants shut down. In this uneasy economic climate, the influence of successful adult role models and stable families declined. The lack of adult supervision gave neighborhood kids a great deal of free time without the moderating influence of prosocial role models. As they matured, local youths had limited access to appealing conventional career lines and high-paying jobs. The lure of the gang and easy profits became irresistible to kids who had nowhere else to turn.[52] **CHECKPOINTS**

CONTEMPORARY GANGS

The gang cannot be viewed as a uniform or homogeneous social concept. Gangs vary by activity, makeup, location, leadership style, and age. The next sections describe some of the most salient features of contemporary gangs.

Extent

The federal government sponsors the National Youth Gang Survey (NYGS) to measure gang activity around the United States.[53] Their most recent effort finds that a significant majority of urban areas report the presence of gangs, and that gangs exist in all levels of the social strata, from rural counties to metropolitan areas.[54] More than one-third of cities and towns with populations of at least 2,500 now experience gang problems. This translates to an estimated 3,550 jurisdictions with gang problems across the United States. Based on law enforcement reports, it is estimated that there arc about 28,000 gangs and 730,000 gang members throughout 3,500 jurisdictions in the United States. The number of jurisdictions with gang problems and the number of gangs has increased about 20 percent since 2002, though the actual number of gang members has remained stable.

Location

As Figure 8.1 indicates, gangs are an urban phenomenon, though a significant number of small towns and suburban areas have a gang presence. As might be expected, rural areas are relatively gang free.

Traditionally, gangs have operated in disorganized neighborhoods experiencing rapid population change. In these so-called "transitional neighborhoods," which house the urban underclass, diverse ethnic and racial groups find themselves in competition with one another.[55] Most typical are the poverty-stricken areas of Eastern and Midwestern cities and the Mexican American barrios of the southwestern states and California. These areas contain large, structured gang clusters that are resistant to change or control by law enforcement agencies. Research by David Pyrooz confirms that cities with greater social and economic deprivation experience higher rates of gang homicide. Communities with fewer resources have limited capacities to regulate human behavior and gangs are naturally occurring deviant

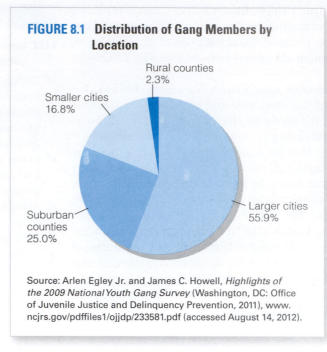

FIGURE 8.1 Distribution of Gang Members by Location

- Rural counties 2.3%
- Smaller cities 16.8%
- Suburban counties 25.0%
- Larger cities 55.9%

Source: Arlen Egley Jr. and James C. Howell, *Highlights of the 2009 National Youth Gang Survey* (Washington, DC: Office of Juvenile Justice and Delinquency Prevention, 2011), www.ncjrs.gov/pdffiles1/ojjdp/233581.pdf (accessed August 14, 2012).

social networks that engage in violence as a result of weakened social controls. It is not, he argues, that these communities are more tolerant of violent gang activities; rather, they lack the collective efficacy to control gangs.[56]

While gangs are disproportionately located in urban phenomenon, thousands of gangs are located in small cities, suburban counties, and even rural areas. Gang activity has been growing in these nontraditional areas at a faster pace than in the urban environment. The growth of gangs in suburban and rural areas has been

Gangs are located in large cities but also in suburban and rural areas. This 16-year-old Lakota Sioux girl is holding an M1 assault rifle. On the reservation, Native American Sioux are the majority, and most live in poverty due to nearly nonexistent job opportunities—the unemployment rate is said to be around 80 percent. Their lifespan used to be around 80 years, but is now 57 years for men and 63 for women. In addition to rampant health problems—diabetes, heart attacks, cancer—from limited and unhealthy dietary options, the reservation also faces contaminated water from uranium mines and rising youth violence. In such an environment, youth gangs flourish.

attributed to a restructuring of the population. There has been a massive movement of people out of the central city to outlying communities and suburbs. In some cities, once-fashionable neighborhoods have declined, whereas in others, downtown areas have undergone extensive renewal. Previously impoverished inner-city districts of major cities, such as New York and Chicago, are now quite fashionable and expensive, devoted to finance, retail stores, high-priced condos, and entertainment. Two aspects of this development inhibit urban gang formation: (1) there are few residential areas and thus few adolescent recruits, and (2) there is intensive police patrol.

Migration

Because of redevelopment, gangs in some areas have relocated or migrated; gang members have organized new chapters when they relocate to new areas. The most recent NYGS found many jurisdictions have experienced gang migration, and in a few areas more than half of all gang members had come from other areas.

Why do gang members migrate? Although the prevailing wisdom is that gang members move for criminal purposes—for example, to sell drugs to new customers at higher prices—the NYGS found that most did so for social reasons. Families relocate in pursuit of legitimate employment opportunities, and teenage sons and daughters are forced to move with them to a new locale. In all, less than 20 percent of gang members move to a new location solely in order to participate in illegal ventures or to start up a new gang branch.

Most migrators are African American or Latino males who maintain close ties with members of their original gangs "back home." Other migrants join local gangs, shedding old ties and gaining new affiliations. Although some experts fear the outcome of migration, it appears the number of migrants is relatively small in proportion to the overall gang population, supporting the contention that most gangs actually are "homegrown."

Formation

Gang formation involves a sense of territoriality. Most gang members live in close proximity to one another, and their sense of belonging extends only to their small area of the city. At first, a gang may form when members of an ethnic minority join together for self-preservation. As the group gains domination over an area, it may view the area as its own territory, or turf, which needs to be defended from outsiders.

Once formed, gangs grow when youths who admire the older gang members "apply" and are accepted for membership. Sometimes the new members will be given a special identity that reflects their apprenticeship status. Joan Moore and her associates found that *klikas*, or youth cliques, in Latino gangs remain together as unique groups with separate names, identities, and experiences; they also have more intimate relationships among themselves than among the general gang membership.[57] She likens *klikas* to a particular class in a university, such as the class of 2013—a group of people who share common interests and backgrounds, gathered together as peers.

Moore also found that gangs can expand by including members' kin, even if they do not live in the neighborhood, and rival gang members who wish to join because they admire the gang's way of doing things. Adding outsiders gives the gang the ability to take over new territory. However, it also brings with it new problems, because it usually results in greater conflicts with rival gangs.

Leadership

Delinquent gangs tend to be small and transitory.[58] Youths often belong to more than a single group or clique and develop an extensive network of delinquent associates. Group roles can vary, and an adolescent who assumes a leadership role in one group may be a follower in another.

klikas Subgroups of same-aged youths in Latino gangs that remain together and have separate names and a unique identity in the gang.

Those who assume leadership roles are described as "cool characters" who have earned their position by demonstrating fighting prowess, verbal quickness, or athletic distinction. They emphasize that leadership is held by one person and varies with particular activities, such as fighting, sex, and negotiations. In fact, in some gangs each age level has its own leaders. Older members are not necessarily considered leaders by younger members. In his analysis of Los Angeles gangs, Malcolm Klein observed that many gang leaders deny leadership. He overheard one gang boy claim, "We got no leaders, man. Everybody's a leader, and nobody can talk for nobody else."[59] The most plausible explanation of this ambivalence is the boy's fear that his decisions will conflict with those of other leaders.

There appear, then, to be diverse concepts of leadership, depending on the structure of the gang. Less organized gangs are marked by diffuse and shifting leadership. More organized gangs have a clear chain of command and leaders who are supposed to plan activities and control members' behavior.[60]

Communication

Gangs seek recognition, both from their rivals and from the community. Image and reputation depend on the ability to communicate to the rest of the world. One major source of communication is **graffiti** (see Figure 8.2).

These wall writings are especially elaborate among Latino gangs, who call them *placasos* or *placa*, meaning sign or plaque. Latino graffiti usually contains the writer's street name and the name of the gang. Strength or power is asserted through the terms *rifa*, which means to rule, and *controllo*, indicating that the gang controls the area. Another common inscription is "p/v," for *por vida*; this refers to the fact that the gang expects to control the area "for life."

Gangs also communicate by means of a secret vocabulary. Members may refer to their *crew*, *posse*, *troop*, or *tribe*. Within larger gangs are "sets," who hang out in particular neighborhoods, and "tips," small groups formed for particular purposes. Exhibit 8.1 contains other slang terms.

Gang communication can also involve hand signs that are quickly displayed with the fingers, hands, and body, and have very specific meanings to gang members. Chicago gangs call this **representing**. Gang members will proclaim their affiliation and ask victims, "Who do you ride?" or "What do you be about?" An incorrect response will provoke an attack. Sometimes, gang members will flash a crowd with the hand signals of a rival gang, called "false flagging," hoping that someone will respond with a rival hand sign so that they can be targeted for a verbal or physical confrontation.

WWW

To access a site that has a good selection of **West Coast gang graffiti**, visit the Criminal Justice CourseMate at CengageBrain.com, then access the Web Links for this chapter.

graffiti Inscriptions or drawings made on a wall or structure and used by delinquents for gang messages and turf definition.
representing Tossing or flashing gang signs in the presence of rivals, often escalating into a verbal or physical confrontation.

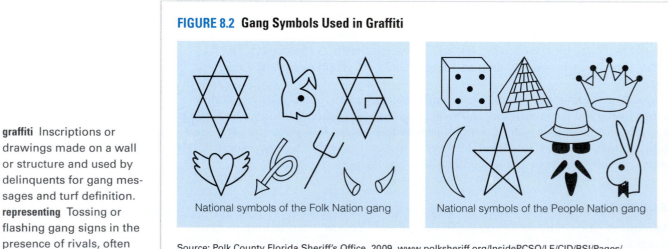

FIGURE 8.2 **Gang Symbols Used in Graffiti**

National symbols of the Folk Nation gang

National symbols of the People Nation gang

Source: Polk County Florida Sheriff's Office, 2009, www.polksheriff.org/InsidePCSO/LE/CID/BSI/Pages/IdentifyingGangMembers.aspx (accessed August 14, 2012).

> **EXHIBIT 8.1** **Common Gang Slang**
>
> - **13, XIII, X3, or *trece*** Thirteenth letter in the alphabet (*M*), which symbolizes or identifies gang affiliation of Mexican heritage. Also may refer to allegiance to Southern California gangs.
> - **14, XIV, or X4** Fourteenth letter of the alphabet (*N*); refers to allegiance to Northern California or *Norte Califas* gangs.
> - **8-ball** A reference to a quantity of cocaine.
> - **5-O** The police.
> - **AK** Used to denote a semi-automatic assault rifle, such as AK47 or SKS rifles.
> - **PV** *Por vida,* Spanish for "for life" or always.

© Cengage Learning

While gang colors, signs, and so on are traditional, law enforcement agents now report that some gang members are becoming more sophisticated and have modified or ceased traditional or stereotypical gang action—for example, no longer displaying their colors, tattoos, or hand signs—in order to remain under the radar. Others are forming hybrid gangs to avoid police attention and make it more difficult for law enforcement to identify and monitor them.[61]

Gangs in Cyberspace. Gang communications have entered the cyber age, and gang members often use cell phones and the Internet to communicate and promote their illicit activities.[62] Street gangs typically use the voice and text messaging capabilities of cell phones to conduct drug transactions and prearrange meetings with customers. Members of street gangs use prepaid cell phones that they discard after conducting their drug trafficking operations. Internet-based methods such as social networking sites, encrypted e-mail, Internet telephony, and instant messaging are commonly used by gang members to communicate with one another and with drug customers. Gang members use the Net to boast about their gang membership and related activities. Take these cases for instance:

- Members of Crips gangs in Hampton, Virginia, use the Internet to intimidate rival gang members and maintain websites to recruit new members. On October 23, 2007, a 15-year-old Crips gang member was arrested for shooting a rival gang member in the leg. Additionally, he was charged with recruiting new members into his street gang through the use of the gang's social networking site.
- Gangs in Oceanside, California, recruit new members and claim new turf from their website. Gang members flash gang signs and wear gang colors in videos and photos posted on the Web. Sometimes, rivals "spar" on Internet message boards.[63]

Types of Gangs and Gang Boys

Gangs have been categorized by their dominant activity: some are devoted to violence and to protecting neighborhood boundaries or turf; others are devoted to theft; some specialize in drug trafficking; others are concerned with recreation rather than crime.[64] Jeffrey Fagan found that most gangs fall into one of these four categories:

- *Social gang.* Involved in few delinquent activities and little drug use other than alcohol and marijuana. Members are more interested in social activities.
- *Party gang.* Concentrates on drug use and sales but forgoes most delinquent behavior. Drug sales are designed to finance members' personal drug use.
- *Serious delinquent gang.* Engages in serious delinquent behavior while avoiding drug dealing and usage. Drugs are used only on social occasions.

- *Organized gang.* Heavily involved in criminality. Drug use and sales are related to other criminal acts. Gang violence is used to establish control over drug sale territories. This gang is on the verge of becoming a formal criminal organization.[65]

Not only are there different types of gangs, there may be different roles played by gang boys within each type of gang. When Avelardo Valdez and Stephen Sifaneck studied the role that Mexican American gangs and gang members play in southwest Texas drug markets, they found that the gangs and gang members could be separated into four distinct categories, so that using the term "drug gang" or "gang boy" to describe gang activity/members was too simplistic.[66]

The format and structure of gangs may be changing. They are now commonly described as having a *hybrid gang culture*, meaning they do not follow a single code of rules or method of operation. Today's gangs do have several common characteristics:

- Symbols and graffiti associated with different gangs
- Wearing colors traditionally associated with a rival gang
- Less concern over turf or territory
- Members who sometimes switch from one gang to another[67]

Cohesion

The standard definition of a gang implies that it is a cohesive group. However, some experts refer to gangs as **near-groups**, which have limited cohesion, impermanence, minimal consensus of norms, shifting membership, disturbed leadership, and limited definitions of membership expectations.[68] Gangs maintain a small core of committed members, who work constantly to keep the gang going, and a much larger group of affiliated youths, who participate in gang activity only when the mood suits them. James Diego Vigil found that boys in **barrio** gangs (Latino neighborhood gangs) could be separated into regular members and those he describes as "peripheral," "temporary," and "situational."[69] The more embedded a boy becomes in the gang and its processes the less likely they are to leave. When David Pyrooz and his research team interviewed gang members, they found that about half of less involved gang boys leave within 6 months of their first contact, while more involved kids stay at least 2 more years.[70]

Current research indicates that some gangs remain near-groups, others lack overall organization but do have pockets or members who are structured and organized, while still others have become quite organized and stable.[71] These gangs resemble traditional organized crime families more than temporary youth groups. Some, such as Chicago's Latin Kings and Gangster Disciples, have members who pay regular dues, are expected to attend gang meetings regularly, and carry out political activities to further gang ambitions.

Age

The ages of gang members range widely, perhaps from as young as 8 to as old as 55.[72] Traditionally, most members of offending groups were usually no more than a few years apart in age, with a leader who may have been a few years older than most other members. However, because members are staying in gangs longer than in the past, the age spread between gang members has widened considerably. Gang experts believe the average age of gang members has been increasing yearly, a phenomenon explained in part by the changing structure of the U.S. economy.[73]

Why Are Gang Members Aging? Gang members are getting older, and the majority are now legal adults. As noted earlier, relatively high-paid, low-skilled factory jobs that would entice older gang members to leave the gang have been lost to overseas competition. A transformed U.S. economy now prioritizes information and services over heavy industry. This shift in emphasis undermines labor unions that might have attracted former gang boys. Equally damaging has been the embrace of social

near-groups Clusters of youth who outwardly seem unified, but actually have limited cohesion, impermanence, minimal consensus of norms, shifting membership, disturbed leadership, and limited definitions of membership expectations.
barrio A Spanish word meaning "district."

policies that stress security and the needs of the wealthy, weakening the economic safety net for the poor—for example, by reducing welfare eligibility. William Julius Wilson found that the inability of inner-city males to obtain adequate jobs means that they cannot afford to marry and raise families. Criminal records acquired at an early age quickly lock these youths out of the job market so that remaining in a gang becomes an economic necessity.[74] In the wake of reduced opportunity for unskilled labor, gangs have become an important ghetto employer that offers low-level drug-dealing opportunities that are certainly not available in the nongang world.[75]

Gender

Traditionally, gangs were considered a male-dominated enterprise. Of the more than 1,000 groups included in Thrasher's original survey, only half a dozen were female gangs. Females were involved in gangs in three ways: as auxiliaries (or branches) of male gangs, as part of sexually mixed gangs, or as autonomous gangs. Auxiliaries are a feminized version of the male gang name, such as the Lady Disciples rather than the Devil's Disciples

During early adolescence, roughly one-third of all gang members are female, but studies show that females leave gangs at an earlier age than males, so that their representation declines in later adolescence. Gender-mixed gangs are also more commonly reported now than in the past. There is evidence that gender composition shapes the nature of gang delinquency rates: females in all-female or majority-female gangs exhibit the lowest delinquency rates, while those in majority-male gangs exhibit the highest delinquency rates (including higher rates than males in all-male gangs).[76] Today some locales report that females make up almost half of all gang members.[77]

Girls in the Gang. Why do girls join gangs? There are a variety of reasons, including (but not limited to) financial opportunity, identity and status, peer pressure, family dysfunction, and protection.[78] Some admit that they join because they are bored and look to gangs for a social life; they are seeking fun and excitement and a means to find parties and meet boys. Others join simply because gangs are there in the neighborhood and are viewed as part of their way of life. And some are the children of gang members and are just following in their parents' footsteps.[79]

What benefits does gang membership offer to females? According to the "liberation" view, ganging can provide girls with a sense of sisterhood, independence, and solidarity, as well as a chance to earn profit through illegal activities.

Mark Fleisher and Jessie Krienert's research in Illinois found that girls from tough inner-city neighborhoods drift into gangs to escape the turmoil of their home lives, characterized by abuse, parental crime, and fatherless homes. Their affiliation begins when they hang around the street with gang boys, signaling their gang affiliation and symbolizing a lifestyle shift away from their home and school and into the street culture. The shift causes rifts with parents, leading to more time on the street and closer gang ties.[80] These young girls, typically aged 14 or 15, are targets for sexual and criminal exploitation. Although initial female gang participation may be forged by links to male gang members, once in gangs girls form close ties with other female members and engage in group criminal activity.[81] In contrast, the "social injury" view suggests that female members are still sexually exploited by male gang boys and are sometimes forced to exploit other females.

Girls who are members of male gang auxiliaries report that males control them by determining the arenas within which they can operate (i.e., the extent to which they may become involved in intergang violence). Males also play a divisive role in the girls' relationships with each other; this manipulation is absent for girls in independent gangs.[82] When criminologist Jody Miller studied female gangs in St. Louis, Missouri, and Columbus, Ohio, she found that girls in mixed gangs expressed little

Looking Back at Luis's Story

Unlike Luis, many kids are not helped and remain in gangs longer than ever before.

CRITICAL THINKING   Considering the global information economy, do you see a way to wean kids out of gangs? Are there any alternatives? What about easing entry requirements for the military?

evidence of sisterhood and solidarity with other female gang members.[83] Rather, female gang members expressed hostility to other women in the gang—believing, for example, that those who suffered sexual assault by males in the same gang actually deserved what they got. Instead of trying to create a sense of sisterhood, female gang members tried to identify with males and viewed themselves as thereby becoming "one of the guys" in the gang.

Why then do girls join gangs if they are exploitive and provide little opportunities for sisterhood? Miller found that even though being a gang member is not a walk in the park, most girls join gangs in an effort to cope with their turbulent personal lives, which may provide them with an even harsher reality; they see the gang as an institution that can increase their status and improve their lives. The gang provides them with an alternative to a tough urban lifestyle filled with the risk of violence and victimization. Many of the girl gang members had early exposure to neighborhood violence, had encounters with girl gangs while growing up, experienced severe family problems (violence or abuse), and had close family members who were gang involved.[84] Did they experience life benefits after they joined the gang? The evidence is mixed. Miller found that female gang members increased their delinquent activities and increased their risk of becoming a crime victim; they were more likely to suffer physical injury than girls who shunned gang membership. The risk of being sexually assaulted by male members of their own gang was also not insignificant. However, female gang membership did have some benefits: it protected female gang members from sexual assault by nongang neighborhood men, which they viewed as a more dangerous and deadly risk.

Why do girls leave the gang? One not-so-surprising answer is that female gang members begin to drift away from gangs when they become young mothers. Fleisher and Krienert found that a majority of the Illinois gang girls they studied became inactive members soon after getting pregnant. Pregnancy leads to a disinterest in hanging around the streets and an interest in the safety of the fetus. Other girls became inactive after they decided to settle down and raise a family. But pregnancy seemed to be the primary motivating factor for leaving the gang life.[85]

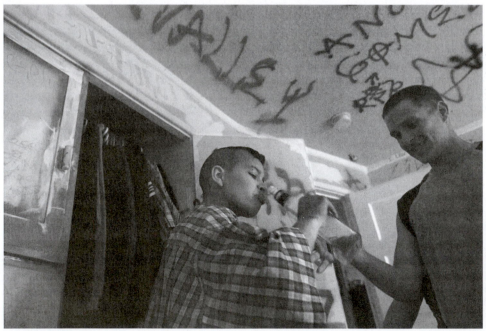

Females make up a small but growing element of gang membership. Here, Maria Ball takes a swig of liquor from a bottle in her home in Yakima, Washington, as her friend Randy reaches for the bottle. Ball is one of the few girls in the male-dominated *Chicanos Por Vida* (CPV, Chicanos for Life) gang. Because she is female, 17-year-old Maria says she has to prove to the guys in the gang that she is ready to take punches and bullets, as well as demonstrate her loyalty for CPV and her toughness.

Ethnic and Racial Composition

According to the National Youth Gang Survey, African American and/or Latino youth predominate among documented gang members. About half are Hispanic/Latino, one-third African American, and about 10 percent European American, with the rest being other races, such as Asian. This association applies to all types of environments except rural counties, where African American gang members predominate. There is an association between gang membership size, gang-problem onset, and race/ethnicity characteristics. Areas with smaller numbers of gang members or a relatively new emergence of gang problems are significantly more likely to report a greater percentage of European American gang members. Larger cities with newer gang problems are more than twice as likely to report greater variation in racial/ethnic composition of gang members (that is, proportionally fewer African American and/or Hispanic/Latino gang members) than larger cities with long-standing gang problems.

The ethnic distribution of gangs corresponds to their geographic location; the racial/ethnic composition of gangs is an extension of the characteristics of the larger community. In Philadelphia and Detroit, the overwhelming number of gang members are African American. In New York and Los Angeles, Latino gangs predominate. Newly emerging immigrant groups are making their presence felt in gangs. Authorities in Buffalo, New York, estimate that 10 percent of their gang population is Jamaican. A significant portion of Honolulu's gangs are Filipinos.

African American Gangs. The first African American youth gangs were organized in the early 1920s.[86] Because they had few rival organizations, they were able to concentrate on criminal activity rather than defending their turf. By the 1930s, the expanding number of rival gangs spawned inner-city gang warfare. Today a number of African American gangs have a national presence across the United States. Three of the largest include:

- The Black P. Stone Nation consists of seven highly structured street gangs with a single leader and a common culture. It has an estimated 6,000 to 8,000 members, most of whom are African American males from the Chicago metropolitan area. The gang's main source of income is the street-level distribution of cocaine, heroin, marijuana, and, to a lesser extent, methamphetamine. Members also are involved in many other types of criminal activity, including assault, drive-by shootings, robbery, burglary, auto theft and carjacking, extortion, and homicide.

- Bloods are an association of structured and unstructured gangs that have adopted a single-gang culture. The original Bloods were formed in the early 1970s to provide protection from the Crips street gang in Los Angeles. Large, national-level Bloods gangs include Bounty Hunter Bloods and Crenshaw Mafia Gangsters. Bloods membership is estimated to be 7,000 to 30,000 nationwide; most members are African American males. Bloods gangs are active in 123 cities in 33 states. The main source of income for Bloods gangs is street-level distribution of cocaine and marijuana. Bloods members also are involved in transporting and distributing methamphetamine, heroin, and PCP (phencyclidine), but to a much lesser extent. The gangs are involved in other criminal activity, including assault, auto theft and carjacking, burglary and robbery, identity fraud, drive-by shootings, extortion, and homicide.

- Crips are a collection of structured and unstructured gangs that have adopted a common gang culture. Crips membership is estimated at 30,000 to 35,000; most members are African American males from the Los Angeles metropolitan area. Large, national-level Crips gangs include 107 Hoover Crips, Insane Gangster Crips, and Rolling 60s Crips. Crips gangs operate in 221 cities in 41 states. The main source of income for Crips gangs is the street-level distribution of powder cocaine, crack cocaine, marijuana, and PCP. The gangs also are involved in other criminal activity such as assault, burglary, auto theft, and homicide.[87]

African American gang members have some unique characteristics. They frequently use nicknames. "Lil 45" might be used by someone whose favorite weapon is a large handgun. The three most popular categories of black gang members' nicknames in Las Vegas are combinations of any single letter of the alphabet with a Loc, Mac, or Wak, for example, X-Loc, P-Mac, D-Wak. The next most popular nicknames are Dre and then Baby with any letter following—Baby-X, for example.[88]

Although TV shows portray gangs as wearing distinctive attire, members usually favor nondescript attire to reduce police scrutiny. However, gang members frequently have distinctive hairstyles, such as shaving or braids, which are designed to look like their leaders'. Tattooing is popular, and members often wear colored head scarves or "rags" to identify their gang affiliation. It is also common for African American gang members to mark their territory with distinctive graffiti: drawings of guns, dollar signs, proclamations of individual power, and profanity.

Latino Gangs. The popularity of gangs and gang culture is relatively high among youth of Latino background, explaining in part their disproportionate participation in gang membership.[89] Many join Sureño gangs (Southerners), which are groups of loosely affiliated street gangs. Even though they have a common heritage, Sureño gangs may be rivals in the streets, but become allies for mutual aid when they enter the prison system. Among the most popular gangs under the Sureño umbrella, the Mara Salvatrucha (MS-13), 18th Street, and Florencia 13 are expanding faster than other national-level gangs, both in membership and geographically. Twenty states and the District of Columbia report an increase of Sureño migration into their region. California has experienced a substantial migration of Sureño gangs into Northern California and the neighboring states of Arizona, Nevada, and Oregon.

Latino gangs are made up of youths whose ethnic ancestry can be traced to one of several Spanish-speaking cultures. They are known for their fierce loyalty to their home gang. Admission to the gang usually involves an initiation ritual in which boys are required to prove their *machismo*. The most common test requires novices to fight several established members or to commit some crime, such as a robbery. The code of conduct associated with membership means never ratting on a brother or even a rival.

In some areas, Latino gangs have a fixed leadership hierarchy. However, in Southern California, which has the largest concentration of Latino youth gangs, leadership is fluid. During times of crisis, those with particular skills will assume command. One boy will lead in combat, while another negotiates drug deals.

Latino gang members are known for their dress codes. Some wear dark-colored caps pulled down over the ears with a small roll at the bottom. Others wear a folded bandana over the forehead and tied in back. Another popular headpiece is the "stingy brim" fedora or a baseball cap with the wearer's nickname and gang affiliation written on the bill. Members favor tank-style T-shirts that give them quick access to weapons.

Members mark off territory with colorful and intricate graffiti. Latino gang graffiti has very stylized lettering and frequently uses three-dimensional designs. Latino gangs, especially local ones, have a strong sense of turf, and a great deal of gang violence is directed at warding off any threat to their control. Slights by rivals, including put-downs, stare-downs ("mad-dogging"), defacing gang insignia, and territorial intrusions, can set off a violent confrontation, often with high-powered automatic weapons. However, there are intragang differences: some, such as the Sur-13 gang, are more rooted in the community, while others, including the Mexican Mafia and MS-13, are more mobile. There may also be differences between national and local gangs. National gangs are significantly larger, more organized, and more criminally active; local gangs may be more turf-oriented, visible in the community, and more involved in drug-related activities.[90]

Mara Salvatrucha (MS-13) A violent, international gang begun in southern California by immigrants from El Salvador. Engages in such crimes as burglaries, narcotic sales, weapons smuggling, murder, rape, and witness intimidation.

Mara Salvatrucha (MS-13). One of the most feared Latino gangs, **Mara Salvatrucha (MS-13)** was started in Los Angeles by immigrants from El Salvador fleeing a civil war.[91] MS-13 was formed as a means of self-protection from preexisting Mexican gangs. *Mara* is El Salvadoran slang for "posse," or gang, *Salvatruchas* is local slang for being alert and ready to take action; the "13" is a reference to their beginnings on 13th street in Los Angeles.

When law enforcement cracked down and deported MS-13 members, the deportees quickly created outposts in El Salvador and throughout Central America. The Salvadoran government responded by criminalizing gang membership and arresting thousands.[92] Nonetheless, gang membership has continued to grow, and the Salvadoran gangs have actually returned to set up branches in the United States. Some experts believe that the MS-13 is now the nation's most dangerous gang. Members are involved in burglaries, auto thefts, narcotic sales, home invasion robberies, weapons smuggling, carjacking, extortion, murder, rape, witness intimidation, illegal firearm sales, car theft, aggravated assaults, and drug trafficking. They also have been known to place a "tax" on prostitutes and nongang member drug dealers who are working on MS-13 turf. Failure to pay up will most likely result in violence.

Asian Gangs. Asian gangs are prominent in New York, Los Angeles, San Francisco, Seattle, and Houston. The earliest gangs, the Wah Ching, were formed in the nineteenth century by Chinese youths affiliated with adult crime groups (*tongs*). In the 1960s, two other gangs formed in San Francisco, the Joe Boys and Yu Li. The Tiny Rascal Gangsters is one of the largest and most violent Asian street gang associations in the United States, and is now composed of at least 60 structured and unstructured gangs, commonly referred to as sets, with an estimated 5,000 to 10,000 members and associates who have adopted a common gang culture. The sets are most active in the southwestern, Pacific, and New England regions of the United States. The street-level distribution of powder cocaine, marijuana, MDMA, and methamphetamine is a primary source of income for the sets. Members also are involved in other criminal activity, including theft, robbery, assault, drive-by shootings, home invasion, extortion, and homicide.[93]

There are also regional gangs. Samoan gangs have operated on the West Coast, as have Vietnamese gangs. The formation of Vietnamese gangs can be tied to external factors, such as racism and economic problems, and to internal problems, including family stress and failure to achieve the success enjoyed by other Asians. Vietnamese gangs are formed when youths feel they need their *ahns*, or brothers, for protection.[94]

Asian gangs are unique and do not share many qualities with other ethnically centered groups. They tend to victimize members of their own ethnic group. They are more organized, have recognizable leaders, and are far more secretive than African American or Latino groups. They also tend to be far less territorial and less openly visible. Asian gangs are also known for the strict control gang elders have over younger members. Elders, some of whom may be in their 30s and 40s, are no longer engaged in street crime and violence, but may instead be involved in other forms of illegal activities such as running gambling parlors. They use the younger gang members to protect their business interests and to collect any unpaid gambling debts. In some jurisdictions, police can pressure the elders to control the violent tendencies of the younger members by threatening to crack down on their illegitimate business enterprises—for example, by parking patrol cars in front of suspected gambling locations.[95]

Anglo Gangs. The first American youth gangs were made up of European American youths. During the 1950s, they competed with African American and Latino gangs in the nation's largest cities. Today less than 10 percent of all gang members are white. European American gang members are often alienated middle-class youths rather than poor lower-class youths. They include "punkers" and "stoners," who dress in heavy-metal fashions and engage in drug- and violence-related activities. Some are obsessed with occult themes, suicide, ritual killings, and animal mutilations. They get involved in devil worship, tattoo themselves with occult symbols, and gouge their bodies to draw blood for satanic rituals.[96] Some **skinhead** youth groups are devoted to European American supremacist activities and are being actively recruited by adult hate groups. `CHECKPOINTS`

skinhead Member of a European American supremacist gang, identified by a shaved skull and Nazi or Ku Klux Klan markings.

LO3 Describe the makeup of gangs.

✔ There are different types of gangs—some are social, others criminal.

✔ Gang membership seems to be aging; kids are staying longer in gangs.

✔ Many gangs are involved in drug dealing, whereas others specialize in violence.

✔ The number of female gang members and female gangs is rapidly increasing.

✔ Many girls join gangs in an effort to cope with their turbulent personal lives.

✔ Once in gangs, girls form close ties with other female members and engage in group criminal activity.

✔ The ethnic distribution of gangs corresponds to their geographic location.

✔ The first black youth gangs were organized in the early 1920s.

✔ Latino gangs such as MS-13 have continued to grow and now constitute the largest number of gangs and gang memberships.

✔ White gang members are often alienated middle-class youths rather than poor lower-class youths.

Criminality and Violence

Regardless of their type, gang members typically commit more crimes than any other youths in the social environment.[97] Members self-report significantly more crime than nonmembers, and the more enmeshed a youth is in a gang, the more likely he is to report criminal behavior, to have an official record, and to get sent to juvenile court. The gang membership–crime relationship begins as early as middle school.[98] Recent research by Chris Melde and Finn-Aage Esbensen found that active gang members experienced a significant increase in violent behavior activities. After leaving the gang, their propensity for violence declined significantly, becoming no different than that of kids who had never been in a gang.[99]

Although the association between gang membership and delinquency is unquestioned, there are three different explanations for the relationship:

- *Selection hypothesis.* Kids with a history of crime and violence join gangs and maintain their persistent delinquency once they become members.

- *Facilitation hypothesis.* Gang membership facilitates deviant behavior because it provides the structure and group support for antisocial activities.

- *Enhancement hypothesis.* Selection and facilitation work interactively, increasing the likelihood of enhanced criminality.[100]

Gang criminality has numerous patterns.[101] Some gangs specialize in drug dealing. But not all gangs are major players in drug trafficking: many are only weakly or sporadically involved in drug dealing, and some who are tend to distribute small amounts of drugs at the street level.[102] The world of major dealing belongs to adults, not to gang youths.[103] Other gangs engage in a wide variety of criminal activity, ranging from felony assaults to drug dealing.[104] Gang members are most commonly involved in such crimes as larceny or theft, aggravated assault, and burglary or breaking and entering. Drug use is quite common. Most female gang members report multiple-drug use, using drugs such as cocaine, crack, LSD, PCP, methamphetamine, heroin, glue/inhalants, MDMA, and Quaaludes.[105]

Do gang kids increase their involvement in criminal activity after they join gangs or do gangs recruit kids who are already high-rate offenders? Data from the Rochester Youth Development Study (RYDS), a longitudinal cohort study of 1,000 youths in upstate New York, support the gang–crime association theory. The RYDS data show that gang members account for a significant portion of all violent and drug crimes; two-thirds (66 percent) of the chronic violent offenders were gang members.[106]

Gang Violence. Not surprisingly, research shows that gang members are more violent than nonmembers. One reason is that kids who join gangs are more likely to carry weapons than nonmembers.[107] The RYDS found that young gang members in Rochester were about 10 times more likely to carry handguns than nongang juvenile offenders, and gun-toting gang members committed about 10 times more violent crimes than nonmembers.[108] These findings are supported by Richard Spano and John Bolland's analysis of data collected on gang boys in Mobile, Alabama. Over a one-year period, youth who were both gang members and exposed to violence were 549 percent more likely to initiate gun carrying. Gang members who engaged in violent behavior were 575 percent more likely to initiate gun carrying. Gang members who were exposed to violence and engaged in violent behavior themselves increased the likelihood of initiation of gun carrying by 665 percent.[109]

It is not surprising, then, that youth gangs are responsible for a disproportionate number of homicides. In two cities, Los Angeles and Chicago—considered the most gang-populated cities in the United States—over half of the annual homicides are attributed to gangs. Nationally, approximately one-fourth of all homicides are considered gang-related, and the numbers are increasing.[110]

Research indicates that gang violence is impulsive and therefore happens in spurts. It usually involves defense of the gang and gang members' reputations. Once the threat ends, the level of violence may recede, but it remains at a level higher than it was previously. Peaks in gang homicides tend to correspond to a series of escalating confrontations, usually over control of gang turf or a drug market.[111] The most dangerous areas are along disputed boundaries where a drug hot spot intersects with a turf hot spot. There are also "marauder" patterns in which members of rival gangs travel to their enemy's territory in search of victims.[112]

Violence is a core fact of gang formation and life.[113] Gang members feel threatened by other gangs and are wary of encroachments on their turf. It is not surprising that gangs try to recruit youths who are already gun owners; new members are likely to increase gun ownership and possession.[114] Gang members face a far greater chance of death at an early age than do nonmembers.[115]

Revenge, Honor, Courage, and Prestige. When criminologist Scott Decker interviewed gang boys, he found that violence is essential to the transformation of a peer group into a gang. When asked why he calls the group he belongs to a gang, one member replied: "There is more violence than a family. With a gang it's like fighting all the time, killing, shooting."[116]

When joining the gang, members may be forced to partake in violent rituals to prove their reliability. Gang members are ready to fight when others attack them or when they believe their territory or turf is being encroached upon. Violence may be directed against rival gang members accused of insults or against those involved in personal disputes. Gang members also expect to fight when they go to certain locations that are off limits or attend events where violence is routine. Girl gang members may fight when they sense that a member of a rival gang is trying to hook up with their boyfriend. Gini Sykes spent two years hanging with girl gangs in New York City in order to develop an understanding of their lives and lifestyle. One girl, Tiny, told Sykes how ferociousness made up for lack of stature:

Tiny fixed me with a cold stare that wiped away any earlier impression of childish cuteness. "See, we smaller girls, we go for your weak spot." Her gaze moved across my features. "Your face. Your throat. Your eyes, so we can blind you. I don't care if you have more weight on me. I'll still try to kill you because, you know, I have a bad temper."[117]

Tiny related the story of how she attacked a rival involved in a sexual encounter with her boyfriend:

"She was crying and begging, but she'd disrespected me in front of everybody. We started fighting and she pulled that blade out—." Tiny shrugged. "I just wasn't prepared. You can't tell when someone's got a razor in their mouth."

After she was cut, Tiny went into a defensive rage, and

frantically felt for [her] wound, blood seeping between her fingers. Suddenly, in self-preservation, she grabbed [her rival's] neck, and blinded by her own blood, began smashing [the girl's] head into the concrete until [another gang member], hearing a siren, dragged her away. The girl had slashed Tiny's face eleven times.

Gang members are sensitive to any rivals who question their honor. Once an insult is perceived, the gang's honor cannot be restored until the "debt" is repaid. Police efforts to cool down gang disputes only delay the revenge, which can be a beating or a drive-by shooting. Random acts of revenge have become so common that physicians now consider them a significant health problem—a major contributor to early morbidity and mortality among adolescents and children in major gang cities.[118]

Violence is used to maintain the gang's internal discipline. If subordinates disobey orders, perhaps by using rather than selling drugs, they may be subject to disciplinary action by other gang members.

Another common gang crime is extortion, called "turf tax," which involves forcing people to pay the gang to be protected from dangerous neighborhood youths. **Prestige crimes** occur when a gang member steals or assaults someone to gain prestige in the gang. These crimes may be part of an initiation rite or an effort to establish a special reputation, a position of responsibility, or a leadership role; to prevail in an internal power struggle; or to respond to a challenge from a rival.

WHY DO YOUTHS JOIN GANGS?

Although gangs flourish in inner-city areas, gang membership cannot be assumed to be solely a function of lower-class identity. Many lower-class youths do not join gangs, and middle-class youths are found in suburban skinhead groups. Let's look at some of the suspected causes of gang delinquency.

WHAT DOES THIS MEAN TO ME?

▶ **Music and Gangs** Gang expert John Hagedorn has noted that music is not often discussed in gang studies, although it has a strong influence on gangs in the United States and abroad. In Nigeria, he notes, gangs of Muslim youth enforce Sharia (Islamic law), while wearing gold chains, using and selling drugs, and listening to rap music. Throughout Africa, Latin America, and Asia, rap music has captured the imagination of youth who find that embracing hip-hop helps them identity with African American youth in the United States who are rebelling against authority. Among the founders of hip-hop were former gang members, like Afrika Bambaataa in the South Bronx, who consciously saw hip-hop as a way to pull youth away from gangs.

Do you believe that listening to rap and hip-hop encourages kids to join gangs and embrace the gang lifestyle and culture? Or conversely, do you think that gang kids like to listen to music that symbolizes their beliefs? What would you expect them to listen to—Bach and Beethoven?

The Anthropological View

In the 1950s, Herbert Block and Arthur Niederhoffer suggested that gangs appeal to adolescents' longing for the tribal process that sustained their ancestors.[119] They found that gang processes do seem similar to the puberty rites of some tribal cultures; gang rituals help the child bridge the gap between childhood and adulthood. For example, tattoos and other identifying marks are an integral part of gang culture. Gang initiation ceremonies are similar to the activities of young men in Pacific Island cultures. Many gangs put new members through a hazing to make sure they have "heart," a feature similar to tribal rites. In tribal societies, initiation into a cult is viewed as the death of childhood. By analogy, boys in lower-class urban areas yearn to join the gang and "really start to live." Membership in the gang "means the youth gives up his life as a child and assumes a new way of life."[120] Gang names are suggestive of "totemic ancestors," because they usually are symbolic (Cobras, Jaguars, and Kings, for example).

James Diego Vigil has described the rituals of gang initiation, which include pummeling to show that the boy is ready to leave his matricentric (mother-dominated) household; this is reminiscent of tribal initiation rites.[121] These rituals become an important part of gang activities.[122]

The Social Disorganization/Sociocultural View

Sociologists have commonly viewed the destructive sociocultural forces in poor inner-city areas as the major cause of gang formation.[123] Irving Spergel's classic study *Racketville, Slumtown, and Haulburg* found that Slumtown—the area with the lowest income and the largest population—had the highest number of violent gangs.[124] According to Spergel, the gang gives lower-class youths a means of attaining status. Malcolm Klein's research of the late 1960s and 1970s also found that typical gang members came from dysfunctional and destitute families and lacked adequate role models.[125]

prestige crimes. Stealing or assaulting someone to gain prestige in the neighborhood; often part of gang initiation rites.

The sociocultural view assumes that gangs are a natural response to lower-class life and a status-generating medium for boys whose aspirations cannot be realized by legitimate means. Youths who join gangs may hold conventional goals, but are either unwilling or unable to accomplish them through conventional means.

While gang membership is highest in disorganized areas, in a classic work, Richard Cloward and Lloyd Ohlin suggested that some disadvantaged neighborhoods are so deteriorated that they cannot even support gang membership.[126] According to Cloward and Ohlin, the opportunity to become a successful gang member is limited in the most deteriorated areas. Recent research by criminologists Charles Katz and Stephen Schnebly support Cloward and Ohlin's ideas. They find that neighborhood disadvantage does promote gang membership, but that the association is not linear: at extreme levels of structural disadvantage gang membership begins to decline. They find that some neighborhoods are so disadvantaged and disorganized, and social networks in them are so sparse, that they no longer possess the basic social structures necessary for youth residents to coalesce and form into gangs. These communities lack the resources to support conventional youth activities. The disorganized nature of their communities also prohibits them from transmitting unconventional norms and behaviors—such as gang culture—to youth residents.[127]

The Anomie/Alienation View

According to this view, conditions of anomie/alienation encourage gang formation on both a cultural and individual level. On a cultural level, youths are encouraged to join gangs during periods of social, economic, and cultural turmoil.[128] Immigration or emigration, rapidly expanding or contracting populations, and the incursion of different racial/ethnic groups, or even different segments or generations of the same racial/ethnic population, can create fragmented communities and gang problems.[129]

On an individual level, the gang is a coalition of troubled youths who are socialized mainly by the streets rather than by conventional institutions.[130] Gang

© Daniel Rosenthal/laif/Redux

Some experts believe that the destructive sociocultural forces in poor inner-city areas prompt kids to join gangs. Gangs provide these kids with a means to obtain status. Here, Pete, a former gang activist, stands in front of his house in Roseland, on the south side of Chicago. This area is mainly poor and troubled by drugs, violence, and a lack of opportunity.

membership has appeal to adolescents who are alienated from their families as well as the mainstream of society. It is not surprising that (a) kids who have had problems with the law and suffer juvenile justice processing are more likely to join gangs than nonstigmatized kids, and (b) joining gangs further involves them in criminal activities.[131]

Once kids join gangs, feelings of alienation may be exacerbated. Chris Melde and Finn-Aage Esbensen found that the onset of gang involvement was associated with a number of escalating social problems not limited to association with antisocial peers and a lowered commitment to educational achievement. Melde and Esbensen conclude that joining a gang is a type of "turning point" that changes the direction of people's lives. Their findings suggest that the onset of gang membership is associated with a substantial change in emotions, attitudes, and social controls conducive to delinquency and helps explain why adolescents significantly increase their delinquent involvement after they assume gang membership.[132]

The Psychological View

Some experts believe that kids who live in deteriorated, disorganized areas are prone to suffer from elements of an antisocial personality defect; they may also be the ones most likely to join gangs.[133] Gangs recruit from among the more sociopathic youths living in poverty-stricken communities. Lacking in remorse and concern for others, they make perfect vehicles to carry out the gang's violent missions.[134]

A number of prominent research efforts have linked personality disturbance with gang membership. Malcolm Klein found that Los Angeles gang members suffer from a variety of personal deficits, including low self-concept, poor impulse control, and limited life skills.[135]

The Rational Choice View

Some youths may make a rational choice to join a gang. Members of the underclass turn to gangs as a method of obtaining desired goods and services, either directly through theft and extortion or indirectly through drug dealing and weapons sales. In this case, joining a gang can be viewed as an "employment decision." Mercer Sullivan's study of Brooklyn gangs found that members call success at crime "getting paid." Gang boys also refer to the rewards of crime as "getting over," which refers to their pride at "beating the system" even though they are far from the economic mainstream.[136] According to this view, the gang boy has long been involved in criminal activity *prior* to his gang membership, and he joins the gang as a means of improving his illegal "productivity."[137]

Gang membership is *not* a necessary precondition for delinquency. Felix Padilla found this when he studied the Diamonds, a Latino gang in Chicago.[138] The decision to join the gang was made after an assessment of legitimate opportunities. The Diamonds made collective business decisions, and individuals who made their own deals were penalized. The gang maintained a distinct structure and carried out other functions similar to those of legitimate enterprises, including recruiting personnel and financing business ventures.

Drug use is a big part of the gang experience, and drug users may join gangs to enhance availability of drugs and support for their use.[139] Terence Thornberry and his colleagues at the Rochester Youth Development Study (RYDS) found that before youths join gangs, their substance abuse and delinquency rates are no higher than

those of nongang members. When they are in the gang, their crime and drug abuse rates increase, only to decrease when they leave the gang. Thornberry concludes that gangs facilitate criminality rather than provide a haven for youths who are disturbed or already highly delinquent. This research is important, because it lends support to the life course model: events that take place during the life cycle, such as joining a gang, have a significant impact on criminal behavior and drug abuse.[140] The Focus on Delinquency feature explores this concept further.

Personal Safety. According to Spergel, some adolescents choose to join gangs from a "rational calculation" to achieve safety.[141] Youths who are new to a community may believe they will be harassed or attacked if they remain "unaffiliated." Girls also join gangs for protection. Though they may be exploited by male gang members, they are protected from assaults by nongang males in the neighborhood.[142]

Motivation may have its roots in inter-race or interethnic rivalry; youths who reside in an area dominated by a different racial or ethnic group may be persuaded that gang membership is a means of protection. Ironically, gang members are more likely to be attacked than nonmembers.

Fun and Support. Some youths join gangs simply to have fun.[143] They enjoy hanging out with others like themselves and want to get involved in exciting experiences. There is evidence that youths learn pro-gang attitudes from their peers and that these attitudes direct them to join gangs.[144]

Some experts suggest that youths join gangs in an effort to obtain a family-like atmosphere. Many gang members report that they have limited contact with their parents, many of whom are unemployed and have substance abuse problems.[145] Those members who have strained family relations are also the ones most likely to be involved in the most serious and frequent criminal activity.[146] Kids may join gangs, then, to compensate for the lack of a family life they have experienced at home. Concept Summary 8.1 summarizes these views. **CHECKPOINTS**

CONCEPT SUMMARY 8.1 | Views of Gang Formation

View	Premise	Evidence
Anthropological	Gangs appeal to kids' tribal instincts.	Use of totems, signs, secret languages, and symbols.
Sociocultural	Gangs form because of destructive sociocultural forces in disorganized inner-city areas.	Concentration of gangs in inner-city areas.
Anomie/ alienation	Alienated kids join gangs. Anomic, social, and economic conditions encourage gang activity.	Upswing in gang activities after market forces create anomic situations. Gang activity increases with globalization.
Psychological	Kids with personality problems form gangs and become leaders.	Antisocial, destructive behavior patterns. Increase in violence.
Rational choice	Kids join gangs for protection, fun, and survival.	Presence of party gangs, gang members protect one another.

GANG MEMBERSHIP OVER THE LIFE COURSE

In a recent study, Marvin Krohn, Jeffrey Ward, Terence Thornberry, Alan Lizotte, and Rebekah Chu used a life-course perspective to understand the long-term impact of gang membership on individual achievement and success. They note that decisions, behaviors, and outcomes during the teenage years have effects on outcomes well past adolescence, and choosing to be part of a particular group or social network is one of those decisions that may be of particular importance in determining the life trajectory of youth. Do these findings apply to juvenile street gang? Using data from a sample of males from the Rochester Youth Development Study, the research did indeed find that adolescent membership in gangs has important, long-lasting effects not only on continuation of criminal behaviors but also on the opportunities for adult success in major conventional social roles.

Krohn and his associates note that by the late 20s or early 30s, most people find that their financial outlook and family situations have stabilized, and projections about their future life course are clearer. Most have completed their formal education, met life partners, and selected a trade or occupation. If gang membership has an enduring effect on their lives, it will be evident in these years.

When they looked at the lives of former gang members who had turned 30, the research team found that gang involvement did indeed have a significant impact on adult behavior through a developmental process they call "precocious transitions," composed of factors that can affect a person's life chances, such as dropping out of

CONTROLLING GANG ACTIVITY

Two methods are used to control gang activity. One involves targeting by criminal justice agencies, and the other involves social service efforts. These methods will be discussed in the next sections.

Law Enforcement Efforts

In recent years, gang control has often been left to local police departments. Gang control takes three basic forms:

- *Youth services programs*, in which traditional police personnel, usually from the youth unit, are given responsibility for gang control
- *Gang details*, in which one or more police officers, usually from youth or detective units, are assigned exclusively to gang-control work
- *Gang units*, established solely to deal with gang problems, to which one or more officers are assigned exclusively to gang-control work[147]

The most recent NYGS found that about one in four law enforcement agencies with a gang problem now operates a gang unit, including more than half of larger cities. Across all area types, agencies with long-standing gang problems and/or higher numbers of documented gang members are more likely to report operating a gang unit.[148]

school and teenage parenthood. Gang members are more likely to fail to graduate from high school, father a child during their teenage years, leave the parental home before finishing high school, and/or engage in early co-habitation. By the time they reached 30, those who experience these precocious transitions had more problematic home lives and are more financially disadvantaged than those who do not experience problematic transitions. The longer the adolescent stayed in the gang, the more disruption he or she experienced during emerging adulthood and in adulthood itself.

The results also show that gang involvement is indirectly related to continued participation in street crime and to the probability of being arrested. The decision to join a gang decreases one's life chances; diminished life chances in both the family and economic arenas are related to persistence in criminal activities and experiences with criminal justice system contact in adulthood.

Ironically, most of the gang boys in their sample were only in the gang for two years or less. However, although membership in a gang is short-lived, it typically occurs during a stage in the development of youth that is critical in determining the course of their lives. It is during this period of time that they are expected to acquire necessary human and social capital, such as completing their education, so that they are prepared to orient themselves toward a career and family life. Not accomplishing those developmental tasks (e.g., high school completion) or experiencing problems in those areas has important long-term effects on both crime and noncrime outcomes.

These findings provide new insights into the effects that gang membership can have on criminal behavior and involvement with the criminal justice system. The research shows that the crime-enhancing effects of gang membership are not merely confined to periods of active gang membership but can have long-term consequences even when gang members are no longer actively involved.

CRITICAL THINKING

Consider the groups you have joined and belonged to in your life. Did they have a long-term effect on your attitudes and behavior? If they did, why should gangs be any different? What does this tell you about how to direct gang prevention or control efforts?

Writing Assignment The Krohn research puts the focus on the long-term effects of gang membership. Write an essay that lists and discusses all the possible negative influences related to gang membership and try to find research that supports your view.

Source: Marvin Krohn, Jeffrey Ward, Terence Thornberry, Alan Lizotte, and Rebekah Chu, "The Cascading Effects of Adolescent Gang Involvement Across the Life Course," *Criminology* 49:991–1028 (2011).

The Chicago Police Department's gang crime section maintains intelligence on gang problems and trains its more than 400 officers to deal with gang problems. Officers identify street gang members and enter their names in a computer bank that is programmed to alert the unit if the youths are picked up or arrested. Other police departments engage in "gang-breaking" activities. They attempt to arrest, prosecute, convict, and incarcerate gang leaders. For example, Los Angeles police conduct sweeps, in which more than 1,000 officers are put on the street to round up gang members. Police say the sweeps let the gangs know "who the streets belong to" and show neighborhood residents that someone cares.[149]

Community Control Efforts

During the late nineteenth century, social workers of the YMCA worked with youths in Chicago gangs.[150] During the 1950s, the **detached street worker** program was developed in major centers of gang activity. Social workers went into the community to work with gangs on their own turf. They participated in gang activities and tried to get to know their members. The purpose was to act as advocates for the youths, to provide them with positive role models, and to treat individual problems. Today, a number of jurisdictions still use gang outreach programs. For example, the city of Stockton, California, employs Peacekeepers Youth Outreach Workers, who are street-wise young men and women, trained in conflict resolution, mediation, community organizing, mentoring, and case management. They work in

detached street workers Social workers who went out into the community and established close relationships with juvenile gangs with the goal of modifying gang behavior to conform to conventional behaviors and helping gang members get jobs and educational opportunities.

Today, there are numerous community-level programs designed to limit gang activity. While most involve institutions such as police and community agencies, individuals can also be of help. Here, Pastor Mike Cummings (left), a former gang member turned community activist, asks a pedestrian to move along as students leave David Starr Jordan High School in the Watts district of Los Angeles. Walking to and from the school is a perilous journey that winds through one of the city's deadliest ganglands. Safely navigating the turf of the West Side Varrios, the Grape Street Crips, and several smaller factions is a matter of street smarts, luck, and, for some, guidance from Cummings, widely known as "Big Mike." He escorts girls past groups of men beckoning from the stoops of housing projects. He rides a crammed public bus to make sure a bump or a push doesn't escalate into a fight. He breaks up groups waiting to brawl on the corners of 103rd Street, the main thoroughfare to school.

neighborhood settings wherever young people at risk of violence are found, including schools, parks, street corners, and apartment complexes.[151]

Detached street worker programs are sometimes credited with curbing gang activities in the 1950s and 1960s, although some critics claimed that they turned delinquent groups into legitimate neighborhood organizations. Today, there are numerous community-level programs designed to limit gang activity. Some employ recreation areas open in the evening hours that provide supervised activities.[152] In some areas, citywide coordinating groups help orient gang-control efforts. Some police departments also sponsor prevention programs such as school-based lectures, police–school liaisons, recreation programs, and street worker programs that offer counseling, assistance to parents, and other services.

Still another approach has been to involve schools in gang-control programs. Some invite law enforcement agents to lecture students on the dangers of gang involvement and teach them gang-resistance techniques. Others provide resources that can help parents prevent their children from joining gangs, or if they already are members, get them out. One of the most ambitious programs is the Gang Resistance Education And Training (G.R.E.A.T.)

Looking Back at Luis's Story

Luis was put in an aftercare plan that included ongoing drug counseling and support, individual counseling, intensive supervision and monitoring, group support, and placement in an alternative educational setting.

CRITICAL THINKING Can such measures turn kids living in high-risk neighborhoods around or was Luis's success a fluke?

program that is a gang and violence prevention program built around school-based, law enforcement officer-instructed classroom curricula. According to the program, G.R.E.A.T. is intended to prevent delinquency, youth violence, and gang membership for children in the years immediately before the prime ages for recruitment and entry into gangs and delinquent behavior. G.R.E.A.T. will be discussed further in Chapter 12.[153]

Why Gang Control Is Difficult

Gang control can be difficult to attain. While aggressive police tactics can work, they also run the risk of becoming overzealous and alienating the community. Social and economic solutions seem equally challenging. Experts suggest that to reduce the gang problem, hundreds of thousands of high-paying jobs are needed. This solution does not seem practical in an economy where the unemployment rate has trended upward, and it's unlikely that employers would prefer a former gang member for a job coveted by hundreds without a criminal record. Many of the jobs for which undereducated gang boys can qualify are now being shipped overseas. Highly paid manufacturing jobs are particularly hard to obtain. It is unlikely that a youth who has five years as a Crip on his résumé will be in demand for legitimate work opportunities. The more embedded youths become in criminal enterprise, the less likely they are to find meaningful adult work. It is unlikely that gang members can suddenly be transformed into highly paid professionals.

Although social solutions to the gang problem seem elusive, the evidence shows that gang involvement is a socio-ecological phenomenon and must be treated as such. Youths who live in areas where their needs cannot be met by existing institutions join gangs when gang members are there to recruit them.[154] Social causes demand social solutions. Programs that enhance the lives of adolescents are the key to reducing gang delinquency. A more effective alternative would be to devote more resources to the most deteriorated urban areas where gangs are likely to recruit and to reach out to children with school-based programs at the earliest age possible.[155] The Prevention/Intervention/Treatment feature focuses on a strategy for gang prevention. **CHECKPOINTS**

Looking Back at Luis's Story

Through the alternative school, Luis got involved in a program that offered troubled youth the experience of building homes for underprivileged families.

CRITICAL THINKING Write a memorandum outlining the best way for probation officers and social workers to assist young people who may be gang affiliated. Make sure you address what can be done to prevent young people from joining gangs and/or help them get out of gang involvement.

CHECKPOINTS

LO5 Describe the various forms of gang-control efforts that are in use today.

✔ A number of states have created laws specifically designed to control gang activity.

✔ Police departments have responded by creating specialized gang-control units.

✔ Detached street workers were social workers who went out into the community and established close relationships with juvenile gangs. Outreach programs are still being used today.

✔ Another approach has been to involve schools in gang-control programs.

Strategies to Prevent Gang Delinquency

Recently, Dr. James Howell from the National Gang Center conducted research on why youth join gangs and how a community can build gang prevention and intervention services. He found that in general youth join gangs for protection, enjoyment, respect, money, or because a friend is in a gang. Youth are at higher risk of joining a gang if they engage in delinquent behaviors, are aggressive or violent, experience multiple caretaker transitions, have many problems at school, associate with other gang-involved youth, or live in communities where they feel unsafe and where many youth are in trouble.

To prevent youth from joining gangs, Howell finds that communities must strengthen families and schools, improve community supervision, train teachers and parents to manage disruptive youth, and teach students interpersonal skills. Preventing youth from joining gangs is challenging, and most programs have not shown noteworthy results. Several factors contribute to this challenge. Gang boys seek a place where they are accepted socially, and they find it in the streets. Most youth who join gangs experience many risk factors and family, school, and community problems. Joining a gang can be a natural process for many youth in socially and economically deprived areas of large cities. The gang may already be in their neighborhood, and their friends and relatives often belong to it. The gang's promises of protection gradually envelop these youth. Another major problem is the lack of gang awareness in schools, among community leaders, and among parents.

Despite obstacles, communities can take steps to prevent youth from joining gangs. The first level of prevention involves changing the experiences that propel children and adolescents into gangs. It involves strengthening the core social institutions, such as schools and families, which sometimes let youth down in the early years of their lives. Moreover, communities must provide interventions for youth at high risk for delinquency and gang involvement early in life, specifically targeting areas where gang problems are serious and more permanent. Programs should target girls and boys and both white and minority youth. Interventions such as effective school-based gang prevention programs are much in demand, and practical steps in integrating them with other measures that increase school safety have been identified. To prevent youth from joining gangs, communities must employ multiple strategies and services, including:

- Addressing elevated risk factors for joining a gang
- Strengthening families
- Reducing youth's conflicts
- Improving community-level supervision of youth
- Providing training for teachers on how to manage disruptive students
- Providing training for parents of disruptive and delinquent youth
- Reviewing and softening school "zero tolerance" policies to reduce suspensions and expulsions
- Ensuring that punitive sanctions target delinquent gang behaviors, not gang apparel, signs, and symbols
- Providing tutoring for students who are performing poorly in school
- Increasing adult supervision of students after school
- Providing interpersonal skills training to students to help resolve conflicts
- Providing a center for youth recreation and referrals for services
- Providing gang awareness training for school personnel, parents, and students
- Teaching students that gangs can be dangerous
- Providing training for school resource officers in mediating conflicts

Source: James C. Howell, *Gang Prevention: An Overview of Research and Programs*, Office of Juvenile Justice and Delinquency Prevention, *Juvenile Justice Bulletin, 2010*, www.ncjrs.gov/pdffiles1/ojjdp/231116.pdf (accessed August 14, 2012).

SUMMARY

In adolescence, friends begin to have a greater influence over decision making than parents. As they go through adolescence, children form cliques, small groups of friends who share activities and confidences. In mid-adolescence, kids strive for peer approval and to impress their closest friends. Adolescents who maintain delinquent friends are more likely to engage in antisocial behavior and drug abuse.

There are a number of theoretical views on the peer–delinquency linkage. According to the social control theory approach, delinquents are as detached from their peers as they are from other elements of society. Delinquent friends cause law-abiding youth to get in trouble. Antisocial youths join up with like-minded friends; deviant peers sustain and amplify delinquent careers.

Gangs are groups of youths who engage in delinquent behaviors. Members have self-recognition of their gang status and use special vocabulary, clothing, signs, colors, graffiti, and names. There is a commitment to criminal activity, although even the most criminal gang members spend the bulk of their time in noncriminal activities.

Gangs first formed in the 1600s, when London was terrorized by organized gangs that called themselves Hectors, Bugles, Dead Boys, and other colorful names. Gangs appeared in America in the late 1780s, when prison reformers noted the presence of gangs of young people hanging out on Philadelphia's street corners. In the nineteenth century, gangs were common in New York's Bowery and Five Points districts, Boston's North End and Fort Hill, and the outlying Southwark and Moyamensing sections of Philadelphia

In the 1950s and early 1960s, the threat of gangs and gang violence swept the public consciousness. By the mid-1960s, the gang menace seemed to have disappeared, only to reemerge in the 1970s. Gang formation was the natural consequence of the economic and social dislocation that occurred when the economy shifted from a relatively high-paying manufacturing to low-wage service economy.

At recent count, there are an estimated more than 700,000 gang members in the United States. Traditionally, gangs have operated in large urban areas experiencing rapid population change. Because of redevelopment, gangs in some areas have relocated or migrated; gang members have organized new chapters when they relocate to new areas.

The number of female gang members and female gangs is rapidly increasing. There are a variety of reasons why girls join gangs, including but not limited to financial opportunity, identity and status, peer pressure, family dysfunction, and protection. Many girls join gangs in an effort to cope with their turbulent personal lives. Ganging can provide girls with a sense of sisterhood, independence, and solidarity, as well as a chance to earn profit through illegal activities. Once in gangs, girls form close ties with other female members and engage in group criminal activity.

The ethnic distribution of gangs corresponds to their geographic location. The first black youth gangs were organized in the early 1920s. Latino gangs such as MS-13 have continued to grow and now constitute the largest number of gangs and gang memberships. White gang members are often alienated middle-class youths rather than poor lower-class youths.

Some gangs specialize in drug dealing. Youth gangs are responsible for a disproportionate number of homicides. Research indicates that gang violence is impulsive and therefore happens in spurts. Violence is a core fact of gang formation and life.

There are a number of views of gang formation. The anthropological view is that gangs appeal to adolescents longing for the tribal process that sustained their ancestors. Conditions of anomie/alienation encourage gang formation on both a cultural and individual level. Some believe that gangs serve as an outlet for disturbed youths who suffer a multitude of personal problems and deficits. Some kids make a rational choice to join gangs in order to have fun, receive protection, and garner prestige.

A number of states have created laws specifically designed to control gang activity. Police departments have responded by creating specialized gang-control units. Detached street workers were social workers who went out into the community and established close relationships with juvenile gangs. Today, outreach programs are still being used. Another approach has been to involve schools in gang-control programs.

KEY TERMS

cliques, p. 212

crowds, p. 212

controversial status
   youth, p. 212

gang, p. 215

interstitial area, p. 216

klikas, p. 219

graffiti, p. 220

representing, p. 220

near-groups, p. 222

barrio, p. 222

Mara Salvatrucha (MS-13), p. 226

skinhead, p. 227

prestige crimes, p. 230

detached street workers, p. 235

QUESTIONS FOR REVIEW

1. Describe how peer relations influence antisocial behaviors.

2. List and discuss how the various theories of delinquency explain gang behavior.

3. Describe the history of gangs and their early development.

4. Discuss the relationship between peer relations and delinquency.

5. Compare and contrast Thrasher's, Klein's, and Miller's definitions of gangs. Discuss their similarities or differences.

6. List the social and economic factors that support gang delinquency.

7. Explain why changing social and economic conditions in the post-globalization world have caused the age of gang members to steadily increase.

8. Discuss ethnic, racial, and gender differences in gangs and gang members.

9. List the various views of gang formation and discuss their similarities and differences.

10. Compare community and law enforcement efforts at gang control.

QUESTIONS FOR DISCUSSION

1. Do gangs serve a purpose? Differentiate between a gang and a fraternity.

2. Discuss the differences between violent, criminal, and drug-oriented gangs.

3. How do gangs in suburban areas differ from inner-city gangs?

4. Do delinquents have cold and distant relationships with their peers?

5. Can gangs be controlled without changing the economic opportunity structure of society? Are there any truly meaningful alternatives to gangs today for lower-class youths?

APPLYING WHAT YOU HAVE LEARNED

You are a professor at a local state university who teaches courses on delinquent behavior. One day you are approached by the director of the president's National Task Force on Gangs (NTFG). This group has been formed to pool resources from a variety of federal agencies, ranging from the FBI to Health and Human Services, in order to provide local jurisdictions with a comprehensive plan to fight gangs. The director claims that the gang problem is big and becoming bigger. Thousands of gangs are operating around the country, with hundreds of thousands of members. Government sources, he claims, indicate that there has been a significant growth in gang membership over the past 20 years. So far, the government has not been able to do anything at either the state or national level to stem this growing tide of organized criminal activity. The NTFG would like you to be part of the team that provides state and local jurisdictions with a gang-control activity model, which, if implemented, would provide a cost-effective means of reducing both gang membership and gang activity.

Writing Assignment: Write a memo to the NTFG giving them your vision of a gang-control project. Would you take a hard-line approach and recommend that police employ anti-gang units that use tactics developed in the fight against organized crime families or a more liberal one by recommending the redevelopment of deteriorated neighborhoods in which gangs flourish? Make sure to cover all the bases in your report.

GROUPWORK

Have the group make a list of rituals used in contemporary society that reflect an affinity or longing for more tribal times. Describe our totemic symbols. Hint: Why do brides wear white at weddings? Why do so many students have piercings and tattoos?

Schools and Delinquency

© The Republican/Landov

LEARNING OBJECTIVES

After reading this chapter you should:

1. Discuss the role the educational experience plays in human development over the life course.
2. Be familiar with the problems facing the educational system in the United States.
3. Describe the association between school failure and delinquency.
4. Know about the nature and extent of school crime and its control.
5. Be familiar with the legal rights of students.

Graduate Jose Perales at Commencement of Roger L. Putnam Vocational Technical High School.

Meisha's Story

Meisha was referred to the juvenile justice system after receiving a harassment charge for sending threatening text and other electronic messages to several girls at her high school. Meisha had also been referred a number of times for fighting at her middle school, but that was a few years ago. She was an average student in terms of grades and did not participate in any extracurricular activities. Meisha lived with her aunt, uncle, and their three children. Her parents were killed in a car accident when she was four and she had no siblings. Meisha had been struggling with bulimia for several years but had managed to keep it hidden from her family. Her symptoms of depression were not as easy to hide, but she had refused to attend counseling.

Meisha had been dating a young man she liked very much. She considered him her boyfriend, and when she discovered he had been out with another girl, Meisha began harassing and threatening to hurt her and her friends. Meisha also spread nasty rumors about the girls and made it very clear she was planning to harm them if she had the chance. She made her threats and spread the rumors using text messages and social websites during school hours and while at home. A few of the girls became frightened and told their parents, which resulted in police intervention, a charge of harassment and making threats, and suspension from school.

Meisha and her aunt attended the initial hearing and meeting with the juvenile delinquency social worker. Meisha was defensive and unwilling to take responsibility for her actions. She blamed the other girls, stating

they "should have know better than to mess with my boyfriend." It was clear to the social worker that Meisha had a number of serious errors in her thought processes. The worker was able to get Meisha into a therapy group that specifically focused on juvenile female offenders. The core focus of the group was on self-esteem issues, family relations, building empathy, risk factors such as substance abuse, eating disorders, independent living skills, and sexual, physical, and emotional abuse. By participating in a therapy group with her female peers experiencing similar issues, Meisha had an opportunity to address many aspects of her negative behavior.

When the therapy group concluded, Meisha, her aunt, and teachers were all asked to complete a survey regarding improvements and areas for continued improvement as it related to Meisha's behavior and attitude. Areas of increased skills included social skills and learning new ways of coping with her frustrations. Meisha also agreed to work with a therapist regarding her bulimia and depression, as she began to realize that talking with others was improving her willingness to address these areas of her life. Meisha is still working on taking full responsibility for her actions and coping with her frustrations but has been permitted back in school. She is not allowed to have a cell phone at school or have access to the school computers. Meisha meets with the school social worker twice a week and has weekly meetings at school with her aunt and school staff. She has not made any further threats and has not had any further referrals to the juvenile delinquency system.

School officials must make daily decisions about discipline and crime prevention. When kids like Meisha begin acting out and bullying other students, it is up to school officials to control their behavior, something that is often difficult to achieve. Because so much of an adolescent's time is spent in school, it would seem logical that some relationship exists between delinquent behavior and what is happening—or not happening—in classrooms. Numerous studies have confirmed that delinquency is related to **academic achievement**, and experts have concluded that many of the underlying problems of delinquency, as well as their prevention and control, are intimately connected with the nature and quality of the school experience.[1] Although there are differences of opinion, most experts agree that problems associated with the educational system bear some responsibility for the relatively high rate of juvenile crime.

In this chapter, we first explore how educational achievement and delinquency are related and what factors in the school experience appear to contribute to delinquent behavior. Next, we turn to delinquency in the school setting—vandalism, theft, violence, and so on. Finally, we look at the attempts made by schools to prevent delinquency.

academic achievement Being successful in a school environment.

THE SCHOOL IN MODERN AMERICAN SOCIETY

The school plays a significant role in shaping the values of children.[2] In contrast to earlier periods, when formal education was a privilege of the upper classes, the U.S. system of compulsory public education has made schooling a legal obligation. Today, more than 90 percent of school-age children attend school, compared with only 7 percent in 1890.[3] In contrast to the earlier, agrarian days of U.S. history, when most adolescents shared in the work of the family, today's young people spend most of their time in school. The school has become the primary instrument of socialization, the "basic conduit through which the community and adult influences enter into the lives of adolescents."[4]

Because young people spend a longer time in school, their adolescence is prolonged. As long as students are still dependent on their families and have not entered the work world, they are not considered adults. The responsibilities of adulthood come later to modern-day youths than to those in earlier generations, and some experts see this prolonged childhood as one factor contributing to the irresponsible and often irrational behavior of many juveniles who commit delinquent acts.

Socialization and Status

Another significant aspect of the educational experience is that children spend their school hours with their peers, and most of their activities after school take place with school friends. Young people rely increasingly on school friends and become less interested in adult role models. The norms of the peer culture are often at odds with those of adult society, and a pseudoculture with a distinct social system develops. Law-abiding behavior may not be among the values promoted in such an atmosphere. Kids enmeshed in this youth culture may admire bravery, defiance, and having fun much more than adults do.

The school has become a primary determinant of economic and social status. In this technological age, education is the key to a job that will mark its holder as successful. No longer can parents ensure the status of their children through social class alone. Educational achievement has become of equal, if not greater, importance as a determinant of economic success. This emphasis on the value of education is fostered by parents, the media, and the schools themselves. Regardless of their social or economic background, most children grow up believing education is the key to success. However, many youths do not meet acceptable standards of school achievement. Whether failure is measured by test scores, not being promoted, or dropping out, the incidence of school failure continues to be a major problem for U.S. society. A single school failure often leads to a pattern of chronic failure. The links between school failure and delinquency will be explored more fully in the next sections.

The school itself has become an engine of social change and improvement. School desegregation efforts have heralded a new age of improved race relations, which in the long run may help reduce crime rates. African American youth educated in states where a higher proportion of their classmates are European American experience significantly lower incarceration rates later as adults. The constructive effects of racial inclusiveness in the school setting have grown stronger over time, highlighting the need for further educational integration.[5]

Education Trends and Issues

The role schools play in adolescent development is underscored by the problems faced by the U.S. education system. There has been some improvement in reading, math,

CHECKPOINTS

LO1 Discuss the role the educational experience plays in human development over the life course.

✔ The school environment has been found to have a significant effect on a child's emotional well-being.

✔ Young people rely increasingly on school friends and become less interested in adult role models.

✔ The school has become a primary determinant of economic and social status.

✔ Children spend their school hours with their peers, and most of their activities after school take place with school friends.

✔ The school itself has become an engine of social change and improvement.

and science achievement during the past decade, but in some cases improvements have been minimal. The latest data from the National Assessment of Educational Progress (NAEP) on math achievement show there has been significant improvement in math ability over this 20-year period and significantly more fourth-graders are considered proficient at math today than they were in 1990.

While these findings are encouraging, some significant problems still remain. For example, reading scores have not had a significant improvement during this time, and racial and ethnic differences in reading and math achievement have proven difficult to erase.[6]

It is also troubling that cross-national surveys that compare academic achievement show that students in the United States trail those in other nations (e.g., Russia, Japan, China) in critical academic areas such as science and math achievement as measured by standardized math tests.[7] One reason may be that many secondary school math and science teachers did not major in the subjects they teach. Another reason is that the United States, the richest country in the world, devotes less of its resources to education than do many other nations. Spending on elementary and secondary education (as a percentage of the U.S. gross domestic product) is less than that of other nations. And budget cutting has reduced educational resources in many communities and curtailed state support for local school systems.

Economic Disadvantage and Educational Achievement

Economically disadvantaged children enter school lagging behind their more advantaged peers in terms of the knowledge and social competencies that are widely recognized as enabling children to perform at even the most basic level.[8] They face substantial gaps in measures of reading and mathematics proficiency, in prosocial

© Brian Harkin/*New York Times*/Redux

Some kids drop out because they are alienated from school or struggle academically. Ivan Lucero, 28, was expelled from his Bronx high school when he was 18, still in the 10th grade. Ivan, who emigrated illegally from Mexico with his mother when he was 6 and grew up in the Belmont area of the Bronx, said his parents urged him to stay in school and study. But his father was distracted by long workdays, and his mother, who did not speak English, had no contact with the school. Ivan began skipping classes to hang out with other young Mexicans who had formed a gang. In high school, Ivan began working as a busboy, which further distracted him from school work. He was forced to repeat 10th grade twice, though he lied to his parents about how he was doing. Most of his friends from high school dropped out and entered the workforce, and so did one of his younger brothers.

behaviors and behavior problems, and in readiness to learn. Many children are not familiar with basic rules of print or writing (for example, knowing that English is read from left to right and top to bottom, or where a story ends). About one-third of children whose mothers have less than a high school education suffer educational deficiencies, compared to only 8 percent for children whose mothers have a college degree or higher. Many children from disadvantaged backgrounds fail to meet grade-level expectations on core subjects. As a consequence they face higher rates of special education placement and grade repetition.[9] As the Focus on Delinquency feature shows, these disadvantages often fall directly on minority youth. These disadvantages may increase their risk of leaving school early and becoming dropouts.

DROPPING OUT

When kids are alienated from school, they may want to **drop out**, a step that may make them even more prone to antisocial behaviors. Though dropout rates have been in decline, dropping out is still a serious issue.[10] Nearly one-third of all high school students leave the public school system before graduating, and the problem is particularly severe among students of color and students with disabilities.

There are a few high schools, mostly in inner-city neighborhoods, where the high school completion rate is 40 percent or less—the so-called **dropout factories**. There are still more than 1700 of these failing schools in the United States. While they represent a small fraction of all public high schools in America, they account for about half of all high school dropouts each year.[11]

Dropping out of high school has severe long-term financial and personal consequences. The median income of persons ages 18 through 67 who have not completed high school is now about $23,000 per year; in comparison high school completers averaged $42,000. Over a person's lifetime, this translates into a loss of approximately $630,000 in income for dropouts. Among adults ages 25 and older, a lower percentage of dropouts are in the labor force and those that are face a greater risk of unemployment. Dropouts also face personal problems. They report being in worse health than adults who completed high school. Dropouts also make up disproportionately higher percentages of the nation's prison and death row inmates. High school dropouts cost the economy approximately $240,000 over their lifetime in terms of lower tax contributions, higher reliance on Medicaid and Medicare, higher rates of criminal activity, and higher reliance on welfare.[12]

Even though one might assume dropouts commit more crime than graduates, research on the effect of dropping out on crime and delinquency is a mixed bag: while some efforts show that school dropouts face a significant chance of entering a criminal way of life, others fail to find a link between dropping out and crime.[13] Recent research by Gary Sweeten and his associates found that those who do leave school early have a long history of poor school performance and antisocial behaviors. It is possible, then, that social problems suffered over the life course lead to dropping out and also explain involvement in criminal activity after a student leaves school.[14]

Why Do Kids Drop Out?

There seem to be two distinct paths to dropping out, one educational and the other social.

Educational Factors. Kids who show disinterest in school are prone to dropping out.[15] Most kids who drop out show danger signs as early as the fourth grade, and serious problems begin to manifest in their first year of high school. Educational indicators of potential dropping out include:[16]

- *Failed courses.* Research indicates that students who fail one or more courses in the fall semester of their first year of high school are less likely to graduate than students who do not. Research done in Chicago public schools found that

drop out To leave school before completing the required program of education.
dropout factories Schools in which the graduation rate is 40 percent or less.

SCHOOL DISCIPLINE, SCHOOL OPPORTUNITIES, AND MINORITY YOUTH

In March 2012, the U.S. Department of Education released a report containing data from a national survey of more than 72,000 public schools (serving 85 percent of the nation's students) showing that minority students, especially boys, face much harsher discipline in public schools than other students. One in five African American boys and more than one in ten African American girls received an out-of-school suspension, and black students (especially males) are three and a half times as likely to be suspended or expelled than white students. Over

85 percent of students with zero semester course failures in their freshman year graduated four years later, but only 70 percent of students with one semester F and only 55 percent of students with two semester Fs graduated in four years. Students with three or more semester Fs are not likely to graduate high school.

- *Grade point average.* Grades earned are clearly related to students' likelihood of successfully graduating from high school. On average, students who earn a 2.0 GPA or less in their freshman year have significantly lower graduation rates than students who earn a 2.5 or higher (on a 4-point scale).

- *Absences.* Kids who miss more than 10 percent of instructional time are at risk. This percentage translates to roughly 2 weeks (10 days) of school per semester in most high schools.

- *Pushed out.* Some kids are pushed out of school because they lack attention or have poor attendance records. Teachers label them as troublemakers, and school administrators use suspensions, transfers, and other means to "convince" them that leaving school is their only option. Because minority students often come from circumstances that interfere with their attendance, they are more likely to be labeled disobedient.

Exhibit 9.1 sets out some indicators of risk for dropping out.

Looking Back at Meisha's Story

Meisha's counselor was concerned that she was having difficulty in her thought processes.

CRITICAL THINKING Did the counseling program Meisha attended shield her from the problems she may have encountered in school? Can you think of other types of nonstigmatizing alternatives?

Social Factors. There are also social causes for dropping out. When surveyed, most dropouts say they left either because they did not like school or because they wanted to get a job. Some dropouts could not get along with teachers, had been expelled, or were under suspension. Almost half of all female dropouts left school because they were pregnant or had already given birth.

Poverty and family dysfunction increase the chances of dropping out among all racial and ethnic groups. Dropouts are more likely than graduates to have lived in single-parent families headed by parents who were educational

70 percent of the students involved in school-related arrests or referred to law enforcement were Hispanic or black. Black and Hispanic students—particularly those with disabilities—are also disproportionately subject to seclusion or restraints.

Many of the nation's largest districts had very different disciplinary rates for students of different races. In Los Angeles, for example, black students made up 9 percent of those enrolled, but 26 percent of those suspended; in Chicago, they made up 45 percent of the students, but 76 percent of the suspensions.

The data revealed a wide range of other racial and ethnic disparities. Though black and Hispanic students made up 44 percent of the students in the survey, they were only 26 percent of the students in gifted and talented programs. The data also showed that schools with a lot of black and Hispanic students were likely to have relatively inexperienced and low-paid teachers. On average, teachers in high-minority schools were paid $2,251 less per year than their colleagues elsewhere.

CRITICAL THINKING

Any form of institutional racial disparity is intolerable in contemporary society, and the fact that the differences uncovered by the U.S. Department of Education still exist illustrates one of the most significant problems facing the American school system. Should every child be entitled to an equal education? Is it fair that kids in wealthy suburbs enjoy better school systems than those kids living in poor neighborhoods?

Writing Assignment Write an essay that describes a model school system in which educational advantages are available to all students regardless of race or income.

Source: U.S. Department of Education press release, "New Data from U.S. Department of Education Highlights Educational Inequities Around Teacher Experience, Discipline and High School Rigor," March 6, 2012, www.ed.gov/news/press-releases/new-data-us-department-education-highlights-educational-inequities-around-teache (accessed August 15, 2012).

EXHIBIT 9.1 **Indicators of Risk for School Dropout**

Type of Information	Indicator	Brief Description	Benchmark
Attendance	Absenteeism rate	Number of days absent during the first 20 days, and each quarter of the first year of high school	The equivalent of more than 10 percent instructional time missed during the first year indicates student may be at risk.
Course performance	Course failures	Number of Fs in any semester-long course during the first year of high school	Even one failed course indicates student may be at risk.
	Grade point average (GPA)	GPA for each semester and cumulative GPA	GPA under 2.0 indicates student may be at risk.
	on-track indicator	Combination of the number of Fs in core academic courses and credits earned during the first year of high school	Two or more Fs in core academic courses *and/or* fewer than one-fourth of the credits required to graduate minus one indicate that student is off-track to graduate.

Source: Jessica B. Heppen and Susan Bowles Therriault, *Developing Early Warning Systems to Identify Potential High School Dropouts*, National High School Center, www.betterhighschools.org/pubs/ews_guide.asp (accessed August 15, 2012).

underachievers themselves. Other social risk factors include poor problem-solving ability, low self-esteem, difficulty getting along with teachers, dissatisfaction with school, substance abuse, and being too old for their grade level.[17]

Race and Dropping Out

Race-based disciplinary practices may help sustain high minority dropout rates. Although the African American dropout rate has declined faster than the European American dropout rate over the past three decades, minority students still drop out at a higher rate than European American students.

In his thoughtful book *Creating the Dropout*, Sherman Dorn shows that graduation rates slowly but steadily rose during the twentieth century, whereas regional, racial, and ethnic differences in graduation rates declined.[18] Nonetheless, Dorn argues that the relatively high dropout rate among minorities is the legacy of disciplinary policies instituted more than 40 years ago when educational administrators opposed to school desegregation employed a policy of race-based suspension and expulsion directed at convincing minority students to leave previously all–European American high school districts. This legacy still affects contemporary school districts. Dorn believes that the dropout problem is a function of inequality of educational opportunity rather than the failure of individual students. The proportion of African Americans who fail to graduate from high school remains high compared with the proportion of European Americans who fail to graduate, because the educational system still fails to provide minority group members with the services and support they need.

As noted earlier, African American children receive more disciplinary infractions than children from other racial categories, despite the fact that their behavior is quite similar. Having a higher percentage of black students in a school translates into a greater use of disciplinary tactics, a factor that may explain why minority students fare less well and are more likely to disengage from schools at a younger age than whites.[19] Allison Payne and Kelly Welch recently found that in disadvantaged, urban schools in minority areas, administrators and teachers are more likely to respond to misbehavior in a punitive manner and less likely to respond in a restorative manner as they do in suburban, mostly white schools.[20] **CHECKPOINTS**

ACADEMIC PERFORMANCE AND DELINQUENCY

Whether they drop out or not, kids who do poorly in school are at risk for delinquent behavior; students who are chronic **underachievers** in school are among the most likely to be delinquent.[21] In fact, researchers find that school failure is a stronger predictor of delinquency than variables such as economic class membership, racial or ethnic background, or peer-group relations. Studies that compare the academic records of delinquents and nondelinquents—including their scores on standardized tests, failure rate, and other academic measures—have found that delinquents are often academically deficient, a condition that may lead to their leaving school and becoming involved in antisocial activities.[22] Children who report that they do not like school and do not do well in school are most likely to self-report delinquent acts.[23] In contrast, at-risk youths who do well in school are often able to avoid delinquent involvement.[24]

An association between academic failure and delinquency is commonly found among chronic offenders. Those leaving school without a diploma are more likely to become involved in chronic delinquency than high school graduates.[25] Only 9

underachievers Those who fail to meet expected levels of school achievement.

percent of the chronic offenders in Marvin Wolfgang's Philadelphia *Delinquency in a Birth Cohort* study graduated from high school, compared with 74 percent of nonoffenders.[26] Chronic offenders also had more disciplinary actions than nonoffenders.[27]

The relationship between school achievement and persistent offending is supported by surveys that indicate that only 40 percent of incarcerated felons had 12 or more years of education, compared with about 80 percent of the general population.[28] In sum, the school experience can be a significant factor in shaping the direction of an adolescent's life course.

School Failure and Delinquency

Although there is general agreement that school failure and delinquency are related, some questions remain concerning the nature and direction of this relationship. There are actually three independent views on the association:

- *School failure is a direct cause of delinquent behavior.* Children who fail at school soon feel frustrated and rejected. Believing they will never achieve success through conventional means, they seek out like-minded companions and together engage in antisocial behaviors. Educational failure evokes negative responses from important people in the child's life, including teachers, parents, and prospective employers. These reactions help solidify feelings of inadequacy, and in some cases, lead to a pattern of chronic delinquency.

- *School failure leads to emotional and psychological problems that are the actual cause of antisocial behavior.* Academic failure reduces self-esteem, and reduced self-esteem is the actual cause of delinquency. Studies using a variety of measures of academic competence and self-esteem demonstrate that good students have a better attitude about themselves than poor students.[29] The association then runs from school failure to low self-concept to delinquency. Schools may mediate these effects by taking steps to improve the self-image of academically challenged children.

- *School failure and delinquency share a common cause.* Both are caused by personal or social problems so that although it appears that school failure precedes and causes delinquency, the association is actually spurious. For example, kids often fail in inner-city schools, neighborhoods that also produce high crime rates.

Correlates of School Failure

Despite disagreement over the direction the relationship takes, there is little argument that delinquent behavior is influenced by educational experiences. A number of factors have been linked to school failure; the most prominent are discussed in the next sections.

Personal Problems. Some kids have personal problems that they bring with them to school. Because of their deprived background and ragged socialization, some lack the verbal skills that are a prerequisite of educational success.[30] Others live in a dysfunctional family; a turbulent family life has been linked to academic underachievement.

Still others suffer psychological abnormality. The adolescent who both fails at school and engages in delinquency may be experiencing depression and other mental deficits that are associated with both their school failure and their involvement in antisocial activities.[31] Personality structure may also be a key factor. Kids who have low self-control are more likely to engage in delinquent behavior *and* fail in school. An impulsive personality can cause both school failure and delinquency.[32]

Social Class. During the 1950s, research by Albert Cohen indicated that delinquency was a phenomenon of working-class students who were poorly equipped to function in middle-class schools. Cohen referred to this phenomenon as a failure to live up to "middle-class measuring rods."[33] Jackson Toby reinforced this concept,

WWW

To learn more about math and science education, visit the **Eisenhower National Clearinghouse for Mathematics and Science Education (ENC)** by going to the Criminal Justice CourseMate at CengageBrain.com, then accessing the Web Links for this chapter.

WWW

To get more educational data from the **National Center for Education Statistics**, visit the Criminal Justice CourseMate at CengageBrain.com, then access the Web Links for this chapter.

contending that the disadvantages lower-class children have in school (for example, lack of verbal skills) are a result of their position in the social structure and that these disadvantages foster delinquency.[34] These views have been supported by the higher-than-average dropout rates among lower-class children.

One reason why lower-class children may do poorly in school is that economic problems require them to take part-time jobs. Working while in school seems to lower commitment to educational achievement and is associated with higher levels of delinquent behavior.[35]

Not all experts agree with the social class–school failure–delinquency hypothesis. There is evidence that boys who do poorly in school, regardless of their socioeconomic background, are more likely to be delinquent than those who perform well.[36] Affluent students may be equally affected by school failure as lower-class youths, and middle-class youths who do poorly in school are more likely to become delinquent than their lower-class peers who also have academic performance problems.[37] In fact, because expectations are so much higher for affluent youth, their failure to achieve in school may have a more profound effect on their behavior and well-being than it does on lower-class youth, who face so many other social problems. Not surprisingly, middle-class kids who are involved in antisocial behaviors are more likely to experience school failure than lower-class youth who experience similar social problems.[38]

Tracking. Most researchers have looked at academic **tracking**—dividing students into groups according to ability and achievement level—as a contributor to school failure. Placement in a non-college track means consignment to educational oblivion without apparent purpose. Studies indicate that non–college-track students experience greater academic failure and progressive deterioration of achievement, participate less in extracurricular activities, have an increased tendency to drop out, and commit more delinquent acts.

Some school officials begin tracking students in the lowest grade levels. Educators separate youths into groups that have innocuous names ("special enrichment program"), but may carry the taint of academic incompetence. High school students may be tracked within individual subjects based on ability. Classes may be labeled in descending order: advanced placement, academically enriched, average, basic, and remedial. It is common for students to have all their courses in only one or two tracks.[39]

The effects of school labels accumulate over time. If students fail academically, they are often destined to fail again. Repeated instances of failure can help produce the career of the misfit or dropout. Using a tracking system keeps certain students from having any hope of achieving academic success, thereby causing lack of motivation, which may foster delinquent behavior.[40]

Alienation. Student alienation has also been identified as a link between school failure and delinquency. Students who report they neither like school nor care about their teachers' opinions are more likely to exhibit delinquent behaviors.[41] Alienation may be a function of students' inability to see the relevance of what they are taught. The gap between their education and the real world leads some students to feel that the school experience is a waste of time.[42]

Many students, particularly those from low-income families, believe schooling has no payoff. Because this legitimate channel appears to be meaningless, delinquent acts become increasingly more attractive. This middle- and upper-class bias is evident in the preeminent role of the college preparatory curriculum in many school systems. Furthermore, methods of instruction and curriculum materials reflect middle-class language and customs that have little meaning for the disadvantaged child.

In contrast, kids who form a bond to school find that this commitment helps them resist delinquency-producing factors in the environment, such as antisocial peers.[43] Youths who report liking school and being involved in school activities are also less likely to engage in delinquent behaviors.[44] Involvement is especially beneficial in schools where students are treated fairly and where rules are laid out clearly.[45] Schools might lower delinquency rates if they can develop programs that counteract student alienation. **CHECKPOINTS**

tracking Dividing students into groups according to their ability and achievement levels.

DELINQUENCY IN SCHOOLS

In its pioneering study of school crime, *Violent Schools–Safe Schools* (1977),[46] the federal government found that, although teenagers spend only 25 percent of their time in school, 40 percent of the robberies and 36 percent of the physical attacks involving this age group occur there. School crime has remained a national concern since the *Safe Schools* study was published.

Research still shows that a significant portion of all juvenile crime and victimization occurs during the school day. One effort by David Soulé and his colleagues found that juvenile victimization and delinquency peak during school hours, whereas substance use peaks over the weekend. While the most serious violent offenses do occur after school, the crimes that kids are most likely to get involved in, such as simple assault offenses, take place at school.

The latest data from the National Center for Educational Statistics (Figure 9.1), find that there are about 820,000

FIGURE 9.1 Rate of Nonfatal Crime by Type of Crime and Age

Rate of nonfatal victimizations against students ages 12–18 per 1,000 students, by type of victimization and location: 1992–2010

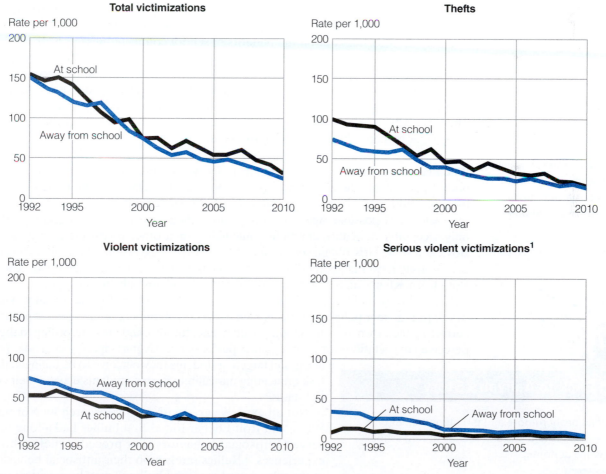

[1]Serious violent victimization is also included in violent victimization.

Source: National Center for Educational Statistics, *Indicators of School Crime and Safety: 2011*, http://nces.ed.gov/programs/crimeindicators/crimeindicators2011/ (accessed August 21, 2012).

crimes committed at school each year and that the school crime rate has declined significantly during the past two decades, reflecting the general drop in delinquency. Among students ages 12 to 18, there were about 470,000 thefts and 359,000 acts of violence; about 33 students are now being killed on school grounds each year.[47]

Bullying

In Chapter 1, we discussed the phenomenon of **bullying**, both in the school yard and online, and the toll it takes on its targets. Experts define bullying among children as repeated, negative acts committed by one or more children against another. These negative acts may be physical or verbal in nature—for example, hitting or kicking, teasing, or taunting—or they may involve indirect actions such as manipulating friendships or purposely excluding other children from activities. Implicit in this definition is an imbalance in real or perceived power between the bully and victim.

National data indicate that in a single year about one-quarter of all public schools report that bullying occurred among students on a daily or weekly basis, and 9 percent reported widespread disorder in classrooms on a daily or weekly basis.[48] Six percent of students ages 12 to 18 report being cyberbullied, and about 3 percent reported being subject to harassing text messages; girls are twice as likely to be subject to harassing text messages than boys. It is disturbing to find that 30 to 50 percent of gay, lesbian, and bisexual young people experience harassment in an educational setting.[49]

Studies of bullying suggest that there are short- and long-term consequences for both the perpetrators and the victims of bullying.[50] Students who are chronic victims of bullying experience more physical and psychological problems than their peers who are not harassed by other children, and they tend not to grow out of the role of victim. Young people mistreated by peers may not want to be in school and may thereby miss out on the benefits of school connectedness as well as educational advancement. Longitudinal studies have found that victims of bullying in early grades also reported being bullied several years later. Studies also suggest that chronically victimized students may, as adults, be at increased risk for depression, poor self-esteem, and other mental health problems, including schizophrenia.[51] There have been numerous recent cases, including Eden Wormer (see Preface), that show clear evidence linking bullying to suicide.[52]

Who Becomes a Bully? There are a number of views on this issue. According to a recent book by sociologist Jessie Klein, boys who bully are motivated by the need to prove their masculinity, and terrorizing others is a contrivance that allows them to do so in the easiest way possible. Acting the bully allows them to express anger and rage, the only acceptable masculine emotions, while hiding their other, unacceptable, emotions. Boys, and some girls, obtain social status by displaying aggression and a willingness to demonstrate power at another's expense. Some bullying is directed at the opposite sex. Boys learn, Klein claims, that they can assert manhood not only by being popular with girls but also by wielding power over them, physically, emotionally, and sexually. What develops is **gender policing**. Students tend to become members of the "gender police," correcting their own and one another's behaviors, attitudes, and dress according to their perceived expectations for proper gender performance. By participating in gender policing, and targeting students they perceive to be failing in the task of meeting masculinity norms, students elevate their social status.[53]

Not all experts agree with Klein: research by Norman White and Rolf Loeber found that bullies had a long history of antisocial behaviors that precedes their school experiences.[54] Bullies rarely stop their antisocial behavior at the school yard gate, and bullying may be a critical risk factor in the development of future problems with violence and delinquency. Bullies are more likely to carry weapons in and out of school and get involved with substance

bullying Repeated, negative acts committed by one or more children against another, which may be physical or verbal.

gender policing Pressure to conform to gender expectations.

Looking Back to Aaliyah's Story

Meisha spread nasty rumors and threatened other girls using text messages and social websites during school hours and while at home.

CRITICAL THINKING Meisha used the Internet to harass other students whom she disliked. What can schools do to restrict Internet bullying?

Preventing School Bullying

The first and best-known intervention to reduce bullying among schoolchildren was launched by Dan Olweus in Norway and Sweden in the early 1980s. Prompted by the suicides of several severely victimized children, Norway supported the development and implementation of a comprehensive program to address bullying among children in school. The program involved interventions at multiple levels:

- *Schoolwide interventions.* A survey of bullying problems at each school, increased supervision, schoolwide assemblies, and teacher in-service training to raise the awareness of children and school staff regarding bullying.
- *Classroom-level interventions.* The establishment of classroom rules against bullying, regular class meetings to discuss bullying at school, and meetings with all parents.
- *Individual-level interventions.* Discussions with students to identify bullies and victims.

A number of research studies have found the program to be highly effective in reducing bullying and other antisocial behavior among students in primary and junior high schools. In some studies, within two years of implementation, both boys and girls report that bullying has decreased by half. These changes in behavior were more pronounced the longer the program was in effect. Moreover, students reported significant decreases in rates of truancy, vandalism, and theft, and indicate that their school's climate was significantly more positive as a result of the program. Not surprisingly, those schools that had implemented more of the program's components experienced the most marked changes in behavior.

The core components of the Olweus anti-bullying program have been adapted for use in several other cultures, including Canada, England, and the United States, and the results have been similar: schools that were more active in implementing the program observed the most marked changes in reported behaviors. Maria Ttofi and her associates recently conducted a meta-analysis of 59 studies of the effectiveness of bullying prevention programs around the world and found that while many were successful, the Olweus system worked best.

Can bullying be stopped? Recent research by Ann Marie Popp shows that a student's exposure to motivated bullies and the school's lack of guardianship efforts were associated with the student's risk of experiencing bullying victimization. Ken Seeley, Martin L. Tombari, Laurie J. Bennett, and Jason B. Dunkle suggest the following measures can help stop bullying:

- Increase student engagement.
- Model caring behavior for students.
- Offer mentoring programs.
- Provide students with opportunities for service learning as a means of improving school engagement.
- Address the difficult transition between elementary and middle school (from a single classroom teacher to teams of teachers with periods and class changes in a large school).
- Start prevention programs early.
- Resist the temptation to use prefabricated curriculums that are not aligned to local conditions.

Clearly, schools that make an effort to protect kids from their more aggressive classmates can help lower the incidence of school yard bullying.

CRITICAL THINKING

Should schoolyard bullies be expelled from school? Would such a measure make a bad situation worse? For example, might expelled bullies shift their aggressive behavior from the schoolyard to the community?

Sources: Ken Seeley, Martin L. Tombari, Laurie J. Bennett, and Jason B. Dunkle, "Bullying in Schools: An Overview," *OJJDP Juvenile Justice Bulletin*, December 2011, www.ojjdp.gov/pubs/234205.pdf (accessed August 15, 2012); Maria Ttofi, David Farrington, and Anna Baldry, "Effectiveness of Programmes to Reduce School Bullying," Swedish National Council for Crime Prevention, Stockholm, Sweden, 2008; Ann Marie Popp, "The Effects of Exposure, Proximity, and Capable Guardians on the Risk of Bullying Victimization," *Youth Violence and Juvenile Justice*, first published online February 23, 2012; Dan Olweus, "A Useful Evaluation Design, and Effects of the Olweus Bullying Prevention Program," *Psychology, Crime and Law* 11:389–402 (2005); Dan Olweus, "Victimization by Peers: Antecedents and Long-Term Outcomes," in *Social Withdrawal, Inhibitions, and Shyness*, ed. K. H. Rubin and J. B. Asendorf (Hillsdale, NJ: Erlbaum, 1993), pp. 315–341.

abuse. And in addition to threatening other children, bullies are several times more likely than their non-bullying peers to commit antisocial acts, including vandalism, fighting, theft, drunkenness, and truancy, and to have an arrest by young adulthood. So whether bullying is a social phenomenon or a matter of general psychological malaise is still being debated. Regardless of its cause, schools are trying hard to end this phenomenon, as the Prevention/Intervention/Treatment feature indicates.

Bullying is not unique to the United States. When 16-year-old Australian Casey Heynes was shown on YouTube slamming his playground bully to the ground, he became a global Internet sensation and a hero for bullying victims everywhere. Now the Sydney teenager is joining forces with boxing trainer Christian Marchegiani to launch a statewide anti-bullying campaign, called Underdog, which will see the duo speak at schools and workplaces across New South Wales. "I'm sick and tired of people getting picked on. I've seen it my whole life and I want it to stop," says Casey. The YouTube video that went viral showed fellow Chifley High School student Ritchard Gale punching Casey several times in the face, before Casey snapped, lifted his tormentor in the air, and threw him to the ground.

School Shootings

Although incidents of school-based crime and violence are not uncommon, it is the highly publicized incidents of fatal school shootings that have helped focus attention on school crime. Upward of 10 percent of students report bringing weapons to school on a regular basis, and, knowing this, many of their peers report being afraid of school-based gun violence.[55]

Who brings guns to schools? Jessie Klein and others closely link shootings to a history of bullying.[56] Many of these kids have a history of being abused and bullied; many perceive a lack of support from peers, parents, and teachers.[57] Kids who have been the victims of crime themselves and who hang with peers who carry weapons are the ones most likely to bring guns to school.[58] A troubled kid who has little social support and carries deadly weapons makes for an explosive situation.

Nature and Extent of Shootings. Social scientists are now conducting studies of these events in order to determine their trends and patterns.[59] Research shows that most shooting incidents occurred around the start of the school day, the lunch period, or the end of the school day. In most shootings, a note, threat, or other action indicating risk for violence occurred prior to the event. Shooters were also likely to have expressed some form of suicidal behavior prior to the event and to report having been bullied by their peers. These patterns may help school officials one day to identify potential risk factors and respond in a timely fashion.

Who Is the School Shooter? The U.S. Secret Service has developed a profile of school shootings and shooters.[60] They found that most attacks were neither spontaneous nor impulsive. Shooters typically developed a plan of attack well in advance; more than half had considered the attack for at least two weeks and had a plan for at least two days.

The attackers' mental anguish was well known, and these kids had come to the attention of someone (school officials, police, fellow students) because of their bizarre and disturbing behavior prior to the attack taking place. One student told more than 20 friends beforehand about his plans, which included killing students and planting bombs. Threats were communicated in more than three-fourths of the cases, and in more than half the incidents the attacker told more than one person. Some people knew detailed information, whereas others knew "something spectacular" was going to happen on a particular date. In less than one-fourth of the cases, the attacker made a direct threat to the target.

The Secret Service found that the shooters came from such a wide variety of backgrounds that no accurate or useful profile of at-risk kids could be developed. They ranged in age from 11 to 21 and came from a wide variety of ethnic and racial backgrounds; about 25 percent of the shooters were minority-group members. Some lived in intact families with strong ties to the community, whereas others were reared in foster homes with histories of neglect. Some were excellent students, whereas others were poor academic performers. Shooters could not be characterized as isolated and alienated; some had many friends and were considered popular. There was no evidence that shootings were a result of the onset of mental disorder. Drugs and alcohol seemed to have little involvement in school violence.

What the Secret Service did find, however, was that many of the shooters had a history of feeling extremely depressed or desperate, because they had been picked on or bullied. About three-fourths of the shooters either threatened to kill themselves, made suicidal gestures, or tried to kill themselves before the attack; six of the students studied killed themselves during the incident. The most frequent motivation was revenge. More than three-fourths were known to hold a grievance, real or imagined, against the target or others. In most cases, this was the first violent act against the target. Two-thirds of the attackers described feeling persecuted, and in more than three-fourths of the incidents the attackers had difficulty coping with a major change in a significant relationship or a loss of status, such as a lost love or a humiliating failure. Not surprisingly, most shooters had experience with guns and weapons and had access to them at home.

The Causes of School Crime

What are the suspected causes of school violence? Research indicates that they may be found at the individual, school, and community level.

School-Level Causes. Schools with a high proportion of students behind grade level in reading, with many students from families on welfare, and located in a community with high unemployment, crime, and poverty rates, are at risk for delinquency.[61] Research shows that the perpetrators and victims of school crime cannot be neatly divided into separate groups and that many offenders have been victims of delinquency themselves.[62] It is possible that school-based crimes have "survival value": striking back against a weaker victim is a method of regaining lost possessions or self-respect.[63]

Research also shows that school climate—the social and educational atmosphere of a school—is one of the most important predictors of campus crime and violence levels.[64]

Individual-Level Causes. School crime may be a function of the number of students with emotional and psychological problems. Kids who feel isolated and alone with little parental attention may be the most prone to alienation and substance abuse.[65] As substance abuse increases among the student body, so too may school violence rates. The level of student drinking may increase violent crime rates.[66] Because heavy drinking reduces cognitive ability, information processing skills, and the ability to process and react to verbal and nonverbal behavior, a student argument may quickly turn into a full-scale

School shootings have become a continuing saga in American schools. Here, Hammad Memon, 16, leaves a bond revocation hearing under heavy security in the Madison County Courthouse in Huntsville, Alabama. Memon is charged in the fatal shooting death of 14-year-old Todd Brown, who was shot inside Discovery Middle School in Madison. While profiles of school shooters exist, it remains extremely difficult to predict who will participate in school violence before it occurs.

AP Photo/Huntsville Times, Dave Dieter, File

RACE, ETHNICITY, ACTIVITIES, AND SCHOOL VIOLENCE

In a recent study using longitudinal survey data collected from a national sample of more than 12,000 youths as they progressed from 10th grade through high school, Anthony Peguero, Ann Marie Popp, and Dixie Koo found that race, ethnicity, and activities played a significant role in producing high school victimization. Minority students who are involved in academic extracurricular activities are more likely to be selected as suitable targets for violent victimization than those who shun such programs.

How can these unusual findings be explained? The authors rely on an interpretation based on Anderson's "code of the street" concept.

WHAT DOES THIS MEAN TO ME?

▶ **"Bully for You!"** Research indicates that more than 80 percent of school kids say their behavior includes physical aggression, social ridicule, teasing, name-calling, and issuing threats over the previous 30 days. Some kids seem proud of being bullies and think their behavior, no matter how destructive, is just having fun at another's expense. Many of us have been the targets of bullies, but felt unsure of how to cope with the problem. If you told the teacher or your parents, you were a wimp; if you did nothing, you remained a target.

1. Did you ever find yourself having to confront this dilemma, and if so, what did you do to solve the problem?
2. Do you believe there is a link between being the victim of bullying and engaging in school violence? The Columbine shooters were believed to be targets of bullying. Could this have been the spark that caused them to snap?

battle.[67] Schools with high-achieving students, a drug-free environment, strong discipline, and involved parents have fewer behavioral problems in the student body.[68]

Community-Level Causes. Schools experiencing drug abuse and crime are most likely to be found in socially disorganized neighborhoods. A number of researchers have observed that school crime is a function of the community in which the school is located. Schools in high-crime areas experience more crime than schools in safer areas; there is less fear in schools in safer neighborhoods than in high-crime ones. Students who report being afraid in school are actually more afraid of being in city parks, streets, or subways.[69]

Delinquency experts Rod Brunson and Jody Miller have found that school violence often starts in the community and then migrates to the school. A great many of these incidents revolve around gang membership: gang affiliations carry over into the school and cause conflicts. Tensions escalate during school hours and then turn violent just after school ends. The school experience amplifies gang conflicts; while rival gang members could avoid each other in the community, they are forced to be in close proximity at school. Gang rivalry caused by a particular violent incident or long-standing feud may fuel conflicts at school.[70]

Who Are the Victims of School Crime?

School crime is not a random event, and some kids are targeted because of their personal status and behavior. Recent research by Marie Skubak Tillyer and her associates found that kids who take risks themselves may be the most likely target. Those who self-report criminal behavior and associate with delinquent peers were more likely to become victims, in contrast to kids who were attached to school and peers, which seem to be protective factors against violent victimization at school. Their findings suggest that risky behaviors do in fact increase students' exposure to motivated offenders and heighten the likelihood of violent victimization. In addition, impulsivity significantly increased the risk of violent victimization, a finding that supports Gottfredson and Hirschi's General Theory of Crime. Kids with

Within a school context, education is controlled by the dominant social group, who believe that their peers who pursue academic achievement are weak and vulnerable; they are acting "white." In primarily black inner-city schools, academically successful kids are perceived to be "selling out to whites." They are often less popular, verbally harassed, taunted, and isolated. In contrast, those kids who are prepared to use violence to defend themselves are less likely to be victimized.

The code of the street emphasizes maintaining the respect of others through a violent identity and toughness. As a result, inner-city kids who are tough do not get disrespected or victimized. Students in these schools may feel pressured to engage in misbehavior to establish a tough social identity and reduce their risk of victimization.

This research shows that, ironically, inner-city schools that create extracurricular programs to encourage academic achievement may actually be putting students who participate in them at risk. The only way for them to escape the increased risk of victimization is to adopt a super-tough demeanor, neutralizing any benefit of program participation.

CRITICAL THINKING

What can be done to reshape student attitudes to respect education and achievement? Are adults able to have any impact on teens or are they viewed merely as annoying people who are simply ignored?

Writing Assignment Write an essay entitled, "The Zen of Ferris Bueller: Ways of Gaining Respect in High School."

Source: Anthony A. Peguero, Ann Marie Popp, and Dixie J. Koo, "Race, Ethnicity, and School-Based Adolescent Victimization," *Crime and Delinquency*, first published online February 28, 2011.

low self-control may be viewed by offenders as antagonistic or particularly suitable targets because of their impulsive behaviors.[71]

The Tillyer research also founds that involvement in school sports increased the risk of victimization, indicating that involvement in after-school activities may increase risk. This topic is discussed further in the Focus on Delinquency feature.

The local high school can be the single most dangerous area in the neighborhood. Brawls, fights, theft, and drug use are not uncommon. Schools have designed a number of security measures to crack down on crime. Here, students at Thomas Jefferson High School in Los Angeles are ordered to tuck in their shirts before entering school in the aftermath of two apparently racially motivated student brawls. A number of students suffered injuries while fleeing from a lunch period fight involving about 200 Hispanic and African American students. Stepped-up school police and Los Angeles police presence, strict regulation of clothing styles that could be associated with gangs, and a tightened school bell schedule that leaves little time to linger between classes are in effect to curb the violence.

© David McNew/Getty Images

Reducing School Crime

Schools around the country have mounted campaigns to reduce the incidence of delinquency on campus. Nearly all states have developed some sort of crime-free, weapon-free, or safe-school zone statute. Most have defined these zones to include school transportation and school-sponsored functions. Schools are also cooperating with court officials and probation officers to share information and monitor students who have criminal records. School districts are formulating crisis prevention and intervention policies and are directing individual schools to develop safe-school plans.

Some schools have instituted strict controls over student activity—for example, performing locker searches, preventing students from having lunch off campus, and using patrols to monitor drug use. According to one national survey, a majority of schools have adopted a **zero tolerance policy** that mandates predetermined punishments for specific offenses, most often possession of drugs, weapons, and tobacco, and also for engaging in violent behaviors.[72]

School Security Efforts

School systems have increased security efforts in an attempt to control crime and bullying. Certain practices, such as locked or monitored doors or gates, are intended to limit or control access to school campuses, while others, such as metal detectors, security cameras, and limiting access to social networking websites, are intended to monitor or restrict students' and visitors' behavior on campus.

Limiting Access. Almost every school attempts to restrict entry of dangerous persons by having visitors sign in before entering, and most close the campus for lunch. Schools have attempted to ensure the physical safety of students and staff by using mechanical security devices such as surveillance cameras, metal detectors, and electronic barriers to keep out intruders, and have also employed roving security guards. Security measures include the following:

- *Access control.* About 75 percent of all schools control access to school buildings by locking or monitoring doors.
- *Lighting control.* Some administrators keep buildings dark at night, believing that brightly illuminated schools give the buildings too high a profile and attract vandals who might have not bothered with the facility, or even noticed it, if the premises were not illuminated.[73]
- *Gates.* About one-third of schools control access to school grounds with locked or monitored gates.
- *Picture IDs.* About one-quarter of schools require faculty or staff to wear picture IDs. and a number now require students to have badges or picture IDs.
- *Security cameras.* About 84 percent of high schools, 73 percent of middle schools, and 51 percent of primary schools report that they use security cameras to monitor their schools.

Monitoring Students. In addition to controlling access, school systems are also introducing methods to control student behaviors in an effort to reduce crime:

- *Book bag control.* Some schools require transparent book bags or ban book bags altogether.
- *Random checks.* About 15 percent of secondary schools use random metal detector checks, half use random dog sniffs, and one-quarter use random sweeps for contraband.

zero tolerance policy Mandating specific consequences or punishments for delinquent acts and not allowing anyone to avoid these consequences.

- *Computer and electronic device monitoring.* More than 90 percent of schools now limit access to social networking websites from school computers and prohibit the use of cell phones and text messaging devices during school hours.
- *Threat reporting.* More than one-third of schools have a structured, anonymous threat reporting system in place.

Figure 9.2 shows the percentage of schools using safety and security measures.

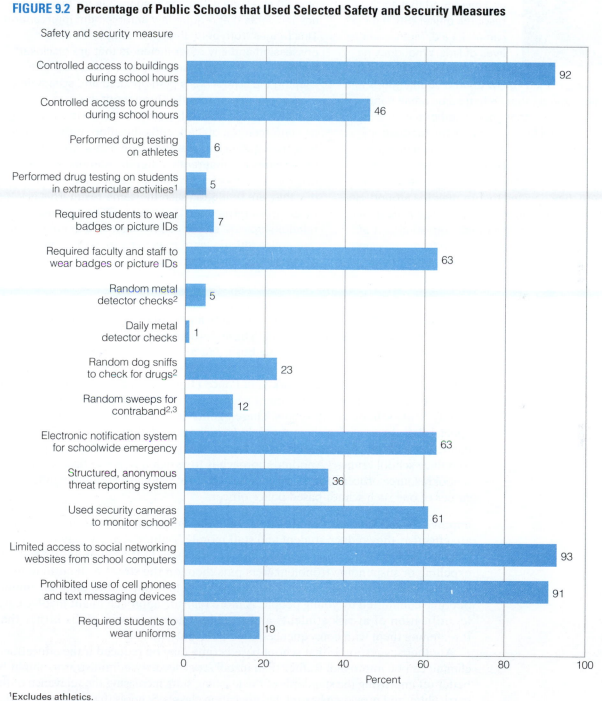

FIGURE 9.2 **Percentage of Public Schools that Used Selected Safety and Security Measures**

Safety and security measure

Measure	Percent
Controlled access to buildings during school hours	92
Controlled access to grounds during school hours	46
Performed drug testing on athletes	6
Performed drug testing on students in extracurricular activities[1]	5
Required students to wear badges or picture IDs	7
Required faculty and staff to wear badges or picture IDs	63
Random metal detector checks[2]	5
Daily metal detector checks	1
Random dog sniffs to check for drugs[2]	23
Random sweeps for contraband[2,3]	12
Electronic notification system for schoolwide emergency	63
Structured, anonymous threat reporting system	36
Used security cameras to monitor school[2]	61
Limited access to social networking websites from school computers	93
Prohibited use of cell phones and text messaging devices	91
Required students to wear uniforms	19

Percent

[1]Excludes athletics.
[2]One or more checks, sweeps, or cameras.
[3]For example, drugs or weapons. Does not include dog sniffs.

Source: National Center for Education Statistics, *Indicators of School Crime and Safety: 2011*, http://nces.ed.gov/programs/crimeindicators/crimeindicators2011/figures/figure_20_1.asp (accessed August 21, 2012).

© Kevin Quinn

Kevin Quinn

*School Resource Officer,
Chandler Police Department,
Chandler, Arizona*

Kevin Quinn works in the largest high school in the city and has found that a school resource officer (SRO) officer can make a difference in the lives of kids. What does he find most rewarding about the job? Watching the kids grow up into young adults and then graduate, knowing that he had some small hand in helping them achieve that goal, whether they realize it or not. He has seen kids walk across the graduation stage whom he thought would never finish high school, even some he had to arrest. He is pleased when they thank him on graduation day, to say the arrest was the moment where they decided to turn their life around. He has also helped some students get out of abusive dating relationships. Quinn thinks the most interesting part of the job is seeing the educational system from the inside. Being a part of the administration team and attending staff meetings has given him real insight into what goes on behind the scenes in schools and why school administrators do the things they do.

While Quinn does not follow a regular routine, there are some tasks that occur on a daily basis. Since he is the only police officer on the campus and it spans more than 80 acres, he is the one responsible for taking care of any incidents that require law enforcement intervention. This ranges from petty thefts on campus to drug possession and any other incidents that are disclosed by students. He also assists the administration with keeping the school crisis plan updated and scheduling emergency response drills throughout the year. Quinn believes that his biggest challenge is trying to get law enforcement officers and education professionals to work together to meet the same goals. Since the professions are inherently different, sometimes there is a conflict between the two, but at the end of the day they are trying to reach the same result. This is where having trainings that cover SRO–administration relationships are so critical, to be sure both educators and police officers learn how to cooperate for the good of the school community.

Employing Law Enforcement. Some districts have gone so far as to place undercover detectives on school grounds. These detectives attend classes, mingle with students, contact drug dealers, make buys, and arrest campus dealers.[74] Other cities, such as New York, maintain a significant uniformed police presence within the educational system. The New York City Police Department School Safety Division is one of the largest law enforcement agencies in the United States, with approximately 5,000 school safety agents. These agents are designated as New York City Special Patrolmen, giving them the right to make warrantless arrests, carry and use handcuffs, and use physical and deadly force.[75] They also carry out special programs to reduce school crime.[76] Another approach is to assign a police officer known as a school resource officer to work on campus. The Professional Spotlight highlights the career of one such school-based police officer.

Improve School Climate. Some critics complain that even when security methods are effective, they reduce student and staff morale. Tighter security may reduce acts of crime and violence in school, only to displace them to the community. Similarly, expelling or suspending troublemakers puts them on the street with nothing to do, so in the end, lowering the level of crime in schools may not reduce the total amount of crime committed by young people. A more realistic approach might involve early identification of at-risk students and teaching them prosocial skills rather than threatening them with consequence-based punishments.[77]

Another suggestion is that school-based crime may be reduced if the educational climate can be improved. Rather than install strict security, administrators might be better off improving the standards of the teaching staff, increasing the relevance of the curriculum, and providing law-related education classes. Schools that encourage order, organization, and student bonding have experienced a decline in disorder and crime.[78] In addition to controlling gangs and drugs in the school, administrators who apply school rules evenly and increase the certainty of punishment for breaking those rules can create the multifaceted approach needed provide a safer school environment.[79]

THE ROLE OF THE SCHOOL IN DELINQUENCY PREVENTION

Numerous organizations and groups have called for reforming the educational system to make it more responsive to the needs of students. Educational leaders now recognize that children undergo enormous pressures while in school that can lead to emotional and social problems. At one extreme are the pressures to succeed academically; at the other are the crime and substance abuse students face on school grounds. It is difficult to talk about achieving academic excellence in a deteriorated school dominated by gang members.

One way of improving schools and reducing delinquency is through sponsored educational reform. The No Child Left Behind Act of 2001 (NCLB) (Public Law 107-110) authorizes federal programs aimed at improving America's primary and secondary schools by increasing the accountability for states, school districts, and schools and also providing parents more flexibility in choosing which schools their children will attend.[80] The NCLB increases focus on reading and relies on outcome-based education or the belief that high expectations and setting of goals will result in success for all students.[81] The NCLB has proven quite controversial.

School-Based Prevention Programs

Education officials have instituted numerous programs to make schools more effective instruments of delinquency prevention.[82] Some of the most prevalent strategies are as follows:

- *Cognitive.* Increase students' awareness about the dangers of drug abuse and delinquency.
- *Affective.* Improve students' psychological assets and self-image to give them the resources to resist antisocial behavior.

AP Photo/Jacquelyn Martin

School systems have become active in delinquency prevention efforts. Some programs are classroom based, while others take students off campus. Some contract out services to local community groups, and others are run by the school system itself. Here, Brendan Fox (left) passes a level to Dontike Miller as they work on a construction project as part of Miller's vocational training in the YouthBuild program in Washington. YouthBuild prepares students who have not completed high school to take the GED and gives them vocational training in construction.

- *Behavioral.* Train students in techniques to resist peer pressure.
- *Environmental.* Establish school management and disciplinary programs that deter crime, such as locker searches.
- *Therapeutic.* Treat youths who have already manifested problems.

More specific suggestions include creating special classes or schools with individualized programs that foster success for nonadjusting students. Efforts can be made to help students deal constructively with academic failure when it does occur.

More personalized student–teacher relationships have been recommended. This effort to provide young people with a caring, accepting adult role model will, it is hoped, strengthen the controls against delinquency. Counselors acting as liaisons between the family and the school might also be effective in preventing delinquency. These counselors try to ensure cooperation between the parents and the school and to secure needed services for troubled students. Some programs that help families and schools develop conflict-avoidance skills have proven effective in reducing violence levels and disciplinary measures, such as suspensions and expulsions.[83]

Experiments have been proposed to integrate job training and experience with classroom instruction, allowing students to see education as a relevant prelude to their careers. Job training programs emphasize public service, encouraging students to gain a sense of attachment to their communities.

Because three out of four mothers with school-age children are employed, and two-thirds of them work full time, there is a growing need for after-school programs. Today, after-school options include child-care centers, tutoring programs at school, dance groups, basketball leagues, and drop-in clubs. State and federal budgets for education, public safety, crime prevention, and childcare provide some funding for after-school programs. Research shows that younger children (ages 5 to 9) and those in low-income neighborhoods gain the most from after-school programs, showing improved work habits, behavior with peers and adults, and performance in school. Young teens who attend after-school activities achieve higher grades in school and engage in less risky behavior. These findings must be interpreted with caution. Because after-school programs are voluntary, participants may be the more motivated youngsters in a given population and the least likely to engage in antisocial behavior.[84]

Schools may not be able to reduce delinquency single-handedly, but a number of alternatives to their present operations could aid a community-wide effort to lessen juvenile crime. And reviews of some of the more successful programs show that the savings in terms of reduced delinquency, school costs, and so on far outweigh the amount of money spent on prevention. **CHECKPOINTS**

CHECKPOINTS

LO4 Know about the nature and extent of school crime and its control.

✔ Kids who feel isolated and alone with little parental attention may be the most prone to alienation and substance abuse.

✔ The level of student drinking and substance abuse may increase violent crime rates.

✔ School crime is a function of the community in which the school is located.

✔ Shooting incidents typically occur around the start of the school day.

✔ Many shooters have a history of feeling extremely depressed or desperate because they have been picked on or bullied.

✔ Almost every school attempts to restrict entry of dangerous persons by having visitors sign in before entering, and most close the campus for lunch.

✔ Most schools control access to school buildings by locking or monitoring doors.

✔ Schools use random metal detector checks and one or more security cameras to monitor the school.

LEGAL RIGHTS IN THE SCHOOL

The actions of education officials often run into opposition from the courts, which are concerned with maintaining the legal rights of minors. The U.S. Supreme Court has sought to balance the civil liberties of students with the school's mandate to provide a safe environment. Three of the main issues involved are privacy issues, free speech in school, and school discipline.

The Right to Personal Privacy

One major issue is the right of school officials to search students and their possessions on school grounds. Drug abuse, theft, assault and battery, and racial conflicts in schools have increased the need to take action against troublemakers. School administrators have questioned students about their illegal activities, conducted searches of students' persons and possessions, and reported suspicious behavior to the police.

In 1984, in *New Jersey v. T.L.O.*, the Supreme Court helped clarify a vexing problem: whether the Fourth Amendment's prohibition against unreasonable searches and seizures applies to school officials as well as to police officers.[85] In this case, the Court found that students are in fact constitutionally protected from illegal searches, but that school officials are not bound by the same restrictions as law enforcement agents. Police need "probable cause" before they can conduct a search, but educators can legally search students when there are reasonable grounds to believe the students have violated the law or broken school rules. In creating this distinction, the Court recognized the needs of school officials to preserve an environment conducive to education and to secure the safety of students.

Drug Testing. The Supreme Court has allowed school authorities to conduct random drug tests on the grounds that they are less intrusive than a search of a student's body. In the 1995 case *Vernonia School District 47J v. Acton*, the Court allowed the testing of student athletes who were going off campus to engage in events.[86] Underlying this decision is the recognition that drug use is a serious threat to public safety that interferes with the right of children to receive a decent and safe education. While drug tests are intrusive, maintaining school safety was viewed as outweighing the minor inconvenience and loss of personal privacy. In a subsequent case, *Board of Education of Independent School District No. 92 of Pottawatomie County et al. v. Earls et al.*, the Court extended the right to test for drugs without probable cause to all students as long as the drug-testing policies were "reasonable." In this instance, the need for maintaining swift and informal disciplinary procedures to maintain order in a public school outweighs the right to personal privacy. Because the school's responsibility for children cannot be disregarded, it would not be unreasonable to search students for drug usage even if no single student was suspected of abusing drugs.

The Court also ruled that, within this context, students have a limited expectation of privacy. In their complaint, the students argued that children participating in nonathletic extracurricular activities have a stronger expectation of privacy than athletes who regularly undergo physicals as part of their participation in sports. The Court disagreed, maintaining that students who participate in competitive extracurricular activities voluntarily subject themselves to many of the same intrusions on their privacy as do athletes.[87]

Limiting Drug Searches. But how far can school officials go in their efforts to preserve a safe school environment? The Court clarified this issue in *Safford Unified School District v. Redding*, a 2009 case that drew national headlines. Savana Redding was a 13-year-old eighth-grade honors student at Safford Middle School, located about 127 miles from Tucson, Arizona, when on October 3, 2003, she was taken out of class by the school's vice principal. It seems that one of Redding's classmates had been caught possessing four prescription-strength ibuprofen pills (400 mg, the strength of two Advils) and when asked where she got the pills blamed Redding, who had no history of disciplinary issues or drug abuse.

Though Redding claimed that she had no knowledge of the pills, she was subjected to a strip search by the school nurse and another female employee because the school has a zero tolerance policy for all over-the-counter medication (which students could not possess without prior written permission). During the search, Redding was forced to strip to her underwear and her bra, and her underpants were pulled away from her body. No drugs were found. Redding later told authorities, "The strip search was the most humiliating experience I have ever had. I held my head down so that they could not see that I was about to cry."

After a trial court ruled that the search was legal, Redding sought help from the American Civil Liberties Union, whose attorneys brought an appeal before the Ninth Circuit Court. Here the judges ruled that the search was "traumatizing" and illegal, stating that: "Common sense informs us that directing a 13-year-old girl to remove her clothes, partially revealing her breasts and pelvic area, for allegedly possessing ibuprofen was excessively intrusive." It further went on to say, "The overzealousness of school administrators in efforts to protect students has the tragic impact of traumatizing those they claim to serve. And all this to find prescription-strength ibuprofen." Rather than let the appellate court decision stand, the school district appealed the case to the U.S. Supreme Court, complaining that restrictions on conducting student searches would cast a "roadblock to the kind of swift and effective response that is too often needed to protect the very safety of students, particularly from the threats posed by drugs and weapons."[88]

On June 25, 2009, the Supreme Court held that Redding's Fourth Amendment rights were indeed violated by the search.[89] With Justice David Souter writing for the majority, the Court agreed that search measures used by school officials to root out contraband must be "reasonably related to the objectives of the search and not excessively intrusive in light of the age and sex of the student and the nature of the infraction." In Redding's case, school officials did not have sufficient suspicion to extend the search to her underwear. In a separate opinion, Justice John Paul Stevens agreed that the strip search was unconstitutional and that the school administrators should be held personally liable for damages: "[i]t does not require a constitutional scholar to conclude that a nude search of a 13-year old child is an invasion of constitutional rights of some magnitude." (His opinion was in response to the majority ruling that school officials could not be held personally liable because the law was unclear prior to the *Safford* decision). The only justice to disagree with the main finding was Clarence Thomas, who concluded that the judiciary should not meddle with decisions of school administrators that are intended to be in the interest of school safety.

This photo shows Savana Redding standing outside the Supreme Court in Washington, D.C., after the Court heard her appeal on a case in which she was strip searched when she was 13 years old by school officials looking for prescription-strength ibuprofen pills. In a landmark decision, the Court ruled that the school's strip search was illegal. The justices said school officials violated the law because their search violated Redding's personal privacy and was traumatic and offensive to a young girl.

Academic Privacy. Students have the right to expect that their records will be kept private. Although state laws govern the disclosure of information from juvenile court records, a 1974 federal law—the Family Educational Rights and Privacy Act (FERPA)—restricts disclosure of information from a student's education records without parental consent.[90] The act defines an education record to include all records, files, and other materials, such as photographs, containing information related to a student that an education agency maintains. In 1994, Congress passed the Improving America's Schools Act, which allowed educational systems to disclose education records under these circumstances: (a) state law authorizes the disclosure, (b) the disclosure is to a juvenile justice agency, (c) the disclosure relates to the justice system's ability to provide preadjudication services to a student, and (d) state or local officials certify in writing that the institution or individual receiving the information has agreed not to disclose it to a third party other than another juvenile justice system agency.[91]

Free Speech

Freedom of speech is guaranteed by the First Amendment to the U.S. Constitution. This right has been divided into two categories as it affects children in schools: passive speech and active speech.

Passive speech is a form of expression not associated with actually speaking words, such as wearing armbands or political protest buttons. The most important U.S. Supreme Court decision concerning a student's right to passive speech was in 1969 in the case of *Tinker v. Des Moines Independent Community School District*.[92] This case involved the right to wear black armbands to protest the war in Vietnam. Three high school students, ages 16, 15, and 13, were suspended for wearing the armbands in school. According to the Court, to justify prohibiting an expression of opinion, the school must be able to show that its action was caused by something more than a desire to avoid the unpleasantness that accompanies the expression of an unpopular view. Unless it can be shown that the forbidden conduct will interfere with the discipline required to operate the school, the prohibition cannot be sustained.[93]

The concept of free speech articulated in *Tinker* was used again in 1986 in *Bethel School District No. 403 v. Fraser*.[94] This case upheld a school system's right to discipline a student who uses obscene or profane language and gestures. The Court found that a school has the right to control offensive speech that undermines the educational mission. In a 1988 case, *Hazelwood School District v. Kuhlmeier*, the Court extended the right of school officials to censor **active speech** when it ruled that the principal could censor articles in a student publication.[95] In this case, students had written about their experiences with pregnancy and parental divorce. The majority ruled that censorship was justified, because school-sponsored publications were part of the curriculum and therefore designed to impart knowledge. Control over such activities could be differentiated from the action of the *Tinker* defendants' passive protests. In a dissent, Justice William J. Brennan accused school officials of favoring "thought control."

Off-Campus Speech. Does the school have a right to control off-campus speech? It depends. In what has come to be known as the "Bong Hits for Jesus" case, the Supreme Court ruled that school officials can control student speech at off-campus events. In 2002, Joseph Frederick unveiled a 14-foot paper sign on a public sidewalk outside his high school in Juneau, Alaska, that linked marijuana smoking and Jesus. The school principal confiscated it and suspended Frederick. He sued, and his case went all the way to the Supreme Court, where the justices concluded that Frederick's free speech rights were not violated because it was reasonable to conclude that the banner promoted illegal drug use, and that had the principal failed to act, it would send a powerful message to the students that the school condoned pro-drug messages.[96]

Speech in Cyberspace. Free speech has become a significant issue because the cyberage provides numerous opportunities for students to test the limits of free speech, whether it be through personal websites, Twitter messages, texts and emails that are quickly spread among the student body, and YouTube postings that show secretly made recordings of teachers in unflattering poses. While the Supreme Court has not yet ruled on this issue, a number of cases have gone to federal appellate courts. The most prominent cases took place in Pennsylvania, when a federal judge ruled in two cases involving off-campus speech. In the first, high school senior Justin Layshock sued Mercer County's Hermitage School District after he was suspended for 10 days for creating what he called a "parody profile" of his school principal. The MySpace page largely consisted of jokes about the principal's size and weight. The Third Circuit Court ruled the suspension violated Layshock's right to freedom of speech, finding that self-expression "that originated outside of the schoolhouse, did not disturb the school environment and was not related to any school-sponsored event" could not be punished. In the second case, J.S., an eighth-grader, sued the Blue Mountain School District after she was suspended for 10 days

passive speech A form of expression protected by the First Amendment, but not associated with actually speaking words; examples include wearing symbols or protest messages on buttons or signs.
active speech Expressing an opinion by speaking or writing; freedom of speech is a protected right under the First Amendment to the U.S. Constitution.

in 2007 for creating a fake online profile of her school principal. Her profile did not list the principal's name, but contained his picture and copy that stated he was a pedophile and a sex addict. The Court noted that legal precedent has already been set that so long as the online content created by a student on their own time, using their own resources, is not disruptive to the learning environment, they cannot be disciplined. But if the content disrupts the learning environment, it becomes a "school issue" and is subject to disciplinary action. However, the Court left the door open to controlling students who publish off-campus material that is disruptive, saying, "We decline to say that simply because the disruption to the learning environment originates from a computer located off campus, the school should be left powerless to discipline the student."[97]

The clash between a student's right to free speech and the school's ability to maintain security and discipline has not been settled and will continue to grow as the cyberage provides new venues of expression.

School Prayer. One of the most divisive issues involving free speech is school prayer. Although some religious-minded administrators, parents, and students want to have prayer sessions in schools or hold religious convocations, others view the practice both as a violation of the principle of separation of church and state and as an infringement on the First Amendment right to freedom of religion. The case of *Santa Fe Independent School District, Petitioner v. Jane Doe* (2000) helps clarify the issue.[98]

Prior to 1995, the Santa Fe High School student who occupied the school's elective office of student council chaplain delivered a prayer over the public address system before each varsity football game for the entire season. After the practice was challenged in federal district court, the school district adopted a different policy that permitted, but did not require, prayer initiated and led by a student at each of the home games. The district court entered an order modifying that policy to permit only nonsectarian, nonproselytizing prayer. However, a federal appellate court held that, even as modified, the football prayer policy was invalid. This decision was upheld when the case was appealed to the U.S. Supreme Court. They ruled that prayers led by an "elected" student undermine the protection of minority viewpoints. Such a system encourages divisiveness along religious lines and threatens the imposition of coercion upon those students not desiring to participate in a religious exercise. The *Santa Fe* case severely limits school-sanctioned prayer at public events.

Despite the *Santa Fe* decision, the Supreme Court has not totally ruled out the role of religion in schools. In its ruling in *Good News Club v. Milford Central School* (2001), the Court required an upstate New York school district to provide space for an after-school Bible club for elementary students.[99] The Court ruled that it was a violation of the First Amendment's free speech clause to deny the club access to the school space on the ground that the club was religious in nature; the school routinely let secular groups use its space. The Court reasoned that because the club's meetings were to be held after school hours, were not sponsored by the school, and were open to any student who obtained parental consent, it could not be perceived that the school was endorsing the club or that students might feel coerced to participate in its activities.

In *Elk Grove Unified School District v. Newdow*, the Court refused to hear a case brought by a California father contesting the recital of the Pledge of Allegiance because it contains the phrase "under God."[100] Although the Court refused the case on a technical issue, some of the justices felt the issue should have been dealt with and dismissed for substantive reasons:

> To give the parent of such a child a sort of "heckler's veto" over a patriotic ceremony willingly participated in by other students, simply because the Pledge of Allegiance contains the descriptive phrase "under God," is an unwarranted extension of the establishment clause, an extension which would have the unfortunate effect of prohibiting a commendable patriotic observance.[101]

School Discipline

About 20 states have statutes permitting teachers to use corporal punishment in public school systems. Under the concept of **in loco parentis**, discipline is one of the parental duties given to the school system. In the 1977 case *Ingraham v. Wright*, the Court held that neither the Eighth nor the Fourteenth Amendment was violated by a teacher's use of corporal punishment to discipline students.[102] The Court established the standard that only reasonable discipline is allowed in school systems. Despite the *Ingraham* decision, the use of corporal punishment remains controversial. According to a recent study conducted by the American Civil Liberties Union and Human Rights Watch, almost a quarter of a million U.S. public school children are now being subjected to corporal punishment each school year, and a disproportionate number of them are students with mental or physical disabilities. The research found that students with disabilities made up about 19 percent of students who suffered corporal punishment at school, although they constituted just 14 percent of the total nationwide student population. More than 40,000 students with disabilities are subjected to corporal punishment in U.S. schools each year, and this tally probably undercounts the actual rate of physical discipline, since not all instances are reported or recorded. The report found that some students were punished for conduct related to their disabilities: students with Tourette syndrome were paddled for exhibiting involuntary tics, and students with autism were punished for repetitive behaviors such as rocking. Opponents charge that corporal punishment may harm kids with disabilities, leading to a worsening of their conditions. For instance, some parents reported that students with autism became violent toward themselves or others following corporal punishment.[103]

With regard to suspension and expulsion, in 1976, in the case of *Goss v. Lopez*, the Supreme Court ruled that any time a student is to be suspended for more than 10 days, he or she is entitled to a hearing.[104] In summary, schools have the right to discipline students, but students are protected from unreasonable, excessive, and arbitrary discipline.

CHECKPOINTS

in loco parentis In the place of the parent; rights given to schools that allow them to assume parental duties in disciplining students.

CHECKPOINTS

LO5 Be familiar with the legal rights of students.

✔ Educators can legally search students when there are reasonable grounds to believe the students have violated the law or broken school rules.

✔ The search must be reasonable and there are limits to how far school officials can go when searching students.

✔ Children have the right to free speech in school as long as it does not interfere with the educational process.

✔ *Ingraham v. Wright* upheld the right of teachers to use corporal punishment.

✔ Schools can control off-campus and on-campus speech under some circumstances.

SUMMARY

The school environment has been found to have a significant effect on a child's emotional well-being. The school has become a primary determinant of economic and social status. Despite its importance, the United States trails other nations in critical academic areas.

Many children are at risk for educational problems and school failure, which have been linked to delinquency. There are a number of factors that are correlated with school failure. Tracking (dividing students into groups according to ability and achievement level) may be a contributor, as are feelings of isolation, alienation, and substance abuse.

Crimes of violence on school grounds are both troubling and frequent. Shooting incidents occur all too frequently. As a result, almost every school attempts to restrict entry of dangerous persons by controlling access to school buildings and using security systems to monitor students. Some schools are now employing uniformed police officers on school grounds, typically called school safety officers.

The U.S. Supreme Court has sought to balance the civil liberties of students with the school's mandate to provide a safe environment. Despite legal protections, educators can legally search students when there are reasonable grounds to believe the students have violated the law or broken school rules. Children have the right to free speech in school as long as it does not interfere with the educational process. *Ingraham v. Wright* upheld the right of teachers to use corporal punishment.

KEY TERMS

academic achievement, p. 242

drop out, p. 245

dropout factories, p. 245

underachievers, p. 248

tracking, p. 250

bullying, p. 252

gender policing, p. 252

zero tolerance policy, p. 258

passive speech, p. 265

active speech, p. 265

in loco parentis, p. 267

QUESTIONS FOR REVIEW

1. How does the Supreme Court distinguish between active and passive speech on school grounds?

2. In what significant ways does the school experience become a factor in shaping the direction of an adolescent's life course?

3. What is the relationship between school failure and persistent offending?

4. Do police need probable cause before they can conduct a search on school grounds? When can educators legally search students?

5. What effect do socialization and status have on a student's educational experience?

6. What are the differences between social and educational reasons for dropping out of school?

7. What are the three independent views on the association between school failure and delinquency? What are the similarities and differences between these views?

8. What are the four sources of student alienation?

9. What are the reasons some youth become school bullies?

10. What are the factors linked to children who engage in serious school violence?

11. What security measures do schools utilize to control crime and delinquency on campus?

QUESTIONS FOR DISCUSSION

1. Was there a delinquency problem in your high school? If so, how was it dealt with?

2. Should disobedient youths be suspended from school? Does this solution hurt or help?

3. What can be done to improve the delinquency prevention capabilities of schools?

4. Is school failure responsible for delinquency, or are delinquents simply school failures?

APPLYING WHAT YOU HAVE LEARNED

You are the principal of a suburban high school. It seems that one of your students, Steve Jones, has had a long-running feud with Mr. Metcalf, an English teacher whom he blames for giving him a low grade unfairly and for being too strict with other students. Steve set up a home-based website that posted insulting images of Metcalf and contained messages describing him in unflattering terms ("a slob who doesn't bathe often enough," for example). He posted a photo of the teacher with the caption "Public Enemy Number One." Word of the website has gotten out around school. Even though the students think it's funny and "cool," the faculty is outraged. You bring Steve into your office and ask him to take down the site, explaining that its existence has had a negative effect on school discipline and morale. He refuses, arguing that the site is home-based and you have no right to ask for its removal. Besides, he claims, it is just in fun and not really hurting anyone.

School administrators are asked to make these kinds of decisions every day, and the wrong choice can prove costly. You are aware that a case very similar to this one resulted in a $30,000 settlement in a damage claim against a school system when the principal suspended a student for posting an insulting website and the student later sued for violating his right to free speech.

Writing Assignment: Write an essay on how you would handle this case. Make sure to address the issue of whether you would suspend Steve if he refuses your request to take down the site, or whether you would allow him to leave it posted and try to placate Mr. Metcalf.

GROUPWORK

Divide the class into three groups. Have each draw up a school security program designed to reduce crime on campus. Compare notes and see where there is overlap.

Drug Use and Delinquency

© David Klammer/laif/Redux

LEARNING OBJECTIVES

After reading this chapter you should:

1. Understand the drug problem among American youth today and over time.

2. Know the main explanations for why youths take drugs.

3. Recognize the different behavior patterns of drug-involved youths.

4. Understand the relationship between drug use and delinquency.

5. Be familiar with the major drug-control strategies.

Nature One music festival, August 2006.

Fernando's Story

Fernando Ellis is a 15-year-old young man of Latino heritage who was referred to the local health/substance abuse agency after he attempted to jump out of his father's moving vehicle during a verbal argument. Fernando had been using and was high on drugs at the time. He was skipping school, using marijuana on a daily basis, and had numerous drug-related police contacts and charges. He was also on probation for selling drugs on school grounds.

Fernando's father worked long hours and drank to excess when he was at home. He introduced his son to alcohol and drugs at an early age, and offered little supervision or guidance. Fernando's mother was killed in an accident when Fernando was 12 years old, leaving his father to care for him and his three older siblings. In addition, Fernando was born with a birth defect that had often resulted in teasing by other children. At times, it was difficult to understand his speech and he walked with a significant limp. It appeared Fernando was trying to fit in, "be cool," and gain acceptance by engaging in criminal activity.

At the juvenile court hearing, Fernando was ordered to complete community service and individual counseling, and referred to the community mental health center for an alcohol and drug assessment, as well as a suicide risk assessment. He reluctantly cooperated with the order to avoid a more serious disposition.

Fernando's assessments indicated that although he did try to jump out of a moving car, he did not appear to be a suicide risk. He was under the influence at the time and in a very heated argument with his father. There was concern about his daily use of drugs and alcohol, and Fernando was referred to an outpatient drug treatment program at the center. In addition, Fernando met weekly with his counselor for individual counseling. They worked on his drug and alcohol issues, changing his behavior and habits, and the grief and loss issues related to the sudden death of his mother. This loss was a turning point for Fernando. Up to that time, he had been a good student who was not involved with drugs. Everything changed when his mother was killed.

Over the course of his work with his counselor, Fernando began to process this loss, as well as make positive changes in his life. A team of professionals, including his teachers, probation officer, drug and alcohol counselor, and a mentor provided by the school, all worked with Fernando to help him realize his goals. He began to attend school on a more regular basis and worked to improve his relationships with his father and siblings. Fernando continued to occasionally use alcohol, but eliminated his drug use. He also struggled with his home situation and sometimes ran away from home to stay with friends. Overall, Fernando significantly reduced his criminal activity, although he remained on probation for the duration of the court order.

There is little question that adolescent **substance abuse** and its association with delinquency is a vexing problem. Almost every city, town, and village in the United States has confronted some type of teenage substance abuse problem.

Self-report surveys indicate that just under half of high school seniors have tried drugs and 70 percent have used alcohol.[1] Adolescents at high risk for drug abuse often come from the most impoverished communities and experience a multitude of problems, including school failure and family conflict.[2] Equally troubling is the association between drug use and crime.[3] Research indicates that between 5 and 8 percent of all juvenile male arrestees in some cities test positive for cocaine.[4] Self-report surveys show that drug abusers are more likely to become delinquents than are nonabusers.[5] The pattern of drug use and crime makes teenage substance abuse a key national concern.

This chapter addresses some important issues involving teenage substance abuse, beginning with a review of the kinds of drugs children and adolescents are using and how often they are using them. Then we discuss who uses drugs and what causes substance abuse. After describing the association between drug abuse and delinquent behavior, the chapter concludes with a review of efforts to prevent and control the use of drugs in the United States.

substance abuse Using drugs or alcohol in such a way as to cause physical harm to oneself.

FREQUENTLY ABUSED DRUGS

A wide variety of substances referred to as drugs are used by teenagers. Some are addicting, others not. Some create hallucinations, others cause a depressed stupor, and a few give an immediate uplift. In this section, we will identify the most widely used substances and discuss their effects. All of these drugs can be abused, and because of the danger they present, many have been banned from private use. Others are available legally only with a physician's supervision, and a few are available to adults but prohibited for children.

Marijuana and Hashish

Commonly called "pot" or "grass," **marijuana** is produced from the leaves of *Cannabis sativa*. **Hashish** (hash) is a concentrated form of cannabis made from unadulterated resin from the female plant. The main active ingredient in both marijuana and hashish is tetrahydrocannabinol (THC), a mild hallucinogen. Marijuana is the drug most commonly used by teenagers.

Smoking large amounts of pot or hash can cause distortions in auditory and visual perception, even producing hallucinatory effects. Small doses produce an early excitement ("high") that gives way to drowsiness. Pot use is also related to decreased activity, overestimation of time and space, and increased food consumption. When the user is alone, marijuana produces a dreamy state. In a group, users become giddy and lose perspective.

Marijuana is not physically addicting, but its long-term effects have been the subject of much debate. During the 1970s, it was reported that smoking pot caused a variety of physical and mental problems, including brain damage and mental illness. Although the dangers of pot and hash may have been overstated, use of these drugs does present some health risks, including an increased risk of lung cancer, chronic bronchitis, and other diseases. Prospective parents should avoid smoking marijuana, because it lowers sperm counts in male users and females experience disrupted ovulation and a greater chance of miscarriage.[6]

Cocaine

Cocaine is an alkaloid derivative of the coca plant. When first isolated in 1860, it was considered a medicinal breakthrough that could relieve fatigue, depression, and other symptoms, and it quickly became a staple of patent medicines. When its addictive qualities and dangerous side effects became apparent, its use was controlled by the Pure Food and Drug Act of 1906.

Cocaine is the most powerful natural stimulant. Its use produces euphoria, restlessness, and excitement. Overdoses can cause delirium, violent manic behavior, and possible respiratory failure. The drug can be sniffed, or "snorted," into the nostrils, or it can be injected. The immediate feeling of euphoria, or "rush," is short-lived, and heavy users may snort coke as often as every 10 minutes. Another dangerous practice is "speedballing"—injecting a mixture of cocaine and heroin.

Crack is processed street cocaine. Its manufacture involves using ammonia or baking soda (sodium bicarbonate) to remove the hydrochlorides and create a crystalline form of cocaine that can be smoked. (Crack gets its name from the fact that the sodium bicarbonate often emits a crackling sound when the substance is smoked.) Also referred to as "rock," "gravel," and "roxanne," crack gained popularity in the mid-1980s. It is relatively inexpensive, can provide a powerful high, and is highly addictive psychologically. Crack cocaine use has been in decline in recent years. Heavy criminal penalties, tight enforcement, and social disapproval have helped to lower crack use.

marijuana The dried leaves of the cannabis plant.

hashish A concentrated form of cannabis made from unadulterated resin from the female cannabis plant.

cocaine A powerful natural stimulant derived from the coca plant.

crack A highly addictive crystalline form of cocaine containing remnants of hydrochloride and sodium bicarbonate; it makes a crackling sound when smoked.

Heroin

Narcotic drugs have the ability to produce insensibility to pain and to free the mind of anxiety and emotion. Users experience relief from fear and apprehension, release of tension, and elevation of spirits. This short period of euphoria is followed by a period of apathy, during which users become drowsy and may nod off. **Heroin**, the most commonly used narcotic in the United States, is produced from opium, a drug derived from the opium poppy flower. Dealers cut the drug with neutral substances (sugar or lactose), and street heroin is often only 1 percent to 4 percent pure.

Heroin is probably the most dangerous commonly abused drug. Users rapidly build up a tolerance for it, fueling the need for increased doses to obtain the desired effect. At first, heroin is usually sniffed or snorted. As tolerance builds, it is "skin popped" (shot into skin, but not into a vein), and finally it is injected into a vein, or "mainlined."[7] Through this progressive use, the user becomes an **addict**—a person with an overpowering physical and psychological need to continue taking a particular substance by any means possible. If addicts cannot get enough heroin to satisfy their habit, they will suffer withdrawal symptoms, which include irritability, depression, extreme nervousness, and nausea.

Alcohol

Alcohol remains the drug of choice for most teenagers. A little under two-thirds (64 percent) of high school seniors reported using alcohol in the past year, and 70 percent say they have tried it at some time during their lifetime; by the 12th grade, just over half (51 percent) of American youths report that they have been drunk.[8]

Alcohol may be a factor in nearly half of all murders, suicides, and accidental deaths.[9] Alcohol-related deaths number 100,000 a year, far more than all other illegal drugs combined. Just over 1.4 million drivers are arrested each year for driving under the influence (including 9,300 teen drivers), and about 840,000 more are arrested for other alcohol-related violations.[10] The economic cost is staggering. An estimated $185 billion is lost each year, including $36 billion from premature deaths, $88 billion in reduced work effort, and $19 billion arising from short- and long-term medical problems.[11]

heroin A narcotic made from opium and then cut with sugar or some other neutral substance until it is only 1 to 4 percent pure.

addict A person with an overpowering physical or psychological need to continue taking a particular substance or drug.

alcohol Fermented or distilled liquids containing ethanol, an intoxicating substance.

Youths who use alcohol report that it provides a number of benefits. But these benefits may result from limited use of alcohol; its use in higher doses has been shown to act as a depressant.

Considering these problems, why do so many youths drink to excess? Youths who use alcohol report that it reduces tension, enhances pleasure, improves social skills, and transforms experiences for the better.[12] Although these reactions may follow the limited use of alcohol, alcohol in higher doses acts as a depressant. Long-term use has been linked with depression and physical ailments ranging from heart disease to cirrhosis of the liver. Many teens also think drinking stirs their romantic urges, but scientific evidence indicates that alcohol decreases sexual response.[13]

Other Drug Categories

Other drug categories include anesthetic drugs, inhalants, sedatives and barbiturates, tranquilizers, hallucinogens, stimulants, steroids, designer drugs, and cigarettes.

Anesthetic Drugs. **Anesthetic drugs** are central nervous system (CNS) depressants. Local anesthetics block nervous system transmissions; general anesthetics act on the brain to produce loss of sensation, stupor, or unconsciousness. The most widely abused anesthetic drug is *phencyclidine* (*PCP*), known as "angel dust." Angel dust can be sprayed on marijuana or other leaves and smoked, drunk, or injected. Originally developed as an animal tranquilizer, PCP creates hallucinations and a spaced-out feeling that causes heavy users to engage in violent acts. The effects of PCP can last up to two days, and the danger of overdose is high.

Inhalants. Some youths inhale vapors from lighter fluid, shoe polish, paint thinner, cleaning fluid, or model airplane glue to reach a drowsy, dizzy state that is sometimes accompanied by hallucinations. **Inhalants** produce a short-term euphoria followed by a period of disorientation, slurred speech, and drowsiness. Amyl nitrite ("poppers") is a commonly used volatile liquid packaged in capsule form that is inhaled when the capsule is broken open.

Sedatives and Barbiturates. **Sedatives**, the most commonly used drugs of the barbiturate family, depress the central nervous system into a sleeplike condition. On the illegal market, sedatives are called "goofballs" or "downers" and are often known by the color of the capsules: "reds" (Seconal), "blue devils" (Amytal), and "rainbows" (Tuinal).

Sedatives can be prescribed by doctors as sleeping pills. Illegal users employ them to create relaxed, sociable feelings; overdoses can cause irritability, repellent behavior, and unconsciousness. Barbiturates are the major cause of drug-overdose deaths.

Tranquilizers. **Tranquilizers** reduce anxiety and promote relaxation. Legally prescribed tranquilizers, such as Ampazine, Thorazine, Pacatal, and Sparine, were originally designed to control the behavior of people suffering from psychoses, aggressiveness, and agitation. Less powerful tranquilizers, such as Valium, Librium, Miltown, and Equanil, are used to combat anxiety, tension, fast heart rate, and headaches. The use of illegally obtained tranquilizers can lead to addiction, and withdrawal can be painful and hazardous.

Hallucinogens. **Hallucinogens,** either natural or synthetic, produce vivid distortions of the senses without greatly disturbing the viewer's consciousness. Some produce hallucinations, and others cause psychotic behavior in otherwise normal people.

One common hallucinogen is mescaline, named after the Mescalero Apaches, who first discovered its potent effect. Mescaline occurs naturally in the peyote, a small cactus that grows in Mexico and the southwestern United States. After initial discomfort, mescaline produces vivid hallucinations and out-of-body sensations.

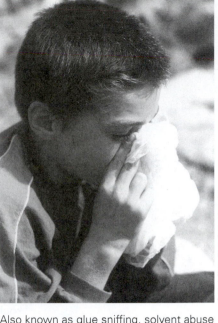

Also known as glue sniffing, solvent abuse is highly dangerous and can have fatal consequences. A wide range of volatile substances such as gasoline, nail polish remover, aerosols, various glues, and lighter fluid can all be abused in this fashion. The fumes from these inhalants can cause dizziness, hallucinations, memory loss, long-term brain and liver damage, and sometimes death.

anesthetic drugs Nervous system depressants.

inhalants Volatile liquids that give off a vapor, which is inhaled, producing short-term excitement and euphoria followed by a period of disorientation.

sedatives Drugs of the barbiturate family that depress the central nervous system into a sleeplike condition.

tranquilizers Drugs that reduce anxiety and promote relaxation.

hallucinogens Natural or synthetic substances that produce vivid distortions of the senses without greatly disturbing consciousness.

A second group of hallucinogens are synthetic alkaloid compounds, such as psilocybin. These can be transformed into lysergic acid diethylamide, commonly called LSD. This powerful substance stimulates cerebral sensory centers to produce visual hallucinations, intensify hearing, and increase sensitivity. Users often report a scrambling of sensations; they may "hear colors" and "smell music." Users also report feeling euphoric and mentally superior, although to an observer they appear disoriented. Anxiety and panic may occur, and overdoses can produce psychotic episodes, flashbacks, and even death.

Stimulants. **Stimulants** ("uppers," "speed," "pep pills," "crystal") are synthetic drugs that stimulate action in the central nervous system. They increase blood pressure, breathing rate, and bodily activity, and elevate mood. Commonly used stimulants include Benzedrine ("bennies"), Dexedrine ("dex"), Dexamyl, Biphetamine ("whites"), and Methedrine ("meth," "speed," "crystal meth"). Methedrine is probably the most widely used and most dangerous amphetamine. Some people swallow it; heavy users inject it. Long-term heavy use can result in exhaustion, anxiety, prolonged depression, and hallucinations.

One form of methamphetamine is a crystallized substance with the street name of "ice" or "crystal." Ice methamphetamine looks like shards of ice or chunks of rock salt and is highly pure and extremely addictive.[14] Smoking this ice or crystal causes weight loss, kidney damage, heart and respiratory problems, and paranoia.[15]

Methamphetamines in general, in its three main forms of powder, ice, or tablets, have become an increasingly important priority of United States law enforcement authorities. Although its use among secondary school students has shown a downward trend in the 13 years it has been investigated (1999–2011),[16] authorities are concerned because it has spread from its origins in the rural West to other parts of the country and into urban and suburban areas. According to the U.S. Department of Justice's National Drug Intelligence Center, methamphetamine availability is highest in the Southeast region, followed by the Great Lakes, West Central, and Southwest regions.[17] Other problems arise from the majority of it being produced domestically, either in "Mom and Pop" laboratories or super labs, which are mostly found in the Central Valley and southern areas of California. It can be made with many household products that are difficult or not feasible to regulate, and its production presents many dangers to people and the environment.[18] A number of states, including Oklahoma and Iowa, have banned over-the-counter cold medicines (such as Sudafed) that contain pseudoephedrine, an essential ingredient of methamphetamine, making them only available by prescription.[19] One study estimates that the economic cost of methamphetamine use in the United States exceeds $23 billion annually.[20]

Steroids. Teenagers use highly dangerous **anabolic steroids** to gain muscle bulk and strength.[21] Black market sales of these drugs approach $1 billion annually. Although not physically addicting, steroids can become a kind of obsession among teens who desire athletic success. Long-term users may spend up to $400 a week on steroids and may support their habit by dealing the drug.

Steroids are dangerous because of the health problems associated with their long-term use: liver ailments, tumors, kidney problems, sexual dysfunction, hypertension, and mental problems such as depression. Steroid use runs in cycles, and other drugs—Clomid, Teslac, and Halotestin, for example—that carry their own dangerous side effects are often used to curb the need for high dosages of steroids. Finally, steroid users often share needles, which put them at high risk for contracting HIV, the virus that causes AIDS.

Designer Drugs. **Designer drugs** are lab-created synthetics that are designed at least temporarily to get around existing drug laws. The most widely used designer drug is Ecstasy, which is derived from speed and methamphetamine. After being swallowed, snorted, injected, or smoked, it acts simultaneously as a stimulant and a hallucinogen, producing mood swings, disturbing sleeping and eating habits, altering

stimulants Synthetic substances that produce an intense physical reaction by stimulating the central nervous system.

anabolic steroids Drugs used by athletes and bodybuilders to gain muscle bulk and strength.

designer drugs. Lab-made drugs designed to avoid existing drug laws.

thinking processes, creating aggressive behavior, interfering with sexual function, and affecting sensitivity to pain. The drug can also increase blood pressure and heart rate. Teenage users taking Ecstasy at raves have died from heat stroke because the drug can cause dehydration.

Cigarettes. Many countries around the world have established laws to prohibit the sale of cigarettes to minors. The reality, however, is that in many countries children and adolescents have easy access to tobacco products.[22] In the United States, the Synar Amendment, enacted in 1992, requires states to enact and enforce laws restricting the sale of tobacco products to youths under the age of 18. States were required to reduce rates of illegal sales to minors to no more than 20 percent within several years of the amendment's passing. The FDA rules require age verification for anyone under the age of 27 who is purchasing tobacco products. The FDA has also banned vending machines and self-service displays except in adult-only facilities. The signing of the Master Tobacco Settlement Agreement between 46 states and the tobacco industry in 1998 placed further restrictions on the advertising and marketing of cigarettes to young people and allocated substantial sums to antismoking campaigns.[23] Some efforts to enforce compliance with these restrictions and educate tobacco retailers about the new laws have produced promising results.[24] Despite all of these measures, four out of every ten high school seniors in America (40 percent) report having smoked cigarettes in their lifetime. However, in recent years, cigarette use by high school students has been on a consistent decline.[25]

DRUG USE TODAY

Has America's long-standing war on drugs paid off? Has drug use declined, or is it on the upswing? A number of national surveys conduct annual reviews of teen drug use by interviewing samples of teens around the nation. What do national surveys tell us about the extent of drug use, and what have been the recent trends in teen usage?

The Monitoring the Future (MTF) Survey

One of the most important and influential surveys of teen substance abuse is the annual Monitoring the Future survey conducted by the Institute for Social Research at the University of Michigan. In all, more than 50,000 students located in 433 secondary schools participate in the study.

The most recent MTF survey in 2011 indicates that, with few exceptions, drug use among American adolescents continued to decline from the peak levels reached in 1996 and 1997. Annual drug use was down by almost two-fifths (38 percent) for 8th graders during this time period, while reductions have been considerably lower for those in the 10th (19 percent) and 12th (6 percent) grades.[26] As Figure 10.1 shows, drug use peaked in the late 1970s and early 1980s and then began a decade-long decline until showing an up-tick in the mid-1990s; usage for most drugs has been stable or in decline since then. Especially encouraging has been a significant drop in the use of alcohol by the youngest kids in the survey—a 15 percent drop in annual rates in the last five years (from 31.8 percent in 2007 to 26.9 percent in 2011) and a 30 percent drop in the last 10 years (from 38.7 percent in 2002). There has also been a continuing decline in cigarette smoking, as well as the use of smokeless tobacco products. In recent years, a great deal of attention has been paid to the use of prescription-type drugs such as narcotics, tranquilizers, and sedatives among youths.[27] From 2010 to 2011, annual use of OxyContin, a prescription painkiller narcotic, was marginally lower among 12th graders (5.1 percent to 4.9 percent), 10th graders (4.6 percent to 3.9 percent), and 8th graders (2.1 percent to 1.8 percent). Annual use among all grades combined (3.4 percent in 2011) was also marginally lower from the peak year of 2009, when it was 3.9 percent.[28]

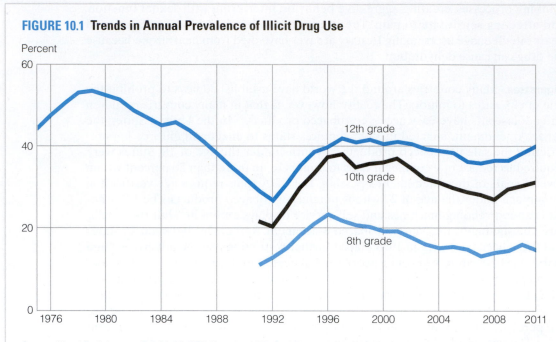

FIGURE 10.1 Trends in Annual Prevalence of Illicit Drug Use

Source: Lloyd D. Johnston, Patrick M. O'Malley, Jerald G. Bachman, and John E. Schulenberg, *Monitoring the Future: National Results on Adolescent Drug Use: Overview of Key Findings, 2011* (Ann Arbor, MI: Institute for Social Research, University of Michigan, 2012), Table 6, p. 56.

The PRIDE Survey

A second source of information on teen drug and alcohol abuse is the national Parents' Resource Institute for Drug Education (PRIDE) survey, which up until recently was also conducted annually.[29] Typically, findings from the PRIDE survey correlate highly with the MTF drug survey. The most recent PRIDE survey (for the 2009–2010 school year) indicates small to moderate reductions in drug activity over the previous school year, but substantial decreases over the last 10 years. For example, just over 21 percent of students in grades 6 to 12 claimed to have used drugs during the past year, down from around 25 percent in the 2000–2001 school year (Table 10.1). Cigarette smoking and alcohol use are also down from 10 years ago. The fact that two surveys generate roughly the same pattern in drug abuse helps bolster their validity and give support to a decline in teenage substance abuse.

The National Survey on Drug Use and Health

Sponsored by the U.S. Department of Health and Human Services' Substance Abuse and Mental Health Services Administration, the National Survey on Drug Use and Health (NSDUH, formerly called the National Household Survey on Drug Abuse) interviews approximately 70,000 people at home each year.[30] Like the MTF and PRIDE surveys, the latest NSDUH (2010) shows that drug and alcohol use, although still a problem, has stabilized or declined.

Although overall illicit drug use by youths ages 12 to 17 has shown impressive declines in recent years (a significant 13 percent reduction between 2002 and 2010),[31] it still remains a considerable problem. For example, *heavy drinking* (defined as having five or more alcoholic drinks on the same occasion on at least five different days in the past 30 days) was reported by about 7 percent of the population ages 12 and older, or 17 million people. Among youths ages 12 to 17, about 2 percent were heavy drinkers and 8 percent engaged in *binge drinking*, defined as having five or more alcoholic beverages on the same occasion at least once in the past 30 days.[32]

TABLE 10.1 Annual Drug Use, 2000–2001 versus 2009–2010, Grades 6–12

	2000–01 (%)	2009–10 (%)	Rate of Decrease (%)
Cigarettes	30.5	18.9	38.0
Any alcohol	52.1	40.3	22.6
Any illicit drug	24.6	21.4	13.0

Source: *PRIDE Questionnaire Report for Grades 6 to 12: National Summary Statistics for 2009–10* (Bowling Green, KY: PRIDE Surveys, September 27, 2010), Tables 1.5–1.7.

The latest NSDUH results show that rates of illicit drug use in the past month by adolescent males and females are similar for overall illicit drug use (10.4 percent for males and 9.8 percent for females).[33] Previous surveys (2002–2004) found that adolescent females were closing the gap with their male counterparts in terms of usage of marijuana, alcohol, and cigarettes.[34] The most recent survey shows that current marijuana use is more common among male youths (8.3 percent) compared to their female counterparts (6.4 percent), while female youths are more likely to self-report nonmedical use of prescription psychotherapeutic drugs (3.7 percent compared to 2.3 percent for males) and prescription pain relievers (3.0 percent compared to 2.0 percent for males).[35]

Are the Survey Results Accurate?

Student drug surveys must be interpreted with caution. First, it may be overly optimistic to expect that heavy users are going to cooperate with a drug-use survey, especially one conducted by a government agency. Even if they were willing, these students are likely to be absent from school during testing periods. Also, drug abusers are more likely to be forgetful and to give inaccurate accounts of their substance abuse.

Another problem is the likelihood that the most drug-dependent portion of the adolescent population is omitted from the sample. In some cities, almost half of all youths arrested dropped out of school before the 12th grade, and more than half of these arrestees are drug users.[36] Juvenile detainees (those arrested and held in a lockup) test positive for cocaine at a rate many times higher than those reporting recent use in the MTF and PRIDE surveys.[37] The inclusion of eighth-graders in the MTF sample is one way of getting around the dropout problem. Nonetheless, high school surveys may be excluding some of the most drug-prone young people in the population.

There is evidence that the accuracy of reporting may be affected by social and personal traits: girls are more willing than boys to admit taking drugs; kids from two-parent homes are less willing to admit taking drugs than kids growing up in single-parent homes. Julia Yun Soo Kim, Michael Fendrich, and Joseph Wislar speculate that it is culturally unacceptable for some subgroups in the population, such as Hispanic families, to use drugs, and therefore, in self-report surveys, they may underrepresent their involvement.[38]

Although these problems are serious, they are consistent over time and therefore do not hinder the *measurement of change* or trends in drug usage. That is, prior surveys also omitted dropouts and other high-risk individuals. However, because these problems are built into every wave of the survey, any change recorded in the annual substance-abuse rate is probably genuine. So, although the *validity* of these surveys may be questioned, they are probably reliable indicators of trends in substance abuse.

CHECKPOINTS

CHECKPOINTS

LO1 Understand the drug problem among American youth today and over time.

✔ Just under half of all high school seniors have tried drugs.

✔ Use of alcohol and cigarettes is on the decline.

✔ Alcohol remains the drug of choice for most teens.

✔ Prescription drugs and inhalants have become popular in recent years.

✔ Teenage drug use is measured by three main national surveys: MTF, PRIDE, and NSDUH.

✔ Each of these surveys shows that overall illicit drug use has remained relatively stable in recent years.

WHY DO YOUTHS TAKE DRUGS?

Why do youths engage in an activity that is sure to bring them overwhelming problems? It is hard to imagine that even the youngest drug users are unaware of the problems associated with substance abuse. Although it is easy to understand dealers' desires for quick profits, how can we explain users' disregard for long- and short-term consequences? Concept Summary 10.1 reviews some of the most likely reasons.

Social Disorganization

One explanation ties drug abuse to poverty, social disorganization, and hopelessness. Drug use by young minority group members has been tied to factors such as racial prejudice, low self-esteem, poor socioeconomic status, and the stress of living in a harsh urban environment.[39] The association between drug use, race, and poverty has been linked to the high level of mistrust and defiance found in lower socioeconomic areas.[40]

Despite the long-documented association between social disorganization and drug use, and even some specific drugs like methamphetamine,[41] the empirical data on the relationship between class and crime have been inconclusive. For example, the National Youth Survey (NYS), a longitudinal study of delinquent behavior conducted by Delbert Elliott and his associates, found little if any association between drug use and social class. The NYS found that drug use is higher among urban youths, but there was little evidence that minority youths or members of the lower class were more likely to abuse drugs than European American youths and the more affluent.[42] Research by the RAND Corporation indicates that many drug-dealing youths had legitimate jobs at the time they were arrested for drug trafficking.[43] Therefore, it would be difficult to describe drug abusers simply as unemployed dropouts.

Peer Pressure

Research shows that adolescent drug abuse is highly correlated with the behavior of best friends, especially when parental supervision is weak.[44] Youths in inner-city areas where feelings of alienation run high often come in contact with drug users who teach them that drugs provide an answer to their feelings of inadequacy and stress.[45] Perhaps they join with peers to learn the techniques of drug use; their friendships with other drug-dependent youths give them social support for their habit. Empirical research efforts show that a youth's association with friends who are substance abusers increases the probability of drug use.[46] The relationship is reciprocal: adolescent substance abusers seek out friends who engage in these behaviors, and associating with drug abusers leads to increased levels of drug abuse. Recent research by Gregory Zimmerman and Bob Edward Vásquez also finds that

CONCEPT SUMMARY 10.1	Key Reasons Why Youths Take Drugs
Social disorganization	Poverty, growing up in disorganized urban environment
Peer pressure	Associating with youths who take drugs
Family factors	Poor family life, including harsh punishment, neglect
Genetic factors	Parents abuse drugs
Emotional problems	Feelings of inadequacy; blaming others for failures
Problem behavior syndrome	Drug use just one of many problem behaviors
Rational choice	Perceived benefits, including relaxation, greater creativity

Young people may take drugs for many reasons, including peer pressure, growing up in a rough neighborhood, poor family life, living with parents who abuse drugs, or to escape reality. Here, Misty Croslin, age 18, appears before Judge Charles Tinlin at the St. Johns County (Florida) Jail for her first appearance for felony drug trafficking charges. Distraught throughout her appearance, she told the judge about her parents' long-term abuse of drugs and alcohol, homelessness, and being left alone to care for her two younger brothers.

the peer effect on adolescent substance use may be nonlinear; that is, it decreases at higher levels of substance use, which suggests a "saturation" effect. The researchers also found that the peer influence on substance use is partially mediated by the perceptions of the health consequences of substance use and that neighborhood context plays a more important role than previously suggested.[47]

Peer networks may be the most significant influence on long-term substance abuse. Shared feelings and a sense of intimacy lead youths to become enmeshed in what has been described as the "drug-use subculture."[48] Research indicates that drug users do in fact have warm relationships with substance-abusing peers who help support their behaviors.[49] This lifestyle provides users with a clear role, activities they enjoy, and an opportunity for attaining status among their peers.[50] One reason it is so difficult to treat hard-core users is that quitting drugs means leaving the "fast life" of the streets.

Family Factors

Another explanation is that drug users have a poor family life. Studies have found that the majority of drug users have had an unhappy childhood, which included harsh punishment and parental neglect.[51] The drug abuse and family quality association may involve both racial and gender differences: females and European Americans who were abused as children are more likely to have alcohol and drug arrests as adults; abuse was less likely to affect drug use in males and African Americans.[52] It is also common to find substance abusers in large families and with parents who are divorced, separated, or absent.[53]

Social psychologists suggest that drug abuse patterns may also result from observation of parental drug use.[54] Youths who learn that drugs provide pleasurable sensations may be most likely to experiment with illegal substances; a habit may develop if the user experiences lower anxiety and fear.[55] Research shows, for example, that gang members raised in families with a history of drug use were more likely than other gang members to use cocaine and to use it seriously. And even among gang members, parental drug abuse was a key factor in the onset of adolescent drug use.[56] Observing drug abuse may be a more important cause of drug abuse than other family-related problems.

Other family factors associated with teen drug abuse include parental conflict over childrearing practices, failure to set rules, and unrealistic demands followed by harsh punishments. Low parental attachment, rejection, and excessive family conflict have all been linked to adolescent substance abuse.[57]

Genetic Factors

The association between parental drug abuse and adolescent behavior may have a genetic basis.[58] Research has shown that biological children of alcoholics reared by non-alcoholic adoptive parents more often develop alcohol problems than the natural children of the adoptive parents.[59] A number of studies comparing alcoholism among identical and fraternal twins have found that the degree of concordance (that is, both siblings behaving identically) is twice as high among the identical twin groups.[60]

A genetic basis for drug abuse is also supported by evidence showing that future substance abuse problems can be predicted by behavior exhibited as early as 6 years of age. The traits predicting future abuse are independent from peer relations and environmental influences.[61]

Emotional Problems

As we have seen, not all drug-abusing youths reside in lower-class urban areas. To explain drug abuse across social classes, some experts have linked drug use to emotional problems that can strike youths in any economic class. Psychodynamic explanations of substance abuse suggest that drugs help youths control or express unconscious needs. Some psychoanalysts believe adolescents who internalize their problems may use drugs to reduce their feelings of inadequacy. Introverted people may use drugs as an escape from real or imagined feelings of inferiority.[62] Another view is that adolescents who externalize their problems and blame others for their perceived failures are likely to engage in antisocial behaviors, including substance abuse. Research exists to support each of these positions.[63]

Drug abusers are also believed to exhibit psychopathic or sociopathic behavior characteristics, forming what is called an **addiction-prone personality**.[64] Drinking alcohol may reflect a teen's need to remain dependent on an overprotective mother or an effort to reduce the emotional turmoil of adolescence.[65]

Research on the psychological characteristics of narcotics abusers does, in fact, reveal the presence of a considerable degree of pathology. Personality testing of users suggests that a significant percentage suffer from psychotic disorders. Studies have found that addicts suffer personality disorders characterized by a weak ego, low frustration tolerance, and fantasies of omnipotence. Up to half of all drug abusers may also be diagnosed with antisocial personality disorder (ASPD), which is defined as a pervasive pattern of disregard for the rights of others.[66]

Problem Behavior Syndrome

For some adolescents, substance abuse is one of many problem behaviors that begin early in life and remain throughout the life course.[67] Longitudinal studies show that youths who abuse drugs are maladjusted, emotionally distressed, and have many social problems.[68] Having a deviant lifestyle means associating with delinquent peers, living in a family in which parents and siblings abuse drugs, being alienated from the dominant values of society, and engaging in

Looking Back to Fernando's Story

Although there was progress in the case, involved team members continued to have concerns for Fernando and his siblings.

CRITICAL THINKING Discuss what could have been done to address these concerns, including whether Fernando (and his siblings) should have been removed from his parental home. Make sure to weigh the advantages and disadvantages over both the short and long term.

WWW

The **Psychedelic Library** is a collection of leading studies and reports on drug use internationally. To read more about the concept of addiction, visit the Criminal Justice CourseMate at CengageBrain.com, then access the Web Links for this chapter.

addiction-prone personality The view that the cause of substance abuse can be traced to a personality that has a compulsion for mood-altering drugs.

Looking Back to Fernando's Story

Understanding why young people take drugs is not always straightforward, and Fernando's situation was no different.

CRITICAL THINKING Based on the information you read in this chapter, make a list of the reasons why Fernando may have abused alcohol and drugs. For example, what were the significant family factors that may have played a role?

delinquent behaviors at an early age.[69] Youths who abuse drugs lack commitment to religious values, disdain education, and spend most of their time in peer activities.[70] Youths who take drugs do poorly in school, have high dropout rates, and maintain their drug use after they leave school.[71] (Chapter 5 provides an in-depth discussion of problem behavior syndrome.)

Rational Choice

Youths may choose to use drugs because they want to get high, relax, improve their creativity, escape reality, or increase their sexual responsiveness. Research indicates that adolescent alcohol abusers believe getting high will increase their sexual performance and facilitate their social behavior; they care little about negative consequences.[72] Substance abuse, then, may be a function of the rational, albeit mistaken, belief that substance abuse benefits the user. **CHECKPOINTS**

PATHWAYS TO DRUG ABUSE

There is no single path to becoming a drug abuser, but it is generally believed that most users start at a young age using alcohol as a **gateway drug** to harder substances. That is, drug involvement begins with drinking alcohol at an early age, which progresses to experimentation with marijuana, and finally to using cocaine and even heroin. Research on adolescent drug users in Miami found that youths who began their substance abuse careers early—by experimenting with alcohol at age 7, getting drunk at age 8, having alcohol with an adult present by age 9, and becoming regular drinkers by the time they were 11 years old—later became crack users.[73] Drinking with an adult present was a significant precursor of substance abuse and delinquency.[74]

WAW

Above the Influence is a web-based anti-drug education campaign for teens. It was created for the National Youth Anti-Drug Media Campaign, a program of the White House Office of National Drug Control Policy. For more information, visit the Criminal Justice CourseMate at CengageBrain.com, then access the Web Links for this chapter.

CHECKPOINTS

LO2 Know the main explanations for why youths take drugs.

✔ Some kids take drugs because they live in disorganized areas in which there is a high degree of hopelessness, poverty, and despair.

✔ There is peer pressure to take drugs and to drink.

✔ Kids whose parents take drugs are more likely to become abusers themselves.

✔ Some experts believe that drug dependency is a genetic condition.

✔ Youngsters with emotional problems may be drug prone.

✔ Drug use may be part of a general problem behavior syndrome.

✔ Drug use may also be rational: kids take drugs and drink alcohol simply because they enjoy the experience.

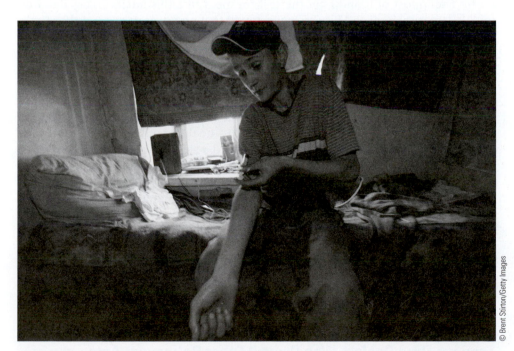

© Brent Stirton/Getty Images

According to the gateway model of drug abuse, drug involvement begins with drinking alcohol at an early age, which progresses to experimentation with recreational drugs such as marijuana, and, finally, to using hard drugs such as cocaine and even heroin, as pictured here. Although most recreational users do not progress to addictive drugs, few addicts begin their drug involvement with narcotics.

gateway drug A substance that leads to use of more serious drugs; alcohol use has long been thought to lead to more serious drug abuse.

Although the gateway concept is still being debated, there is little disagreement that serious drug users begin their involvement with alcohol.[75] Though most recreational users do not progress to "hard stuff," most addicts first experiment with recreational alcohol and recreational drugs before progressing to narcotics. By implication, if teen drinking could be reduced, the gateway to hard drugs would be narrowed.

What are the patterns of teenage drug use? Are all abusers similar, or are there different types of drug involvement? Research indicates that drug-involved youths do take on different roles, lifestyles, and behavior patterns, some of which are described in the next sections.[76]

Adolescents Who Distribute Small Amounts of Drugs

Many adolescents who use and distribute small amounts of drugs do not commit any other serious delinquent acts. They occasionally sell marijuana, crystal, and PCP to support their own drug use. Their customers include friends, relatives, and acquaintances. Deals are arranged over the phone, in school, or at public meeting places; however, the actual distribution occurs in more private arenas, such as at home or in cars. Petty dealers do not consider themselves seriously involved in drugs.

Adolescents Who Frequently Sell Drugs

A small number of adolescents are high-rate dealers who bridge the gap between adult drug distributors and the adolescent user. Though many are daily users, they take part in many normal activities, including going to school and socializing with friends.

Frequent dealers often have adults who "front" for them—that is, sell them drugs for cash. The teenagers then distribute the drugs to friends and acquaintances. They return most of the proceeds to the supplier, keeping a commission for themselves. They may also keep drugs for their personal use, and in fact, some consider their dealing as a way of "getting high for free." One young user, Winston, age 17, told investigators, "I sell the cracks for money and for cracks. The man, he give me this *much*. I sell most of it and I get the rest for me. I like this much. Every day I do this."[77] James Inciardi and his associates found that about 80 percent of the youths who dealt crack regularly were daily users.[78]

Frequent dealers are more likely to sell drugs in parks, schools, or other public places. Deals occur irregularly, so the chance of apprehension is not significant, nor is the payoff substantial. In the first study of its kind, conducted in the early 1990s, Robert MacCoun and Peter Reuter found that drug dealers made about $30 per hour when they were working and cleared on average about $2,000 per month. These amounts were greater than most dealers could hope to earn in legitimate jobs, but they were not enough to afford a steady stream of luxuries. Most small-time dealers also hold conventional jobs.[79]

In a more recent analysis of the financial activities of a drug-selling street gang over a four-year period in which the gang was active, economist Steven Levitt and sociologist Sudhir Venkatesh found that the average hourly wage of drug dealers or "foot soldiers" was between $2.50 and $7.10 (see Table 10.2).[80] As an average wage per month, this comes to $140 to $470.[81] In a typical month, drug dealers worked just over 50 hours. As shown in Table 10.2, the hourly wage of drug dealers is substantially lower than the average wage for all gang members and the gang leader. These more recent findings suggest that, at least for drug dealers, factors other than income may explain participation in this activity.

Teenage Drug Dealers Who Commit Other Delinquent Acts

A more serious type of drug-involved youth is the one who distributes multiple substances and commits both property and violent crimes. These youngsters make up about 2 percent of the teenage population, but they may commit up to 40 percent

TABLE 10.2 Estimated Hourly Wages of Members in a Drug-Selling Gang

	Drug Dealers	All Gang Members	Gang Leader
Year 1	$2.50	$5.90	$32.50
Year 2	$3.70	$7.40	$47.50
Year 3	$3.30	$7.10	$65.90
Year 4	$7.10	$11.10	$97.20

Notes: Estimated hourly wages include both official and unofficial income sources. All wages are in 1995 dollars.

Source: Adapted from Steven D. Levitt and Sudhir A. Venkatesh, "An Economic Analysis of a Drug-Selling Gang's Finances," *Quarterly Journal of Economics* 115:755–789 (2000), Table III.

of the robberies and assaults and about 60 percent of all teenage felony thefts and drug sales. Few gender or racial differences exist among these youths: girls are as likely as boys to become persistent drug-involved offenders, European American youths as likely as African American youths, and middle-class adolescents raised outside cities as likely as lower-class city children.[82]

In cities, these youths frequently are hired by older dealers to act as street-level drug runners. Each member of a crew of 3 to 12 youths will handle small quantities of drugs; the supplier receives 50 percent to 70 percent of the drug's street value. The crew members also act as lookouts, recruiters, and guards. Although they may be recreational drug users themselves, crew members refrain from using addictive drugs such as heroin. Between drug sales, the young dealers commit robberies, burglaries, and other thefts.

Some experts question whether gangs are responsible for as much drug dealing as the media would have us believe. Some believe that the tightly organized "super" gangs are being replaced with loosely organized neighborhood groups. The turbulent environment of drug dealing is better handled by flexible organizations than by rigid, vertically organized gangs with a leader who is far removed from the action.[83]

Losers and Burnouts

Some drug-involved youths do not have the savvy to join gangs or groups and instead begin committing unplanned crimes that increase their chances of arrest. Their heavy drug use increases their risk of apprehension and decreases their value for organized drug distribution networks. Drug-involved "losers" can earn a living by steering customers to a seller in a "copping" area, touting drug availability for a dealer, or acting as a lookout. However, they are not considered trustworthy or deft enough to handle drugs or money. Although these offenders get involved in drugs at an early age, they receive little attention from the justice system until they have developed an extensive arrest record. By then they are approaching the end of their minority and will either desist or become so entrapped in the drug-crime subculture that little can be done to deter their illegal activities.

Persistent Offenders

About two-thirds of substance-abusing youths continue to use drugs in adulthood, but about half desist from other criminal activities. Those who persist in both substance abuse and crime maintain these characteristics:

- They come from poor families.
- Their family members include other criminals.
- They do poorly in school.

LO3 Recognize the different behavior patterns of drug-involved youths.
✔ There are a number of pathways to drug abuse.
✔ Some users distribute small amounts of drugs, others are frequent dealers, whereas another group supplements drug dealing with other crimes.
✔ Some users are always in trouble and are considered burnouts.

- They started using drugs and committing other delinquent acts at an early age.
- They use multiple types of drugs and commit crimes frequently.
- They have few opportunities in late adolescence to participate in legitimate and rewarding adult activities.[84]

Some evidence exists that these drug-using persisters have low nonverbal IQs and poor physical coordination. Nonetheless, there is little evidence to explain why some drug-abusing youths drop out of crime, whereas others remain active. CHECKPOINTS

DRUG USE AND DELINQUENCY

An association between drug use and delinquency has been established, and this connection can take a number of forms.[85] Crime may be an instrument of the drug trade: violence erupts when rival gangs use weapons to settle differences and establish territorial monopolies. In New York City, authorities report that crack gangs will burn down their rivals' headquarters. In the 1990s, it was estimated that between 35 and 40 percent of New York's homicides are drug-related.[86] This figure has come down somewhat since then.

Drug users may also commit crimes to pay for their habits.[87] One study conducted in Miami found that 573 narcotics users *annually* committed more than 200,000 crimes to obtain cash. Similar research with a sample of 356 addicts accounted for 118,000 crimes annually.[88] If such proportions hold true, then the nation's estimated 700,000 heroin addicts alone may be committing more than 100 million crimes each year.

Drug users may be more willing to take risks, because their inhibitions are lowered by substance abuse. Cities with high rates of cocaine abuse are also more likely to experience higher levels of armed robbery. It is possible that crack and cocaine users are more willing to engage in a risky armed robbery to get immediate cash than a burglary, which requires more planning and effort.[89]

The relationship between alcohol and drug abuse and delinquency has been substantiated by a number of studies. Some have found that youths who abuse alcohol are most likely to engage in violence; as adults, those with long histories of drinking are more likely to report violent offending patterns.[90]

The National Institute of Justice's Arrestee Drug Abuse Monitoring (ADAM) program tracked trends in drug use among arrestees in urban areas. Some, but not all, of its 36 sites collected data on juveniles. Due to lack of funding, the Department of Justice ended this program in 2004.[91] The most recent report (2002) found that, among juvenile detainees, almost 60 percent of juvenile males and 30 percent of juvenile females tested positive for marijuana, the most commonly used drug, and its prevalence was 10 and 6 times higher than cocaine use for juvenile males and females, respectively. With the exception of methamphetamines, male detainees were more likely to test positive for the use of any drug than were female detainees.[92]

Juvenile justice researchers Carl McCurley and Howard Snyder found that higher levels of youth problem behaviors and delinquency, ranging from school suspensions to major theft to gun carrying, are associated with drug use as well as selling drugs.[93] This finding held up for younger and older teens (see Table 10.3). For example, among youths ages 12 to 14, 31 percent who reported drinking alcohol in the past month were suspended from school compared to 18 percent who did not drink alcohol. Similarly, for youths ages 15 to 17, school suspensions were significantly higher for those who drank alcohol compared to those who did not (38 percent versus 27 percent). These findings are based on data from the National Longitudinal Survey of Youth, a self-report survey administered to a nationally

TABLE 10.3 Drug Use, Problem Behaviors, and Delinquency

Behavior	Drank Alcohol (Past 30 Days)		Used Marijuana (Past 30 Days)		Sold Drugs (Ever)	
	No	Yes	No	Yes	No	Yes
Youths ages 12–14						
Suspended from school	18%	31%	19%	46%	19%	55%
Vandalize property	13	37	14	50	14	56
Major theft	2	11	2	20	2	27
Attack/assault	8	28	9	36	9	53
Belong to a gang	1	7	1	16	1	18
Carry handgun	4	12	4	20	4	25
Arrested	2	8	3	15	2	22
Youths ages 15–17						
Suspended from school	27%	38%	27%	52%	27%	63%
Vandalize property	10	23	11	33	11	40
Major theft	3	10	4	17	3	23
Attack/assault	8	21	10	29	9	37
Belong to a gang	1	5	1	9	1	12
Carry handgun	4	10	5	15	5	18
Arrested	5	12	5	21	5	26

Note: The timeframe for "suspended from school" was ever; for the other items, it was the past 12 months. The value in the "yes" column differs significantly ($p < 0.05$) from the value in the "no" column for all column pairs within substance behavior and age groups.

Source: Carl McCurley and Howard Snyder, *Co-occurrence of Substance Use Behaviors in Youth* (Washington, DC: Office of Juvenile Justice and Delinquency Prevention, U.S. Department of Justice, 2008), p. 3.

representative sample of youths ages 12 to 17. The researchers found that the difference in the prevalence of problem behaviors is even greater among youths, both younger and older, who used marijuana in the past month compared to their counterparts who did not: a twofold increase in school suspensions (19 percent versus 46 percent and 27 percent versus 52 percent), a threefold increase in vandalizing property (14 percent versus 50 percent and 11 percent versus 33 percent), and a five- and threefold increase in gun carrying (4 percent versus 20 percent and 5 percent versus 15 percent).

Drugs and Chronic Offending

It is possible that most delinquents are not drug users, but that police are more likely to apprehend muddle-headed substance abusers than clear-thinking abstainers. A second, more plausible, interpretation of the existing data is that the drug abuse–crime connection is so powerful because many criminals are in fact substance abusers.[94] Research by Bruce Johnson and his associates confirms this suspicion. Using data from a national self-report survey, these researchers found that less than 2 percent of the youths who responded to the survey (a) report using cocaine or heroin, and (b) commit two or more index crimes each year. However, these drug-abusing adolescents accounted for 40 percent to 60 percent of all the index crimes reported in the sample. Less than one-quarter of these delinquents committed crimes solely to support a drug habit. These data suggest that a small core of substance-abusing adolescents commit a significant proportion of all serious crimes. It is also evident that a behavior—drug abuse—that develops late in adolescence influences the extent of delinquent activity through the life course.[95]

Explaining Drug Use and Delinquency

The association between delinquency and drug use has been established in a variety of cultures.[96] It is far from certain, however, whether (a) drug use *causes* delinquency, (b) delinquency *leads* youths to engage in substance abuse, or (c) both drug abuse and delinquency are *functions* of some other factor.[97]

Some of the most sophisticated research on this topic has been conducted by Delbert Elliott and his associates at the Institute of Behavioral Science at the University of Colorado.[98] Using data from the National Youth Survey, the longitudinal study of self-reported delinquency and drug use mentioned earlier in this chapter, Elliott and his colleagues David Huizinga and Scott Menard found a strong association between delinquency and drug use.[99] However, the direction of the relationship is unclear. As a general rule, drug abuse appears to be a *type* of delinquent behavior and not a *cause* of delinquency.[100] Most youths become involved in delinquent acts *before* they are initiated into drugs; it is difficult therefore to conclude that drug use causes crime. In other research involving the National Youth Survey, Jason Ford found that there is a reciprocal and ongoing relationship between alcohol use and delinquency during adolescence, and that part of the reason for this reciprocal relationship is that both behaviors have the effect of weakening youths' bonds with society, thereby promoting continued alcohol use and delinquency.[101]

According to the Elliott research, both drug use and delinquency seem to reflect developmental problems; they are both part of a disturbed lifestyle. This research reveals some important associations between substance abuse and delinquency:

- Alcohol abuse seems to be a cause of marijuana and other drug abuse, because most drug users started with alcohol, and youths who abstain from alcohol almost never take drugs.

- Marijuana use is a cause of multiple drug use: about 95 percent of youths who use more serious drugs started on pot; only 5 percent of serious drug users never smoked pot.

- Youths who commit felonies started off with minor delinquent acts. Few delinquents (1 percent) report committing only felonies.

CHECKPOINTS

LO4 Understand the relationship between drug use and delinquency.

✔ There is a strong association between drug use and delinquency.

✔ Juvenile arrestees often test positive for drugs.

✔ Chronic offenders are often drug abusers.

✔ Although drug use and delinquency are associated, it is difficult to show that abusing drugs leads kids into a delinquent way of life.

CHECKPOINTS

DRUG-CONTROL STRATEGIES

Billions of dollars are spent each year to reduce the importation of drugs, deter drug dealers, and treat users. Yet although the overall incidence of drug use has declined, drug use has concentrated in the nation's poorest neighborhoods, with a consequent association between substance abuse and crime.

A number of drug-control strategies have been tried. Some are designed to deter drug use by stopping the flow of drugs into the country, apprehending dealers, and cracking down on street-level drug deals. Another approach is to prevent drug use by educating would-be users and convincing them to "say no" to drugs. A third approach is to treat users so that they can terminate their addictions. These and other drug control efforts are discussed in the following sections. Concept Summary 10.2 reviews the key strategies.

Law Enforcement Efforts

Law enforcement strategies are aimed at reducing the supply of drugs and, at the same time, deterring would-be users from drug abuse.

Source Control. One approach to drug control is to deter the sale of drugs through apprehension of large-volume drug dealers coupled with enforcement of drug laws that carry heavy penalties. This approach is designed to punish known dealers and users and to deter those who are considering entering the drug trade.

CONCEPT SUMMARY 10.2 | Key Drug-Control Strategies

Law enforcement	Preventing drugs from entering the country; destroying crops used to make drugs; arresting members of drug cartels and street-level dealers
Education	Informing children about the dangers of drug use; teaching children to resist peer pressure
Community-based	Community organizations and residents taking action to deter drug dealing; engaging youth in prosocial activities
Treatment	Intervening with drug users, including counseling and experiential activities
Harm reduction	Minimizing the harmful effects caused by drug use and some of the more punitive responses to drug use

A great effort has been made to cut off supplies of drugs by destroying overseas crops and arresting members of drug cartels; this approach is known as *source control*. The federal government has been encouraging exporting nations to step up efforts to destroy drug crops and prosecute dealers. Other less aggressive source control approaches, such as crop substitution and alternative development programs for the largely poor farmers in other countries, have also been tried, and a review of international efforts suggests that "some success can be achieved in reduction of narcotic crop production."[102] Three South American nations—Peru, Bolivia, and Colombia—have agreed to coordinate control efforts with the United States. However, translating words into deeds is a formidable task. Drug lords fight back through intimidation, violence, and corruption. The United States was forced to invade Panama with 20,000 troops in 1989 to stop its leader, General Manuel Noriega, from trafficking in cocaine.

Even when efforts are successful in one area, they may result in a shift in production to another area or in the targeted crop being replaced by another. For example, enforcement efforts in Peru and Bolivia were so successful that they altered cocaine cultivation patterns. As a consequence, Colombia became the premier coca-cultivating country when the local drug cartels encouraged growers to cultivate coca plants. When the Colombian government mounted an effective eradication campaign in the traditional growing areas, the cartel linked up with rebel groups in remote parts of the country for their drug supply.[103] Leaders in neighboring countries expressed fear when the United States announced $1.3 billion in military aid—under the program known as Plan Columbia—to fight Colombia's rural drug dealers/rebels, assuming that success would drive traffickers over the border.[104] Another unintended effect of this campaign has been a recent shift by drug cartels to exploit new crops, from a traditional emphasis on coca to opium poppy, the plant used to make heroin. It is estimated that Latin American countries, including Mexico, now supply upwards of 80 percent of the heroin consumed in the United States.[105]

On the other side of the world, Afghanistan has since reclaimed its position as the world leader in opium production, accounting for 92 percent of the global market.[106] This has come about after the fall of the Taliban government in 2001, which had banned poppy growing. Now, almost all of the heroin sold in Russia and three-quarters of that sold in Europe comes from Afghanistan. This has occurred despite new laws against poppy growing, law enforcement efforts, and crop substitution efforts on the part of agricultural aid organizations. Breaking with religious beliefs, Taliban forces are now promoting the growing of poppy—in some areas distributing leaflets that order farmers to grow the crop—and providing protection to drug smugglers, all in an effort to finance their operations against the United States

WHAT DOES THIS MEAN TO ME?

▶ **Reducing Drug Activity** There is no easy solution to reduce drug-related activities. Some experts argue that less serious drugs like marijuana should be decriminalized, others call for the continued use of police stings and long sentences for drug violations, and some advocate for more education and treatment. Suppose in your community you have witnessed the harms associated with teenage drug use and drug selling, but have also seen the need for some users to get treatment rather than punishment.

1. What do you recommend be done to address the drug problem more effectively? Explain.
2. What are some things you could do in your community to help prevent children and youths from getting involved in drug-related activities?

military and coalition forces in the country.[107] The United Nations estimates that in 2010 almost 250,000 households in Afghanistan were involved in opium production, which equates to six percent of the country's population.[108]

Border Control. Law enforcement efforts have also been directed at interdicting drug supplies as they enter the country. Border patrols and military personnel have been involved in massive interdiction efforts, and many billion-dollar seizures have been made. It is estimated that between one-quarter and one-third of the annual cocaine supply shipped to the United States is seized by drug enforcement agencies. Yet U.S. borders are so vast and unprotected that meaningful interdiction is impossible. In 2010 (most recent data available), U.S. federal law enforcement agencies seized more than 8,500 pounds of cocaine and 335 pounds of heroin along the southwest border alone.[109] Global rates of interception of heroin and cocaine indicate that only 26 percent and 42 percent of all imports are being seized by law enforcement.[110]

In recent years, another form of border control to interdict drugs entering the country has emerged: targeting Internet drug traffickers in foreign countries. With the widespread use of the Internet, some offenders are now turning to this source to obtain designer-type drugs. In Buffalo, New York, U.S. Customs discovered that a steady flow of packages containing the drug gamma-butyrolactone (GBL), an ingredient of GBH (gamma hydroxybutyrate), also known as the date-rape drug, were entering the country from Canada; the drug was disguised as a cleaning product. Operation Webslinger, a joint investigation of federal law enforcement agencies in the United States and Canada, was put in place to track down the suppliers. Within a year, Operation Webslinger had shut down four Internet drug rings operating in the United States and Canada, made 115 arrests in 84 cities, and seized the equivalent of 25 million doses of GBH and other related drugs.[111] Shortly following this, another federal task force, known as Operation Gray Lord and involving the Food and Drug Administration (FDA) and the Drug Enforcement Administration (DEA), was set up to combat illegal sales of narcotics on the Internet.[112]

If all importation were ended, homegrown marijuana and lab-made drugs such as Ecstasy could become the drugs of choice. Even now, their easy availability and relatively low cost are increasing their popularity; they are a $10 billion business in the United States today. But there have been some signs of success. In 2010 (most recent data available), 6,768 illegal methamphetamine laboratories were seized by authorities across the United States. This is down considerably from the peak in 2003 when more than 10,000 labs were seized nationwide, but represents a 12 percent increase from 2009. The DEA attributes this success to state restrictions on retail sales of ephedrine and pseudoephedrine products.[113] Many of these labs were operated out of homes, putting children—3,300 children were found in 8,000 of these labs—at grave risk of being burned or injured, not to mention exposing them to illegal drugs.[114]

Targeting Dealers. Law enforcement agencies have also made a concerted effort to focus on drug trafficking. Efforts have been made to bust large-scale drug rings. The long-term consequence has been to decentralize drug dealing and to encourage teenage gangs to become major suppliers. Ironically, it has proven easier for federal agents to infiltrate traditional organized crime groups than to take on drug-dealing gangs.

Police can also intimidate and arrest street-level dealers and users in an effort to make drug use so much of a hassle that consumption is cut back. Some street-level enforcement efforts have had success, but others are considered failures. A review of more than 300 international studies on police crackdowns on drug users and dealers found that this approach more often than not leads to increased violence; 87 percent of the studies reported an increase in violence due to these law enforcement practices.[115]

"Drug sweeps" have clogged correctional facilities with petty offenders while draining police resources. These sweeps are also suspected of creating a displacement effect: stepped-up efforts to curb drug dealing in one area or city may encourage dealers to seek out friendlier territory.[116]

Nick Smith (second from right) and other inmates from the West Central Community Correctional Facility in Marysville, Ohio, perform an interpretative show about the dangers of drugs at Marysville High School. The dance was followed by their testimonials.

Education Strategies

Another approach to reducing teenage substance abuse relies on educational programs. Drug education now begins in kindergarten and extends through the 12th grade. An overwhelming majority of public school districts across the United States have implemented drug education programs with various components, including teaching students about the causes and effects of alcohol, drug, and tobacco use; teaching students to resist peer pressure; and referring students for counseling and treatment.[117] In a Texas survey of drug use among secondary school students that found drug use in rural school districts to be fast approaching usage rates in urban schools, the researchers speculate that funding cutbacks for drug education programs in the rural schools may be partly to blame.[118] Education programs—such as Project ALERT, which now operates in all 50 states—have been shown to be successful in training middle-school youths to avoid recreational drugs and to resist peer pressure to use cigarettes and alcohol.[119] The latest survey of evidence-based drug use prevention programs in general shows that they are increasingly being implemented in middle schools across the country.[120] While not considered to be evidence-based, D.A.R.E. (Drug Abuse Resistance Education) continues to be widely used across the country and has recently undergone a large-scale evaluation of its new curriculum, "Take Charge of Your Life." Because of its continued widespread use and influence, D.A.R.E. is the subject of the accompanying Focus on Delinquency feature.

One large-scale study demonstrates the effectiveness of anti-drug messages targeted at youth. An evaluation of the National Youth Anti-Drug Media Campaign, which features ads showing the dangers of marijuana use, reported that 41 percent of students in grades 7 to 12 "agree a lot" that the ads made them less likely to try or use drugs. Importantly, the study also reported that past-year marijuana use among the students was down 6 percent.[121] However, the National Survey on Drug Use and Health, which asked young people ages 12 to 17 about anti-drug messages they had heard or seen outside of school hours, reported that past-month drug use by those exposed to the messages was not significantly different than those who had not been exposed to the messages (10.1 percent compared to 10.0 percent).[122]

WWW

To learn more about **Drug Abuse Resistance and Education (D.A.R.E.),** visit the Criminal Justice CourseMate at CengageBrain.com, then access the Web Links for this chapter.

D.A.R.E.: ON THE ROAD TO RECOVERY?

A landmark study of "Take Charge of Your Life," touted as the new D.A.R.E., found that the new curriculum reduced the use of marijuana among teens who reported using it at the start of the study, but increased the initiation of smoking and drinking among teens. The end result: D.A.R.E. America, the organization that oversees the program, will no longer use the new curriculum.

Over the last 15 years, national evaluations and independent reviews, including a study by the General Accountability Office (GAO), have repeatedly questioned the effectiveness of D.A.R.E., the most popular and widespread school-based substance abuse prevention program, leading many communities to discontinue its use. This was also due to the program not meeting U.S. Department of Education effectiveness standards. To meet these criticisms head-on, D.A.R.E. began testing a new curriculum for middle and high school programs called "Take Charge of Your Life" (TCYL). The program focuses on older students and relies more on having them question their assumptions about drug use than on listening to lectures on the subject. The program works largely on changing social norms, teaching students to question whether they really have to use drugs to fit in with their peers. Emphasis shifted from fifth-grade students to those in the seventh grade and a booster program was added in ninth grade, when kids are more likely to experiment with drugs. Police officers serve more as coaches than as lecturers, encouraging students to challenge the social norm of drug use in discussion groups. Students do more role-playing in an effort to learn decision-making skills. There is also an emphasis on the role of media and advertising in shaping behavior.

A large-scale experimental study was launched to test the effectiveness of the new program. The study was led by researchers at the University of Akron with $14 million in funding from the Robert Wood Johnson Foundation.

Community Strategies

Community-based programs reach out to some of the highest-risk youths, who are often missed by the well-known education programs that take place in schools.[123] Community programs try to get youths involved in after-school programs; offer counseling; deliver clothing, food, and medical care when needed; and encourage school achievement. Community programs also sponsor drug-free activities involving the arts, clubs, and athletics. In many respects, these evaluations of community programs have shown that they may encourage anti-drug attitudes and help insulate participating youths from an environment that encourages drugs.[124]

One of the most successful community-based programs to prevent substance abuse and delinquency is provided by the Boys and Girls Clubs (BGCs) of America. One study examined the effectiveness of BGCs for high-risk youths in public housing developments at five sites across the country. The usual services of BGCs, which include reading classes, sports, and homework assistance, were offered, as well as a program to prevent substance abuse, known as SMART Moves (Skills Mastery and Resistance Training). This program targets the specific pressures that young people face to try drugs and alcohol and provides education to parents and the community at large to assist youths in learning about the dangers of substance abuse and strategies for resisting these pressures.[125] Evaluation results showed that housing

Eighty-three school districts in six metropolitan areas from across the country—Detroit, Houston, Los Angeles, Newark, New Orleans, and St. Louis—involving nearly 20,000 seventh grade students, were randomly assigned to the program (41 school districts) or to a control group that used the schools' existing substance abuse prevention education program (42 school districts). Five years later and two years after the program ended—when students were in 11th grade—researchers once again interviewed the students about their past-month and past-year use of tobacco, alcohol, and marijuana. Study results showed that there was a significant decrease in marijuana use among teens enrolled in the TCYL program compared to those who were not, but this only applied to those who were already using marijuana at the start of the study. The program had no effect on the initiation or onset of marijuana use. More problematic was the finding that 3 to 4 percent more students who took part in the TCYL program, compared to those in the control group, used alcohol and tobacco by the 11th grade.

The main conclusion of the researchers was that the TCYL program should not be implemented in schools as a universal prevention intervention. This was the original designation of the program, and it was to be achieved by altering students' intentions to use drugs—preventing them from trying drugs in the first place. Further analyses suggested that "both the content and intensity of the specific lessons around the targeted messages may not have been powerful enough to affect student substance using behaviors."

CRITICAL THINKING

1. What do these study results mean for the future of D.A.R.E.? Should schools continue to use it? What are the implications of its continued use in schools?

2. Are the reasons for teenage drug use so complex that a single school-based program is doomed to fail? Explain.

Writing Assignment Put yourself in the place of a school principal faced with having to make a decision about the continued use or replacement of D.A.R.E. in your school. In an essay, write about what steps you would take to improve the effectiveness of D.A.R.E. or what type of program you would use in its place.

Sources: Zili Sloboda, Richard C. Stephens, Peggy C. Stephens, Scott F. Grey, Brent Teasdale, Richard D. Hawthorne, Joseph Williams, and Jesse F. Marquette, "The Adolescent Substance Abuse Prevention Study: A Randomized Field Trial of a Universal Substance Abuse Prevention Program," *Drug and Alcohol Dependence* 102:1–10 (2009); Peggy C. Stephens, Zili Sloboda, Richard C. Stephens, Brent Teasdale, Scott F. Grey, Richard D. Hawthorne, and Joseph Williams, "Universal School-Based Substance Abuse Prevention Programs: Modeling Targeted Mediators and Outcomes for Adolescent Cigarette, Alcohol and Marijuana Use," *Drug and Alcohol Dependence* 102:19–29 (2009); Brent Teasdale, Peggy C. Stephens, Zili Sloboda, Scott F. Grey, and Richard C. Stephens, "The Influence of Program Mediators on Eleventh Grade Outcomes for Seventh Grade Substance Users and Nonusers," *Drug and Alcohol Dependence* 102:11–18 (2009); University of Akron, "Landmark Substance-Abuse Study Completed," press release, March 31, 2009; Dennis P. Rosenbaum, "Just Say No to D.A.R.E.," *Criminology and Public Policy* 6:815–824 (2007); Carol H. Weiss, Erin Murphy-Graham, and Sarah Birkeland, "An Alternative Route to Policy Influence: How Evaluations Affect D.A.R.E.," *American Journal of Evaluation* 26:12–30 (2005); General Accountability Office, *Youth Illicit Drug Use Prevention: D.A.R.E. Long-Term Evaluations and Federal Efforts to Identify Effective Programs* (Washington, DC: Author, 2003).

---

developments with BGCs, with and without SMART Moves, produced a reduction in substance abuse, drug trafficking, and other drug-related delinquency activity.[126]

multisystemic therapy (MST) Addresses a variety of family, peer, and psychological problems by focusing on problem-solving and communication skills training.

Treatment Strategies

Each year, more than 130,000 youths ages 12 to 17 are admitted to treatment facilities in the United States, with just over half (52 percent) being referred through the juvenile justice system. Almost two-thirds (between 61 and 66 percent, depending on age group) of all admissions involved marijuana as the primary drug of abuse.[127]

Several approaches are available to treat these users. Some efforts stem from the perspective that users have low self-esteem and employ various techniques to build up their sense of self. Some use psychological counseling, and others, such as the **multisystemic therapy (MST)** technique developed by Scott Henggeler, direct attention to family, peer, and psychological problems by focusing on problem solving and communication skills.[128] Because of its importance and effectiveness as a drug and delinquency treatment strategy, MST is the subject of the accompanying Prevention/Intervention/Treatment feature.

Looking Back to Fernando's Story

Multisystemic therapy has proven effective in treating juvenile substance abuse, serious and violent offending, and other problem behaviors.

CRITICAL THINKING If you were going to use a multisystemic treatment approach with Fernando, identify whom would you involve and what issues you would address. Do you think this approach could be successful in the case? Discuss why or why not.

Multisystemic Therapy

MST is an increasingly popular multimodal treatment approach that is designed for serious juvenile offenders. The particular type of treatment is chosen according to the needs of the young person; therefore, the nature of the treatment is different for each youth. The treatment may include individual, family, peer, school, and community interventions, including parent training and skills training; more often, though, it is referred to as a family-based treatment.

MST has proven successful in reducing delinquency, substance abuse, and other problematic behaviors in many experiments with serious juvenile offenders. Scott Henggeler and his colleagues carried out a long-term follow-up of a randomized experiment to test the efficacy of MST compared to traditional counseling services for 118 substance-abusing juvenile offenders. The average age at treatment was 16 years and the average age at follow-up was 19.5 years. Compared to those who received traditional counseling services (the control group), MST participants had significantly lower yearly conviction rates for aggressive criminal activity (15 percent versus 57 percent), but not for property crimes. Treatment effects on long-term illicit drug use were mixed, with biological measures (for example, urine analysis) indicating significantly higher rates of marijuana abstinence for MST participants compared to control group participants (55 percent versus 28 percent), but no effect on cocaine use.

In another randomized experiment, Cindy Schaeffer and Charles Borduin carried out an even longer-term follow-up to test the efficacy of MST compared to individualized therapy for 176 serious and violent juvenile offenders. The average age at treatment was 14 years and the average age at follow-up was about 29 years. Compared to those who received individual therapy, MST participants had significantly lower recidivism rates (50 percent versus 81 percent), including lower rates of rearrest for violent offenses (14 percent versus 30 percent). As well, MST participants had 54 percent fewer arrests and 57 percent fewer days of confinement in adult detention facilities compared to their control counterparts.

MST has also been shown to be highly cost-effective. According to the Washington State Institute for Public Policy, for every dollar spent on MST, more than eight dollars are saved in victim costs and juvenile justice and criminal justice costs. This finding has proven particularly influential with policymakers and legislators across the country who are grappling with how best to keep juvenile crime rates from going up in tough economic times.

Critical Thinking

1. What factors account for MST's success in reducing delinquency, substance abuse, and other problematic behaviors? Explain.
2. How does MST compare with other treatment strategies to reduce juvenile drug use? Do you think more communities should use it to address juvenile drug use? If so, what are the most important challenges the program will need to address?

Sources: Elizabeth K. Drake, Steve Aos, and Marna G. Miller, "Evidence-Based Public Policy Options to Reduce Crime and Criminal Justice Costs: Implications in Washington State," *Victims and Offenders* 4:170–190 (2009); Cindy M. Schaeffer and Charles M. Borduin, "Long-Term Follow-Up to a Randomized Clinical Trial of Multisystemic Therapy with Serious and Violent Juvenile Offenders," *Journal of Consulting and Clinical Psychology* 73:445–453 (2005); Scott W. Henggeler, W. Glenn Clingempeel, Michael J. Brondino, and Susan G. Pickrel, "Four-Year Follow-Up of Multisystemic Therapy with Substance-Abusing and Substance-Dependent Juvenile Offenders," *Journal of the American Academy of Child and Adolescent Psychiatry* 41:868–874 (2002); Scott W. Henggeler, Sonja K. Schoenwald, Charles M. Borduin, Melisa D. Rowland, and Phillippe B. Cunningham, *Multisystemic Treatment of Antisocial Behavior in Children and Adolescents* (New York: Guilford Press, 1998).

Another approach is to involve users in outdoor activities, wilderness training, and after-school community programs.[129] More intensive efforts use group therapy, in which leaders try to give users the skills and support to help them reject social pressure to use drugs. These programs are based on the Alcoholics Anonymous (and Narcotics Anonymous) philosophy that users must find the strength to stay clean and that support from those who understand their experiences can be a successful way to achieve a drug-free life.

Residential programs are used with more heavily involved drug abusers. Some are detoxification units that use medical procedures to wean patients from the more addicting drugs. Others are therapeutic communities that attempt to deal with the psychological causes of drug use. Hypnosis, aversion therapy (getting users to associate drugs with unpleasant sensations, such as nausea), counseling, biofeedback, and other techniques are often used.

PROFESSIONAL SPOTLIGHT

© Mai Ferrell

Mai Ferrell
Juvenile Substance Abuse Counselor

Mai Ferrell is a juvenile substance abuse counselor at a program called Sun-Hawk Adolescent Recovery Center in Utah, Arizona. She decided to work in this area of juvenile justice because she feels drawn to work with children and adolescents—something she has done for some time now—as they are the most open to change. There is a real chance to make a difference in their lives and help them achieve their dreams. Ferrell prepared for her career in juvenile substance abuse recovery by first getting an undergraduate degree in psychology and then earning her master's degree in social work.

Ferrell's routine can vary from day to day. On most days, she facilitates a group therapy session in the morning. Some of the topics they deal with include the processing of feelings, relapse recovery, and the benefits of psycho-educational classes. Throughout much of the remainder of the day, she is in contact with the parents of the juveniles, preparing individual counseling sessions, and staying on top of case management duties.

What does Ferrell find to be the most rewarding part of her job? She says that without a doubt it is being able to see the internal change that takes place in her clients. The adolescents she works with come into the facility angry, broken, and completely oblivious about the lifestyles they were leading. It makes her feel fulfilled when they "get it," when they accept responsibility and accountability for their choices.

The most challenging part of Mai Ferrell's job is the parents of her juvenile clients. For her, it seems that sometimes parents do not get exactly what addiction is and how it affects their children as well the family as a whole. There are many parents who are not willing to invest themselves in the process of helping their families get healthy. Also, from time to time there are parents who are just not willing to accept accountability and responsibility for their part in their children's choices and behaviors.

There is little evidence that these residential programs can effectively terminate teenage substance abuse.[130] Many are restricted to families whose health insurance will pay for short-term residential care; when the coverage ends, the children are released. Adolescents do not often enter these programs voluntarily, and most have little motivation to change.[131] A stay can stigmatize residents as "addicts" even though they never used hard drugs; while in treatment, they may be introduced to hard-core users with whom they will associate upon release. One residential program that holds promise for reducing teenage substance abuse is UCLA's Comprehensive Residential Education, Arts, and Substance Abuse Treatment (CREASAT) program, which integrates "enhanced substance abuse services" (group therapy, education, vocational skills) and visual and performing arts programming.[132] Because of the importance of these programs, we discuss the career of a juvenile substance abuse counselor in the Professional Spotlight feature.

Harm Reduction

A **harm reduction** approach involves lessening the harms caused to youths by drug use and by some of the more punitive responses to drug use. Harm reduction encapsulates some of the efforts advanced under the community and treatment strategies noted above, but maintains as its primary focus efforts to minimize the harmful effects of drug use. This approach includes the following components:

- The availability of drug treatment facilities so that all addicts who wish to do so can overcome their habits and lead drug-free lives.
- The use of health professionals to administer drugs to addicts as part of a treatment and detoxification program.
- Needle exchange programs that will slow the transmission of HIV and educate drug users about how HIV is contracted and spread.
- Special drug courts or pretrial diversion programs that compel drug treatment.[133] (Juvenile drug courts are discussed in Chapter 11.)

WWW

The **Harm Reduction Coalition** is a national advocacy and capacity-building organization that promotes the health and dignity of individuals and communities impacted by drug use. To learn more about the harm reduction approach to teenage drug use, visit the Criminal Justice CourseMate at CengageBrain.com, then access the Web Links for this chapter.

harm reduction Efforts to minimize the harmful effects caused by drug use.

Needle exchange programs—providing drug users with clean needles in exchange for used ones—have been shown to maintain the low prevalence of HIV transmission among drug users and lower rates of hepatitis C. Methadone maintenance clinics in which heroin users receive doctor-prescribed methadone (a nonaddictive substance that satisfies the cravings caused by heroin) have been shown to reduce illegal heroin use and criminal activity.[134]

Critics of the harm reduction approach warn that it condones or promotes drug use, "encouraging people either to continue using drugs or to start using drugs, without recognizing the dangers of their addiction."[135] Advocates, on the other hand, refer to harm reduction as a valuable interim measure in dealing with drug use: "There are safer ways of using drugs, and harm reduction for patients is a valuable interim measure to help them make informed choices and improve their overall health."[136] Advocates also call for this approach to replace the "War on Drugs," and claim that this change in drug policy will go a long way toward solving two key problems caused by punitive responses. First, it will reduce the number of offenders, both juvenile and adult, being sent to already overcrowded institutionalized settings for what amounts to less serious offenses. Second, it will discourage police crackdowns in minority neighborhoods that result in racial minorities being arrested and formally processed at much higher rates for drug offenses.[137]

The War on Drugs has been a major source of the racial discrimination that occurs in the juvenile justice system. (For more on racial discrimination in the juvenile justice system, see Chapters 12, 13, and 14.) The latest data (2008) show that African Americans make up 17 percent of the juvenile population, but account for 24 percent (43,000) of all drug law violations referred to juvenile court. This is down from 27 percent in 1999 and slightly up from 23 percent in 2004. African American juveniles involved in drug offense cases are also more likely to be detained (held in a detention facility or in shelter care to await court appearances) than European American juveniles.[138] **CHECKPOINTS**

A harm reduction approach to juvenile drug use emphasizes ways to reduce the harms caused by drug use as well as overly punitive responses to drug use. Needle exchange programs are one example of harm reduction. Here, Life Works Program Coordinator Genny Fulco (center) talks with an unidentified intravenous drug user (far right) at the needle exchange program location in Camden, New Jersey, as the Camden Area Health Education Center's mobile health unit coordinator Sadia Sanchez looks on.

AP Photo/Joseph Kaczmarek

WHAT DOES THE FUTURE HOLD?

The United States appears willing to go to great lengths to fight the drug war.[139] The financial cost alone of the 40-year War on Drugs has been considerable. A detailed study by the Associated Press puts the government price tag at $1 trillion.[140] Innovative prevention and treatment programs have been stepped up. Indeed, the National Research Council's scientific panel on the demand for illegal drugs concluded that the short-term effectiveness of many treatment modalities have been "repeatedly and convincingly demonstrated," and called for greater research to investigate the long-term benefits.[141] Yet all drug-control strategies are doomed to fail as long as youths want to take drugs and drugs remain widely available and accessible. Prevention, deterrence, and treatment strategies ignore the core reasons for the drug problem: poverty, alienation, and family disruption. As the gap between rich and poor widens and the opportunities for legitimate advancement decrease, it should come as no surprise that adolescent drug use continues.

Some commentators have called for the **legalization of drugs**. This approach can have the short-term effect of reducing the association between drug use and crime (because, presumably, the cost of drugs would decrease), but it may have grave consequences. Drug use would most certainly increase, creating an overflow of unproductive people who must be cared for by the rest of society. The problems of teenage alcoholism should serve as a warning of what can happen when controlled substances are made readily available. However, the implications of decriminalization should be further studied: What effect would a policy of partial decriminalization (for example, legalizing small amounts of marijuana) have on drug use rates? Does a get-tough policy on drugs "widen the net"? Are there alternatives to the criminalization of drugs that could help reduce their use?[142] Studies of drug dealing in Philadelphia and Washington, D.C., suggest that law enforcement efforts may have little influence on drug-abuse rates as long as dealers can earn more than the minimal salaries they might earn in the legitimate business world. Only by giving youths legitimate future alternatives can hard-core users be made to forgo drug use willingly.[143]

WWW

The **White House Office of National Drug Control Policy (ONDCP)**, a component of the Executive Office of the President, establishes policies, priorities, and objectives for the nation's drug control program. To find out more about the federal government's drug-control strategies, visit the Criminal Justice CourseMate at CengageBrain.com, then access the Web Links for this chapter.

legalization of drugs Decriminalizing drug use to reduce the association between drug use and crime.

SUMMARY

Alcohol is the drug most frequently abused by American teens. Other popular drugs include marijuana and prescription drugs. Self-report surveys indicate that just under half of all high school seniors have tried drugs. Surveys of arrestees indicate that a significant proportion of teenagers are drug users and many are high school dropouts. The number of drug users may be even higher than surveys suggest, because surveys of teen abusers may be missing the most delinquent youths. The national survey conducted by PRIDE, the Monitoring the Future survey, and the National Survey on Drug Use and Health report that drug and alcohol use are much lower today than 5 and 10 years ago.

There are many explanations for why youths take drugs, including growing up in disorganized areas in which there is a high degree of hopelessness, poverty, and despair; peer pressure; parental substance abuse; emotional problems; and suffering from general problem behavior syndrome. Also, a variety of youths use drugs. Some are occasional users who might sell to friends. Others are seriously involved in both drug abuse and delinquency; many of these are gang members. There are also "losers" who filter in and out of the juvenile justice system. A small percentage of teenage users remain involved with drugs into adulthood. It is not certain whether drug abuse causes delinquency. Some experts believe there is a common cause for both delinquency and drug abuse—perhaps alienation and rage.

Many attempts have been made to control the drug trade. Some try to inhibit the importation of drugs, others to close down major drug rings, and a few to stop street-level dealing. There are also attempts to treat users through rehabilitation programs, reduce juvenile use by educational efforts, and implement harm reduction measures. Some communities have mounted grassroots drives. These efforts have not been totally successful, although overall use of drugs may have declined somewhat.

It is difficult to eradicate drug abuse because there is much profit to be made from the sale of drugs. One suggestion: legalize drugs. But critics warn that such a step may produce greater numbers of substance abusers. Supporters of legalization argue that it would greatly reduce the violence and other criminal activity associated with drug dealing.

KEY TERMS

QUESTIONS FOR REVIEW

1. What are some of the health risks associated with smoking marijuana?

2. What are some of the features of the Monitoring the Future survey that make it such an authoritative source on teen drug use in America?

3. How do social psychologists explain the family influence on teens who take drugs?

4. What is the meaning of *gateway drug*? Give one or two examples.

5. What does the research say about the role of gangs in dealing drugs?

6. List the most important problem and delinquent behaviors associated with drug selling.

7. Why is multisystemic therapy such an effective treatment for juveniles with substance abuse problems?

8. List the pros and cons of a harm reduction approach to reducing drug use.

QUESTIONS FOR DISCUSSION

1. Discuss the differences between the various categories and types of substances of abuse. Is the term *drugs* too broad to have real meaning?

2. Why do you think youths take drugs? Do you know anyone with an addiction-prone personality?

3. What policy do you think might be the best strategy to reduce teenage drug use? Source control? Reliance on treatment? National education efforts? Community-level enforcement? Harm reduction measures?

4. Do you consider alcohol a drug? Should greater controls be placed on the sale of alcohol?

5. Do TV shows and films glorify drug usage and encourage youths to enter the drug trade? Should all images of drinking and smoking be banned from TV? What about advertisements that try to convince youths how much fun it is to drink beer or smoke cigarettes?

APPLYING WHAT YOU HAVE LEARNED

The president has appointed you as the new "drug czar." You have $10 billion under your control with which to wage your campaign. You know that drug use is unacceptably high, especially among poor, inner-city kids, that a great deal of criminal behavior is drug-related, and that drug-dealing gangs are expanding around the United States.

At an open hearing, drug-control experts express their policy strategies. One group favors putting the money into hiring new law enforcement agents who will patrol borders, target large dealers, and make drug raids here and abroad. They also call for such get-tough measures as the creation of strict drug laws and the mandatory waiver of young drug dealers to the adult court system.

A second group believes the best way to deal with drugs is to spend the money on community treatment programs, expanding the number of beds in drug detoxification units, and funding research on how to reduce drug dependency clinically.

A third group argues that neither punishment nor treatment can restrict teenage drug use and that the best course is to educate at-risk kids about the dangers of substance abuse and then legalize all drugs, but control their distribution. This course of action will help reduce crime and violence among drug users and also balance the national debt because drugs could be heavily taxed.

Writing Assignment: Write a policy statement setting out the course of action you would recommend to the president.

After outlining the need for action, select one of the three strategies that you believe will be the most effective in reducing juvenile drug use now and in the years to come. Identify five to seven key points that make the case for your strategy.

GROUPWORK

Divide the class into seven groups and assign each group one of the main explanations for why youths take drugs: social disorganization, peer pressure, family factors, genetic factors, emotional problems, problem behavior syndrome, and rational choice. Have each group identify at least five reasons to support why their explanation is the most important and should be the focus of public policy efforts to reduce substance abuse.

CHAPTER ELEVEN

Delinquency Prevention and Juvenile Justice Today

© Chassenet/age footstock

LEARNING OBJECTIVES

After reading this chapter you should:

1. Understand key features of delinquency prevention.
2. Be familiar with effective delinquency prevention programs for children.
3. Be familiar with effective delinquency prevention programs for teens.
4. Know how children are processed by the juvenile justice system.
5. Understand the key elements of a comprehensive juvenile justice strategy.

Martin's Story

Martin was a 13-year-old male who was in eighth grade. He was the youngest of four boys and lived with his mother and father. Martin's mother worked very long hours and his father had been laid off and was not able to find work for some time. His father was depressed and irritable most of the time. Finances were a huge struggle for the family and a source of constant stress and verbal fighting between the parents. Martin was described as a smart young man in terms of academics, but a follower in terms of friends and social life. He tried many sports and activities, but showed little interest. During the second semester of school Martin's grades significantly declined. Martin also started sleeping more than usual and had a difficult time getting up for school on most days. His parents tried to talk with Martin and the school, but nothing proved helpful. His mother felt her time at home was very limited when she began working to support the family.

During this time, Martin was arrested for possession of marijuana with the intent to distribute. He explained to his parents that he was only "helping out his friends" by carrying the duffel bag full of drugs to another location. He also received a drug screen and tested positive for marijuana use, but he denied he ever used. Martin seemed concerned about the arrest and exhibited signs of depression.

At Martin's dispositional hearing at the juvenile court, he was ordered to complete a drug and alcohol assessment as well as participate in individual and family therapy. Additionally, he was required to complete 50 hours of community service and participate in a local community supervision program for teens involved in criminal activity. Martin struggled with many of the court-ordered requirements, as did the family. Martin's drug use and poor school achievement continued and he was not cooperative with the assigned social workers and juvenile justice authorities. As a result, Martin received a series of weekend incarcerations in the juvenile correctional facility as well as stricter curfews and more intensive supervision. While Martin's struggles continued, his parents were encouraged to seek support from involved systems and utilize counseling.

During the summer, Martin's parents separated for a short period of time. This prompted the father to get help for his depression, and he also received additional support in finding a job, which he successfully did. Eventually, the parents got back together with a renewed vision for their family and were better able to focus on the needs of Martin and their other children. During the second semester of Martin's freshman year, things began to turn around. Martin has begun a new program where he receives tutoring, attends a weekly support meeting, and is linked with a mentor. He is also beginning to more actively engage in his drug treatment program and improve his grades; he has hopes of attending a local technical school upon graduation.

Public officials faced with the problem of juvenile delinquency in their cities have many options. For some, it will be a clear choice of getting tough on juvenile delinquency and implementing punitive or justice-oriented measures. For others, it will be a matter of getting tough on the causes of juvenile delinquency and implementing prevention programs to ward off delinquency before it takes place. Still others will combine justice and nonjustice measures to combat the problem. Ideally, decisions about which approach or which combination of measures to use will be based on the needs of the community and the highest quality available evidence on what works best in preventing juvenile delinquency.

This chapter looks at the role of prevention programs and juvenile justice in contemporary American society. It begins with an overview of key features of delinquency prevention and reviews the effectiveness of delinquency prevention programs for children and adolescents. This is followed with a description of the juvenile justice process, beginning with arrest and concluding with reentry into society. A comprehensive juvenile justice strategy, which combines elements of delinquency prevention and intervention and justice approaches, is discussed in the next section. The chapter concludes with a look at key issues facing the future of delinquency prevention and juvenile justice.

DELINQUENCY PREVENTION

Preventing juvenile delinquency means many different things to many different people. Programs or policies designed to prevent juvenile delinquency can include the police making an arrest as part of an operation to address gang problems, a juvenile court sanction to a secure correctional facility, or, in the extreme case, a death penalty sentence. These measures are often referred to as **delinquency control** or **delinquency repression**. More often, though, **delinquency prevention** refers to intervening in young people's lives before they engage in delinquency in the first place—that is, preventing the first delinquent act. Both forms of delinquency prevention have a common goal of trying to prevent the occurrence of a future delinquent act, but what distinguishes delinquency prevention from delinquency control is that prevention typically does not involve the juvenile justice system. Instead, programs or policies designed to prevent delinquency involve day care providers, nurses, teachers, social workers, recreation staff at the YMCA, counselors at Boys and Girls Clubs of America, other young people in school, and parents. This form of delinquency prevention is sometimes referred to as nonjustice delinquency prevention or alternative delinquency prevention. Exhibit 11.1 lists examples of programs to prevent and control delinquency.

Delinquency prevention programs are not designed with the intention of excluding juvenile justice personnel. Many types of delinquency prevention programs, especially those that focus on adolescents, involve juvenile justice personnel such as the police. In these cases, the juvenile justice personnel work in close collaboration with those from such areas as education, health care, recreation, and social services.

Classifying Delinquency Prevention

Just as there are a number of different ways to define delinquency prevention and very little agreement on the best way to do so,[1] the organization or classification of delinquency prevention is equally diverse, and there is very little agreement on the most effective way to do this.

Public Health Approach. One of the first efforts to classify the many different types of delinquency prevention activities drew upon the public health approach to preventing diseases and injuries.[2] This method divided delinquency prevention activities into three categories: primary prevention, secondary prevention, and tertiary prevention.

- *Primary prevention* focuses on improving the general well-being of individuals through such measures as access to health care services and general prevention education, and modifying conditions in the physical environment that are conducive to delinquency through such measures as removing abandoned vehicles and improving the appearance of buildings.

- *Secondary prevention* focuses on intervening with children and young people who are potentially at risk for becoming offenders, as well as the provision of neighborhood programs to deter known delinquent activity.

delinquency control or delinquency repression Involves any justice program or policy designed to prevent the occurrence of a future delinquent act.

delinquency prevention Involves any nonjustice program or policy designed to prevent the occurrence of a future delinquent act.

EXHIBIT 11.1 Delinquency Prevention vs. Control

Prevention	Control
Home visitation	Antigang police task force
Preschool	Boot camps
Child skills training	Wilderness programs
Mentoring	Probation
After-school recreation	Electronic monitoring
Job training	Secure confinement

© Cengage Learning 2013

- *Tertiary prevention* focuses on intervening with adjudicated juvenile offenders through such measures as substance abuse treatment and imprisonment. Here, the goal is to reduce repeat offending or recidivism.[3]

Developmental Perspective. Another popular approach to classifying delinquency prevention activities is the developmental perspective. Developmental prevention refers to interventions, especially those targeting **risk and protective factors**, designed to prevent the development of criminal potential in individuals.[4] Developmental prevention of juvenile delinquency is informed generally by motivational or human development theories on juvenile delinquency, and specifically by longitudinal studies that follow samples of young persons from their early childhood experiences to the peak of their involvement with delinquency in their teens and crime in their 20s.[5] The developmental perspective claims that delinquency in adolescence (and later criminal offending in adulthood) is influenced by "behavioral and attitudinal patterns that have been learned during an individual's development."[6] Concept Summary 11.1 lists key features of the developmental perspective. From this perspective, prevention activities are organized around different stages of the life course. We divide our discussion of developmental prevention of juvenile delinquency into two stages: childhood and adolescence.

For the most part, we have adopted the developmental perspective in discussing the effectiveness of different types of delinquency prevention programs in the next two sections. This approach has several advantages: it allows for assessing the success of programs at different life-course stages; its coverage of the types of delinquency prevention programs that have been implemented is vast; and it is a well-recognized approach that has been used by other social scientists in reviews of the effectiveness of delinquency prevention.[7] CHECKPOINTS

EARLY PREVENTION OF DELINQUENCY

In the effort to address juvenile delinquency, early childhood interventions—initiated before delinquency occurs—have received much interest and have come to be seen as an important part of an overall strategy to reduce the harm caused by juvenile delinquency. Recent research shows that the general public is highly supportive of delinquency prevention programs and is even willing to pay more in taxes for these programs compared to more punitive options like military-style boot camps and prison. (This is discussed in the Focus on Delinquency box entitled "Public Support for Delinquency Prevention.") Early childhood delinquency prevention programs aim at positively influencing the early risk factors or "root causes" of delinquency and criminal offending that may continue into the adult years. These early risk factors are many, some of which include growing up in poverty, a high level of hyperactivity or impulsiveness, inadequate parental supervision, and harsh or inconsistent discipline. Early childhood interventions are often multidimensional, targeted at more

risk factor A negative prior factor in an individual's life that increases the risk of occurrence of a future delinquent act.

protective factor A positive prior factor in an individual's life that decreases the risk of occurrence of a future delinquent act.

PUBLIC SUPPORT FOR DELINQUENCY PREVENTION

Politicians who support "get-tough" responses to juvenile offenders have long claimed to have the full backing of the general public, and that it is indeed the public that demands tougher dispositions (or sentences) such as military-style boot camps and longer terms in institutions to hold youth accountable for their transgressions. To be sure, there is public support for get-tough responses to juvenile delinquency, especially violent acts. But this support is not at the levels often claimed and, more importantly, not as high when compared to alternatives such as rehabilitation or treatment for juvenile offenders or early childhood or youth prevention programs. This overestimate of the punitiveness of the general public on the part of politicians and others has become known as the "mythical punitive public."

New, cutting-edge research provides more evidence to substantiate the mythical punitive public—that is,

that citizens are highly supportive of delinquency prevention and are even willing to pay more in taxes to support these programs compared to other responses. In a review of the public opinion literature, criminologist Frank Cullen and his colleagues found that the American public is generally supportive of delinquency prevention programs, especially for at-risk children and youth. They also found that public opinion is no longer a barrier—as it once was perceived to be—to the implementation of delinquency prevention programs in communities across the country.

In a study of public preferences of responses to juvenile offending, criminologist Daniel Nagin and his colleagues found that the public values early prevention and offender rehabilitation or treatment more than increased incarceration. As shown in Table 11-A, households were willing to pay an average of $125.71 in addi-

tional taxes on nurse home visitation programs to prevent delinquency compared to $80.97 on longer sentences, a difference of $44.74 per year. Support for paying more in taxes for rehabilitation was also higher than for longer sentences: $98.10 versus $80.97. At the state level, public support for the prevention option translated into $601 million that hypothetically could be used to prevent delinquency, compared to $387 million for longer sentences for juvenile offenders.

This study was based on a large sample of residents in Pennsylvania and used a highly rigorous methodology of public opinion polling known as contingent valuation (CV), which has many advantages over conventional polling methods. The contingent valuation approach allows for the "comparison of respondents' willingness to pay for competing policy alternatives."

In another innovative study to gauge the public's preferences for a

than one risk factor, because they take a variety of different forms, including cognitive development, child skills training, and family support. The following examines early childhood delinquency prevention programs that have been implemented in influential settings. Most of the programs have been carried out in the United States.

Home-Based Programs

In a supportive and loving home environment, parents care for their children's health and general well-being, help instill in their children positive values such as honesty and respect for others, and nurture prosocial behaviors. One of the most important types of home-based programs to prevent juvenile delinquency involves the provision of support for families. Support for families in their homes can take many different forms. A popular and effective form of family support is home visitation.[8]

TABLE 11.A Public Willingness to Pay for Delinquency Prevention versus Other Measures

Program	Average WTP per Household per Year	Statewide WTP per Year
Longer sentence	$80.97	$387 million
Rehabilitation	$98.10	$468 million
Nurse visitation	$125.71	$601 million

Note: WTP = willingness to pay.

Source: Adapted from Daniel S. Nagin, Alex R. Piquero, Elizabeth S. Scott, and Laurence Steinberg, "Public Preferences for Rehabilitation versus Incarceration of Juvenile Offenders: Evidence from a Contingent Valuation Survey," *Criminology and Public Policy* 5:627–652 (2006), Table 2.

range of alternative responses to crime, Mark Cohen, Ronald Rust, and Sara Steen found the public overwhelmingly supported increased spending of tax dollars on youth prevention programs compared to building more prisons. Public support for spending more taxes on drug treatment for nonviolent offenders as well as police also ranked higher than support for building more prisons, but not as high as for youth prevention programs.

While the mythical punitive public appears to be just that, there is no denying that the general public do see some value in get-tough policies to tackle juvenile crime. But this new crop of public opinion research reveals—even more convincingly than past research—that there is a growing demand for early prevention programs and little demand for increased use of incarceration.

CRITICAL THINKING

1. If you were a politician, would these research findings influence your decision on the policy positions you take on juvenile crime? Explain.

2. Public opinion is one important consideration in implementing delinquency prevention programs. What are some other key factors?

Writing Assignment Write an essay about the strengths and limitations of using public opinion research as the basis for supporting a strategy that emphasizes prevention over punishment. Make sure to consider your answers to the Critical Thinking questions.

Sources: Francis T. Cullen, Brenda A. Vose, Cheryl N. Lero, and James D. Unnever, "Public Support for Early Intervention: Is Child Saving a 'Habit of the Heart'?" *Victims and Offenders* 2:108–124 (2007); Mark A. Cohen, Ronald T. Rust, and Sara Steen, "Prevention, Crime Control or Cash? Public Preferences Toward Criminal Justice Spending Priorities," *Justice Quarterly* 23:317–335 (2006); Daniel S. Nagin, Alex R. Piquero, Elizabeth S. Scott, and Laurence Steinberg, "Public Preferences for Rehabilitation versus Incarceration of Juvenile Offenders: Evidence from a Contingent Valuation Survey," *Criminology and Public Policy* 5:627–652 (2006); Julian V. Roberts, "Public Opinion and Youth Justice," in *Youth Crime and Youth Justice: Comparative and Cross-National Perspectives. Crime and Justice: A Review of Research*, vol. 31, ed. Michael Tonry and Anthony N. Doob (Chicago: University of Chicago Press, 2004).

Home Visitation. The best-known home visitation program is the Nurse-Family Partnership (formerly Prenatal/Early Infancy Project) that was started in Elmira, New York.[9] This program was designed with three broad objectives:

1. To improve the outcomes of pregnancy
2. To improve the quality of care that parents provide to their children (and their children's subsequent health and development)
3. To improve women's own personal life-course development (completing their education, finding work, and planning future pregnancies)[10]

The program targeted first-time mothers-to-be who were under 19 years of age, unmarried, or poor. In all, 400 women were enrolled in the program. The mothers-to-be received home visits from nurses during pregnancy and during the first two years of the child's life. Each home visit lasted about one and one-quarter hours, and the mothers were visited on average every two weeks. The home visitors gave advice to the mothers about care of the child, infant development, and the importance of proper nutrition and avoiding smoking and drinking during pregnancy. Fifteen years after the program started, children of the mothers who received home visits had half as many arrests as children of mothers who received no home visits (the control group).[11] It was also found that these children, compared to those in the control group, had fewer convictions and violations of probation, were less likely to run away from home, and were less likely to drink alcohol. In addition to the program's success in preventing juvenile crime and other delinquent activities, it also produced a number of improvements in the lives of the mothers, such as lower rates of child abuse and neglect, crime in general, and substance abuse, as well as less reliance on welfare and social services.[12]

A Rand study found that the program's desirable effects, for both the children and the mothers, translated into substantial financial benefits for government and taxpayers, and that the total amount of these benefits was more than four times the cost of the program (see Figure 11.1).[13] In the latest follow-up of the program, when the children were 19 years old, girls incurred significantly fewer arrests and convictions compared to their control counterparts, while few program effects were observed for the boys.[14]

Two other experiments of the Nurse-Family Partnership (NFP) program in Memphis, Tennessee, and Denver, Colorado, have produced similar benefits for the mothers and their children, including a reduction in child abuse and neglect. The success of the program has resulted in its use in almost 400 counties in 32 states across the country, serving more than 21,000 families each year.[15] In Colorado, the program was established in law, and in its first year of operation served almost 1,400 families in 49 of the state's 64 counties.[16] It is also now being replicated throughout England.[17] The use of nurses instead of paraprofessionals, its intensity (a minimum of two years), and its targeted nature (for first time, disadvantaged mothers only) are critical features that distinguish it from other, less effective home visitation programs such as Hawaii Healthy Start.[18]

WW

Nurse-Family Partnership, a maternal and early childhood health program, fosters long-term success for first-time moms, their babies, and society. To read more, visit the Criminal Justice CourseMate at CengageBrain.com, then access the Web Links for this chapter.

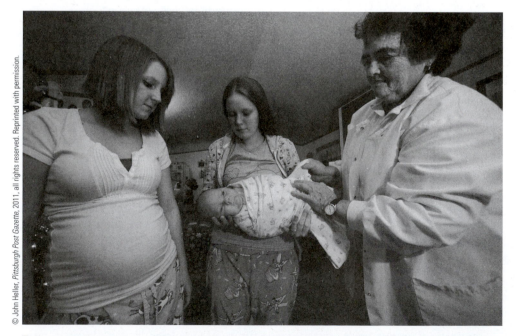

Early prevention programs that stress family support can reduce child abuse and neglect and juvenile delinquency. The most effective early family support programs provide infants with regular pediatrician checkups and provide parents with advice about care for the child, infant development, and local services. Here, Molly Walters watches her sister, Billie Joe Walters, swaddle Billie Joe's month-old son, Hayden, with the help of "coach" Janet DeBolt, director of the Nurse-Family Partnership in Uniontown, Pennsylvania.

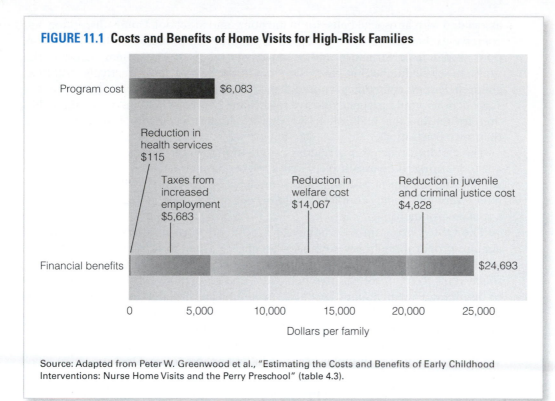

FIGURE 11.1 Costs and Benefits of Home Visits for High-Risk Families

Program cost $6,083

Reduction in
health services
$115

Taxes from
increased
employment
$5,683

Reduction in
welfare cost
$14,067

Reduction in juvenile
and criminal justice cost
$4,828

Financial benefits $24,693

0   5,000   10,000   15,000   20,000   25,000

Dollars per family

Source: Adapted from Peter W. Greenwood et al., "Estimating the Costs and Benefits of Early Childhood
Interventions: Nurse Home Visits and the Perry Preschool" (table 4.3).

Improving Parenting Skills

Another form of family support that has shown some success in preventing juvenile
delinquency is improving parenting skills. Although the main focus of parent training programs is on the parents, many of these programs also involve children, with
the aim of improving the parent–child bond.

Two reviews capture the broad-scale effectiveness of family-based prevention
programs. The first one involved a meta-analysis of the effects of early prevention
programs that included parents and children up to age 5.[19] Eleven high-quality studies were included that covered a variety of program modalities, including home
visitation, family support services, and parental education (improvement of core
parenting skills). Results showed significant effects across a number of important
domain outcomes, including educational success, delinquency, cognitive development, involvement in the justice system, and family well-being. Program duration
and intensity were associated with larger effects, but not multicomponent programs.
This latter finding goes against much past research, including the latest results on
the effectiveness of the Fast Track multicomponent, multisite prevention program.[20]

The second one involved a systematic review and meta-analysis of the effects of
early family/parent training programs for children up to age 5 years on antisocial behavior and delinquency.[21] It included 55 **randomized controlled experiments** and investigated the full range of these programs, including home visits, parent education
plus daycare, and parent training. Results indicated that early family/parent training
is an effective intervention for reducing antisocial behavior and delinquency. These
programs also produce a wide range of other important benefits for families, including improved school readiness and school performance on the part of children and
greater employment and educational opportunities for parents. Significant differences were not detected across program type, such as traditional parent training
versus home visiting.

Oregon Social Learning Center. The most widely cited parenting skills program is
one created at the Oregon Social Learning Center (OSLC) by Gerald Patterson and
his colleagues.[22] Patterson's research convinced him that poor parenting skills were

randomized controlled experiment
Considered the "gold standard" of evaluation designs
to measure the effect of a
program on delinquency or
other outcomes. Involves
randomly assigning subjects
either to receive the program
(the experimental group) or not
receive it (the control group).

associated with antisocial behavior in the home and at school. Family disruption and coercive exchanges between parents and children led to increased family tension, poor academic performance, and negative peer relations. The primary cause of the problem seemed to be that parents did not know how to deal effectively with their children. Parents sometimes ignored their children's behavior, but at other times the same actions would trigger explosive rage. Some parents would discipline their children for reasons that had little to do with the children's behavior, instead reflecting their own frustrations.

The children reacted in a regular progression, from learning to be noncompliant to learning to be assaultive. Their coercive behavior, which included whining, yelling, and temper tantrums, would sometimes be acquired by other family members. Eventually family conflict would flow out of the home and into the school and social environment.

The OSLC program uses behavior modification techniques to help parents acquire proper disciplinary methods. Parents are asked to select several behaviors for change and to count the frequency of their occurrence. OSLC personnel teach social skills to reinforce positive behaviors, and constructive disciplinary methods to discourage negative ones. Incentive programs are initiated in which a child can earn points for desirable behaviors. Points can be exchanged for allowance, prizes, or privileges. Parents are also taught disciplinary techniques that stress firmness and consistency rather than "nattering" (low-intensity behaviors, such as scowling or scolding) or explosive discipline, such as hitting or screaming. One important technique is the "time out," in which the child is removed for brief isolation in a quiet room. Parents are taught the importance of setting rules and sticking to them. A number of evaluation studies carried out by Patterson and his colleagues showed that improving parenting skills can lead to reductions in juvenile delinquency.[23]

The parent training method used by the OSLC may be the most cost-effective method of early intervention. A Rand study found that parent training costs about one-twentieth what a home visit program costs and is more effective in preventing serious crimes. The study estimates that 501 serious crimes could be prevented for every million dollars spent on parent training (or $2,000 per crime), a far cheaper solution than long-term incarceration, which would cost about $16,000 to prevent a single crime.[24]

Preschool

Typically provided to children ages 3 to 5, preschool programs are geared toward preparing children for grade school. These are the formative years of brain development; more learning takes place during this developmental stage than at any other stage over the life course. Low intelligence and school failure are important risk factors for juvenile delinquency.[25] (See Chapter 5 for why these are risk factors for juvenile delinquency.) For these reasons, highly structured, cognitive-based preschool programs give young children a positive start in life. Some of the key features of preschool programs include the provision of:

- Developmentally appropriate learning curricula
- A wide array of cognitive-based enriching activities
- Activities for parents, usually of a less intensive nature, so that they may be able to support the school experience at home[26]

A preschool program in Michigan and another in Chicago provide some positive findings on the benefits of early prevention of delinquency.

Started in the mid-1960s, the Perry Preschool in Ypsilanti, Michigan, provided disadvantaged children with a program of educational enrichment supplemented with weekly home visits. The main hypothesis of the program was that "good preschool programs can help children in poverty make a better start in their transition from home to community and thereby set more of them on paths to becoming economically self-sufficient, socially responsible adults."[27] The main intervention was high-quality, active-learning preschool programming administered by professional teachers for two years. Preschool sessions were half a day long and were provided

WWW

For more information on the **Oregon Social Learning Center (OSLC)**, visit the Criminal Justice CourseMate at CengageBrain.com, then access the Web Links for this chapter.

five days a week for the duration of the 30-week school year. The educational approach focused on supporting the development of the children's cognitive and social skills through individualized teaching and learning.

A number of assessments were made of the program at important stages of development. The first assessment of juvenile delinquency, when the participants were age 15, found that those who received the program reported one-third fewer offenses than a control group.[28] By the age of 27, program participants had accumulated half the arrests of the control group. The researchers also found that the preschoolers had achieved many other significant benefits compared to their control group counterparts, including higher monthly earnings, higher percentages of home ownership and second car ownership, a higher level of schooling completed, and a lower percentage receiving welfare benefits.[29] All of these benefits translated into substantial dollar cost savings. It was estimated that for each dollar it cost to run and administer the program, more than $7 was saved to taxpayers, potential crime victims, and program participants.[30] An independent study by Rand also found that Perry Preschool was a very worthwhile investment.[31]

The most recent assessment of the effectiveness of Perry Preschool—when the subjects were age 40—found that it continues to make an important difference in the lives of those who were enrolled in the program. Compared to the control group, program group members had achieved many significant benefits, including:

- Fewer lifetime arrests for violent crimes (32 percent vs. 48 percent), property crimes (36 percent vs. 58 percent), and drug crimes (14 percent vs. 34 percent)
- Higher levels of schooling completed (77 percent vs. 60 percent graduated from high school)
- Higher annual earnings (57 percent vs. 43 percent had earnings in the top half of the sample)[32]

An assessment of the costs and benefits at age 40 found that for every dollar spent on the program, more than $17 was returned to society—in the form of savings in crime, education, welfare, and increased tax revenue.

The Child-Parent Center (CPC) program in Chicago, like Perry Preschool, provided disadvantaged children ages 3 to 4 years with high-quality, active-learning preschool supplemented with family support. However, unlike Perry, CPC continued to provide the children with the educational enrichment component into elementary school, up to the age of 9 years. Just focusing on the effect of the preschool, it was found that, compared to a control group, those who received the program were less likely to be arrested for nonviolent offenses (17 percent vs. 25 percent) and violent offenses (9 percent vs. 15 percent) by the time they were 18. Preschool participants, compared to a control group, were also less likely to be arrested more than once (10 percent vs. 13 percent). Other significant benefits realized by the preschool participants compared to the control group included:

- A higher rate of high school completion (50 percent vs. 39 percent)
- More years of completed education (11 vs. 10)
- A lower rate of dropping out of school (47 percent vs. 55 percent)[33]

A more recent evaluation when participants were age 24 found that the experimental group, compared to the control group members, had significantly lower rates of felony arrest (17 percent vs. 21 percent) and lower rates of incarceration (21 percent vs. 26 percent).[34] Positive results were found for official justice contact in a follow-up at age 28 as well.[35] The success of the CPC program in preventing juvenile delinquency and improving other life-course outcomes produced substantial cost savings. For each dollar spent on the program, $7.14 was saved to taxpayers, potential crime victims, and program participants.[36]

Overall, high-quality, intensive preschool programs show strong support for preventing delinquency and improving the lives of young people.[37] The provision of family support services combined with preschool programming likely adds to the strength of the Perry and CPC programs in preventing delinquency, but it is clear that preschool was the most important element. The intellectual enrichment component of preschool helps prepare children for the academic challenges of elementary and later grades; reducing the chances of school failure is a significant factor in reducing delinquency. Another notable point about the positive findings of Perry and CPC is that these two programs were implemented many years apart, yet the CPC, as a semi-replication of Perry, demonstrates that preschool programs today can still be effective in preventing delinquency. **CHECKPOINTS**

PREVENTION OF DELINQUENCY IN THE TEENAGE YEARS

Like early childhood interventions, delinquency prevention programs started in the teenage years also play an important role in an overall strategy to reduce juvenile delinquency. A wide range of non–juvenile justice delinquency prevention programs attempt to address such risk factors as parental conflict and separation, poor housing, dropping out of high school, and antisocial peers. The following sections examine a number of key delinquency prevention approaches targeted at teenagers: mentoring, school-based programs, and job training.

Mentoring

Mentoring programs usually involve nonprofessional volunteers spending time with young people at risk for delinquency, dropping out of school, school failure, and other social problems. Mentors behave in a supportive, nonjudgmental manner while acting as role models.[38] In recent years, there has been a large increase in the number of mentoring programs, many of which are aimed at preventing delinquency.[39]

Federal Mentoring Programs. The Office of Juvenile Justice and Delinquency Prevention (OJJDP) has supported mentoring for many years in all parts of the United States, most notably through the Juvenile Mentoring Program (JUMP), now called the Mentoring Initiative for System Involved Youth (MISIY). The new initiative provides funding to faith- and community-based agencies to mentor youth involved in the juvenile justice system, foster care, and reentry programs.[40] Under JUMP, thousands of at-risk youths were provided with mentors. The mentors were responsible and caring adults who volunteered their time to work with young people exposed to one or more risk factors, including delinquency, dropping out of school, and problems in school.

The most common areas of increased risk, based on a large number of male and female youths enrolled in the program, are school and social/family domains. (See Table 11.1.) Mentors work one-on-one with young people.[41] Research has shown that mentoring and other types of delinquency prevention programs offered in group settings, particularly for high-risk youths, may end up causing more harm than good. By participating in these types of programs in groups, young people who are more chronically involved in delinquency may negatively affect those who are marginally involved in delinquency.[42] An evaluation of JUMP found significant reductions in risk in three critical areas: aggressive behavior/delinquency, peer relationships, and mental health.[43]

Effectiveness of Mentoring. The overall effectiveness of mentoring in preventing delinquency is reported in two comprehensive reviews of the literature. In one systematic review and meta-analysis that included 18 mentoring programs, British

Mentoring is one of many types of interventions that have been used with teens considered to be at high risk for engaging in delinquent acts. These two juniors at North High School in Evansville, Indiana, are part of a mentor program to help incoming freshmen.

TABLE 11.1 Risk Factors of Young People in the Juvenile Mentoring Program (JUMP)

	Percentage of Enrolled Youth*	
Risk Domain	Male (n = 3,592)	Female (n = 3,807)
School problems	74.6%	63.0%
School behavior	39.5	23.5
Poor grades	53.6	45.9
Truancy	10.4	9.1
Social/family problems	51.7	56.4
Delinquency	17.7	8.5
Fighting	12.8	6.3
Property crime	2.8	0.5
Gang activity	3.0	1.0
Weapons	1.1	0.4
Alcohol use	3.2	1.5
Drug use	4.0	1.8
Tobacco use	2.3	1.9
Pregnancy/early parenting	0.2	1.5

*Percentage of total JUMP enrollment for each gender. For 23 youths, no gender was reported in the database.

Source: Laurence C. Novotney, Elizabeth Mertinko, James Lange, and Tara Kelly Baker, *Juvenile Mentoring Program: A Progress Review* (Washington, DC: *OJJDP Juvenile Justice Bulletin*, 2000), p. 5.

criminologists Darrick Jolliffe and David Farrington found that the average effect across the studies corresponded to a significant 10 percent reduction in delinquency.[44] The authors also found that mentoring was more effective in reducing delinquency when the average duration of each contact between mentor and mentee was greater, in smaller scale studies, and when mentoring was combined with other interventions. A second systematic review and meta-analysis by Patrick Tolan and his colleagues examined the effects of mentoring on a wide range of areas, including delinquency, academic achievement, drug use, and aggression.[45] The review included 39 programs, some of which were included in the first review. The authors found that mentoring had a positive effect in all four areas, but the largest effects involved reductions in delinquency and aggression.

It is important to note that not all mentoring programs are effective in preventing delinquency. Why is it that some work and not others? The biggest issue has to do with what the mentors actually do and how they do it. Mentors should be a source of support and guidance to help young people deal with a broad range of issues that have to do with their family, school, and future career. They work one-on-one with young people, in many cases forming strong bonds. Care is taken in matching the mentor and young person. Other research on effective mentoring relationships between adults and teens points to the need for the mentors to display empathy, pay particular attention to and nurture the strengths of the young person, and treat them "as a person of equal worth and value."[46]

School Programs

Schools are a critical social context for delinquency prevention efforts, from the early to later grades.[47] (See Chapter 9.) All schools work to produce vibrant and productive members of society. The school's role in preventing delinquency in general, which is the focus of this section, differs from measures taken to make the school a safer place. In this case, a school may adopt a greater security orientation and implement such measures as metal detectors, police in school, and closed-circuit television cameras.

Schools may not be able to reduce delinquency single-handedly, but a number of viable alternatives to their present operations could aid a communitywide effort to reduce the problem of juvenile crime. A comprehensive review of school-based programs was conducted by Denise Gottfredson and her colleagues as part of a study to determine the best methods of delinquency prevention. Some of their findings are contained in Exhibit 11.2. The main difference between the programs that work and those that do not is that successful programs target an array of important risk factors.

Often it is not enough to improve only the school environment or only the family environment; for example, a youth who has a troubled family life may find it more difficult to do well at school, regardless of the improvements made at school. Some effective school-based delinquency prevention programs also show that greater gains are made with those who are at the highest risk for future delinquency. An evaluation of Peace-Builders, a school-based violence prevention program for young and older children, found that decreases in aggression and improvements in social competence were larger for the highest-risk kids compared to those at medium and low levels of risk.[48] School-based programs also need to be intensive; two or three sessions a semester often does not cut it. Two additional components of successful school-based delinquency prevention programs—especially in the later grades—are improving the family environment by engaging parents in helping the student to learn, and reducing negative peer influences through information about the downsides of gun carrying, drug use, and gang involvement.

Job Training

The effects of having an after-school job can be problematic (see Chapter 3). Some research indicates that it may be associated with delinquency and substance abuse. However, helping kids to prepare for the adult workforce is an important aspect of

> **EXHIBIT 11.2** **School-Based Delinquency Prevention Programs**
>
> **What Works?**
> - Programs aimed at building school capacity to initiate and sustain innovation
> - Programs aimed at clarifying and communicating norms about behaviors by establishing school rules, improving the consistency of their enforcement (particularly when they emphasize positive reinforcement of appropriate behavior), or communicating norms through school-wide campaigns (for example, anti-bullying campaigns) or ceremonies
> - Comprehensive instructional programs that focus on a range of social competency skills (such as developing self-control and skills in stress management, responsible decision making, social problem solving, and communication) and that are delivered over a long period of time to continually reinforce skills
>
> **What Does Not Work?**
> - Instructional programs that do not focus on social competency skills or do not make use of cognitive-behavioral teaching methods
>
> **What Is Promising?**
> - Programs that group youths into smaller "schools within schools" to create smaller units, more supportive interactions, or greater flexibility in instruction
> - Classroom or instructional management
>
> Source: Denise C. Gottfredson, David B. Wilson, and Stacy Skroban Najaka, "School-Based Crime Prevention," in *Evidence-Based Crime Prevention*, ed. Lawrence W. Sherman, David P. Farrington, Brandon C. Welsh, and Doris Layton MacKenzie (New York: Routledge, 2006, rev. ed.).

delinquency prevention. Job training programs play an important role in improving the chances of young people obtaining jobs in the legal economy and thereby may reduce delinquency.[49] The developmental stage of transition to work is difficult for many young people.[50] Coming from a disadvantaged background, having poor grades in school or perhaps dropping out of school, and having some involvement in delinquency can all pose difficulties in securing a steady, well-paying job in early adulthood. Programs like the two described here are concerned not only with providing young people with employable skills, but also with helping them overcome some of these immediate obstacles.

Job Corps. The best-known and largest job training program in the United States is Job Corps, which was established in 1964 as a federal training program for disadvantaged, unemployed youths. The designers of the national program, the Department of Labor, were hopeful that spin-off benefits in the form of reduced dependence on social assistance and a reduction in delinquency would occur as a result of empowering at-risk youth to achieve stable, long-term employment opportunities. The program is still active today, operating out of 124 centers across the nation, and each year provides services to more than 100,000 young people at a cost of over $1.5 billion.[51]

The main goal of Job Corps is to improve the employability of participants by offering a comprehensive set of services that largely includes vocational skills training, basic education (the ability to obtain graduate equivalent degrees), and health care. Job Corps is provided to young people between the ages of 16 and 24 years. Most of the young people enrolled in the program are at high risk for delinquency, substance abuse, and social assistance dependency. Almost all of the Job Corps centers require the participants to live there while taking the program.

A large-scale evaluation of Job Corps, involving 15,400 young people, found that participation in the program resulted in significant reductions in criminal activity, improvements in educational attainment, and greater earnings. Program

Job Corps is a national program serving more than 100,000 at-risk young people each year. It seeks to help them improve their vocational skills and education, find sustainable jobs, serve their communities, and avoid lives of crime. Pictured here are teen Job Corps students removing graffiti from the Tatum Waterway near Biscayne, Florida.

WWW

To learn more about **Job Corps**, visit the Criminal Justice Course-Mate at CengageBrain.com, then access the Web Links for this chapter.

participants had an average arrest rate of 29 percent compared to 33 percent for their control counterparts. An analysis of tax data showed that earnings gains were sustained for the oldest participants eight years after they had left the program.[52] An earlier evaluation of Job Corps found it to be a worthwhile investment of public resources: for each dollar that was spent on the program, $1.45 was saved to government or taxpayers, crime victims, and program participants.[53] A later analysis of the program's costs and benefits also found it to be a worthwhile investment of public resources, saving society at large $2 for each dollar spent on the program.[54]

YouthBuild U.S.A. Another job training program for disadvantaged, unemployed youths is YouthBuild U.S.A. Started in 1978 by a group of young people in New York City, YouthBuild has become a national program with offices in 45 states, Washington, D.C., and the Virgin Islands. Since 1994, it has helped more than 100,000 youths between the ages of 16 and 24 years in the 273 programs across the country.[55] The program's focus is on building or renovating affordable housing—more than 20,000 units have been built since 1994—and through this young people learn skills in carpentry and construction. YouthBuild also provides educational services—for example, to achieve a high school diploma or prepare for college—and promotes the development of leadership skills. The program's impact on delinquency varies from site to site, with some sites reporting reductions as high as 40 percent among youths enrolled in the program compared to similar youths who did not receive the program.[56] The latest, most rigorous evaluation of YouthBuild so far, which involved an 18-month follow-up after the completion of the program, reports significant reductions in offending and improvements in educational attainment (graduating from high school or obtaining a GED) for those who graduated from the program compared to those who dropped out.[57]

CHECKPOINTS

LO3 Be familiar with effective delinquency prevention programs for teens.

✔ Mentoring programs are playing an increasingly important role in preventing delinquency in the community.

✔ There are a number of effective school programs for elementary, middle, and high school students.

✔ Job Corps is an effective job training program for youths that has also shown reductions in juvenile crime.

CHECKPOINTS

JUVENILE JUSTICE TODAY

Today the juvenile justice system exercises jurisdiction over two distinct categories of offenders—delinquents and status offenders.[58] *Delinquent children* are those who fall under a jurisdictional age limit, which varies from state to state, and who commit an act in violation of the penal code. *Status offenders* are commonly characterized in state statutes as persons or children in need of supervision (PINS or CHINS). Most states distinguish such behavior from delinquent conduct to lessen the effect of any stigma on children as a result of their involvement with the juvenile court. In addition, juvenile courts generally have jurisdiction over situations involving conduct directed at (rather than committed by) juveniles, such as parental neglect, deprivation, abandonment, and abuse.

The states have also set different maximum ages below which children fall under the jurisdiction of the juvenile court. Most states (and the District of Columbia) include all children under 18, others set the upper limit at 17, and still others include children under 16 (see Table 11.2).

Today's juvenile justice system exists in all states by statute. Each jurisdiction has a juvenile code and a special court structure to accommodate children in trouble. Nationwide, the juvenile justice system consists of thousands of public and private agencies, with a total budget amounting to billions of dollars. Most of the nation's police agencies have juvenile components, and there are more than 3,000 juvenile courts and about an equal number of juvenile correctional facilities.

Figure 11.2 depicts the numbers of juvenile offenders removed at various stages of the juvenile justice process. These figures do not take into account the large number of children who are referred to community diversion and mental health programs. There are thousands of these programs throughout the nation. This multitude of agencies and people dealing with juvenile delinquency has led to the development of what professionals view as an incredibly expansive and complex system.

The Juvenile Justice Process

How are children processed by the juvenile justice system?[59] Most children come into the justice system as a result of contact with a police officer. When a juvenile commits a serious crime, the police are empowered to make an arrest. Less serious offenses may also require police action, but in these instances, instead of being arrested, the child may be warned or a referral may be made to a social service program. About two-thirds (68 percent) of all children arrested are referred to the

---

TABLE 11.2 **Oldest Age for Juvenile Court Jurisdiction in Delinquency Cases**

Age	State (Total Number)
15	New York, North Carolina (2)
16	Georgia, Illinois, Louisiana, Massachusetts, Michigan, Missouri, New Hampshire, South Carolina, Texas, Wisconsin (10)
17	Alabama, Alaska, Arizona, Arkansas, California, Colorado, Connecticut, Delaware, Florida, Hawaii, Idaho, Indiana, Iowa, Kansas, Kentucky, Maine, Maryland, Minnesota, Mississippi, Montana, Nebraska, Nevada, New Jersey, New Mexico, North Dakota, Ohio, Oklahoma, Oregon, Pennsylvania, Rhode Island, South Dakota, Tennessee, Utah, Vermont, Virginia, Washington, West Virginia, Wyoming (38 and the District of Columbia)

Source: Linda Szymanski, "Upper and Lower Age of Delinquency Jurisdiction," *NCJJ Snapshot*, 16(7) (Pittsburgh: National Center for Juvenile Justice, 2011).

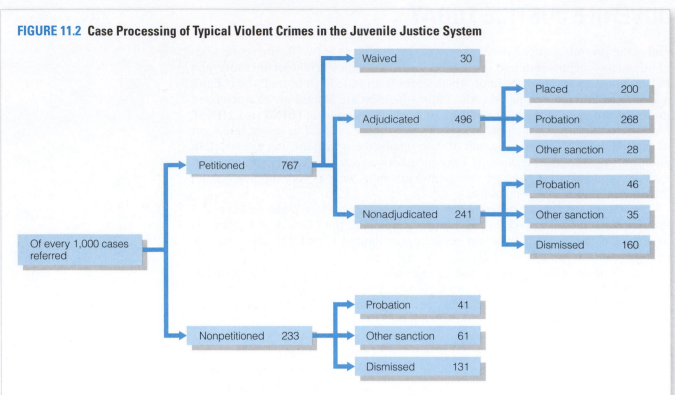

FIGURE 11.2 Case Processing of Typical Violent Crimes in the Juvenile Justice System

Note: Cases are categorized by their most severe or restrictive sanction. Detail may not add to totals because of rounding.

Source: Office of Juvenile Justice and Delinquency Prevention, *OJJDP Statistical Briefing Book*, May 1, 2012, http://ojjdp.gov/ojstatbb/court/JC-SCF_Display.asp?ID=qa06603 (accessed August 17, 2012).

juvenile court.[60] Figure 11.3 outlines the **juvenile justice process** and a detailed analysis of this process is presented in the next sections.

Police Investigation. When youths commit a crime, police have the authority to investigate the incident and decide whether to release the youths or commit them to the juvenile court. This is often a discretionary decision, based not only on the nature of the offense, but also on conditions existing at the time of the arrest. Such factors as the seriousness of the offense, the child's past contacts with the police, and whether the child denies committing the crime determine whether a petition is filed. As you may recall, juveniles in custody today have constitutional rights similar to those of adult offenders. They are protected against unreasonable search and seizure under the Fourth and Fourteenth Amendments of the Constitution. The Fifth Amendment places limitations on police interrogation procedures.

Detention. If the police decide to file a petition, the child is referred to juvenile court. The primary decision at this point is whether the child should remain in the community or be placed in a detention facility or in shelter care (temporary foster homes, detention boarding homes, programs of neighborhood supervision). In the past, children were routinely held in detention facilities to await court appearances. Normally, a **detention hearing** is held to determine whether to remand the child to a shelter. At this point, the child has a right to counsel and other procedural safeguards. A child who is not detained is usually released to a parent or guardian. Most state juvenile court acts provide for a child to return home to await further court action, except when it is necessary to protect the child, when the child presents a serious danger to the public, or when it is not certain that the child will return to court. In many cases, the police will refer the child to a community service program instead of filing a formal charge.

juvenile justice process Under the parens patriae philosophy, juvenile justice procedures are informal and nonadversarial, invoked for juvenile offenders rather than against them. A petition instead of a complaint is filed, courts make findings of involvement or adjudication of delinquency instead of convictions, and juvenile offenders receive dispositions instead of sentences.

detention hearing A hearing by a judicial officer of a juvenile court to determine whether a juvenile is to be detained or released while proceedings are pending in the case.

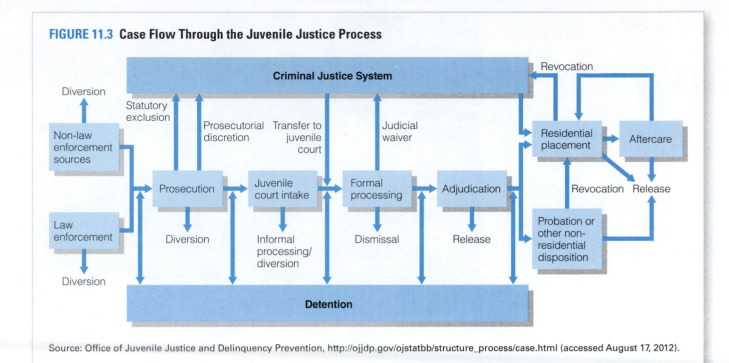

FIGURE 11.3 Case Flow Through the Juvenile Justice Process

Source: Office of Juvenile Justice and Delinquency Prevention, http://ojjdp.gov/ojstatbb/structure_process/case.html (accessed August 17, 2012).

Pretrial Procedures. In most jurisdictions, the adjudication process begins with some sort of hearing. At this hearing, juvenile court rules normally require that juveniles be informed of their right to a trial, that the plea or admission be voluntary, and that they understand the charges and consequences of the plea. The case will often not be further adjudicated if a child admits to the crime at the initial hearing.

In some cases, youths may be detained at this stage pending a trial. Juveniles who are detained are eligible for bail in a handful of jurisdictions. Plea bargaining may also occur at any stage of the proceedings. A plea bargain is an agreement between the prosecution and the defense by which the juvenile agrees to plead guilty for certain considerations, such as a lenient sentence. This issue is explored more thoroughly in Chapter 13, which discusses pretrial procedures.

If the child denies the allegation of delinquency, an **adjudicatory hearing** or trial is scheduled. Under extraordinary circumstances, a juvenile who commits a serious crime may be waived to adult court. Today, most jurisdictions have laws providing for such transfers. Whether such a transfer occurs depends on the type of offense, the youth's prior record, the availability of treatment services, and the likelihood that the youth will be rehabilitated in the juvenile court system.

Adjudication. Adjudication is the trial stage of the juvenile court process. If the child does not admit guilt at the initial hearing and is not waived to an adult court, the adjudication hearing is held to determine the facts of the case. The court hears evidence on the allegations in the delinquency petition. This is a trial on the merits (dealing with issues of law and facts), and rules of evidence similar to those of criminal proceedings generally apply. At this stage, the juvenile offender is entitled to many of the procedural guarantees given adult offenders. These include the right to counsel, freedom from self-incrimination, the right to confront and cross-examine witnesses, and in certain instances, the right to a jury trial. In addition, many states have their own procedures concerning rules of evidence, competence of witnesses, pleadings, and pretrial motions. At the end of the adjudicatory hearing, the court enters a judgment against the juvenile.

Disposition. If the adjudication process finds the child guilty, the court must decide what should be done to treat the child. Most juvenile court acts require a dispositional hearing separate from the adjudication. This two-stage decision is

adjudicatory hearing The fact-finding process wherein the juvenile court determines whether there is sufficient evidence to sustain the allegations in a petition.

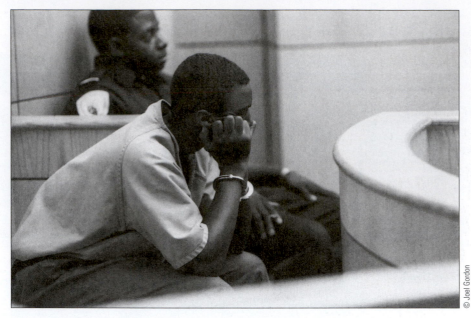

Many critical decisions are made before a juvenile trial begins. Known as pretrial procedures, they range from the juvenile entering a plea to the judge making a decision on detention or the prosecution filing a motion to waive the juvenile to adult court. Here, a handcuffed teen awaits a preliminary hearing in juvenile court at the Juvenile Justice Center, part of the Ninth Judicial Circuit Court of Florida in Orlando.

often referred to as a **bifurcated process**. The dispositional hearing is less formal than adjudication. Here, the judge imposes a **disposition** on the offender in light of the offense, the youth's prior record, and his or her family background. The judge can prescribe a wide range of dispositions, ranging from a reprimand to probation to institutional commitment. In theory, the judge's decision serves the best interests of the child, the family, and the community.

Treatment. After disposition in juvenile court, delinquent offenders may be placed in some form of correctional treatment. Probation is the most commonly used formal sentence for juvenile offenders, and many states require that a youth fail on probation before being sent to an institution (unless the criminal act is extremely serious). Probation involves placing the child under the supervision of the juvenile probation department for the purpose of community treatment. Because of the importance of probation to the juvenile justice system, we discuss the career of one juvenile probation officer in the accompanying Professional Spotlight feature.

The most severe of the statutory dispositions available to the juvenile court involves commitment of the child to an institution. The committed child may be sent to a state training school or a private residential treatment facility. These are usually minimum-security facilities with small populations and an emphasis on treatment and education. Some states, however, maintain facilities with populations of over 1,000 youths. Currently there are more than 70,000 youths in some form of correctional institution in the United States.[61]

Some jurisdictions allow for a program of juvenile aftercare or parole. A youth can be paroled from an institution and placed under the supervision of a parole officer. This means that he or she will complete the period of confinement in the community and receive assistance from the parole officer in the form of counseling, school referral, and vocational training.

Juveniles who are committed to treatment programs or control programs have a legal right to treatment. States are required to provide suitable rehabilitation programs that include counseling, education, and vocational services. Appellate courts have ruled that if such minimum treatment is not provided individuals must be released from confinement.

bifurcated process The procedure of separating adjudicatory and dispositionary hearings so different levels of evidence can be heard at each.

disposition For juvenile offenders, the equivalent of sentencing for adult offenders; juvenile dispositions should be more rehabilitative than retributive.

PROFESSIONAL SPOTLIGHT

© Carla Stalnaker

Carla Stalnaker
Juvenile Probation Officer

Carla Stalnaker is a juvenile probation officer at the Fourth Judicial Circuit Court in Clinton County, Illinois. She chose this career because she has always been interested in working with adolescents in some capacity. Stalnaker believes that adolescents are at a pivotal point in life to make positive life changes. They are old enough to have the cognitive skills necessary for making positive change and they are young enough that their habits are changeable.

Stalnaker prepared for her career by first getting a bachelor's degree in psychology with a specialization in adolescent development. Prior to becoming a juvenile probation officer, she worked for eight years in a long-term residential group home for behavior disordered and developmentally delayed youth. She points to this experience as the key to preparing her to be a juvenile probation officer.

For Stalnaker, the most rewarding part of being a juvenile probation officer is having the ability to help youths who are overlooked or pushed aside by society. Many times these young people are labeled as the "bad kids," so they tend to become lost and hopeless. She feels very strongly that these youths need someone to provide appropriate discipline, support, and reinforcement to help them get on the right path.

What does Stalnaker feel is the biggest challenge in her job? She says it is the lack of sufficient funding. There are many programs and services available to youths that provide much needed treatment and support. However, there is rarely (if ever) funding to be able to access these programs and services. She finds it especially difficult to cope with this issue. Another challenge is the parent component of juvenile probation. While the youth committed the offense, the role of the parents is crucial in both why their son or daughter committed the offense and putting a plan in place to best help them.

Stalnaker finds that there are a number of important misconceptions about a job in juvenile probation. One is that juvenile probation eventually sends all the offenders to jail, boot camp, or tries to scare kids straight. This could not be further from the truth. Another misconception is that youths on probation are all "bad kids." Yet another misconception is that the probation department has unlimited resources. Importantly, it is doing a far better job at targeting resources and connecting youths to the services they need so that they will stay out of trouble once they leave probation.

© Joel Gordon

Although juvenile offenders have a legal right to treatment, is correctional treatment more rhetoric than reality? Many experts argue that there is more punishment than rehabilitation in juvenile treatment programs. Shown here are juveniles adjudicated as adults who are enrolled in a GED residential youthful offender program in Orange County, California.

Conflicting Values in Juvenile Justice. This overview of the juvenile justice process hints at the often-conflicting values at the heart of the system. Efforts to ensure that juveniles are given appropriate treatment are consistent with the doctrine of *parens patriae* that predominated in the first half of the twentieth century. Over the past century, the juvenile court has struggled to provide treatment for juvenile offenders while guaranteeing them constitutional due process. But the system has been so overwhelmed by the increase in violent juvenile crime and family breakdown that some judges and politicians have suggested abolishing the juvenile system. Even those experts who want to retain an independent juvenile court have called for its restructuring. Crime-control advocates want to reduce the court's jurisdiction over juveniles charged with serious crimes and liberalize the prosecutor's ability to try them in adult courts. In contrast, child advocates suggest that the court scale back its judicial role and transfer its functions to community groups and social service agencies.[62] **CHECKPOINTS**

Looking Back to Martin's Story

Some might argue that Martin's disposition, which included a drug and alcohol assessment, family therapy, community service, and community supervision, was too lenient given the nature of his offense.

CRITICAL THINKING Assess if this was an appropriate treatment consistent with *parens patriae*.

CHECKPOINTS

LO4 Know how children are processed by the juvenile justice system.

✔ There are a number of stages in the juvenile justice process, beginning with police investigation.

✔ One critical decision is whether a child should be detained prior to trial.

✔ The adjudicatory hearing is the trial stage of the process.

✔ If a juvenile is found to be delinquent, a proper sentence, or disposition, must be found.

Criminal Justice versus Juvenile Justice

The components of the adult and juvenile criminal processes are similar. However, the juvenile system has a separate organizational structure. In many communities, juvenile justice is administered by people who bring special skills to the task. Also, more kinds of facilities and services are available to juveniles than to adults.

One concern of the juvenile court reform movement was to make certain that the stigma attached to a convicted offender would not be affixed to young people in juvenile proceedings. Thus, even the language used in the juvenile court differs from that used in the adult criminal court. Juveniles are not indicted for a crime; they have a **petition** filed against them. Secure pretrial holding facilities are called *detention centers* rather than jails. Similarly, the criminal trial is called a *hearing* in the juvenile justice system. Exhibit 11.3 compares the two systems.

A COMPREHENSIVE JUVENILE JUSTICE STRATEGY

At a time when much attention is focused on serious juvenile offenders, a comprehensive strategy has been called for to deal with all aspects of juvenile crime. This strategy focuses on delinquency prevention and expanding options for handling juvenile offenders. It addresses the links among crime and poverty, child abuse, drugs, weapons, and school behavior. Programs are based on a continuum of care that begins in early childhood and progresses through late adolescence. The components of this strategy include prevention in early childhood; intervention for at-risk teenage youths; graduated sanctions to hold juvenile offenders accountable for crimes; proper utilization of detention and confinement; and placement of serious juvenile offenders in adult courts.[63] There are many expected benefits from the use of this comprehensive strategy, including fewer youths entering the juvenile justice system, decreased costs of juvenile corrections, and fewer delinquents becoming adult offenders.[64] Proponents of this strategy have called for an expanded framework that focuses on youths facing a wider range of problem behaviors, including mental health, school, and drug use problems, and a greater integration of services across juvenile justice, child welfare, and other youth-serving agencies.[65]

petition Document filed in juvenile court alleging that a juvenile is a delinquent, a status offender, or a dependent and asking that the court assume jurisdiction over the juvenile.

EXHIBIT 11.3 Similarities and Differences Between Juvenile and Adult Justice Systems

Since its creation, the juvenile justice system has sought to maintain its independence from the adult justice system. Yet there are a number of similarities and differences that characterize the institutions, processes, and law of the two systems.

Similarities

- Police officers, judges, and correctional personnel use discretion in decision making in both the adult and the juvenile systems.
- The right to receive *Miranda* warnings applies to juveniles as well as to adults.
- Juveniles and adults are protected from prejudicial lineups or other identification procedures.
- Similar procedural safeguards protect juveniles and adults when they make an admission of guilt.
- Prosecutors and defense attorneys play equally critical roles in juvenile and adult advocacy.
- Juveniles and adults have the right to counsel at most key stages of the court process.
- Pretrial motions are available in juvenile and criminal court proceedings.
- Negotiations and plea bargaining exist for juvenile and adult offenders.
- Juveniles and adults have a right to a hearing and an appeal.
- The standard of evidence in juvenile delinquency adjudications, as in adult criminal trials, is proof beyond a reasonable doubt.
- Juveniles and adults can be placed on probation by the court.
- Both juveniles and adults can be placed in pretrial detention facilities.
- Juveniles and adults can be kept in detention without bail if they are considered dangerous.
- After trial, both can be placed in community treatment programs.
- Juveniles and adults can be required to undergo drug testing.
- Boot camp correctional facilities are now being used for both juveniles and adults.

Differences

- The primary purposes of juvenile procedures are protection and treatment. With adults, the aim is to punish the guilty.
- Age determines the jurisdiction of the juvenile court. The nature of the offense determines jurisdiction in the adult system. Juveniles can be ordered to the criminal court for trial as adults.
- Juveniles can be apprehended for acts that would not be criminal if they were committed by an adult (status offenses).
- Juvenile proceedings are not considered criminal; adult proceedings are.
- Juvenile court procedures are generally informal and private. Those of adult courts are more formal and are open to the public.
- Courts cannot release identifying information about a juvenile to the press, but they must release information about an adult.
- Parents are highly involved in the juvenile process but not in the adult process.
- The standard of arrest is more stringent for adults than for juveniles.
- Juveniles are released into parental custody. Adults are generally given the opportunity for bail.
- Juveniles have no constitutional right to a jury trial. Adults have this right. Some state statutes provide juveniles with a jury trial.
- Juveniles can be searched in school without probable cause or a warrant.
- A juvenile's record is generally sealed when the age of majority is reached. The record of an adult is permanent.
- A juvenile court cannot sentence juveniles to county jails or state prisons; these are reserved for adults.

Prevention

Research has identified an array of early risk factors that may suggest future delinquency. For young children, some of the most important risk factors include low intelligence and attainment, impulsiveness, poor parental supervision, parental conflict, and living in crime-ridden and deprived neighborhoods.[66] A number of early childhood programs have been shown to be effective in tackling these risk factors and preventing delinquency and later criminal offending, including preschool intellectual enrichment, child skills training, parent management training, and parent education programs such as home visiting.[67] Some of these programs can pay back program costs and produce substantial monetary benefits for the government and taxpayers.[68] As discussed earlier, recent research also shows that the general public is highly supportive of delinquency prevention programs and is even willing to pay more in taxes for these programs compared to punitive options like military-style boot camps and prison.

There are also a number of promising federal early childhood programs. Head Start provides children in poverty with, among other things, an enriched educational environment to develop learning and cognitive skills to be better prepared for the early school years. One study found that children who attended Head Start at ages 3 to 5 were significantly less likely to report being arrested or referred to court for a crime by ages 18 to 30 compared to their siblings who did not attend the program.[69] Smart Start is designed to make sure children are healthy before starting school. State-funded home-visiting programs like those in Hawaii and Colorado are especially concerned with reducing child abuse and neglect and bettering the lives of at-risk families and their children.[70]

Intervention

Intervention programs focus on teenage youths considered to be at higher risk for engaging in petty delinquent acts, using drugs or alcohol, or associating with antisocial peers.[71] Interventions at this stage are designed to ward off involvement in more serious delinquency. Many jurisdictions are developing intervention programs for teenage youths. An example is the Big Brothers/Big Sisters program, which matches a volunteer adult with a youngster.[72] Another example is CASASTART or the Center on Addiction and Substance Abuse's Striving Together to Achieve Rewarding Tomorrows.[73] This program was set up to help improve the lives of young people at high risk for delinquency, gang involvement, substance abuse, and other problem behaviors. It was delivered to a large number of young people in poor and high-crime neighborhoods in five cities across the country. It involved a wide range of preventive measures, including case management and family counseling, family skills training, tutoring, mentoring, after-school activities, and community policing. The program was different in each neighborhood. A study of all five cities showed that one year after the program ended the young people who received the program, compared to a control group, were less likely to have committed violent delinquent acts and to have used or sold drugs. Some of the other beneficial results for those in the program included less association with delinquent peers, less peer pressure to engage in delinquency, and more positive peer support.[74]

Graduated Sanctions

Another solution being explored by states across the country is graduated sanctions. Types of graduated sanctions include immediate sanctions for nonviolent offenders (these consist of community-based diversion and day treatment); intermediate sanctions, such as probation and electronic monitoring, which target repeat minor offenders and first-time serious offenders; and secure institutional care, which is reserved for repeat serious offenders and violent offenders. The philosophy behind this approach is to limit the most restrictive sanctions to the most dangerous offenders, while increasing restrictions and intensity of treatment services as offenders move from minor to serious offenses.[75]

Institutional Programs

Another key to a comprehensive strategy is improving institutional programs. Many experts believe that juvenile incarceration is overused, particularly for nonviolent offenders. That is why the concept of *deinstitutionalization*—removing as many youths from secure confinement as possible—was established by the Juvenile Justice and Delinquency Act of 1974. Considerable research supports the fact that warehousing juveniles without proper treatment does little to deter criminal behavior. The most effective secure corrections programs are those that provide individual services for a small number of participants.[76]

Alternative Courts

New venues of juvenile justice that provide special services to youths while helping to alleviate the case flow problems that plague overcrowded juvenile courts are being implemented across the United States. For example, as of 2010 (latest data available) there were 457 juvenile **drug courts** (another 51 are in the planning process) operating in 49 states and the District of Columbia, Guam, and Northern Mariana Islands.[77] These special courts have jurisdiction over the burgeoning number of cases involving substance abuse and trafficking. Although juvenile drug courts operate under a number of different frameworks, the aim is to place nonviolent first offenders into intensive treatment programs rather than in a custodial institution.[78]

In a **systematic review** and **meta-analysis** of the effects of drug courts, Ojmarrh Mitchell and his colleagues found that drug courts are an effective alternative crime control measure to reducing recidivism rates among drug-involved offenders. Of the 154 independent evaluations included in the review, only 34 (22 percent) were of juvenile drug courts.[79] This small number is explained, in part, by the relatively recent interest of juvenile justice agencies in experimenting with drug courts.[80] The findings of the 34 juvenile drug court evaluations show that this is an effective intervention for reducing juvenile recidivism, but the effects are substantially smaller compared to adult drug courts.[81] A long-term follow-up of juveniles who successfully completed drug court in Tennessee found that their involvement in adult crime was lower for felonies but not for misdemeanors.[82]

Teen courts, also called youth courts, are another alternative to traditional forms of juvenile court that has received increased attention of late in an effort to relieve overcrowding and provide a more effective response to reducing recidivism. The Prevention/Intervention/Treatment feature discusses this alternative. **CHECKPOINTS**

Looking Back to Martin's Story

Martin's case may have benefited from the application of the comprehensive juvenile justice strategy.

CRITICAL THINKING Beginning with the intervention component, examine how the different components could help him get back on track and avoid further contact with the juvenile and adult systems.

WWW

The Bureau of Justice **Drug Court Clearinghouse Project** at American University serves as a national clearinghouse for drug court information and activity. For more information, visit the Criminal Justice CourseMate at CengageBrain.com, then access the Web Links for this chapter.

In teen courts, which are increasingly being used across the country as alternatives to traditional forms of juvenile courts, young people rather than adults determine the disposition in a case. Shown here is the swearing-in ceremony for participants at Onslow County's teen court annual training session in Jacksonville, North Carolina.

AP Photo/The Daily News/Randy Davey

drug courts Courts whose focus is providing treatment for youths accused of drug-related acts.

systematic review A type of review that uses rigorous methods for locating, appraising, and synthesizing evidence from prior evaluation studies.

meta-analysis A statistical technique that synthesizes results from prior evaluation studies.

teen courts Courts that make use of peer juries to decide nonserious delinquency cases.

Teen Courts

To relieve overcrowding and provide an alternative to traditional forms of juvenile courts, jurisdictions across the country are now experimenting with teen courts, also called youth courts. These differ from other juvenile justice programs because young people rather than adults determine the disposition in a case. Cases handled in these courts typically involve young juveniles (ages 10 to 15) with no prior arrest records who are being charged with minor law violations, such as shoplifting, vandalism, and disorderly conduct. Usually, young offenders are asked to volunteer to have their case heard in a teen court instead of the more formal court of the traditional juvenile justice system.

As in a regular juvenile court, teen court defendants may go through an intake process, a preliminary review of charges, a court hearing, and disposition. In a teen court, however, other young people are responsible for much of the process. Charges may be presented to the court by a 15-year-old "prosecutor." Defendants may be represented by a 16-year-old "defense attorney." Other youths may serve as jurors, court clerks, and bailiffs. In some teen courts, a youth "judge" (or panel of youth judges) may choose the best disposition or sanction for each case. In a few teen courts, teens even determine whether the facts in a case have been proven by the prosecutor (similar to a finding of guilt). Offenders are often ordered to pay restitution or perform community service. Some teen courts require offenders to write formal apologies to their victims; others require offenders to serve on a subsequent teen court jury.

Although decisions are made by juveniles, adults are also involved in teen courts. They often administer the programs, and they are usually responsible for essential functions, such as budgeting, planning, and personnel. In some programs, adults act as the judges.

Proponents of teen court argue that the process takes advantage of one of the most powerful forces in the life of an adolescent—the desire for peer approval and the reaction to peer pressure. According to this argument, youths respond better to prosocial peers than to adult authority figures. Teen courts offer at least four potential benefits:

- *Accountability.* Teen courts may help to ensure that young offenders are held accountable for their illegal behavior, even when their offenses are relatively minor and would not likely result in sanctions from the traditional juvenile justice system.
- *Timeliness.* An effective teen court can move young offenders from arrest to sanctions within a matter of days rather than the months that may pass with traditional juvenile courts. This rapid response may in-

crease the positive impact of court sanctions, regardless of their severity.
- *Cost savings.* Teen courts usually depend heavily on youth and adult volunteers. If managed properly, they may handle a substantial number of offenders at relatively little cost to the community.
- *Community cohesion.* A well-structured and expansive teen court program may affect the entire community by increasing public appreciation of the legal system, enhancing community–court relationships, encouraging greater respect for the law among youths, and promoting volunteerism among both adults and youths.

The teen court movement is one of the fastest growing delinquency intervention programs in the country, with more than 1,050 of these courts in operation in 49 states and the District of Columbia, serving an estimated 110,000 to 125,000 young offenders each year; another 100,000 youths benefit from their participation as volunteers. Some recent evaluations (but not all) of teen courts have found that they did not "widen the net" of justice by handling cases that in the absence of the teen court would have been subject to a lesser level of processing. Also, in the OJJDP Evaluation of Teen Courts Project, which covered four states—Alaska, Arizona, Maryland, and Missouri—and compared 500 first-time offending youths referred to teen court with 500 similar youths handled by the regular juvenile justice system, it was found that six-month recidivism rates were lower for those who went through the teen court program in three of the four jurisdictions. Importantly, in these three teen courts, the six-month recidivism rates were under 10 percent. Similar findings were reported in a rigorous evaluation of a teen court in Florida, and in one for repeat offenders in Washington State. However, other recent evaluations of teen courts in Kentucky, New Mexico, and Delaware indicate that short-term recidivism rates range from 25 percent to 30 percent. A couple of recent evaluations report no effects or gender differences in effects on delinquency. The conclusions from the OJJDP teen court evaluation may be the best guide for future experimentation with teen courts:

> Teen courts and youth courts may be preferable to the normal juvenile justice process in jurisdictions that do not, or cannot, provide meaningful sanctions for all young, first-time juvenile offenders. In jurisdictions that do not provide meaningful sanctions and services for these offenders, youth court may still perform just as well as a more traditional, adult-run program.

THE FUTURE OF DELINQUENCY PREVENTION AND JUVENILE JUSTICE

The National Research Council and Institute of Medicine's Panel on Juvenile Crime expressed alarm over an increasingly punitive juvenile justice system and called for a number of changes to uphold the importance of treatment for juveniles. One of their recommendations is particularly noteworthy:

> The federal government should assist the states through federal funding and incentives to reduce the use of secure detention and secure confinement, by developing community-based alternatives. The effectiveness of such programs both for the protection of the community and the benefit of the youth in their charge should be monitored.[83]

Although calling for reforms to the juvenile justice system was a key element of this national panel's final report, panel members were equally—and perhaps more—concerned with the need to prevent delinquency before it occurs and intervene with at-risk children and adolescents. As previously discussed, there is growing public support for prevention and intervention programs designed to reduce delinquency,[84] not to mention a high level of public disapproval for abolishing the juvenile justice system in favor of a harsher, criminal justice response.[85] The panel also called attention to the need for more rigorous experimentation with prevention and intervention programs with demonstrated success in reducing risk factors associated with delinquency.[86] Some states, such as Washington, have begun to incorporate a research-based approach to guide juvenile justice programming and policy.[87]

It should be noted that there is some, albeit limited, evidence that points to a slowdown of sorts in recent years in a get-tough approach toward juvenile offenders. In an analysis of state juvenile transfer laws, Patrick Griffin reports that there has been a considerable reduction in the number of states that have expanded their transfer provisions. At the same time, very few states have reversed their restrictive transfer laws.[88]

Those who support the juvenile justice concept believe it is too soon to write off the rehabilitative ideal that has always underpinned the separate treatment of juvenile offenders. They note that fears of a juvenile crime wave are misplaced and that the actions of a few violent children should not mask the needs of millions who can benefit from solicitous treatment rather than harsh punishments. And although a get-tough approach may be able to reduce the incidence of some crimes, economic analysis indicates that the costs incurred by placing children in more punitive secure facilities outweigh the benefits accrued in crime reduction.[89]

CHECKPOINTS

LO5 Understand the key elements of a comprehensive juvenile justice strategy.

✔ Prevention and intervention are key components to keeping youths out of the juvenile justice system.

✔ Graduated sanctions are designed to increase in intensity and control for the most serious juvenile offenders.

✔ Almost all of the states are experimenting with juvenile drug courts and peer-run teen courts.

SUMMARY

Prevention is distinguished from control or repression in that prevention seeks to reduce the risk factors for delinquency before antisocial behavior or delinquency becomes a problem. Delinquency control programs, which involve the juvenile justice system, intervene in the lives of juvenile offenders with the aim of preventing the occurrence of future delinquent acts.

There are a number of different ways to classify or organize delinquency prevention programs, including the public health approach and the developmental perspective. Key features of the developmental perspective of delinquency prevention include: targeting of risk factors and the promotion of protective factors; provision of services to children and families; and programs provided over the life course.

Some of the most effective delinquency prevention programs for children and teens include: home visits for new mothers; parent training; enriched preschool programs; school-based programs that are intensive, cognitive-oriented, and targeted on high-risk kids; mentoring; and job training. Many of these programs also show positive results in reducing other problem behaviors, such as substance abuse, and leading to improvements in other areas of life, such as educational achievement, health, and employment. These benefits often translate into substantial cost savings for the government and taxpayers.

The juvenile justice process consists of a series of steps: police investigation; intake procedure in the juvenile court; pretrial procedures used for juvenile offenders; and adjudication, disposition, and postdispositional procedures.

There are conflicting values in contemporary juvenile justice. Some experts want to get tough with young criminals, while others want to focus on treatment. Crime-control advocates want to reduce the court's jurisdiction over juveniles charged with serious crimes and liberalize the prosecutor's ability to try them in adult courts. Child advocates suggest that the court scale back its judicial role and transfer its functions to community groups and social service agencies.

A comprehensive juvenile justice strategy has been developed to preserve the need for treatment services for juveniles while at the same time using appropriate sanctions to hold juveniles accountable for their actions. Elements of this strategy include delinquency prevention, intervention programs, graduated sanctions, improvement of institutional programs, and treating juveniles like adults. New courts, such as drug courts and teen courts, are used extensively across the nation.

The future of delinquency prevention and the juvenile justice system continues to be debated. A number of state jurisdictions are revising their juvenile codes to restrict eligibility in the juvenile justice system and to remove the most serious offenders. At the same time, there are some promising signs, such as juvenile crime rates being lower than in decades past, public support for prevention and intervention programs, and some states beginning to incorporate research-based initiatives to guide delinquency prevention and juvenile justice programming and policy.

KEY TERMS

delinquency control or delinquency repression, p. 300

delinquency prevention, p. 300

risk factor, p. 301

protective factor, p. 301

randomized controlled experiment, p. 305

juvenile justice process, p. 314

detention hearing, p. 314

adjudicatory hearing, p. 315

bifurcated process, p. 316

disposition, p. 316

petition, p. 318

drug courts, p. 321

systematic review, p. 321

meta-analysis, p. 321

teen courts, p. 321

QUESTIONS FOR REVIEW

1. What are the most important risk factors that early delinquency prevention programs should target?

2. What does public opinion research conclude about delinquency prevention?

3. List the key factors behind the effectiveness of the Nurse-Family Partnership program.

4. How do you explain why some mentoring programs work and others do not?

5. What is the intake procedure in juvenile court?

6. Does the right to receive the *Miranda* warning apply to juveniles?

7. What does the research evidence say about juvenile drug courts?

8. What are some of the potential benefits of teen courts?

QUESTIONS FOR DISCUSSION

1. Prevention and control are the two broad-based approaches that can be used to reduce delinquency. How do these approaches differ?

2. What are some of the benefits of implementing prevention programs in childhood compared to adolescence?

3. Many programs have been successful in preventing delinquency, but many have not been successful. What are some of the reasons why a program may fail to reduce delinquency?

4. The formal components of the criminal justice system are often considered to be the police, the court, and the correctional agency. How do these components relate to the major areas of the juvenile justice system? Is the operation of justice similar in the juvenile and adult systems?

5. What are some of the potential advantages as well as disadvantages of the comprehensive juvenile justice strategy?

APPLYING WHAT YOU HAVE LEARNED

Fourteen-year-old Daphne, a product of the city's best private schools, lives with her wealthy family in a fashionable neighborhood. Her father is an executive at a local financial services conglomerate and earns close to a million dollars per year. Daphne, however, is always in trouble at school, and teachers report she is impulsive and has poor self-control. At times she can be kind and warm, but on other occasions she is obnoxious, unpredictable, insecure, and demanding of attention. She is overly self-conscious about her body and has a drinking problem.

Despite repeated promises to get her life together, Daphne likes to hang out at night in a local park, drinking with neighborhood kids. On more than one occasion she has gone to the park with her friend Chris, a quiet boy with his own personal problems. His parents have separated and he is prone to severe anxiety attacks. He has been suspended from school, and diagnosed with depression, for which he takes two drugs—an antidepressant and a sedative.

One night, the two meet up with Michael, a 44-year-old man with a long history of alcoholism. After a night of drinking, a fight breaks out and Michael is stabbed, his throat cut, and his body dumped in a pond. Soon after the attack, Daphne calls 911, telling police that a friend "jumped in the lake and didn't come out." Police search the area and find the slashed and stabbed body in the water; the body had been disemboweled in an attempt to sink it. When the authorities trace the call, Daphne is arrested, and she confesses to police that she helped Chris murder the victim.

During an interview with court psychiatrists, Daphne admits she participated in the killing, but cannot articulate what caused her to get involved. She had been drinking and remembers little of the events. She says she was flirting with Michael, and Chris stabbed him in a jealous rage. She speaks in a flat, hollow voice and shows little remorse for her actions. It was a spur-of-the-moment thing, she claims, and after all, it was Chris who had the knife and not she. Later, Chris claims that Daphne instigated the fight, egged him on, taunting him that he was too scared to kill someone. Chris says that Daphne, while drunk, often talked of killing an adult because she hates older people, especially her parents.

If Daphne is tried as a juvenile, she can be kept in institutions until she is 17; the sentence could be expanded to age 21, but only if she is a behavior problem in custody and demonstrates conclusive need for further secure treatment.

Writing Assignment: Write an essay explaining how the concept of *parens patriae* applies in the case of Daphne. Also, give your assessment of what reforms are needed to aid the juvenile justice system in treating adolescents like her.

GROUPWORK

Divide the class into five or more groups and assign each group one of the five components of the comprehensive juvenile justice strategy: prevention, intervention, graduated sanctions, institutional programs, and alternative courts. Have each group identify up to 10 reasons to support how their component can contribute to greater reductions in serious offending in the teenage years as well as early adulthood.

Police Work with Juveniles

CHAPTER OUTLINE

© Jeff Greenberg/Alamy

Policewoman talks to youth at Florida Miami Drug Free Youth In Town Annual HS Summit.

LEARNING OBJECTIVES

After reading this chapter you should:

1. Be able to identify key historical events that have shaped juvenile policing in America today.

2. Understand key roles and responsibilities of the police in responding to juvenile offenders.

3. Understand key legal aspects of police work and how they apply to juveniles.

4. Be able to describe police use of discretion and factors that influence discretion.

5. Be familiar with the major policing strategies to prevent delinquency.

Rico's Story

Rico grew up in Harlem, one of 12 children raised primarily by their mother, a strong and determined African American woman who struggled daily to provide for the basic needs and safety of her family. Rico's father, a man of Puerto Rican descent, was heavily involved in criminal activity and drifted in and out of their lives for brief periods of time.

Rico attended a large New York public high school with approximately 8,000 students. Violence and gang activity were common in both his community and in the school setting; sexual assaults took place in school stairwells, fights occurred on a daily basis, young drug dealers did business in the hallways, and there had been murders in school. Rico found it difficult to focus on academics with such chaos and fear all around him. The school, like many in the area, enlisted the assistance of the New York City Police Department in an effort to create a safer learning environment. Eight full-time uniformed and armed police officers patrolled the school daily. They had the ability and discretion to arrest on site and to intervene as needed, and they worked in collaboration with the educators and administrators to reduce violence and crime on school grounds. In the lunchroom, halls, and school auditorium, police officers were dressed in full uniform and acted clearly as authority figures. The officers also worked hard to be approachable and friendly to the students. They made efforts to have relationships with the students so that they could be a resource during challenging times.

Rico was a brilliant and gifted young man who, despite being in some trouble during his younger years, aspired to go to college and make a better life for himself. Several of his teachers encouraged him in his studies and although he was thriving academically, he needed a safer environment where he could focus on his education.

During his freshman year, Rico and some other students were playing cards in front of the school during a lunch break when another student threw a glass bottle at Rico's head and threatened his life. Rico went after the young man and a fight ensued. The police at the school intervened to stop the fight and address the young men's behavior. Although both teens could have been arrested for disorderly conduct or battery, Rico explained to them that he was defending himself, and the officers agreed. Knowing he was an excellent student who did not typically engage in this type of conduct, the officers chose to talk with Rico and try to encourage him in a more positive direction, rather than arresting him.

After graduating from high school, Rico attended the University of Cincinnati on a full athletic scholarship for football and track, and he also became a member of the U.S. Boxing Team. Upon completing his undergraduate degree, Rico attended medical school. Today he is Dr. Richard Larkin, professor at a community college in Illinois. In addition to crediting the New York Police Department and his teachers for their efforts, he credits his mother's hard work, strict discipline, and tremendous drive for his success.

HISTORY OF JUVENILE POLICING

Providing specialized police services for juveniles is a relatively recent phenomenon. At one time, citizens were responsible for protecting themselves and maintaining order.

The origin of police agencies can be traced to early English society.[1] Before the Norman Conquest, the **pledge system** assumed that neighbors would protect each other from thieves and warring groups. Individuals were entrusted with policing themselves and resolving minor problems. By the thirteenth century, however, the **watch system** was created to police larger communities. Men were organized in church parishes to patrol areas at night and guard against disturbances and breaches of the peace. This was followed by establishment of the constable, who was responsible for dealing with more serious crimes. By the seventeenth century, the constable, the justice of the peace, and the night watchman formed the nucleus of the police system in England.

pledge system Early English system in which neighbors protected each other from thieves and warring groups.

watch system Replaced the pledge system in England; watchmen patrolled urban areas at night to provide protection from harm.

Modern policing began in England. This nineteenth-century photo shows Tom Smith, a well-known "peeler." English policemen became known as peelers in reference to Home Secretary Sir Robert Peel, who organized the police force in 1829. They were also referred to as "bobbies" after their creator—a name that has stuck to the present day.

WNW

The website for the **London Metropolitan Police** contains descriptions of famous and lesser known cases from 1829 to the present day, as well as biographies of key figures. To learn more, visit the Criminal Justice Course-Mate at CengageBrain.com, then access the Web Links for this chapter.

When the Industrial Revolution brought thousands of people from the countryside to work in factories, the need for police protection increased. As a result, the first organized police force was established in London in 1829. The British "bobbies" (so called after their founder, Sir Robert Peel) were not successful at stopping crime and were influenced by the wealthy for personal and political gain.[2]

In the American colonies, the local sheriff became the most important police official. By the mid-1800s, city police departments had formed in Boston, New York, and Philadelphia. Officers patrolled on foot, and conflicts often arose between untrained officers and the public.

When children violated the law, they were often treated the same as adult offenders. But even at this stage a belief existed that the enforcement of criminal law should be applied differently to children. (See Chapter 1 for more on the development of the concept of a separate status of childhood in America.)

During the late nineteenth century and into the first half of the twentieth, the problem of how to deal with growing numbers of unemployed and homeless youths increased. Groups such as the Wickersham Commission of 1931 and the International Association of Chiefs of Police became the leading voices for police reform.[3] Their efforts resulted in the creation of specialized police units, known as *delinquency control squads*.

The most famous police reformer of the 1930s was August Vollmer. As the police chief in Berkeley, California, Vollmer instituted numerous reforms, including university training, modern management techniques, and prevention programs, as well as juvenile aid bureaus.[4] These bureaus were the first organized police services for juvenile offenders.

In the 1960s, policing entered a turbulent period.[5] The U.S. Supreme Court handed down decisions designed to restrict police operations and discretion. Civil unrest produced growing tensions between police and the public. Urban police departments were unable to handle the growing crime rate. Federal funding from the Law Enforcement Assistance Administration (LEAA), an agency set up to fund justice-related programs, was a catalyst for developing hundreds of new police programs and enhancing police services for children. By the 1980s, most urban police departments recognized that the problem of juvenile delinquency required special attention.

Today, the role of the juvenile police officer—an officer assigned to juvenile work—has taken on added importance. Most of the nation's urban law enforcement agencies now have specialized juvenile police programs. Typically, such programs involve prevention (police athletic leagues, community outreach) and law enforcement work (juvenile court, school policing, gang control). Other concerns of the programs include child abuse, domestic violence, and missing children.

CHECKPOINTS

CHECKPOINTS

LO1 Be able to identify key historical events that have shaped juvenile policing in America today.

✔ Modern policing developed in England at the beginning of the nineteenth century.

✔ The Industrial Revolution, recognition of the need to treat children as a distinguishable group, and growing numbers of unemployed and homeless youths were among the key events that helped shape juvenile policing in America.

POLICE AND JUVENILE OFFENDERS

In the minds of most citizens, the primary responsibility of the police is to protect the public. Based on films, books, and TV shows that depict the derring-do of police officers, the public has obtained an image of crime fighters who always get their man. Since the 1960s, however, the public has become increasingly aware that the reality of police work is substantially different from its fictional glorification. When police departments failed to bring the crime rate down despite massive government subsidies, when citizens complained of civil rights violations, and when tales of police corruption became widespread, it was evident that a crisis was imminent in American policing.

Over the last three decades, a new view of policing has emerged. Discarding the image of crime fighters who track down serious criminals or stop armed robberies in progress, many police departments have adopted the concept that the police role should be to maintain order and be a visible and accessible component of the community. The argument is that police efforts can be successful only when conducted in partnership with concerned citizens. This movement is referred to as **community policing**.[6]

Interest in community policing does not mean that the crime-control model of law enforcement is history. An ongoing effort is being made to improve the crime-fighting capability of police agencies, and there are some indications that the effort is paying off.[7] Some research suggests that police innovation in crime-fighting techniques contributed to the substantial reduction in crime rates during the 1990s, whereas other research suggests that the reduction simply had more to do with cities hiring more police.[8]

Working with juvenile offenders may be especially challenging for police officers, because the desire to help young people and to steer them away from crime seems to conflict with the traditional police duties of crime prevention and maintenance of order. In addition, the police are faced with a nationwide adolescent drug problem and renewed gang activity. Although the need to help troubled youths may conflict with traditional police roles, it fits nicely with the newly emerging community policing models. Improving these relationships is critical, because many juveniles do not have a high regard for the police.[9] Because of its importance, this is discussed in more detail in the accompanying Focus on Delinquency box.

Police Roles

Juvenile officers operate either as specialists in a police department or as part of the juvenile unit of a police department. Their role is similar to that of officers working with adult offenders: to intervene if the actions of a citizen produce public danger or disorder. Most juvenile officers are appointed after having had some general patrol experience. A desire to work with juveniles as well as an aptitude for the work are considered essential for the job. Officers must also have a thorough knowledge of the law, especially the constitutional protections available to juveniles. Some officers undergo special training in the handling of aggressive or potentially aggressive juveniles.[10]

Most officers regard the violations of juveniles as nonserious unless they are committed by chronic troublemakers or involve significant damage to persons or property. Police encounters with juveniles are generally the result of reports made by citizens, and the bulk of such encounters pertain to matters of minor legal consequence.[11] Of course, police must also deal with serious juvenile offenders whose criminal acts are similar to those of adults, but these are a small minority of the offender population. Thus, police who deal with delinquency must concentrate on being peacekeepers and crime preventers.[12]

Handling juvenile offenders can produce major **role conflicts** for police. They may experience a tension between their desire to perform what they consider their primary duty, law enforcement, and the need to aid in the rehabilitation of youthful offenders. Police officers' actions in cases involving adults are usually controlled by the law and their own judgment or discretion. (The concept of *discretion* is discussed later in this chapter.) In contrast, a case involving a juvenile often demands that the officer consider the "best interests of the child" and how the officer's actions will influence the child's future well-being. However, in recent years police have become more likely to refer juvenile offenders to courts. It is estimated that two-thirds

community policing Police strategy that emphasizes fear reduction, community organization, and order maintenance rather than crime fighting.

juvenile officers Police officers who specialize in dealing with juvenile offenders; they may operate alone or as part of a juvenile police unit in the department.

role conflicts Conflicts police officers face that revolve around the requirement to perform their primary duty of law enforcement and a desire to aid in rehabilitating youthful offenders.

JUVENILE VIEWS ABOUT POLICE: A CALL TO ACTION

In study after study, from Phoenix to Chicago to Philadelphia, police get mixed to less-than-favorable reviews from juveniles, and minority teens are especially critical of police performance in their community. One large-scale study carried out in 11 cities across the country found that African American teens rated the police less favorably than all other racial groups for all questions asked (for example, "Are police friendly? Are police courteous?"). The most striking racial differences pertained to the question about police honesty: only 15 percent of African American youths said the police were honest. In contrast, 57 percent of European Americans, 51 percent of Asians, 31 percent of Hispanics, and 30 percent of Native Americans said they were.

Another study, carried out in Cincinnati, Ohio, focused exclusively on the attitudes of female juveniles toward the police and found similar results. Of the more than 400 female high school students interviewed, African Americans compared to their European American counterparts were significantly more likely to report having an overall negative attitude toward police. When asked about police honesty ("In general, I trust the police"), the difference was even greater: only 22 percent of African American female juveniles either agreed or strongly agreed with the statement compared to 56 percent of European American female juveniles.

(68 percent) of all juvenile arrests are referred to juvenile court, whereas 23 percent of all juvenile arrests are handled informally within the police department or are referred to a community-service agency (Figure 12.1). These informal dispositions are the result of the police officer's discretionary authority.

Police intervention in situations involving juveniles can be difficult and emotional. The officer often encounters hostile behavior from the juvenile offender, as well as agitated witnesses. Overreaction by the officer can result in a violent incident. Even if the officer succeeds in quieting or dispersing the witnesses, they will probably reappear the next day, often in the same place.[13]

Role conflicts are common because most encounters between police and juveniles are brought about by loitering and rowdiness rather than by serious law violations. Public concern has risen about out-of-control youth. Yet, because of legal constraints and family interference, the police are often limited in the ways in which they can respond to such offenders.[14]

Another role conflict arises in the use of juveniles as police **informants**. Informants are individuals who have access to criminal networks and who, under conditions of anonymity, provide information to authorities in exchange for money or special treatment.[15] Police rely on informants, both adult and juvenile, to obtain evidence to make arrests in serious cases that the police may otherwise not be able to solve, such as gun and drug trafficking. Juvenile informants are also used in less serious cases where age is important to the crime—for example, when retailers sell cigarettes or alcohol to minors. Police must balance the need to obtain evidence and the vulnerabilities of and extra safeguards that are needed for juveniles in these cases. As criminologist Mary Dodge notes, there is a need for a higher degree of scrutiny in the use of juvenile police informants, and this practice should not be warranted in all circumstances.[16]

informant A person who has access to criminal networks and shares information with authorities in exchange for money or special treatment under conditions of anonymity.

Some studies have looked specifically at the influence of police contact on juvenile perceptions toward the police. Not surprisingly, juveniles who have had prior contact with the police hold less favorable attitudes toward the police compared to their counterparts who have not had any prior contact. This is a consistent finding across studies. Less well known is what may explain this relationship. In a national study it was found that police contact, with the exception of arrest, did not predict negative attitudes toward the police when involvement in delinquent peer groups and community ties were controlled.

In addition to the importance these results hold for improving police relations with juveniles, especially minorities, in order to prevent crime, the results may also hold special significance for the reporting of crimes to the police to address juvenile victimization. Research shows that juvenile crime victims are much less likely than adult victims to contact the police. This disparity in reporting crimes to the police holds true even after taking account of a number of important factors, such as crime severity, school victimization, and reporting crimes to officials other than police.

CRITICAL THINKING

1. What are the key factors that are driving the poor views of police by minority youths?

2. What might explain the differences between male and female juveniles in their unfavorable views toward the police?

Writing Assignment It is likely that no one measure will help improve police–juvenile relations. Write an essay about the key efforts that you believe the police can adopt to help address the negative views held by young people.

Sources: Joanna M. Lee, Laurence Steinberg, and Alex R. Piquero, "Ethnic Identity and Attitudes Toward the Police Among African American Juvenile Offenders," *Journal of Criminal Justice* 38:781–789 (2010); Bradley T. Brick, Terrance J. Taylor, and Finn-Aage Esbensen, "Juvenile Attitudes Towards the Police: The Importance of Subcultural Involvement and Community Ties," *Journal of Criminal Justice* 37:488–495 (2009); Jamie L. Flexon, Arthur J. Lurigio, and Richard G. Greenleaf, "Exploring the Dimensions of Trust in the Police Among Chicago Juveniles," *Journal of Criminal Justice* 37:180–189 (2009); Kenneth Dowler and Raymond Sparks, "Victimization, Contact with Police, and Neighborhood Conditions: Reconsidering African American and Hispanic Attitudes Toward the Police," *Police Practice and Research* 9:395–415 (2008); Yolander G. Hurst, M. Joan McDermott, and Deborah L. Thomas, "The Attitudes of Girls Toward the Police: Differences by Race," *Policing* 28:578–593 (2005), pp. 585–586; Adam M. Watkins, "Examining the Disparity Between Juvenile and Adult Victims in Notifying the Police: A Study of Mediating Variables," *Journal of Research in Crime and Delinquency* 42:333–353 (2005); Terrance J. Taylor, K. B. Turner, Finn-Aage Esbensen, and L. Thomas Winfree, Jr., "'Coppin' an Attitude: Attitudinal Differences Among Juveniles Toward Police," *Journal of Criminal Justice* 29:295–305 (2001).

What role should the police play in mediating problems with youths: law enforcer or delinquency prevention worker? The answer may lie somewhere between the two. Most police departments operate juvenile programs that combine law enforcement and delinquency prevention, and the police work with the juvenile court to determine a role most suitable for their community.[17] Police officers may even act as prosecutors in some rural courts when attorneys are not available. Thus, the police role with juveniles extends from the on-the-street encounter to the station house to the courtroom. For juvenile matters involving minor criminal conduct or incorrigible behavior, the police ordinarily select the least restrictive alternative, which includes such measures as temporary assistance or referral to community agencies. In contrast, violent juvenile crime requires that the police arrest youths while providing constitutional safeguards similar to those available for adult offenders.

Police and Violent Juvenile Crime

Violent juvenile offenders are defined as those adjudicated delinquent for crimes of homicide, rape, robbery, aggravated assault, and kidnapping. Juveniles account for 13 percent of all violent crime arrests.[18] Since the mid-1990s, the juvenile violence rate has declined rather substantially, leveling off in more recent years. Many experts predicted a surge of violence as children of baby boomers entered their "prime crime" years, whereas others predicted that juvenile arrests for violent crime would double by the year 2010.[19] (See Chapter 2 for more on juvenile crime rates.)

As a result of these predictions, police and other justice agencies are experimenting with different methods of controlling violent youth. Some of these

FIGURE 12.1 Police Response to Juvenile Crime

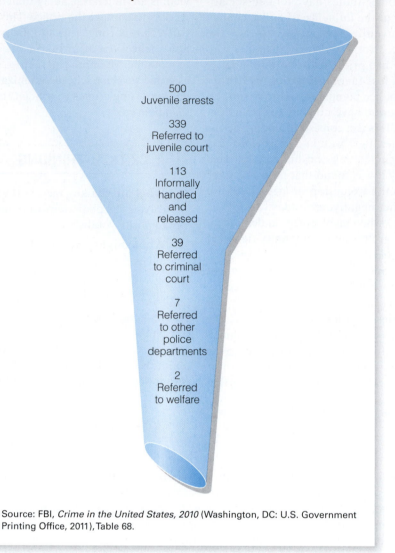

500
Juvenile arrests

339
Referred to
juvenile court

113
Informally
handled
and
released

39
Referred
to criminal
court

7
Referred
to other
police
departments

2
Referred
to welfare

Source: FBI, *Crime in the United States, 2010* (Washington, DC: U.S. Government Printing Office, 2011), Table 68.

problem-oriented policing Law enforcement that focuses on addressing the problems underlying incidents of juvenile delinquency rather than the incidents alone.

methods, such as placing more officers on the beat, have existed for decades; others rely on state-of-the-art technology to pinpoint the locations of violent crimes and develop immediate countermeasures. Research shows that there are a number of effective policing practices, including increased directed patrols in street-corner hot spots of crime, proactive arrests of serious repeat offenders, and **problem-oriented policing**.[20] These strategies address problems of community disorganization and can be effective deterrents when combined with other laws and policies, such as targeting illegal gun carrying.[21] Although many of these policing strategies are not new, implementing them as one element of an overall police plan may have an impact on preventing juvenile violence.

Finally, one key component of any innovative police program dealing with violent juvenile crime is improved communications between the police and the community. Community policing is discussed in more detail at the conclusion of this chapter. **CHECKPOINTS**

CHECKPOINTS

LO2 Understand key roles and responsibilities of the police in responding to juvenile offenders.

✔ Most modern police agencies have specialized units or officers who interface with teens.

✔ Most juvenile cases are referred to juvenile court.

✔ Police who work with juvenile offenders usually have skills and talents that go beyond those associated with regular police work.

✔ The number of police officers assigned to juvenile work has increased in recent years.

✔ Most juvenile officers are appointed after they have had some general patrol experience.

POLICE AND THE RULE OF LAW

When police are involved with the criminal activity of juvenile offenders, their actions are controlled by statute, constitutional case law, and judicial review. Police methods of investigation and control include the arrest procedure, search and seizure, and custodial interrogation.

The Arrest Procedure

When a juvenile is apprehended, the police must decide whether to release him or her or make a referral to the juvenile court. Cases involving serious crimes against property or persons are often referred to court. Less serious cases, such as disputes between juveniles, petty shoplifting, runaways, and assaults of minors, are often diverted from court action.

Most states require that the law of **arrest** be the same for both adults and juveniles. To make a legal arrest, an officer must have probable cause to believe that an offense took place and that the suspect is the guilty party. **Probable cause** is usually defined as falling somewhere between a mere suspicion and absolute certainty. In misdemeanor cases, the police officer must personally observe the crime to place a suspect in custody. For a felony, the police officer may make the arrest without having observed the crime if the officer has probable cause to believe the crime occurred and the person being arrested committed it. A felony is a serious offense; a misdemeanor is a minor or petty crime. Crimes such as murder, rape, and robbery are felonies; crimes such as petty larceny and disturbing the peace are misdemeanors.

The main difference between arrests of adult and juvenile offenders is the broader latitude police have to control youthful behavior. Most juvenile codes, for instance, provide broad authority for the police to take juveniles into custody.[22] Such statutes are designed to give the police the authority to act *in loco parentis* (Latin for "in place of the parent"). Accordingly, the broad power granted to police is consistent with the notion that a juvenile is not arrested, but rather taken into custody—which implies a protective rather than a punitive form of detention.[23] Once a juvenile is arrested, however, the constitutional safeguards of the Fourth and Fifth Amendments available to adults are applicable to the juvenile as well.

Police officers must deal with serious offenders whose violent acts are similar to those of adults, but these are a small minority of the offender population. Shown here is Javier De La Rosa and one of his defense attorneys, Rick Canales, as the sentence is read in the Cameron County State District Court in Brownsville, Texas, on May 3, 2012. Two years earlier, at age 16, De La Rosa fatally stabbed high school student Tiffany Galvan. He pleaded guilty to the murder and received a sentence of 90 years in prison.

AP Photo/*Brownsville Herald*, Brad Doherty

Most states require that the law of arrest be the same for both adults and juveniles. In this photo, Chicago police arrest a 9-year-old boy after shots were fired at the police.

© Carlos Javier Ortiz/Redux

arrest Taking a person into the custody of the law to restrain the accused until he or she can be held accountable for the offense in court proceedings.

probable cause Reasonable grounds to believe the existence of facts that an offense was committed and that the accused committed that offense.

As you may recall, there is currently a trend toward treating juvenile offenders more like adults. Related to this trend are efforts by the police to provide a more legalistic and less informal approach to the arrest process, and a more balanced approach to case disposition.[24]

Search and Seizure

Do juveniles have the same right to be free from unreasonable **search and seizure** as adults? In general, a citizen's privacy is protected by the Fourth Amendment of the Constitution, which states:

> *The right of the people to be secure in their persons, houses, papers, and effects, against unreasonable searches and seizures, shall not be violated, and no warrants shall issue, but upon probable cause, supported by oaths or affirmation, and particularly describing the place to be searched, and the persons or things to be seized.*[25]

Most courts have held that the Fourth Amendment ban against unreasonable search and seizure applies to juveniles and that illegally seized evidence is inadmissible in a juvenile trial. To exclude incriminating evidence, a juvenile's attorney makes a pretrial motion to suppress the evidence, the same procedure used in the adult criminal process.

A full discussion of search and seizure is beyond the scope of this text, but it is important to note that the Supreme Court has ruled that police may stop a suspect and search for evidence without a warrant under certain circumstances. In an important 2009 case, *Arizona v. Gant*, the Court limited a police officer's ability to search a vehicle for evidence.[26] After Rodney Gant was arrested for driving with a suspended sentence, he was handcuffed and locked in the back of a patrol car. A police officer noticed a jacket on the backseat of Gant's vehicle, searched the jacket, and found cocaine. The Court ruled that police may search a vehicle incident to a recent occupant's arrest only if the arrestee is within reaching distance of the passenger compartment at the time of the search or it is reasonable to believe the vehicle contains evidence of the offense of arrest. The search of Gant's jacket was deemed unreasonable since he could not gain access to it and the cocaine was therefore inadmissible at trial. The *Gant* case is important because controlling a suspect after arrest is critical to police safety. Some officers may now sacrifice safety concerns in order to search suspects or their vehicles.

In general, a person may be searched after a legal arrest, but then only in the immediate area of the suspect's control. For example, after an arrest for possession of drugs, the pockets of a suspect's jacket may be searched;[27] an automobile may be searched if there is probable cause to believe a crime has taken place;[28] a suspect's outer garments may be frisked if police are suspicious of his or her activities;[29] and a search may be conducted if a person volunteers for the search.[30] These rules are usually applied to juveniles as well as to adults. Concept Summary 12.1 reviews when warrantless searches are allowed.

Custodial Interrogation

In years past, police often questioned juveniles without their parents or even an attorney present. Any incriminating statements arising from such **custodial interrogation** could be used at trial. However, in the 1966 case *Miranda v. Arizona*, the Supreme Court placed constitutional limitations on police interrogation procedures with adult offenders. *Miranda* held that persons in police custody must be told the following:

- They have the right to remain silent.
- Any statements they make can be used against them.
- They have the right to counsel.
- If they cannot afford counsel, it will be furnished at public expense.[31]

search and seizure The U.S. Constitution protects citizens from any search and seizure by police without a lawfully obtained search warrant; such warrants are issued when there is probable cause to believe that an offense has been committed.

custodial interrogation Questions posed by the police to a suspect held in custody in the prejudicial stage of the juvenile justice process. Juveniles have the same rights as adults against self-incrimination when being questioned.

Action	Scope of Search
Stop-and-frisk	Pat-down of a suspect's outer garments.
Search incident to arrest	Full body search after a legal arrest.
Automobile search	If probable cause exists, full search of car, including driver, passengers, and closed containers found in trunk. Search must be reasonable.
Consent search	Warrantless search of person or place is justified if suspect knowingly and voluntarily consents to search.
Plain view	Suspicious objects seen in plain view can be seized without a warrant.
Electronic surveillance	Material can be seized electronically without a warrant if suspect has no expectation of privacy.
Home entry	A home can be entered without a warrant if there is reason to believe that evidence of a crime is being destroyed.

The *Miranda* **warning** has been made applicable to children taken into custody. The Supreme Court case of *in re Gault* stated that constitutional privileges against self-incrimination are applicable in juvenile cases too. Because *in re Gault* implies that *Miranda* applies to custodial interrogation in criminal procedure, state court jurisdictions apply the requirements of *Miranda* to juvenile proceedings as well. Since the *Gault* decision in 1967, virtually all courts that have ruled on the question of the *Miranda* warning have concluded that the warning does apply to the juvenile process. More recently (in 2011), the Supreme Court, in *J.D.B. v. North Carolina*, ruled that age does matter and that greater care must be taken by the police when questioning children in their custody.[32]

One problem associated with custodial interrogation of juveniles has to do with waiver of *Miranda* rights: Under what circumstances can juveniles knowingly and willingly waive the rights given them by *Miranda v. Arizona*? Does a youngster, acting alone, have sufficient maturity to appreciate the right to remain silent?

Most courts have concluded that parents or attorneys need not be present for children effectively to waive their rights.[33] In a frequently cited California case, *People v. Lara*, the court said that the question of a child's waiver is to be determined by the *totality of the circumstances doctrine*.[34] This means that the validity of the waiver rests not only on the age of the child, but also on a combination of other factors, including the child's education, the child's knowledge of the charge, whether the child was allowed to consult with family or friends, and the method of interrogation.[35] The general rule is that juveniles can waive their rights to protection from self-incrimination, but that the validity of this waiver is determined by the circumstances of each case.

Research by University of Minnesota law professor Barry Feld suggests that older juveniles (16- and 17-year-olds) sufficiently understand their *Miranda* rights, but younger ones do not. He argues that mandating recordings of all police interrogations would go some way toward ensuring that juveniles of all ages do in fact understand their rights and minimize the risk of false confessions, which is especially problematic among younger juveniles.[36]

The waiver of *Miranda* rights by a juvenile is one of the most controversial legal issues addressed in the state courts. It has also been the subject of federal constitutional review. In two cases, *Fare v. Michael C.* and *California v. Prysock*, the Supreme Court has attempted to clarify children's rights when they are interrogated

WW

The Public Broadcasting Services provides a detailed look at the landmark Supreme Court decision in *Miranda v. Arizona*. To learn more, visit the Criminal Justice CourseMate at CengageBrain .com, then access the Web Links for this chapter.

Miranda **warning** Supreme Court decisions require police officers to inform individuals under arrest of their constitutional rights. Warnings must also be given when suspicion begins to focus on an individual in the accusatory stage.

✔ Most states require that the law of arrest be the same for both adults and juveniles.

✔ The main difference between arrests of adult and juvenile offenders is the broader latitude police have to control youthful behavior.

✔ Most courts have held that the Fourth Amendment ban against unreasonable search and seizure applies to juveniles.

✔ Most courts have concluded that parents or attorneys need not be present for children effectively to waive their right to remain silent.

by the police. In *Fare v. Michael C.*, the Court ruled that a child asking to speak to his probation officer was not the equivalent of asking for an attorney; consequently, statements he made to the police absent legal counsel were admissible in court.[37] In *California v. Prysock*, the Court was asked to rule on the adequacy of a *Miranda* warning given Randall Prysock, a young murder suspect.[38] After reviewing the taped exchange between the police interrogator and the boy, the Court upheld Prysock's conviction when it ruled that even though the *Miranda* warning was given in slightly different language and out of exact context, its meaning was easily understandable, even to a juvenile.

Taken together, *Fare* and *Prysock* make it seem indisputable that juveniles are at least entitled to receive the same *Miranda* rights as adults. *Miranda v. Arizona* is a historic decision that continues to protect the rights of all suspects placed in custody.[39] CHECKPOINTS

DISCRETIONARY JUSTICE

Today, juvenile offenders receive nearly as much procedural protection as adult offenders. However, the police have broader authority in dealing with juveniles than with adults. Granting such **discretion** to juvenile officers raises some important questions: Under what circumstances should an officer arrest status offenders? Should a summons be used in lieu of arrest? Under what conditions should a juvenile be taken into protective custody?

When police confront a case involving a juvenile offender, they rely on their discretion to choose an appropriate course of action. *Police discretion* is selective enforcement of the law by authorized police agents. Discretion gives officers a choice among possible courses of action within the limits of their power.[40] It is a prime example of low-visibility decision making, or decisions by public officials, that the public is not in a position to regulate or criticize.[41]

Much discretion is exercised in juvenile work because of the informality that has been built into the system in an attempt to individualize justice.[42] Furthermore, officials in the juvenile justice system make decisions about children that often are without oversight or review. The daily procedures of juvenile personnel are rarely subject to judicial review, except when they clearly violate a youth's constitutional rights. As a result, discretion sometimes deteriorates into discrimination and other abuses on the part of the police. The real danger in discretion is that it allows the law to discriminate against precisely those elements in the population—the poor, the ignorant, the unpopular—who are least able to draw attention to their plight.[43]

The problem of discretion in juvenile justice is one of extremes. Too little discretion provides insufficient flexibility to treat juvenile offenders as individuals. Too much discretion can lead to injustice. Guidelines and controls are needed to structure the use of discretion.

discretion Use of personal decision making and choice in carrying out operations in the criminal justice system, such as deciding whether to make an arrest or accept a plea bargain.

Generally, the first contact a youth has with the juvenile justice system is with the police. Research indicates that most police decisions arising from this initial contact involve discretion.[44] These studies show that many juvenile offenders are never referred to juvenile court.

In a classic 1963 study, Nathan Goldman examined the arrest records of more than 1,000 juveniles from four communities in Pennsylvania.[45] He concluded that more than 64 percent of police contacts with juveniles were handled informally. Subsequent research offered additional

Looking Back to Rico's Story

In Rico's case, he did not receive any serious consequences for his actions. The police exercised their discretion.

CRITICAL THINKING Discuss the basis of the officers' decision making. Also discuss if you agree with what the officers did.

evidence of informal disposition of juvenile cases.[46] For example, in the 1970s, Paul Strasburg found that about 50 percent of all children who come in contact with the police do not get past the initial stage of the juvenile justice process.[47]

A more recent study analyzed juvenile data collected as part of the Project on Policing Neighborhoods—a comprehensive study of police patrols in Indianapolis, Indiana, and St. Petersburg, Florida. This study indicated that police still use discretion.[48] It found that 13 percent of police encounters with juveniles resulted in arrest.[49]

After arrest, the most current data show an increase in the number of cases referred to the juvenile court. The FBI estimates that two-thirds (68 percent) of all juvenile arrests are referred to juvenile court.[50] Despite the variations between the estimates, these studies indicate that the police use significant discretion in their decisions regarding juvenile offenders. Research shows that differential decision making goes on without clear guidance.

If all police officers acted in a fair and just manner, the seriousness of the crime, the situation in which it occurred, and the legal record of the juvenile would be the factors that affected their decision making. Research does show that police are much more likely to take formal action if the crime is serious and has been reported by a victim who is a respected member of the community, and if the offender is well known to them.[51] However, there are other factors that are believed to shape police discretion; they are discussed next.

Environmental Factors

How does a police officer decide what to do with a juvenile offender? The norms of the community affect the decision. Some officers work in communities that tolerate a fair amount of personal freedom. In liberal environments, the police may be inclined to release juveniles rather than arrest them. Other officers work in conservative communities that expect a no-nonsense approach to police enforcement. Here, police may be more inclined to arrest a juvenile.

Police officers may be influenced by their perception of community alternatives to police intervention. Some officers may make an arrest because they believe nothing else can be done.[52] Others may favor referring juveniles to social service agencies, particularly if they believe the community has a variety of good resources. These referrals save time and effort, records do not have to be filled out, and court appearances can be avoided. The availability of such options allows for greater latitude in police decision making.[53]

Police Policy

The policies and customs of the local police department also influence decisions. Juvenile officers may be pressured to make more arrests or to refrain from making arrests under certain circumstances. Directives instruct officers to be alert to certain types of juvenile violations. The chief of police might initiate policies governing the arrest practices of the juvenile department. For example, if local merchants complain that youths congregating in a shopping center parking lot are inhibiting business, police may be called on to make arrests. Under other circumstances, an informal warning might be given. Similarly, a rash of deaths caused by teenage drunk driving may galvanize the local media to demand police action. The mayor and the police chief, sensitive to possible voter dissatisfaction, may then demand that formal police action be taken in cases of drunk driving.

Another source of influence is pressure from supervisors. Some supervising officers may believe it is important to curtail disorderly conduct or drug use. In addition, officers may be influenced by the discretionary decisions made by their peers.

Justice in Policing. A growing body of research shows that by exercising a greater degree of fairness or **procedural justice** in making arrests and handling offenders after arrest, police can better gain offenders' cooperation as well as deter them from further involvement in criminal activity.[54] One of the first studies to assess the effect

WWW

The Office of Juvenile Justice and Delinquency Prevention provides the latest update on **trends in juvenile arrests**. To learn more, visit the Criminal Justice Course-Mate at CengageBrain.com, then access the Web Links for this chapter.

procedural justice An evaluation of the fairness of the manner in which an offender's or another group's problem or dispute was handled by police.

of police fairness on criminal offending was carried out by criminologist Ray Paternoster and his colleagues. As part of the Milwaukee domestic assault experiment, they found that men who were arrested for assaulting their female spouses were much less likely—by almost 40 percent—to commit another act of assault against their spouses if they were handled by police in a fair and just manner compared to a similar group of men who were not handled in a fair way.[55]

Perceptions of police fairness are not just limited to the arrest procedure; they include other, less formal contacts with police. In a recent study of procedural justice and order maintenance policing in St. Louis, Missouri, 45 high-risk, young male adolescents were questioned about their experiences with and perceptions of the police.[56] Thirty-five of them (or 78 percent) reported that they had been stopped and frisked by the police at least one time in their lives; many reported multiple occasions. Most of them held a negative view of this interaction, which was often accompanied by the police being "discourteous and even verbally abusive." The authors concluded that, in the absence of strict codes of conduct, the growing use of stop-and-frisks by police in inner cities across the country could substantially erode procedural justice and "undermine police legitimacy."[57] Another study reveals that youths who view the police as legitimate are more willing to assist the police.[58]

Although it is difficult to know if this research is leading police departments to implement policies on procedural fairness and train their officers appropriately, police scholars have called for more research on the subject to better understand the mechanisms that result in crime control effectiveness.[59]

Situational Factors

In addition to the environment, a variety of situational factors affect a police officer's decisions. Situational factors are those attached to a particular crime, such as specific traits of offenders. Traditionally, it was believed that police officers relied heavily on the demeanor and appearance of the juvenile in making decisions. Some research shows that the decision to arrest is often based on factors such as dress, attitude, speech, and level of hostility toward the police.[60] Kids who displayed "attitude" were believed to be the ones more likely to be arrested than those who were respectful and contrite.[61] However, more recent research has challenged the influence of demeanor on police decision making, suggesting that it is delinquent behavior and actions that occur during police detention that influence the police decision to take formal action.[62] For example, a person who struggles or touches police during a confrontation is a likely candidate for arrest, but those who merely sport a bad attitude or negative demeanor are as likely to suffer an arrest as the polite and contrite.[63] In a recent study that found that juveniles are significantly more likely to be arrested than adults, disrespectful demeanor on the part of juveniles toward police did not increase their likelihood of arrest. Disrespectful adults, on the other hand, were more likely to be arrested.[64]

It is possible that the earlier research reflected a time when police officers demanded absolute respect and were quick to take action when their authority was challenged. The more recent research may indicate that police, through training or experience, are now less sensitive to slights and confrontational behavior and view them as just part of the job. Most studies conclude that the following variables are important in the police discretionary process:

- The attitude of the complainant
- The type and seriousness of the offense
- The race, sex, and age of the offender
- The attitude of the offender
- The offender's prior contacts with the police
- The perceived willingness of the parents to assist in solving the problem (in the case of a child)
- The setting or location in which the incident occurs

- Whether the offender denies the actions or insists on a court hearing (in the case of a child)
- The likelihood that a child can be served by an agency in the community[65]

Bias and Police Discretion

Do police allow bias to affect their decisions on whether to arrest youths? Do they routinely use racial profiling when they decide to make an arrest? A great deal of debate has been generated over this issue. Some experts believe that police decision making is deeply influenced by the offender's personal characteristics, whereas others maintain that crime-related variables are more significant.

Racial Bias. It has long been charged that police are more likely to act formally with African American suspects and use their discretion to benefit European Americans.[66] In the context of traffic stops by police, the phrase "Driving While Black" has been coined to refer to the repeated findings of many studies that African American drivers are disproportionately stopped by police and that race is the primary reason for this practice.[67] As Table 12.1 shows, African American youth are arrested at a rate disproportionate to their representation in the population. Research on this issue has yielded mixed conclusions. One view is that although discrimination may have existed in the past, there is no longer a need to worry about racial discrimination because minorities now possess sufficient political status to protect them within the justice system.[68] As Harvard University law professor Randall Kennedy forcefully argues, even if a law enforcement policy exists that disproportionately affects African American suspects, it might be justified as a "public good" because law-abiding African Americans are statistically more often victims of crimes committed by other African Americans.[69]

In contrast to these views, several research efforts do show evidence of police discrimination against African American youths.[70] Donna Bishop and Charles Frazier found that race can have a direct effect on decisions made at several junctures of the juvenile justice process.[71] According to Bishop and Frazier, African Americans are more likely than European Americans to be recommended for formal processing,

TABLE 12.1 African American Representation in Arrest Statistics

Most Serious Offense	African American Juvenile Arrests in 2010 (%)
Murder	56
Forcible rape	36
Robbery	67
Aggravated assault	42
Burglary	37
Larceny/theft	32
Motor vehicle theft	42
Weapons	36
Drug abuse violations	24
Curfew and loitering	38

Note: Percentage is of all juvenile arrests.
Source: FBI, *Crime in the United States, 2010* (Washington, DC: U.S. Government Printing Office, 2011), Table 43b.

referred to court, adjudicated delinquent, and given harsher dispositions for comparable offenses. In the arrest category, specifically, being African American increases the probability of formal police action.[72] (For more on racial bias, see Chapter 2.)

Gender Bias. Is there a difference between police treatment of male and female offenders? Some experts favor the *chivalry hypothesis*, which holds that police are likely to act paternally toward young girls and not arrest them. Others believe that police may be more likely to arrest female offenders because their actions violate officers' stereotypes of the female.

There is some research support for various forms of gender bias. The nature of this bias may vary according to the seriousness of the offense and the age of the offender. Studies offer a variety of conclusions, but there seems to be general agreement that police are less likely to process females for delinquent acts and that they discriminate against them by arresting them for status offenses. Examples of the conclusions reached by some of these studies follow:

- Police tend to be more lenient toward females than males with regard to acts of delinquency. Merry Morash found that boys who engage in "typical male" delinquent activities are much more likely to develop police records than females.[73]

- Females who have committed minor or status offenses seem to be referred to juvenile court more often than males. Meda Chesney-Lind has found that adolescent female status offenders are arrested for less serious offenses than boys.[74]

- Recent evidence has confirmed earlier studies showing that the police, and most likely the courts, apply a double standard in dealing with male and female juvenile offenders. Bishop and Frazier found that both female status offenders and male delinquents are differently disadvantaged in the juvenile justice system in that, for status offenses, females are more likely to be arrested, and for other offenses, males are more likely to be arrested.[75] Chesney-Lind and Shelden report that in many other countries female teens are also more likely than male teens to be arrested for status offenses and referred to juvenile court for status offenses.[76] (Gender bias is discussed in more detail in Chapter 6.)

Organizational Bias. The policies of some police departments may result in biased practices. Research has found that police departments can be characterized by their professionalism (skills and knowledge) and bureaucratization.[77] Departments that are highly bureaucratized (with a high emphasis on rules and regulations) and at the same time unprofessional are most likely to be insulated from the communities they serve. Organizational policy may be influenced by the perceptions of police decision makers. A number of experts have found that law enforcement administrators have a stereotyped view of the urban poor as troublemakers who must be kept under control.[78]

Consequently, lower-class neighborhoods experience much greater police scrutiny than middle-class areas, and their residents face a proportionately greater chance of arrest. For example, there is a significant body of literature that shows that police are more likely to "hassle" or arrest African American males in poor neighborhoods.[79] It is therefore not surprising, as Harvard criminologist Robert Sampson has found, that teenage residents of neighborhoods with low socioeconomic status have a significantly greater chance of acquiring police records than youths living in higher socioeconomic areas, regardless of the actual crime rates in these areas.[80] Sampson's research indicates that, although police officers may not discriminate on an individual level, departmental policy that focuses on lower-class areas may result in class and racial bias in the police processing of delinquent youth. **CHECKPOINTS**

POLICE WORK AND DELINQUENCY PREVENTION

Police have taken the lead in delinquency prevention. They have used a number of strategies: some rely on their deterrent powers; others rely on their relationship with schools, the community, and other juvenile justice agencies; and others rely on a problem-solving model. Concept Summary 12.2 lists the main police strategies to prevent delinquency.

Looking Back to Rico's Story

Although controversial, especially in schools, police officer discretion is not bound by setting or place.

CRITICAL THINKING Discuss any special advantages that police have to use their discretion in school settings and how this may have been beneficial in Rico's case.

Aggressive Law Enforcement

One method of contemporary delinquency prevention relies on aggressive patrolling targeted at specific patterns of delinquency. Police departments in Chicago and Los Angeles have at one time used *saturation patrol*, targeting gang areas and arresting members for any law violations. These tactics have not proven to be effective against gangs according to the findings of a large-scale review of law enforcement and other responses to the country's gang problems.[81] Conducted by the Justice Policy Institute, the review also found that "heavy-handed suppression efforts" results in increased rather than decreased cohesion among gang members and further exacerbates the sometimes-fragile relations that exist between the police and some communities.[82]

Police in Schools

One of the most important institutions playing a role in delinquency prevention is the school (see Chapter 9). In schools across the country, there are an estimated 13,000 full-time police working as school resource officers. In addition to helping to make the school environment safe for students and teachers, school resource officers work closely with staff and administrators in developing delinquency prevention programs.[83] For example, these officers and liaison officers from schools and police departments have played a leadership role in developing recreational programs for juveniles. In some instances, police have actually operated such programs. In others, they have encouraged community support for recreational activities, including Little League baseball, athletic clubs, camping outings, and police athletic and scouting programs.

The Gang Resistance Education and Training (G.R.E.A.T.) program is one example of a police and school partnership to prevent delinquency. Modeled after D.A.R.E. (Drug Abuse Resistance Education; see Chapter 10), G.R.E.A.T. was developed among a number of Arizona police departments in an effort to reduce adolescent involvement in criminal behavior. Today the program is in school curricula in all 50 states and the District of Columbia.[84] The program's primary objective is the prevention of delinquency and gang involvement. Trained police officers administer

WWW

To learn more about **G.R.E.A.T. (Gang Resistance, Education, and Training)**, visit the Criminal Justice CourseMate at CengageBrain.com, then access the Web Links for this chapter.

CONCEPT SUMMARY 12.2	Police Strategies to Prevent Delinquency
Strategy	**Scope**
Aggressive law enforcement	High visibility; make arrests for minor and serious infractions.
Police in schools	Collaborate with school staff to create a safer school environment and develop programs.
Community policing	Engage citizens and community-based organizations.
Problem-oriented policing	Focus on problems underlying criminal incidents; often engage community and other juvenile justice agencies.

Youth gang and violence problems have given rise to many innovative police-led delinquency prevention programs. One of these is the Gang Resistance Education and Training (G.R.E.A.T.) program, which aims to reduce gang activity. Partnering with schools across the country, trained police officers and other juvenile justice officials instruct students on conflict resolution, social responsibility, and the dangers of gang life. Shown here are senior parole officer Raymond Vonderheide and Sgt. Daniel Riccardo speaking with third-grade students during a G.R.E.A.T. presentation at St. Rose of Lima School in Newark, New Jersey.

the program in school classrooms about once a week. The program consists of four components: a 13-week middle-school curriculum, a six-week elementary school curriculum, a summer program, and family training.

Evaluations of G.R.E.A.T. when it was just an eight-week program for middle-school students showed mixed results in reducing delinquency and gang involvement. One evaluation found that students who completed the curriculum developed more prosocial attitudes and had lower rates of gang membership and delinquency than those in a comparison group who were not exposed to G.R.E.A.T.[85] Another evaluation of the program, four years after students completed the curriculum, did not find any significant differences for gang membership or delinquency compared to a control group. The evaluation did find that those who took the program held more prosocial attitudes than those who were not in the program.[86] These evaluations contributed to the new and more comprehensive program, which was implemented on a national scale in 2003.

In 2006, the National Institute of Justice awarded a five-year grant to the University of Missouri–St. Louis to evaluate the new version of G.R.E.A.T. The evaluation was carried out in seven cities across the country and includes 31 public middle schools, 195 classrooms (102 received G.R.E.A.T. and 93 did not receive the program), and approximately 4,000 students. Short-term results—one year after the program ended—were very promising. Compared to the group of students who did not receive the program, G.R.E.A.T. students self-reported lower rates of gang membership and more prosocial attitudes on a range of outcomes related to the program.[87]

Another example of police working in close collaboration with schools is the Community Outreach through Police in Schools program. This program brings together Yale University's Child Study Center and the New Haven Police Department to address the mental health and emotional needs of middle-school students who

WHAT DOES THIS MEAN TO ME?

▶ **The Debate over Police in Schools** Police have long played a role in working with schools to improve their safety and prevent delinquency in the community through the organization of various programs. But some view police in schools as an infringement on students' personal freedom. Others call for greater use of police in schools, especially in those that have experienced violent incidents by students against other students and teachers.

1. Do you feel all high schools should have a police presence? What about elementary and middle schools?
2. In looking back on your high school years, can you recall an event when a school resource officer made a difference in your life or a friend's life?

have been exposed to violence in the community. Specifically, the program aims to help these students:

- Better understand the way their feelings affect their behavior
- Develop constructive means of responding to violence and trauma
- Change their attitudes toward police and learn how to seek help in their community[88]

An evaluation of the program found that students benefited from it in a number of ways, including improved emotional and psychological functioning (for example, feeling less nervous, having fewer thoughts of death), as well as improved attitudes toward and relationships with the police.[89]

Community Policing

One of the most important changes in U.S. law enforcement is the emergence of the community policing model of delinquency prevention. This concept is based on the premise that the police can carry out their duties more effectively if they gain the trust and assistance of concerned citizens. Under this model, the main police role should be to increase feelings of community safety and encourage area residents to cooperate with their local police agencies.[90]

The community policing model has been translated into a number of policy initiatives. It has encouraged police departments to get officers out of patrol cars, where they were insulated from the community, and onto the streets via foot or bicycle patrol.[91] The official survey of policing in the United States—the Law Enforcement Management and Administrative Statistics (LEMAS) survey—reports that 47 percent of local police departments have full-time community policing officers. Across the country, local police departments employ about 47,000 community policing officers.[92] However, the use of community policing officers has decreased in recent years. Between 2000 and 2007 (the most recent data available), the percentage of local police departments using community policing officers was lower, sometimes substantially, in all sizes of cities, from rural to large urban, with 54 percent fewer community policing officers overall.[93] The main reason for this has been a dramatic reduction in federal funding.

The federal Office of Community Oriented Policing Services (COPS) is involved in a number of initiatives to reduce gun violence by serious juvenile offenders.[94] One of these initiatives is Project Safe Neighborhoods, which brings together federal, state, and local law enforcement, prosecutors, and community leaders to deter and punish gun crime.[95]

Efforts are being made by police departments to involve citizens in delinquency control. Community policing is a philosophy that promotes community, government, and police partnerships that address juvenile crime, as well as adult crime.[96] Although there is not a great deal of evidence that these efforts can lower crime rates,[97] they do seem to be effective methods of improving perceptions of community safety and the quality of community life,[98] and involving citizens in the juvenile justice network. Under the community policing philosophy, prevention programs may become more effective crime control measures. Programs that combine the reintegration of youths into the community after institutionalization with police surveillance and increased communication are vital for improving police effectiveness with juveniles.

Problem-Oriented Policing

Also referred to as *problem-solving policing*, problem-oriented policing involves a systematic analysis and response to the problems or conditions underlying criminal incidents rather than the incidents themselves.[99] The theory is that by attending to the underlying problems that cause criminal incidents, the police will have a greater chance of preventing the crimes from recurring—the main problem with reactive or "incident-driving policing."[100] However, as noted by Harvard criminologist Mark Moore, "This is not the same as seeking out the root causes of the crime problem in general. It is a much shallower, more situational approach."[101]

WWW

To learn about other **community policing programs,** visit the Criminal Justice CourseMate at CengageBrain.com, then access the Web Links for this chapter.

The systematic nature of problem-oriented policing is characterized by its adherence to a four-step model, often referred to as SARA, which stands for scanning, analysis, response, and assessment. Descriptions of the four steps are as follows:

1. *Scanning* involves identifying a specific crime problem through various data sources (for example, victim surveys, 911 calls).
2. *Analysis* involves carrying out an in-depth analysis of the crime problem and its underlying causes.
3. *Response* brings together the police and other partners to develop and implement a response to the problem based on the results produced in the analysis stage.
4. *Assessment* is the stage in which the response to the problem is evaluated.[102]

Like community policing, problem-oriented policing is viewed as a proactive delinquency prevention strategy. Unlike community policing, however, the engagement of the community in problem-oriented policing is not imperative, but more often than not these operations involve close collaborations with the community. Collaborations with other juvenile justice agencies, such as probation, are also common in problem-oriented policing operations.[103]

As you may recall, problem-oriented policing has been shown to be effective in reducing juvenile delinquency in some circumstances.[104] A number of successful practices resulted in the federal COPS office initiating a national Problem-Solving Partnership (PSP) program with the objective of assisting police agencies to "solve recurrent crime and disorder problems by helping them form community partnerships and engage in problem-solving activities."[105] Various case studies to emerge out of a national evaluation of this program by the Police Executive Research Forum identify a wide range of successful efforts to reduce delinquency.[106] The COPS Office also initiated a series of guides to aid police in addressing specific crime problems, with one focusing on underage drinking[107] and another on gun violence among serious young offenders.[108]

Closely related to problem-oriented policing is another strategy commonly referred to as **pulling levers policing**. It is described as a highly focused deterrence strategy that involves communicating to offenders direct and explicit messages about the responses they can expect if certain illegal behavior (e.g., gun violence) is not ceased.[109] One of the most successful applications of this policing strategy is Boston's Operation Ceasefire,[110] which is the subject of this chapter's Prevention/Intervention/Treatment feature.

Today, many experts consider delinquency prevention efforts to be crucial to the development of a comprehensive approach to youth crime. Although such efforts cut across the entire juvenile justice system, police programs have become increasingly popular. CHECKPOINTS

WWW

To learn about other **problem-oriented policing programs**, visit the Criminal Justice CourseMate at CengageBrain.com, then access the Web Links for this chapter.

CHECKPOINTS

LO5 Be familiar with the major policing strategies to prevent delinquency.

✔ Police departments have used aggressive saturation patrol, targeting gang areas and arresting members for any law violations.

✔ Prevention programs between the police and the schools have been implemented in many communities.

✔ Police are now identifying the needs of youth in the community and helping the community meet those needs.

✔ Problem-oriented or problem-solving policing, which very often involves community groups and other juvenile justice agencies, is an innovative and successful approach to preventing delinquency.

✔ Many experts consider police-based delinquency prevention efforts to be crucial to the development of a comprehensive approach to youth crime

FUTURE OF JUVENILE POLICING

Many challenges confront the police response to juvenile offending today and will continue to do so in the years to come. Witness intimidation, charges of racial profiling, and poor relations with some communities and groups of young people who are distrustful of the police are some of the key challenges. The police are making progress in dealing with many of these and other challenges, and in the years ahead it will be even more important that the police implement greater transparency in their operations, be more accountable to those they serve, especially young people, and exercise a greater degree of fairness or procedural justice in arresting juvenile offenders and handling them after arrest. It is very likely that future success in controlling as well as preventing juvenile offending will come to depend even more on these factors.

pulling levers policing A focused deterrence strategy that involves applying all available measures or "levers" to police as well as communicating with offenders to reduce a targeted delinquent problem.

JUVENILE DELINQUENCY

Pulling Levers Policing

Closely related to problem-oriented policing, pulling levers policing is about activating or pulling every deterrent "lever" available to reduce the targeted delinquency problem. If it is juvenile gang violence, responses may include shutting down drug markets, serving warrants, enforcing probation restrictions, and making disorder arrests. Also important to this approach is communicating direct and explicit messages to offenders about the responses they can expect if this behavior is not stopped.

In a recent systematic review and meta-analysis of pulling levers policing, Anthony Braga and David Weisburd found that it is an effective approach to reducing a wide range of crime problems, including homicides, gang violence, gun assaults, and illegal drug possession. The review included 11 high-quality studies of programs from across the country, including Los Angeles, Chicago, Indianapolis, and Newark.

One of the most successful examples of this policing strategy is in Boston. Known as Operation Ceasefire, this program aims to reduce youth homicide victimization and youth gun violence. Although it is a police-led program, Operation Ceasefire involves many other juvenile and criminal justice and social agencies, including probation and parole, the Bureau of Alcohol, Tobacco, Firearms, and Explosives (ATF), gang outreach and prevention street workers, and the Drug Enforcement Administration (DEA). (This is another key component of the pulling levers approach.) This group of agencies has become known as the Ceasefire Working Group.

The program has two main elements:

- A direct law enforcement focus on illicit gun traffickers who supply youth with guns
- An attempt to generate a strong deterrent to gang violence

A wide range of measures have been used to reduce the flow of guns to youths, including pooling the resources of local, state, and federal justice authorities to track and seize illegal guns, and targeting traffickers of the types of guns most used by gang members. The response to gang violence has been equally comprehensive. The Ceasefire Working Group delivered its message clearly to gang members: "We're ready, we're watching, we're waiting: Who wants to be next?"

An evaluation from before the program started to the time it ended showed a 63 percent reduction in the mean monthly number of youth homicide victims across the city. The program was also associated with significant decreases in the mean monthly number of gun assaults and overall gang violence across the city. In a comparison with other New England cities and large cities across the United States, most of which also experienced a reduction in youth homicides over the same period, it was found that the significant reduction in youth homicides in Boston was due to Operation Ceasefire.

Maintaining the level of intensity of this program and the cooperation of the many agencies involved, which are essential ingredients of its success, has not been easy. In recent years, there have been cutbacks in local policing, fewer federal criminal justice resources made available to the program, and a perception that the deterrence strategy is no longer focused on the most dangerous suspects. Recent research suggests that in order for the program to maintain its success it will also have to adapt to changes in the nature of gang and youth violence across the city.

The Los Angeles Operation Ceasefire took place in the Hollenbeck area, which suffers from exceptionally high rates of gang-related gun violence. Organized by 19 public and private agencies, it too was designed to send gang members the message that serious consequences would result for all gang members if guns were used. The researchers found that the intervention was most effective in reducing gun crimes during the suppression phase, with slightly smaller effects evidenced in the deterrence phase. As with Boston, the long-term success of the Los Angeles initiative will depend on sufficient resources, continued collaboration among the many participating agencies, and the ability to adapt to changing conditions in gang behavior.

Critical Thinking

1. What is the importance of having a multidisciplinary team as part of the program?
2. With comprehensive programs it is often difficult to assess the independent effects of the different program elements. In your opinion, what is the most important element of this program? Why?

Sources: Anthony A. Braga and David Weisburd, "The Effects of Focused Deterrence Strategies on Crime: A Systematic Review and Meta-Analysis of the Empirical Evidence," *Journal of Research in Crime and Delinquency*, 49:323–358 (2012); George E. Tita, K. Jack Riley, Greg Ridgeway, and Peter W. Greenwood, *Reducing Gun Violence: Operation Ceasefire in Los Angeles* (Washington, DC: National Institute of Justice, 2005); Jack McDevitt, Anthony A. Braga, Dana Nurge, and Michael Buerger, "Boston's Youth Violence Prevention Program: A Comprehensive Community-Wide Approach," in *Policing Gangs and Youth Violence*, ed. Scott H. Decker (Belmont, CA: Wadsworth, 2003); Anthony A. Braga, David M. Kennedy, Elin J. Waring, and Anne Morrison Piehl, "Problem-Oriented Policing, Deterrence, and Youth Violence: An Evaluation of Boston's Operation Ceasefire," *Journal of Research in Crime and Delinquency* 38:195–225 (2001); David M. Kennedy, "Pulling Levers: Chronic Offenders, High-Crime Settings, and a Theory of Prevention," *Valparaiso University Law Review* 31:449–484 (1997).

The integration of "soft" and "hard" technologies into police work with juveniles will also become more important in the years to come. Soft technology involves information technology (IT) systems to enhance police operational and administrative decision making, such as in analyses of city crime patterns and deployment of resources to the most crime-prone areas.[111] Hard technology involves nonlethal weapons, such as the Taser or stun gun, and other alternative weapons systems used by police.[112] Increasingly, the police are also turning to various forms of surveillance technology, such as closed-circuit television (CCTV), to deter juvenile and other crime in public places. Although evaluations have shown CCTV systems to be rather ineffective in reducing crime, real-time communication links between police and CCTV operators and their use in high-crime areas may improve effectiveness.[113]

As we have seen throughout this chapter, some new approaches to policing juvenile delinquency show promising results in reducing serious offenses, such as gang activity and gun crimes. These include community-based policing services, police in schools, and—one of the most successful approaches—problem-oriented policing. Versions of Operation Ceasefire in Boston, which brought together a broad range of juvenile justice and social agencies and community groups and produced substantial reductions in youth violence, are now being replicated in other cities across the country. With the research evidence demonstrating that targeted problem-solving policing strategies of this type are the most effective in reducing serious urban crime problems,[114] continued use of these strategies holds much promise in maintaining record low rates of juvenile violence.

SUMMARY

Modern policing developed in England at the beginning of the nineteenth century. The Industrial Revolution, recognition of the need to treat children as a distinguishable group, and growing numbers of unemployed and homeless youths were among the key events that helped shape juvenile policing in America.

The role of juvenile officers is similar to that of officers working with adult offenders: to intervene if the actions of a citizen produce public danger or disorder. Juvenile officers must also have a thorough knowledge of the law, especially the constitutional protections available to juveniles. Juvenile officers operate either as specialists in a police department or as part of the juvenile unit of a police department. The organization of juvenile work depends on the size of the police department, the kind of community in which the department is located, and the amount and quality of resources available in the community.

Most courts have held that the Fourth Amendment ban against unreasonable search and seizure applies to juveniles and that illegally seized evidence is inadmissible in a juvenile trial. Most courts have concluded that parents or attorneys need not be present for children effectively to waive their right to remain silent.

Discretion is a low-visibility decision made in the administration of adult and juvenile justice. Discretionary decisions are made without guidelines from the police administrator. Numerous factors influence the decisions police make about juvenile offenders, including the seriousness of the offense, the harm inflicted on the victim, and the likelihood that the juvenile will break the law again. Problems with discretion include discrimination, unfairness, and bias toward particular groups of juveniles.

The major policing strategies to prevent delinquency include aggressive law enforcement, police in schools, community policing, and problem-oriented policing. Innovation in policing strategies can address the ever-changing nature of juvenile delinquency. Tailoring policing activities to local conditions and engaging the community and other stakeholders show promise in reducing delinquency. Saturation patrols that include targeting gang areas and arresting members for any law violations have not proven to be effective against gangs. Maintaining the level of intensity and cooperation of the many agencies involved in problem-oriented policing strategies, which are essential to their success, is not easy and requires sustainable funding.

KEY TERMS

pledge system, p. 327
watch system, p. 327
community policing, p. 329
juvenile officers, p. 329
role conflicts, p. 329

informant, p. 330
problem-oriented policing, p. 332
arrest, p. 333
probable cause, p. 333
search and seizure, p. 334

custodial interrogation, p. 334
Miranda warning, p. 335
discretion, p. 336
procedural justice, p. 337
pulling levers policing, p. 344

QUESTIONS FOR REVIEW

1. When were the first police departments formed in American cities?

2. What are some of the major role conflicts that police may experience in dealing with juvenile offenders?

3. Discuss how police currently deal with juvenile offenders; for example, what percent of juvenile arrests are referred to juvenile court?

4. What conditions must be met for an officer to make an arrest for a felony offense?

5. When can the police conduct warrantless searches?

6. Explain procedural justice and give an example of how it is used by the police.

7. What does the research say about police discrimination against minority youths?

8. What are the four steps that serve as the foundation to problem-oriented policing?

QUESTIONS FOR DISCUSSION

1. The term *discretion* is often defined as selective decision making by police and others in the juvenile justice system who are faced with alternative modes of action. Discuss some of the factors affecting the discretion of the police when dealing with juvenile offenders.

2. What role should police organizations play in delinquency prevention and control? Is it feasible to expect police departments to provide social services to children and families? How could police departments be better organized to provide for the control of juvenile delinquency?

3. What qualities should a juvenile police officer have? Should a college education be a requirement?

4. Can the police and community be truly effective in forming a partnership to reduce juvenile delinquency? Discuss the role of the juvenile police officer in preventing and investigating juvenile crime.

5. The experience of Boston's successful Operation Ceasefire program suggests that it may be difficult to sustain the needed intensity and problem-solving partnerships to keep violent juvenile crime under control over the long term. What other innovative problem-oriented policing measures could be employed to achieve this?

APPLYING WHAT YOU HAVE LEARNED

You are a newly appointed police officer assigned to a juvenile unit of a medium-size urban police department. Wayne is an 18-year-old European American male who was caught shoplifting with two male friends of the same age. Wayne attempted to leave a large department store with a $25 shirt and was apprehended by a police officer in front of the store.

Wayne seemed quite remorseful about the offense. He said several times that he didn't know why he did it and that he had not planned to do it. He seemed upset and scared, and although admitting the offense, did not want to go to court. Wayne had three previous contacts with the police as a juvenile: one for malicious mischief when he destroyed some property, another involving a minor assault on a boy, and a third involving another shoplifting charge. In all three cases, Wayne promised to refrain from ever committing such acts again, and as a result was not required to go to court. The other shoplifting incident involved a baseball worth only $3.

Wayne appears at the police department with his mother. His parents are divorced. The mother does not seem overly concerned about the case and feels that her son was not really to blame. She argues that he is always getting in trouble and she is not sure how to control him. She blames most of his troubles with the law on his being in the wrong crowd. Besides, a $25 shirt is "no big deal" and she offers to pay back the store. The store has left matters in the hands of the police and will support any decision you make.

Writing Assignment: Deciding what to do in a case like Wayne's is a routine activity for most police officers. When dealing with juveniles, they must consider not only the nature of the offense, but also the needs of the juvenile. Write an essay about the best course of action for this case, weighing the advantages and disadvantages of prosecution, release with a warning, and other options available to the police.

GROUPWORK

Divide the class into four or more groups and assign each group one of the four major police strategies to prevent delinquency: aggressive law enforcement, police in schools, community policing, and problem-oriented policing. Have each group identify the potential advantages and limitations of their strategy. Each group should consider not just crime reduction, but also police relations with youths and the community and other important issues.

CHAPTER THIRTEEN

Juvenile Court Process: Pretrial, Trial, and Sentencing

LEARNING OBJECTIVES

After reading this chapter you should:

1. Understand the roles and responsibilities of the main players in the juvenile court.

2. Be able to discuss key issues of the preadjudicatory stage of juvenile justice.

3. Be able to argue the pros and cons of transferring youths to adult court.

4. Understand key issues of the trial stage of juvenile justice and the major U.S. Supreme Court decisions that have influenced the handling of juveniles at the preadjudicatory and trial stages.

5. Know the most common dispositions for juvenile offenders.

Cliff's Story

Cliff is a 16-year-old European American being raised by his grandparents in a small rural community. He and his younger sisters were removed from their parental home when Cliff was 7 due to domestic violence and parental drug abuse. Although Cliff was well cared for by his grandparents, he engaged in several delinquent behaviors. He was charged with disorderly conduct for breaking windows in the family home and for threatening to physically assault his grandfather. Doing poorly in school, his grades dropped dramatically and several times concerned family members called the police worried that Cliff was using drugs.

Cliff began dating a girl he met at school, but her parents did not approve and they refused to allow her to go out with him. Upset about the situation, Cliff reacted by taking his anger out on his family and by threatening suicide. He was hospitalized for an evaluation and diagnosed with bipolar disorder. He was at risk for being removed from the family home and placed in detention. Fortunately for Cliff, he received juvenile probation and was ordered by the court to receive a mental health assessment and treatment. Cliff also received medications and a referral for a Functional Family Therapy (FFT) intervention.

The FFT program has three phases that target juvenile delinquents and their families. During FFT intervention, other services to the family are stopped in order for the family to focus on the FFT process and plan. During the first phase of the program, attempts are made to engage and motivate all family members to participate in the process. Also during this initial phase, the family therapists focus on redefining the problem (Cliff's problematic behavior and mental health concerns) as a family issue, and encouraging family members to view the issues in a new light. Everyone has a part in the problem and thus in the solution. They create real and obtainable goals and provide assistance to increase the family's problem-solving skills. This again takes the focus off the adolescent and distributes the responsibility among all family members. In the last phase, the therapists worked with Cliff's family to generalize their new skills to many different situations.

The FFT therapists worked with Cliff's family for four months, and then did a follow-up call at six and twelve months. They saw a reduction in Cliff's problematic behavior and criminal activity, as well as fewer calls to the police over the course of the intervention.

THE JUVENILE COURT AND ITS JURISDICTION

Today's juvenile delinquency cases are sometimes handled as part of a criminal trial court jurisdiction or even within the probate court. Also called surrogate court in some states, probate court is a court of special jurisdiction that handles wills, administration of estates, and guardianship of minors and incompetents. However, in most jurisdictions they are treated in the structure of a family court or an independent juvenile court (14 states use more than one method to process juvenile cases).[1] The independent juvenile court is a specialized court for children, designed to promote rehabilitation of youth in a framework of procedural due process. It is concerned with acting both in the best interest of the child and in the best interest of public protection, two often incompatible goals. Family courts, in contrast, have broad jurisdiction over a wide range of personal and household problems, including delinquency, paternity, child support, and custody issues. The major advantages of such a system are that it can serve sparsely populated areas, permits judicial personnel and others to deal exclusively with children's matters, and can obtain legislative funding more readily than other court systems.

Court Case Flow

In 2008 (the latest data available), approximately 1,650,000 delinquency cases were referred to juvenile court. This represents a 12 percent decrease in court case flow from the peak year in 1997. This recent downward trend comes after a steady increase or upward trend in court case flow that began in the mid-1980s.[2]

There were distinct gender- and race-based differences in the juvenile court population. In 2008, almost three-quarters (73 percent) of delinquency cases involved a male. However, the number of females processed by juvenile courts has increased in the last two decades, when about 19 percent of the cases involved females. Similarly, 34 percent of the juvenile court population was made up of African American youth, although African Americans make up only 16 percent of the general population.[3]

The Actors in the Juvenile Courtroom

The key players in the juvenile court are the defense attorneys, prosecutors, and judges.

The Defense Attorney. As the result of a series of Supreme Court decisions, the right of a delinquent youth to have counsel at state trials has become a fundamental part of the juvenile justice system.[4] Today, courts must provide counsel to indigent defendants who face the possibility of incarceration. Over the past three decades, the rules of juvenile justice administration have become extremely complex. Preparation of a case for juvenile court often involves detailed investigation of a crime, knowledge of court procedures, use of rules of evidence, and skills in trial advocacy. The right to counsel is essential if children are to have a fair chance of presenting their cases in court.[5]

In many respects, the role of the **juvenile defense attorney** is similar to that in the criminal and civil areas. Defense attorneys representing children in the juvenile court play an active and important part in virtually all stages of the proceedings. For example, the defense attorney helps to clarify jurisdictional problems and to decide whether there is sufficient evidence to warrant filing a formal petition. The defense attorney helps outline the child's position regarding detention hearings and bail, and explores the opportunities for informal adjustment of the case. If no adjustment or diversion occurs, the defense attorney represents the child at adjudication, presenting evidence and cross-examining witnesses to see that the child's position is made clear to the court. Defense attorneys also play a critical role in the disposition hearing. They present evidence bearing on the treatment decision and help the court formulate alternative plans for the child's care. Finally, defense attorneys pursue any appeals from the trial, represent the child in probation revocation proceedings, and generally protect the child's right to treatment.

© Shelley Gazin/Corbis

Juvenile defense attorneys play an active and important part in virtually all stages of juvenile court proceedings, ranging from representing youths in police custody to filing their final appeals.

juvenile defense attorney Represents children in juvenile court and plays an active role at all stages of the proceedings.

Important to these roles is the attorney–juvenile relationship and the competence of the attorney. Some studies report that many juvenile offenders do not trust their attorney,[6] but juvenile offenders represented by private attorneys are more trusting in their attorney than those represented by court-appointed attorneys.[7] One possible reason for this difference may be the belief among juveniles that because court-appointed attorneys work for the "system" they might share information with the judge, police, or others.[8] Another important dimension of the attorney–juvenile relationship is effective participation of the juvenile as a defendant, which "requires a personally relevant understanding of the lawyer's advocacy role and the confidential nature of the attorney–client relationship."[9] A recent study investigating effective participation among juvenile and adult defendants concluded that juveniles are in need of extra procedural safeguards, such as training for lawyers on how to be more effective counselors.[10] There may also be a need to improve the competency of juvenile defense attorneys, as well as to overcome some of the time constraints they face in case preparation. In a study of legal representation of juveniles charged with felonies in three juvenile courts in Missouri, it was found that they were more likely to receive an out-of-home placement disposition (instead of a less punitive disposition) if they had an attorney, even after controlling for other legal and individual factors.[11] Two other studies found that youth not represented by an attorney were more likely to have the charges dismissed than similar youth represented by an attorney,[12] and in one of these studies the effect was more pronounced for minorities.[13] Yet another study, the largest to date, which compared the case processing of almost 70,000 juvenile offenders in Minnesota, found that legal representation—next to an extensive prior record—was the strongest predictor of an out-of-home placement disposition.[14] (See the following section for other problems specific to public defenders.)

In some cases, a **guardian *ad litem*** may be appointed by the court.[15] The guardian *ad litem*—ordinarily seen in abuse, neglect, and dependency cases—may be appointed in delinquency cases when there is a question of a need for a particular treatment (for example, placement in a mental health center) and offenders and their attorneys resist placement. The guardian *ad litem* may advocate for the commitment on the ground that it is in the child's best interests. The guardian *ad litem* fulfills many roles, ranging from legal advocate to concerned individual who works with parents and human service professionals in developing a proper treatment plan that best serves the interests of the minor child.[16]

Court-Appointed Special Advocates (CASA). Court-Appointed Special Advocates (CASA) are volunteers who advise the juvenile court about child placement. The CASA programs (*casa* is Spanish for "home") have demonstrated that volunteers can investigate the needs of children and provide a vital link among the judge, the attorneys, and the child in protecting the juvenile's right to a safe placement.[17]

Public Defender Services for Children. To satisfy the requirement that indigent children be provided with counsel, the federal government and the states have expanded **public defender** services. Three alternatives exist for providing children with legal counsel: an all-public defender program, an appointed private-counsel system, and a combination system of public defenders and appointed private attorneys.

The public defender program is a statewide program established by legislation and funded by the state government to provide counsel to children at public expense. This program allows access to the expertise of lawyers who spend a considerable amount of time representing juvenile offenders every day. Defender programs generally provide separate office space for juvenile court personnel, as well as support staff and training programs for new lawyers.

In many rural areas where individual public defender programs are not available, defense services are offered through appointed private counsel. Private lawyers are assigned to individual juvenile court cases and receive compensation for the time and services they provide. When private attorneys are used in large urban areas, they are generally selected from a list established by the court, and they often operate in conjunction with a public defender program. The weaknesses of a system

WWW

Volunteer **Court-Appointed Special Advocates (CASA)** are appointed by judges to advocate for the best interests of abused and neglected children. To read more about the CASA program, visit the Criminal Justice Course-Mate at CengageBrain.com, then access the Web Links for this chapter.

guardian *ad litem* A court-appointed attorney who protects the interests of the child in cases involving the child's welfare.

public defender An attorney who works in a public agency or under private contractual agreement as defense counsel to indigent defendants.

of assigned private counsel include assignment to cases for which the lawyers are unqualified, inadequate compensation, and lack of support or supervisory services.

Although efforts have been made to supply juveniles with adequate legal representation, many juveniles still go to court unrepresented or with an overworked lawyer who provides inadequate representation. Many juvenile court defense lawyers work on more than 500 cases per year, and more than half leave their jobs in under two years.[18] Other problems facing juvenile public defenders include lack of resources for independent evaluations, expert witnesses, and investigatory support; lack of computers, telephones, files, and adequate office space; inexperience, lack of training, low morale, and salaries lower than those of their counterparts who defend adults or serve as prosecutors; and inability to keep up with rapidly changing juvenile codes.[19] In a six-state study of access to counsel and quality of legal representation for indigent juveniles, the American Bar Association found these and many other problems.[20] With juvenile offenders facing the prospect of much longer sentences, mandatory minimum sentences, and time in adult prisons, the need for quality defense attorneys for juveniles has never been greater.

The Prosecutor. The **juvenile prosecutor** is the attorney responsible for bringing the state's case against the accused juvenile. Depending on the level of government and the jurisdiction, the prosecutor can be called a *district attorney*, *county attorney*, *state attorney*, or *United States attorney*. Prosecutors are members of the bar selected for their positions by political appointment or popular election.

For the first 60 years of its existence, the juvenile court did not include a prosecutor because the concept of an adversary process was seen as inconsistent with the philosophy of treatment. The court followed a social-service helping model, and informal proceedings were believed to be in the best interests of the child. Today, in a more legalistic juvenile court, almost all jurisdictions require by law that a prosecutor be present in the juvenile court.

A number of states have passed legislation giving prosecutors control over intake and waiver decisions. Some have passed concurrent-jurisdiction laws that allow prosecutors to decide in which court to bring serious juvenile cases. In some jurisdictions, it is the prosecutor and not the juvenile court judge who is entrusted with the decision of whether to waive a case to adult court.

The prosecutor has the power either to initiate or to discontinue delinquency or status-offense allegations. Like police officers, prosecutors have broad discretion in the exercise of their duties. Because due process rights have been extended to juveniles, the prosecutor's role in the juvenile court has in some ways become similar to the prosecutor's role in the adult court.

Because children are committing more serious crimes and because the courts have granted juveniles constitutional safeguards, the prosecutor is likely to play an increasingly significant role in the juvenile court system. According to authors James Shine and Dwight Price, the prosecutor's involvement will promote a due process model that should result in a fairer, more just system for all parties. But they also point out that, to meet current and future challenges, prosecutors need more information on such issues as how to identify repeat offenders, how to determine which programs are most effective, how early-childhood experiences relate to delinquency, and what measures can be used in lieu of secure placements without reducing public safety.[21]

Today, prosecutors are addressing the problems associated with juvenile crime. A balanced approach has been recommended—one that emphasizes enforcement, prosecution, and detention of serious offenders, and the use of proven prevention and intervention programs.[22]

The Juvenile Court Judge. Even with the elevation of the prosecutor's role, the **juvenile court judge** is still the central character in a court of juvenile or family law. The responsibilities of this judge have become far more extensive and complex in recent years. Because of the importance of the juvenile court judge in the juvenile justice system, we discuss the career of one of these judges in the accompanying Professional Spotlight feature.

juvenile prosecutor Government attorney responsible for representing the interests of the state and bringing the case against the accused juvenile.

juvenile court judge A judge elected or appointed to preside over juvenile cases whose decisions can only be reviewed by a judge of a higher court.

Lamont Christian Berecz
Juvenile Court Judge

Lamont Christian Berecz is a juvenile court judge assigned to the Ada County Juvenile Court Services in Boise, Idaho. Judge Berecz decided to work in the juvenile justice system because of the vast potential to impact society in a positive way. He often tells people that the juvenile courts are one of the few places in the criminal justice system where you can see hope. He believes that in dealing with adult offenders you also hope for change, but juveniles are at such a vital stage of their lives that if you can reach them now, you can greatly affect their futures.

Judge Berecz prepared for his career as a juvenile court judge by first getting an undergraduate degree and then a law degree. After his first year of law school, he interned in a prosecuting attorney's office over the summer and was assigned to the juvenile division. It was that exposure to juvenile justice that opened his eyes to the possibilities and challenges of working with troubled youth within the legal system.

After law school, he served as a prosecutor for several years before taking the bench as a juvenile court judge. While that study of the law prepared him for the legal aspects of his job, Judge Berecz says that he values his experience working with kids over the years as a vital component to his success as a juvenile court judge.

What does Judge Berecz feel is the most rewarding part of his job? It is seeing kids change for the better. To see a child from a dysfunctional home or abusive past turn the corner and begin to realize their potential is what keeps him going in this line of work. Not all of the juveniles he sees take advantage of the services, programs, and accountability that the juvenile court provides, but the ones who do bring him the most reward and satisfaction.

For Judge Berecz, the biggest challenge he faces is dealing with the emotional toll that comes from daily seeing the heartache, trauma, neglect, and failure that surrounds so many juvenile offenders. Parents often present quite a challenge as well. He has seen cases where a parent started their child on drugs, abandoned them, or otherwise sabotaged the juvenile's future. On the other end of the spectrum, there are parents who view their child as a victim, who instill a sense of entitlement and resist efforts to hold their child accountable. Nevertheless, Judge Berecz finds that it is imperative that he engages the family and their unique challenges in impacting that child for positive change.

Judge Berecz finds that a common misconception people hold about his job is that there is some sort of power trip or rush that comes from being a judge and having so much authority. Quite to the contrary, he finds it to be a grave responsibility that at times can weigh on him. He says that it is not always easy to have to be the final word. On the other hand, he adds, you have the opportunity to implement great change. Judge Berecz believes that the judges who are successful in juvenile justice are those who view their position as a sacred trust given to them by the people in their community.

In addition, judges often have extensive influence over other agencies of the court: probation, the court clerk, the law enforcement officer, and the office of the juvenile prosecutor. Juvenile court judges exercise considerable leadership in developing solutions to juvenile justice problems. In this role, they must respond to the pressures the community places on juvenile court resources. According to the *parens patriae* philosophy, the juvenile judge must ensure that the necessary community resources are available so that the children and families who come before the court can receive the proper care and help.[23] This may be the most untraditional role for the juvenile court judge, but it may also be the most important.

In some jurisdictions, juvenile court judges handle family-related cases exclusively. In others, they preside over criminal and civil cases as well. Traditionally, juvenile court judges have been relegated to a lower status than other judges. The National Council of Juvenile and Family Court Judges, as part of a larger effort to improve juvenile courts, took up this issue by recommending that, "Juvenile delinquency court judges should have the same status as the highest level of trial court in the state and should have multiple year or permanent assignments."[24] Furthermore, judges assigned to juvenile courts have not ordinarily been chosen from the highest levels of the legal profession. Such groups as the American Judicature Society have noted that the field of juvenile justice has often been shortchanged by the appointment of unqualified judges. In some jurisdictions, particularly major urban areas,

WWW

The American Judicature Society is a nonpartisan organization with a membership of judges, lawyers, and other citizens interested in the administration of justice. Visit this organization's website by going to the Criminal Justice CourseMate at CengageBrain.com, and accessing the Web Links for this chapter.

LO1 Understand the roles and responsibilities of the main players in the juvenile court.

✔ In most jurisdictions, kids are adjudicated within the structure of either a family court or an independent juvenile court.

✔ All juveniles must be provided with legal counsel if they face the possibility of incarceration.

✔ A guardian *ad litem* is an attorney who represents the child during special legal proceedings, including abuse, neglect, and dependency cases.

✔ Court-Appointed Special Advocates (CASA) are volunteers who advise the juvenile court about child placement.

✔ The juvenile prosecutor is the attorney responsible for bringing the state's case against the accused juvenile.

✔ The juvenile judge must ensure that the children and families who come before the court can receive the proper care and help.

juvenile court judges may be of the highest caliber, but many courts continue to function with mediocre judges.

Inducing the best-trained individuals to accept juvenile court judgeships is a very important goal. Where the juvenile court is part of the highest general court of trial jurisdiction, the problem of securing qualified personnel is not as great. However, if the juvenile court is of limited or specialized jurisdiction and has the authority to try only minor cases, it may attract only poorly trained personnel. Lawyers and judges who practice in juvenile court receive little respect. The juvenile court has a negative image because even though what it does is of great importance to parents, children, and society in general, it has been placed at the lowest level of the judicial hierarchy. **CHECKPOINTS**

JUVENILE COURT PROCESS

Now that we have briefly described the setting of the juvenile court and the major players who control its operations, we turn to a discussion of the procedures that shape the contours of juvenile justice: the pretrial process and the juvenile trial and disposition. Many critical decisions are made at this stage of the juvenile justice system: whether to detain or release the youth to the community; whether to waive youths to the adult court or retain them in the juvenile justice system; whether to treat them in the community or send them to a secure treatment center. Each of these can have a profound influence on the child, with effects lasting throughout the life course. What are these critical stages, and how are decisions made within them?

Release or Detain?

After a child has been taken into custody and a decision is made to treat the case formally (that is, with a juvenile court hearing), a decision must be made either to release the child into the custody of his or her parents or to detain the child in the temporary care of the state in physically restrictive facilities pending court disposition or transfer to another agency.

Detention can be a traumatic experience because many facilities are prison-like, with locked doors and barred windows. Consequently, most experts in juvenile justice advocate that detention be limited to alleged offenders who require secure custody for the protection of themselves and others. However, children who are neglected and dependent, runaways, or homeless may under some circumstances be placed in secure detention facilities along with violent and dangerous youth until more suitable placements can be found.[25] Others have had a trial, but have not been sentenced or are awaiting the imposition of their sentence. Some may have violated probation and are awaiting a hearing while being kept alongside severely mentally ill adolescents for whom no appropriate placement can be found. Another group are adjudicated delinquents awaiting admittance to a correctional training school.[26] Consequently, it is possible for nonviolent status offenders to be housed in the same facility with delinquents who have committed felony-type offenses. A study of child detention centers in New Jersey found that one out of every four youths in the centers (about 2,500 out of 10,000) were placed there inappropriately and should have instead been placed in hospitals, foster care homes, or other noncustodial settings. Because of the inappropriate placement in detention facilities, many of these youths were preyed upon by violent youths, did not receive much needed medical or mental care, or resorted to self-harm or suicide attempts as a way to cope or escape from the dangerous and chaotic setting.[27]

Looking Back to Cliff's Story

Cliff was not placed in detention.

CRITICAL THINKING Discuss how this decision may have benefited Cliff as well as his family.

To remedy these situations, an ongoing effort has been made to remove status offenders, neglected or abused children, and foster care youths from detention facilities that also house juvenile delinquents, as well as develop alternatives to detention centers, such as temporary foster homes, detention boarding homes, and programs of neighborhood supervision. These alternatives, referred to as **shelter care**, enable youths to live in a more homelike setting while the courts dispose of their cases.

Project Confirm in New York City is one example of an effort to reduce the detention of foster care youths who have been arrested. Very often these youths who otherwise would have been released are placed in detention facilities because their guardians fail to appear in court, a result of a breakdown in communication between (and within) the child welfare and juvenile justice systems. The project involves two main strategies to overcome this problem: notifying project staff upon a youth's arrest to allow for a search of child welfare databases, and court conferencing among child welfare and juvenile justice authorities. An evaluation of the project found that disparity in detention experienced by foster care youths compared to a similar group of non–foster care youths was reduced among those charged with minor offenses and with no prior detentions, but increased among those charged with more serious offenses and prior police contact. The authors speculate that the improved quality of information provided by the project to the court, especially prior detentions, coupled with court officials' preconceived notions of the likelihood of these youths to commit another crime or fail to appear in court, resulted in more serious cases being detained.[28]

National Detention Trends. Despite an ongoing effort to limit detention, juveniles are still being detained in just over one out of every five delinquency cases (21 percent), with some variation across the major offense categories: violent (27 percent), property (17 percent), drugs (18 percent), and public order (23 percent). Although the detention rate for delinquency cases is down from 1990, in which the percent of cases detained was highest (23 percent), between 1990 and 2008 the total number of juveniles held in short-term detention facilities increased 15 percent, from 302,800 to 347,800.[29]

The typical delinquent detainee is male, 16 years of age, and charged with a violent crime.[30] Racial minorities are heavily overrepresented in detention, especially those who are indigent and whose families may be receiving public assistance. Minority overrepresentation is particularly vexing, considering that detention may increase the risk of a youth's being adjudicated and eventually confined.[31]

In a study of the extent of racial discrimination and disparity among male juvenile property offenders in six Missouri counties at four stages of juvenile justice (decision to file a petition, pretrial detention, adjudication, and disposition), it was found that African American youth were more likely than European American youth to be detained prior to adjudication (40 percent compared to 22 percent).[32] The study also found that African American youth were more likely to be formally referred and European American youth were more likely to be adjudicated. The authors speculate that a "correction of biases" may be one of the reasons for European American youth being more likely than African American youth to be adjudicated; that is, "judges may dismiss black youths because they feel that a detained youth has been punished enough already."[33] In another study, being African American was one of the key factors that predicted longer time spent in detention. Also important were prior mental health service, neglect, physical abuse, personal crime offense, and early age of first delinquency adjudication.[34]

The Decision to Detain. Most children taken into custody by the police are released to their parents or guardians. Some are held overnight until their parents can be notified. Police officers normally take a child to a place of detention only after other alternatives have been exhausted. Many juvenile courts in urban areas have staff members, such as intake probation officers, on duty 24 hours a day to screen detention admissions.

Ordinarily, delinquent children are detained if the police believe they are inclined to run away while awaiting trial, or if they are likely to commit an offense dangerous to the parent. There is evidence that some decision makers are more likely to detain

shelter care A place for temporary care of children in physically unrestricting facilities.

minority youth, especially if they dwell in dangerous lower-class areas.[35] The use of screening instruments to determine the need for detention has proven useful.[36]

Generally, children should not be held in a detention facility or shelter-care unit for more than 24 hours without a formal petition (a written request to the court) being filed to extend the detention period. To detain a juvenile, there must be clear evidence of probable cause that the child has committed the offense and will flee if not detained. Although the requirements for detention hearings vary, most jurisdictions require that they occur almost immediately after the child's admission to a detention facility and provide the youth with notice and counsel.

New Approaches to Detention. Efforts have been ongoing to improve the process and conditions of detention. Experts maintain that detention facilities should provide youths with education, visitation, private communications, counseling, continuous supervision, medical and health care, nutrition, recreation, and reading. Detention should also include, or provide, a system for clinical observation and diagnosis that complements the wide range of helpful services.[37]

The consensus today is that juvenile detention centers should be reserved for youths who present a clear threat to the community. In some states, nonsecure facilities are being used to service juveniles for a limited period. Alternatives to secure detention include in-home monitoring, home detention, day-center electronic monitoring, high-intensity community supervision, and comprehensive case management programs.

Undoubtedly, juveniles pose special detention problems, but some efforts are being made to improve programs and to reduce pretrial detention use, especially in secure settings. Of all the problems associated with detention, however, none is as critical as the issue of placing youths in adult jails.

Restricting Detention in Adult Jails. A significant problem in juvenile justice is placing youths in adult jails. This is usually done in rural areas where no other facility exists. Almost all experts agree that placing children under the age of 18 in any type of jail facility should be prohibited because youngsters can easily be victimized by other inmates and staff, be forced to live in squalid conditions, and be subject to physical and sexual abuse.

Until a number of years ago, placing juveniles in adult facilities was common, but efforts have been made to change this situation. In 1989, the Juvenile Justice and Delinquency Prevention Act (JJDPA) of 1974 was amended to require that states remove all juveniles from adult jails and lockups. According to federal guidelines, all juveniles in state custody must be separated from adult offenders or the state could lose federal juvenile justice funds. The Office of Juvenile Justice and Delinquency Prevention (OJJDP) defines separation as the condition in which juvenile detainees have either totally independent facilities or shared facilities that are designed so that juveniles and adults neither have contact nor share programs or staff.[38]

Much debate has arisen over whether the initiative to remove juveniles from adult jails has succeeded. Most indications are that the number of youths being held in adult facilities has declined significantly from the almost 500,000 a year recorded in 1979.

Removing Status Offenders. Along with removing all juveniles from adult jails, the OJJDP has made deinstitutionalization of status offenders a cornerstone of its policy. The Juvenile Justice and Delinquency Prevention Act of 1974 prohibits the placement of status offenders in secure detention facilities.

Bail for Children. One critical detention issue is whether juveniles can be released on **bail**. Adults retain the right, via the Eighth Amendment to the Constitution, to reasonable bail in noncapital cases. Most states, however, refuse juveniles the right to bail. They argue that juvenile proceedings are civil, not criminal, and that detention is rehabilitative, not punitive. In addition, they argue that juveniles do not need a constitutional right to bail, because statutory provisions allow children to be released into parental custody.

bail Amount of money that must be paid as a condition of pretrial release to ensure that the accused will return for subsequent proceedings. Bail is normally set by the judge at the initial appearance, and if unable to make bail the accused is detained in jail.

State juvenile bail statutes fall into three categories: those guaranteeing the right to bail, those that grant the court discretion to give bail, and those that deny a juvenile the right to bail.[39] This disparity may be a function of the lack of legal guidance on the matter. The U.S. Supreme Court has never decided the issue of juvenile bail. Some courts have stated that bail provisions do not apply to juveniles. Others rely on the Eighth Amendment against cruel and unusual punishment, or on state constitutional provisions or statutes, and conclude that juveniles do have a right to bail.

Preventive Detention. Although the U.S. Supreme Court has not yet decided whether juveniles have a right to traditional money bail, it has concluded that the state has a right to detain dangerous youth until their trial, a practice called **preventive detention**. On June 4, 1984, the U.S. Supreme Court dealt with this issue in *Schall v. Martin*, when it upheld the state of New York's preventive detention statute.[40] Because this is a key case in juvenile justice, it is the subject of Exhibit 13.1. Today, most states allow "dangerous" youths to be held indefinitely before trial. Because preventive detention may attach a stigma of guilt to a child presumed innocent, the practice remains a highly controversial one, and the efficacy of such laws remains unknown.[41]

The Intake Process

The term **intake** refers to the screening of cases by the juvenile court system. The child and the child's family are screened by intake officers to determine whether the services of the juvenile court are needed. Intake officers may send the youth home with no further action, divert the youth to a social agency, petition the youth to the juvenile court, or file a petition and hold the youth in detention. The intake process reduces demands on court resources, screens out cases that are not in the court's jurisdiction,

preventive detention Keeping the accused in custody prior to trial, because the accused is suspected of being a danger to the community.

intake Process during which a juvenile referral is received and a decision made to file a petition in juvenile court to release the juvenile, to place the juvenile under supervision, or to refer the juvenile elsewhere.

EXHIBIT 13.1 *Schall v. Martin*

Facts

Gregory Martin, age 14, was arrested in New York City on December 13, 1977, on charges of robbery, assault, and criminal possession of a weapon. Because he was arrested at 11:30 p.m. and lied about his residence, Martin was kept overnight in detention and brought to juvenile court the next day for an "initial appearance," accompanied by his grandmother. The family court judge, citing possession of a loaded weapon, the false address given to police, and the fact that Martin was left unsupervised late in the evening, ordered him detained before trial. Later, at trial, Martin was found to be a delinquent and sentenced to two years' probation.

During the time he was in pretrial detention, Martin's attorneys filed a class action on behalf of all youths subject to preventive detention in New York, charging that this form of detention was a denial of due process rights under the Fifth and Fourteenth Amendments. The New York appellate courts upheld Martin's claim on the ground that because, at adjudication, most delinquents are released or placed on probation, it was unfair to incarcerate them before trial. The prosecution brought the case to the U.S. Supreme Court for final judgment.

Decision

The U.S. Supreme Court upheld the state's right to place juveniles in preventive detention, holding that the practice serves the legitimate objective of protecting both the juvenile and society from pretrial crime. Pretrial detention need not be considered punishment merely because the juvenile is eventually released or put on probation. The Court also found that detention based on prediction of future behavior was not a violation of due process.

Significance of the Case

Schall v. Martin established the right of juvenile court judges to deny youths pretrial release if they perceive them to be dangerous. However, the case also established a due process standard for detention hearings that includes notice and a statement of substantial reasons for the detention. Despite these measures, opponents hold that preventive detention deprives offenders of their freedom because guilt has not been proven. It is also unfair, they claim, to punish people for what judicial authorities believe they may do in the future because it is impossible to predict who will be a danger to the community.

Source: *Schall v. Martin*, 467 U.S. 253 (1984).

The intake process refers to the screening of cases by the juvenile court system. Intake officers, who are often probation staff members, determine whether the services of the juvenile court are needed. Here, juvenile offenders beginning the intake process are searched by a correctional officer at the Department of Youth Services Detention Center in Rathbone, Ohio.

and enables assistance to be obtained from community agencies without court intervention. Juvenile court intake is provided for by statute in almost all the states.

Eighteen percent (305,600) of all delinquency cases in 2008 were dismissed at intake, often because they were not legally sufficient. An additional 26 percent (423,300) were processed informally, with the juvenile voluntarily agreeing to the recommended disposition (for example, voluntary treatment).[42] Intake screening allows juvenile courts to enter into consent decrees with juveniles without filing petitions and without formal adjudication. The *consent decree* is a court order authorizing disposition of the case without a formal label of delinquency. It is based on an agreement between the intake department of the court and the juvenile who is the subject of the complaint.

But intake also suffers from some problems. Although almost all state juvenile court systems provide intake and diversion programs, there are few formal criteria for selecting children for such alternatives. There are also legal problems associated with the intake process. Among them are whether the child has a right to counsel, whether the child is protected against self-incrimination, and to what degree the child needs to consent to nonjudicial disposition as recommended by the intake officer. Finally, intake dispositions are often determined by the prior record rather than by the seriousness of the offense or the social background of the child. Race has also been shown to influence intake decisions. A study of juvenile males in one county court in Iowa found that African American juveniles were more likely than their Caucasian counterparts to receive a court referral.[43] This is part of the widely documented (but understudied) problem of disproportionate minority contact that extends from first contact with police throughout the entire juvenile justice process.[44]

Diversion

One of the most important alternatives chosen at intake is *nonjudicial disposition*, or as it is variously called, *nonjudicial adjustment*, *handling or processing*, *informal disposition*, *adjustment*, or (most commonly) **diversion**. Juvenile diversion is the process of placing youths suspected of law-violating behavior into treatment programs prior to formal trial and disposition to minimize their penetration into the justice system and thereby avoid stigma and labeling.

diversion Officially halting or suspending a formal criminal or juvenile justice proceeding at any legally prescribed processing point after a recorded justice system entry, and referral of that person to a treatment or care program, or a recommendation that the person be released.

Diversion implies more than simply screening out cases for which no additional treatment is needed. Screening involves abandoning efforts to apply coercive measures to a defendant. In contrast, diversion encourages an individual to participate in some specific program or activity to avoid further prosecution.

Most court-based diversion programs employ a particular formula for choosing youths. Criteria, such as being a first offender, a nonviolent offender, or a status offender, or being drug- or alcohol-dependent, are used to select clients. In some programs, youths are asked to partake of services voluntarily in lieu of a court appearance. In other programs, prosecutors agree to defer, and then dismiss, a case once a youth has completed a treatment program. Finally, some programs can be initiated by the juvenile court judge after an initial hearing. Concept Summary 13.1 lists the factors considered in diversion decisions.

In sum, diversion programs have been created to remove nonserious offenders from the justice system, provide them with nonpunitive treatment services, and help them avoid the stigma of a delinquent label.

Issues in Diversion: Widening the Net. Diversion has been viewed as a promising alternative to official procedures, but over the years its basic premises have been questioned.[45] The most damaging criticism has been that diversion programs are involving those children in the juvenile justice system who previously would have been released without official notice. This is referred to as **widening the net**. Various studies indicate that police and court personnel are likely to use diversion programs for youths who ordinarily would have been turned loose at the intake or arrest stage.[46] Why does this "net widening" occur? One explanation is that police and prosecutors find diversion a more attractive alternative than either official processing or outright release—diversion helps them resolve the conflict between doing too much and doing too little.

Diversion has also been criticized as ineffective; that is, youths being diverted make no better adjustment in the community than those who go through official channels. However, not all experts are critical of diversion. Some challenge the net-widening concept as naive: How do we know that diverted youths would have had less interface with the justice system if diversion didn't exist?[47] Even if juveniles escaped official labels for their current offense, might they not eventually fall into the hands of the police? The rehabilitative potential of diversion should not be overlooked.[48] There is some evidence that diversion with a treatment component for juveniles suffering from mental health problems can delay or prevent further delinquent activity.[49]

Some experts even argue that diversion has been the centerpiece or at least a core element of the juvenile justice system's success in limiting the growth of juvenile incarceration rates over the last three decades, which were dwarfed by the dramatic increase in incarceration rates among young adult offenders (ages 18 to 24) over the same period of time.[50] In the words of legal scholar Franklin Zimring,

> . . . the angry assaults on juvenile courts throughout the 1990s are a tribute to the efficacy of juvenile justice in protecting delinquents from the incarcerative explosion that had happened everywhere else.[51]

CONCEPT SUMMARY 13.1 | Who Gets Diversion?

Factors Considered	Criteria for Eligibility
Past criminal record	It is the juvenile's first offense.
Type of offense	It is a nonviolent or status offense.
Other circumstances	The juvenile abuses drugs or alcohol.

widening the net Phenomenon that occurs when programs created to divert youths from the justice system actually involve them more deeply in the official process.

The Petition

A **complaint** is the report made by the police or some other agency to the court to initiate the intake process. Once the agency makes a decision that judicial disposition is required, a petition is filed. The petition is the formal complaint that initiates judicial action against a juvenile charged with delinquency or a status offense. The petition includes basic information, such as the name, age, and residence of the child; the parents' names; and the facts alleging the child's delinquency. The police officer, a family member, or a social service agency can file a petition.

If after being given the right to counsel, the child admits the allegation in the petition, an initial hearing is scheduled for the child to make the admission before the court, and information is gathered to develop a treatment plan. If the child does not admit to any of the facts in the petition, a date is set for a hearing on the petition. This hearing, whose purpose is to determine the merits of the petition, is similar to the adult trial. Once a hearing date has been set, the probation department is normally asked to prepare a social study report. This predisposition report contains relevant information about the child, along with recommendations for treatment and service.

When a date has been set for the hearing on the petition, parents or guardians and other persons associated with the petition (witnesses, the arresting police officer, and victims) are notified. On occasion, the court may issue a summons—a court order requiring the juvenile or others involved in the case to appear for the hearing. The statutes in a given jurisdiction govern the contents of the petition. Some jurisdictions, for instance, allow for a petition to be filed based on the information of the complainant alone. Others require that the petition be filed under oath or that an affidavit accompany the petition. Some jurisdictions authorize only one official, such as a probation officer or prosecutor, to file the petition. Others allow numerous officials, including family and social service agencies, to set forth facts in the petition.

The Plea and Plea Bargaining

In the adult criminal justice system, the defendant normally enters a plea of guilty or not guilty. More than 90 percent of all adult defendants plead guilty. A large proportion of those pleas involve **plea bargaining**, the exchange of prosecutorial and judicial concessions for guilty pleas.[52] Plea bargaining, which involves a discussion between the child's attorney and the prosecutor, permits a defendant to plead guilty to a less-serious charge in exchange for an agreement by the prosecutor to recommend a reduced sentence to the court.

Few juvenile codes require a guilty or not-guilty plea when a petition is filed against a child. In most jurisdictions, an initial hearing is held at which the child either submits to a finding of the facts or denies the petition.[53] If the child admits to the facts, the court determines an appropriate disposition. If the child denies the allegations, the case normally proceeds to trial. When a child enters no plea, the court ordinarily imposes a denial of the charges. This may occur when a juvenile doesn't understand the nature of the complaint or isn't represented by an attorney.

A high percentage of juvenile offenders enter guilty pleas—that is, they admit to the facts of the petition. How many of these pleas involve plea bargaining is unknown. In the past it was believed that plea bargaining was unnecessary in the juvenile justice system because there was little incentive to bargain in a system that does not have jury trials or long sentences. In addition, because the court must dispose of cases in the best interests of the child, plea negotiation seemed unnecessary. Consequently, there has long been a debate over the appropriateness of plea bargaining in juvenile justice. The arguments in favor of plea bargaining include lower court costs and efficiency. Counterarguments hold that plea bargaining with juveniles is an unregulated and unethical process. When used, experts believe the process requires the highest standards of good faith by the prosecutor.[54]

There is little clear evidence on how much plea bargaining occurs in the juvenile justice system, but it is apparent that such negotiations do take place and seem to be increasing. Joseph Sanborn found that about 20 percent of the cases processed in Philadelphia resulted in a negotiated plea. Most were for reduced sentences,

complaint Report made by the police or some other agency to the court that initiates the intake process.

plea bargaining The exchange of prosecutorial and judicial concessions for a guilty plea by the accused; plea bargaining usually results in a reduced charge or a more lenient sentence.

Plea bargaining involves the exchange of prosecutorial and judicial concessions for a guilty plea that usually results in a reduced charge or a more lenient disposition. Here, Charles Erickson testifies at an evidentiary hearing for convicted murder defendant Ryan Ferguson in Cole County Circuit Court in Jefferson City, Missouri, on April 18, 2012. Erickson is serving a 25-year sentence as part of a plea bargain for testifying against Ferguson in the killing of *Columbia Daily Tribune* editor Kent Heitholt in 2008.

typically probation in lieu of incarceration. Sanborn found that plea bargaining was a complex process, depending in large measure on the philosophy of the judge and the court staff. In general, he found it to have greater benefit for the defendants than for the court.[55]

In summary, the majority of juvenile cases that are not adjudicated seem to be the result of admissions to the facts rather than actual plea bargaining. Plea bargaining is less common in juvenile courts than in adult courts because incentives, such as dropping multiple charges or substituting a misdemeanor for a felony, are unlikely. Nonetheless, plea bargaining is firmly entrenched in the juvenile process. Any plea bargain, however, must be entered into voluntarily and knowingly; otherwise, the conviction may be overturned on appeal. **CHECKPOINTS**

TRANSFER TO THE ADULT COURT

One of the most significant actions that can occur in the early court processing of a juvenile offender is the **transfer process**. Otherwise known as *waiver*, *bind over*, or *removal*, this process involves transferring a juvenile from the juvenile court to the criminal court. Virtually all state statutes allow for this kind of transfer.

The number of delinquency cases judicially waived to criminal court peaked in 1994 at 13,200 cases, an increase of 83 percent over the number of cases waived in 1985 (7,200). From 1994 to 2008 (the latest data available), however, the number of cases waived to criminal court actually declined by one-third (33 percent) to

transfer process Transferring a juvenile offender from the jurisdiction of juvenile court to adult criminal court.

8,900 cases, representing about 0.5 percent of the formally processed delinquency caseload. Between 1985 and 2008, person offense cases were the most likely to be waived to criminal court.[56] Figure 13.1 shows numbers of delinquency cases waived to criminal court from 1985 to 2008.

Waiver Procedures

Today, all states allow juveniles to be tried as adults in criminal courts in one of three ways:

- *Concurrent jurisdiction.* In 14 states and the District of Columbia, the prosecutor has the discretion of filing charges for certain offenses in either juvenile or criminal court.

- *Statutory exclusion policies.* In 29 states, certain offenses are automatically excluded from juvenile court. These offenses can be minor, such as traffic violations, or serious, such as murder or rape. Statutory exclusion accounts for the largest number of juveniles tried as adults.

- *Judicial waiver.* In the waiver (or bind over or removal) of juvenile cases to criminal court, a hearing is held before a juvenile court judge, who then decides whether jurisdiction should be waived and the case transferred to criminal court. Forty-four states and the District of Columbia (not Connecticut, Massachusetts, Montana, Nebraska, New Mexico, or New York) offer provisions for juvenile waivers.[57]

Due Process in Transfer Proceedings

The standards for transfer procedures are set by state statute. Some jurisdictions allow for transfer between the ages of 14 and 17. Others restrict waiver proceedings to mature juveniles and specify particular offenses. In a few jurisdictions, any child can be transferred to the criminal court system, regardless of age.

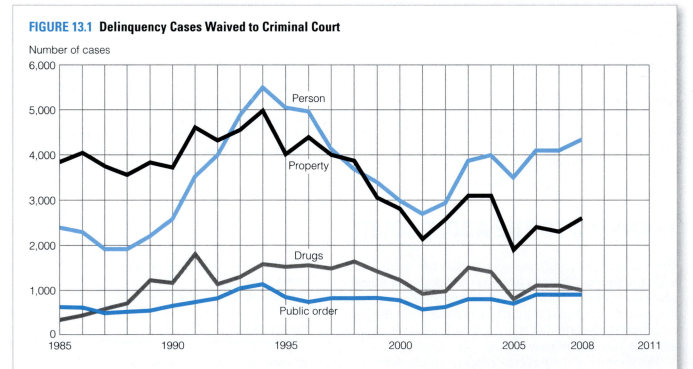

FIGURE 13.1 **Delinquency Cases Waived to Criminal Court**

Source: Charles Puzzanchera, Benjamin Adams, and Melissa Sickmund, *Juvenile Court Statistics, 2008* (Pittsburgh: National Center for Juvenile Justice, 2011), pp. 60–61.

Those states that have amended their waiver policies with statutory exclusion policies now exclude certain serious offenses from juvenile court jurisdiction. For example, Indiana excludes cases involving 16- and 17-year-olds charged with murder, drug and weapons offenses, and certain felonies and other person offenses. In Illinois, youths ages 13 and older who are charged with murder, and youths ages 15 and older who are charged with drug and weapons offenses and certain felonies and other person offenses are automatically sent to criminal court. In Nevada and Pennsylvania, any child accused of murder, regardless of age, is tried before the criminal court.[58] Other jurisdictions use exclusion to remove traffic offenses and public-ordinance violations.

The trend toward excluding serious violent offenses from juvenile court jurisdictions grew in response to the demand to get tough on crime. In addition, large numbers of youths under age 18 are tried as adults in states where the upper age of juvenile court jurisdiction is 15 or 16.

In a small number of states, statutes allow prosecutors to file particularly serious cases in either the juvenile court or the adult court.[59] Prosecutor discretion may occasionally be a more effective transfer mechanism than the waiver process because the prosecutor can file a petition in criminal or juvenile court without judicial approval.

Since 1966, the U.S. Supreme Court and other federal and state courts have attempted to ensure fairness in the waiver process by handing down decisions that spell out the need for due process. Two Supreme Court decisions, *Kent v. United States* (1966) and *Breed v. Jones* (1975), are relevant.[60] The *Kent* case declared a District of Columbia transfer statute unconstitutional and attacked the subsequent conviction of the child by granting him the specific due process rights of having an attorney present at the hearing and access to the evidence that would be used in the case. In *Breed v. Jones*, the U.S. Supreme Court declared that the child was to be granted the protection of the double-jeopardy clause of the Fifth Amendment after he was tried as a delinquent in the juvenile court: once found to be a delinquent, the youth could no longer be tried as an adult. Exhibit 13.2 discusses these two important cases in more detail.

Today, as a result of *Kent* and *Breed*, states that have transfer hearings provide a legitimate transfer hearing, sufficient notice to the child's family and defense attorney, the right to counsel, and a statement of the reason for the court order regarding transfer. These procedures recognize that the transfer process is critical in determining the statutory rights of the juvenile offender.

Should Youths Be Transferred to Adult Court?

Most juvenile justice experts oppose waiver because it clashes with the rehabilitative ideal. Basing waiver decisions on type and seriousness of offense rather than on the rehabilitative needs of the child has advanced the *criminalization* of the juvenile court and interfered with its traditional mission of treatment and rehabilitation.[61] And despite this sacrifice, there is little evidence that strict waiver policies

Some youths who commit the most serious crimes are routinely waived to adult court. Pictured here is Gary Flakes, age 31, at a park in downtown Colorado Springs on March 6, 2012. At 16, Flakes was tried as an adult and sentenced to 15 years in prison for criminally negligent homicide and accessory to murder. Flakes argues that he should have been sentenced as a juvenile because he was not convicted of the original charge. Colorado lawmakers are reexamining their juvenile transfer laws.

AP Photo/Ed Andrieski

EXHIBIT 13.2 *Kent v. United States* and *Breed v. Jones*

Kent v. United States: Facts

Morris Kent was arrested at age 16 in connection with charges of housebreaking, robbery, and rape. As a juvenile, he was subject to the exclusive jurisdiction of the District of Columbia juvenile court. The District of Columbia statute declared that the court could transfer the petitioner "after full investigation" and remit him to trial in the U.S. District Court. Kent admitted his involvement in the offenses and was placed in a receiving home for children. Subsequently, his mother obtained counsel, and they discussed with the social service director the possibility that the juvenile court might waive its jurisdiction.

Kent was detained at the receiving home for almost a week. There was no arraignment, no hearing, and no hearing for petitioner's apprehension. Kent's counsel arranged for a psychiatric examination, and a motion requesting a hearing on the waiver was filed. The juvenile court judge did not rule on the motion and entered an order that stated: "After full investigation, the court waives its jurisdiction and directs that a trial be held under the regular proceedings of the criminal court." The judge made no finding and gave no reasons for his waiver decision.

After the juvenile court waived its jurisdiction, Kent was indicted by the grand jury and was subsequently found guilty of housebreaking and robbery and not guilty by reason of insanity on the charge of rape. Kent was sentenced to serve a period of 30 to 90 years on his conviction.

Decision

The petitioner's lawyer appealed the decision on the basis of the infirmity of the proceedings by which the juvenile court waived its jurisdiction. He further attacked the waiver on statutory and constitutional grounds, stating: "(1) no hearing occurred, (2) no findings were made, (3) no reasons were stated before the waiver, and (4) counsel was denied access to the social service file." The U.S. Supreme Court found that the juvenile court order waiving jurisdiction and remitting the child to trial in the district court was invalid.

Significance of the Case

This case examined for the first time the substantial degree of discretion associated with a transfer proceeding in the District of Columbia. Thus, the Supreme Court significantly limited its holding to the statute involved but justified its reference to constitutional principles relating to due process and the assistance of counsel. In addition, it said that the juvenile court waiver hearings need to measure up to the essentials of due process and fair treatment. Furthermore, in an appendix to its opinion, the Court set up criteria concerning waiver of the jurisdictions. Some of these included:

- Whether the alleged offense was committed in an aggressive, violent, or willful manner
- The sophistication and maturity of the juvenile
- The record and previous history of the juvenile
- Prospects for adequate protection of the public and the likelihood of reasonable rehabilitation

Breed v. Jones: Facts

In 1971, a petition in the juvenile court of California was filed against Jones, who was then 17, alleging that he had committed an offense that, if committed by an adult, would constitute robbery. At a hearing, the juvenile court took testimony, found that the allegations were true, and sustained the petition. The proceedings were continued for a disposition hearing, at which point Jones was found unfit for treatment in the juvenile court. It was ordered that he be prosecuted as an adult offender. Jones was subsequently tried and found guilty and committed to the California Youth Authority.

Petitioner Jones sought an appeal in the federal district court on the basis of the double-jeopardy argument that jeopardy attaches at the juvenile delinquency proceedings. The writ of *habeas corpus* was denied.

Decision

The U.S. Supreme Court held that the prosecution of Jones as an adult in the California Superior Court violated the double-jeopardy clause of the Fifth Amendment to the U.S. Constitution as applied to the states through the Fourteenth Amendment. Thus, Jones's trial in the California Superior Court for the same offense as that for which he was tried in the juvenile court violated the policy of the double-jeopardy clause, even if he never faced the risk of more than one punishment. *Double jeopardy* refers to the risk or potential risk of trial and conviction, not punishment.

Significance of the Case

The *Breed* case provided answers on several important transfer issues: (a) it prohibits trying a child in an adult court when there has been a prior adjudicatory juvenile proceeding; (b) probable cause may exist at a transfer hearing, and this does not violate subsequent jeopardy if the child is transferred to the adult court; (c) because the same evidence is often used in both the transfer hearing and subsequent trial in either the juvenile or adult court, a different judge is often required for each hearing.

Sources: *Kent v. United States*, 383 U.S. 541, 86 S.Ct. 1045, 16 L.Ed.2d 84 (1966); *Breed v. Jones*, 421 U.S. 519, 95 S.Ct. 1779 (1975).

can lower crime rates.[62] This particularly important issue is the subject of the Focus on Delinquency feature on pages 366–367.

Some experts also question whether juveniles waived to adult court, particularly younger ones, are competent to be tried as adults. Adjudicative competency pertains to the mental capacity or cognitive skills of the youth to understand the nature and object of the proceedings against him or her. Two studies found that the mental competency of youths under the age of 16 to stand trial is far below that of similarly charged adults, with one study comparing the competency of young juvenile offenders to that of severely mentally impaired adults.[63]

Waiver can also create long-term harm. Waived children may be stigmatized by a conviction in the criminal court. Labeling children as adult offenders early in life may seriously impair their future educational, employment, and other opportunities. Youthful offenders convicted in adult courts are more likely to be incarcerated and to receive longer sentences than if they remained in the juvenile court. This is the conclusion of a growing number of high-quality studies.[64] In one study in New York and New Jersey, juveniles transferred to criminal court were almost three times more likely to receive sentences of incarceration than juvenile court defendants (36 percent versus 14 percent).[65] In another study in Pennsylvania, the average sentence length for juvenile offenders sentenced in adult court was found to be significantly longer than for a similar group of young adult offenders (18 months compared to six months).[66] And these children may be incarcerated under conditions so extreme, and in institutions where they may be physically and sexually exploited, that they will become permanently damaged.[67] In a small-scale study of female youths transferred to criminal court and subsequently placed in a prison for adult women, it was found that the prison was severely limited in its ability to care for and provide needed treatment services for these youths compared with the adults.[68]

Waivers don't always support the goal of increased public protection. Because juveniles may only serve a fraction of the prison sentence imposed by the criminal court, the actual treatment of delinquents in adult court is similar to what they might have received had they remained in the custody of juvenile authorities.[69] This has prompted some critics to ask: why bother transferring these children?

Sometimes waiver can add an undue burden to youthful offenders. Studies have found that, although transfer to criminal court was intended for the most serious juvenile offenders, many transferred juveniles were not violent offenders, but repeat property offenders.[70] Cases involving waiver take significantly longer than comparable juvenile court cases, during which time the waived youth is more likely to be held in a detention center.

Transfer decisions are not always carried out fairly or equitably, and there is evidence that minorities are waived at a rate that is greater than their representation in the population.[71] Forty-two percent of all waived youth are African Americans, even though they represent 34 percent of the juvenile court population.[72] A federal study of juveniles waived to criminal court in the nation's 40 largest counties found that 62 percent of waived youth were African American.[73] Between the peak years of 1994 and 2008, the total number of judicially waived cases involving African American youth decreased by just over one-third (36 percent, from 5,800 to 3,700 cases); a similar decrease was reported for European American youth (35 percent, from 7,500 to 4,900 cases).[74]

In Support of Waiver. Not all experts challenge the waiver concept. Waiver is attractive to conservatives because it jibes with the get-tough policy that is currently popular. Some have argued that the increased use of waiver can help get violent offenders off the streets and should be mandatory for juveniles committing serious violent crimes.[75] Others point to studies that show that, for the most part, transfer is reserved for the most serious cases and the most serious juvenile offenders. Kids are most likely to be transferred to criminal court if they have injured someone with a weapon or if they have a long juvenile court record.[76] The most recent federal study of waiver found that 27 percent of juveniles tried in criminal court were sent to prison. This outcome might be expected because those waived to criminal court were more likely (64 percent) than adults (24 percent) to be charged with a violent

QUESTIONS RAISED ABOUT EFFECTIVENESS OF JUVENILE TRANSFERS TO ADULT COURT IN REDUCING VIOLENCE

In all the debate surrounding transfers of juvenile offenders to adult or criminal court, one of the most important issues—for some, it is the bottom line on this matter—concerns whether transfers are effective in reducing crime rates. One of the pressing questions: are juveniles who are transferred to and convicted in adult court less likely to recidivate than similar youths who are convicted in juvenile court? This pertains to a specific or individual deterrent effect of transfers. Another key question, which pertains to a general deterrent effect, can be framed as such: do transfers decrease crime rates in the juvenile population as a whole? This could be for a city or state, for example. In recent years, a number of high-quality studies have investigated the effectiveness of transfers on these two fronts.

The Task Force on Community Preventive Services, an independent group that receives support from the U.S. Department of Health and Human Services and the Centers for Disease Control and Prevention, conducted the first comprehensive, methodologically rigorous review of the literature—known as a systematic review—on the effects of transfer laws and policies on crime rates.

The review identified six high-quality evaluation studies (each had experimental and comparable control groups) that measured the specific deterrent effect of transfers on violent crime rates. Not one of the studies found that transfers produced lower violent crime rates. In fact, four of the studies found a harmful effect, meaning that juveniles transferred to adult court had higher violent rearrest rates than their counterparts who were retained in juvenile court. For these four studies, rearrest rates for the transferred juveniles were between 27 and 77 percent higher than the nontransferred juveniles. The authors of the review also reported that these studies found harmful effects for total crime rates as well. The Washington State study found that transfers to adult court made no difference: violent crime rearrest rates were neither higher nor lower for transferred juveniles compared to retained juveniles 18 months after release from prison.

On the matter of a general deterrent effect of transfers, less could be said. The review identified three high-quality evaluation studies that measured whether transfer laws deter juveniles in the general population from violent crime. Inconsistent results were found across the studies: one study reported no effect, one reported mixed effects, and one reported harmful effects. Based on these inconsistent results, the task force concluded that there was insufficient evidence at present to make a determination on the effectiveness of transfer laws and policies in reducing juvenile violence generally.

A more recent study on the general deterrent effects of transfer, the largest and perhaps most rigorous one yet to investigate this question, may shed some light on these inconsistent results. (This study was not included in the systematic review because it was outside of the review's publication date cutoff.) Criminologists Benjamin Steiner, Craig Hemmens, and Valerie Bell examined 22 states that enacted statutory exclusion or automatic transfer laws after 1979. The study found no reduction in arrest rates for violent juvenile crime in 21 of the 22 states over a period of five years following the introduction of the transfer law. Only Maine experienced a reduction in its juvenile arrest rate for violent crime, a reduction that was both immediate and permanent, and thus could be said to provide support for

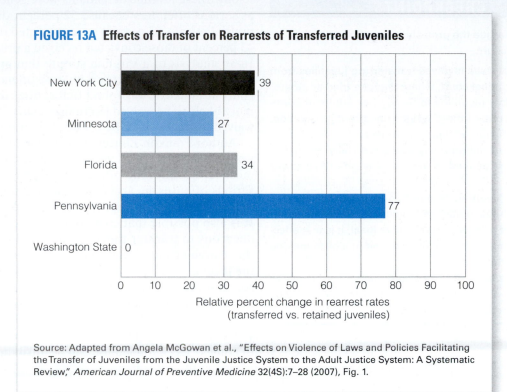

FIGURE 13A Effects of Transfer on Rearrests of Transferred Juveniles

Relative percent change in rearrest rates
(transferred vs. retained juveniles)

New York City — 39
Minnesota — 27
Florida — 34
Pennsylvania — 77
Washington State — 0

Source: Adapted from Angela McGowan et al., "Effects on Violence of Laws and Policies Facilitating the Transfer of Juveniles from the Juvenile Justice System to the Adult Justice System: A Systematic Review," *American Journal of Preventive Medicine* 32(4S):7–28 (2007), Fig. 1.

a general deterrent effect of the transfer law.

Based on the overall findings, the Task Force on Community Preventive Services concluded that transferring juvenile offenders to the adult system is "counterproductive for the purpose of reducing juvenile violence and enhancing public safety." They did not go so far as to recommend that states repeal their transfer laws and discontinue the practice of transfers altogether, possibly because of the inconsistent results found for general deterrent effects. Legal scholar Michael Tonry, in commenting on the task force's report, says it is time that some of these changes take place. He also calls for more individualized treatment for juvenile offenders, noting that, "One-size-fits-all policies inevitably produce anomalies, injustices, and unwanted side effects (including increased violent reoffending)." Research on the perceptions of the public as well as practitioners

backs up some of these views, indicating that they want transfers used sparingly and selectively and when there is a balance between effective rehabilitation and punishment.

CRITICAL THINKING

1. Should the practice of transferring juvenile offenders to adult court be ceased altogether or should transfers be used only in isolated cases involving extreme violence? Explain.

2. While the effects of transfers on crime rates are important, what are some other key issues that need to be considered?

Writing Assignment Based on this research evidence, write an essay on what you would recommend to your state legislator. Conversely, if you remain unconvinced by this research, explain

its shortcomings and recommend what the state legislator should do.

Sources: David L. Myers, Daniel Lee, Dennis Giever, and Jay Gilliam, "Practitioner Perceptions of Juvenile Transfer in Pennsylvania," *Youth Violence and Juvenile Justice* 9:222–240 (2011); Brandon K. Applegate, Robin King Davis, and Francis T. Cullen, "Reconsidering Child Saving: The Extent and Correlates of Public Support for Excluding Youths from Juvenile Courts," *Crime and Delinquency* 55:51–77 (2009); Jeffrey Fagan, "Juvenile Crime and Criminal Justice: Resolving Border Disputes," *The Future of Children* 18(2):81–118 (2008); Angela McGowan, Robert Hahn, Akiva Liberman, Alex Crosby, Mindy Fullilove, Robert Johnson, Eve Mosciki, LeShawndra Price, Susan Snyder, Farris Tuma, Jessica Lowy, Peter Briss, Stella Cory, Glenda Stone, and the Task Force on Community Preventive Services, "Effects on Violence of Laws and Policies Facilitating the Transfer of Juveniles from the Juvenile Justice System to the Adult Justice System: A Systematic Review," *American Journal of Preventive Medicine* 32(4S):7–28 (2007); Michael Tonry, "Treating Juveniles as Adult Criminals: An Iatrogenic Violence Prevention Strategy if Ever There Was One," *American Journal of Preventive Medicine* 32(4S):3–4 (2007); Benjamin Steiner, Craig Hemmens, and Valerie Bell, "Legislative Waiver Reconsidered: General Deterrent Effects of Statutory Exclusion Laws Enacted Post-1979," *Justice Quarterly* 23:34–59 (2006).

✔ The waiver process involves transferring juveniles from juvenile to criminal court, where they are tried as adults.

✔ All states allow juveniles to be tried as adults in criminal courts in one of three ways: concurrent jurisdiction, statutory exclusion, and judicial waiver.

✔ The number of delinquency cases judicially waived to criminal court peaked in 1994 and is one-third lower today.

✔ Transfers of juveniles to adult court are opposed on a number of philosophical and factual grounds, including that it clashes with the rehabilitative ideal, it is ineffective in reducing juvenile violence, and juveniles may be subject to further harm.

✔ There is some support for the continuation of the waiver concept, including that it is reserved for the most serious juvenile offenders.

felony. These juvenile defendants were generally regarded as serious offenders because 52 percent did not receive pretrial release, 63 percent were convicted of a felony, and 43 percent of those convicted received a prison sentence.[77] In an analysis of a Virginia statute that grants prosecutors the authority to certify a juvenile offender to criminal court at intake, it was found that serious offenders were more likely to be waived to criminal court.[78] Clearly, many waived juveniles might be considered serious offenders.

Author Franklin Zimring argues that, despite its faults, waiver is superior to alternative methods for handling the most serious juvenile offenders.[79] Some cases involving serious offenses, he argues, require a minimum criminal penalty greater than that available to the juvenile court. It is also possible that some juveniles take advantage of decisions to transfer them to the adult court. Although the charge against a child may be considered serious in the juvenile court, the adult criminal court will not find it so; consequently, a child may have a better chance for dismissal of the charges, or acquittal, after a jury trial.

In sum, though the use of waiver has declined in recent years, it is still being used today as an important strategy for attacking serious youth crime.[80] Its continued use can be attributed to concerns about the most serious and violent juvenile offenders. **CHECKPOINTS**

JUVENILE COURT TRIAL

If the case cannot be decided during the pretrial stage, it will be brought for trial in the juvenile court. An adjudication hearing is held to determine the merits of the petition claiming that a child is either a delinquent youth or in need of court supervision. The judge is required to make a finding based on the evidence and arrive at a judgment. The adjudication hearing is comparable to an adult trial. Rules of evidence in adult criminal proceedings are generally applicable in juvenile court, and the standard of proof used—*beyond a reasonable doubt*—is similar to that used in adult trials.

State juvenile codes vary with regard to the basic requirements of due process and fairness. Most juvenile courts have bifurcated hearings—that is, separate hearings for adjudication and disposition (sentencing). At disposition hearings, evidence can be submitted that reflects nonlegal factors, such as the child's home life.

Most state juvenile codes provide specific rules of procedure. These rules require that a written petition be submitted to the court, ensure the right of a child to have an attorney, provide that the adjudication proceedings be recorded, allow the petition to be amended, and provide that a child's plea be accepted. Where the child admits to the facts of the petition, the court generally seeks assurance that the plea is voluntary. If plea bargaining is used, prosecutors, defense counsel, and trial judges take steps to ensure the fairness of such negotiations.

At the end of the adjudication hearing, most juvenile court statutes require the judge to make a factual finding on the legal issues and evidence. In the criminal court, this finding is normally a prelude to reaching a verdict. In the juvenile court, however, the finding itself is the verdict, and the case is resolved in one of three ways:

- The juvenile court judge makes a finding of fact that the child or juvenile is not delinquent or in need of supervision.
- The juvenile court judge makes a finding of fact that the juvenile is delinquent or in need of supervision.
- The juvenile court judge dismisses the case because of insufficient or faulty evidence.

In some jurisdictions, informal alternatives are used, such as filing the case with no further consequences or continuing the case without a finding for a period of time (for example, six months). If the juvenile does not get into further difficulty during that time, the case is dismissed. These alternatives involve no determination of delinquency or noncriminal behavior. Because of the philosophy of the juvenile court that emphasizes rehabilitation over punishment, a delinquency finding is not the same thing as a criminal conviction. The disabilities associated with conviction, such as disqualifications for employment or being barred from military service, do not apply in an adjudication of delinquency.

There are other differences between adult and juvenile proceedings. For instance, whereas adults are entitled to public trials by a jury of their peers, these rights are not extended to juveniles.[81] Because juvenile courts treat some defendants similarly to adult criminals, an argument can be made that the courts should extend to these youths the Sixth Amendment right to a public jury trial.[82] For the most part, however, state juvenile courts operate without recognizing a juvenile's constitutional right to a jury trial.

Constitutional Rights at Trial

In addition to mandating state juvenile code requirements, the U.S. Supreme Court has mandated the application of constitutional due process standards to the juvenile trial. **Due process** is addressed in the Fifth and Fourteenth Amendments to the U.S. Constitution. It refers to the need for rules and procedures to ensure that no person can be deprived of life, liberty, or property without protections, such as legal counsel, an open and fair hearing, and an opportunity to confront those making accusations against him or her.

For many years, children were deprived of their due process rights because the *parens patriae* philosophy governed their relationship to the juvenile justice system. Such rights as having counsel and confronting one's accusers were deemed unnecessary. After all, why should children need protection from the state when the state was seen as acting in their interest? As we have seen, this view changed in the 1960s, when the U.S. Supreme Court began to grant due process rights and procedures to minors. The key case was that of Gerald Gault; it articulated the basic requirements of due process that must be satisfied in juvenile court proceedings. Because *in re Gault* (1967) remains the key constitutional case in the juvenile justice system, it is discussed in depth in Exhibit 13.3.

The *Gault* decision reshaped the constitutional and philosophical nature of the juvenile court system, and with the addition of legal representation, made it more similar to the adult system.[83] Following the *Gault* case, the U.S. Supreme Court decided in *in re Winship* that the amount of proof required in juvenile delinquency adjudications is "beyond a reasonable doubt," a level equal to the requirements in the adult system.[84]

Although the ways in which the juvenile court operates were altered by *Gault* and *Winship*, the trend toward increased rights for juveniles was somewhat curtailed by the U.S. Supreme Court's decision in *McKeiver v. Pennsylvania* (1971), which held that trial by jury in a juvenile court's adjudicative stage is not a constitutional requirement.[85] This decision does not prevent states from giving the juvenile a trial by jury, but in most states a child has no such right.

Once an adjudicatory hearing has been completed, the court is normally required to enter a judgment or finding against the child. This may take the form of declaring the child delinquent, adjudging the child to be a ward of the court, or possibly even suspending judgment so as to avoid the stigma of a juvenile record. After a judgment has been entered, the court can begin its determination of possible dispositions. **CHECKPOINTS**

W∧W

To get information on **juvenile courts**, go to the website of the National Center for State Courts by visiting the Criminal Justice CourseMate at CengageBrain.com, then accessing the Web Links for this chapter.

W∧W

For a review of **due process issues in juvenile justice**, visit the Criminal Justice CourseMate at CengageBrain.com, then access the Web Links for this chapter.

CHECKPOINTS

LO4 Understand key issues of the trial stage of juvenile justice and the major U.S. Supreme Court decisions regarding the handling of juveniles at the preadjudicatory and trial stages.

✔ Most juvenile courts have bifurcated hearings—that is, separate hearings for adjudication and disposition (sentencing).

✔ Whereas adults are entitled to public trials by a jury of their peers, these rights are not extended to juveniles.

✔ *In re Gault* is the key legal case that set out the basic requirements of due process that must be satisfied in juvenile court proceedings.

due process Basic constitutional principle based on the concept of the primacy of the individual and the complementary concept of limitation on governmental power; safeguards the individual from unfair state procedures in judicial or administrative proceedings; due process rights have been extended to juvenile trials.

EXHIBIT 13.3 *In Re Gault*

Facts

Gerald Gault, 15 years of age, was taken into custody by the sheriff of Gila County, Arizona, because a woman complained that he and another boy had made an obscene telephone call to her. At the time, Gault was under a six-month probation disposition after being found delinquent for stealing a wallet. As a result of the woman's complaint, the boy was taken to a children's home. His parents were not informed that he was being taken into custody. His mother appeared in the evening and was told by the superintendent of detention that a hearing would be held in the juvenile court the following day. On the day in question, the police officer who had taken Gault into custody filed a petition alleging his delinquency. Gault, his mother, and the police officer appeared before the judge in his chambers. Mrs. Cook, the complainant, was not at the hearing. The boy was questioned about the telephone calls and sent back to the detention home and subsequently released a few days later.

On the day of his release, Mrs. Gault received a letter indicating that a hearing would be held subsequently on his delinquency. A hearing was held, and the complainant again was not present. There was no transcript or recording of the proceedings, and the juvenile officer stated that Gault had admitted making the lewd telephone calls. Neither the boy nor his parents were advised of any right to remain silent, right to be represented by counsel, or any other constitutional rights. At the conclusion of the hearing, the juvenile court committed Gault as a juvenile delinquent to the state industrial school for the period of his minority. This meant that, at age 15, Gerald Gault was sentenced to remain in the state school until he reached the age of 21, unless he was discharged sooner. An adult charged with the same crime would have received a maximum punishment of no more than a $50 fine or two months in prison.

Decision

Gault's attorneys filed a writ of *habeas corpus*, which was denied by the Superior Court of the State of Arizona. That decision was subsequently affirmed by the Arizona Supreme Court. On appeal to the U.S. Supreme Court, Gault's counsel argued that the juvenile code of Arizona under which the boy was found delinquent was invalid because it was contrary to the due process clause of the Fourteenth Amendment.

The Court, in a far-reaching opinion, agreed that Gerald Gault's constitutional rights had been violated. Notice of charges was an essential ingredient of due process of law, as was the right to counsel, the right to cross-examine and to confront witnesses, and the privilege against self-incrimination.

Significance of the Case

The *Gault* case established that a child has due process constitutional rights in delinquency adjudication proceedings, where the consequences were that the child could be committed to a state institution.

This decision was also significant because of its far-reaching impact throughout the entire juvenile justice system. *Gault* instilled in juvenile proceedings the development of due process standards at the pretrial, trial, and post-trial stages of the juvenile process. Although recognizing the history and development of the juvenile court, it sought to accommodate the motives of rehabilitation and treatment with children's rights. It recognized the principle of fundamental fairness of the law for children as well as for adults. Judged in the context of today's juvenile justice system, *Gault* redefined the relationships among juveniles, their parents, and the state. It remains the single most significant constitutional case in the area of juvenile justice.

Source: *In re Gault*, 387 U.S. 1; 87 S.Ct. 1248 (1967).

Disposition

The sentencing step of the juvenile justice process is called *disposition*. At this point, the court orders treatment for the juvenile.[86] According to prevailing juvenile justice philosophy, dispositions should be in the *best interest of the child*, which in this context means providing the help necessary to resolve or meet the youth's personal needs while also meeting society's needs for protection.

As already noted, in most jurisdictions, adjudication and disposition hearings are bifurcated so that evidence that could not be entered during the juvenile trial can be considered at the dispositional hearing. At the hearing, the defense counsel represents the child, helps the parents understand the court's decision, and influences the direction of the disposition. Others involved at the dispositional stage include representatives of social service agencies, psychologists, social workers, and probation personnel.

The appeal of Gerald Gault (center) heralded in the due process revolution in juvenile justice. The *Gault* case redefined the relationships among juveniles, their parents, and the state. It remains the single most significant constitutional case in the area of juvenile justice.

The Predisposition Report. After the child has admitted to the allegations, or the allegations have been proved in a trial, the judge normally orders the probation department to complete a predisposition report. The predisposition report, which is similar to the presentence report of the adult justice system, has a number of purposes:

- It helps the judge decide which disposition is best for the child.
- It aids the juvenile probation officer in developing treatment programs when the child is in need of counseling or community supervision.
- It helps the court develop a body of knowledge about the child that can aid others in treating the child.[87]

Some state statutes make the predisposition report mandatory. Other jurisdictions require the report only when there is a probability that the child will be institutionalized. Some appellate courts have reversed orders institutionalizing children where the juvenile court did not use a predisposition report in reaching its decision. Access to predisposition reports is an important legal issue.

In the final section of the predisposition report, the probation department recommends a disposition to the presiding judge. This is a critical aspect of the report, because it has been estimated that the court follows more than 90 percent of all probation department recommendations.

Juvenile Court Dispositions. Historically, the juvenile court has had broad discretionary power to make dispositional decisions. The major categories of dispositional choices are community release, out-of-home placement, fines or restitution, community service, and institutionalization. A more detailed list of the dispositions open to the juvenile court judge appears in Exhibit 13.4.[88]

Looking Back to Cliff's Story

Cliff was ordered to take part in an intervention known as Functional Family Therapy (FFT).

CRITICAL THINKING Discuss the short- and long-term benefits of FFT for juvenile offenders. Also, identify if there are any situations where this type of intervention may not be appropriate or successful and explain why.

EXHIBIT 13.4 Common Juvenile Dispositions

Disposition	Action Taken
Informal consent decree	In minor or first offenses, an informal hearing is held, and the judge will ask the youth and his or her guardian to agree to a treatment program, such as counseling. No formal trial or disposition hearing is held.
Probation	A youth is placed under the control of the county probation department and required to obey a set of probation rules and participate in a treatment program.
Home detention	A child is restricted to his or her home in lieu of a secure placement. Rules include regular school attendance, curfew observance, avoidance of alcohol and drugs, and notification of parents and the youth worker of the child's whereabouts.
Court-ordered school attendance	If truancy was the problem that brought the youth to court, a judge may order mandatory school attendance. Some courts have established court-operated day school and court-based tutorial programs staffed by community volunteers.
Financial restitution	A judge can order the juvenile offender to make financial restitution to the victim. In most jurisdictions, restitution is part of probation (see Chapter 14), but in some states restitution can be a sole order.
Fines	Some states allow fines to be levied against juveniles age 16 and older.
Community service	Courts in many jurisdictions require juveniles to spend time in the community working off their debt to society. Community service orders are usually reserved for victimless crimes, such as vandalism of school property. Community service orders are usually carried out in schools, hospitals, or nursing homes.
Outpatient psychotherapy	Youths who are diagnosed with psychological disorders may be required to undergo therapy at a local mental health clinic.
Drug and alcohol treatment	Youths with drug- or alcohol-related problems may be allowed to remain in the community if they agree to undergo drug or alcohol therapy.
Commitment to secure treatment	In the most serious cases, a judge may order an offender admitted to a long-term treatment center, such as a training school, camp, ranch, or group home. These may be either state-run or privately run institutions, and are usually located in remote regions. Training schools provide educational, vocational, and rehabilitation programs in a secure environment (see Chapter 14).
Commitment to a residential community	Youths who commit crimes of a less serious nature, but who still need to be removed from their homes, can be placed in community-based group homes or halfway houses. They attend school or work during the day and live in a controlled, therapeutic environment at night.
Foster home placement	Foster homes are usually sought for dependent or neglected children and status offenders. Judges may also place delinquents with insurmountable problems at home in state-licensed foster care homes.

Most state statutes allow the juvenile court judge to select whatever disposition seems best suited to the child's needs, including institutionalization. In some states, the court determines commitment to a specific institution; in other states, the youth corrections agency determines where the child will be placed. In addition to the dispositions shown in Exhibit 13.4, some states grant the court the power to order parents into treatment or suspend a youth's driver's license.

Today it is common for juvenile court judges to employ a graduated sanction program for juveniles: (1) immediate sanctions for nonviolent offenders, which consist of community-based diversion and day treatment imposed on first-time nonviolent offenders; (2) intermediate sanctions, which target repeat minor offenders and first-time serious offenders; and (3) secure care, which is reserved for repeat serious offenders and violent offenders.[89]

In 2008 (the latest data available), juveniles were adjudicated delinquent in 61 percent of the 924,400 cases brought before a judge. Once adjudicated, the majority of these juveniles (57 percent or 322,900 cases) were placed on formal probation, just over one quarter (28 percent or 157,700 cases) were placed in a residential facility, and 15 percent (or 83,200 cases) were given another disposition, such as referral to an outside agency, community service, or restitution.[90]

Although the juvenile court has been under pressure to get tough on youth crime, these figures show that probation is the disposition of choice, even in the most serious cases,[91] and its use has grown in recent years. Between 1985 and 2008, the number of cases in which the court ordered an adjudicated delinquent to be placed on formal probation increased by a full two-thirds (67 percent, from 193,100 to 322,900), whereas the number of cases involving placement in a residential facility increased 51 percent (from 104,500 to 157,700).[92]

least detrimental alternative Choosing a program that will best foster a child's growth and development.

indeterminate sentence Does not specify the length of time the juvenile must be held; rather, correctional authorities decide when the juvenile is ready to return to society.

Juvenile Sentencing Structures

For most of the juvenile court's history, disposition was based on the presumed needs of the child. Although critics have challenged the motivations of early reformers in championing rehabilitation, there is little question that the rhetoric of the juvenile court has promoted that ideal.[93] For example, in their classic work *Beyond the Best Interest of the Child*, Joseph Goldstein, Anna Freud, and Albert Solnit said that placement of children should be based on the **least detrimental alternative** available in order to foster the child's development.[94] Most states have adopted this ideal in their sentencing efforts, and state courts usually insist that the purpose of disposition must be rehabilitation and not punishment.[95] Consequently, it is common for state courts to require judges to justify their sentencing decisions if it means that juveniles are to be incarcerated in a residential treatment center: they must set forth in writing the reasons for the placement, address the danger the child poses to society, and explain why a less restrictive alternative has not been used.[96]

Traditionally, states have used the **indeterminate sentence** in juvenile court. In about half the states, this means having the judge place the offender with the state department of juvenile corrections until correctional authorities consider the youth ready to return to society or until the youth reaches legal majority. A preponderance of states consider 18 to be the age of release; others peg the termination age at 19; a few can retain minority status until the 21st birthday. In practice, few youths remain in custody for the entire statutory period, but juveniles are usually released if their rehabilitation has been judged to have progressed satisfactorily. This practice is referred to as the *individualized treatment model*.

© AP Photo/*Daytona Beach News-Journal*/David Tucker

When making disposition decisions, juvenile court judges have a wide range of options, including referral to programs that will enhance life skills and help youths form a positive bond to society. Here, 16-year-old Warren Messner fights back tears after being sentenced to 22.8 years in prison by Circuit Judge Joseph Will in Daytona Beach, Florida. Messner, along with three other teens, pleaded guilty to the beating murder of Michael Roberts, a homeless man.

Another form of the indeterminate sentence allows judges to specify a maximum term. Under this form of sentencing, youths may be released when the corrections department considers them to be rehabilitated or they reach the automatic age of termination (usually 18 or 21). In states that stipulate a maximum sentence, the court may extend the sentence, depending on the youth's progress in the institutional facility.

A number of states have changed from an indeterminate to a **determinate sentence**. This means sentencing juvenile offenders to a fixed term of incarceration that must be served in its entirety. Other states have passed laws creating **mandatory sentences** for serious juvenile offenders. Juveniles receiving mandatory sentences are usually institutionalized for the full sentence and are not eligible for early parole. The difference between mandatory and determinate sentences is that the mandatory sentence carries a statutory requirement that a certain penalty be set in all cases on conviction for a specified offense.

The Death Penalty for Juveniles

On March 1, 2005, the U.S. Supreme Court, in the case of *Roper v. Simmons*, put an end to the practice of the death penalty for juveniles in the United States. At issue was the minimum age that juveniles who were under the age of 18 when they committed their crimes could be eligible for the death penalty.[97] At the time, 16- and 17-year-olds were eligible for the death penalty, and 21 states permitted the death penalty for juveniles,[98] with a total of 72 juvenile offenders on death row.[99] In a 5–4 decision, the Court ruled that the juvenile death penalty was in violation of the Eighth Amendment's ban on cruel and unusual punishment.[100]

The execution of minor children has not been uncommon in our nation's history; at least 366 juvenile offenders have been executed since 1642.[101] This represents about 2 percent of the more than 18,000 executions carried out since colonial times. Between the reinstatement of the death penalty in 1976 and the last execution of a juvenile in 2003, 22 juvenile offenders were executed in seven states; Texas accounted for 13 of these executions. All 22 of the executed juvenile offenders were male, 21 committed their crimes at age 17, and just over half (13 of them) were minorities.[102]

Past Legal Issues. In *Thompson v. Oklahoma* (1988), the U.S. Supreme Court prohibited the execution of persons under age 16, but left open the age at which execution would be legally appropriate.[103] They then answered this question in two 1989 cases, *Wilkins v. Missouri* and *Stanford v. Kentucky*, in which they ruled that states were free to impose the death penalty for murderers who committed their crimes after they reached age 16 or 17.[104] According to the majority opinion, society at that time had not formed a consensus that the execution of such minors constitutes cruel and unusual punishment.

Those who oppose the death penalty for children find that it has little deterrent effect on youngsters who are impulsive and do not have a realistic view of the destructiveness of their misdeeds or their consequences. Victor Streib, the leading critic of the death penalty for children, argues that such a practice is cruel and unusual punishment for four primary reasons: the condemnation of children makes no measurable contribution to the legitimate goals of punishment; condemning any minor to death violates contemporary standards of decency; the capacity of the young for change, growth, and rehabilitation makes the death penalty particularly harsh and inappropriate; and both legislative attitudes and public opinion reject juvenile executions.[105] Those who oppose the death penalty for children also refer to a growing body of research that shows that the brain continues to develop through the late teen years, affecting important mental functions such as planning, judgment, and emotional control.[106] Opposition to the juvenile death penalty is also backed up by declining public support for the death penalty in general in the

determinate sentence Specifies a fixed term of detention that must be served.

mandatory sentences Sentences are defined by a statutory requirement that states the penalty to be set for all cases of a specific offense.

United States (at least for the execution of juveniles) and world opinion.[107] Supporters of the death penalty hold that, regardless of their age, people can form criminal intent and therefore should be responsible for their actions. If the death penalty is legal for adults, they assert, then it can also be used for children who commit serious crimes.

Life Without Parole for Juveniles

Closely tied to the end of the practice of the death penalty for juveniles is a debate that concerns juveniles sentenced to life without the possibility of parole. In a provocatively titled article, "A Slower Form of Death: Implications of *Roper v. Simmons* for Juveniles Sentenced to Life without Parole," legal scholar Barry Feld argues that the Supreme Court's diminished responsibility standard—used in their decision to end the juvenile death penalty—should also be applicable to cases in which juvenile offenders are receiving life sentences without the possibility of parole.[108] The main reasons for this view center on the overly punitive nature of this sentence and the need to differentiate between juvenile and adult culpability.[109] To achieve this end, Feld proposes that "states formally recognize youthfulness as a mitigating factor by applying a 'youth discount' to adult sentence lengths."[110] This could have implications for thousands of juvenile offenders now and in the future. Amnesty International and Human Rights Watch estimate that there are more than 2,225 prisoners in the United States who "have been sentenced to spend the rest of their lives in prison for the crimes they committed as children." Of this total, more than 356 (or 16 percent) were between 13 and 15 years old at the time they committed their crimes.[111] A recent survey of 1,579 of these juveniles by the Washington, D.C.-based organization The Sentencing Project found that these youths have endured socioeconomic disadvantages, education failure, and abuse; the life sentences were characterized by extreme racial disparities; and state prison policies preclude many from receiving treatment programs.[112] While sentencing juveniles to life without parole raises any number of legal, moral, and social issues for some—others argue that "death is different" and the standards applied in *Roper v. Simmons* should not apply here[113]—the more controversial matter concerns juveniles who have received this sentence for crimes other than murder.

In 2009, the United States Supreme Court agreed to take up the matter of juveniles sentenced to life without the possibility of parole. The court accepted appeals from two individuals, both from Florida, who were serving life sentences for nonhomicide crimes committed when they were juveniles. In the first case, which goes back to 1989, Joe Sullivan, then 13, was convicted of raping a 72-year-old woman. In the other case, Terrance Graham, who was 17 years old, was convicted of a probation violation for a home invasion robbery in 2004. In their briefs to the Court, both petitioners argued that the sentence of life without the possibility of parole violates the Eighth Amendment's prohibition of cruel and unusual punishment. In oral arguments before the Court, the justices did not revisit the question that "juveniles generally are psychologically less mature than adults," but instead focused on "whether the mitigating trait of immaturity justified a categorical exclusion of juveniles from the sentence of life without parole."[114]

On May 17, 2010, the U.S. Supreme Court, in the case of *Graham v. Florida*, put an end to the practice of life sentences without the possibility of parole for juveniles convicted of non-homicide crimes.[115] The Court agreed that this sentence violated the Eighth Amendment's ban on cruel and unusual punishment. The Court did leave in place the prospect that juveniles could continue to receive a life sentence without parole for crimes in which someone is killed.

In two separate cases involving 14-year-olds convicted of homicide and sentenced to life without parole, *Miller v. Alabama* and *Jackson v. Hobbs*, the U.S. Supreme Court subsequently decided to revisit this issue.[116] On June 25, 2012, the Court struck down the sentence of life without the possibility of parole for all juvenile offenders, including those convicted of homicide.[117] The Court ruled that the sentence violated the Eighth Amendment's ban on cruel and unusual punishment.

The Child's Right to Appeal

Regardless of the sentence imposed, juveniles may want to appeal the decision made by the juvenile court judge. Juvenile court statutes normally restrict appeals to cases where the juvenile seeks review of a **final order**, one that ends the litigation between two parties by determining all their rights and disposing of all the issues.[118] The **appellate process** gives the juvenile the opportunity to have the case brought before a reviewing court after it has been heard in the juvenile or family court. Today, the law does not recognize a federal constitutional right of appeal. In other words, the U.S. Constitution does not require any state to furnish an appeal to a juvenile charged and found to be delinquent in a juvenile or family court. Consequently, appellate review of a juvenile case is a matter of statutory right in each jurisdiction. However, the majority of states do provide juveniles with some method of statutory appeal.

The appeal process was not always part of the juvenile law system. In 1965, few states extended the right of appeal to juveniles.[119] Even in the *Gault* case in 1967, the U.S. Supreme Court refused to review the Arizona juvenile code, which provided no appellate review in juvenile matters. It further rejected the right of a juvenile to a transcript of the original trial record.[120] Today, however, most jurisdictions that provide a child with some form of appeal also provide for counsel and for securing a record and transcript, which are crucial to the success of any appeal.

Because juvenile appellate review is defined by individual statutes, each jurisdiction determines for itself what method of review will be used. There are two basic methods of appeal: the direct appeal and the collateral attack.

The *direct appeal* normally involves an appellate court review to determine whether, based on the evidence presented at the trial, the rulings of law and the judgment of the court were correct. The second major area of review involves the collateral attack of a case. The term *collateral* implies a secondary or indirect method of attacking a final judgment. Instead of appealing the juvenile trial because of errors, prejudice, or lack of evidence, *collateral attack* uses extraordinary legal writs to challenge the lower-court position. One such procedural device is the writ of *habeas corpus*. Known as the *Great Writ*, the **writ of *habeas corpus*** refers to a procedure for determining the validity of a person's custody. In the context of the juvenile court, it is used to challenge the custody of a child in detention or in an institution. This writ is often the method by which the Supreme Court exercises its discretionary authority to hear cases involving constitutional issues. Even though there is no constitutional right to appeal a juvenile case and each jurisdiction provides for appeals differently, juveniles have a far greater opportunity for appellate review today than in years past. CHECKPOINTS

Confidentiality in Juvenile Proceedings

Along with the rights of juveniles at adjudication and disposition, the issue of **confidentiality** in juvenile proceedings has also received attention in recent years. The debate on confidentiality in the juvenile court deals with two areas: open versus closed hearings, and privacy of juvenile records. Confidentiality has become moot in some respects because many legislatures have broadened access to juvenile records.

final order Order that ends litigation between two parties by determining all their rights and disposing of all the issues.

appellate process Allows the juvenile an opportunity to have the case brought before a reviewing court after it has been heard in juvenile or family court.

writ of *habeas corpus* Judicial order requesting that a person detaining another produce the body of the prisoner and give reasons for his or her capture and detention.

confidentiality Restricting information in juvenile court proceedings in the interest of protecting the privacy of the juvenile.

Open versus Closed Hearings. Generally, juvenile trials are closed to the public and the press, and the names of the offenders are kept secret. The U.S. Supreme Court has ruled on the issue of privacy in three important decisions. In *Davis v. Alaska*, the Court concluded that any injury resulting from the disclosure of a juvenile's record is outweighed by the right to completely cross-examine an adverse witness.[121] The *Davis* case involved an effort to obtain testimony from a juvenile probationer who was a witness in a criminal trial. After the prosecutor was granted a court order preventing the defense from making any reference to the juvenile's record, the Supreme Court reversed the state court, claiming that a juvenile's interest in confidentiality was secondary to the constitutional right to confront adverse witnesses.

The decisions in two subsequent cases, *Oklahoma Publishing Co. v. District Court* and *Smith v. Daily Mail Publishing Co.*, sought to balance juvenile privacy with freedom of the press. In the *Oklahoma* case, the Supreme Court ruled that a state court was not allowed to prohibit the publication of information obtained in an open juvenile proceeding.[122] The case involved an 11-year-old boy suspected of homicide, who appeared at a detention hearing where photographs were taken and published in local newspapers. When the local district court prohibited further disclosure, the publishing company claimed that the court order was a restraint in violation of the First Amendment, and the Supreme Court agreed.

The *Smith* case involved the discovery and publication of the identity of a juvenile suspect in violation of a state statute prohibiting publication. The Supreme Court, however, declared the statute unconstitutional, because it believed the state's interest in protecting the child's identity was not of such a magnitude as to justify the use of such a statute.[123] Therefore, if newspapers lawfully obtain pictures or names of juveniles, they may publish them. Based on these decisions, it appears that the Supreme Court favors the constitutional rights of the press over the right to privacy of the juvenile offender.

Privacy of Juvenile Records. For most of the twentieth century, juvenile records were kept confidential.[124] Today, however, the record itself, or information contained in it, can be opened by court order in many jurisdictions on the basis of statutory exception. The following groups can ordinarily gain access to juvenile records: law enforcement personnel, the child's attorney, parents or guardians, military personnel, and public agencies such as schools, court-related organizations, and correctional institutions.

Today, most states recognize the importance of juvenile records in sentencing. Many first-time adult offenders committed numerous crimes as juveniles, and evidence of these crimes may not be available to sentencing for the adult offenses unless states pass statutes allowing access. Knowledge of a defendant's juvenile record may help prosecutors and judges determine appropriate sentencing for offenders ages 18 to 24, the age group most likely to be involved in violent crime.

According to experts such as Ira Schwartz, the need for confidentiality to protect juveniles is far less than the need to open up the courts to public scrutiny.[125] The problem of maintaining confidentiality of juvenile records will become more acute in the future as electronic information storage makes these records both more durable and more accessible.

In conclusion, virtually every state provides prosecutors and judges with access to the juvenile records of adult offenders. There is great diversity, however, regarding provisions for the collection and retention of juvenile records.[126]

FUTURE OF THE JUVENILE COURT

The future of the juvenile court is subject to wide-ranging and sometimes contentious debate. Some experts, including legal scholar Barry Feld, believe that over the years the juvenile justice system has taken on more of the characteristics of the adult courts, which he refers to as the "criminalizing" of the juvenile court,[127] or in a more stern admonition: "Despite juvenile courts' persisting rehabilitative rhetoric, the reality of *treating* juveniles closely resembles *punishing* adult criminals."[128] Robert Dawson suggests that because the legal differences between the juvenile and criminal systems are narrower than they ever have been, it may be time to abolish the juvenile court.[129]

Other juvenile justice experts, such as Peter Greenwood, contend that, despite these and other limitations, the treatment programs that the modern juvenile court currently provides play a central role in society's response to the most serious delinquents.[130] Greenwood argues that this comes with a number of specific responsibilities that juvenile courts must take on so as to ensure that these programs are indeed effective, including: awareness of the most up-to-date scientific evidence on

the effectiveness of court-based programs, diversion of cases that can be handled informally outside of the system, disposition of cases to appropriate programs, and quality control.[131]

Part of the answer to making this happen and overcoming the often default position of getting tough on juvenile offenders,[132] argue criminologists Daniel Mears, Carter Hay, Marc Gertz, and Christina Mancini, is that the juvenile court and the juvenile justice system in general need to be guided by a core set of rational and science-based principles such as "systematic assessments of culpability and treatment needs and a consistent balancing of punishment and treatment."[133] These become the overriding considerations in how the juvenile court can best serve society, a course of action that the public finds to be much more appealing than the wholesale criminalization of children.[134]

SUMMARY

Prosecutors, judges, and defense attorneys are the key players in the juvenile court. The juvenile prosecutor is the attorney responsible for bringing the state's case against the accused juvenile. The juvenile judge must ensure that the children and families who come before the court receive the proper help. Defense attorneys representing children in the juvenile court play an active and important part in virtually all stages of the proceedings.

Many decisions about what happens to a child may occur prior to adjudication. Due to personnel limitations, the juvenile justice system is not able to try every child accused of a crime or status offense. Therefore, diversion programs seem to hold greater hope for the control of delinquency. As a result, such subsystems as statutory intake proceedings, plea bargaining, and other informal adjustments are essential ingredients in the administration of the juvenile justice system.

Each year, thousands of youths are transferred to adult courts because of the seriousness of their crimes. This process, known as waiver, is an effort to remove serious offenders from the juvenile process and into the more punitive adult system. Most juvenile experts oppose waiver because it clashes with the rehabilitative ideal and has proven ineffective in reducing juvenile violence. Supporters argue that its increased use can help get violent juvenile offenders off the street, and they point to studies that show that, for the most part, transfer is reserved for the most serious cases and the most serious juvenile offenders.

Most jurisdictions have a bifurcated juvenile code system that separates the adjudication hearing from the dispositional hearing. Juveniles alleged to be delinquent have virtually all the constitutional rights given a criminal defendant at trial— except possibly the right to a trial by jury. Juvenile proceedings are generally closed to the public.

A number of U.S. Supreme Court decisions have influenced the handling of juveniles at the preadjudicatory and trial stages. *In re Gault* is the key legal case that set out the basic requirements of due process that must be satisfied in juvenile court proceedings. In *Roper v. Simmons*, the U.S. Supreme Court ruled that the death penalty for juveniles is prohibited, because it constitutes cruel and unusual punishment. In *Graham v. Florida*, the Court put an end to the practice of life sentences without the possibility of parole for juveniles convicted of nonhomicide crimes.

The major categories of dispositional choice in juvenile cases are community release, out-of-home placements, fines or restitution, community service, and institutionalization. Although the traditional notion of rehabilitation and treatment as the proper goals for disposition is being questioned, many juvenile codes do require that the court consider the least-restrictive alternative.

Many state statutes require that juvenile hearings be closed and that the privacy of juvenile records be maintained. This is done to protect the child from public scrutiny and to provide a greater opportunity for rehabilitation. This approach may be inconsistent with the public's interest in taking a closer look at the juvenile justice system.

juvenile defense attorney, p. 350

guardian *ad litem*, p. 351

public defender, p. 351

juvenile prosecutor, p. 352

juvenile court judge, p. 352

shelter care, p. 355

bail, p. 356

preventive detention, p. 357

intake, p. 357

diversion, p. 358

widening the net, p. 359

complaint, p. 360

plea bargaining, p. 360

transfer process, p. 361

due process, p. 369

least detrimental alternative, p. 373

indeterminate sentence, p. 373

determinate sentence, p. 374

mandatory sentences, p. 374

final order, p. 376

appellate process, p. 376

writ of *habeas corpus*, p. 376

confidentiality, p. 376

QUESTIONS FOR REVIEW

1. What are some of the key duties of the juvenile court judge?

2. What are some of the most important factors for detaining a youth once he or she is taken into custody by the police?

3. What is the purpose of the intake process?

4. Under what conditions is it possible to transfer juveniles to adult court?

5. When is a predisposition report used?

6. What is the most widely used disposition in juvenile court?

7. What are blended sentences?

8. When is it possible to appeal a juvenile court case?

QUESTIONS FOR DISCUSSION

1. Discuss and identify the major participants in the juvenile adjudication process. What are each person's role and responsibilities in the course of a juvenile trial?

2. The criminal justice system in the United States is based on the adversarial process. Does the same principle apply in the juvenile justice system?

3. Children have certain constitutional rights at adjudication, such as the right to an attorney and the right to confront and cross-examine witnesses. But they do not have the right to a trial by jury. Should juvenile offenders have a constitutional right to a jury trial? Should each state make that determination? Discuss the legal decision that addresses this issue.

4. What is the point of obtaining a predisposition report in the juvenile court? Is it of any value in cases where the child is released to the community? Does it have a significant value in serious juvenile crime cases?

5. The standard of proof in juvenile adjudication is to show that the child is guilty beyond a reasonable doubt. Explain the meaning of this standard of proof in the U.S. judicial system.

6. Should states adopt get-tough sentences in juvenile justice or adhere to the individualized treatment model?

7. Do you agree with the Supreme Court's 2005 ruling that prohibits the death penalty for juvenile offenders?

APPLYING WHAT YOU HAVE LEARNED

As an experienced family court judge, you are often faced with difficult decisions, but few are more difficult than the case of John, arrested at age 14 for robbery and rape. His victim, a young neighborhood girl, was badly injured in the attack and needed extensive hospitalization; she is now in counseling. Even though the charges are serious, because of his age, John can still be subject to the jurisdiction of the juvenile division of the state family court. However, the prosecutor has filed a petition to waive jurisdiction to the adult court.

Under existing state law, a hearing must be held to determine whether there is sufficient evidence that John cannot be successfully treated in the juvenile justice system and therefore warrants transfer to the adult system; the final decision on the matter is yours alone.

At the waiver hearing, you discover that John is the oldest of three siblings living in a single-parent home. He has had no contact with his father for more than 10 years. His psychological evaluation showed hostility, anger toward females, and great feelings of frustration. His intelligence is below average, and his behavioral and academic records are poor. In addition, he seems to be involved with a local youth gang, although he denies any formal association with them. This is his first formal involvement with the juvenile court. Previous contact was limited to an informal complaint for disorderly conduct at age 13, which was dismissed by the court's intake department. During the hearing, John verbalizes what you interpret to be superficial remorse for his offenses.

To the prosecutor, John seems to be a youth with poor controls who is likely to commit future crimes. The defense attorney argues that there are effective treatment opportunities within the juvenile justice system that can meet John's needs. Her views are supported by an evaluation of the case con-ducted by the court's probation staff, which concludes that the case can be dealt with in the confines of juvenile corrections.

If the case remains in the juvenile court, John can be kept in custody in a juvenile facility until age 18; if transferred to felony court, he could be sentenced to up to 20 years in a maximum-security prison. As judge, you recognize the seriousness of the crimes committed by John and realize that it is very difficult to predict or assess his future behavior and potential dangerousness.

Writing Assignment Write an essay discussing the best course of action for this case, weighing the individualized need for treatment and public protection. Include in your discussion whether a juvenile court judge should consider the victim in making a disposition decision.

GROUPWORK

Diversion is one of the most important alternatives that can be implemented at the intake process. Divide the class into an equal number of groups. Assign one set of groups to identify the benefits of diversion and the others to identify its limitations and challenges. The groups may wish to use the categories of "individual juvenile," "family," and "society" as a way to focus on benefits or limitations.

CHAPTER FOURTEEN

Juvenile Corrections:

Probation, Community Treatment, and Institutionalization

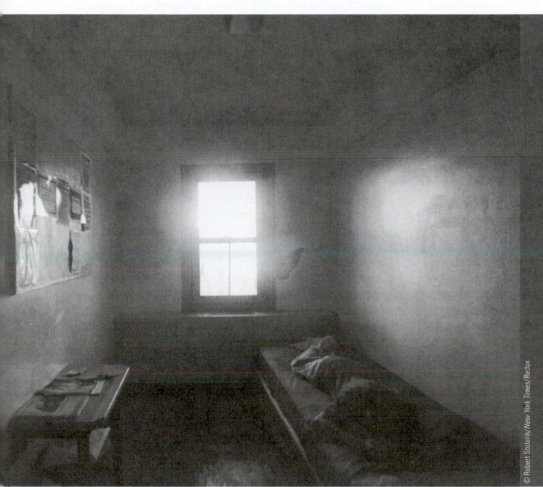

© Robert Stolarik/New York Times/Redux

LEARNING OBJECTIVES

After reading this chapter you should:

1. Be familiar with juvenile probation.

2. Know about new approaches for providing probation services to juvenile offenders.

3. Understand past and current trends in the use of juvenile institutions and key issues facing the institutionalized juvenile offender.

4. Be able to identify current juvenile correctional treatment approaches and comment on their effectiveness in reducing recidivism.

5. Know about aftercare and re-entry for juvenile offenders.

Karen's Story

Karen Gilligan, age 16, was the oldest of four children living with their parents in a small rural community. Her mother worked two jobs, her father was unemployed, and both parents drank heavily. Karen's high school attendance was sporadic. She started to experiment with alcohol and vandalized local businesses. After being arrested in a stolen car on several occasions, Karen was referred to juvenile court and was put on community supervision and probation. An initial assessment was provided by her probation officer, and formal dispositional recommendations were made to the court. She would remain at home on house arrest for 60 days, attend school regularly and maintain at least a C average, follow an alcohol and drug assessment program, and participate in weekly family therapy with her parents. Karen was also ordered to cooperate with the juvenile restitution program, pay her restitution in full within six months, and participate in the Community Adolescent Intensive Supervision Program, as arranged by her probation officer.

Not used to being accountable to anyone, Karen struggled initially with all the new rules and expectations. She missed some of her initial appointments and skipped some classes at school. Karen's probation officer began making unannounced visits to her at school, trying to help her understand the consequences of her

behavior. It was clear to the probation officer that Karen possessed many strengths and positive attributes. She enjoyed dancing and singing, and even liked school at times. The team of professionals encouraged her to focus on these qualities.

In addition to Karen's individual counseling, her family participated in weekly family therapy to talk about their issues and to address how to best support the children. Initially, the sessions were very challenging and stressful for the entire family. They blamed each other for their difficulties, and Karen seemed to be the target of much of the anger expressed by her parents.

During the many months of intensive supervision, treatment, and family therapy, Karen was able to stop her delinquent behavior, pay her restitution, attend school regularly, and improve her communication with her parents. Through therapy, Karen's mother also acknowledged that she needed some assistance with her drinking and entered treatment. Karen's probation officer provided the court with regular monthly progress reports showing significant improvement in Karen's behavior and lifestyle choices. Karen has proven her success and remains living with her parents and siblings. She plans to attend a local college after graduation to prepare for a career in the medical field.

There are many choices of correctional treatments available for juveniles, all of which can be subdivided into two major categories: community treatment and institutional treatment. **Community treatment** refers to efforts to provide care, protection, and treatment for juveniles in need. These efforts include probation, treatment services (such as individual and group counseling), restitution, and other programs. The term *community treatment* also refers to the use of privately maintained residences, such as foster homes, small-group homes, and boarding schools, which are located in the community. Nonresidential programs, where youths remain in their own homes, but are required to receive counseling, vocational training, and other services, also fall under the rubric of community treatment.

Institutional treatment facilities are correctional centers operated by federal, state, and county governments; these facilities restrict the movement of residents through staff monitoring, locked exits, and interior fence controls. There are several types of institutional facilities in juvenile corrections, including reception centers that screen juveniles and assign them to an appropriate facility; specialized facilities that provide specific types of care, such as drug treatment; training schools or reformatories for youths needing a long-term secure setting; ranch or forestry camps that provide long-term residential care; and boot camps, which seek to rehabilitate youths through the application of rigorous physical training.

Choosing the proper mode of juvenile corrections can be difficult. Some experts believe that any hope for rehabilitating juvenile offenders and resolving the problems of juvenile crime lies in community treatment programs.[1] Such programs are

community treatment Using nonsecure and noninstitutional residences, counseling services, victim restitution programs, and other community services to treat juveniles in their own communities.

Mark Ryan (left), the principal of Community Prep in Manhattan, New York City's first public high school for students who have been recently released from juvenile prisons and jails, speaks with Joshua Brignoni about wearing his hat in class.

smaller than secure facilities for juveniles, operate in a community setting, and offer creative approaches to treating the offender. In contrast, institutionalizing young offenders may do more harm than good. It exposes them to prison-like conditions and to more experienced delinquents without giving them the benefit of constructive treatment programs.[2]

Those who favor secure treatment are concerned about the threat that violent young offenders present to the community and believe that a stay in a juvenile institution may have a long-term deterrent effect. They point to the findings of Charles Murray and Louis B. Cox, who uncovered what they call a **suppression effect**, a reduction in the number of arrests per year following release from a secure facility, which is not achieved when juveniles are placed in less punitive programs.[3] Murray and Cox concluded that the justice system must choose the outcome it wants to achieve: prevention of delinquency, or the care and protection of needy youths. If the former is a proper goal, institutionalization or the threat of institutionalization is desirable. Not surprisingly, secure treatment is still being used extensively, and the populations of these facilities continue to grow as state legislators pass more stringent and punitive sentencing packages aimed at repeat juvenile offenders.

JUVENILE PROBATION

Probation and other forms of community treatment generally refer to nonpunitive legal dispositions for delinquent youths, emphasizing treatment without incarceration. Probation is the primary form of community treatment used by the juvenile justice system. A juvenile who is on probation is maintained in the community under the supervision of an officer of the court. Probation also encompasses a set of rules and conditions that must be met for the offender to remain in the community. Juveniles on probation may be placed in a wide variety of community-based treatment programs that provide services ranging from group counseling to drug treatment.

suppression effect A reduction of the number of arrests per year for youths who have been incarcerated or otherwise punished.

probation Nonpunitive, legal disposition of juveniles emphasizing community treatment in which the juvenile is closely supervised by an officer of the court and must adhere to a strict set of rules to avoid incarceration.

Community treatment is based on the idea that the juvenile offender is not a danger to the community and has a better chance of being rehabilitated in the community. It provides offenders with the opportunity to be supervised by trained personnel who can help them reestablish forms of acceptable behavior in a community setting. When applied correctly, community treatment maximizes the liberty of the individual and at the same time vindicates the authority of the law and protects the public; promotes rehabilitation by maintaining normal community contacts; avoids the negative effects of confinement, which often severely complicate the reintegration of the offender into the community; and greatly reduces the financial cost to the public.[4]

Historical Development

Although the major developments in community treatment have occurred in the twentieth century, its roots go back much further. In England, specialized procedures for dealing with youthful offenders were recorded as early as 1820, when the magistrates of the Warwickshire quarter sessions (periodic court hearings held in a county, or shire, of England) adopted the practice of sentencing youthful criminals to prison terms of one day, then releasing them conditionally under the supervision of their parents or masters.[5]

In the United States, juvenile probation developed as part of the wave of social reform characterizing the latter half of the nineteenth century. Massachusetts took the first step. Under an act passed in 1869, an agent of the state board of charities was authorized to appear in criminal trials involving juveniles, to find them suitable homes, and to visit them periodically. These services were soon broadened, so that by 1890, probation had become a mandatory part of the court structure.[6]

Probation was a cornerstone in the development of the juvenile court system. In fact, in some states, supporters of the juvenile court movement viewed probation as the first step toward achieving the benefits that the new court was intended to provide. The rapid spread of juvenile courts during the first decades of the twentieth century encouraged the further development of probation. The two were closely related, and to a large degree, both sprang from the conviction that the young could be rehabilitated and that the public was responsible for protecting them.

Expanding Community Treatment

By the mid-1960s, juvenile probation had become a complex institution that touched the lives of an enormous number of children. To many experts, institutionalization of even the most serious delinquent youths was a mistake. Reformers believed that confinement in a high-security institution could not solve the problems that brought a youth into a delinquent way of life, and that the experience could actually help amplify delinquency once the youth returned to the community.[7] Surveys indicating that 30 to 40 percent of adult prison inmates had prior experience with the juvenile court, and that many had been institutionalized as youths, gave little support to the argument that an institutional experience could be beneficial or reduce recidivism.[8]

Contemporary Juvenile Probation

Traditional probation is still the backbone of community-based corrections. As Figure 14.1 shows, 322,900 juveniles were placed on formal probation in 2008 (latest data available), which amounts to more than half (57 percent) of all juvenile dispositions. The use of probation has increased significantly since 1993, when 224,500 adjudicated youths were placed on probation, but in recent years has remained relatively stable.[9] These figures show that, regardless of public sentiment, probation

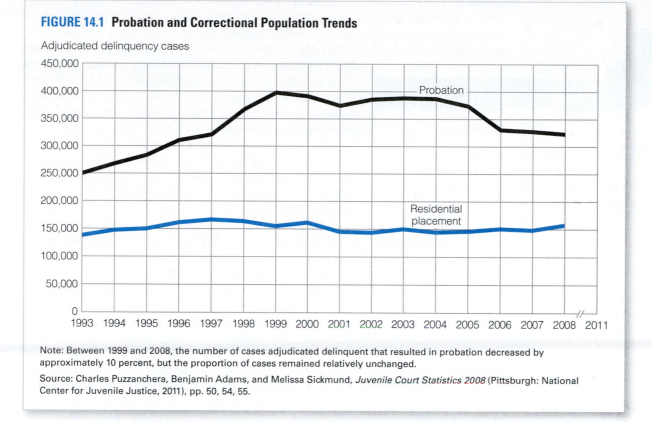

FIGURE 14.1 Probation and Correctional Population Trends

Adjudicated delinquency cases

Note: Between 1999 and 2008, the number of cases adjudicated delinquent that resulted in probation decreased by approximately 10 percent, but the proportion of cases remained relatively unchanged.

Source: Charles Puzzanchera, Benjamin Adams, and Melissa Sickmund, *Juvenile Court Statistics 2008* (Pittsburgh: National Center for Juvenile Justice, 2011), pp. 50, 54, 55.

continues to be a popular dispositional alternative for judges. Here are the arguments in favor of probation:

- For youths who can be supervised in the community, probation represents an appropriate disposition.
- Probation allows the court to tailor a program to each juvenile offender, including those involved in interpersonal offenses. Research, however, raises questions about the adequacy of the present system to attend to the specific needs of female youths on probation.[10]
- The justice system continues to have confidence in rehabilitation while accommodating demands for legal controls and public protection, even when caseloads may include many more serious offenders than in the past.
- Probation is often the disposition of choice, particularly for status offenders.[11]

The Nature of Probation. In most jurisdictions, probation is a direct judicial order that allows a youth who is found to be a delinquent or status offender to remain in the community under court-ordered supervision. A probation sentence implies a contract between the court and the juvenile. The court promises to hold a period of institutionalization in abeyance; the juvenile promises to adhere to a set of rules mandated by the court. The rules of probation vary, but they typically involve conditions such as attending school or work, keeping regular hours, remaining in the jurisdiction, and staying out of trouble.

In the juvenile court, probation is often ordered for an indefinite period. Depending on the statutes of the jurisdiction, the seriousness of the offense, and the juvenile's adjustment on probation, youths can remain under supervision until the court no longer has jurisdiction over them (that is, when they reach the age of majority). State statutes determine if a judge can specify how long a juvenile may be placed under an order of probation. In most jurisdictions, the status of probation is reviewed regularly to ensure that a juvenile is not kept on probation needlessly. Generally, discretion lies with the probation officer to discharge youths who are adjusting to the treatment plan.

Conditions of Probation. **Conditions of probation** are rules mandating that a juvenile on probation behave in a particular way. They can include restitution or reparation, intensive supervision, intensive counseling, participation in a therapeutic program, or participation in an educational or vocational training program. In addition to these specific conditions, state statutes generally allow courts to insist that probationers lead law-abiding lives, maintain a residence in a family setting, refrain from associating with certain types of people, and remain in a particular area unless they have permission to leave.

Although probation conditions vary, they are never supposed to be capricious, cruel, or beyond the capacity of the juvenile to satisfy. Furthermore, conditions of probation should relate to the crime that was committed and to the conduct of the child.

Courts have invalidated probation conditions that were harmful or that violated the juvenile's due process rights. Restricting a child's movement, insisting on a mandatory program of treatment, ordering indefinite terms of probation, and demanding financial reparation where this is impossible are all grounds for appellate court review. For example, it would not be appropriate for a probation order to bar a youth from visiting his girlfriend (unless he had threatened or harmed her) merely because her parents objected to the relationship.[12] However, courts have ruled that it is permissible to bar juveniles from such sources of danger as a "known gang area" in order to protect them from harm.[13] If a youth violates the conditions of probation—and especially if the juvenile commits another offense—the court can revoke probation. In this case, the contract is terminated and the original commitment order may be enforced. The juvenile court ordinarily handles a decision to revoke probation upon recommendation of the probation officer. Today, as a result of Supreme Court decisions dealing with the rights of adult probationers, a juvenile is normally entitled to legal representation and a hearing when a violation of probation occurs.[14]

Duties of Juvenile Probation Officers

The **juvenile probation officer** plays an important role in the justice process, beginning with intake and continuing throughout the period in which a juvenile is under court supervision. Their role is so important and influence so great that it has generated much research over the years on how juvenile probation officers perform their duties, including their approach to treatment and punishment.[15] Probation officers are involved at four stages of the court process. At *intake*, they screen complaints by deciding to adjust the matter, refer the child to an agency for service, or refer the case to the court for judicial action. During the *predisposition* stage, they participate in release or detention decisions. At the *postadjudication* stage, they assist the court in reaching its dispositional decision. During *postdisposition*, they supervise juveniles placed on probation.

At intake, the probation staff has preliminary discussions with the child and the family to determine whether court intervention is necessary or whether the matter can be better resolved by some form of social service. If the child is placed in a detention facility, the probation officer helps the court decide whether the child should continue to be held or be released pending the adjudication and disposition of the case.

The probation officer exercises tremendous influence over the child and the family by developing a **social investigation or predisposition report** and submitting it to the court. This report is a clinical diagnosis of the child's problems and the need for court assistance based on an evaluation of social functioning, personality, and environmental issues. The report includes an analysis of the child's feelings about the violations and the child's capacity for change. It also examines the influence of family members, peers, and other environmental influences in producing and possibly resolving the problems. All of this information is brought together in a

---

conditions of probation Rules and regulations mandating that a juvenile on probation behave in a particular way.

juvenile probation officer Officer of the court involved in all four stages of the court process—intake, predisposition, postadjudication, and postdisposition—who assists the court and supervises juveniles placed on probation.

social investigation report (also known as predisposition report). Developed by the juvenile probation officer, this report includes clinical diagnosis of the juvenile and the need for court assistance, relevant environmental and personality factors, and other information to assist the court in developing a treatment plan.

complex but meaningful picture of the offender's personality, problems, and environment.[16]

Juvenile probation officers also provide the child with supervision and treatment in the community. Treatment plans vary in approach and structure. Some juveniles simply report to the probation officer and follow the conditions of probation. In other cases, the probation officer may need to provide extensive counseling to the child and family, or more often, refer them to other social service agencies, such as a drug treatment center. Performance of such a broad range of functions requires good training. Today, juvenile probation officers have legal or social work backgrounds or special counseling skills. **CHECKPOINTS**

PROBATION INNOVATIONS

Community corrections have traditionally emphasized offender rehabilitation. The probation officer has been viewed as a caseworker or counselor whose primary job is to help the offender adjust to society. Offender surveillance and control have seemed more appropriate for law enforcement, jails, and prisons than for community corrections.[17] Since 1980, a more conservative justice system has reoriented toward social control. Although the rehabilitative ideals of probation have not been abandoned, new programs have been developed that add a control dimension to community corrections. In some cases this has involved the use of police officers, working in collaboration with probation officers, to enhance the supervision of juvenile probationers.[18] These programs can be viewed as "probation plus," because they add restrictive penalties and conditions to community-service orders. More punitive than probation, this kind of intermediate sanction can be politically attractive to conservatives while still appealing to liberals as alternatives to incarceration. What are some of these new alternative sanctions? (See Concept Summary 14.1.)

CONCEPT SUMMARY 14.1 | Community-Based Corrections

Although correctional treatment in the community generally refers to nonpunitive legal dispositions, in most cases there are still restrictions designed to protect the public and hold juvenile offenders accountable for their actions.

Type	Main Restrictions
Probation	Regular supervision by a probation officer; youths must adhere to conditions such as attend school or work, stay out of trouble.
Intensive supervision	Almost daily supervision by a probation officer; adhere to similar conditions as regular probation.
House arrest	Remain at home during specified periods; often there is monitoring through random phone calls, visits, or electronic devices.
Restorative justice	Restrictions may be prescribed by community members to help repair harm done to victim.
Balanced probation	Restrictions tailored to the risk the juvenile offender presents to the community.
Restitution	None.
Residential programs	Placement in a residential, nonsecure facility, such as group home or foster home; adhere to conditions; close monitoring.

Intensive Supervision

Juvenile intensive probation supervision (JIPS) involves treating offenders who would normally have been sent to a secure treatment facility as part of a very small probation caseload that receives almost daily scrutiny.[19] The primary goal of JIPS is *decarceration*; without intensive supervision, youngsters would normally be sent to secure juvenile facilities that are already overcrowded. The second goal is control; high-risk juvenile offenders can be maintained in the community under much closer security than traditional probation efforts can provide. A third goal is maintaining community ties and reintegration; offenders can remain in the community and complete their education while avoiding the pains of imprisonment.

Intensive probation programs get mixed reviews. Some jurisdictions find that they are more successful than traditional probation supervision and come at a much cheaper cost than incarceration.[20] However, some studies indicate that the failure rate is high and that younger offenders who commit petty crimes are the most likely to fail when placed in intensive supervision programs.[21] It is not surprising that intensive probation clients fail more often, because, after all, they are more serious offenders who might otherwise have been incarcerated and are now being watched and supervised more closely than probationers. In one experimental study of intensive probation supervision plus a coordinated team approach for high-risk juveniles, known as the Los Angeles County Repeat Offender Prevention Program (ROPP), mixed results were found for those who received the program compared to a similar group of youths who received regular probation only: recidivism was reduced in the short term, but not over the long term, school performance was increased, and there was no difference in probation technical violations.[22] In another recent California experiment of juvenile intensive probation supervision, no significant differences were observed in recidivism rates among those youths who received intensive probation compared to a similar group of youths who received regular probation.[23] Further analyses of this program revealed no effects on key family and peer relationship measures.[24]

An innovative experiment in three Mississippi counties examined the differential effects on juvenile justice costs for intensive supervision and monitoring, regular probation, and cognitive behavioral treatment, which involved sessions on problem solving, social skills, negotiation skills, the management of emotion, and values enhancement, to improve the thinking and reasoning ability of juvenile offenders. After one year of the program, the intensive supervision treatment was found to be less cost-effective than the other two treatments, with the cognitive behavioral treatment imposing the fewest costs on the juvenile justice system.[25]

Electronic Monitoring

Another program, which has been used with adult offenders and is finding its way into the juvenile justice system, is **house arrest**, which is often coupled with **electronic monitoring**. This program allows offenders sentenced to probation to remain in the community on condition that they stay at home during specific periods (for example, after school or work, on weekends, and in the evenings). Offenders may be monitored through random phone calls, visits, or in some jurisdictions, electronic devices.

Most systems employ radio transmitters that receive a signal from a device worn by the offender and relay it back to the computer via telephone lines. Probationers are fitted with an irremovable monitoring device that alerts the probation department's computers if they leave their place of confinement.[26]

Currently, there is widespread belief that electronic monitoring can be effective, with some evaluations showing that recidivism rates are no higher than in traditional programs, costs are lower, and institutional overcrowding is reduced. Some studies also reveal that electronic monitoring seems to work better with some individuals than others: serious felony offenders, substance abusers, repeat offenders, and people serving the longest sentences are the most likely to fail.[27]

juvenile intensive probation supervision (JIPS) A true alternative to incarceration that involves almost daily supervision of the juvenile by the probation officer assigned to the case.

house arrest Offender is required to stay home during specific periods of time; monitoring is done by random phone calls and visits or by electronic devices.

electronic monitoring Active monitoring systems consist of a radio transmitter worn by the offender that sends a continuous signal to the probation department computer; passive systems employ computer-generated random phone calls that must be answered in a certain period of time from a particular phone.

However, in a review on the effects of electronic monitoring on recidivism, criminologists Marc Renzema and Evan Mayo-Wilson found that the results do not support the claim that it works at the present time. This conclusion was largely based on there being too few high-quality studies available and a difficulty in isolating the independent effects of programs that combine electronic monitoring with other interventions. Importantly, the researchers did not call for an end to the use of electronic monitoring, but rather for new and better experiments.[28]

Restorative Justice

Restorative justice is a nonpunitive strategy for delinquency control that attempts to address the issues that produce conflict between two parties (offender and victim) and, hence, reconcile the parties. Restoration rather than retribution or punishment is at the heart of the restorative justice approach. Seven core values characterize restorative justice:

- Crime is an offense against human relationships.
- Victims and the community are central to justice processes.
- The first priority of justice processes is to assist victims.
- The second priority of justice processes is to restore the community, to the degree possible.
- The offender has a personal responsibility to victims and to the community for crimes committed.
- The offender will develop improved competency and understanding as a result of the restorative justice experience.
- Stakeholders share responsibilities for restorative justice through partnerships for action.[29]

Criminologists Heather Strang and Lawrence Sherman carried out a systematic review and meta-analysis of the effects of restorative justice on juvenile reoffending and victim satisfaction. The review involved two studies from Australia and one from the United States that evaluated the restorative justice practice of face-to-face conferences. (The main reason for the small number of studies is that the authors used only those studies that employed randomized controlled designs to assess program effects.) The conferences proceeded as follows:

> Any victims (or their representatives) present have the opportunity to describe the full extent of the harm a crime has caused, offenders are required to listen to the victims and to understand the consequences of their own actions, and all participants are invited to deliberate about what actions the offender could take to repair them. The precondition of such a conference is that the offender does not dispute the fact that he is responsible for the harm caused, and the conference cannot and will not become a trial to determine what happened.[30]

The review found evidence that this form of restorative justice can be an effective strategy in reducing repeat offending by juveniles who have committed violent crimes. The type of violence includes minor offenses of battery to middle-level offenses of assault and aggravated assault. The review also found that face-to-face conferences can be effective in preventing victims from committing crimes of retaliation against their perpetrators. Perhaps not surprisingly, across all studies, victim satisfaction levels strongly favored restorative justice compared to traditional juvenile justice proceedings.[31] Successful results have also been demonstrated in other restorative justice programs for juvenile offenders.[32]

Looking Back to Karen's Story

While electronic monitoring was not used in Karen's case, she was placed on house arrest in her parent's home.

CRITICAL THINKING Discuss the pros and cons of placing Karen on house arrest. As part of this, give some thought to what crimes would justify an automatic removal from the home as well as what would need to be accomplished for the youth to return.

Balanced Probation

Some jurisdictions have also turned to a **balanced probation** approach in an effort to enhance the success of probation.[33] Balanced probation systems integrate community protection, the accountability of the juvenile offender, and individualized attention to the offender. These programs are based on the view that juveniles are responsible for their actions and have an obligation to society whenever they commit an offense. The probation officer establishes a program tailored to the offender while helping the offender accept responsibility for his or her actions. The balanced approach is promising, because it specifies a distinctive role for the juvenile probation system.[34]

One innovative program that adheres to a balanced probation approach is the California 8% Solution, which is run by the Orange County Probation Department. The "8 percent" refers to the percentage of juvenile offenders who are responsible for the majority of crime: in the case of Orange County, 8 percent of first-time offenders were responsible for 55 percent of repeat cases over a three-year period. This 8 percent problem has become the 8 percent solution thanks to the probation department initiating a comprehensive, multiagency program targeting this group of offenders.[35]

Once the probation officer identifies an offender for the program—the 8% Early Intervention Program—the youth is referred to the Youth and Family Resource Center. Here the youth's needs are assessed and an appropriate treatment plan is developed. Some of the services provided to youths include these:

- An outside school for students in junior and senior high school
- Transportation to and from home
- Counseling for drug and alcohol abuse
- Employment preparation and job placement services
- At-home, intensive family counseling for families[36]

Restitution

Victim restitution is another widely used method of community treatment. In most jurisdictions, restitution is part of a probationary sentence and is administered by the county probation staff. In many jurisdictions, independent restitution programs have been set up by local governments; in others, restitution is administered by a private nonprofit organization.[37]

Restitution can take several forms. A juvenile can reimburse the victim of the crime or donate money to a charity or public cause; this is referred to as **monetary restitution**. In other instances, a juvenile may be required to provide some service directly to the victim (**victim service restitution**) or to assist a community organization (**community service restitution**).

Requiring youths to reimburse the victims of their crimes is the most widely used method of restitution in the United States. Less widely used, but more common in Europe, is restitution to a charity. In the past few years, numerous programs have been set up to enable juvenile offenders to provide a service to the victim or participate in community programs—for example, working in schools for mentally challenged children. In some cases, juveniles are required to contribute both money and community service. Other programs emphasize employment.[38]

Restitution programs can be employed at various stages of the juvenile justice process. They can be part of a diversion program prior to conviction, a method of informal adjustment at intake, or a condition of probation. Restitution has a number of advantages: it provides alternative sentencing options; it offers monetary compensation or service to crime victims; it allows the juvenile the opportunity to compensate the victim and take a step toward becoming a productive member of society; it helps relieve overcrowded juvenile courts, probation caseloads, and detention facilities. Finally, like other alternatives to incarceration, restitution has the potential for allowing vast savings in the operation of the juvenile justice system.

balanced probation A program that integrates community protection, accountability of the juvenile offender, competency, and individualized attention to the juvenile offender, based on the principle that juvenile offenders must accept responsibility for their behavior.

monetary restitution Offenders compensate crime victims for out-of-pocket losses caused by the crime, including property damage, lost wages, and medical expenses.

victim service restitution Offenders provide some service directly to the crime victim.

community service restitution Offenders assist some worthwhile community organization for a period of time.

Monetary restitution programs in particular may improve the public's attitude toward juvenile justice by offering equity to the victims of crime and ensuring that offenders take responsibility for their actions.

The use of restitution is increasing. In 1977, there were fewer than 15 formal restitution programs around the United States. By 1985, formal programs existed in 400 jurisdictions, and 35 states had statutory provisions that gave courts the authority to order juvenile restitution.[39] Today, all 50 states, as well as the District of Columbia, have statutory restitution programs.

Does Restitution Work? How successful is restitution as a treatment alternative? Most evaluations have shown that it is reasonably effective and should be expanded.[40] In an analysis of restitution programs across the country, Peter Schneider and Matthew Finkelstein found that about 74 percent of youths who received restitution as a condition of probation successfully completed their orders. The researchers also found that juvenile restitution programs that reported a reduction in recidivism rates were the ones that had high successful completion rates.[41]

Anne Schneider conducted a thorough analysis of restitution programs in four states and found that participants had lower recidivism rates than youths in control groups (regular probation caseloads).[42] Although Schneider's data indicate that restitution may reduce recidivism, the number of youths who had subsequent involvement in the justice system still seemed high. In short, there is evidence that most restitution orders are successfully completed and that youths who make restitution are less likely to become recidivists; however, the number of repeat offenses committed by juveniles who made restitution suggests that, by itself, restitution is not the answer to the delinquency problem.

Another criticism of restitution programs is that they foster involuntary servitude. Indigent clients may be unfairly punished when they are unable to make restitution payments or face probation violations. To avoid such bias, probation officers should first determine why payment has stopped and then suggest appropriate action, rather than simply treating nonpayment as a matter of law enforcement.

Residential Community Treatment

Many experts believe that institutionalization of even the most serious delinquent youth is a mistake. Confinement in a high-security institution usually cannot solve the problems that brought a youth into a delinquent way of life, and the experience may actually amplify delinquency once the youth returns to the community. Many agree that warehousing juveniles without attention to their treatment needs does little to prevent their return to criminal behavior. Research has shown that the most effective secure-corrections programs provide individualized services for a small number of participants. Large training schools have not proved to be effective.[43] This realization has produced a wide variety of residential community-treatment programs to service youths who need a more secure environment than can be provided by probation services, but who do not require a placement in a state-run juvenile correctional facility.

How are community corrections implemented? In some cases, youths are placed under probation supervision, and the probation department maintains a residential treatment facility. Placement can also be made to the department of social services or juvenile corrections with the direction that the youth be placed in a residential facility. **Residential programs** are generally divided into four major categories: group homes, including boarding schools and apartment-type settings; foster homes; family group homes; and rural programs.

Group homes are nonsecure residences that provide counseling, education, job training, and family living. They are staffed by a small number of qualified persons, and generally house 12 to 15 youngsters. The institutional quality of the environment is minimized, and the kids are given the opportunity to build a close relationship with the staff. They reside in the home, attend public schools, and participate in community activities.

residential programs Residential nonsecure facilities, such as a group home, foster home, family group home, or rural home, where the juvenile can be closely monitored and develop close relationships with staff members.

group homes Nonsecured structured residences that provide counseling, education, job training, and family living.

Foster care programs involve one or two juveniles who live with a family—usually a husband and wife who serve as surrogate parents. The juveniles enter into a close relationship with the foster parents and receive the attention and care they did not receive in their own homes. The quality of the foster home experience depends on the foster parents. Foster care for adjudicated juvenile offenders has not been extensive in the United States. Welfare departments generally handle foster placements, and funding of this treatment option has been a problem for the juvenile justice system. However, foster home services have expanded as a community treatment approach.

One example of a successful foster care program is the multidimensional treatment foster care (MTFC) program, developed by social scientists at the Oregon Social Learning Center. Designed for the most serious and chronic young offenders, this program combines individual therapy, such as skill building in problem solving for the youths, and family therapy for the biological or adoptive parents. The foster care families receive training by program staff so they can provide the young people with close supervision, fair and consistent limits and consequences, and a supportive relationship with an adult.[44] Foster care families also receive close supervision and are consulted regularly on the progress of the youth by program staff. An experiment of MTFC found that one year after the completion of the program, participating male youths were significantly less likely to be arrested than a control group.[45] Another test of MTFC that involved only serious and chronic female juvenile offenders found that it was more effective than group care, as measured by days in locked settings, number of criminal referrals, and self-reported delinquency.[46]

Family group homes combine elements of foster care and group home placements. Juveniles are placed in a group home that is run by a family rather than by a professional staff. Troubled youths have an opportunity to learn to get along in a family-like situation, and at the same time the state avoids the startup costs and neighborhood opposition often associated with establishing a public institution.

Rural programs include forestry camps, ranches, and farms that provide recreational activities or work for juveniles. Programs usually handle from 30 to 50 youths. Such programs have the disadvantage of isolating juveniles from the community, but reintegration can be achieved if a youth's stay is short and if family and friends are allowed to visit.

Most residential programs use group counseling as the main treatment tool. Although group facilities have been used less often than institutional placements, there is a trend toward developing community-based residential facilities. As jurisdictions continue to face ever-increasing costs for juvenile justice services, community-based programs will play an important role in providing rehabilitation of juvenile offenders and ensuring public safety. **CHECKPOINTS**

CHECKPOINTS

LO2 Know about new approaches for providing probation services to juvenile offenders.

✔ There are new programs being developed that are "probation plus" because they add restrictive penalties and conditions to community service orders.

✔ Juvenile intensive probation supervision involves treatment as part of a very small probation caseload that receives almost daily scrutiny.

✔ Electronic monitoring combined with house arrest is being implemented in juvenile correction policy.

✔ Balanced probation systems integrate community protection, accountability of the juvenile offender, and individualized attention to the offender.

✔ Monetary restitution allows a juvenile to reimburse the victim of the crime or donate money to a charity or public cause.

✔ Community service restitution allows juveniles to engage in public works as part of their disposition.

✔ Residential community programs are usually divided into four major categories: group homes, foster homes, family group homes, and rural programs.

foster care programs Placement of juveniles with families who provide attention, guidance, and care.

family group homes A combination of foster care and group home; they are run by a single family rather than by professional staff.

rural programs Specific recreational and work opportunities provided for juveniles in a rural setting, such as a forestry camp, a farm, or a ranch.

SECURE CORRECTIONS

When the court determines that community treatment can't meet the special needs of a delinquent youth, a judge may refer the juvenile to a secure treatment program. Today, correctional institutions operated by federal, state, and county governments are generally classified as secure or open facilities. *Secure facilities* restrict the movement of residents through staff monitoring, locked exits, and interior fence controls.

Open institutions generally do not restrict the movement of the residents and allow much greater freedom of access to the facility.[47]

History of Juvenile Institutions

Until the early 1800s, juvenile offenders, as well as neglected and dependent children, were confined in adult prisons. The inhumane conditions in these institutions were among the factors that led social reformers to create a separate children's court system in 1899.[48] Early juvenile institutions were industrial schools modeled after adult prisons, but designed to protect children from the evil influences in adult facilities. The first was the New York House of Refuge, established in 1825. Not long after, states began to establish **reform schools** for juveniles. Massachusetts was the first, opening the Lyman School for Boys in Westborough in 1846. New York opened the State Agricultural and Industrial School in 1849, and Maine opened the Maine Boys' Training School in 1853. By 1900, 36 states had reform schools.[49] Although it is difficult to determine the exact population of these institutions, by 1880 there were approximately 11,000 youths in correctional facilities, a number that more than quadrupled by 1980.[50] Early reform schools were generally punitive in nature and were based on the concept of rehabilitation (or reform) through hard work and discipline.

In the second half of the nineteenth century, emphasis shifted to the **cottage system**. Juvenile offenders were housed in compounds of cottages, each of which could accommodate 20 to 40 children. A set of "parents" ran each cottage, creating a homelike atmosphere. This setup was believed to be more conducive to rehabilitation.

The first cottage system was established in Massachusetts in 1855, the second in Ohio in 1858.[51] The system was held to be a great improvement over reform schools. The belief was that, by moving away from punishment and toward rehabilitation, not only could offenders be rehabilitated but also crime among unruly children could be prevented.[52]

Twentieth-Century Developments. The early twentieth century witnessed important changes in juvenile corrections. Because of the influence of World War I, reform schools began to adopt a militaristic style. Living units became barracks, cottage groups became companies, house fathers became captains, and superintendents became majors or colonels. Military-style uniforms were standard wear.

In addition, the establishment of the first juvenile court in 1899 reflected the expanded use of confinement for delinquent children. As the number of juvenile offenders increased, the forms of juvenile institutions varied to include forestry camps, ranches, and vocational schools. Beginning in the 1930s, camps modeled after the camps run by the Civilian Conservation Corps became a part of the juvenile correctional system. These camps centered on conservation activities and work as a means of rehabilitation.

Los Angeles County was the first to use camps during this period.[53] Southern California was experiencing problems with transient youths who came to California with no money and then got into trouble with the law. Rather than filling up the jails, the county placed these offenders in conservation camps, paid them low wages, and released them when they had earned enough money to return home. The camps proved more rehabilitative than training schools, and by 1935, California had established a network of forestry camps for delinquent boys. The idea soon spread to other states.[54]

Also during the 1930s, the U.S. Children's Bureau sought to reform juvenile corrections. The bureau conducted studies to determine the effectiveness of the training school concept. Little was learned from these programs because of limited funding and bureaucratic ineptitude, and the Children's Bureau failed to achieve any significant change. But such efforts recognized the important role of positive institutional care.[55]

Another innovation came in the 1940s with passage of the American Law Institute's Model Youth Correction Authority Act. This act emphasized reception/classification centers. California was the first to try out this idea, opening the

reform schools Institutions in which educational and psychological services are used in an effort to improve the conduct of juveniles who are forcibly detained.

cottage system Housing in a compound of small cottages, each of which can accommodate 20 to 40 children.

Northern Reception Center and Clinic in Sacramento in 1947. Today, there are many such centers scattered around the United States.

Since the 1970s, a major change in institutionalization has been the effort to remove status offenders from institutions housing juvenile delinquents. This includes removing status offenders from detention centers and removing all juveniles from contact with adults in jails. This decarceration policy mandates that courts use the **least restrictive alternative** in providing services for status offenders. A noncriminal youth should not be put in a secure facility if a community-based program is available. In addition, the federal government prohibits states from placing status offenders in separate facilities that are similar in form and function to those used for delinquent offenders. This is to prevent states from merely shifting their institutionalized population around so that one training school houses all delinquents, and another houses all status offenders, but actual conditions remain the same.

Throughout the 1980s and into the 1990s, admissions to juvenile correctional facilities grew substantially.[56] Capacities of juvenile facilities also increased, but not enough to avoid overcrowding. Training schools became seriously overcrowded in some states, causing private facilities to play an increased role in juvenile corrections. Reliance on incarceration became costly to states: inflation-controlled juvenile corrections expenditures for public facilities grew to more than $2 billion in 1995, an increase of 20 percent from 1982.[57] A 1994 report issued by the Office of Juvenile Justice and Delinquency Prevention (OJJDP) said that crowding, inadequate health care, lack of security, and poor control of suicidal behavior was widespread in juvenile corrections facilities. Despite new construction, crowding persisted in more than half the states.[58]

JUVENILE INSTITUTIONS TODAY: PUBLIC AND PRIVATE

Most juveniles are housed in public institutions that are administered by state agencies: child and youth services, health and social services, corrections, or child welfare.[59] In some states these institutions fall under a centralized system that covers adults as well as juveniles. Recently, a number of states have removed juvenile corrections from an existing adult corrections department or mental health agency. However, the majority of states still place responsibility for the administration of juvenile corrections within social service departments.

Supplementing publicly funded institutions are private facilities that are maintained and operated by private agencies funded or chartered by state authorities. Most of today's private institutions are relatively small facilities holding fewer than 30 youths. Many have a specific mission or focus (for example, treating females who display serious emotional problems). Although about 80 percent of public institutions can be characterized as secure, only 20 percent of private institutions are high-security facilities.

Population Trends

Whereas most delinquents are held in public facilities, most status offenders are held in private facilities. At last count (2010), there were 70,792 juvenile offenders being held in public (69 percent) and private (31 percent) facilities in the United States. Between 1991 and 1999, the number of juveniles held in custody increased 41 percent, followed by a 34 percent drop from 1999 to 2010.[60] The juvenile custody

least restrictive alternative A program with the least restrictive or secure setting that will benefit the child.

rate varies widely among states: South Dakota makes the greatest use of custodial treatment, incarcerating 575 delinquents in juvenile facilities per 100,000 juveniles in the population, whereas Vermont and Hawaii have the lowest juvenile custody rates (53 and 90, respectively). South Dakota's juvenile custody rate is more than twice the national average.[61] Some states rely heavily on privately run facilities, whereas others place many youths in out-of-state facilities.

This wide variation in state-level juvenile custody rates has been the subject of much speculation but little empirical research. In an important study, criminologist Daniel Mears found that there are three main explanations for why some states incarcerate juveniles at a much higher rate than others: (1) they have high rates of juvenile property crime and adult violent crime; (2) they have higher adult custody rates; and (3) there is a "cultural acceptance of punitive policies" in some parts of the country. Interestingly, Mears found that western and midwestern states were more likely to have higher juvenile incarceration rates than southern states, thus calling into question the widely held view that the South is disproportionately punitive.[62]

Although the number of institutionalized youths appears to have stabilized in the last few years, the data may reveal only the tip of the iceberg. The data do not include many minors who are incarcerated after they are waived to adult courts or who have been tried as adults because of exclusion statutes. Most states place underage juveniles convicted of adult charges in youth centers until they reach the age of majority, whereupon they are transferred to an adult facility. In addition, there may be a hidden, or subterranean, correctional system that places wayward youths in private mental hospitals and substance-abuse clinics for behaviors that might otherwise have brought them a stay in a correctional facility or community-based program.[63] These data suggest that the number of institutionalized children may be far greater than reported in the official statistics.[64] Studies also show that large numbers of youths are improperly incarcerated because of a lack of appropriate facilities. A nationwide survey carried out by congressional investigators as part of the House Committee on Government Reform found that 15,000 children with psychiatric disorders who were awaiting mental health services were improperly incarcerated in secure juvenile detention facilities.[65] In New Jersey, investigations into the state's child welfare system found that large numbers of teenage foster children were being held in secure juvenile detention facilities. Other states resort to similar practices, citing a lack of appropriate noncorrectional facilities.[66]

Physical Conditions

The physical plans of juvenile institutions vary in size and quality. Many of the older training schools still place all offenders in a single building, regardless of the offense. More acceptable structures include a reception unit with an infirmary, a security unit, and dormitory units or cottages. Planners have concluded that the most effective design for training schools is to have facilities located around a community square. The facilities generally include a dining hall and kitchen area, a storage warehouse, academic and vocational training rooms, a library, an auditorium, a gymnasium, an administration building, and other basic facilities.

The individual living areas also vary, depending on the type of facility and the progressiveness of its administration. Most traditional training school conditions were appalling. Today, however, most institutions provide toilet and bath facilities, beds, desks, lamps, and tables. New facilities usually try to provide a single room for each individual. However, the Juvenile Residential Facility Census, which collects information about the facilities in which juvenile offenders are held, found that one-quarter (25 percent) of the 2,860 facilities that reported information were either at capacity or overcrowded, with the latter defined as having more residents than available standard beds.[67]

The physical conditions of secure facilities for juveniles have come a long way from the training schools of the turn of the twentieth century. However, many administrators realize that more modernization is necessary to comply with national standards for juvenile institutions.[68] Although some improvements have been made, there are still enormous problems to overcome.[69]

WWW

If you want to learn more about **improving the conditions of children in custody,** visit the Criminal Justice CourseMate at CengageBrain.com, then access the Web Links for this chapter.

THE INSTITUTIONALIZED JUVENILE

The typical resident of a juvenile facility is a 17-year-old European American male incarcerated for an average stay of three and a half months in a public facility or four months in a private facility. Private facilities tend to house younger youths, whereas public institutions provide custodial care for older ones, including a small percentage between 18 and 21 years of age. Most incarcerated youths are person, property, or drug offenders.[70]

Minority youths are incarcerated at a rate two to four times that of European American youths. The difference is greatest for African American youths, with a custody rate of 605 per 100,000 juveniles; for European American youths the rate is 127.[71] In a number of states, such as California, New Jersey, New York, and Pennsylvania, the difference in custody rates between African American and European American youths is considerably greater (Table 14.1). Research has found that this overrepresentation is not a result of differentials in arrest rates, but often stems from disparity at early stages of case processing.[72] Of equal importance, minorities are more likely to be confined in secure public facilities rather than in open, private facilities that might provide more costly and effective treatment,[73] and among minority groups African American youths are more likely to receive more punitive treatment—throughout the juvenile justice system—compared with others.[74]

Minority youths accused of delinquent acts are less likely than European American youths to be diverted from the court system into informal sanctions and are more likely to receive sentences involving incarceration.[75] Today, more than 7 in 10 juveniles in custody belong to racial or ethnic minorities.[76] Racial disparity in juvenile disposition is an ongoing problem that demands immediate public scrutiny.[77] In response, many jurisdictions have initiated studies of racial disproportion in their juvenile justice systems, along with federal requirements to reduce disproportionate minority confinement (DMC), as contained in the Juvenile Justice and Delinquency Prevention Act of 2002.[78] A report on state compliance to reduce DMC demonstrates that some progress has been made but that many challenges remain, including the basic need to identify factors that contribute to DMC (at least 18 states have yet to initiate this process), incomplete and inconsistent data systems, and the need for ongoing evaluation of focused interventions and system-wide efforts to reduce DMC.[79] Some promising practices in reducing DMC, such as cultural competency training and increasing community-based detention alternatives, are beginning to emerge.[80]

Across all races and ethnicities, mental health needs are particularly acute among institutionalized juveniles.[81] Because of the importance of this topic, it is featured in the accompanying Focus on Delinquency box.

For more than two decades, shocking exposés, sometimes resulting from investigations by the U.S. Department of Justice's civil rights division, have focused public attention on the problems of juvenile corrections.[82] Today, more so than in years past, some critics believe public scrutiny has improved conditions in training schools. There is greater professionalism among the staff, and staff brutality seems to have diminished. Status offenders and delinquents are, for the most part, held in separate facilities. Confinement length is shorter, and rehabilitative programming has increased. However, there are significant differences in the experiences of male and female delinquents in institutions.

WWW

To learn more about **Columbia University's Center for the Promotion of Mental Health in Juvenile Justice,** visit the Criminal Justice CourseMate at CengageBrain.com, then access the Web Links for this chapter.

Male Inmates

Males make up the great bulk of institutionalized youth, accounting for seven out of every eight juvenile offenders in residential placement,[83] and most programs are directed toward their needs. In many ways their experiences mirror those of adult

TABLE 14.1 State Comparison of Custody Rates between European American and African American Juvenile Offenders, 2010

State of Offense	White	Black	State of Offense	White	Black
United States	**127**	**605**	Missouri	140	586
Alabama	131	392	Montana	131	581
Alaska	228	649	Nebraska	217	1,716
Arizona	114	334	Nevada	155	723
Arkansas	142	534	New Hampshire	84	389
California	115	984	New Jersey	26	538
Colorado	204	1,202	New Mexico	159	652
Connecticut	27	360	New York	77	538
Delaware	89	703	North Carolina	60	249
District of Columbia	172	501	North Dakota	178	452
Florida	202	650	Ohio	128	712
Georgia	76	461	Oklahoma	90	576
Hawaii	48	84	Oregon	274	1,214
Idaho	240	257	Pennsylvania	111	1,316
Illinois	106	476	Rhode Island	123	961
Indiana	207	717	South Carolina	128	450
Iowa	165	864	South Dakota	317	2,109
Kansas	172	1,040	Tennessee	64	293
Kentucky	135	577	Texas	123	529
Louisiana	96	472	Utah	154	666
Maine	131	446	Vermont	31	0
Maryland	47	321	Virginia	112	583
Massachusetts	54	403	Washington	137	625
Michigan	105	625	West Virginia	254	1,173
Minnesota	85	673	Wisconsin	109	1,062
Mississippi	38	189	Wyoming	402	1,103

Note: The rate is the number of juvenile offenders in residential placement in 2010 per 100,000 juveniles in the population.

Source: Melissa Sickmund, T. J. Sladky, Wei Kang, and Charles Puzzanchera, "Easy Access to the Census of Juveniles in Residential Placement," 2011, www.ojjdp.gov/ojstatbb/ezacjrp/ (accessed August 30, 2012).

offenders. In an important paper, Clemens Bartollas and his associates identified an inmate value system that they believed was common in juvenile institutions:

"Exploit whomever you can."

"Don't play up to staff."

"Don't rat on your peers."

"Don't give in to others."[84]

MENTAL HEALTH NEEDS OF JUVENILE INMATES ON THE RISE

Research suggests that as many as two out of every three (65 percent) juvenile offenders in juvenile correctional facilities suffer from mental health problems, and a large proportion of these youths enter the system without previously having been diagnosed or receiving treatment. Incarcerated youths suffering from mental health problems may find it harder to adjust to their new environment, which may in turn lead to acting-out behaviors, disciplinary problems, and trouble participating in treatment programs. All of these problems increase the risk of recidivism upon release to the community.

These findings are cause for concern on their own, but have become more pressing as many states, in an effort to trim their budgets, are cutting back on funding for community- and school-based mental health programs. In a survey of state mental health offices, at least 32 states reported funding cuts—by an average of 5 percent—to these programs in fiscal year 2009. These same states are planning to double these reductions in funding in the years to come. According to Joseph Penn, a child psychologist at the Texas Youth Commission, "We're seeing more and more mentally ill kids who couldn't find community programs that were intensive enough to treat them. Jails and juvenile justice facilities are the new asylums."

Even with a diagnosis, treatment services can be scarce in juvenile correctional facilities; culturally competent programs are even rarer. One study found that only one out of four (23 percent) juvenile offenders diagnosed with a mental disorder received any treatment. Contributing to the problem is that there is little information on what treatment works best for these juveniles. Columbia University's Center for the Promotion of Mental Health in Juvenile Justice and the National Center for Mental Health and Juvenile Justice are leading a national effort to improve this state of affairs, as well as the need for improved mental health assessments beginning as early as intake.

In addition to these general rules, the researchers found that there were separate norms for African American inmates ("exploit whites," "no forcing sex on blacks," "defend your brother") and for European Americans ("don't trust anyone," "everybody for himself").

Other research efforts confirm the notion that residents do in fact form cohesive groups and adhere to an informal inmate culture.[85] The more serious the youth's record and the more secure the institution, the greater the adherence to the inmate social code. Male delinquents are more likely to form allegiances with members of their own racial group and attempt to exploit those outside the group. They also scheme to manipulate staff and take advantage of weaker peers. However, in institutions that are treatment-oriented, and where staff-inmate relationships are more intimate, residents are less likely to adhere to a negativistic inmate code.

Female Inmates

The growing involvement of female youths in criminal behavior and the influence of the feminist movement have drawn more attention to the female juvenile offender. This attention has revealed a double standard of justice. For example, girls

CRITICAL THINKING

1. Is mental health treatment in the community a realistic option? Explain.

2. What should states be doing to plan for the long-term needs of this population?

Writing Assignment Many experts are calling for immediate attention to the mental health needs of incarcerated juveniles. Write an essay that outlines the short-term measures that can be taken to help this population. Also discuss the potential benefits associated with these measures.

Sources: Lisa Rapp-Paglicci, Chris Stewart, William Rowe, and J. Mitchell Miller, "Addressing the Hispanic Delinquency and Mental Health Relationship Through Cultural Arts Programming: A Research Note from the Prodigy Evaluation," *Journal of Contemporary Criminal Justice* 27:110–121 (2011); Solomon Moore, "Mentally Ill Offenders Strain Juvenile System," *New York Times*, August 10, 2009; Thomas Grisso, "Adolescent Offenders with Mental Disorders," *The Future of Children* 18(2):143–164 (2008); Kathleen R. Skowyra and Joseph J. Cocozza, *Blueprint for Change: A Comprehensive Model for the Identification and Treatment of Youth with Mental Health Needs in Contact with the Juvenile Justice System* (Delmar, NY: National Center for Mental Health and Juvenile Justice, 2007); Deborah Shelton, "Patterns of Treatment Services and Costs for Young Offenders with Mental Disorders," *Journal of Child and Adolescent Psychiatric Nursing* 18:103–112 (2005).

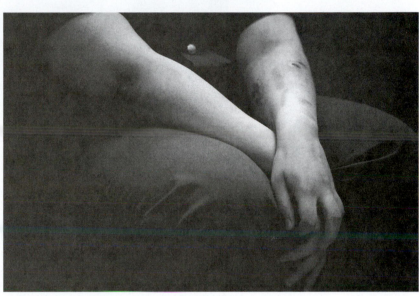

Mental health needs are particularly acute among institutionalized juveniles. As much as 65 percent of youths in the juvenile justice system suffer from mental health problems. Shown here is an inmate at the Scioto Juvenile Correctional Facility in Delaware, Ohio. The facility recently added therapy programs to address inmates' self-mutilation.

© Kirk Irwin/*New York Times*/Redux

are more likely than boys to be incarcerated for status offenses. Institutions for girls are generally more restrictive than those for boys, and they have fewer educational and vocational programs and fewer services. Institutions for girls also do a less-than-adequate job of rehabilitation. It has been suggested that this double standard operates because of a male-dominated justice system that seeks to "protect" young girls from their own sexuality.[86]

Over the years, the number of females held in public institutions has declined, albeit less so in the past few years. This represents the continuation of a long-term trend to remove girls, many of whom are nonserious offenders, from closed institutions and place them in private or community-based facilities. It is estimated that 33 percent of all female youths in residential placement are held in private facilities; for male youths it is 30 percent.[87]

The same double standard that brings a girl into an institution continues to exist once she is in custody. Institutional programs for girls tend to be oriented toward reinforcing traditional roles for women. Most of these programs also fail to take account of the different needs of African American and European American females, as in the case of coping with past abuse.[88] How well these programs rehabilitate girls is questionable. The one exception to this double standard is that female youths are incarcerated for similar terms as male youths.[89]

The girls' unit at a class in the San Jose, California, Juvenile Hall.

Many of the characteristics of juvenile female offenders are similar to those of their male counterparts, including poor social skills and low self-esteem. Other problems are more specific to the female juvenile offender (sexual abuse issues, victimization histories, lack of placement options).[90] Female juvenile offenders also have higher rates of mental health problems than their male counterparts.[91] In addition, there have been numerous allegations of emotional and sexual abuse by correctional workers, who either exploit vulnerable young women or callously disregard their emotional needs. An interview survey conducted by the National Council on Crime and Delinquency uncovered numerous incidents of abuse, and bitter resentment by the young women over the brutality of their custodial treatment.[92]

Although there are more coed institutions for juveniles than in the past, most girls remain incarcerated in single-sex institutions that are isolated in rural areas and rarely offer adequate rehabilitative services. Several factors account for the different treatment of girls. One is sexual stereotyping by administrators, who believe that teaching girls "appropriate" sex roles will help them function effectively in society. These beliefs are often held by the staff as well, many of whom have highly sexist ideas of what is appropriate behavior for adolescent girls. Another factor that accounts for the different treatment of girls is that staff members often are not adequately trained to understand and address the unique needs of this population.[93] Girls' institutions tend to be smaller than boys' institutions and lack the money to offer as many programs and services as the larger male institutions.[94]

It appears that although society is more concerned about protecting girls who act out, it is less concerned about rehabilitating them because the crimes they commit are not serious. These attitudes translate into fewer staff, older facilities, and poorer educational and recreational programs than those found in boys' institutions.[95] To help address these and other problems facing female juveniles in institutions, the American Bar Association and the National Bar Association recommend a number of important changes, including these:

- Identify, promote, and support effective gender-specific, developmentally sound, culturally sensitive practices with girls
- Promote an integrated system of care for at-risk and delinquent girls and their families based on their competencies and needs

- Assess the adequacy of services to meet the needs of at-risk or delinquent girls and address gaps in service
- Collect and review state and local practices to assess the gender impact of decision making and system structure[96]

Some of these recommendations are starting to garner serious attention, notably with the emergence of a growing body of evidence of effective programs for female juveniles in institutions and at other stages in the juvenile justice system.[97] **CHECKPOINTS**

CORRECTIONAL TREATMENT FOR JUVENILES

Nearly all juvenile institutions implement some form of treatment program: counseling, vocational and educational training, recreational programs, and religious counseling. In addition, most institutions provide medical programs as well as occasional legal service programs. Generally, the larger the institution, the greater the number of programs and services offered.

The purpose of these programs is to rehabilitate youths to become well-adjusted individuals and send them back into the community to be productive citizens. Despite good intentions, however, the goal of rehabilitation is sometimes not attained, due in large part to poor implementation of the programs.[98] A significant number of juvenile offenders commit more crimes after release,[99] and some experts believe that correctional treatment has little effect on recidivism.[100] However, a large scale empirical review of institutional treatment programs found that serious juvenile offenders who receive treatment have recidivism rates about 10 percent lower than similar untreated juveniles, and that the best programs reduced recidivism by as much as 40 percent.[101] The most successful of these institutional treatment programs provide training to improve interpersonal skills and family-style teaching to improve behavioral skills. Also important is the need to foster healthy, supportive relationships between incarcerated youth and juvenile care workers.[102]

What are the drawbacks to correctional rehabilitation? One of the most common problems is the lack of well-trained staff members. Budgetary limitations are a primary concern. It costs a substantial amount of money per year to keep a child in an institution, which explains why institutions generally do not employ large professional staffs.

However, some correctional programs are highly cost-efficient, producing monetary benefits that outweigh the costs of running the program.[103] In a recent study with the provocative title, "Are Violent Delinquents Worth Treating?" researchers Michael Caldwell, Michael Vitacco, and Gregory Van Rybroek found that an institutional treatment program for violent juvenile offenders that was effective in reducing recidivism rates produced cost savings to taxpayers that were seven times greater than what it cost to run the program. These findings can be particularly influential on policy makers and government funding agencies.[104]

The most glaring problem with treatment programs is that they are not administered as intended. Although the official goals of many may be treatment and rehabilitation, the actual programs may center around security and punishment. The next sections describe some treatment approaches that aim to rehabilitate offenders.

Individual Treatment Techniques: Past and Present

In general, effective individual treatment programs are built around combinations of psychotherapy, reality therapy, and behavior modification. **Individual counseling**

individual counseling Counselors help juveniles understand and solve their current adjustment problems.

WWW

To learn more about **reality therapy,** visit the Criminal Justice CourseMate at CengageBrain.com, then access the Web Links for this chapter.

is one of the most common treatment approaches, and virtually all juvenile institutions use it to some extent. This is not surprising because psychological problems such as depression are prevalent in juvenile institutions.[105] Individual counseling does not attempt to change a youth's personality. Rather, it attempts to help individuals understand and solve their current adjustment problems. Some institutions employ counselors who are not professionally qualified, which subjects offenders to a superficial form of counseling.

Professional counseling may be based on **psychotherapy**. Psychotherapy requires extensive analysis of the individual's childhood experiences. A skilled therapist attempts to help the individual make a more positive adjustment to society by altering negative behavior patterns learned in childhood. Another frequently used treatment is **reality therapy**.[106] This approach, developed by William Glasser during the 1970s, emphasizes current, rather than past, behavior by stressing that offenders are completely responsible for their own actions. The object of reality therapy is to make individuals more responsible people. This is accomplished by giving them confidence through developing their ability to follow a set of expectations as closely as possible. The success of reality therapy depends greatly on the warmth and concern of the counselor.

Behavior modification is used in many institutions.[107] It is based on the theory that all behavior is learned and that current behavior can be shaped through rewards and punishments. This type of program is easily used in an institutional setting that offers privileges as rewards for behaviors, such as work, study, or the development of skills. It is reasonably effective, especially when a contract is formed with the youth to modify certain behaviors. When youths are aware of what is expected of them, they plan their actions to meet these expectations and then experience the anticipated consequences. In this way, youths can be motivated to change.

Group Treatment Techniques

Group therapy is more economical than individual therapy, because one therapist can counsel more than one individual at a time. Also, the support of the group is often valuable to individuals in the group, and individuals derive hope from other members of the group who have survived similar experiences. Another advantage of group therapy is that a group can often solve a problem more effectively than an individual.

One disadvantage of group therapy is that it provides little individual attention. Everyone is different, and some group members may need more individualized treatment. Also, there is the concern that by providing therapy in a group format, those who are more chronically involved in delinquency may negatively affect those who are marginally involved.[108]

Guided group interaction (GGI) is a fairly common method of group treatment. It is based on the theory that, through group interactions, a delinquent can acknowledge and solve personal problems. A leader facilitates interaction, and a group culture develops. Individual members can be mutually supportive and reinforce acceptable behavior. In the 1980s, a version of GGI called **positive peer culture (PPC)** became popular. These programs use groups in which peer leaders encourage other youths to conform to conventional behaviors. The rationale is that if negative peer influence can encourage youths to engage in delinquent behavior, then positive peer influence can help them conform.[109] Though research results are inconclusive, there is evidence that PPC may facilitate communication ability for incarcerated youth.[110]

Another common group treatment approach, **milieu therapy**, seeks to make all aspects of the inmates' environment part of their treatment and to minimize differences between custodial staff and treatment personnel. Milieu therapy, based on psychoanalytic theory, was developed during the late 1940s and early 1950s by Bruno Bettelheim.[111] This therapy attempted to create a conscience, or superego, in delinquent youths by getting them to depend on their therapists to a great extent and then threatening them with loss of the caring relationship if they failed to control their behavior. Today, milieu therapy more often makes use of peer interactions and attempts to create an environment that encourages meaningful change, growth, and satisfactory adjustment. This is often accomplished through peer pressure to conform to group norms.

psychotherapy Highly structured counseling in which a therapist helps a juvenile solve conflicts and make a more positive adjustment to society.

reality therapy A form of counseling that emphasizes current behavior and requires the individual to accept responsibility for all of his or her actions.

behavior modification A technique for shaping desired behaviors through a system of rewards and punishments.

group therapy Counseling several individuals together in a group session.

guided group interaction (GGI) Through group interactions, a delinquent can acknowledge and solve personal problems with support from other group members.

positive peer culture (PPC) Counseling program in which peer leaders encourage other group members to modify their behavior and peers help reinforce acceptable behaviors.

milieu therapy All aspects of the environment are part of the treatment, and meaningful change, increased growth, and satisfactory adjustment are encouraged.

AP Photo/Jeff Roberson

Youth specialist Robert Kofahl, second from left, leads a group session at the Rosa Parks Center, a detention home for female juvenile offenders in Fulton, Missouri. The center stresses group therapy and personal development over isolation and punishment.

Educational, Vocational, and Recreational Programs

Because educational programs are an important part of social development and have therapeutic as well as instructional value, they are an essential part of most treatment programs. What takes place through education is related to all other aspects of the institutional program—work activities, cottage life, recreation, and clinical services.

Educational programs are probably the best-staffed programs in training schools, but even at their best, most of them are inadequate. Educational programs contend with myriad problems. Many of the youths coming into these institutions are mentally challenged, have learning disabilities, and are far behind their grade levels in basic academics. Most have become frustrated with the educational experience, dislike school, and become bored with any type of educational program. Their sense of frustration often leads to disciplinary problems.

Ideally, institutions should allow the inmates to attend a school in the community or offer programs that lead to a high school diploma or GED certificate. In recent years, a growing number of residential facilities have begun offering these types of programs. Almost 9 out of every 10 (87 percent) juvenile residential facility provide high school–level education, 8 of every 10 (81 percent) residential facility provide middle school–level education, and 70 percent provide GED preparation.[112] Secure institutions, because of their large size, are more likely than group homes or day treatment centers to offer programs such as remedial reading, physical education, and tutoring. Some offer computer-based learning and programmed learning modules. The Professional Spotlight discusses the career of one teacher who works in a juvenile correctional facility.

Vocational training has long been used as a treatment technique for juveniles. Early institutions were even referred to as "industrial schools." Today, vocational programs in institutions include auto repair, printing, woodworking, computer training, food service, cosmetology, secretarial training, and data processing. A common drawback of vocational training programs is sex-typing. The recent trend has been to allow equal access to all programs offered in institutions that house both girls and boys. Sex-typing is more difficult to avoid in single-sex institutions, because funds aren't usually available for all types of training.

WWW

To see how **positive peer culture** can be used effectively, visit the Criminal Justice Course-Mate at CengageBrain.com, then access the Web Links for this chapter.

© Kristi Swanson

Kristi Swanson

Teacher, Idaho Prison Juvenile Unit

Kristi Swanson is a teacher in the juvenile unit of an Idaho prison that is run by the Ada County Juvenile Court Services. The program she works for specializes in helping juvenile offenders obtain their high school education. The program serves juveniles who are neither good candidates for traditional school nor any longer allowed in traditional school because of suspension, expulsion, or safety issues.

Swanson started her career in an educational program for adolescents in the neuro-psych unit of a hospital. Although she enjoyed the position, she has always been drawn to working with young people in trouble with the law and in a nontraditional school environment. Her philosophy regarding kids who have broken the law has always been that kids are not bad. They make choices, and some of those choices are not always productive.

Swanson prepared for being a teacher by obtaining a bachelor's degree in English and education. Working at a hospital for a year proved to be an extremely beneficial experience. Mental health issues play a large part when considering the proper course of action to take regarding students in a juvenile correctional facility.

What does Kristi Swanson feel is the most rewarding part of her job? It is found in the stories where a student was able to turn his or her life around and be successful. These kids often have any number of barriers to their education, including substance abuse, parental substance abuse, physical and/or mental abuse, incarcerated parents, coming from disadvantaged homes, and pregnancy. Many times they are referred to Swanson and her colleagues with very little expectation that they will be able to help them where others have failed. That challenge, combined with the capability of each of the young people, keeps the job very interesting.

As a teacher, Swanson's greatest challenge involves dealing with students who continually make poor choices despite the best efforts of staff. Eventually, the time comes when one has to decide how much more energy should be directed toward those students, sometimes to the detriment of others.

The school day at the juvenile unit is divided into three blocks, one hour and 45 minutes apiece. Swanson spends time helping the teens with math, science, English, history, government, economics, and other subjects. Her daily routine also involves responding to inquiries from probation officers, writing letters that accompany students to court, and grading assignments. Notes are needed on each student every day. The notes are sent to the probation department at the end of each week. There are also numerous meetings with parents and probation officers regarding school progress. Swanson is also trained to intervene to deescalate problems and help keep the school a safe place for the students. Sometimes that means providing a listening ear, a shoulder to cry on, or a trip to the social worker's office.

Wilderness Programs

Wilderness probation programs involve troubled youths in outdoor activities as a mechanism to improve their social skills, self-concept, and self-control. Typically, wilderness programs maintain exposure to a wholesome environment; where the concepts of education and the work ethic are taught and embodied in adult role models, troubled youths can regain a measure of self-worth.

A number of wilderness programs for juvenile offenders have been evaluated for their effects on recidivism. In a detailed review of the effects of wilderness programs—those emphasizing physical activity over more therapeutic goals—on recidivism, Doris MacKenzie concludes that these programs do not work.[113] Although some of the programs show success, such as the Spectrum Wilderness Program in Illinois,[114] others had negative effects; that is, the group that received the program had higher arrest rates than the comparison group that did not. Taken together, the programs suffered from poor implementation, weak evaluation designs or problems with too few subjects or large dropout rates, and failure to adhere to principles of successful rehabilitation, such as targeting high-risk youths and lasting for a moderate period of time.[115] However, wilderness programs that include a therapeutic component have been shown to be effective in reducing juvenile offending. Sandra Wilson and Mark Lipsey found that, on average, these programs produced a 20 percent reduction in recidivism rates, with the most successful ones offering more intensive physical activity or therapeutic services.[116]

wilderness probation Programs involving outdoor expeditions that provide opportunities for juveniles to confront the difficulties of their lives while achieving positive personal satisfaction.

Juvenile Boot Camps

Correctional **boot camps** were designed with the idea of combining the get-tough elements of adult programs with education, substance abuse treatment, and social skills training. In theory, a successful boot camp program should rehabilitate juvenile offenders, reduce the number of beds needed in secure institutional programs, and thus reduce the overall cost of care. The Alabama boot camp program for youthful offenders estimated savings of $1 million annually when compared with traditional institutional sentences.[117] However, no one seems convinced that participants in these programs have lower recidivism rates than those who serve normal sentences. Ronald Corbett and Joan Petersilia do note that boot camp participants seem to be less antisocial upon returning to society.[118]

The bottom line for juvenile boot camps, like other correctional sanctions, is whether or not they reduce recidivism. A **meta-analysis** of the effects of juvenile boot camps on recidivism found this to be an ineffective correctional approach to reducing it; from the 17 different program samples, the control groups had, on average, lower recidivism rates than the treatment groups (boot camps).[119] Interestingly, when compared with the effects of 26 program samples of boot camps for adults, the juvenile boot camps had a higher average recidivism rate, although the difference was not significant.[120]

Why do boot camps for juveniles fail to reduce future offending? The main reason is that they provide little in the way of therapy or treatment to correct offending behavior.[121] Also, few are linked to services to help juvenile offenders transition back to the community. One juvenile boot camp program in Quehanna, Pennsylvania, which included a mandatory residential aftercare component, showed a reduction in recidivism rates two years post-release.[122] Experts have also suggested that part of the reason for not finding differences in recidivism between boot camps and other correctional alternatives (the control groups) may be due to juveniles in the control groups receiving enhanced treatment, whereas juveniles in the boot camps are spending more time on physical activities.[123]

The general ineffectiveness of boot camps to reduce reoffending in the community by juvenile offenders (and adult offenders) appears to have resulted in this approach falling into disfavor with some correctional administrators. At the height of its popularity in the mid-1990s, more than 75 state-run boot camps were in operation in more than 30 states across the country.[124] Despite this, boot camps appear to still have a place among the array of sentencing options, if for no other reason than to appease the public with the promise of tougher sentences and lower costs.[125] If boot camps are to become a viable alternative for juvenile corrections, they must be seen not as a panacea that provides an easy solution to the problems of delinquency, but merely part of a comprehensive approach to juvenile care that is appropriate to a select group of adolescents.[126] **CHECKPOINTS**

THE LEGAL RIGHT TO TREATMENT

The primary goal of placing juveniles in institutions is to help them reenter the community successfully. Therefore, lawyers claim that children in state-run institutions have a legal right to treatment.

The concept of a **right to treatment** was introduced to the mental health field in 1960 by Morton Birnbaum, who argued that individuals who are deprived of their liberty because of a mental illness are entitled to treatment to correct that

WWW

To read more about **boot camps,** visit the Criminal Justice CourseMate at CengageBrain .com, then access the Web Links for this chapter.

CHECKPOINTS

LO4 Be able to identify current juvenile correctional treatment approaches and comment on their effectiveness in reducing recidivism.

✔ Nearly all juvenile institutions implement some form of treatment program.

✔ Reality therapy, a commonly used individual approach, emphasizes current, rather than past, behavior by stressing that offenders are completely responsible for their own actions.

✔ Group therapy is more commonly used with kids than individual therapy.

✔ Guided group interaction and positive peer culture are popular group treatment techniques.

✔ Many but not all institutions either allow juveniles to attend a school in the community or offer programs that lead to a high school diploma or GED certificate.

✔ Wilderness programs involve troubled youths using outdoor activities as a mechanism to improve their social skills, self-concepts, and self-control.

✔ Correctional boot camps emphasize the get-tough elements of adult programs.

boot camps Programs that combine get-tough elements with education, substance abuse treatment, and social skills training.

meta-analysis An analysis technique that synthesizes results across many programs over time.

right to treatment Philosophy espoused by many courts that juvenile offenders have a statutory right to treatment while under the jurisdiction of the courts.

condition.[127] The right to treatment has expanded to include the juvenile justice system, an expansion bolstered by court rulings that mandate that rehabilitation and not punishment or retribution be the basis of juvenile court dispositions.[128] It stands to reason then that, if incarcerated, juveniles are entitled to the appropriate social services that will promote their rehabilitation.

One of the first cases to highlight this issue was *Inmates of the Boys' Training School v. Affleck* in 1972.[129] In its decision, a federal court argued that rehabilitation is the true purpose of the juvenile court and that, without this goal, due process guarantees are violated. It condemned such devices as solitary confinement, strip cells, and lack of educational opportunities, and held that juveniles have a statutory right to treatment. The court also established the following minimum standards for all juveniles confined in training schools:

- A room equipped with lighting sufficient for an inmate to read until 10:00 P.M.
- Sufficient clothing to meet seasonal needs
- Bedding, including blankets, sheets, pillows, and pillowcases, to be changed once a week
- Personal hygiene supplies, including soap, toothpaste, towels, toilet paper, and toothbrush
- A change of undergarments and socks every day
- Minimum writing materials: pen, pencil, paper, and envelopes
- Prescription eyeglasses, if needed
- Equal access to all books, periodicals, and other reading materials located in the training school
- Daily showers
- Daily access to medical facilities, including provision of a 24-hour nursing service
- General correspondence privileges[130]

In 1974, in the case of *Nelson v. Heyne*, the First Federal Appellate Court affirmed that juveniles have a right to treatment and condemned the use of corporal punishment in juvenile institutions.[131] In *Morales v. Turman*, the court held that all juveniles confined in training schools in Texas have a right to treatment, including development of education skills, delivery of vocational education, medical and psychiatric treatment, and adequate living conditions.[132] In another case, *Pena v. New York State Division for Youth*, the court held that the use of isolation, hand restraints, and tranquilizing drugs at Goshen Annex Center violated the Fourteenth Amendment right to due process and the Eighth Amendment right to protection against cruel and unusual punishment.[133]

The right to treatment has also been limited. For example, in *Ralston v. Robinson*, the Supreme Court rejected a youth's claim that he should continue to be given treatment after he was sentenced to a consecutive term in an adult prison for crimes committed while in a juvenile institution.[134] In the *Ralston* case, the offender's proven dangerousness outweighed the possible effects of rehabilitation. Similarly, in *Santana v. Callazo,* the U.S. First Circuit Court of Appeals rejected a suit brought by residents at the Maricao Juvenile Camp in Puerto Rico on the grounds that the administration had failed to provide them with an individualized rehabilitation plan or adequate treatment. The circuit court concluded that it was a legitimate exercise of state authority to incarcerate juveniles solely to protect society if they are dangerous.

The Struggle for Basic Civil Rights

Several court cases have led federal, state, and private groups—for example, the American Bar Association, the American Correctional Association, and the National Council on Crime and Delinquency—to develop standards for the juvenile justice system. These standards provide guidelines for conditions and practices in juvenile institutions and call on administrators to maintain a safe and healthy environment for incarcerated youths.

WWW

To learn more about **the right to treatment**, read "Meeting the Needs of the Mentally Ill—A Case Study of the 'Right to Treatment' as Legal Rights Discourse in the USA," by Michael McCubbin and David N. Weisstub. You can find it by visiting the Criminal Justice CourseMate at CengageBrain.com, then accessing the Web Links for this chapter.

For the most part, state-sponsored brutality has been outlawed, although the use of restraints, solitary confinement, and even medication for unruly residents has not been eliminated. The courts have ruled that corporal punishment in any form violates standards of decency and human dignity.

There are a number of mechanisms for enforcing these standards. For example, the federal government's Civil Rights of Institutionalized Persons Act (CRIPA) gives the Civil Rights Division of the U.S. Department of Justice (DOJ) the power to bring actions against state or local governments for violating the civil rights of persons institutionalized in publicly operated facilities.[135] CRIPA does not create any new substantive rights; it simply confers power on the U.S. attorney general to bring action to enforce previously established constitutional or statutory rights of institutionalized persons; about 25 percent of cases involve juvenile detention and correctional facilities.

What provisions does the juvenile justice system make to help institutionalized offenders return to society? The remainder of this chapter is devoted to this topic.

JUVENILE AFTERCARE AND REENTRY

Aftercare in the juvenile justice system is the equivalent of parole in the adult criminal justice system. When juveniles are released from an institution, they may be placed in an aftercare program of some kind, so that those who have been institutionalized are not simply returned to the community without some transitional assistance. Whether individuals who are in aftercare as part of an indeterminate sentence remain in the community or return to the institution for further rehabilitation depends on their actions during the aftercare period. Aftercare is an extremely important stage in the juvenile justice process, because few juveniles age out of custody.[136]

Reentry involves aftercare services but includes preparation for release from confinement, also called prerelease planning.[137] Reentry is further distinguished from aftercare in that reentry is seen as the whole process and experience of the transition of juveniles from "juvenile and adult correctional settings back into schools, families, communities, and society at large."[138] The concept of reentry, which is also the term given to it in the adult criminal justice system, is by no means new.[139] Recently, however, it has come to characterize the larger numbers of juvenile and adult offenders returning to communities each year and the increased needs these offenders exhibit with respect to employment, education, and mental health and substance abuse problems.[140] For juvenile offenders, reentry goes beyond the all-too-common practice of juveniles being placed in aftercare programs that are the same as adult parole programs, which "fail to take account of their unique needs and the challenges they face."[141] Through the Serious and Violent Offender Reentry Initiative (SVORI), the federal government has invested $150 million on reentry programs for adult and juvenile offenders in all 50 states, the District of Columbia, and the Virgin Islands.[142] Promising results are beginning to emerge from this initiative as well as other juvenile reentry programs across the country.[143]

WWW

For more information on **SVORI programs for juvenile offenders,** visit the Criminal Justice CourseMate at CengageBrain .com, then access the Web Links for this chapter.

Supervision

One purpose of aftercare and reentry is to provide support during the readjustment period following release. First, individuals whose activities have been regimented for some time may not find it easy to make independent decisions. Second, offenders may perceive themselves as scapegoats, cast out by society. Finally, the community may view the returning minor with a good deal of prejudice; adjustment problems may reinforce a preexisting need to engage in deviant behavior.

Juveniles in aftercare programs are supervised by parole caseworkers or counselors whose job is to maintain contact with the juvenile, make sure that a corrections plan is followed, and show interest and caring. The counselor also keeps the youth informed of services that may assist in reintegration, and counsels the youth and his or her family. Unfortunately, aftercare caseworkers, like probation officers, often carry such large caseloads that their jobs are next to impossible to do adequately.

aftercare Transitional assistance to juveniles equivalent to adult parole to help youths adjust to community life.
reentry The process and experience of returning to society upon release from a custody facility post-adjudication.

Aftercare—the equivalent of parole in the adult criminal justice system—includes a range of services designed to help juveniles adjust to community life upon release from an institution. Here, Tristan Cassidy, 17, (top) and Scott Epperley, 15, work on a project for their geography class at the Northwest Regional Learning Center (NRLC) in Everett, Washington. The NRLC is a detention school for juveniles on probation or in aftercare that serves as a last chance for some to earn their high school diploma if their former schools will not accept them back.

The Intensive Aftercare Program (IAP) Model. Models of aftercare have been aimed at the chronic or violent offender. The **Intensive Aftercare Program (IAP)** model developed by David Altschuler and Troy Armstrong offers a continuum of intervention for serious juvenile offenders returning to the community following placement.[144] The IAP model begins by drawing attention to five basic principles, which collectively establish a set of fundamental operational goals:

- Preparing youths for progressively increased responsibility and freedom in the community
- Facilitating youth–community interaction and involvement
- Working with both the offender and targeted community support systems (families, peers, schools, employers) on qualities needed for constructive interaction and the youths' successful community adjustment
- Developing new resources and supports where needed
- Monitoring and testing the youths and the community on their ability to deal with each other productively

These basic goals are then translated into practice, which incorporates individual case planning with a family and community perspective. The program stresses a mix of intensive surveillance and services and a balance of incentives and graduated consequences coupled with the imposition of realistic, enforceable conditions. There is also "service brokerage," in which community resources are used and linkage with social networks established.[145]

The IAP initiative was designed to help correctional agencies implement effective aftercare programs for chronic and serious juvenile offenders. After more than 12 years of testing, the program is now being aimed at determining how juveniles are prepared for reentry into their communities, how the transition is handled, and how the aftercare in the community is provided.[146] The Prevention/Intervention/Treatment feature "Using the Intensive Aftercare Program (IAP) Model" illustrates how it is being used in three state jurisdictions and reports on the latest evaluation results.

Intensive Aftercare Program (IAP) A balanced, highly structured, comprehensive continuum of intervention for serious and violent juvenile offenders returning to the community.

Using the Intensive Aftercare Program (IAP) Model

How has the IAP model been used around the nation, and has it proven effective?

Colorado

Although adolescents are still institutionalized, community-based providers begin weekly services (including multi-family counseling and life-skills services) that continue during aftercare. Sixty days prior to release, IAP youths begin a series of step-down measures, including supervised trips to the community, and 30 days before release, there are overnight or weekend home passes. Upon release to parole, most program youths go through several months of day treatment that, in addition to services, provides a high level of structure during the day. As a youth's progress warrants, the frequency of supervision decreases.

Nevada

Once the parole plan is finalized, all IAP youths begin a 30-day prerelease phase, during which IAP staff provide a series of services that continue through the early months of parole. These consist primarily of two structured curricula on life skills and substance abuse. The initial 30 days of release are considered an institutional furlough (that is, the kids are still on the institutional rolls) that involves intensive supervision and service. During furlough, they are involved in day programming and are subject to frequent drug testing and evening and weekend surveillance. Upon successful completion of the furlough, the IAP transition continues through the use of phased levels of supervision. During the first three months, three contacts per week with the case manager or field agent are required. This level of supervision is reduced to two contacts per week for the next two months, and then to once a week during the last month of parole.

Virginia

Virginia's transition differs from the other two states in that its central feature is the use of group home placements as a bridge between the institution and the community. Immediately after release from the institution, youths enter one of two group homes for a 30- to 60-day period. The programs and services in which they will be involved in the community are initiated shortly after placement in the home. Virginia uses a formal step-down system to gradually ease the intensity of parole supervision. In the two months following the youth's release from the group home, staff are required to contact him or her five to seven times per week. This is reduced to three to five times per week during the next two months, and again to three times per week during the final 30 days.

Does the IAP Model Work?

In each state, one site was chosen to assess the effectiveness of the IAP model: Denver, Colorado; Las Vegas, Nevada; and Norfolk, Virginia. An experimental evaluation that randomly assigned juveniles to the program or a control group was used to assess the model's effectiveness on recidivism. As shown in Table 14A, the program produced some benefits in Norfolk, but in Denver, program youths were more likely than their control counterparts to recidivate and to be sentenced to a period of incarceration. The researchers call for caution in interpreting these results. In the case of Denver, control group youths received services similar to those in the IAP. They also note that this was the first test of a "very complex intervention." Suggestions for improvement to the IAP include maximizing parental involvement, emphasizing education and employment skills, and strengthening community support networks.

Critical Thinking

1. What is the importance of reducing the number of supervision contacts with the juvenile offender toward the end of the aftercare program?

2. Should juvenile offenders who have committed less serious offenses also have to go through intensive aftercare programs? Discuss.

Sources: David M. Altschuler, "Juvenile Reentry and Aftercare," *Georgetown Journal on Poverty Law and Policy* 16:655–667 (2009); Richard G. Wiebush, Dennis Wagner, Betsie McNulty, Yanqing Wang, and Thao N. Le, *Implementation and Outcome Evaluation of the Intensive Aftercare Program* (Washington, DC: OJJDP, 2005); Steve V. Gies, *Aftercare Services* (Washington, DC: OJJDP Juvenile Justice Bulletin, 2003).

TABLE 14A **The IAP Model's Effects on Recidivism**

	Denver		Las Vegas		Norfolk	
	IAP	Control	IAP	Control	IAP	Control
Arrested (%)	69	65	77	77	60	67
Convicted (%)	42	33	59	60	44	59
Incarcerated (%)	41	26	45	41	56	58

Aftercare Revocation Procedures

Juvenile parolees are required to meet set standards of behavior, which generally include but are not limited to the following:

- Adhere to a reasonable curfew set by youth worker or parent
- Refrain from associating with persons whose influence would be detrimental
- Attend school in accordance with the law
- Abstain from drugs and alcohol
- Report to the youth worker when required
- Refrain from acts that would be crimes if committed by an adult
- Refrain from operating an automobile without permission of the youth worker or parent
- Refrain from being habitually disobedient and beyond the lawful control of parent or other legal authority
- Refrain from running away from the lawful custody of parent or other lawful authority

If these rules are violated, the juvenile may have his parole revoked and be returned to the institution. Most states have extended the same legal rights enjoyed by adults at parole revocation hearings to juveniles who are in danger of losing their aftercare privileges, as follows:

- Juveniles must be informed of the conditions of parole and receive notice of any obligations.
- Juveniles have the right to legal counsel at state expense if necessary.
- They maintain the right to confront and cross-examine witnesses against them.
- They have the right to introduce documentary evidence and witnesses.
- They have the right to a hearing before an officer who shall be an attorney but not an employee of the revoking agency.[147] **CHECKPOINTS**

CHECKPOINTS

LO5 Know about aftercare and reentry for juvenile offenders.

✔ Aftercare in the juvenile justice system is the equivalent of parole in the adult criminal justice system.

✔ Reentry involves aftercare services but includes preparation for release from confinement.

✔ Supervision is a major component of aftercare services for juvenile offenders.

✔ The Intensive Aftercare Program (IAP) model works with chronic and violent juvenile offenders, and has been evaluated in a number of sites across the country.

FUTURE OF JUVENILE CORRECTIONS

There exists much debate about the effectiveness of community versus institutional treatment. Considerable research shows that warehousing juveniles without proper treatment does little to prevent future delinquent activities.[148] The most effective secure corrections programs are those that provide individual services for a small number of participants.[149] Evaluations of community treatment provide evidence of a number of successful ways to prevent delinquency without jeopardizing the safety of community residents, and members of the public continue to express their support for more treatment over punishment.[150]

There is also a long-standing debate about the effectiveness of correctional treatments compared with other delinquency prevention measures. In their assessment of the full range of interventions to prevent serious and violent juvenile offending, Rolf Loeber and David Farrington found that it is never too early and never too late to make a difference.[151] Though some critics believe that juveniles are being coddled, in the future it is likely that innovative treatment methods will be applied continually within the juvenile justice system.

On another front, deinstitutionalization has become an important goal of the juvenile justice system. The Office of Juvenile Justice and Delinquency Prevention provided funds to encourage this process. In the early 1980s, the deinstitutionalization movement seemed to be partially successful. Admissions to public juvenile correctional facilities declined in the late 1970s and early 1980s. In addition, the number of status offenders being held within the juvenile justice system was reduced. Following a substantial increase in the number of institutionalized children in the 1990s and the early 2000s, numbers have decreased of late. During these years, the majority of states achieved compliance with the DSO mandate (Deinstitutionalizing Status Offenders). Because juvenile crime is a high priority, the challenge to the states will be to retain a focus on prevention despite political, not necessarily public,[152] assertions of the need for more punitive approaches. If that can be achieved, deinstitutionalization will remain a central theme in the juvenile justice system.

A more pressing problem is that a disproportionate number of minority youths continue to be incarcerated in youth facilities. The difference is greatest for African American youths, with the incarceration rate being four times greater than that for Caucasian youths. Of equal importance, minorities are more likely to be placed in secure public facilities rather than in open private facilities that might provide more costly and effective treatment. The OJJDP is committed to ensuring that the nation address situations where there is disproportionate confinement of minority offenders in the juvenile justice system. In the future, it is expected that this initiative will result in a more fair and balanced juvenile justice system.

Aftercare and reentry services represent crucial elements of a juvenile offender's successful transition back to the community. Correctional authorities recognize that juvenile offenders who are released from confinement are at heightened risk for returning to a life of crime without assistance in overcoming barriers with employment, education, and housing, and dealing with mental health, substance abuse, and other problems.[153] Many jurisdictions are experiencing success with halfway houses and reintegration centers and other reentry programs, and the federal government's substantial investment in reentry programs through the Serious and Violent Offender Reentry Initiative is promising.

SUMMARY

Community treatment encompasses efforts to keep offenders in the community and spare them the stigma of incarceration. The primary purpose is to provide a nonrestrictive or home setting, employing educational, vocational, counseling, and employment services. Institutional treatment encompasses provision of these services but in more restrictive and sometimes secure facilities.

Probation is the most widely used method of community treatment. Youths on probation must obey rules given to them by the court and participate in some form of treatment program. If rules are violated, youths may have their probation revoked. Behavior is monitored by probation officers. Formal probation accounts for more than half (57 percent) of all juvenile dispositions.

It is now common to enhance probation with more restrictive forms of treatment, such as intensive supervision and house arrest with electronic monitoring. Residential community treatment programs allow youths to live at home while receiving treatment in a nonpunitive, community-based center. Some of these probation innovations, like intensive supervision, get mixed reviews on their effectiveness in reducing recidivism, while others such as restitution and restorative justice show success.

The secure juvenile institution was developed in the midnineteenth century as an alternative to placing youths in adult prisons. Youth institutions evolved from large, closed institutions to cottage-based education- and rehabilitation-oriented institutions. The concept of *least restrictive alternative* is applicable in decisions on placing juvenile offenders in institutions to ensure that the setting benefits the juvenile's treatment needs.

The juvenile institutional population has decreased in recent years. A large number of youths continue to be "hidden" in private medical centers and drug treatment clinics. There are wide variations in juvenile custody rates across states, and a disproportionate number of minorities are incarcerated in more secure, state-run youth facilities. Compared to males, female juvenile inmates are faced with many hardships.

Most juvenile institutions maintain intensive treatment programs featuring individual or group therapy. Little evidence has been found that any single method is effective in reducing recidivism. Rehabilitation remains an important goal of juvenile practitioners.

The right to treatment is an important issue in juvenile justice. Legal decisions have mandated that a juvenile cannot simply be warehoused in a correctional center but must receive proper care and treatment to aid rehabilitation. What constitutes proper care is still being debated, however.

Juveniles released from institutions are often placed on parole or in aftercare. Many jurisdictions are experiencing success with halfway houses and reintegration centers and other reentry programs.

community treatment, p. 382

suppression effect, p. 383

probation, p. 383

conditions of probation, p. 386

juvenile probation officer, p. 386

social investigation report, predisposition report, p. 386

juvenile intensive probation supervision (JIPS), p. 388

house arrest, p. 388

electronic monitoring, p. 388

balanced probation, p. 390

monetary restitution, p. 390

victim service restitution, p. 390

community service restitution, p. 390

residential programs, p. 391

group homes, p. 391

foster care programs, p. 392

family group homes, p. 392

rural programs, p. 392

reform schools, p. 393

cottage system, p. 393

least restrictive alternative, p. 394

individual counseling, p. 401

psychotherapy, p. 402

reality therapy, p. 402

behavior modification, p. 402

group therapy, p. 402

guided group interaction (GGI), p. 402

positive peer culture (PPC), p. 402

milieu therapy, p. 402

wilderness probation, p. 403

boot camps, p. 405

meta-analysis, p. 405

right to treatment, p. 405

aftercare, p. 407

reentry, p. 407

Intensive Aftercare Program (IAP), p. 408

QUESTIONS FOR REVIEW

1. How does community treatment differ from institutional treatment?

2. What were some of the key events that led to probation becoming a mandatory part of the court structure in 1890?

3. How has the use of juvenile probation changed in recent years?

4. Aside from probation, what are the main community-based alternatives to incarceration?

5. What are the key explanations for the wide variation in state-level juvenile custody rates?

6. Why do African American juvenile offenders have such high custody rates?

7. What are some of the key barriers to providing correctional treatment services for female juvenile offenders?

8. What is the purpose of reentry services for juvenile offenders?

QUESTIONS FOR DISCUSSION

1. Would you want a community treatment program in your neighborhood? Why or why not?

2. Is widening the net a real danger, or are treatment-oriented programs simply a method of helping troubled youths?

3. If youths violate the rules of probation, should they be placed in a secure institution?

4. Is juvenile restitution fair? Should a poor child have to pay back a wealthy victim?

5. What are the most important advantages to community treatment for juvenile offenders?

6. What is the purpose of juvenile probation? Identify some conditions of probation and discuss the responsibilities of the juvenile probation officer.

7. Has community treatment generally proven successful?

8. Why have juvenile boot camps not been effective in reducing recidivism?

APPLYING WHAT YOU HAVE LEARNED

As a local juvenile court judge, you have been assigned the case of Jim Butler, a 13-year-old so short he can barely see over the bench. On trial for armed robbery, the boy has been accused of threatening a woman with a knife and stealing her purse. Barely a teenager, he has already had a long history of involvement with the law. At age 11, he was arrested for drug possession and placed on probation; soon after, he stole a car. At age 12, he was arrested for shoplifting. Jim is accompanied by his legal guardian, his maternal grandmother. His parents are unavailable because his father abandoned the family years ago and his mother is currently undergoing inpatient treatment at a local drug clinic. After talking with his attorney, Jim decides to admit to the armed robbery. At a dispositional hearing, his court-appointed attorney tells you of the tough life Jim has been forced to endure. His grandmother states that, although she loves the boy, her advanced age makes it impossible for her to provide the care he needs to stay out of trouble. She says that Jim is a good boy who has developed a set of bad companions; his current scrape was precipitated by his friends. A representative of the school system testifies that Jim has above-average intelligence and is actually respectful of teachers. He has potential, but his life circumstances have short-circuited his academic success. Jim himself shows remorse and appears to be a sensitive youngster who is easily led astray by older youths.

You must now make a decision. You can place Jim on probation and allow him to live with his grandmother while being monitored by county probation staff. You can place him in a secure incarceration facility for up to three years. You can also put him into an intermediate program such as a community-based facility, which would allow him to attend school during the day while residing in a halfway house and receiving group treatment in the evenings.

Writing Assignment: Jim's crime was serious and involved the use of a weapon. If he remains in the community, he may offend again; if he is sent to a correctional facility, he will interact with older, tougher kids. Write an essay on the best course of action for this case, weighing the costs and benefits of correctional treatment in these different settings.

GROUPWORK

There are a wide range of community-based correctional treatment options for juvenile offenders, including probation, restorative justice, and residential programs. Divide the class into as many as seven groups. Assign each group a different community-based treatment and have the groups come up with a 10-point plan to expand their respective treatment option (i.e., to aid different groups of juvenile offenders) and improve its effectiveness in reducing juvenile recidivism.

NOTES

Chapter 1. Childhood and Delinquency

1. U.S. Bureau of the Census, Table 1, Population by Age and Sex: 2010, www.census.gov/population/www/socdemo/age/age_sex_2010.html (accessed June 14, 2012).
2. Devan Crawford, Les Whitbeck, and Dan R. Hoyt, "Propensity for Violence Among Homeless and Runaway Adolescents: An Event History Analysis," *Crime and Delinquency* 57:950–968 (2011).
3. Nanette Davis, *Youth Crisis: Growing Up in the High-Risk Society* (New York: Praeger/Greenwood, 1998).
4. Steven Martino, Rebecca Collins, Marc Elliott, Amy Strachman, David Kanouse, and Sandra Berry, "Exposure to Degrading Versus Nondegrading Music Lyrics and Sexual Behavior Among Youth" *Pediatrics* 118: 430–441 (2006).
5. Erik Erikson, *Childhood and Society* (New York: Norton, 1963).
6. Roger Gould, "Adult Life Stages: Growth Toward Self-Tolerance," *Psychology Today* 8:74–78 (1975).
7. Rima Shore, *KIDS COUNT Indicator Brief: Reducing the Teen Death Rate* (Baltimore: Annie E. Casey Foundation, 2005).
8. Greg Duncan, W. Jean Yeung, Jeanne Brooks-Gunn, and Judith Smith, "How Much Does Childhood Poverty Affect the Life Chances of Children?" *American Sociological Review* 63:406–423 (1998).
9. Children's Defense Fund, *The Impact of Rising Poverty on the Nation's Young Families and Their Children, 2000–2010*, CDF Policy Brief #1, September 2011, www.childrensdefense.org/child-research-data-publications/the-impact-of-rising-poverty.pdf (accessed June 14, 2012).
10. Ibid.
11. Ibid.
12. Ibid.
13. Childstats,gov, *America's Children: Key National Indicators of Well-Being, 2011*, "Health Insurance Coverage," www.childstats.gov/americaschildren/care1.asp (accessed June 14, 2012).
14. Ibid.
15. Ibid.
16. Children's Defense Fund, *State of America's Children, 2008*.
17. Centers for Disease Control and Prevention, "Marriage and Divorce," www.cdc.gov/nchs/fastats/divorce.htm (accessed June 14, 2012).
18. Childstats,gov, *America's Children: Key National Indicators of Well-Being, 2011*, "Family Structure and Children's Living Arrangements," www.childstats.gov/americaschildren/famsoc1.asp (accessed June 14, 2012).
19. Ibid.
20. Children's Defense Fund, Marian Wright Edelman's Child Watch column, "National Foster Care Month," May 15, 2009, www.childrensdefense.org/newsroom/child-watch-columns/child-watch-documents/national-foster-care-month.html (accessed June 14, 2012).
21. Gary Evans, Nancy Wells, and Annie Moch, "Housing and Mental Health: A Review of the Evidence and a Methodological and Conceptual Critique," *Journal of Social Issues* 59:475–501 (2003).
22. Children's Defense Fund, "Elementary and High School Education," www.childrensdefense.org/helping-americas-children/elementary-high-school-education/ (accessed June 14, 2012).
23. Children's Defense Fund, *Black and White: Black Children Compared to White Children*, www.childrensdefense.org/programs-campaigns/black-community-crusade-for-children-II/bccc-assets/black-and-white-factsheet.pdf (accessed June 14, 2012).
24. Children's Defense Fund, "Elementary and High School Education."
25. Kevin Cullen, "The Untouchable Mean Girls," *Boston Globe*, January 24, 2010, www.boston.com/news/local/massachusetts/articles/2010/01/24/the_untouchable_mean_girls/ (accessed June 14, 2012).
26. Jane Ireland and Rachel Monaghan, "Behaviours Indicative of Bullying Among Young and Juvenile Male Offenders: A Study of Perpetrator and Victim Characteristics," *Aggressive Behavior* 32:172–180 (2006).
27. This section leans heavily on Justin Patchin and Sameer Hinduja, "Bullies Move Beyond the Schoolyard: A Preliminary Look at Cyberbullying," *Youth Violence and Juvenile Justice* 4:148–169 (2006).
28. Justin Patchin, "How Many Teens are Actually Involved in Cyberbullying?" Cyberbullying Research Center blog, April 4, 2012, http://cyberbullying.us/blog/ (accessed June 14, 2012).
29. Justin Patchin and Sameer Hinduja, Cyberbullying Research Center, http://cyberbullying.us/research.php (accessed June 14, 2012).
30. Patchin and Hinduja, "Bullies Move Beyond the Schoolyard."
31. Janis Wolak, David Finkelhor, Kimberly Mitchell, and Michele Ybarra, "Online 'Predators' and Their Victims: Myths, Realities, and Implications for Prevention and Treatment," *American Psychologist* 63 (2008): 111–128.
32. Mike Celizic, "Her Teen Committed Suicide over 'Sexting': Cynthia Logan's Daughter Was Taunted About Photo She Sent to Boyfriend," MSNBC.com, March 6, 2009, www.msnbc.msn.com/id/29546030/ (accessed June 14, 2012).
33. Kimberly Mitchell, David Finkelhor, Lisa Jones, and Janis Wolak, "Prevalence and Characteristics of Youth Sexting: A National Study," *Pediatrics* 129:1–8 (2012).
34. David Eggebeen and Daniel Lichter, "Race, Family Structure, and Changing Poverty Among American Children," *American Sociological Review* 56:801–817 (1991).
35. Tami Videon, "The Effects of Parent-Adolescent Relationships and Parental Separation on Adolescent Well-Being," *Journal of Marriage and the Family* 64:489–504 (2002).
36. National Center for Education Statistics, *Digest of Education Statistics, 2008*, http://nces.ed.gov/programs/digest/d08/ (accessed June 14, 2012).
37. Lloyd Johnston, Patrick O'Malley, Jerald Bachman, and John Schulenberg, "Various Stimulant Drugs Show Continuing Gradual Declines Among Teens in 2008, Most Illicit Drugs Hold Steady," University of Michigan News Service, December 11, 2008, www.monitoringthefuture.org (accessed June 14, 2012).
38. Federal Bureau of Investigation, *Crime in the United States, 2007* (Washington, DC: U.S. Government Printing Office, 2008).
39. Mark Cohen, Alex R. Piquero, and Wesley G. Jennings. "Studying the Costs of Crime Across Offender Trajectories," *Criminology and Public Policy* 9:279–305 (2010); Cohen, Piquero, and Jennings, "Monetary Costs of Gender and Ethnicity Disaggregated Group-Based Offending," *American Journal of Criminal Justice* 35:159–172 (2010).
40. *Sourcebook of Criminal Justice Statistics 2003*, "Attitudes Toward the Treatment of Juveniles Who Commit Violent Crimes, by Demographic Characteristics, United States, 2003," www.albany.edu/sourcebook/pdf/t248.pdf (accessed June 14, 2012).
41. See Lawrence Stone, *The Family, Sex, and Marriage in England: 1500–1800* (New York: Harper & Row, 1977).
42. This section relies on Jackson Spielvogel, *Western Civilization* (St. Paul, MN: West, 1991), pp. 279–286.
43. Ibid.
44. Philippe Aries, *Centuries of Childhood: A Social History of Family Life* (New York: Vintage Books, 1962).
45. Ibid.
46. See Douglas R. Rendleman, "*Parens Patriae*: From Chancery to the Juvenile Court," *South Carolina Law Review* 23:205 (1971).
47. Ibid.
48. See Wiley B. Sanders, *Some Early Beginnings of the Children's Court Movement in England, National Probation Association Yearbook* (New York: National Council on Crime and Delinquency, 1945).

49. Rendleman, "*Parens Patriae*," p. 205.
50. Douglas Besharov, *Juvenile Justice Advocacy—Practice in a Unique Court* (New York: Practicing Law Institute, 1974), p. 2.
51. Rendleman, "*Parens Patriae*," p. 209.
52. Anthony Platt, "The Rise of the Child Saving Movement: A Study in Social Policy and Correctional Reform," *Annals of the American Academy of Political and Social Science* 381:21–38 (1969).
53. Robert Bremmer, ed., and John Barnard, Hareven Tamara, and Robert Mennel, asst. eds., *Children and Youth in America* (Cambridge, MA: Harvard University Press, 1970), p. 64.
54. Elizabeth Pleck, "Criminal Approaches to Family Violence: 640–1980," in *Family Violence*, ed. Lloyd Ohlin and Michael Tonry (Chicago: University of Chicago Press, 1989), pp. 19–58.
55. John R. Sutton, *Stubborn Children: Controlling Delinquency in the United States, 1640–1981* (Berkeley: University of California Press, 1988).
56. Pleck, "Criminal Approaches to Family Violence," p. 29.
57. Graeme Newman, *The Punishment Response* (Philadelphia: Lippincott, 1978), pp. 53–79; Aries, *Centuries of Childhood*. The history of childhood juvenile justice is discussed in detail in Chapter 12.
58. Robert M. Mennel, "Origins of the Juvenile Court: Changing Perspectives on the Legal Rights of Juvenile Delinquents," *Crime and Delinquency* 18:68–78 (1972).
59. Anthony M. Platt, *The Child Savers: The Invention of Delinquency* (Chicago: University of Chicago Press, 1969).
60. See Anne Meis Knupfer, *Reform and Resistance: Gender, Delinquency and America's First Juvenile Court* (New York: Routledge, 2001).
61. Sanford J. Fox, "Juvenile Justice Reform: A Historical Perspective," *Stanford Law Review* 22:1187 (1970).
62. Robert S. Pickett, *House of Refuge—Origins of Juvenile Reform in New York State, 1815–1857* (Syracuse, NY: Syracuse University Press, 1969).
63. Mennel, "Origins of the Juvenile Court," pp. 69–70.
64. Anthony Salerno, "The Child Saving Movement: Altruism or Conspiracy?" *Juvenile and Family Court Journal* 42:37 (1991).
65. Platt, *The Child Savers*.
66. U.S. Department of Justice, Juvenile Justice and Delinquency Prevention, *Two Hundred Years of American Criminal Justice: An LEAA Bicentennial Study* (Washington, DC: Law Enforcement Assistance Administration, 1976).
67. Fox, "Juvenile Justice Reform," p. 1229.
68. Pleck, "Criminal Approaches to Family Violence."
69. Elizabeth Pleck, *Domestic Tyranny: The Making of Social Policy Against Family Violence from Colonial Times to the Present* (New York: Oxford University Press, 1987), pp. 28–30.
70. Linda Gordon, *Family Violence and Social Control* (New York: Viking, 1988).
71. Mary Odem and Steven Schlossman, "Guardians of Virtue: The Juvenile Court and Female Delinquency in Early 20th-Century Los Angeles," *Crime and Delinquency* 37:186–203 (1991).
72. Margueritte Rosenthal, "Reforming the Juvenile Correctional Institution: Efforts of the U.S. Children's Bureau in the 1930s," *Journal of Sociology and Social Welfare* 14:47–74 (1987); see also David Steinhart, "Status Offenses" in *The Future of Children: The Juvenile Court* (Los Altos, CA: David and Lucile Packard Foundation, Center for the Future of Children, 1996).
73. N.Y. Fam. Ct. Act, Art. 7, Sec. 712 (Consol. 1962).
74. *Kent v. United States*, 383 U.S. 541, 86 S.Ct. 1045, 16 L.Ed.2d 84 (1966). *In re Gault*, 387 U.S. 1, 87 S.Ct. 1428, 18 L.Ed.2d 527 (1967): Juveniles have the right to notice, counsel, confrontation, and cross-examination, and to the privileges against self-incrimination in juvenile court proceedings. *In re Winship*, 397 U.S. 358, 90 S.Ct. 1068, 25 L.Ed.2d 368 (1970): Proof beyond a reasonable doubt is necessary for conviction in juvenile proceedings. *Breed v. Jones*, 421 U.S. 519, 95 S.Ct. 1779, 44 L.Ed.2d 346 (1975): Jeopardy attaches in a juvenile court adjudicatory hearing, thus barring subsequent prosecution for the same offense as an adult.
75. Public Law 90-351, Title I—Omnibus Safe Streets and Crime Control Act of 1968, 90th Congress, June 1968.
76. National Advisory Commission on Criminal Justice Standards and Goals, *A National Strategy to Reduce Crime* (Washington, DC: U.S. Government Printing Office, 1973).
77. Juvenile Justice and Delinquency Prevention Act of 1974, Public Law 93-415 (1974). For a critique of this legislation, see Ira Schwartz, *Justice for Juveniles—Rethinking the Best Interests of the Child* (Lexington, MA: D.C. Heath, 1989), p. 175.
78. Stephen J. Morse, "Immaturity and Irresponsibility," *Journal of Criminal Law and Criminology* 88:15–67 (1997).
79. Kareem Jordan and David Myers, "Juvenile Transfer and Deterrence: Reexamining the Effectiveness of a 'Get-Tough' Policy," *Crime and Delinquency* 57:247–270 (2011).
80. Shay Bilchik, "Sentencing Juveniles to Adult Facilities Fails Youths and Society," *Corrections Today* 65:21 (2003).
81. Federal Bureau of Investigation, *Crime in the United States, 2009* (Washington, DC: U.S. Government Printing Office, 2010).
82. Anne Stahl, "Petitioned Status Offense Cases in Juvenile Courts, 2004," Office of Juvenile Justice and Delinquency Prevention, 2008, www.ncjrs.gov/pdffiles1/ojjdp/fs200802.pdf (accessed June 14, 2012).
83. See, generally, David Rothman, *The Discovery of the Asylum* (Boston: Little, Brown, 1971).
84. Reports of the Chicago Bar Association Committee, 1899, cited in Anthony Platt, *The Child Savers: The Invention of Delinquency* (Chicago: University of Chicago Press, 1969), p. 119.
85. Susan Datesman and Mikel Aickin, "Offense Specialization and Escalation Among Status Offenders," *Journal of Criminal Law and Criminology* 75:1246–1275 (1985).
86. Ibid.
87. Wesley Jennings, "Sex Disaggregated Trajectories of Status Offenders: Does CINS/FINS Status Prevent Male and Female Youth From Becoming Labeled Delinquent?" *American Journal of Criminal Justice* 36:177–187 (2011).
88. National Council on Crime and Delinquency, "Juvenile Curfews—A Policy Statement," *Crime and Delinquency* 18:132–133 (1972).
89. *Juvenile Justice and Delinquency Prevention Act (JJDPA)* of 1974, as amended (42 U.S.C. 5601 *et seq.*).
90. Runaway and Homeless Youth Act (RHYA) of 1974 (42 U.S.C. § 5701 *et seq.*).
91. 42 U.S.C.A. 5601B5751 (1983 and Supp. 1987).
92. Gail Robinson and Tim Arnold, "Changes in Laws Impacting Juveniles—An Overview," *The Advocate* 22:14–15 (2000).
93. American Bar Association, Early Interventions for Juvenile Status Offender, *2007*, www.americanbar.org/groups/child_law.html (accessed July 25, 2012).
94. Barry Feld, "Criminalizing the American Juvenile Court," in *Crime and Justice: A Review of Research*, ed. Michael Tonry (Chicago: University of Chicago Press, 1993), p. 232.
95. Sean Kidd, "Factors Precipitating Suicidality Among Homeless Youth: A Quantitative Follow-Up" *Youth and Society* 37:393–422 (2006); Kimberly Tyler, Les Whitbeck, Dan Hoyt, and Kurt Johnson, "Self-Mutilation and Homeless Youth: The Role of Family Abuse, Street Experiences, and Mental Disorders," *Journal of Research on Adolescence*, 13:457–474 (2003).
96. Kimberly Henry and David Huizinga, "Truancy's Effect on the Onset of Drug Use Among Urban Adolescents Placed at-Risk," *Journal of Adolescent Health* 40:9–17 (2007).
97. Tony Favro, "Youth Curfews Popular with American Cities but Effectiveness and Legality Are Questioned," City Mayors Society, July 21, 2009, www.citymayors.com/society/usa-youth-curfews.html (accessed June 14, 2012).
98. Danny Cole, "The Effect of a Curfew Law on Juvenile Crime in Washington, D.C.," *American Journal of Criminal Justice* 27:217–232 (2003).
99. Kenneth Adams, "The Effectiveness of Juvenile Curfews at Crime Prevention," *Annals of the American Academy of Political and Social Science* 587:136–159 (2003); Canadian Parental Responsibility Act, 2000 S.O. 2000, Chapter 4, www.e-laws.gov.on.ca/html/statutes/english/elaws_statutes_00p04_e.htm (accessed June 14, 2012).
100. Michael Luke, "ACLU, Others Take Aim at Expanding Teen Curfew Citywide," WWLTV Eyewitness News, January 18, 2012, www.wwltv.com/news/ACLU-others-take-aim-at-expanding-teen-curfew-citywide-137592918.html (accessed July 24, 2012).
101. Margaret Anne Cleek, John Youril, Michael Youril, and Richard Guarino, "Don't Worry, It's Just a Tool: Enacting Selectively Enforced Laws Such as Curfew Laws Targeting Only the Bad Guys," *Justice Policy Journal* 7:1–23 (2010).
102. *Anonymous vs. City of Rochester* (2009), www.law.cornell.edu/nyctap/I09_0095.htm (accessed July 25, 2012).
103. Jonathon Saltzman, "SJC Sharply Limits Youth Curfew Law: Bars Criminal Charge, Allows Civil Penalty," *Boston Globe*, September 26, 2009.
104. Gilbert Geis and Arnold Binder, "Sins of Their Children: Parental Responsibility for Juvenile Delinquency," *Notre Dame Journal of Law, Ethics, and Public Policy* 5:303–322 (1991).
105. Eve Brank, Edie Greene, and Katherine Hochevar, "Holding Parents Responsible: Is Vicarious Responsibility the Public's Answer to Juvenile Crime?" *Psychology, Public Policy, and Law* 17:507–529 (2011).
106. Elena Laskin, "How Parental Liability Statutes Criminalize and Stigmatize Minority Mothers," *American Criminal Law Review* 37:1195–1217 (2000).

107. Brank, Greene, and Hochevar, "Holding Parents Responsible: Is Vicarious Responsibility the Public's Answer to Juvenile Crime?"

108. Eve Brank and Victoria Weisz, "Paying for the Crimes of Their Children: Public Support of Parental Responsibility" *Journal of Criminal Justice* 32:465–475 (2004).

Chapter 2. The Nature and Extent of Delinquency

1. The data used here are from the FBI, *Crime in the United States, 2010*, www.fbi.gov/about-us/cjis/ucr/crime-in-the-u.s/2010/crime-in-the-u.s.-2010 (accessed June 26, 2012).

2. Fox Butterfield, "Possible Manipulation of Crime Data Worries Top Police," *New York Times*, August 3, 1998, p. 1.

3. Adam Watkins, "Examining the Disparity Between Juvenile and Adult Victims in Notifying the Police: A Study of Mediating Variables," *Journal of Research in Crime and Delinquency* 42:333–353 (2005).

4. Jennifer Truman, *Criminal Victimization, 2010* (Washington, DC: Bureau of Justice Statistics, 2011), http://bjs.ojp.usdoj.gov/content/pub/pdf/cv10.pdf (accessed June 26, 2012).

5. Lynn Addington and Callie Marie Rennison, "Rape Co-occurrence: Do Additional Crimes Affect Victim Reporting and Police Clearance of Rape?" *Journal of Quantitative Criminology* 24:205–226 (2008).

6. L. Edward Wells and Joseph Rankin, "Juvenile Victimization: Convergent Validation of Alternative Measurements," *Journal of Research in Crime and Delinquency* 32:287–307 (1995).

7. A pioneering effort in self-report research is A. L. Porterfield, *Youth in Trouble* (Fort Worth, TX: Leo Potishman Foundation, 1946); for a review, see Robert Hardt and George Bodine, *Development of Self-Report Instruments in Delinquency Research: A Conference Report* (Syracuse, NY: Syracuse University Youth Development Center, 1965).

8. See John Paul Wright and Francis Cullen, "Juvenile Involvement in Occupational Delinquency," *Criminology* 38:863–896 (2000).

9. Christiane Brems, Mark Johnson, David Neal, and Melinda Freemon, "Childhood Abuse History and Substance Use Among Men and Women Receiving Detoxification Services," *American Journal of Drug and Alcohol Abuse* 30:799–821 (2004).

10. David Kirk, "Examining the Divergence Across Self-Report and Official Data Sources on Inferences About the Adolescent Life-Course of Crime," *Journal of Quantitative Criminology* 22:107–129 (2006).

11. Julia Yun Soo Kim, Michael Fendrich, and Joseph S. Wislar, "The Validity of Juvenile Arrestees' Drug Use Reporting: A Gender Comparison," *Journal of Research in Crime and Delinquency* 37:419–432 (2000).

12. Leonore Simon, "Validity and Reliability of Violent Juveniles: A Comparison of Juvenile Self-Reports with Adult Self-Reports Incarcerated in Adult Prisons," paper presented at the annual meeting of the American Society of Criminology, Boston, November 1995, p. 26.

13. Stephen Cernkovich, Peggy Giordano, and Meredith Pugh, "Chronic Offenders: The Missing Cases in Self-Report Delinquency Research," *Journal of Criminal Law and Criminology* 76:705–732 (1985).

14. Terence Thornberry, Beth Bjerregaard, and William Miles, "The Consequences of Respondent Attrition in Panel Studies: A Simulation Based on the Rochester Youth Development Study," *Journal of Quantitative Criminology* 9:127–158 (1993).

15. See Spencer Rathus and Larry Siegel, "Crime and Personality Revisited: Effects of MMPI Sets on Self-Report Studies," *Criminology* 18:245–251 (1980); John Clark and Larry Tifft, "Polygraph and Interview Validation of Self-Reported Deviant Behavior," *American Sociological Review* 31:516–523 (1966).

16. Mallie Paschall, Miriam Ornstein, and Robert Flewelling, "African-American Male Adolescents' Involvement in the Criminal Justice System: The Criterion Validity of Self-Report Measures in Prospective Study," *Journal of Research in Crime and Delinquency* 38:174–187 (2001).

17. Lloyd Johnston, Patrick O'Malley, and Jerald Bachman, *Monitoring the Future, 2010* (Ann Arbor, MI: Institute for Social Research, 2012), http://monitoringthefuture.org/ (accessed June 26, 2012).

18. Jennifer Roberts, Edward Mulvey, Julie Horney, John Lewis, and Michael Arter, "A Test of Two Methods of Recall for Violent Events," *Journal of Quantitative Criminology* 21:175–193 (2005).

19. Lila Kazemian and David Farrington, "Comparing the Validity of Prospective, Retrospective, and Official Onset for Different Offending Categories," *Journal of Quantitative Criminology* 21:127–147 (2005).

20. Barbara Warner and Brandi Wilson Coomer, "Neighborhood Drug Arrest Rates: Are They a Meaningful Indicator of Drug Activity? A Research Note," *Journal of Research in Crime and Delinquency* 40:123–139 (2003).

21. Kirk, "Examining the Divergence Across Self-Report and Official Data Sources on Inferences About the Adolescent Life-Course of Crime."

22. Alfred Blumstein, Jacqueline Cohen, and Richard Rosenfeld, "Trend and Deviation in Crime Rates: A Comparison of UCR and NCVS Data for Burglary and Robbery," *Criminology* 29:237–248 (1991).

23. Kirk, "Examining the Divergence Across Self-Report and Official Data Sources on Inferences About the Adolescent Life-Course of Crime."

24. For example, the following studies have noted the great discrepancy between official statistics and self-report studies: Maynard Erickson and LaMar Empey, "Court Records, Undetected Delinquency, and Decision Making," *Journal of Criminal Law, Criminology, and Police Science* 54:456–469 (1963); Martin Gold, "Undetected Delinquent Behavior," *Journal of Research in Crime and Delinquency* 3:27–46 (1966); James Short and F. Ivan Nye, "Extent of Unrecorded Delinquency, Tentative Conclusions," *Journal of Criminal Law, Criminology, and Police Science* 49:296–302 (1958).

25. Johnston, O'Malley, and Bachman, *Monitoring the Future, 2010.*

26. Steven Levitt, "The Limited Role of Changing Age Structure in Explaining Aggregate Crime Rates," *Criminology* 37:581–599 (1999).

27. Julie Phillips, "The Relationship Between Age Structure and Homicide Rates in the United States, 1970 to 1999," *Journal of Research in Crime and Delinquency* 43:230–260 (2006).

28. Brad Bushman, Morgan Wang, and Craig Anderson, "Is the Curve Relating Temperature to Aggression Linear or Curvilinear? Assaults and Temperature in Minneapolis Reexamined," *Journal of Personality and Social Psychology* 89:62–66 (2005).

29. Paul Bell, "Reanalysis and Perspective in the Heat-Aggression Debate," *Journal of Personality and Social Psychology* 89:71–73 (2005); Ellen Cohn, "The Prediction of Police Calls for Service: The Influence of Weather and Temporal Variables on Rape and Domestic Violence," *Journal of Environmental Psychology* 13:71–83 (1993).

30. Paul Tracy, Kimberly Kempf-Leonard, and Stephanie Abramoske-James, "Gender Differences in Delinquency and Juvenile Justice Processing: Evidence from National Data," Crime and Delinquency 55:171–215 (2009).

31. FBI, *Uniform Crime Reports, 2010,* Table 43, www.fbi.gov/about-us/cjis/ucr/crime-in-the-u.s/2010/crime-in-the-u.s.-2010/tables/table-43 (accessed June 26, 2012).

32. Johnston, O'Malley, and Bachman, *Monitoring the Future, 2010.*

33. Miriam Sealock and Sally Simpson, "Unraveling Bias in Arrest Decisions: The Role of Juvenile Offender Typescripts," *Justice Quarterly* 15:427–457 (1998).

34. Richard Rosenfeld, Jeff Rojek, and Scott Decker, "Age Matters: Race Differences in Police Searches of Young and Older Male Drivers," Journal of Research in Crime and Delinquency 49:31–55 (2011).

35. Hubert Blalock, Jr., *Toward a Theory of Minority-Group Relations* (New York: Capricorn Books, 1967).

36. Rodney Engen, Sara Steen, and George Bridges, "Racial Disparities in the Punishment of Youth: A Theoretical and Empirical Assessment of the Literature," *Social Problems* 49:194–221 (2002).

37. *Karen Parker, Brian* Stults, and Stephen Rice, "Racial Threat, Concentrated Disadvantage and Social Control: Considering the Macro-Level Sources of Variation in Arrests," *Criminology* 43:1111–1134 (2005); Lisa Stolzenberg, J. Stewart D'Alessio, and David Eitle, "A Multilevel Test of Racial Threat Theory," *Criminology* 42:673–698 (2004).

38. Michael Leiber and Kristan Fox, "Race and the Impact of Detention on Juvenile Justice Decision Making," *Crime and Delinquency* 51:470–497 (2005); Traci Schlesinger, "Racial and Ethnic Disparity in Pretrial Criminal Processing," *Justice Quarterly* 22:170–192 (2005).

39. Christina DeJong and Kenneth Jackson, "Putting Race into Context: Race, Juvenile Justice Processing, and Urbanization," *Justice Quarterly* 15:487–504 (1998).

40. Engen, Steen, and Bridges, "Racial Disparities in the Punishment of Youth."

41. David Eitle, Stewart D'Alessio, and Lisa Stolzenberg, "Racial Threat and Social Control: A Test of the Political, Economic, and Threat of Black Crime Hypotheses," *Social Forces* 81:557–576 (2002); Michael Leiber and Jayne Stairs, "Race, Contexts, and the Use of Intake Diversion," *Journal of Research in Crime and Delinquency* 36:56–86 (1999); Darrell Steffensmeier, Jeffery Ulmer, and John Kramer, "The Interaction of Race, Gender, and Age in Criminal Sentencing: The Punishment Cost of Being Young, Black, and Male," *Criminology* 36:763–798 (1998).

42. Bradley Keen and David Jacobs, "Racial Threat, Partisan Politics, and Racial Disparities in Prison Admissions," *Criminology* 47:209–238 (2009).

43. For a general review, see William Wilbanks, *The Myth of a Racist Criminal Justice System* (Pacific Grove, CA: Brooks/Cole, 1987).

44. Samuel Walker, Cassia Spohn, and Miriam DeLone, *The Color of Justice* (Belmont, CA: Wadsworth Publishing, 2003), pp. 47–48.

45. Gary LaFree and Richard Arum, "The Impact of Racially Inclusive Schooling on Adult Incarceration Rates Among U.S. Cohorts of African Americans and Whites Since 1930," *Criminology* 44:73–103 (2006).

46. Julie Phillips, "Variation in African-American Homicide Rates: An Assessment of Potential Explanations," *Criminology* 35:527–559 (1997).

47. Melvin Thomas, "Race, Class, and Personal Income: An Empirical Test of the Declining Significance of Race Thesis, 1968–1988," *Social Problems* 40:328–339 (1993).

48. Julie Phillips, "White, Black, and Latino Homicide Rates: Why the Difference?" *Social Problems* 49:349–374 (2002).

49. Thomas McNulty and Paul Bellair, "Explaining Racial and Ethnic Differences in Adolescent Violence: Structural Disadvantage, Family Well-Being, and Social Capital," *Justice Quarterly* 20:1–32 (2003); Julie Phillips, "White, Black, and Latino Homicide Rates: Why the Difference?" *Social Problems* 49:349–374 (2002).

50. Roy Austin, "Progress toward Racial Equality and Reduction of Black Criminal Violence," *Journal of Criminal Justice* 15:437–459 (1987).

51. Reynolds Farley and William Frey, "Changes in the Segregation of Whites from Blacks During the 1980s: Small Steps toward a More Integrated Society," *American Sociological Review* 59:23–45 (1994).

52. Gary LaFree, Eric Baumer, and Robert O'Brien, "Still Separate and Unequal? A City-Level Analysis of the Black–White Gap in Homicide Arrests Since 1960," *American Sociological Review* 75:75–100 (2010).

53. Charles Tittle and Robert Meier, "Specifying the SES/Delinquency Relationship," *Criminology* 28:271–301 (1990); R. Gregory Dunaway, Francis Cullen, Velmer Burton, and T. David Evans, "The Myth of Social Class and Crime Revisited: An Examination of Class and Adult Criminality," *Criminology* 38:589–632 (2000).

54. G. Roger Jarjoura and Ruth Triplett, "Delinquency and Class: A Test of the Proximity Principle," *Justice Quarterly* 14:765–792 (1997).

55. Nancy Rodriguez, "Concentrated Disadvantage and the Incarceration of Youth: Examining How Context Affects Juvenile Justice," *Journal of Research in Crime and Delinquency*, first published online, December 13, 2011.

56. Judith Blau and Peter Blau, "The Cost of Inequality: Metropolitan Structure and Violent Crime," *American Sociological Review* 147:114–129 (1982); Richard Block, "Community Environment and Violent Crime," *Criminology* 17:46–57 (1979); Robert Sampson, "Structural Sources of Variation in Race-Age-Specific Rates of Offending across Major U.S. Cities," *Criminology* 23:647–673 (1985).

57. Robert J. Sampson, "Disparity and Diversity in the Contemporary City: Social (Dis)order Revisited," *British Journal of Sociology* 60:1–31 (2009)

58. Bonita Veysey and Steven Messner, "Further Testing of Social Disorganization Theory: An Elaboration of Sampson and Groves's 'Community Structure and Crime,'" *Journal of Research in Crime and Delinquency* 36:156–174 (1999).

59. Robert Agnew, "A General Strain Theory of Community Differences in Crime Rates," *Journal of Research in Crime and Delinquency* 36:123–155 (1999).

60. Shawn Bushway, "Economy and Crime," *The Criminologist* 35:1–5 (2010).

61. See, generally, David Farrington, "Age and Crime," in *Crime and Justice: An Annual Review,* vol. 7, ed. Michael Tonry and Norval Morris (Chicago: University of Chicago Press, 1986), pp. 189–250.

62. Travis Hirschi and Michael Gottfredson, "Age and the Explanation of Crime," *American Journal of Sociology* 89:552–584 (1983).

63. Michael Gottfredson and Travis Hirschi, "The True Value of Lambda Would Appear to Be Zero: An Essay on Career Criminals, Criminal Careers, Selective Incapacitation, Cohort Studies, and Related Topics," *Criminology* 24:213–234 (1986); further support for their position can be found in Lawrence Cohen and Kenneth Land, "Age Structure and Crime," *American Sociological Review* 52:170–183 (1987).

64. Lila Kazemian and David Farrington, "Exploring Residual Career Length and Residual Number of Offenses for Two Generations of Repeat Offenders," *Journal of Research in Crime and Delinquency* 43:89–113 (2006).

65. Marvin Wolfgang, Robert Figlio, and Thorsten Sellin, *Delinquency in a Birth Cohort* (Chicago: University of Chicago Press, 1972); Lyle Shannon, *Assessing the Relationship of Adult Criminal Careers to Juvenile Careers: A Summary* (Washington, DC: U.S. Department of Justice, 1982); D. J. West and David P. Farrington, *The Delinquent Way of Life* (London: Heinemann, 1977); Donna Hamparian, Richard Schuster, Simon Dinitz, and John Conrad, *The Violent Few* (Lexington, MA: Lexington Books, 1978).

66. Rolf Loeber and Howard Snyder, "Rate of Offending in Juvenile Careers: Findings of Constancy and Change in Lambda," *Criminology* 28:97–109 (1990).

67. Margo Wilson and Martin Daly, "Life Expectancy, Economic Inequality, Homicide, and Reproductive Timing in Chicago Neighbourhoods," *British Journal of Medicine* 31:1271–1274 (1997).

68. Edward Mulvey and John LaRosa, "Delinquency Cessation and Adolescent Development: Preliminary Data," *American Journal of Orthopsychiatry* 56:212–224 (1986).

69. Timothy Brezina, "Delinquent Problem-Solving: An Interpretive Framework for Criminological Theory and Research," *Journal of Research in Crime and Delinquency* 37:3–30 (2000).

70. Alicia Rand, "Transitional Life Events and Desistance from Delinquency and Crime," in *From Boy to Man, from Delinquency to Crime,* ed. Marvin Wolfgang, Terence Thornberry, and Robert Figlio (Chicago: University of Chicago Press, 1987), pp. 134–163.

71. Marc LeBlanc, "Late Adolescence Deceleration of Criminal Activity and Development of Self- and Social-Control," *Studies on Crime and Crime Prevention* 2:51–68 (1993).

72. Barry Glassner, Margaret Ksander, Bruce Berg, and Bruce Johnson, "Note on the Deterrent Effect of Juvenile vs. Adult Jurisdiction," *Social Problems* 31:219–221 (1983).

73. Kevin Beaver, John Paul Wright, Matt DeLisi, and Michael G. Vaughn, "Desistance from Delinquency: The Marriage Effect Revisited and Extended," *Social Science Research* 37:736–752 (2008).

74. Neal Shover and Carol Thompson, "Age, Differential Expectations, and Crime Desistance," *Criminology* 30:89–104 (1992).

75. D. Wayne Osgood, "The Covariation Among Adolescent Problem Behaviors," paper presented at the annual meeting of the American Society of Criminology, Baltimore, November 1990.

76. Stephen Tibbetts, "Low Birth Weight, Disadvantaged Environment, and Early Onset: A Test of Moffitt's Interactional Hypothesis," paper presented at the annual meeting of the American Society of Criminology, Boston, November 1995.

77. Wolfgang, Figlio, and Sellin, *Delinquency in a Birth Cohort.*

78. Paul Tracy, Marvin Wolfgang, and Robert Figlio, *Delinquency in Two Birth Cohorts, Executive Summary* (Washington, DC: U.S. Department of Justice, 1985).

79. Shannon, *Assessing the Relationship of Adult Criminal Careers to Juvenile Careers*; Howard Snyder, *Court Careers of Juvenile Offenders* (Washington, DC: Office of Juvenile Justice and Delinquency Prevention, 1988); Donald J. West and David P. Farrington, *The Delinquent Way of Life* (London: Heinemann, 1977); Donna Hamparian, Richard Schuster, Simon Dinitz, and John Conrad, *The Violent Few* (Lexington, MA: Lexington Books, 1978).

80. See, generally, Wolfgang, Thornberry, and Figlio, *From Boy to Man.*

81. Paul Tracy and Kimberly Kempf-Leonard, *Continuity and Discontinuity in Criminal Careers* (New York: Plenum, 1996).

82. R. Tremblay, R. Loeber, C. Gagnon, P. Charlebois, S. Larivee, and M. LeBlanc, "Disruptive Boys with Stable and Unstable High Fighting Behavior Patterns During Junior Elementary School," *Journal of Abnormal Child Psychology* 19:285–300 (1991).

83. Peter Jones, Philip Harris, James Fader, and Lori Grubstein, "Identifying Chronic Juvenile Offenders," *Justice Quarterly* 18:478–507 (2001).

84. Jennifer White, Terrie Moffitt, Felton Earls, Lee Robins, and Phil Silva, "How Early Can We Tell? Predictors of Childhood Conduct Disorder and Adolescent Delinquency," *Criminology* 28:507–535 (1990).

85. Kimberly Kempf-Leonard, Paul Tracy, and James Howell, "Serious, Violent, and Chronic Juvenile Offenders: The Relationship of Delinquency Career Types to Adult Criminality," *Justice Quarterly* 18:449–478 (2001).

86. Kimberly Kempf, "Crime Severity and Criminal Career Progression," *Journal of Criminal Law and Criminology* 79:524–540 (1988).

87. Jeffrey Fagan, "Social and Legal Policy Dimensions of Violent Juvenile Crime," *Criminal Justice and Behavior* 17:93–133 (1990).

88. Peter Greenwood, *Selective Incapacitation* (Santa Monica, CA: Rand, 1982).

89. Terence Thornberry, David Huizinga, and Rolf Loeber, "The Prevention of Serious Delinquency and Violence," in *Sourcebook on Serious, Violent, and Chronic Juvenile Offenders*, ed. James Howell, Barry Krisberg, J. David Hawkins, and John Wilson (Thousand Oaks, CA: Sage, 1995).

90. Data here come from Truman, *Criminal Victimization, 2010.*

91. Anthony Peguero, Ann Marie Popp, and Dixie Koo, "Race, Ethnicity, and School-Based Adolescent Victimization" *Crime and Delinquency*, published online February 28, 2011.

92. Dean Kilpatrick, Benjamin Saunders, and Daniel Smith, *Youth Victimization: Prevalence and Implications* (Washington, DC: National Institute of Justice, 2003).

Chapter 3. Individual Views of Delinquency: Choice and Trait

1. Jeremy Bentham, in *A Fragment on Government and an Introduction to the Principles of Morals and Legislation*, ed. Wilfrid Harrison (Oxford, England: Basil Blackwell, 1948).

2. See, generally, Ernest Van den Haag, *Punishing Criminals* (New York: Basic Books, 1975).

3. Timothy Brezina, "Delinquent Problem-Solving: An Interpretive Framework for Criminological Theory and Research," *Journal of Research in Crime and Delinquency* 37:3–30 (2000).

4. Bruce Jacobs and Jody Miller, "Crack Dealing, Gender, and Arrest Avoidance," *Social Problems* 45:550–566 (1998).

5. Pierre Tremblay and Carlo Morselli, "Patterns in Criminal Achievement: Wilson and Abrahamsen Revisited," *Criminology* 38:633–660 (2000).

6. John Petraitis, Brian Flay, and Todd Miller, "Reviewing Theories of Adolescent Substance Use: Organizing Pieces in the Puzzle," *Psychological Bulletin* 117:67–86 (1995).

7. Travis Hirschi, "Rational Choice and Social Control Theories of Crime," in *The Reasoning Criminal*, ed. D. Cornish and R. Clarke (New York: Springer-Verlag, 1986), p. 114.

8. Melanie Wellsmith and Amy Burrell, "The Influence of Purchase Price and Ownership Levels on Theft Targets: The Example of Domestic Burglary," *British Journal of Criminology* 45:741–764 (2005).

9. William Smith, Sharon Glave Frazee, and Elizabeth Davison, "Furthering the Integration of Routine Activity and Social Disorganization Theories: Small Units of Analysis and the Study of Street Robbery as a Diffusion Process," *Criminology* 38:489–521 (2000).

10. Wim Bernasco and Paul Nieuwbeerta, "How Do Residential Burglars Select Target Areas? A New Approach to the Analysis of Criminal Location Choice," *British Journal of Criminology* 45:296–315 (2005).

11. Christopher Uggen and Melissa Thompson, "The Socioeconomic Determinants of Ill-Gotten Gains: Within-Person Changes in Drug Use and Illegal Earnings," *American Journal of Sociology* 109:146–185 (2003).

12. Timothy Brezina, "Delinquent Problem Solving: An Interpretive Framework for Criminological Theory and Research," *Journal of Research in Crime and Delinquency* 37:3–30 (2000); Andy Hochstetler, "Opportunities and Decisions: Interactional Dynamics in Robbery and Burglary Groups," *Criminology* 39:737–763 (2001).

13. Pierre Tremblay and Carlo Morselli, "Patterns in Criminal Achievement: Wilson and Abrahmse Revisited," *Criminology* 38:633–660 (2000).

14. Steven Levitt and Sudhir Alladi Venkatesh, "An Economic Analysis of a Drug-Selling Gang's Finances," NBER Working Papers 6592 (Cambridge, MA: National Bureau of Economic Research, Inc., 1998).

15. Bill McCarthy, " New Economics of Sociological Criminology," *Annual Review of Sociology* 28:417–442 (2002).

16. D. Wayne Osgood, Janet Wilson, Patrick O'Malley, Jerald Bachman, and Lloyd Johnston, "Routine Activities and Individual Deviant Behavior," *American Sociological Review* 61:635–655 (1996).

17. Brenda Sims Blackwell, "Perceived Sanction Threats, Gender, and Crime: A Test and Elaboration of Power-Control Theory," *Criminology* 38:439–488 (2000).

18. Dana Haynie, "Contexts of Risk? Explaining the Link Between Girls' Pubertal Development and Their Delinquency Involvement," *Social Forces* 82:355–397 (2003).

19. Amy Anderson and Lorine Hughes, "Exposure to Situations Conducive to Delinquent Behavior: The Effects of Time Use, Income, and Transportation," *Journal of Research in Crime and Delinquency* 46:5–34 (2009).

20. Raymond Paternoster, Shawn Bushway, Robert Brame, and Robert Apel, "The Effect of Teenage Employment on Delinquency and Problem Behaviors," *Social Forces* 82:297–336 (2003).

21. Matthew Ploeger, "Youth Employment and Delinquency: Reconsidering a Problematic Relationship," *Criminology* 35:659–675 (1997).

22. Jeremy Staff and Christopher Uggen, "The Fruits of Good Work: Early Work Experiences and Adolescent Deviance," *Journal of Research in Crime and Delinquency* 40:263–290 (2003).

23. Michael Hindelang, Michael Gottfredson, and James Garofalo, *Victims of Personal Crime: An Empirical Foundation for a Theory of Personal Victimization* (Cambridge, MA: Ballinger, 1978).

24. Lawrence Cohen and Marcus Felson, "Social Change and Crime Rate Trends: A Routine Activities Approach," *American Sociological Review* 44:588–608 (1979).

25. David Maume, "Inequality and Metropolitan Rape Rates: A Routine Activity Approach," *Justice Quarterly* 6:513–527 (1989).

26. Gordon Knowles, "Deception, Detection, and Evasion: A Trade Craft Analysis of Honolulu, Hawaii's, Street Crack Cocaine Traffickers," *Journal of Criminal Justice* 27:443–455 (1999).

27. Paul Bellair, "Informal Surveillance and Street Crime: A Complex Relationship," *Criminology* 38:137–167 (2000).

28. Denise Osborn, Alan Trickett, and Rob Elder, "Area Characteristics and Regional Variates as Determinants of Area Property Crime Levels," *Journal of Quantitative Criminology* 8:265–282 (1992).

29. Matthew Robinson, "Lifestyles, Routine Activities, and Residential Burglary Victimization," *Journal of Criminal Justice* 22:37–52 (1999).

30. Melanie Wellsmith and Amy Burrell, "The Influence of Purchase Price and Ownership Levels on Theft Targets: The Example of Domestic Burglary," *British Journal of Criminology* 45:741–764 (2005).

31. Brandon Welsh and David Farrington, "Surveillance for Crime Prevention in Public Space: Results and Policy Choices in Britain and America," *Criminology and Public Policy* 3:701–730 (2004).

32. Robert O'Brien, "Relative Cohort Sex and Age-Specific Crime Rates: An Age-Period-Relative-Cohort-Size Model," *Criminology* 27:57–78 (1989).

33. Rolf Becker and Guido Mehlkop, "Social Class and Delinquency: An Empirical Utilization of Rational Choice Theory with Cross-Sectional Data of the 1990 and 2000 German General Population Surveys (Allbus)," *Rationality and Society* 18:193–235 (2006).

34. Daniel Nagin and Greg Pogarsky, "Integrating Celerity, Impulsivity, and Extralegal Sanction Threats into a Model of General Deterrence: Theory and Evidence," *Criminology* 39:865–892 (2001).

35. Ibid.

36. Cesare Beccaria, *On Crimes and Punishments and Other Writings,* Richard Bellamy, ed., Richard Davies, trans. (London: Cambridge University Press, 1995).

37. Daniel Nagin and Greg Pogarsky, "An Experimental Investigation of Deterrence: Cheating, Self-Serving Bias, and Impulsivity," *Criminology* 41:167–195 (2003).

38. Tomislav V. Kovandzic and John J. Sloan, "Police Levels and Crime Rates Revisited: A County-Level Analysis from Florida (1980–1998)," *Journal of Criminal Justice* 30:65–76 (2002).

39. Gordon Bazemore and Mark Umbreit, "Rethinking the Sanctioning Function in Juvenile Court: Retributive or Restorative Responses to Youth Crime," *Crime and Delinquency* 41:296–316 (1995).

40. Michael White, James Fyfe, Suzanne Campbell, and John Goldkamp, "The Police Role in Preventing Homicide: Considering the Impact of Problem-Oriented Policing on the Prevalence of Murder," *Journal of Research in Crime and Delinquency* 40:194–226 (2003).

41. Eric Fritsch, Tory Caeti, and Robert Taylor, "Gang Suppression Through Saturation Patrol, Aggressive Curfew, and Truancy Enforcement: A Quasi-Experimental Test of the Dallas Anti-Gang Initiative," *Crime and Delinquency* 45:122–139 (1999).

42. Bruce Jacobs, "Anticipatory Undercover Targeting in High Schools," *Journal of Criminal Justice* 22:445–457 (1994).

43. Richard Timothy Coupe and Laurence Blake, "The Effects of Patrol Workloads and Response Strength on Arrests at Burglary Emergencies," *Journal of Criminal Justice* 33:239–255 (2005).

44. Cheryl L. Maxson, Kristy N. Matsuda, and Karen Hennigan, "Deterrability Among Gang and Nongang Juvenile Offenders: Are Gang Members More (or Less) Deterrable than Other Juvenile Offenders?" *Crime and Delinquency* 57:516–543 (2011).

45. Ross Matsueda, Derek A. Kreager, and David Huizinga, "Deterring Delinquents: A Rational Choice Model of Theft and Violence," *American Sociological Review* 71:95–122 (2006).

46. Doris Layton MacKenzie and Spencer De Li, "The Impact of Formal and Informal Social Controls on the Criminal Activities of Probationers," *Journal of Research in Crime and Delinquency* 39:243–276 (2002).

47. Shamena Anwar and Thomas Loughran, "Testing a Bayesian Learning Theory of Deterrence Among Serious Juvenile Offenders," *Criminology* 49:667–698 (2011).

48. Christina Dejong, "Survival Analysis and Specific Deterrence: Integrating Theoretical and Empirical Models of Recidivism," *Criminology* 35:561–576 (1997).

49. Pamela Lattimore, Christy Visher, and Richard Linster, "Predicting Rearrest for Violence Among Serious Youthful Offenders," *Journal of Research in Crime and Delinquency* 32:54–83 (1995).

50. Paul Tracy and Kimberly Kempf-Leonard, *Continuity and Discontinuity in Criminal Careers* (New York: Plenum, 1996).

51. Thomas Loughran, Edward Mulvey, Carol Schubert, Jeffrey Fagan, Alex Piquero, and Sandra Losoya, "Estimating a Dose-Response Relationship Between Length of Stay and Future Recidivism in Serious Juvenile Offenders," *Criminology* 47:699–740 (2009).

52. Greg Pogarsky and Alex R. Piquero, "Can Punishment Encourage Offending? Investigating the 'Resetting' Effect," *Journal of Research in Crime and Delinquency* 40:92–117 (2003).

53. Bruce Arrigo and Jennifer Bullock, "The Psychological Effects of Solitary Confinement on Prisoners in Supermax Units: Reviewing What We Know and Recommending What Should Change," *International Journal of Offender Therapy and Comparative Criminology* 52:622–640 (2008).

54. Jeffrey Fagan and Tracey Meares, "Deterrence and Social Control: The Paradox of Punishment in Minority Communities," *Ohio State Journal of Criminal Law* 6:173–229 (2008).

55. Office of Juvenile Justice and Delinquency Prevention, "Reentry," www.ojjdp.gov/mpg/reentry.aspx (accessed July 22, 2012).

56. Eric Jensen and Linda Metsger, "A Test of the Deterrent Effect of Legislative Waiver on Violent Juvenile Crime," *Crime and Delinquency* 40:96–104 (1994).

57. Wanda Foglia, "Perceptual Deterrence and the Mediating Effect of Internalized Norms Among Inner-City Teenagers," *Journal of Research in Crime and Delinquency* 34:414–442 (1997); Donald Green, "Measures of Illegal Behavior in Individual-Level Deterrence Research," *Journal of Research in Crime and Delinquency* 26:253–275 (1989); Charles Tittle, *Sanctions and Social Deviance: The Question of Deterrence* (New York: Praeger, 1980).

58. Greg Pogarsky, KiDeuk Kim, and Ray Paternoster, "Perceptual Change in the National Youth Survey: Lessons for Deterrence Theory and Offender Decision-Making," *Justice Quarterly* 22:1–29 (2005).

59. Bureau of Justice Statistics, *Prisoners and Drugs* (Washington, DC: U.S. Government Printing Office, 1983); Bureau of Justice Statistics, *Prisoners and Alcohol* (Washington, DC: U.S. Government Printing Office, 1983).

60. Robert Apel, Greg Pogarsky, and Leigh Bates, "The Sanctions–Perceptions Link in a Model of School-Based Deterrence," *Journal of Quantitative Criminology* 25:201–226 (2009).

61. Robert Bursik, Harold Grasmick, and Mitchell Chamlin, "The Effect of Longitudinal Arrest Patterns on the Development of Robbery Trends at the Neighborhood Level," *Criminology* 28:431–450 (1990); Theodore Chiricos and Gordon Waldo, "Punishment and Crime: An Examination of Some Empirical Evidence," *Social Problems* 18:200–217 (1970).

62. Laurence Sherman, "Defiance, Deterrence, and Irrelevance: A Theory of the Criminal Sanction," *Journal of Research in Crime and Delinquency* 30:445–473 (1993).

63. Leana Bouffard and Nicole Leeper Piquero, "Defiance Theory and Life Course Explanations of Persistent Offending," *Crime and Delinquency* 56:227–252 (2010).

64. Dieter Dolling, Horst Entorf, Dieter Hermann, and Thomas Rupp, "Deterrence Effective? Results of a Meta-Analysis of Punishment," *European Journal on Criminal Policy and Research* 15:201–224 (2009).

65. Michael Tonry, "Learning from the Limitations of Deterrence Research," *Crime and Justice: A Review of Research* 37:279–311 (2008).

66. Michael Jacobson and Lynn Chancer, "From Left Realism to Mass Incarceration: The Need for Pragmatic Vision in Criminal Justice Policy," *Crime, Law and Social Change* 55:187–196 (2011).

67. Patricia Bratingham, Paul Brantingham, and Wendy Taylor, "Situational Crime Prevention as a Key Component in Embedded Crime Prevention," *Canadian Journal of Criminology and Criminal Justice* 47:271–292 (2005).

68. Marcus Felson, "Routine Activities and Crime Prevention," in National Council for Crime Prevention, *Studies on Crime and Crime Prevention, Annual Review*, vol. 1 (Stockholm: Scandinavian University Press, 1992), pp. 30–34.

69. Andrew Fulkerson, "Blow and Go: the Breath-Analyzed Ignition Interlock Device as a Technological Response to DWI," *American Journal of Drug and Alcohol Abuse* 29:219–235 (2003).

70. Barry Webb, "Steering Column Locks and Motor Vehicle Theft: Evaluations for Three Countries," in *Crime Prevention* Studies, ed. Ronald Clarke (Monsey, NY: Criminal Justice Press, 1994), pp. 71–89.

71. David Farrington and Brandon Welsh, "Improved Street Lighting and Crime Prevention," *Justice Quarterly* 19:313–343 (2002).

72. Brandon Welsh and David Farrington, "Effects of Closed-Circuit Television on Crime," *Annals of the American Academy of Political and Social Science* 587:110–136 (2003).

73. Kenneth Novak, Jennifer Hartman, Alexander Holsinger, and Michael Turner, "The Effects of Aggressive Policing of Disorder on Serious Crime," *Policing* 22:171–190 (1999).

74. Lawrence Sherman, "Police Crackdowns: Initial and Residual Deterrence," in *Crime and Justice: A Review of Research*, vol. 12, ed. Michael Tonry and Norval Morris (Chicago: University of Chicago Press, 1990), pp. 1–48.

75. Anthony Braga, David Weisburd, Elin Waring, Lorraine Green Mazerolle, William Spelman, and Francis Gajewski, "Problem-Oriented Policing in Violent Crime Places: A Randomized Controlled Experiment," *Criminology* 39:541–580 (1999).

76. Fritsch, Caeti, and Taylor, "Gang Suppression Through Saturation Patrol, Aggressive Curfew, and Truancy Enforcement."

77. Bernard Rimland, *Dyslogic Syndrome: Why Today's Children are "Hyper," Attention Disordered, Learning Disabled, Depressed, Aggressive, Defiant, or Violent—and What We Can Do About It* (London, England: Jessica Kingsley Publishers, 2008).

78. Kevin Beaver, John Paul Wright, and Matt Delisi, "Delinquent Peer Group Formation: Evidence of a Gene X Environment Correlation," *Journal of Genetic Psychology* 169:227–244 (2008).

79. For an excellent review of Lombroso's work, as well as that of other well-known theorists, see Randy Martin, Robert Mutchnick, and W. Timothy Austin, *Criminological Thought: Pioneers Past and Present* (New York: Macmillan, 1990).

80. Marvin Wolfgang, "Cesare Lombroso," in *Pioneers in Criminology*, ed. Herman Mannheim (Montclair, NJ: Patterson Smith, 1970), pp. 232–271.

81. Gina Lombroso-Ferrero, *Criminal Man According to the Classification of Cesare Lombroso* (1911; reprint, Montclair, NJ: Patterson Smith, 1972), p. 7.

82. Edwin Driver, "Charles Buckman Goring," in *Pioneers in Criminology*, pp. 429–442.

83. See, generally, Thorsten Sellin, "Enrico Ferri," in *Pioneers in Criminology*, pp. 361–384.

84. Driver, "Charles Buckman Goring," pp. 434–435.

85. Ibid., p. 440.

86. Nicole Hahn Rafter, "Criminal Anthropology in the United States," *Criminology* 30:525–547 (1992).

87. B. R. McCandless, W. S. Persons, and A. Roberts, "Perceived Opportunity, Delinquency, Race, and Body Build Among Delinquent Youth," *Journal of Consulting and Clinical Psychology* 38:281–383 (1972).

88. Edmond O. Wilson, *Sociobiology: The New Synthesis* (Cambridge, MA: Harvard University Press, 1975).

89. For a general review, see John Archer, "Human Sociobiology: Basic Concepts and Limitations," *Journal of Social Issues* 47:11–26 (1991).

90. Arthur Caplan, *The Sociobiology Debate: Readings on Ethical and Scientific Issues* (New York: Harper and Row, 1978).

91. John Paul Wright, Rebecca Schnupp, Kevin M. Beaver, Matt Delisi, and Michael Vaughn, "Genes, Maternal Negativity, and Self-Control: Evidence of a Gene × Environment Interaction," *Youth Violence and Juvenile Justice*, first published on January 11, 2012.

92. Diana Fishbein, "Selected Studies on the Biology of Crime," in *New Perspectives in* Criminology, ed. John Conklin (Needham Heights, MA: Allyn & Bacon, 1996), pp. 26–38.

93. Ronald L. Simons, Man Kit Lei, Eric A. Stewart, Steven R. H. Beach, Gene H. Brody, Robert A. Philibert, and Frederick X. Gibbons, "Social Adversity, Genetic Variation, Street Code, and Aggression: A Genetically Informed Model of Violent Behavior," *Youth Violence and Juvenile Justice* 10:3–24 (2012).

94. See, generally, Adrian Raine, *The Psychopathology of Crime* (San Diego: Academic Press, 1993); see also Leonard Hippchen, *The Ecologic-Biochemical Approaches to Treatment of Delinquents and Criminals* (New York: Van Nostrand Reinhold, 1978).

95. "Diet and the Unborn Child: The Omega Point," *Economist*, January 19, 2006.

96. Amy Schonfeld, Sarah Mattson, and Edward Riley, "Moral Maturity and Delinquency After Prenatal Alcohol Exposure," *Journal of Studies on Alcohol* 66:545–554 (2005).

97. Lilian Calderón-Garcidueñas, "Air Pollution, Cognitive Deficits and Brain Abnormalities: A Pilot Study with Children and Dogs," *Brain and Cognition* 68:117–127 (2008).

98. Paul Stewart, Edward Lonky, Jacqueline Reihman, James Pagano, Brooks Gump, and Thomas Darvill, "The Relationship Between Prenatal PCB Exposure and Intelligence (IQ) in 9-Year-Old Children," *Environmental Health Perspectives* 116:1416–1422 (2008).

99. Emily Oken, Robert O. Wright, Ken P. Kleinman, David Bellinger, Chitra J. Amarasiriwardena, Howard Hu, Janet W. Rich-Edwards, and Matthew W. Gillman, "Maternal Fish Consumption, Hair Mercury, and Infant Cognition in a U.S. Cohort," *Environmental Health Perspectives* 113:1376–1380 (2005).

100. Mark Opler, Alan Brown, Joseph Graziano, Manisha Desai, Wei Zheng, Catherine Schaefer, Pamela Factor-Litvak, and Ezra S. Susser, "Prenatal Lead Exposure, [Delta]-Aminolevulinic Acid, and Schizophrenia," *Environmental Health Perspectives* 112:548–553 (2004).

101. Alexandra Richardson and Paul Montgomery, "The Oxford-Durham Study: A Randomized Controlled Trial of Dietary Supplementation with Fatty Acids in Children with Developmental Coordination Disorder," *Pediatrics* 115:1360–1366 (2005).

102. K. Murata, P. Weihe, E. Budtz-Jorgensen, P. J. Jorgensen, and P. Grandjean, "Delayed Brainstem Auditory Evoked Potential Latencies in 14-Year-Old Children Exposed to Methylmercury," *Journal of Pediatrics* 144:177–183 (2004); Eric Konofal, Samuele Cortese, Michel Lecendreux, Isabelle Arnulf, and Marie Christine Mouren, "Effectiveness of Iron Supplementation in a Young Child with Attention- Deficit/Hyperactivity Disorder," *Pediatrics* 116:732–734 (2005).

103. Wendy Oddy, Monique Robinson, Gina Ambrosini, Therese O'Sullivan, Nicholas de Klerk, Lawrence Beilin, Sven Silburn, Stephen Zubrick, and Fiona Stanley, "The Association Between Dietary Patterns and Mental Health in Early Adolescence," *Preventive Medicine* 49:39–44 (2009).

104. Courtney Van de Weyer, "Changing Diets, Changing Minds: How Food Affects Mental Well-Being and Behaviour," *Sustain: The Alliance for*

Better Food and Farming, available at www.mentalhealth.org.uk (accessed July 22, 2012).

105. Stephen Schoenthaler and Ian Bier, "The Effect of Vitamin–Mineral Supplementation on Juvenile Delinquency Among American Schoolchildren: A Randomized Double-Blind Placebo-Controlled Trial," *Journal of Alternative and Complementary Medicine: Research on Paradigm, Practice, and Policy* 6:7–18 (2000).

106. Christy Miller Buchanan, Jacquelynne Eccles, and Jill Becker, "Are Adolescents the Victims of Raging Hormones? Evidence for Activational Effects of Hormones on Moods and Behavior at Adolescence," *Psychological Bulletin* 111:62–107 (1992).

107. Fishbein, "Selected Studies on the Biology of Crime."

108. Anthony Walsh, "Genetic and Cytogenetic Intersex Anomalies: Can They Help Us to Understand Gender Differences in Deviant Behavior?" *International Journal of Offender Therapy and Comparative Criminology* 39:151–166 (1995).

109. Celina Cohen-Bendahan, Jan Buitelaar, Stephanie van Goozen, Jacob Orlebeke, and Peggy Cohen-Kettenis, "Is There an Effect of Prenatal Testosterone on Aggression and Other Behavioral Traits? A Study Comparing Same-Sex and Opposite-Sex Twin Girls," *Hormones and Behavior* 47:230–237 (2005).

110. Laurence Tancredi, *Hardwired Behavior: What Neuroscience Reveals About Morality* (London: Cambridge University Press, 2005).

111. James Ogilvie, Anna Stewart, Raymond Chan, and David Shum, "Neuropsychological Measures of Executive Function and Antisocial Behavior: A Meta-Analysis," *Criminology* 49:1063–1107 (2011).

112. "McLean Researchers Document Brain Damage Linked to Child Abuse and Neglect," information provided by newsletter of McLean's Hospital, Belmont, MA, December 14, 2000.

113. Brian Perron and Matthew Howard, "Prevalence and Correlates of Traumatic Brain Injury Among Delinquent Youths," *Criminal Behaviour and Mental Health* 18:243–255 (2008).

114. Peer Briken, Niels Habermann, Wolfgang Berner, and Andreas Hill, "The Influence of Brain Abnormalities on Psychosocial Development, Criminal History and Paraphilias in Sexual Murderers," *Journal of Forensic Sciences* 50:1–5 (2005); Yaling Yang, Adrian Raine, Todd Lencz, Susan Bihrle, Lori Lacasse, and Patrick Colletti, "Prefrontal White Matter in Pathological Liars," *British Journal of Psychiatry* 187:320–325 (2005).

115. Alice Jones, Kristin Laurens, Catherine Herba, Gareth Barker, and Essi Viding, "Amygdala Hypoactivity to Fearful Faces in Boys with Conduct Problems and Callous-Unemotional Traits," *American Journal of Psychiatry* 166:95–102 (2009).

116. Thomas. Crowley, Manish S. Dalwani, Susan K. Mikulich-Gilbertson, Yiping P. Du, Carl W. Lejuez, Kristen M. Raymond, and Marie T. Banich, "Risky Decisions and Their Consequences: Neural Processing by Boys with Antisocial Substance Disorder," *PLoS One* 5 (2010), www.ncbi.nlm.nih.gov/pmc/articles/PMC2943904/ (accessed July 22, 2012).

117. Ogilvie, Stewart, Chan, and Shum, "Neuropsychological Measures of Executive Function and Antisocial Behavior."

118. Society for Neuroscience News Release, "Studies Identify Brain Areas and Chemicals Involved in Aggression; May Speed Development of Better Treatment," www.sfn.org/index.cfm?pagename=news_110507d (accessed July 22, 2012).

119. Joseph Biederman, Michael Monuteaux, Eric Mick, Thomas Spencer, Timothy Wilens, Julie Silva, Lindsey Snyder, and Stephen Faraone, "Young Adult Outcome of Attention Deficit Hyperactivity Disorder: A Controlled 10-Year Follow-Up Study," *Psychological Medicine* 36:167–179 (2006); Aldis Putniņš, "Substance Use Among Young Offenders: Thrills, Bad Feelings, or Bad Behavior?" *Substance Use and Misuse* 41:415–422 (2006); Molina Pelham, Jr., "Childhood Predictors of Adolescent Substance Use in a Longitudinal Study of Children with ADHD," *Journal of Abnormal Psychology* 112:497–507 (2003).

120. Joel Zimmerman, William Rich, Ingo Keilitz, and Paul Broder, "Some Observations on the Link Between Learning Disabilities and Juvenile Delinquency," *Journal of Criminal Justice* 9:9–17 (1981).

121. Charles Murray, "The Link Between Learning Disabilities and Juvenile Delinquency: Current Theory and Knowledge" (Washington, DC: U.S. Government Printing Office, 1976).

122. Terrie Moffitt, "The Neuropsychology of Conduct Disorder," mimeo, University of Wisconsin at Madison, 1992.

123. Ibid.

124. National Center for Addiction and Substance Abuse (CASA) at Columbia University, *Substance Abuse and Learning Disabilities: Peas in a Pod or Apples and Oranges?* (New York: CASA, 2000).

125. Jack Katz, *Seduction of Crime: Moral and Sensual Attractions of Doing Evil* (New York: Basic Books, 1988), pp. 12–15.

126. Lee Ellis, "Arousal Theory and the Religiosity-Criminality Relationship," in *Contemporary Criminological Theory*, ed. Peter Cordella and Larry Siegel (Boston: Northeastern University, 1996), pp. 65–84.

127. Adrian Raine, Peter Venables, and Sarnoff Mednick, "Low Resting Heart Rate at Age 3 Years Predisposes to Aggression at Age 11 Years: Evidence from the Mauritius Child Health Project," *Journal of the American Academy of Adolescent Psychiatry* 36:1457–1464 (1997).

128. For a review, see Lisabeth Fisher DiLalla and Irving Gottesman, "Biological and Genetic Contributors to Violence—Widom's Untold Tale," *Psychological Bulletin* 109:125–129 (1991).

129. Anita Thapar, Kate Langley, Tom Fowler, Frances Rice, Darko Turic, Naureen Whittinger, John Aggleton, Marianne Van den Bree, Michael Owen, and Michael O'Donovan, "Catechol O-methyltransferase Gene Variant and Birth Weight Predict Early-Onset Antisocial Behavior in Children with Attention-Deficit/Hyperactivity Disorder," *Archives of General Psychiatry* 62:1275–1278 (2005).

130. Kevin M. Beaver, Chris L. Gibson, Michael G. Turner, Matt Delisi, Michael G. Vaughn, and Ashleigh Holand, "Stability of Delinquent Peer Associations: A Biosocial Test of Warr's Sticky-Friends Hypothesis," *Crime and Delinquency* 57:907–927 (2011).

131. Kevin M. Beaver, "The Effects of Genetics, the Environment, and Low Self-Control on Perceived Maternal and Paternal Socialization: Results from a Longitudinal Sample of Twins," *Journal of Quantitative Criminology* 27:85–105 (2011).

132. For an early review, see Barbara Wooton, *Social Science and Social Pathology* (London: Allen and Unwin, 1959); John Laub and Robert Sampson, "Unraveling Families and Delinquency: A Reanalysis of the Gluecks' Data," *Criminology* 26:355–380 (1988).

133. Donald J. West and David P. Farrington, "Who Becomes Delinquent?" in *The Delinquent Way of Life*, ed. Donald J. West and David P. Farrington (London: Heinemann, 1977), pp. 1–28; D. J. West, *Delinquency: Its Roots, Careers, and Prospects* (Cambridge, MA: Harvard University Press, 1982).

134. West, *Delinquency*, p. 114.

135. David Farrington, "Understanding and Preventing Bullying," in *Crime and Justice*, vol. 17, ed. Michael Tonry (Chicago: University of Chicago Press, 1993), pp. 381–457.

136. To learn more about the RYDS, go to www.albany.edu/hindelang/rydspubs.html (accessed August 6, 2012). Terence Thornberry, Adrienne Freeman-Gallant, Alan Lizotte, Marvin Krohn, and Carolyn Smith, "Linked Lives: The Intergenerational Transmission of Antisocial Behavior," *Journal of Abnormal Child Psychology* 31:171–185 (2003).

137. David Rowe and David Farrington, "The Familial Transmission of Criminal Convictions," *Criminology* 35:177–201 (1997).

138. Edwin J. C. G. van den Oord, Frank Verhulst, and Dorret Boomsma, "A Genetic Study of Maternal and Paternal Ratings of Problem Behaviors in 3-Year-Old Twins," *Journal of Abnormal Psychology* 105:349–357 (1996).

139. Sarnoff Mednick and Jan Volavka, "Biology and Crime," in *Crime and Justice*, ed. Norval Morris and Michael Tonry (Chicago: University of Chicago Press, 1980), pp. 85–159, at 94.

140. Wright, Schnupp, Beaver, Delisi, and Vaughn, "Genes, Maternal Negativity, and Self-Control: Evidence of a Gene × Environment Interaction."

141. Ping Qin, "The Relationship of Suicide Risk to Family History of Suicide and Psychiatric Disorders," *Psychiatric Times* 20:13 (2003).

142. Jane Scourfield, Marianne Van den Bree, Neilson Martin, and Peter McGuffin, "Conduct Problems in Children and Adolescents: A Twin Study," *Archives of General Psychiatry* 61:489–496 (2004); Jeanette Taylor, Bryan Loney, Leonardo Bobadilla, William Iacono, and Matt McGue, "Genetic and Environmental Influences on Psychopathy Trait Dimensions in a Community Sample of Male Twins," *Journal of Abnormal Child Psychology* 31:633–645 (2003).

143. Ginette Dionne, Richard Tremblay, Michel Boivin, David Laplante, and Daniel Perusse, "Physical Aggression and Expressive Vocabulary in 19-Month-Old Twins," *Developmental Psychology* 39:261–273 (2003).

144. Sara R. Jaffee, Avshalom Caspi, Terrie Moffitt, Kenneth Dodge, Michael Rutter, Alan Taylor, and Lucy Tully, "Nature X Nurture: Genetic Vulnerabilities Interact with Physical Maltreatment to Promote Conduct Problems," *Development and Psychopathology* 17:67–84 (2005).

145. Minnesota Study of Twins Reared Apart, http://mctfr.psych.umn.edu/research/UM%20research.html (accessed July 23, 2012).

146. Thomas Bouchard, "Genetic and Environmental Influences on Intelligence and Special Mental Abilities," *American Journal of Human Biology* 70:253–275 (1998).

147. Remi Cadoret, Colleen Cain, and Raymond Crowe, "Evidence for a Gene-Environment Interaction in the Development of Adolescent Antisocial Behavior," *Behavior Genetics* 13:301–310 (1983).

148. David Rowe, *The Limits of Family Influence: Genes, Experiences, and Behavior* (New York: Guilford Press, 1995); Cadoret, Cain, and Crowe, "Evidence for a Gene-Environment Interaction."

149. For a thorough review of this issue, see David Brandt and S. Jack Zlotnick, *The Psychology and Treatment of the Youthful Offender* (Springfield, IL: Charles C. Thomas, 1988).

150. Niranjan Karnik, Marie Soller, Allison Redlich, Melissa Silverman, Helena Kraemer, Rudy Haapanen, and Hans Steiner, "Prevalence of and Gender Differences in Psychiatric Disorders Among Juvenile Delinquents Incarcerated for Nine Months," *Psychiatric Services* 60:838–841 (2009).

151. Spencer Rathus, *Psychology* (New York: Holt, Rinehart and Winston, 1996), pp. 11–21.

152. See, generally, Sigmund Freud, *An Outline of Psychoanalysis*, trans. James Strachey (New York: Norton, 1963).

153. Seymour Halleck, *Psychiatry and the Dilemmas of Crime* (Berkeley: University of California Press, 1971).

154. Robert Krueger, Avshalom Caspi, Phil Silva, and Rob McGee, "Personality Traits Are Differentially Linked to Mental Disorders: A Multitrait-Multidiagnosis Study of an Adolescent Birth Cohort," *Journal of Abnormal Psychology* 105:299–312 (1996).

155. John Bowlby, "Maternal Care and Mental Health," *WHO Monographs Series No. 2* (Geneva: World Health Organization, 1951).

156. Eric Wood and Shelley Riggs, "Predictors of Child Molestation: Adult Attachment, Cognitive Distortions, and Empathy," *Journal of Interpersonal Violence* 23:259–275 (2008).

157. Karen L. Hayslett-McCall and Thomas J. Bernard, "Attachment, Masculinity, and Self-Control: A Theory of Male Crime Rates," *Theoretical Criminology* 6:5–33 (2002).

158. See, generally, Erik Erikson, *Identity, Youth, and Crisis* (New York: Norton, 1968).

159. William Borden, *Contemporary Psychodynamic Theory and Practice: Toward a Critical Pluralism* (Chicago: Lyceum Books, 2008); Gerald Corey, *Theory and Practice of Counseling and Psychotherapy* (Belmont, CA: Cengage, 2009).

160. Michael Pullmann, Jodi Kerbs, Nancy Koroloff, Ernie Veach-White, Rita Gaylor, and DeDe Sieler, "Juvenile Offenders with Mental Health Needs: Reducing Recidivism Using Wraparound," *Crime and Delinquency* 52:375–397 (2006).

161. James Sorrells, "Kids Who Kill," *Crime and Delinquency* 23:312–320 (1977).

162. Beyers and Loeber, "Untangling Developmental Relations."

163. August Aichorn, *Wayward Youth* (New York: Viking Press, 1935).

164. Matt Delisi, Michael G. Vaughn, Kevin M. Beaver, John Paul Wright, Andy Hochstetler, Anna E. Kosloski, and Alan J. Drury, "Juvenile Sex Offenders and Institutional Misconduct: The Role of Thought Psychopathology," *Criminal Behaviour and Mental Health* 18:292–305 (2008).

165. Paige Crosby Ouimette, "Psychopathology and Sexual Aggression in Nonincarcerated Men," *Violence and Victimization* 12:389–397 (1997).

166. Ellen Kjelsberg, "Gender and Disorder Specific Criminal Career Profiles in Former Adolescent Psychiatric In-Patients," *Journal of Youth and Adolescence* 33:261–270 (2004).

167. Richard Rowe, Julie Messer, Robert Goodman, Robert Meltzer, and Howard Meltzer, "Conduct Disorder and Oppositional Defiant Disorder in a National Sample: Developmental Epidemiology," *Journal of Child Psychology and Psychiatry and Allied Disciplines* 45:609–621 (2004).

168. Amy Byrd, Rolf Loeber, and Dustin Pardini, " Understanding Desisting and Persisting Forms of Delinquency: The Unique Contributions of Disruptive Behavior Disorders and Interpersonal Callousness," *Journal of Child Psychology and Psychiatry* 53:371–380 (2012).

169. Minna Ritakallio, Riittakerttu Kaltiala-Heino, Janne Kivivuori, Tiina Luukkaala, and Matti Rimpelä, "Delinquency and the Profile of Offences Among Depressed and Non-depressed Adolescents," *Criminal Behaviour and Mental Health* 16:100–110 (2006).

170. Grégoire Zimmermann, "Delinquency in Male Adolescents: The Role of Alexithymia and Family Structure," *Journal of Adolescence* 29:321–332 (2006).

171. Ching-hua Ho, J. B Kingree, and Martie Thompson, "Associations Between Juvenile Delinquency and Weight-Related Variables: Analyses from a National Sample of High School Students," *International Journal of Eating Disorders* 39:477–483 (2006).

172. Eric Silver, "Mental Disorder and Violent Victimization: The Mediating Role of Involvement in Conflicted Social Relationships," *Criminology* 40:191–212 (2002).

173. Ibid.

174. Stacy DeCoster and Karen Heimer, "The Relationship Between Law Violation and Depression: An Interactionist Analysis," *Criminology* 39:799–836 (2001).

175. B. Lögberg, L-L. Nilsson, M. T. Levander, and S. Levander, "Schizophrenia, Neighbourhood, and Crime," *Acta Psychiatrica Scandinavica* 110:92–97 (2004); DeCoster and Heimer, "The Relationship Between Law Violation and Depression: An Interactionist Analysis."

176. Courtenay Sellers, Christopher Sullivan, Bonita Veysey, and Jon Shane, "Responding to Persons with Mental Illnesses: Police Perspectives on Specialized and Traditional Practices," *Behavioral Sciences and the Law* 23:647–657 (2005).

177. Jennifer Beyers and Rolf Loeber, "Untangling Developmental Relations Between Depressed Mood and Delinquency in Male Adolescents," *Journal of Abnormal Child Psychology* 31:247–267 (2003).

178. Walter Mischel, Yuichi Shoda, and Philip Peake, "The Nature of Adolescent Competencies Predicted by Preschool Delay of Gratification," *Journal of Personality and Social Psychology* 54:687–696 (1988); Albert Bandura and Richard Walters, *Social Learning and Personality Development* (New York: Holt, Rinehart and Winston, 1963).

179. David Perry, Louise Perry, and Paul Rasmussen, "Cognitive Social Learning Mediators of Aggression," *Child Development* 57:700–711 (1986).

180. Bonnie Carlson, "Children's Beliefs About Punishment," *American Journal of Orthopsychiatry* 56:308–312 (1986).

181. See, generally, Jean Piaget, *The Moral Judgment of the Child* (London: Kegan Paul, 1932).

182. Lawrence Kohlberg, *Stages in the Development of Moral Thought and Action* (New York: Holt, Rinehart and Winston, 1969).

183. L. Kohlberg, K. Kauffman, P. Scharf, and J. Hickey, *The Just Community Approach in Corrections: A Manual* (Niantic: Connecticut Department of Corrections, 1973).

184. Quinten Raaijmakers, Rutger Engels, and Anne Van Hoof, "Delinquency and Moral Reasoning in Adolescence and Young Adulthood," *International Journal of Behavioral Development* 29:247–258 (2005); Scott Henggeler, *Delinquency in Adolescence* (Newbury Park, CA: Sage, 1989), p. 26.

185. Eveline Van Vugt, Geert Jan Stams, Maja Dekovic, Daan Brugman, Esther Rutten, and Jan Hendriks "Moral Development of Solo Juvenile Sex Offenders," *Journal of Sexual Aggression* 14:99–109 (2008).

186. K. A. Dodge, "A Social Information Processing Model of Social Competence in Children," in *Minnesota Symposium in Child Psychology*, vol. 18, ed. M. Perlmutter (Hillsdale, NJ: Erlbaum, 1986), pp. 77–125.

187. Elizabeth Cauffman, Laurence Steinberg, and Alex Piquero, "Psychological, Neuropsychological, and Physiological Correlates of Serious Antisocial Behavior in Adolescence: The Role of Self-Control," *Criminology* 43:133–176 (2005).

188. Donald Lynam and Joshua Miller, "Personality Pathways to Impulsive Behavior and Their Relations to Deviance: Results from Three Samples," *Journal of Quantitative Criminology* 20:319–341 (2004).

189. Adrian Raine, Peter Venables, and Mark Williams, "Better Autonomic Conditioning and Faster Electrodermal Half-Recovery Time at Age 15 Years as Possible Protective Factors Against Crime at Age 29 Years," *Developmental Psychology* 32:624–630 (1996).

190. Jean Marie McGloin and Travis Pratt, "Cognitive Ability and Delinquent Behavior Among Inner-City Youth: A Life-Course Analysis of Main, Mediating, and Interaction Effects," *International Journal of Offender Therapy and Comparative Criminology* 47:253–271 (2003).

191. Tony Ward and Claire Stewart, "The Relationship Between Human Needs and Criminogenic Needs," *Psychology, Crime and Law* 9:219–225 (2003).

192. David Ward, Mark Stafford, and Louis Gray, "Rational Choice, Deterrence, and Theoretical Integration," *Journal of Applied Social Psychology* 36:571–585 (2006).

193. Coralijn Nas, Bram Orobio de Castro, and Willem Koops, "Social Information Processing in Delinquent Adolescents," *Psychology, Crime and Law* 11:363–375 (2005).

194. Elizabeth Kubik and Jeffrey Hecker, "Cognitive Distortions About Sex and Sexual Offending: A Comparison of Sex Offending Girls, Delinquent Girls, and Girls from the Community" *Journal of Child Sexual Abuse* 14:43–69 (2005).

195. L. Huesmann and L. Eron, "Individual Differences and the Trait of Aggression," *European Journal of Personality* 3:95–106 (1989).

196. Judith Baer and Tina Maschi, "Random Acts of Delinquency: Trauma and Self-Destructiveness in Juvenile Offenders," *Child and Adolescent Social Work Journal* 20:85–99 (2003).

197. Rolf Loeber and Dale Hay, "Key Issues in the Development of Aggression and Violence from Childhood to Early Adulthood," *Annual Review of Psychology* 48:371–410 (1997).

198. Kathleen Cirillo, B. E. Pruitt, Brian Colwell, Paul M. Kingery, Robert S. Hurley, and Danny Ballard, "School Violence: Prevalence and Intervention Strategies for At-Risk Adolescents," *Adolescence* 33:319–331 (1998).

199. Leilani Greening, "Adolescent Stealers' and Nonstealers' Social Problem-Solving Skills," *Adolescence* 32:51–56 (1997).

200. Graeme Newman, *Understanding Violence* (New York: Lippincott, 1979), pp. 145–146.

201. Cirillo, Pruitt, Colwell, Kingery, Hurley, and Ballard, "School Violence: Prevalence and Intervention Strategies for At-Risk Adolescents."

202. See, generally, Walter Mischel, *Introduction to Personality,* 4th ed. (New York: Holt, Rinehart and Winston, 1986).

203. Sheldon Glueck and Eleanor Glueck, *Unraveling Juvenile Delinquency* (Cambridge, MA: Harvard University Press, 1950).

204. Edelyn Verona and Joyce Carbonell, "Female Violence and Personality," *Criminal Justice and Behavior* 27:176–195 (2000); David Farrington, "Psychobiological Factors in the Explanation and Reduction of Delinquency," *Today's Delinquent* 7:37–51 (1988).

205. See, generally, Hans Eysenck, *Personality and Crime* (London: Routledge and Kegan Paul, 1977).

206. Hans Eysenck and M. W. Eysenck, *Personality and Individual Differences* (New York: Plenum, 1985).

207. Catrien Bijleveld and Jan Hendriks, "Juvenile Sex Offenders: Differences Between Group and Solo Offenders," *Psychology, Crime and Law* 9: 237–246 (2003).

208. Linda Mealey, "The Sociobiology of Sociopathy: An Integrated Evolutionary Model," *Behavioral and Brain Sciences* 18:523–540 (1995).

209. Peter Johansson and Margaret Kerr, "Psychopathy and Intelligence: A Second Look," *Journal of Personality Disorders* 19:357–369 (2005).

210. Sue Kellett and Harriet Gross, "Addicted to Joyriding? An Exploration of Young Offenders' Accounts of Their Car Crime," *Psychology, Crime and Law* 12:39–59 (2006).

211. Lewis Yablonsky, *The Violent Gang* (New York: Penguin Books, 1971), pp. 195–205.

212. Helene Raskin White, Erich Labouvie, and Marsha Bates, "The Relationship Between Sensation Seeking and Delinquency: A Longitudinal Analysis," *Journal of Research in Crime and Delinquency* 2:197–211 (1985).

213. Rathus, *Psychology,* p. 452.

214. Essi Viding, James Blair, Terrie Moffitt, and Robert Plomin, "Evidence for Substantial Genetic Risk for Psychopathy in 7-Year-Olds," *Journal of Child Psychology and Psychiatry* 46:592–597 (2005).

215. Kent Kiehl, Andra Smith, Robert Hare, Adrianna Mendrek, Bruce Forster, Johann Brink, and Peter F. Liddle, *Biological Psychiatry* 5:677–684 (2001).

216. David Lykken, "Psychopathy, Sociopathy, and Crime," *Society* 34:30–38 (1996).

217. L. M. Terman, "Research on the Diagnosis of Predelinquent Tendencies," *Journal of Delinquency* 9:124–130 (1925); L. M. Terman, *Measurement of Intelligence* (Boston: Houghton-Mifflin, 1916); for example, see M. G. Caldwell, "The Intelligence of Delinquent Boys Committed to Wisconsin Industrial School," *Journal of Criminal Law and Criminology* 20:421–428 (1929), and C. Murcheson, *Criminal Intelligence* (Worcester, MA: Clark University, 1926), pp. 41–44.

218. Henry Goddard, *Efficiency and Levels of Intelligence* (Princeton, NJ: Princeton University Press, 1920).

219. William Healy and Augusta Bronner, *Delinquency and Criminals: Their Making and Unmaking* (New York: Macmillan, 1926).

220. Joseph Lee Rogers, H. Harrington Cleveland, Edwin van den Oord, and David Rowe, "Resolving the Debate over Birth Order, Family Size, and Intelligence, "*American Psychologist* 55:599–612 (2000).

221. Kenneth Eels, *Intelligence and Cultural Differences* (Chicago: University of Chicago Press, 1951), p. 181.

222. Sorel Cahahn and Nora Cohen, "Age versus Schooling Effects on Intelligence Development," *Child Development* 60:1239–1249 (1989).

223. Robert McCall and Michael Carriger, "A Meta-Analysis of Infant Habituation and Recognition Memory Performance as Predictors of Later IQ," *Child Development* 64:57–79 (1993).

224. Edwin Sutherland, "Mental Deficiency and Crime," in *Social Attitudes,* ed. Kimball Young (New York: Henry Holt, 1973), ch. 15.

225. H. D. Day, J. M. Franklin, and D. D. Marshall, "Predictors of Aggression in Hospitalized Adolescents," *Journal of Psychology* 132:427–435 (1998); Scott Menard and Barbara Morse, "A Structuralist Critique of the IQ–Delinquency Hypothesis: Theory and Evidence," *American Journal of Sociology* 89:1347–1378 (1984).

226. Travis Hirschi and Michael Hindelang, "Intelligence and Delinquency: A Revisionist Review," *American Sociological Review* 42:471–586 (1977).

227. David Farrington, "Juvenile Delinquency," in *The School Years,* ed. John C. Coleman (London: Routledge, 1992), p. 137.

228. Sheryl Ellis, "It Does Take a Village: A Youth Violence Program in Kincheloe, Michigan, Galvanizes the Community," *Corrections Today* 60:100–103 (1998).

Chapter 4. Sociological Views of Delinquency

1. See, generally, Stephen Cernkovich and Peggy Giordano, "Family Relationships and Delinquency," *Criminology* 25:295–321 (1987).

2. Lance Hannon, "Extremely Poor Neighborhoods and Homicide," *Social Science* Quarterly 86:1418–1434 (2005); Geetanjali Dabral Datta, S. V. Subramanian, Graham Colditz, Ichiro Kawachi, Julie Palmer, and Lynn Rosenberg, "Individual, Neighborhood, and State-Level Predictors of Smoking Among U.S. Black Women: A Multilevel Analysis," *Social Science and Medicine* 63:1034–1044 (2006).

3. Stacey Nofziger and Don Kurtz, "Violent Lives: A Lifestyle Model Linking Exposure to Violence to Juvenile Violent Offending," *Journal of Research in Crime and Delinquency* 42:3–26 (2006); Joanne Kaufman, "Explaining the Race/Ethnicity–Violence Relationship: Neighborhood Context and Social Psychological Processes," *Justice Quarterly* 22:224–251 (2005).

4. Justin Patchin, Beth Huebner, John McCluskey, Sean P. Varano, and Timothy Bynum, "Exposure to Community Violence and Childhood Delinquency," *Crime and Delinquency* 52:307–332 (2006).

5. Gary LaFree, *Losing Legitimacy: Street Crime and the Decline of Social Institutions in America* (Boulder, CO: Westview, 1998).

6. U.S. Census Bureau, Poverty, www.census.gov/hhes/www/poverty/ (accessed July 23, 2012).

7. Edward N. Wolff, *Working Paper No. 589, Recent Trends in Household Wealth in the United States: Rising Debt and the Middle-Class Squeeze,* www.levyinstitute.org/pubs/wp_589.pdf (accessed July 23, 2012).

8. Emilie Andersen Allan and Darrell Steffensmeier, "Youth, Underemployment, and Property Crime: Differential Effects of Job Availability and Job Quality on Juvenile and Young Adult Arrest Rates," *American Sociological Review* 54:107–123 (1989).

9. Kerryn E. Bell, "Gender and Gangs: A Quantitative Comparison," *Crime and Delinquency* 55:363–387 (2009).

10. US Department of Health and Human Services, African American Profile, http://minorityhealth.hhs.gov/templates/browse.aspx?lvl=2&lvlID=51 (accessed July 23, 2012).

11. U.S. Department of Labor, "The Employment Situation," February 2012.

12. National Center for Education Statistics, *Trends in High School Dropout and Completion Rates in the United States: 1972–2009 Compendium Report,* http://nces.ed.gov/pubs2012/2012006.pdf (accessed July 23, 2012).

13. Michael Leiber and Joseph Johnson, "Being Young and Black: What Are Their Effects on Juvenile Justice Decision Making?" *Crime and Delinquency* 54:560–581 (2008).

14. Pew Foundation, "One in 100: Behind Bars in America 2008," www.pewstates.org/uploadedFiles/PCS_Assets/2008/one%20in%20100.pdf (accessed July 23, 2012).

15. Oscar Lewis, "The Culture of Poverty," *Scientific American* 215:19–25 (1966).

16. Julian Chow and Claudia Coulton, "Was There a Social Transformation of Urban Neighborhoods in the 1980s?" *Urban Studies* 35:135–175 (1998).

17. Rodrick Wallace, "Expanding Coupled Shock Fronts of Urban Decay and Criminal Behavior: How U.S. Cities Are Becoming 'Hollowed Out,'" *Journal of Quantitative Criminology* 7:333–355 (1991).

18. William Julius Wilson, *The Truly Disadvantaged* (Chicago: University of Chicago Press, 1987).

19. Bell, "Gender and Gangs."

20. John M. Hagedorn, *A World of Gangs: Armed Young Men and Gangsta Culture* (Minneapolis: University of Minnesota Press, 2008).

21. Clifford R. Shaw and Henry D. McKay, *Juvenile Delinquency and Urban Areas,* rev. ed. (Chicago: University of Chicago Press, 1972).

22. Ibid.

23. Robert Bursik and Harold Grasmick, "Longitudinal Neighborhood Profiles in Delinquency: The Decomposition of Change," *Journal of Quantitative Criminology* 8:247–256 (1992).

24. Delber Elliott, William Julius Wilson, David Huizinga, Robert Sampson, Amanda Elliott, and Bruce Rankin, "The Effects of Neighborhood Disadvantage on Adolescent Development," *Journal of Research in Crime and Delinquency* 33:414 (1996).

25. Robert Bursik and Harold Grasmick, "Economic Deprivation and Neighborhood Crime Rates, 1960–1980," *Law and Society Review* 27:263–278 (1993).

26. For a classic look, see Frederick Thrasher, *The Gang* (Chicago: University of Chicago Press, 1927).

27. Dana Haynie, Eric Silver, and Brent Teasdale, "Neighborhood Characteristics, Peer Networks, and Adolescent Violence," *Journal of Quantitative Criminology* 22:147–169 (2006).

28. National Survey on Drug Use and Health (NSDUH), "Youth Violence and Illicit Drug Use, 2006," available at www.oas.samhsa.gov/2k6/youthViolence/youthViolence.htm (accessed July 23, 2012).

29. Ruth Peterson, Lauren Krivo, and Mark Harris, "Disadvantage and Neighborhood Violent Crime: Do Local Institutions Matter?" *Journal of Research in Crime and Delinquency* 37:31–63 (2000).

30. D. Wayne Osgood and Jeff Chambers, "Social Disorganization Outside the Metropolis: An Analysis of Rural Youth Violence," *Criminology* 38:81–117 (2000).

31. Beverly Stiles, Xiaoru Liu, and Howard Kaplan, "Relative Deprivation and Deviant Adaptations: The Mediating Effects of Negative Self-Feelings," *Journal of Research in Crime and Delinquency* 37:64–90 (2000).

32. Karen Parker and Scott Maggard, "Structural Theories and Race-Specific Drug Arrests: What Structural Factors Account for the Rise in Race-Specific Drug Arrests over Time?" *Crime and Delinquency* 51:521–547 (2005).

33. Ellen Kurtz, Barbara Koons, and Ralph Taylor, "Land Use, Physical Deterioration, Resident-Based Control, and Calls for Service on Urban Street Blocks," *Justice Quarterly* 15:121–149 (1998).

34. Gregory Squires and Charis E. Kubrin, "Privileged Places: Race, Uneven Development and the Geography of Opportunity in Urban America," *Urban Studies* 42:47–68 (2005).

35. Charis E. Kubrin, "Structural Covariates of Homicide Rates: Does Type of Homicide Matter?" *Journal of Research in Crime and Delinquency* 40:139–170 (2003).

36. Micere Keels, Greg Duncan, Stefanie Deluca, Ruby Mendenhall, and James Rosenbaum, "Fifteen Years Later: Can Residential Mobility Programs Provide a Long-Term Escape from Neighborhood Segregation, Crime, and Poverty?" *Demography* 42:51–72 (2005).

37. Allen Liska and Paul Bellair, "Violent-Crime Rates and Racial Composition: Convergence over Time," *American Journal of Sociology* 101:578–610 (1995).

38. Patricia McCall and Karen Parker, "A Dynamic Model of Racial Competition, Racial Inequality, and Interracial Violence," *Sociological Inquiry* 75:273–294 (2005).

39. Steven Barkan and Steven Cohn, "Why Whites Favor Spending More Money to Fight Crime: The Role of Racial Prejudice," *Social Problems* 52:300–314 (2005).

40. Eric Stewart, Eric Baumer, Rod Brunson, and Ronald Simons, "Neighborhood Racial Context and Perceptions of Police-Based Racial Discrimination Among Black Youth," *Criminology* 47:847–887 (2009).

41. John Hipp, George Tita, and Lyndsay Boggess, "Intergroup and Intragroup Violence: Is Violent Crime an Expression of Group Conflict or Social Disorganization?" *Criminology* 47:521–564 (2009).

42. Pamela Wilcox, Neil Quisenberry, and Shayne Jones, "The Built Environment and Community Crime Risk Interpretation," *Journal of Research in Crime and Delinquency* 40:322–345 (2003).

43. Yili Xu, Mora Fiedler, and Karl Flaming, "Discovering the Impact of Community Policing: The Broken Windows Thesis, Collective Efficacy, and Citizens' Judgment," *Journal of Research in Crime and Delinquency* 42:147–186 (2005).

44. Pamela Wilcox Rountree and Kenneth Land, "Burglary Victimization, Perceptions of Crime Risk, and Routine Activities: A Multilevel Analysis Across Seattle Neighborhoods and Census Tracts," *Journal of Research in Crime and Delinquency* 33:147–180 (1996).

45. Jane Sprott and Anthony Doob, "The Effect of Urban Neighborhood Disorder on Evaluations of the Police and Courts," *Crime and Delinquency* 55:339–362 (2009).

46. David Kirk and Andrew Papachristos, "Cultural Mechanisms and the Persistence of Neighborhood Violence," *American Journal of Sociology* 116:1190–1233 (2011).

47. Chris Melde, Terrance J. Taylor, and Finn-Aage Esbensen, "'I Got Your Back': An Examination of the Protective Function of Gang Membership in Adolescence," *Criminology* 47:565–594 (2009).

48. Karen Parker, Brian Stults, and Stephen Rice, "Racial Threat, Concentrated Disadvantage, and Social Control: Considering the Macro-Level Sources of Variation in Arrests," *Criminology* 43:1111–1134 (2005).

49. Patrick Sharkey and Robert Sampson, "Destination Effects: Residential Mobility and Trajectories of Adolescent Violence in a Stratified Metropolis," *Criminology* 48:639–682 (2010).

50. Kyle Crowder and Scott South, "Spatial Dynamics of White Flight: The Effects of Local and Extra-Local Racial Conditions on Neighborhood Out-Migration," *American Sociological Review* 73:792–812 (2008).

51. Paul Jargowsky and Yoonhwan Park, "Cause or Consequence? Suburbanization and Crime in U.S. Metropolitan Areas," *Crime and Delinquency* 55:28–50 (2009).

52. Jackson Goodnight, Benjamin Lahey, Carol Van Hulle, Joseph L. Rodgers, Paul Rathouz, Irwin Waldman, and Brian D'Onofrio, "A Quasi-experimental Analysis of the Influence of Neighborhood Disadvantage on Child and Adolescent Conduct Problems," *Journal of Abnormal Psychology* 121:95–108 (2012).

53. Michael Reisig and Jeffrey Michael Cancino, "Incivilities in Nonmetropolitan Communities: The Effects of Structural Constraints, Social Conditions, and Crime," *Journal of Criminal Justice* 32:15–29 (2004).

54. John Hipp and Daniel Yates, "Ghettos, Thresholds, and Crime: Does Concentrated Poverty Really Have an Accelerating Increasing Effect on Crime?" *Criminology* 49:955–990 (2011).

55. Robert Sampson and Stephen Raudenbush, *Disorder in Urban Neighborhoods: Does It Lead to Crime?* (Washington, DC: National Institute of Justice, 2001).

56. Bridget Freisthler, Elizabeth Lascala, Paul Gruenewald, and Andrew Treno, "An Examination of Drug Activity: Effects of Neighborhood Social Organization on the Development of Drug Distribution Systems," *Substance Use and Misuse* 40:671–686 (2005).

57. Chris Gibson, Jihong Zhao, Nicholas Lovrich, and Michael Gaffney, "Social Integration, Individual Perceptions of Collective Efficacy, and Fear of Crime in Three Cities," *Justice Quarterly* 19:537–564 (2002); Felton Earls, *Linking Community Factors and Individual Development* (Washington, DC: National Institute of Justice, 1998).

58. David S. Kirk, "Unraveling the Contextual Effects on Student Suspension and Juvenile Arrest: The Independent and Interdependent Influences of School, Neighborhood, and Family Social Controls," *Criminology* 47:479–520 (2009).

59. Jennifer Beyers, John Bates, Gregory Pettit, and Kenneth Dodge, "Neighborhood Structure, Parenting Processes, and the Development of Youths' Externalizing Behaviors: A Multilevel Analysis," *American Journal of Community Psychology* 31:35–53 (2003).

60. Ronald Simons, Leslie Gordon Simons, Callie Harbin Burt, Gene Brody, and Carolyn Cutrona, "Collective Efficacy, Authoritative Parenting, and Delinquency: A Longitudinal Test of a Model Integrating Community and Family-Level Processes," *Criminology* 43:989–1029 (2005).

61. Bradley Entner Wright and C. Wesley Younts, "Reconsidering the Relationship Between Race and Crime: Positive and Negative Predictors of Crime Among African American Youth," *Journal of Research in Crime and Delinquency* 46:327–352 (2009).

62. David Maimon and Christopher R. Browning, "Unstructured Socializing, Collective Efficacy, and Violent Behavior Among Urban Youth," *Criminology* 48:443–474 (2010).

63. George Capowich, "The Conditioning Effects of Neighborhood Ecology on Burglary Victimization," *Criminal Justice and Behavior* 30:39–62 (2003).

64. See, for example, Robert Merton, *Social Theory and Social Structure* (Glencoe, IL: Free Press, 1957).

65. Robert Agnew, "Foundation for a General Strain Theory of Crime and Delinquency," *Criminology* 30:47–87 (1992).

66. Ibid., p. 57.

67. Tami Videon, "The Effects of Parent–Adolescent Relationships and Parental Separation on Adolescent Well-Being," *Journal of Marriage and the Family* 64:489–504 (2002).

68. Cesar Rebellon, "Reconsidering the Broken Homes/Delinquency Relationship and Exploring Its Mediating Mechanism(s)," *Criminology* 40:103–135 (2002).

69. Timothy Brezina, "Adolescent Maltreatment and Delinquency: The Question of Intervening Processes," *Journal of Research in Crime and Delinquency* 35:71–99 (1998).

70. Robert Agnew, Timothy Brezina, John Paul Wright, and Francis T. Cullen, "Strain, Personality Traits, and Delinquency: Extending General Strain Theory," *Criminology* 40:43–71 (2002).

71. Lee Ann Slocum, Sally Simpson, and Douglas Smith, "Strained Lives and Crime: Examining Intra-individual Variation in Strain and Offending in a Sample of Incarcerated Women," *Criminology* 43:1067–1110 (2005).

72. Paul Mazerolle, Velmer Burton, Francis Cullen, T. David Evans, and Gary Payne, "Strain, Anger, and Delinquent Adaptations Specifying General Strain Theory," *Journal of Criminal Justice* 28:89–101 (2000).

73. Stephen Cernkovich, Peggy Giordano, and Jennifer Rudolph, "Race, Crime, and the American Dream," *Journal of Research in Crime and Delinquency* 37:131–170 (2000).

74. Robert Agnew, "Experienced, Vicarious, and Anticipated Strain: An Exploratory Study on Physical Victimization and Delinquency," *Justice Quarterly* 19:603–633 (2002).

75. Albert Cohen, *Delinquent Boys* (New York: Free Press, 1955).

76. Richard Cloward and Lloyd Ohlin, *Delinquency and Opportunity* (New York: Free Press, 1960).

77. See, for example, Irving Spergel, *Racketville, Slumtown, and Haulburg* (Chicago: University of Chicago Press, 1964).

78. James Short, "Gangs, Neighborhoods, and Youth Crime," *Criminal Justice Research Bulletin* 5:1–11 (1990).

79. A. Leigh Ingram, "Type of Place, Urbanism, and Delinquency: Further Testing of the Determinist Theory," *Journal of Research in Crime and Delinquency* 30:192–212 (1993).

80. Eric Stewart, Ronald Simons, and Rand Conger, "Assessing Neighborhood and Social Psychological Influences on Childhood Violence in an African-American Sample," *Criminology* 40:801–830 (2002).

81. Ronald Simons, Chyi-In Wu, Kuei-Hsiu Lin, Leslie Gordon, and Rand Conger, "A Cross-Cultural Examination of the Link Between Corporal Punishment and Adolescent Antisocial Behavior," *Criminology* 38:47–79 (2000).

82. Ming Cui and Rand D. Conger, "Parenting Behavior as Mediator and Moderator of the Association Between Marital Problems and Adolescent Maladjustment," *Journal of Research on Adolescence* 18:261–284 (2008).

83. Todd Herrenkohl, Rick Kosterman, David Hawkins, and Alex Mason, "Effects of Growth in Family Conflict in Adolescence on Adult Depressive Symptoms: Mediating and Moderating Effects of Stress and School Bonding," *Journal of Adolescent Health* 44:146–152 (2009).

84. Rand Conger, Institute for Social and Behavioral Research, Iowa State University, www.isbr.iastate.edu/staff/Personals/rdconger/ (accessed July 23, 2012).

85. Kristi Holsinger and Alexander Holsinger, "Differential Pathways to Violence and Self-Injurious Behavior: African American and White Girls in the Juvenile Justice System," *Journal of Research in Crime and Delinquency* 42:211–242 (2005).

86. John Paul Wright and Francis Cullen, "Parental Efficacy and Delinquent Behavior: Do Control and Support Matter?" *Criminology* 39:677–706 (2001).

87. Carter Hay, "Parenting, Self-Control, and Delinquency: A Test of Self-Control Theory," *Criminology* 39:707–736 (2001).

88. Alexander Vazsonyi and Lloyd Pickering, "The Importance of Family and School Domains in Adolescent Deviance: African-American and Caucasian Youth," *Journal of Youth and Adolescence* 32:115–129 (2003).

89. Irving Janis, *Groupthink: Psychological Studies of Policy Decisions and Fiascoes* (Boston: Houghton Mifflin, 1982).

90. Olena Antonaccio, Charles Tittle, Ekaterina Botchkovar, and Maria Kranidioti, "The Correlates of Crime and Deviance: Additional Evidence," *Journal of Research in Crime and Delinquency*, April 28, 2010, http://jrc.sagepub.com/content/47/3/297.abstract (accessed July 23, 2012); Zhang and Messner, "Family Deviance and Delinquency in China."

91. Dana Haynie, Eric Silver, and Brent Teasdale, "Neighborhood Characteristics, Peer Networks, and Adolescent Violence," *Journal of Quantitative Criminology* 22:147–169 (2006).

92. Paul Friday, Xin Ren, Elmar Weitekamp, Hans-Jürgen Kerner, and Terrance Taylor, "A Chinese Birth Cohort: Theoretical Implications," *Journal of Research in Crime and Delinquency* 42:123–146 (2005).

93. Daneen Deptula and Robert Cohen, "Aggressive, Rejected, and Delinquent Children and Adolescents: A Comparison of Their Friendships," *Aggression and Violent Behavior* 9:75–104 (2004); Stephen W. Baron, "Self-Control, Social Consequences, and Criminal Behavior: Street Youth and the General Theory of Crime," *Journal of Research in Crime and Delinquency* 40:403–425 (2003).

94. Amy Anderson and Lorine Hughes, "Exposure to Situations Conducive to Delinquent Behavior: The Effects of Time Use, Income, and Transportation," *Journal of Research in Crime and Delinquency* 46:5–34 (2009).

95. Delbert Elliott, David Huizinga, and Suzanne Ageton, *Explaining Delinquency and Drug Use* (Beverly Hills, CA: Sage, 1985); Helene Raskin White, Robert Padina, and Randy La-Grange, "Longitudinal Predictors of Serious Substance Use and Delinquency," *Criminology* 6:715–740 (1987).

96. Robert Agnew and Timothy Brezina, "Relational Problems with Peers, Gender and Delinquency," *Youth and Society* 29:84–111 (1997).

97. Sylvie Mrug, Betsy Hoza, and William Bukowski, "Choosing or Being Chosen by Aggressive-Disruptive Peers: Do They Contribute to Children's Externalizing and Internalizing Problems?" *Journal of Abnormal Child Psychology* 32:53–66 (2004).

98. Shelley Keith Matthews and Robert Agnew, "Extending Deterrence Theory: Do Delinquent Peers Condition the Relationship Between Perceptions of Getting Caught and Offending?" *Journal of Research in Crime and Delinquency* 45:91–118 (2008).

99. John Paul Wright and Francis Cullen, "Employment, Peers, and Life-Course Transitions," *Justice Quarterly* 21:183–205 (2004).

100. Jean Marie McGloin, "Delinquency Balance: Revisiting Peer Influence," *Criminology* 47:439–477 (2009).

101. Edwin Sutherland, *Principles of Criminology* (Philadelphia: Lippincott, 1939).

102. Paul Vowell and Jieming Chen, "Predicting Academic Misconduct: A Comparative Test of Four Sociological Explanations," *Sociological Inquiry* 74:226–249 (2004).

103. Carlo Morselli, Pierre Tremblay, and Bill McCarthy, "Mentors and Criminal Achievement," *Criminology* 44:17–43 (2006).

104. Terence P. Thornberry, "The Apple Doesn't Fall Far from the Tree (Or Does It?): Intergenerational Patterns of Antisocial Behavior — The American Society of Criminology 2008 Sutherland Address," *Criminology* 47:297–325 (2009); Terence Thornberry, Adrienne Freeman-Gallant, Alan Lizotte, Marvin Krohn, and Carolyn Smith, "Linked Lives: The Intergenerational Transmission of Antisocial Behavior," *Journal of Abnormal Child Psychology* 31:171–184 (2003).

105. Wesley Church II, Tracy Wharton, and Julie Taylor, "An Examination of Differential Association and Social Control Theory: Family Systems and Delinquency," *Youth Violence and Juvenile Justice* 7:3–15 (2009); Jonathan R. Brauer, "Testing Social Learning Theory Using Reinforcement's Residue: A Multilevel Analysis of Self-Reported Theft and Marijuana Use in the National Youth Survey," *Criminology* 47:929–970 (2009).

106. Robert Lonardo, Peggy Giordano, Monica Longmore, and Wendy Manning, "Parents, Friends, and Romantic Partners: Enmeshment in Deviant Networks and Adolescent Delinquency Involvement," *Journal of Youth and Adolescence* 38:367–383 (2009).

107. Wesley Younts, "Status, Endorsement and the Legitimacy of Deviance," *Social Forces* 87:561–590 (2008).

108. Travis C. Pratt, Francis T. Cullen, Christine S. Sellers, L. Thomas Winfree Jr., Tamara D. Madensen, Leah E. Daigle, Noelle E. Fearn, and Jacinta M. Gau, "The Empirical Status of Social Learning Theory: A Meta-Analysis," *Justice Quarterly* 27:765–802 (2010).

109. Travis Hirschi, *Causes of Delinquency* (Berkeley: University of California Press, 1969).

110. Carl Maas, Charles Fleming, Todd Herrenkohl, and Richard Catalano, "Childhood Predictors of Teen Dating Violence Victimization," *Violence and Victims* 25:131–149 (2010).

111. Bobbi Jo Anderson, Malcolm Holmes, and Erik Ostresh, "Male and Female Delinquents' Attachments and Effects of Attachments on Severity of Self-Reported Delinquency," *Criminal Justice and Behavior* 26:425–452 (1999).

112. Patricia Jenkins, "School Delinquency and the School Social Bond," *Journal of Research in Crime and Delinquency* 34:337–367 (1997).

113. Thomas Vander Ven, Francis Cullen, Mark Carrozza, and John Paul Wright, "Home Alone: The Impact of Maternal Employment on Delinquency," *Social Problems* 48:236–257 (2001).

114. Allison Ann Payne, "A Multilevel Analysis of the Relationships Among Communal School Organization, Student Bonding, and Delinquency," *Journal of Research in Crime and Delinquency* 45:429–455 (2008); Norman White and Rolf Loeber, "Bullying and Special Education as Predictors of Serious Delinquency," *Journal of Research in Crime and Delinquency* 45:380–397 (2008).

115. Jennifer Kerpelman and Sondra Smith-Adcock, "Female Adolescents' Delinquent Activity: The Intersection of Bonds to Parents and Reputation Enhancement," *Youth and Society* 37:176–200 (2005).

116. Tiffiney Barfield-Cottledge, "The Triangulation Effects of Family Structure and Attachment on Adolescent Substance Use" *Crime and Delinquency*, published online November 8, 2011; Sonia Cota-Robles and Wendy Gamble, "Parent-Adolescent Processes and Reduced Risk for Delinquency: The Effect of Gender for Mexican American Adolescents," *Youth and Society* 37:375–392 (2006).

117. Jeb Booth, Amy Farrell, and Sean Varano, "Social Control, Serious Delinquency, and Risky Behavior: A Gendered Analysis," *Crime and Delinquency* 54:423–456 (2008).

118. Peggy Giordano, Stephen Cernkovich, and M. D. Pugh, "Friendships and Delinquency," *American Journal of Sociology* 91:1170–1202 (1986).

119. Lisa Stolzenberg and Stewart D'Alessio, "Co-Offending and the Age–Crime Curve," *Journal of Research in Crime and Delinquency* 45:65–86 (2008).

120. Jón Gunnar Bernburg, Marvin Krohn, and Craig Rivera, "Official Labeling, Criminal Embeddedness, and Subsequent Delinquency: A Longitudinal Test of Labeling Theory," *Journal of Research in Crime and Delinquency* 43:67–88 (2006).

121. The self-labeling concept originated in Edwin Lemert, *Social Pathology* (New York: McGraw-Hill, 1951); see also Frank Tannenbaum, *Crime and the Community* (Boston: Ginn, 1936).

122. Harold Garfinkel, "Conditions of Successful Degradation Ceremonies," in *Symbolic Interactionism*, ed. Jerome Manis and Bernard Meltzer (New York: Allyn & Bacon, 1972), pp. 201–208.

123. Edwin Lemert, *Human Deviance, Social Problems, and Social Control* (Englewood Cliffs, NJ: Prentice Hall, 1967), p. 15.

124. Mike Adams, Craig Robertson, Phyllis Gray-Ray, and Melvin Ray, "Labeling and Delinquency, *Adolescence* 38:171–186 (2003).

125. Charles H. Cooley, *Human Nature and the Social Order* (New York: Scribner's, 1902).

126. Ross Matsueda, "Reflected Appraisals, Parental Labeling, and Delinquency: Specifying a Symbolic Interactionist Theory," *American Journal of Sociology* 97:1577–1611 (1992).

127. Raymond Paternoster and Leeann Iovanni, "The Labeling Perspective and Delinquency: An Elaboration of the Theory and an Assessment of the Evidence," *Justice Quarterly* 6:358–394 (1989).

128. Gregg Barak, "Revisionist History, Visionary Criminology, and Needs-Based Justice," *Contemporary Justice Review* 6:217–225 (2003).

129. Kitty Kelley Epstein, "The Whitening of the American Teaching Force: A Problem of Recruitment or a Problem of Racism?" *Social Justice* 32:89–102 (2005).

130. Dawn L. Rothe, Jeffrey Ian Ross, Christopher W. Mullins, David Friedrichs, Raymond Michalowski, Gregg Barak, David Kauzlarich, and Ronald C. Kramer, "That Was Then, This Is Now, What About Tomorrow? Future Directions in State Crime Studies," *Critical Criminology* 17:3–13 (2009).

131. Malcolm Holmes, "Minority Threat and Police Brutality: Determinants of Civil Rights Criminal Complaints in U.S. Municipalities," *Criminology* 38:343–368 (2000).

132. Tammy Rinehart Kochel, David Wilson, and Stephen Mastrofski, "Effect of Suspect Race on Officers' Arrest Decisions," *Criminology* 49:473–512 (2011).

133. Ibid.

134. Robert Gordon, "Capitalism, Class, and Crime in America," *Crime and Delinquency* 19:174 (1973).

135. Richard Quinney, *Class, State, and Crime* (New York: Longman, 1977), p. 52.

136. Anthony Platt, "The Triumph of Benevolence: The Origins of the Juvenile Justice System in the United States," in *Criminal Justice in America: A Critical Understanding*, ed. Richard Quinney (Boston: Little, Brown, 1974), p. 367; see also Anthony Platt, *The Child Savers: The Invention of Delinquency* (Chicago: University of Chicago Press, 1969).

137. Barry Krisberg and James Austin, *Children of Ishmael* (Palo Alto, CA: Mayfield, 1978), p. 2.

138. Herman Schwendinger and Julia Schwendinger, "Delinquency and Social Reform: A Radical Perspective," in *Juvenile Justice*, ed. Lamar Empey (Charlottesville: University of Virginia Press, 1979), p. 250.

139. John F. Wozniak, "Poverty and Peacemaking Criminology: Beyond Mainstream Criminology," *Critical Criminology* 16:209–223 (2008).

140. Operation Weed and Seed Executive Offices, U.S. Department of Justice, Washington, DC, 1998; *Weed and Seed In-sites*, vol. I, no. 5, August–September 1998.

141. Shadd Maruna, Thomas Lebel, Nick Mitchell, and Michelle Maples, "Pygmalion in the Reintegration Process: Desistance from Crime Through the Looking Glass," *Psychology, Crime and Law* 10:271–281 (2004).

142. Arthur L. Kellerman, Dawna Fuqua-Whitley, and Constance S. Parramore, *Reducing Gun Violence: Community Problem Solving in Atlanta* (Washington, DC: National Institute of Justice, 2006); George E. Tita, K. Jack Riley, Greg Ridgeway, and Peter W. Greenwood, *Reducing Gun Violence: Operation Ceasefire in Los Angeles* (Washington, DC: National Institute of Justice, 2005).

143. Jeffrey A. Butts, Janeen Buck, and Mark B. Coggeshall, *The Impact of Teen Court on Young Offenders* (Washington, DC: Urban Institute, 2002).

144. Peter W. Greenwood, "Juvenile Crime and Juvenile Justice," in *Crime: Public Policies for Crime Control*, ed. James Q. Wilson and Joan Petersilia (Oakland, CA: Institute for Contemporary Studies, 2002), pp. 90–91.

145. Doris Layton MacKenzie, *What Works in Corrections: Reducing the Criminal Activities of Offenders and Delinquents* (New York: Cambridge University Press, 2006).

146. Denise C. Gottfredson, Stephanie A. Gerstenblith, David A. Soulé, Shannon C. Womer, and Shaoli Lu, "Do After School Programs Reduce Delinquency?" *Prevention Science* 5:253–266 (2004).

147. David P. Farrington and Brandon C. Welsh, *Saving Children from a Life of Crime: Early Risk Factors and Effective Interventions* (New York: Oxford University Press, 2007).

148. Denise C. Gottfredson and David A. Soulé, "The Timing of Property Crime, Violent Crime, and Substance Abuse Among Juveniles," *Journal of Research in Crime and Delinquency* 42:110–120 (2005).

149. Terence Thornberry, David Huizinga, and Rolf Loeber, "The Prevention of Serious Delinquency and Violence," in *Sourcebook on Serious, Violent, and Chronic Juvenile Offenders*, ed. James Howell, Barry Krisberg, J. David Hawkins, and John Wilson (Thousand Oaks, CA: Sage, 1995).

150. Malcolm Klein, "Deinstitutionalization and Diversion of Juvenile Offenders: A Litany of Impediments," in *Crime and Justice*, vol. 1, ed. Norval Morris and Michael Tonry (Chicago: University of Chicago Press, 1979).

151. Kathleen Daly and Russ Immarigeon, "The Past, Present, and Future of Restorative Justice: Some Critical Reflections," *Contemporary Justice Review* 1:21–45 (1998).

152. Kay Pranis, "Peacemaking Circles: Restorative Justice in Practice Allows Victims and Offenders to Begin Repairing the Harm," *Corrections Today* 59:72–76 (1997).

153. Carol LaPrairie, "The 'New' Justice: Some Implications for Aboriginal Communities," *Canadian Journal of Criminology* 40:61–79 (1998).

154. Gene Stephens, "The Future of Policing: From a War Model to a Peace Model," in *The Past, Present, and Future of American Criminal Justice*, ed. Brendan Maguire and Polly Radosh (Dix Hills, NY: General Hall, 1996), pp. 77–93.

155. This section is based on Gordon Bazemore and Mara Schiff, "Paradigm Muddle or Paradigm Paralysis? The Wide and Narrow Roads to Restorative Justice Reform (or, a Little Confusion May Be a Good Thing)," *Contemporary Justice Review* 7:37–57 (2004).

156. Jay Zaslaw and George Ballance, "The Socio-Legal Response: A New Approach to Juvenile Justice in the '90s," *Corrections Today* 58:72–75 (1996).

157. Gordon Bazemore, "Restorative Justice and Earned Redemption: Communities, Victims, and Offender Reintegration," *American Behavioral Scientist* 41:768–814 (1998).

Chapter 5. Developmental Views of Delinquency: Life Course, Latent Trait, and Trajectory

1. Alex Piquero, "Taking Stock of Developmental Trajectories of Criminal Activity over the Life Course," in *The Long View of Crime: A Synthesis of Longitudinal Research*, ed. Akiva Liberman (New York: Springer. 2008), pp. 23–78.

2. Marvin Krohn, Alan Lizotte, and Cynthia Perez, "The Interrelationship Between Substance Use and Precocious Transitions to Adult Sexuality," *Journal of Health and Social Behavior* 38:88 (1997).

3. Peggy Giordano, Stephen Cernkovich, and Jennifer Rudolph, "Gender, Crime, and Desistance: Toward a Theory of Cognitive Transformation?" *American Journal of Sociology* 107:990–1064 (2002).

4. John Hagan and Holly Foster, "S/He's a Rebel: Toward a Sequential Stress Theory of Delinquency and Gendered Pathways to Disadvantage in Emerging Adulthood," *Social Forces* 82:53–86 (2003).

5. Patrick Lussier, David Farrington, and Terrie Moffitt, "Is the Antisocial Child Father of the Abusive Man? A 40-Year Prospective Longitudinal Study on the Development Antecedents of Intimate Partner Violence," *Criminology* 47:741–780 (2009).

6. See, generally, Sheldon Glueck and Eleanor Glueck, 500 *Delinquent Careers* (New York: Knopf, 1930); Sheldon Glueck and Eleanor Glueck, *One Thousand Juvenile Delinquents* (Cambridge, MA: Harvard University Press, 1934); Sheldon Glueck and Eleanor Glueck, *Predicting Delinquency* (Cambridge, MA: Harvard University Press, 1967), pp. 82–83.

7. Sheldon Glueck and Eleanor Glueck, *Unraveling Juvenile Delinquency* (Cambridge, MA: Harvard University Press, 1950).

8. Ibid., p. 48.

9. Rolf Loeber and Marc LeBlanc, "Toward a Developmental Criminology," in *Delinquency and Justice*, vol. 12, ed. Norval Morris and Michael Tonry (Chicago: University of Chicago Press, 1990), pp. 375–473; Rolf Loeber and Marc LeBlanc, "Developmental Criminology Updated," in *Delinquency and Justice*, vol. 23, ed. Michael Tonry (Chicago: University of Chicago Press, 1998), pp. 115–198.

10. Lila Kazemian, David Farrington, and Marc Le Blanc, "Can We Make Accurate Long-Term Predictions About Patterns of De-escalation in Offending Behavior?" *Journal of Youth and Adolescence* 38:384–400 (2009).

11. Alex R. Piquero and He Len Chung, "On the Relationships Between Gender, Early Onset, and the Seriousness of Offending," *Journal of Delinquent Justice* 29:189–206 (2001).

12. Mary Campa, Catherine Bradshaw, John Eckenrode, and David Zielinski, "Patterns of Problem Behavior in Relation to Thriving and Precocious Behavior in Late Adolescence," *Journal of Youth and Adolescence* 37:627–640 (2008); Alex Mason, Rick Kosterman, J. David Hawkins, Todd Herrenkohi, Liliana Lengua, and Elizabeth McCauley, *Journal of the American Academy of Child and Adolescent Psychiatry* 43:307–315 (2004); Rolf Loeber and David Farrington, "Young Children Who Commit Crime: Epidemiology, Developmental Origins, Risk Factors, Early Interventions, and Policy Implications," *Development and Psychopathology* 12:737–762 (2000); Patrick Lussier, Jean Proulx, and Marc LeBlanc, "Criminal Propensity, Deviant Sexual Interests and Criminal Activity of Sexual Aggressors Against Women: A Comparison of Explanatory Models," *Criminology* 43:249–281 (2005); Glenn Clingempeel and Scott Henggeler, "Aggressive Juvenile Offenders Transitioning into Emerging Adulthood: Factors Discriminating Persistors and Desistors," *American Journal of Orthopsychiatry* 73: 310–323 (2003).

13. David Gadd and Stephen Farrall, "Criminal Careers, Desistance and Subjectivity: Interpreting Men's Narratives of Change," *Theoretical Criminology* 8:123–156 (2004).

14. Rolf Loeber and David Farrington, "Young Children Who Commit Delinquency: Epidemiology, Developmental Origins, Risk Factors, Early

Interventions, and Policy Implications," *Development and Psychopathology* 12:737–762 (2000).

15. W. Alex Mason, Rick Kosterman, J. David Hawkins, Todd Herrenkohi, Liliana Lengua, and Elizabeth McCauley, "Predicting Depression, Social Phobia, and Violence in Early Adulthood from Childhood Behavior Problems," *Journal of the American Academy of Child and Adolescent Psychiatry* 43:307–315 (2004); Rolf Loeber and David Farrington, "Young Children Who Commit Crime: Epidemiology, Developmental Origins, Risk Factors, Early Interventions, and Policy Implications," *Development and Psychopathology* 12:737–762 (2000); Lussier, Proulx, and Leblanc, "Criminal Propensity, Deviant Sexual Interests and Criminal Activity of Sexual Aggressors Against Women."

16. Ronald Prinz and Suzanne Kerns, "Early Substance Use by Juvenile Offenders," *Child Psychiatry and Human Development* 33:263–268 (2003).

17. Magda Stouthamer-Loeber and Evelyn Wei, "The Precursors of Young Fatherhood and Its Effect on Delinquency of Teenage Males," *Journal of Adolescent Health* 22:56–65 (1998); Richard Jessor, John Donovan, and Francis Costa, *Beyond Adolescence: Problem Behavior and Young Adult Development* (New York: Cambridge University Press, 1991).

18. Krohn, Lizotte, and Perez, "The Interrelationship Between Substance Use and Precocious Transitions to Adult Sexuality"; Richard Jessor, "Risk Behavior in Adolescence: A Psychosocial Framework for Understanding and Action," in *Adolescents at Risk: Medical and Social Perspectives*, ed. D. E. Rogers and E. Ginzburg (Boulder, CO: Westview, 1992).

19. Ick-Joong Chung, J. David Hawkins, Lewayne Gilchrist, Karl Hill, and Daniel Nagin, "Identifying and Predicting Offending Trajectories Among Poor Children," *Social Service Review* 76:663–687 (2002).

20. Vladislav Ruchkin, Mary Schwab-Stone, Roman Koposov, Robert Vermeiren, and Robert King, "Suicidal Ideations and Attempts in Juvenile Delinquents," *Child Psychology and Psychiatry and Allied Disciplines* 44:1058–1067 (2003).

21. J. Rayner, T. Kelly, and F. Graham, "Mental Health, Personality and Cognitive Problems in Persistent Adolescent Offenders Require Long-Term Solutions: A Pilot Study," *Journal of Forensic Psychiatry and Psychology* 16:248–262 (2005).

22. Deborah Capaldi and Gerald Patterson, "Can Violent Offenders Be Distinguished from Frequent Offenders? Prediction from Childhood to Adolescence," *Journal of Research in Crime and Delinquency* 33:206–231 (1996).

23. Margit Wiesner and Michael Windle, "Young Adult Substance Use and Depression as a Consequence of Delinquency Trajectories During Middle Adolescence," *Journal of Research on Adolescence* 16:239–264 (2006).

24. Clingempeel and Henggeler, "Aggressive Juvenile Offenders Transitioning into Emerging Adulthood."

25. Marshall Jones and Donald Jones, "The Contagious Nature of Antisocial Behavior," *Criminology* 38:25–46 (2000).

26. Terrie Moffitt, Avshalom Caspi, Michael Rutter, and Phil Silva, *Sex Differences in Antisocial Behavior: Conduct Disorder, Delinquency, and Violence in the Dunedin Longitudinal Study* (London: Cambridge University Press, 2001).

27. Robert Sampson and John Laub, *Crime in the Making: Pathways and Turning Points Through Life* (Cambridge, MA: Harvard University Press, 1993).

28. Terri Orbuch, James House, Richard Mero, and Pamela Webster, "Marital Quality over the Life Course," *Social Psychology Quarterly* 59:162–171 (1996); Lee Lillard and Linda Waite, "'Til Death Do Us Part: Marital Disruption and Mortality," *American Journal of Sociology* 100:1131–1156 (1995).

29. Mark Warr, "Life-Course Transitions and Desistance from Crime," *Criminology* 36:183–216 (1998).

30. Nan Lin, *Social Capital: A Theory of Social Structure and Action* (Cambridge, UK: Cambridge University Press, 2002).

31. Sampson and Laub, *Crime in the Making*, p. 249.

32. John Hagan, Ross MacMillan, and Blair Wheaton, "New Kid in Town: Social Capital and the Life Course Effects of Family Migration on Children," *American Sociological Review* 61:368–385 (1996).

33. Robert Sampson and John Laub, "A Life-Course Theory of Cumulative Disadvantage and the Stability of Delinquency," in *Developmental Theories of Crime and Delinquency*, ed. Terence Thornberry (Somerset, NJ: Transaction Publishing, 1997), pp. 138–162.

34. Raymond Paternoster and Robert Brame, "Multiple Routes to Delinquency? A Test of Developmental and General Theories of Crime," *Criminology* 35:49–84 (1997).

35. Pamela Webster, Terri Orbuch, and James House, "Effects of Childhood Family Background on Adult Marital Quality and Perceived Stability," *American Journal of Sociology* 101:404–432 (1995).

36. Robert Hoge, D. A. Andrews, and Alan Leschied, "An Investigation of Risk and Protective Factors in a Sample of Youthful Offenders," *Journal of Child Psychology and Psychiatry* 37:419–424 (1996).

37. Avshalom Caspi, Terrie Moffitt, Bradley Entner Wright, and Phil Silva, "Early Failure in the Labor Market: Childhood and Adolescent Predictors of Unemployment in the Transition to Adulthood," *American Sociological Review* 63:424–451 (1998).

38. Robert Sampson and John Laub, "Socioeconomic Achievement in the Life Course of Disadvantaged Men: Military Service as a Turning Point, circa 1940–1965," *American Sociological Review* 61:347–367 (1996).

39. Daniel Nagin and Raymond Paternoster, "Personal Capital and Social Control: The Deterrence Implications of a Theory of Offending," *Criminology* 32:581–606 (1994).

40. John Paul Wright, David E. Carter, and Francis T. Cullen, "A Life-Course Analysis of Military Service in Vietnam," *Journal of Research in Crime and Delinquency* 42:55–83 (2005).

41. Bill McCarthy and Teresa Casey, "Love, Sex, and Crime: Adolescent Romantic Relationships and Offending," *American Sociological Review* 73:944–969 (2008).

42. Derek Kreager, Ross Matsueda, and Elena Erosheva, "Motherhood and Criminal Desistance in Disadvantaged Neighborhoods," *Criminology* 48:221–258 (2010).

43. Rand Conger, Institute for Social and Behavioral Research, 2009, www.isbr.iastate.edu/staff/Personals/rdconger/ (accessed July 24, 2012).

44. James Q. Wilson and Richard Herrnstein, *Crime and Human Nature* (New York: Simon and Schuster, 1985).

45. David Rowe, D. Wayne Osgood, and W. Alan Nicewander, "A Latent Trait Approach to Unifying Criminal Careers," *Criminology* 28:237–270 (1990).

46. Lee Ellis, "Neurohormonal Bases of Varying Tendencies to Learn Delinquent and Criminal Behavior," in *Behavioral Approaches to Crime and Delinquency*, ed. E. Morris and C. Braukmann (New York: Plenum, 1988), pp. 499–518.

47. David Rowe, Alexander Vazsonyi, and Daniel Flannery, "Sex Differences in Crime: Do Means and Within-Sex Variation Have Similar Causes?" *Journal of Research in Crime and Delinquency* 32:84–100 (1995).

48. Michael Gottfredson and Travis Hirschi, *A General Theory of Crime* (Stanford, CA: Stanford University Press, 1990).

49. Ibid., p. 27.

50. Christian Seipel and Stefanie Eifler, "Opportunities, Rational Choice, and Self-Control: On the Interaction of Person and Situation in a General Theory of Crime," *Crime and Delinquency* 56:167–197 (2010).

51. Gottfredson and Hirschi, *A General Theory of Crime*, p. 90.

52. Ibid., p. 89.

53. Marianne Junger and Richard Tremblay, "Self-Control, Accidents, and Delinquency," *Criminal Justice and Behavior* 26:485–501 (1999).

54. Gottfredson and Hirschi, *A General Theory of Crime*, p. 112.

55. Ibid.

56. Chris L. Gibson, Christopher J. Sullivan, Shayne Jones, and Alex R. Piquero, "Does It Take a Village? Assessing Neighborhood Influences on Children's Self-Control," *Journal of Research in Crime and Delinquency* 47:31–62 (2010).

57. Dennis Giever, "An Empirical Assessment of the Core Elements of Gottfredson and Hirschi's General Theory of Crime," paper presented at the annual meeting of the American Society of Criminology, Boston, November 1995.

58. Brian Boutwell and Kevin Beaver, "The Intergenerational Transmission of Low Self-control," *Journal of Research in Crime and Delinquency* 47:174–209 (2010).

59. David Farrington, Darrick Jolliffe, Rolf Loeber, Magda Stouthamer-Loeber, and Larry Kalb, "The Concentration of Offenders in Families, and Family Criminality in the Prediction of Boys' Delinquency," *Journal of Adolescence* 24:579–596 (2001).

60. Daniel Nagin and Greg Pogarsky, "Time and Punishment: Delayed Consequences and Criminal Behavior," *Journal of Quantitative Criminology* 20:295–317 (2004); Peter Muris and Cor Meesters, "The Validity of Attention Deficit Hyperactivity and Hyperkinetic Disorder Symptom Domains in Nonclinical Dutch Children," *Journal of Clinical Child and Adolescent Psychology* 32:460–466 (2003); David Brownfield and Ann-Marie Sorenson, "Self-Control and Juvenile Delinquency: Theoretical Issues and an Empirical Assessment of Selected Elements of a General Theory of Crime," *Deviant Behavior* 14:243–264 (1993); Harold Grasmick, Charles Tittle, Robert Bursik, and Bruce Arneklev, "Testing the Core Empirical Implications of Gottfredson and Hirschi's General Theory of Crime," *Journal of Research in Crime and Delinquency* 30:5–29 (1993).

61. Alexander Vazsonyi, Janice Clifford Wittekind, Lara Belliston, and Timothy Van Loh, "Extending the General Theory of Crime to 'The East': Low Self-Control in Japanese Late Adolescents," *Journal of Quantitative Criminology* 20:189–216 (2004); Alexander Vazsonyi, Lloyd Pickering, Marianne Junger, and Dick Hessing, "An Empirical Test of a General Theory of Crime: A Four-Nation Comparative Study of Self-Control and the

Prediction of Deviance," *Journal of Research in Crime and Delinquency* 38:91–131 (2001).

62. Christopher Sullivan, Jean Marie McGloin, Travis Pratt, and Alex Piquero, "Rethinking the 'Norm' of Offender Generality: Investigating Specialization in the Short-Term," *Criminology* 44:199–233 (2006).

63. Annemaree Carroll, Francene Hemingway, Julie Bower, Adrian Ashman, Stephen Houghton, and Kevin Durkin, "Impulsivity in Juvenile Delinquency: Differences Among Early-Onset, Late-Onset, and Non-Offenders," *Journal of Youth and Adolescence* 35:517–527 (2006).

64. Christopher Schreck, "Criminal Victimization and Low Self-Control: An Extension and Test of a General Theory of Crime," *Justice Quarterly* 16:633–654 (1999).

65. Ronald Akers, "Self-Control as a General Theory of Crime," *Journal of Quantitative Criminology* 7:201–211 (1991).

66. Richard Wiebe, "Reconciling Psychopathy and Low Self-Control," *Justice Quarterly* 20:297–336 (2003).

67. Alan Feingold, "Gender Differences in Personality: A Meta-Analysis," *Psychological Bulletin* 116:429–456 (1994).

68. Charles Tittle, David Ward, and Harold Grasmick, "Gender, Age, and Crime/Deviance: A Challenge to Self-Control Theory," *Journal of Research in Crime and Delinquency* 40:426–453 (2003).

69. Dana Haynie, Peggy Giordano, Wendy Manning, and Monica Longmore, "Adolescent Romantic Relationships and Delinquency Involvement," *Criminology* 43:177–210 (2005).

70. Brent Benda, "Gender Differences in Life-Course Theory of Recidivism: A Survival Analysis," *International Journal of Offender Therapy and Comparative Criminology* 49:325–342 (2005).

71. Gottfredson and Hirschi, *A General Theory of Crime*, p. 153.

72. Scott Menard, Delbert Elliott, and Sharon Wofford, "Social Control Theories in Developmental Perspective," *Studies on Crime and Delinquency Prevention* 2:69–87 (1993).

73. Dustin Pardini, Jelena Obradovic, and Rolf Loeber, "Interpersonal Callousness, Hyperactivity/Impulsivity, Inattention, and Conduct Problems as Precursors to Delinquency Persistence in Boys: A Comparison of Three Grade-Based Cohorts," *Journal of Clinical Child and Adolescent Psychology* 35:46–59 (2006).

74. Ojmarrh Mitchell and Doris Layton MacKenzie, "The Stability and Resiliency of Self-Control in a Sample of Incarcerated Offenders," *Crime and Delinquency* 52:432–449 (2006).

75. Charles R. Tittle and Harold G. Grasmick, "Delinquent Behavior and Age: A Test of Three Provocative Hypotheses," *Journal of Criminal Law and Criminology* 88:309–342 (1997).

76. Callie Harbin Burt, Ronald Simons, and Leslie Simons, "A Longitudinal Test of the Effects of Parenting and the Stability of Self-Control: Negative Evidence for the General Theory of Crime," *Criminology* 44:353–396 (2006).

77. Alex Piquero, John MacDonald, Adam Dobrin, Leah Daigle, and Francis Cullen, "Self-Control, Violent Offending, and Homicide Victimization: Assessing the General Theory of Crime," *Journal of Quantitative Criminology* 21:55–71 (2005).

78. Gregory Zimmerman, "Impulsivity, Offending, and the Neighborhood: Investigating the Person–Context Nexus," *Journal of Quantitative Criminology* 26:301–332 (2010).

79. Chris Gibson, "An Investigation of Neighborhood Disadvantage, Low Self-Control, and Violent Victimization Among Youth" *Youth Violence and Juvenile Justice* 10:41–63 (2012).

80. Ick-Joong Chung, Karl G Hill, J. David Hawkins, Lewayne Gilchrist, and Daniel Nagin, "Childhood Predictors of Offense Trajectories," *Journal of Research in Crime and Delinquency* 39:60–91 (2002).

81. Amy D'Unger, Kenneth Land, Patricia McCall, and Daniel Nagin, "How Many Latent Classes of Delinquent/Criminal Careers? Results from Mixed Poisson Regression Analyses," *American Journal of Sociology* 103:1593–1630 (1998).

82. George E. Higgins, Melissa L. Ricketts, Catherine D. Marcum, and Margaret Mahoney, "Primary Socialization Theory: An Exploratory Study of Delinquent Trajectories," *Criminal Justice Studies* 23:133–146 (2010).

83. Nicole Leeper Piquero and Terrie E. Moffitt, "Can Childhood Factors Predict Workplace Deviance?" *Justice Quarterly*, published online February 21, 2012.

84. Chung et al., "Childhood Predictors of Offense Trajectories."

85. Sarah Bacon, Raymond Paternoster, and Robert Brame, "Understanding the Relationship Between Onset Age and Subsequent Offending During Adolescence," *Journal of Youth and Adolescence* 38:301–311 (2009).

86. Victor van der Geest, Arjan Blokland, and Catrien Bijleveld, "Delinquent Development in a Sample of High-Risk Youth: Shape, Content, and Predictors of Delinquent Trajectories from Age 12 to 32," *Journal of Research in Crime and Delinquency* 46:111–143 (2009).

87. Donald Lynam, Alex Piquero, and Terrie Moffitt, "Specialization and the Propensity to Violence: Support from Self-Reports but Not Official Records," *Journal of Contemporary Criminal Justice* 20:215–228 (2004).

88. Jennifer Reingle, Wesley Jennings, and Mildred Maldonado-Molina, "Risk and Protective Factors for Trajectories of Violent Delinquency Among a Nationally Representative Sample of Early Adolescents," *Youth Violence and Juvenile Justice*, published online February 16, 2012.

89. Georgia Zara and David Farrington, "Childhood and Adolescent Predictors of Late Onset Criminal Careers," *Journal of Youth and Adolescence* 38:287–300 (2009).

90. Alex Piquero, Robert Brame, Paul Mazerolle, and Rudy Haapanen, "Crime in Emerging Adulthood," *Criminology* 40:137–170 (2002).

91. D'Unger et al., "How Many Latent Classes of Delinquent/Criminal Careers?"

92. Alex R. Piquero, David P. Farrington, Daniel S. Nagin and Terrie E. Moffitt, "Trajectories of Offending and Their Relation to Life Failure in Late Middle Age: Findings from the Cambridge Study in Delinquent Development," *Journal of Research in Crime and Delinquency* 47:151–173 (2010).

93. Margit Wiesner and Ranier Silbereisen, "Trajectories of Delinquent Behaviour in Adolescence and Their Covariates: Relations with Initial and Time-Averaged Factors," *Journal of Adolescence* 26:753–771 (2003).

94. Rolf Loeber, Phen Wung, Kate Keenan, Bruce Giroux, Magda Stouthamer-Loeber, Wemoet Van Kammen, and Barbara Maughan, "Developmental Pathways in Disruptive Behavior," *Development and Psychopathology* 23:12–48 (1993).

95. Alex Piquero and Timothy Brezina, "Testing Moffitt's Account of Adolescent-Limited Delinquency," *Criminology* 39:353–370 (2001).

96. Terrie Moffitt, "Adolescence-Limited and Life-Course Persistent Antisocial Behavior: A Developmental Taxonomy," *Psychological Review* 100:674–701 (1993).

97. Terrie Moffitt, "Natural Histories of Delinquency," in *Cross-National Longitudinal Research on Human Development and Criminal Behavior*, ed. Elmar Weitekamp and Hans-Jurgen Kerner (Dordrecht, Netherlands: Kluwer, 1994), pp. 3–65.

98. Andrea Donker, Wilma Smeenk, Peter van der Laan, and Frank Verhulst, "Individual Stability of Antisocial Behavior from Childhood to Adulthood: Testing the Stability Postulate of Moffitt's Developmental Theory," *Criminology* 41:593–609 (2003).

99. Robert Vermeiren, "Psychopathology and Delinquency in Adolescents: A Descriptive and Developmental Perspective," *Clinical Psychology Review* 23:277–318 (2003); Paul Mazerolle, Robert Brame, Ray Paternoster, Alex Piquero, and Charles Dean, "Onset Age, Persistence, and Offending Versatility: Comparisons Across Sex," *Criminology* 38:1143–1172 (2000).

100. Margit Wiesner, Deborah Capaldi, and Hyoun Kim, "General versus Specific Predictors of Male Arrest Trajectories: A Test of the Moffitt and Patterson Theories," *Journal of Youth and Adolescence* 42:217–228 (2012).

101. Adrian Raine, Rolf Loeber, Magda Stouthamer-Loeber, Terrie Moffitt, Avshalom Caspi, and Don Lynam, "Neurocognitive Impairments in Boys on the Life-Course Persistent Antisocial Path," *Journal of Abnormal Psychology* 114:38–49 (2005).

102. Per-Olof Wikstrom and Rolf Loeber, "Do Disadvantaged Neighborhoods Cause Well-Adjusted Children to Become Adolescent Delinquents? A Study of Male Juvenile Serious Offending, Individual Risk and Protective Factors, and Neighborhood Context," *Criminology* 38:1109–1142 (2000).

103. Nicole Buck, Frank Verhulst, Hjalmar van Marle, and Jan van der Ende, "Childhood Psychopathology Predicts Adolescence-Onset Offending: A Longitudinal Study," *Crime and Delinquency*, first published online July 22, 2009.

104. Dawn Jeglum Bartusch, Donald Lynam, Terrie Moffitt, and Phil Silva, "Is Age Important? Testing a General versus a Developmental Theory of Antisocial Behavior," *Criminology* 35:13–48 (1997).

105. Daniel Nagin and Richard Tremblay, "What Has Been Learned from Group-Based Trajectory Modeling? Examples from Physical Aggression and Other Problem Behaviors," *Annals of the American Academy of Political and Social Science* 602:82–117 (2005).

106. Terrie Moffitt, "A Review of Research on the Taxonomy of Life-Course Persistent versus Adolescence-Limited Antisocial Behavior," in *Taking Stock: The Status of Criminological Theory*, vol. 15, ed. F. T. Cullen, J. P. Wright, and K. R. Blevins (New Brunswick, NJ: Transaction Publications, 2006), pp. 277–311.

107. David Farrington, "Key Results from the First Forty Years of the Cambridge Study in Delinquent Development," in *Taking Stock of Delinquency: An Overview of Findings from Contemporary Longitudinal Studies*, ed. Terence Thornberry and Marvin Krohn (New York: Kluwer, 2002), pp. 137–185.

108. Xiaojin Chen and Michele Adam, "Are Teen Delinquency Abstainers Social Introverts? A Test of Moffitt's Theory," *Journal of Research in Crime and Delinquency* 47:439–468 (2010).

109. C. Barnes, Kevin Beaver, and Brian Boutwell, "Examining the Genetic Underpinnings to Moffitt's Developmental Taxonomy: A Behavioral Genetic Analysis," *Criminology* 49:923–954 (2011).

110. Chen and Adams, "Are Teen Delinquency Abstainers Social Introverts?"

111. Jennifer Gatewood Owens and Lee Ann Slocum, "Abstainers in Adolescence and Adulthood: Exploring the Correlates of Abstention Using Moffitt's Developmental Taxonomy," *Crime and Delinquency*, published online February 7, 2012.

112. Bradley Entner Wright, Avshalom Caspi, Terrie Moffitt, and Phil Silva, "Low Self-Control, Social Bonds, and Delinquency: Social Causation, Social Selection, or Both?" *Criminology* 37:479–514 (1999).

113. Ibid., p. 504.

114. Stephen Cernkovich and Peggy Giordano, "Stability and Change in Antisocial Behavior: The Transition from Adolescence to Early Adulthood," *Criminology* 39:371–410 (2001).

115. Gerald R. Patterson, Patricia Chamberlain, and John B. Reid, "A Comparative Evaluation of a Parent-Training Program," *Behavior Therapy* 13:638–650 (1982); Gerald R. Patterson, John B. Reid, and Thomas J. Dishion, *Antisocial Boys* (Eugene, OR: Castalia, 1992).

116. Peter W. Greenwood, Karyn E. Model, C. Peter Rydell, and James Chiesa, *Diverting Children from a Life of Crime: Measuring Costs and Benefits* (Santa Monica, CA: Rand, 1996).

117. Alex Mason, Rick Kosterman, J. David Hawkins, Kevin P. Haggerty, and Richard L. Spoth. "Reducing Adolescents' Growth in Substance Use and Delinquency: Randomized Trial Effects of a Parent-Training Prevention Intervention," *Prevention Science* 4:203–212 (2003).

118. Heather Lonczk, Robert Abbott, J. David Hawkins, Rick Kosterman, and Richard Catalano, "Effects of the Seattle Social Development Project on Sexual Behavior, Pregnancy, Birth, and Sexually Transmitted Disease Outcomes by Age 21 Years," *Archive of Pediatrics and Adolescent Medicine* 156:438–447 (2002).

119. Kathleen Bodisch Lynch, Susan Rose Geller, and Melinda G. Schmidt, "Multi-Year Evaluation of the Effectiveness of a Resilience-Based Prevention Program for Young Children," *Journal of Primary Prevention* 24:335–353 (2004).

120. This section leans on Thomas Tatchell, Phillip Waite, Renny Tatchell, Lynne Durrant, and Dale Bond, "Substance Abuse Prevention in Sixth Grade: The Effect of a Prevention Program on Adolescents' Risk and Protective Factors," *American Journal of Health Studies* 19:54–61 (2004).

121. Nancy Tobler and Howard Stratton, "Effectiveness of School Based Drug Prevention Programs: A Meta-Analysis of the Research," *Journal of Primary Prevention* 18:71–128 (1997).

122. Office of Juvenile Justice and Delinquency Prevention, *Model Programs Guide*, www.ojjdp.gov/mpg/ (accessed July 24, 2012).

Chapter 6. Gender and Delinquency

1. Cesare Lombroso and William Ferrero, *The Female Offender* (New York: Philosophical Library, 1895).

2. Cesare Lombroso, *The Female Offender* (New York: Appleton, 1920); W. I. Thomas, *The Unadjusted Girl* (New York: Harper & Row, 1923).

3. Cheryl Maxson and Monica Whitlock, "Joining the Gang: Gender Differences in Risk Factors for Gang Membership," in *Gangs in America III*, ed. C. Ronald Huff (Thousand Oaks, CA: Sage, 2002), pp. 19–35.

4. This section relies on Spencer Rathus, *Psychology in the New Millennium* (Fort Worth, TX: Harcourt, Brace, 1996); see also Darcy Miller, Catherine Trapani, Kathy Fejes-Mendoza, Carolyn Eggleston, and Donna Dwiggins, "Adolescent Female Offenders: Unique Considerations," *Adolescence* 30:429–435 (1995).

5. Rolf Loeber and Dale Hay, "Key Issues in the Development of Aggression and Violence from Childhood to Early Adulthood," *Annual Review of Psychology* 48:371–410 (1997).

6. Danielle Boisvert, Jamie Vaske, Justine Taylor, and John Wright, "The Effects of Differential Parenting on Sibling Differences in Self-Control and Delinquency Among Brother-Sister Pairs," *Criminal Justice Review* 37:5–23 (2012).

7. Allison Morris, *Women, Crime, and Criminal Justice* (Oxford, England: Basil Blackwell, 1987).

8. Elizabeth Burgess Dowdell, "Risky Internet Behaviors of Middle-School Students: Communication with Online Strangers and Offline Contact," *CIN: Computers, Informatics, Nursing* 29:352–359 (2011).

9. Loeber and Hay, "Key Issues in the Development of Aggression and Violence," p. 378.

10. John Mirowsky and Catherine Ross, "Sex Differences in Distress: Real or Artifact?" *American Sociological Review* 60:449–468 (1995).

11. Philip Cook and Susan Sorenson, "The Gender Gap Among Teen Survey Respondents: Why Are Boys More Likely to Report a Gun in the Home than Girls?" *Journal of Quantitative Criminology* 22:61–76 (2006).

12. Mirowsky and Ross, "Sex Differences in Distress: Real or Artifact?" pp. 460–465.

13. For a review of this issue, see Anne Campbell, *Men, Women, and Aggression* (New York: Basic Books, 1993).

14. Thomas Parsons, Albert Rizzo, Cheryl Van Der Zaag, Jocelyn McGee, and J. Galen Buckwalter, "Gender Differences and Cognition Among Older Adults," *Aging, Neuropsychology and Cognition* 12:78–88 (2005).

15. Diane Halpern and Mary LaMay, "The Smarter Sex: A Critical Review of Sex Differences in Intelligence," *Educational Psychology Review* 12: 229–246 (2000).

16. Parsons, Rizzo, Van Der Zaag, McGee, and Buckwalter, "Gender Differences and Cognition Among Older Adults."

17. James Messerschmidt, *Masculinities and Crime: Critique and Reconceptualization of Theory* (Lanham, MD: Rowman & Littlefield, 1993).

18. Debra Kaysen, Miranda Morris, Shireen Rizvi, and Patricia Resick, "Peritraumatic Responses and Their Relationship to Perceptions of Threat in Female Crime Victims," *Violence Against Women* 11:1515–1535 (2005).

19. D. J. Pepler and W. M. Craig, "A Peek Behind the Fence: Naturalistic Observations of Aggressive Children with Remote Audiovisual Recording," *Developmental Psychology* 31:548–553 (1995).

20. Daniel Mears, Matthew Ploeger, and Mark Warr, "Explaining the Gender Gap in Delinquency: Peer Influence and Moral Evaluations of Behavior," *Journal of Research in Crime and Delinquency* 35:251–266 (1998).

21. John Gibbs, Dennis Giever, and Jamie Martin, "Parental Management and Self-Control: An Empirical Test of Gottfredson and Hirschi's General Theory," *Journal of Research in Crime and Delinquency* 35:40–70 (1998); Velmer Burton, Francis Cullen, T. David Evans, Leanne Fiftal Alarid, and R. Gregory Dunaway, "Gender, Self-Control, and Crime," *Journal of Research in Crime and Delinquency* 35:123–147 (1998).

22. Ann Beutel and Margaret Mooney Marini, "Gender and Values," *American Sociological Review* 60:436–448 (1995).

23. American Association of University Women, *Shortchanging Girls, Shortchanging America: Executive Summary* (Washington, DC: American Association of University Women, 1991).

24. Spencer Rathus, *Voyages in Childhood* (Belmont, CA: Wadsworth, 2004).

25. Carol Gilligan, *In a Different Voice* (Cambridge, MA: Harvard University Press, 1982).

26. David Roalf, Natasha Lowery, and Bruce Turetsky, "Behavioral and Physiological Findings of Gender Differences in Global-Local Visual Processing," *Brain and Cognition* 60:32–42 (2006).

27. Audrey Zakriski, Jack Wright, and Marion Underwood, "Gender Similarities and Differences in Children's Social Behavior: Finding Personality in Contextualized Patterns of Adaptation," *Journal of Personality and Social Psychology* 88:844–855 (2005).

28. David Rowe, Alexander Vazsonyi, and Daniel Flannery, "Sex Differences in Crime: Do Means and Within-Sex Variation Have Similar Causes?" *Journal of Research in Crime and Delinquency* 32:84–100 (1995).

29. Sandra Bem, *The Lenses of Gender* (New Haven: Yale University Press, 1993).

30. Walter DeKeseredy and Martin Schwartz, "Male Peer Support and Woman Abuse," *Sociological Spectrum* 13:393–413 (1993).

31. Janet Shibley Hyde, "The Gender Similarities Hypothesis," *American Psychologist* 60:581–592 (2005).

32. John Archer, "The Importance of Theory for Evaluating Evidence on Sex Differences," *American Psychologist* 61:638–639 (2006); Richard Lippa, "The Gender Reality Hypothesis," *American Psychologist* 61:639–640 (2006).

33. Shari Miller, Patrick Malone, and Kenneth Dodge, "Developmental Trajectories of Boys' and Girls' Delinquency: Sex Differences and Links to Later Adolescent Outcomes," *Journal of Abnormal Child Psychology* 38:1021–1032 (2010).

34. Johannes Landsheer and C. van Dijkum, "Male and Female Delinquency Trajectories from Pre- Through Middle Adolescence and Their Continuation in Late Adolescence," *Adolescence* 40:729–748 (2005).

35. Eleanor Maccoby, "Gender and Group Process: A Developmental Perspective," *Current Directions in Psychological Science* 11:54–58 (2002).

36. Jean Bottcher, "Social Practices of Gender: How Gender Relates to Delinquency in the Everyday Lives of High-Risk Youths," *Criminology* 39:893–932 (2001).

37. Arrest data from FBI, *Crime in the United States, 2010*, Table 33, www.fbi.gov/about-us/cjis/ucr/crime-in-the-u.s/2010/crime-in-the-u.s.-2010/tables/10tbl33.xls (accessed July 27, 2012).

38. *Monitoring the Future, 2010* (Ann Arbor, MI: Institute for Social Research, 2012).

39. Sara Goodkind, John Wallace, Jeffrey Shook, Jerald Bachman, and Patrick O'Malley, "Are Girls Really Becoming More Delinquent? Testing the

Gender Convergence Hypothesis by Race and Ethnicity, 1976–2005," *Children and Youth Services Review* 31:885–895 (2009).

40. Margaret Zahn, Susan Brumbaugh, Darrell Steffensmeier, Barry Feld, Merry Morash, Meda Chesney-Lind, Jody Miller, Allison Ann Payne, Denise C. Gottfredson, and Candace Kruttschnitt, *Violence by Teenage Girls: Trends and Context* (Washington, DC: Office of Juvenile Justice and Delinquency Prevention, 2008, www.ncjrs.gov/pdffiles1/ojjdp/218905.pdf (accessed August 10, 2012).

41. Lombroso and Ferrero, *The Female Offender.*

42. Ibid., p. 122.

43. Ibid., pp. 51–52.

44. For a review, see Anne Campbell, *Girl Delinquents* (Oxford, England: Basil Blackwell, 1981), pp. 41–48.

45. Cyril Burt, *The Young Delinquent* (New York: Appleton, 1925); see also Warren Middleton, "Is There a Relation Between Kleptomania and Female Periodicity in Neurotic Individuals?" *Psychology Clinic* (December 1933), pp. 232–247.

46. William Healy and Augusta Bronner, *Delinquents and Criminals: Their Making and Unmaking* (New York: Macmillan, 1926).

47. Ibid., p. 10.

48. Miriam Sealock and Sally Simpson, "Unraveling Bias in Arrest Decisions: The Role of Juvenile Offender Typescripts," *Justice Quarterly* 15:427–457 (1998); Christina Polsenberg and Kenneth Jackson, "Putting Race into Context: Race, Juvenile Justice Processing, and Urbanization," paper presented at the annual meeting of the American Society of Criminology, Boston, November 1995 (rev. version, January 1996); for a general review, see Carl Pope and William Feyerherm, "Minority Status and Juvenile Justice Processing (Part I)," *Criminal Justice Abstracts* 22:327–335 (1990); see also Douglas Smith and Jody Klein, "Police Control of Interpersonal Disputes," *Social Problems* 31:468–481 (1984).

49. Sigmund Freud, *An Outline of Psychoanalysis*, trans. James Strachey (New York: Norton, 1949), p. 278.

50. Dorie Klein, "The Etiology of Female Crime: A Review of the Literature," in *The Criminology of Deviant Women*, ed. Freda Adler and Rita Simon (Boston: Houghton Mifflin, 1979), pp. 69–71.

51. Peter Blos, "Pre-Oedipal Factors in the Etiology of Female Delinquency," *Psychoanalytic Studies of the Child* 12:229–242 (1957).

52. Sheldon Glueck and Eleanor Glueck, *Five Hundred Delinquent Women* (New York: Knopf, 1934).

53. J. Cowie, V. Cowie, and E. Slater, *Delinquency in Girls* (London: Heinemann, 1968).

54. Anne Campbell, "On the Invisibility of the Female Delinquent Peer Group," *Women and Criminal Justice* 2:41–62 (1990).

55. Carolyn Smith, "Factors Associated with Early Sexual Activity Among Urban Adolescents," *Social Work* 42:334–346 (1997).

56. For a review, see Christy Miller Buchanan, Jacquelynne Eccles, and Jill Becker, "Are Adolescents the Victims of Raging Hormones? Evidence for Activational Effects of Hormones on Moods and Behavior at Adolescence," *Psychological Bulletin* 111:63–107 (1992).

57. L. Kris Gowen, S. Shirley Feldman, Rafael Diaz, and Donnovan Somera Yisrael, "A Comparison of the Sexual Behaviors and Attitudes of Adolescent Girls with Older vs. Similar-Aged Boyfriends," *Journal of Youth and Adolescence* 33:167–176 (2004).

58. Rona Carter, James Jaccard, Wendy Silverman, and Armando Pina, "Pubertal Timing and Its Link to Behavioral and Emotional Problems Among 'At-Risk' African American Adolescent Girls," *Journal of Adolescence* 32:467–481 (2009).

59. Dana Haynie, "Contexts of Risk? Explaining the Link Between Girls' Pubertal Development and Their Delinquency Involvement," *Social Forces* 82:355–397 (2003).

60. Margaret A. Zahn, Robert Agnew, Diana Fishbein, Shari Miller, Donna-Marie Winn, Gayle Dakoff, Candace Kruttschnitt, Peggy Giordano, Denise C. Gottfredson, Allison A. Payne, Barry C. Feld, and Meda Chesney-Lind, *Causes and Correlates of Girls' Delinquency Justice and Delinquency Prevention* (OJJDP, April 2010), www.ncjrs.gov/pdffiles1/ojjdp/226358.pdf (accessed July 27, 2012).

61. Dana Haynie and Alex Piquero, "Pubertal Development and Physical Victimization in Adolescence," *Journal of Research in Crime and Delinquency* 43:3–35 (2006).

62. Eleanor Maccoby and Carol Jacklin, *The Psychology of Sex Differences* (Stanford, CA: Stanford University Press, 1974).

63. Kathleen Pajer, William Gardner, Robert Rubin, James Perel, and Stephen Neal, "Decreased Cortisol Levels in Adolescent Girls with Conduct Disorder," *Archives of General Psychiatry* 58:297–302 (2001).

64. Alan Booth and D. Wayne Osgood, "The Influence of Testosterone on Deviance in Adulthood: Assessing and Explaining the Relationship," *Criminology* 31:93–118 (1993).

65. D. H. Baucom, P. K. Besch, and S. Callahan, "Relationship Between Testosterone Concentration, Sex Role Identity, and Personality Among Females," *Journal of Personality and Social Psychology* 48:1218–1226 (1985).

66. Lee Ellis, "Evidence of Neuroandrogenic Etiology of Sex Roles from a Combined Analysis of Human, Nonhuman Primate, and Nonprimate Mammalian Studies," *Personality and Individual Differences* 7:519–552 (1986).

67. Diana Fishbein, "The Psychobiology of Female Aggression," *Criminal Justice and Behavior* 19:99–126 (1992).

68. Spencer Rathus, *Psychology*, 3rd ed. (New York: Holt, Rinehart & Winston, 1987), p. 88.

69. See, generally, Katharina Dalton, *The Premenstrual Syndrome* (Springfield, IL: Charles C. Thomas, 1971).

70. Julie Horney, "Menstrual Cycles and Criminal Responsibility," *Law and Human Nature* 2:25–36 (1978).

71. Lee Ellis, "The Victimful-Victimless Crime Distinction and Seven Universal Demographic Correlates of Victimful Criminal Behavior," *Personality and Individual Differences* 9:525–548 (1988).

72. Lee Ellis, "Evolutionary and Neurochemical Causes of Sex Differences in Victimizing Behavior: Toward a Unified Theory of Criminal Behavior and Social Stratification," *Social Science Information* 28:605–636 (1989).

73. Kathleen Pajer, "What Happens to 'Bad' Girls? A Review of the Adult Outcomes of Antisocial Adolescent Girls," *American Journal of Psychiatry* 155:862–870 (1998).

74. Zahn et al., *Causes and Correlates of Girls' Delinquency Justice and Delinquency Prevention.*

75. Jan ter Laak, Martijn de Goede, Liesbeth Aleva, Gerard Brugman, Miranda van Leuven, and Judith Hussmann, "Incarcerated Adolescent Girls: Personality, Social Competence, and Delinquency," *Adolescence* 38:251–265 (2003).

76. Dorothy Espelage, Elizabeth Cauffman, Lisa Broidy, Alex Piquero, Paul Mazerolle, and Hans Steiner, "A Cluster-Analytic Investigation of MMPI Profiles of Serious Male and Female Juvenile Offenders," *Journal of the American Academy of Child and Adolescent Psychiatry* 42:770–777 (2003).

77. Kristen McCabe, Amy Lansing, Ann Garland, and Richard Hough, "Gender Differences in Psychopathology, Functional Impairment, and Familial Risk Factors Among Adjudicated Delinquents," *Journal of the American Academy of Child and Adolescent Psychiatry* 41:860–867 (2002).

78. Paul Frick, Amy Cornell, Christopher Barry, Doug Bodin, and Heather Dane, "Callous-Unemotional Traits and Conduct Problems in the Prediction of Conduct Problem Severity, Aggression, and Self-Report of Delinquency," *Journal of Abnormal Child Psychology* 31:457–470 (2003).

79. Alex Mason and Michael Windle, "Gender, Self-Control, and Informal Social Control in Adolescence: A Test of Three Models of the Continuity of Delinquent Behavior," *Youth and Society* 33:479–514 (2002).

80. Thomas, *The Unadjusted Girl.*

81. Ibid., p. 109.

82. Elaine Eggleston Doherty, Kerry Green, and Margaret Ensminger, "The Impact of Adolescent Deviance on Marital Trajectories," *Deviant Behavior* 33:185–206 (2012).

83. Ruth Morris, "Female Delinquents and Relational Problems," *Social Forces* 43:82–89 (1964).

84. Cowie, Cowie, and Slater, *Delinquency in Girls*, p. 27.

85. Morris, "Female Delinquency and Relational Problems."

86. Clyde Vedder and Dora Somerville, *The Delinquent Girl* (Springfield, IL: Charles C. Thomas, 1970).

87. Ames Robey, Richard Rosenwal, John Small, and Ruth Lee, "The Runaway Girl: A Reaction to Family Stress," *American Journal of Orthopsychiatry* 34:763–767 (1964).

88. William Wattenberg and Frank Saunders, "Sex Differences Among Juvenile Court Offenders," *Sociology and Social Research* 39:24–31 (1954).

89. Don Gibbons and Manzer Griswold, "Sex Differences Among Juvenile Court Referrals," *Sociology and Social Research* 42:106–110 (1957).

90. Gordon Barker and William Adams, "Comparison of the Delinquencies of Boys and Girls," *Journal of Criminal Law, Criminology, and Police Science* 53:470–475 (1962).

91. George Calhoun, Janelle Jurgens, and Fengling Chen, "The Neophyte Female Delinquent: A Review of the Literature," *Adolescence* 28:461–471 (1993).

92. Angela Dixon, Pauline Howie and Jean Starling, "Trauma Exposure, Posttraumatic Stress, and Psychiatric Comorbidity in Female Juvenile Offenders," *Journal of the American Academy of Child and Adolescent Psychiatry* 44:798–806 (2005).

93. Veronica Herrera and Laura Ann McCloskey, "Sexual Abuse, Family Violence, and Female Delinquency: Findings from a Longitudinal Study," *Violence and Victims* 18:319–334 (2003).

94. Sherry Hamby, David Finkelhor, and Heather Turner, "Teen Dating Violence: Co-occurrence with Other Victimizations in the National Survey of Children's Exposure to Violence (NatSCEV)," *Psychology of Violence* 2:111–124 (2012).

95. Emily Gaarder and Joanne Belknap, "Tenuous Borders: Girls Transferred to Adult Court," *Criminology* 40:481–518 (2002).

96. Zahn et al., *Causes and Correlates of Girls' Delinquency Justice and Delinquency Prevention.*

97. Pernilla Johansson and Kimberly Kempf-Leonard, "A Gender-Specific Pathway to Serious, Violent, and Chronic Offending? Exploring Howell's Risk Factors for Serious Delinquency," *Crime Delinquency* 55:216–240 (2009).

98. Julie Messer, Barbara Maughan, and David Quinton, "Precursors and Correlates of Criminal Behaviour in Women," *Criminal Behaviour and Mental Health* 14:82–107 (2004).

99. Dominique Eve Roe-Sepowitz, "Comparing Male and Female Juveniles Charged with Homicide: Child Maltreatment, Substance Abuse, and Crime Details," *Journal of Interpersonal Violence* 24:601–617 (2009).

100. Kristin Carbone-Lopez and Jody Miller, "Precocious Role Entry as a Mediating Factor in Women's Methamphetamine Use: Implications for Life-Course and Pathways Research," *Criminology* 50:187–220 (2012).

101. Joan Moore, *Going Down to the Barrio: Homeboys and Homegirls in Change* (Philadelphia: Temple University Press, 1991), p. 93.

102. Ibid., p. 101.

103. Gaarder and Belknap, "Tenuous Borders."

104. Jennifer Kerpelman and Sondra Smith-Adcock, "Female Adolescents" Delinquent Activity: The Intersection of Bonds to Parents and Reputation Enhancement," *Youth and Society* 37:176–200 (2005).

105. D. Wayne Osgood, Janet Wilson, Patrick O'Malley, Jerald Bachman, and Lloyd Johnston, "Routine Activities and Individual Deviant Behaviors," *American Sociological Review* 61:635–655 (1996).

106. Girls Inc. Friendly PEERsuasion, www.girlsinc.org/about/programs/friendly-peersuasion.html (accessed July 27, 2012).

107. Freda Adler, *Sisters in Crime* (New York: McGraw-Hill, 1975).

108. Ibid., pp. 10–11.

109. Rita James Simon, "Women and Crime Revisited," *Social Science Quarterly* 56:658–663 (1976).

110. Ibid., pp. 660–661.

111. Roy Austin, "Women's Liberation and Increase in Minor, Major, and Occupational Offenses," *Criminology* 20:407–430 (1982).

112. Sarah Goodkind, John Wallace, Jeffrey Shook, Jerald Bachman, and Patrick O'Malley, "Are Girls Really Becoming More Delinquent? Testing the Gender Convergence Hypothesis by Race and Ethnicity, 1976–2005," *Children and Youth Services Review* 31:885–895 (2009).

113. Darrell Steffensmeier and Dana Haynie, "Gender, Structural Disadvantage, and Urban Crime: Do Macrosocial Variables Also Explain Female Offending Rates?" *Criminology* 38:403–438 (2000); Beth Bjerregaard and Carolyn Smith, "Gender Differences in Gang Participation and Delinquency," *Journal of Quantitative Criminology* 9:329–350 (1993).

114. Julia Schwendinger and Herman Schwendinger, *Rape and Inequality* (Beverly Hills, CA: Sage, 1983).

115. For a review of feminist theory, see Sally Simpson, "Feminist Theory, Crime and Justice," *Criminology* 27:605–632 (1989).

116. Victoria Titterington, "A Retrospective Investigation of Gender Inequality and Female Homicide Victimization," *Sociological Spectrum* 26:205–236 (2006).

117. Messerschmidt, *Masculinities and Crime.*

118. Center for Research on Women, *Secrets in Public: Sexual Harassment in Our Schools* (Wellesley, MA: Wellesley College, 1993).

119. Jody Miller, *Getting Played: African American Girls, Urban Inequality, and Gendered Violence* (New York: NYU Press 2008).

120. Joanne Belknap, Kristi Holsinger, and Melissa Dunn, "Understanding Incarcerated Girls: The Results of a Focus Group Study," *Prison Journal* 77:381–404 (1997).

121. Kathleen Daly and Meda Chesney-Lind, "Feminism and Criminology," *Justice Quarterly* 5:497–538 (1988).

122. Jane Siegel and Linda Williams, "The Relationship Between Child Sexual Abuse and Female Delinquency and Crime: A Prospective Study," *Journal of Research in Crime and Delinquency* 40:71–94 (2003).

123. John Hagan, A. R. Gillis, and John Simpson, "The Class Structure and Delinquency: Toward a Power-Control Theory of Common Delinquent Behavior," *American Journal of Sociology* 90:1151–1178 (1985); John Hagan, John Simpson, and A. R. Gillis, "Class in the Household: A Power-Control Theory of Gender and Delinquency," *American Journal of Sociology* 92:788–816 (1987).

124. John Hagan, A. R. Gillis, and John Simpson, "Clarifying and Extending Power-Control Theory," *American Journal of Sociology* 95:1024–1037 (1990).

125. Gary Jensen and Kevin Thompson, "What's Class Got to Do with It? A Further Examination of Power-Control Theory," *American Journal of Sociology* 95:1009–1023 (1990); Kevin Thompson, "Gender and Adolescent Drinking Problems: The Effects of Occupational Structure," *Social Problems* 36:30–44 (1989); for some critical research, see Simon Singer and Murray Levine, "Power-Control Theory, Gender, and Delinquency: A Partial Replication with Additional Evidence on the Effects of Peers," *Criminology* 26:627–648 (1988).

126. Christopher Uggen, "Class, Gender, and Arrest: An Intergenerational Analysis of Workplace Power and Control," *Criminology* 38:835–862 (2001).

127. Hagan, Gillis, and Simpson, "Clarifying and Extending Power-Control Theory."

128. Brenda Sims Blackwell and Mark Reed, "Power-Control as a Between—and Within—Family Model: Reconsidering the Unit of Analysis," *Journal of Youth and Adolescence* 32:385–400 (2003).

129. Linda Williams and Jennifer Ngo, "Human Trafficking," in *Encyclopedia of Interpersonal Violence*, ed. Claire M. Renzetti and Jeffrey I. Edelson (Thousand Oaks, CA: Sage Publications, 2007); U.S. Department of State, *Trafficking in Persons Report* (Washington, DC: U.S. Department of State, 2005), www.state.gov/g/tip/rls/tiprpt/2005/ (accessed July 27, 2012).

130. *Victims of Trafficking and Violence Protection Act of 2000,* www.state.gov/documents/organization/10492.pdf (accessed July 27, 2012).

131. *Trafficking Victims Protection Reauthorization Act of 2005,* www.lexisnexis.com/documents/pdf/20090504045724_large.pdf (accessed July 27, 2012).

132. Paul E. Tracy, Kimberly Kempf-Leonard, and Stephanie Abramoske-James, "Gender Differences in Delinquency and Juvenile Justice Processing," *Crime Delinquency* 55:171–215 (2009).

133. Meda Chesney-Lind, "Judicial Enforcement of the Female Sex Role: The Family Court and the Female Delinquent," *Issues in Criminology* 8:51–59 (1973).

134. Meda Chesney-Lind and Randall Shelden, *Girls, Delinquency, and Juvenile Justice* (Belmont, CA: West/Wadsworth, 1998).

135. Meda Chesney-Lind and Vickie Paramore, "Are Girls Getting More Violent? Exploring Juvenile Robbery Trends," *Journal of Contemporary Criminal Justice* 17:142–166 (2001).

136. Meda Chesney-Lind and Katherine Irwin, *Beyond Bad Girls: Gender, Violence and Hype* (London: Routledge, 2007).

137. Tracy, Kempf-Leonard, and Abramoske-James, "Gender Differences in Delinquency and Juvenile Justice Processing."

138. Holly Hartwig and Jane Myers, "A Different Approach: Applying a Wellness Paradigm to Adolescent Female Delinquents and Offenders," *Journal of Mental Health Counseling* 25:57–75 (2003).

139. Sealock and Simpson, "Unraveling Bias in Arrest Decisions."

140. Tia Stevens, Merry Morash, and Meda Chesney-Lind, "Are Girls Getting Tougher, or Are We Tougher on Girls? Probability of Arrest and Juvenile Court Oversight in 1980 and 2000," *Justice Quarterly* 28: 719–744 (2011).

141. Chesney-Lind and Shelden, *Girls, Delinquency, and Juvenile Justice,* p. 243.

Chapter 7. The Family and Delinquency

1. Tracy Harachi, Charles Fleming, Helene White, Margaret Ensminger, Robert Abbott, Richard Catalano, and Kevin Haggerty, "Aggressive Behavior Among Girls and Boys During Middle Childhood: Predictors and Sequelae of Trajectory Group Membership," *Aggressive Behavior* 32:279–293 (2006).

2. Rolf Loeber and Magda Stouthamer-Loeber, "Development of Juvenile Aggression and Violence," *American Psychologist* 53:250 (1998).

3. Callie Harbin Burt, Ronald Simons, and Leslie Simons, "A Longitudinal Test of the Effects of Parenting and the Stability of Self-Control: Negative Evidence for the General Theory of Crime," *Criminology* 44:353–396 (2006).

4. Peggy C. Giordano, *Legacies of Crime, A Follow-Up of the Children of Highly Delinquent Girls and Boys* (London: Cambridge University Press, 2010).

5. Joan McCord, "Family Relationships, Juvenile Delinquency, and Adult Criminality," *Criminology* 29:397–417 (1991); Scott Henggeler, ed., *Delinquency and Adolescent Psychopathology: A Family Ecological Systems Approach* (Littleton, MA: Wright–PSG, 1982).

6. Rolf Loeber and Magda Stouthamer-Loeber, "Family Factors as Correlates and Predictors of Juvenile Conduct Problems and Delinquency," in *Crime and Justice,* vol. 7, ed. Michael Tonry and Norval Morris (Chicago: University of Chicago Press, 1986), pp. 29–151.

7. Ruth Inglis, *Sins of the Fathers: A Study of the Physical and Emotional Abuse of Children* (New York: St. Martin's Press, 1978), p. 131.

8. National Vital Statistics Report, *Births, Marriages, Divorces, and Deaths: Provisional Data for 2005*, July 21, 2006, www.cdc.gov/nchs/data/nvsr/nvsr54/nvsr54_20.pdf (accessed July 31, 2012).

9. See Joseph J. Costa and Gordon K. Nelson, *Child Abuse and Neglect: Legislation, Reporting, and Prevention* (Lexington, MA: Heath, 1978), p. xiii.

10. Bureau of Labor Statistics, *Employment Characteristics of Families in 2008*, www.bls.gov/news.release/famee.nr0.htm (accessed July 31, 2012).

11. Tamar Lewin, "Men Assuming Bigger Role at Home, New Survey Shows," *New York Times*, April 15, 1998, p. A18.

12. U.S. Census Bureau press release, "More Young Adults Are Living in Their Parents' Home," Census Bureau Reports, November 3, 2011, www.census.gov/newsroom/releases/archives/families_households/cb11-183.html (accessed July 31, 2012).

13. *America's Children: Key National Indicators of Well-Being, 2011,* http://childstats.gov/pdf/ac2011/ac_11.pdf (accessed July 31, 2012).

14. William S. Comanor and Llad Phillips, "The Impact of Income and Family Structure on Delinquency," *Journal of Applied Economics* 5:209–232 (2002).

15. Mary Shaw, Debbie Lawlor, and Jake Najman, "Teenage Children of Teenage Mothers: Psychological, Behavioural and Health Outcomes from an Australian Prospective Longitudinal Study," *Social Science and Medicine* 62:2526–2539 (2006).

16. *America's Children: Key National Indicators of Well-Being, 2012, Child Care,* www.childstats.gov/americaschildren/tables/fam3a.asp (accessed July 31, 2012).

17. Nancy Cambria, "Missouri Prosecutors Face Limits on Punishing Illegal Day Cares," *St. Louis Post-Dispatch*, October 10, 2011, www.stltoday.com/news/special-reports/daycares/missouri-prosecutors-face-limits-on-punishing-illegal-day-cares/article_132aead4-f05d-11e0-a77c-0019bb30f31a.html (accessed July 31, 2012).

18. Annie E. Casey Foundation, *Kids Count Survey 1998*, press release.

19. Valerie Polakow, *Who Cares for Our Children? The Child Care Crisis in the Other America* (New York: Teachers College Press, 2007).

20. U.S. Census Bureau, *Projected Population of the United States, by Age and Sex: 2000 to 2050*, www.census.gov/population/www/projections/usinterim-proj/natprojtab02a.pdf (accessed July 31, 2012).

21. Christopher Sullivan, "Early Adolescent Delinquency: Assessing the Role of Childhood Problems, Family Environment, and Peer Pressure," *Youth Violence and Juvenile Justice* 4:291–313 (2006).

22. Loeber and Stouthamer-Loeber, "Family Factors," pp. 39–41.

23. Paul Howes and Howard Markman, "Marital Quality and Child Functioning: A Longitudinal Investigation," *Child Development* 60:1044–1051 (1989).

24. Andre Sourander, Henrik Elonheimo, Solja Niemelä, Art-Matti Nuutila, Hans Helenius, Lauri Sillanmäki, Jorma Piha, Tuulk Tamminen, Kirsti Kumpulkinen, Irma Moilanen, and Frederik Almovist, "Childhood Predictors of Male Criminality: A Prospective Population-Based Follow-up Study from Age 8 to Late Adolescence," *Journal of the American Academy of Child and Adolescent Psychiatry* 45:578–586 (2006).

25. Barbara Dafoe Whitehead, "Dan Quayle Was Right," *Atlantic Monthly* 271:47–84 (1993).

26. C. Patrick Brady, James Bray, and Linda Zeeb, "Behavior Problems of Clinic Children: Relation to Parental Marital Status, Age, and Sex of Child," *American Journal of Orthopsychiatry* 56:399–412 (1986).

27. Scott Henggeler, *Delinquency in Adolescence* (Newbury Park, CA: Sage, 1989), p. 48.

28. Terence P. Thornberry, Carolyn A. Smith, Craig Rivera, David Huizinga, and Magda Stouthamer-Loeber, *Family Disruption and Delinquency*, Office of Juvenile Justice and Delinquency Prevention, *Juvenile Justice Bulletin*, September 1999, www.ncjrs.gov/pdffiles1/ojjdp/178285.pdf (accessed July 31, 2012).

29. Sara McLanahan, "Father Absence and the Welfare of Children," working paper (Chicago: John D. and Catherine T. MacArthur Research Foundation, 1998).

30. Cesar Rebellon, "Reconsidering the Broken Homes/Delinquency Relationship and Exploring Its Mediating Mechanism(s)," *Criminology* 40:103–135 (2002).

31. Nicholas Wolfinger, "Parental Divorce and Offspring Marriage: Early or Late?" *Social Forces* 82:337–354 (2003); Paul Amato and Bruce Keith, "Parental Divorce and the Well-Being of Children: A Meta-Analysis," *Psychological Bulletin* 110:26–46 (1991).

32. Ronald Simons, Kuei-Hsiu Lin, Leslie Gordon, Rand Conger, and Frederick Lorenz, "Explaining the Higher Incidence of Adjustment Problems Among Children of Divorce Compared with Those in Two-Parent Families," *Journal of Marriage and the Family* 61:131–148 (1999).

33. En-Ling Pan and Michael Farrell, "Ethnic Differences in the Effects of Intergenerational Relations on Adolescent Problem Behavior in U.S. Single-Mother Families," *Journal of Family Issues* 27:1137–1158 (2006).

34. Sara Jaffee, Terrie Moffitt, Avshalom Caspi, and Alan Taylor, "Life with (or without) Father: The Benefits of Living with Two Biological Parents Depend on the Father's Antisocial Behavior," *Child Development* 74:109–117 (2003).

35. Judith Smetena, "Adolescents' and Parents' Reasoning About Actual Family Conflict," *Child Development* 60:1052–1067 (1989).

36. F. Ivan Nye, "Child Adjustment in Broken and Unhappy Unbroken Homes," *Marriage and Family* 19:356–361 (1957); Nye, *Family Relationships and Delinquent Behavior* (New York: Wiley, 1958).

37. Michael Hershorn and Alan Rosenbaum, "Children of Marital Violence: A Closer Look at the Unintended Victims," *American Journal of Orthopsychiatry* 55:260–266 (1985).

38. Peter Jaffe, David Wolfe, Susan Wilson, and Lydia Zak, "Similarities in Behavior and Social Maladjustment Among Child Victims and Witnesses to Family Violence," *American Journal of Orthopsychiatry* 56:142–146 (1986).

39. Veronica Herrera, "Equals in Risk? The Differential Impact of Family Violence on Male and Female Delinquency," paper presented at the annual meeting of the American Society of Criminology, San Diego, November 1997; Henggeler, *Delinquency in Adolescence*, p. 39.

40. Lynette Renner, "Single Types of Family Violence Victimization and Externalizing Behaviors Among Children and Adolescents," *Journal of Family Violence* 27:177–186 (2012).

41. Diana Formoso, Nancy Gonzales, and Leona Aiken, "Family Conflict and Children's Internalizing and Externalizing Behavior: Protective Factors," *American Journal of Community Psychology* 28:175–199 (2000).

42. Jill Leslie Rosenbaum, "Family Dysfunction and Female Delinquency," *Crime and Delinquency* 35:31–44 (1989).

43. Paul Robinson, "Parents of 'Beyond Control' Adolescents," *Adolescence* 13:116–119 (1978).

44. Loeber and Stouthamer-Loeber, "Development of Juvenile Aggression and Violence," p. 251.

45. Carolyn Smith, Sung Joon Jang, and Susan Stern, "The Effect of Delinquency on Families," *Family and Corrections Network Report* 13:1–11 (1997).

46. Amato and Keith, "Parental Divorce and the Well-Being of Children."

47. Christopher Kierkus and Douglas Baer, "A Social Control Explanation of the Relationship Between Family Structure and Delinquent Behaviour," *Canadian Journal of Criminology*, 44:425–458 (2002).

48. David Huh, Jennifer Tristan, Emily Wade, and Eric Stice, "Does Problem Behavior Elicit Poor Parenting? A Prospective Study of Adolescent Girls," *Journal of Adolescent Research* 21:185–204 (2006).

49. Martha Gault-Sherman, "The Bidirectional Relationship Between Parenting and Delinquency," *Journal of Youth and Adolescence* 41:121–145 (2012).

50. Sonja Siennick, "Tough Love? Crime and Parental Assistance in Young Adulthood," *Criminology* 49:163–196 (2011).

51. Judith Rich Harris, *The Nurture Assumption, Why Children Turn Out the Way They Do* (New York: Free Press, 1998).

52. John Paul Wright and Francis Cullen, "Parental Efficacy and Delinquent Behavior: Do Control and Support Matter?" *Criminology* 39:677–706 (2001).

53. Rick Trinkner, Ellen S. Cohn, Cesar J. Rebellon, and Karen Van Gundy, "Don't Trust Anyone over 30: Parental Legitimacy as a Mediator Between Parenting Style and Changes in Delinquent Behavior over Time," *Journal of Adolescence* 35:119–132 (2012).

54. Carter Hay, "Parenting, Self-Control, and Delinquency: A Test of Self-Control Theory," *Criminology* 39:707–736 (2001).

55. Sonia Cota-Robles and Wendy Gamble, "Parent–Adolescent Processes and Reduced Risk for Delinquency: The Effect of Gender for Mexican American Adolescents," *Youth and Society* 37:375–392 (2006).

56. Stephanie Hicks-Pass, "Corporal Punishment in America Today: Spare the Rod, Spoil the Child? A Systematic Review of the Literature," *Best Practices in Mental Health* 5:71–88 (2009).

57. Eric Slade and Lawrence Wissow, "Spanking in Early Childhood and Later Behavior Problems: A Prospective Study of Infants and Young Toddlers," *Pediatrics* 113:1321–1330 (2004).

58. Loeber and Stouthamer-Loeber, "Development of Juvenile Aggression and Violence," p. 251.

59. Nathaniel Pallone and James Hennessy, "Brain Dysfunction and Criminal Violence," *Society* 35:21–27 (1998).

60. Nye, *Family Relationships and Delinquent Behavior.*

61. Laurence Steinberg, Ilana Blatt-Eisengart, and Elizabeth Cauffman, "Patterns of Competence and Adjustment Among Adolescents from Authoritative, Authoritarian, Indulgent, and Neglectful Homes: A Replication in a Sample of Serious Juvenile Offenders," *Journal of Research on Adolescence* 26:47–58 (2006).

62. Lisa Broidy, "Direct Supervision and Delinquency: Assessing the Adequacy of Structural Proxies," *Journal of Criminal Justice* 23:541–554 (1995).

63. James Unnever, Francis Cullen, and Robert Agnew, "Why Is "Bad" Parenting Criminogenic? Implications from Rival Theories," *Youth Violence and Juvenile Justice* 4:3–33 (2006).

64. Bill McCarthy and John Hagan, "Mean Streets: The Theoretical Significance of Situational Delinquency Among Homeless Youth," *American Journal of Sociology* 98:597–627 (1992).

65. Jennifer Wainright and Charlotte Patterson, "Delinquency, Victimization, and Substance Use Among Adolescents with Female Same-Sex Parents," *Journal of Family Psychology* 20:526–530 (2006); Carolyn Smith, Alan Lizotte, Terence Thornberry, and Marvin Krohn, "Resilience to Delinquency," *Prevention Researcher* 4:4–7 (1997).

66. Jacinta Bronte-Tinkew, Kristin Moore, and Jennifer Carrano, "The Father–Child Relationship, Parenting Styles, and Adolescent Risk Behaviors in Intact Families," *Journal of Family Issues* 27:850–881 (2006).

67. Jang and Smith, "A Test of Reciprocal Causal Relationships Among Parental Supervision, Affective Ties, and Delinquency"; Linda Waite and Lee Lillard, "Children and Marital Disruption," *American Journal of Sociology* 96:930–953 (1991).

68. Jennifer Beyers, John Bates, Gregory Pettit, and Kenneth Dodge, "Neighborhood Structure, Parenting Processes, and the Development of Youths' Externalizing Behaviors: A Multilevel Analysis," *American Journal of Community Psychology* 31:35–53 (2003).

69. Joongyeup Lee, Hyunseok Jang, and Leana A. Bouffard, "Maternal Employment and Juvenile Delinquency: A Longitudinal Study of Korean Adolescents," *Crime and Delinquency*, first published online December 7, 2011.

70. Thomas Vander Ven and Francis Cullen, "The Impact of Maternal Employment on Serious Youth Crime: Does the Quality of Working Conditions Matter?" *Crime and Delinquency* 50:272–292 (2004); Thomas Vander Ven, Francis Cullen, Mark Carrozza, and John Paul Wright, "Home Alone: The Impact of Maternal Employment on Delinquency," *Social Problems* 48:236–257 (2001).

71. Douglas Downey, "Number of Siblings and Intellectual Development," *American Psychologist* 56:497–504 (2001); Downey, "When Bigger Is Not Better: Family Size, Parental Resources, and Children's Educational Performance," *American Sociological Review* 60:746–761 (1995).

72. G. Rahav, "Birth Order and Delinquency," *British Journal of Criminology* 20:385–395 (1980); D. Viles and D. Challinger, "Family Size and Birth Order of Young Offenders," *International Journal of Offender Therapy and Comparative Criminology* 25:60–66 (1981).

73. For an early review, see Barbara Wooton, *Social Science and Social Pathology* (London: Allen and Unwin, 1959).

74. Daniel Shaw, "Advancing Our Understanding of Intergenerational Continuity in Antisocial Behavior," *Journal of Abnormal Child Psychology* 31:193–199 (2003).

75. Marieke van de Rakt, Joseph Murray, and Paul Nieuwbeerta, "The Long-Term Effects of Paternal Imprisonment on Criminal Trajectories of Children," *Journal of Research in Crime and Delinquency* 49:81–108 (2012).

76. Joseph Murray, Rolf Loeber, and Dustin Pardini, "Parental Involvement in the Criminal Justice System and the Development of Youth Theft, Marijuana Use, Depression, and Poor Academic Performance," *Criminology* 50:255–312 (2012).

77. Michael Roettger and Raymond Swisher, ""Associations of Fathers' History of Incarceration with Sons' Delinquency and Arrest Among Black, White, and Hispanic Males in the United States," *Criminology* 49: 1109–1148 (2011).

78. Donald J. West and David P. Farrington, eds., "Who Becomes Delinquent?" in *The Delinquent Way of Life* (London: Heinemann, 1977); Donald J. West, *Delinquency: Its Roots, Careers, and Prospects* (Cambridge, MA: Harvard University Press, 1982).

79. David Farrington, "Understanding and Preventing Bullying," in *Crime and Justice*, vol. 17, ed. Michael Tonry (Chicago: University of Chicago Press, 1993), pp. 381–457.

80. Carolyn Smith and David Farrington, "Continuities in Antisocial Behavior and Parenting Across Three Generations," *Journal of Child Psychology and Psychiatry* 45:230–247 (2004).

81. John Paul Wright and Kevin Beaver, "Do Parents Matter in Creating Self-Control in Their Children? A Genetically Informed Test of Gottfredson and Hirschi's Theory of Low Self-Control," *Criminology* 43: 1169–1202 (2005).

82. Leonore Simon, "Does Criminal Offender Treatment Work?" *Applied and Preventive Psychology* 7:1–22 (1998).

83. Nancy Day, Lidush Goldschmidt, and Carrie Thomas, "Prenatal Marijuana Exposure Contributes to the Prediction of Marijuana Use at Age 14," *Addiction* 101:1313–1322 (2006).

84. Philip Harden and Robert Pihl, "Cognitive Function, Cardiovascular Reactivity, and Behavior in Boys at High Risk for Alcoholism," *Journal of Abnormal Psychology* 104:94–103 (1995).

85. Anne Dannerbeck, "Differences in Parenting Attributes, Experiences, and Behaviors of Delinquent Youth with and Without a Parental History of Incarceration," *Youth Violence and Juvenile Justice* 3:199–213 (2005).

86. Joseph Murray and David Farrington, "Parental Imprisonment: Effects on Boys' Antisocial Behaviour and Delinquency Through the Life-Course," *Journal of Child Psychology and Psychiatry* 46:1269–1278 (2005).

87. David P. Farrington, Gwen Gundry, and Donald J. West, "The Familial Transmission of Criminality," in *Crime and the Family*, ed. Alan Lincoln and Murray Straus (Springfield, IL: Charles C Thomas, 1985), pp. 193–206.

88. Peggy Giordano, *Legacies of Crime: A Follow-Up of the Children of Highly Delinquent Girls and Boys* (Cambridge, U.K.: Cambridge University Press, 2010).

89. Abigail Fagan and Jake Najman, "Sibling Influences on Adolescent Delinquent Behaviour: An Australian Longitudinal Study," *Journal of Adolescence* 26:546–558 (2003).

90. David Rowe and Bill Gulley, "Sibling Effects on Substance Use and Delinquency," *Criminology* 30:217–232 (1992); see also David Rowe, Joseph Rogers, and Sylvia Meseck-Bushey, "Sibling Delinquency and the Family Environment: Shared and Unshared Influences," *Child Development* 63:59–67 (1992).

91. Richard Gelles and Claire Pedrick Cornell, *Intimate Violence in Families*, 2nd ed. (Newbury Park, CA: Sage, 1990), p. 33.

92. Lois Hochhauser, "Child Abuse and the Law: A Mandate for Change," *Harvard Law Journal* 18:200 (1973); see also Douglas J. Besharov, "The Legal Aspects of Reporting Known and Suspected Child Abuse and Neglect," *Villanova Law Review* 23:458 (1978).

93. C. Henry Kempe, F. N. Silverman, B. F. Steele, W. Droegemueller, and H. K. Silver, "The Battered-Child Syndrome," *Journal of the American Medical Association* 181:17–24 (1962).

94. Brian G. Fraser, "A Glance at the Past, a Gaze at the Present, a Glimpse at the Future: A Critical Analysis of the Development of Child Abuse Reporting Statutes," *Chicago-Kent Law Review* 54:643 (1977–1978).

95. Centers for Disease Control and Prevention, "Heads Up: Prevent Shaken Baby Syndrome," www.cdc.gov/concussion/HeadsUp/sbs.html (accessed August 14, 2012).

96. See, especially, Inglis, *Sins of the Fathers*, Ch. 8.

97. William Downs and Brenda Miller, "Relationships Between Experiences of Parental Violence During Childhood and Women's Self-Esteem," *Violence and Victims* 13:63–78 (1998).

98. Ruth S. Kempe and C. Henry Kempe, *Child Abuse* (Cambridge, MA: Harvard University Press, 1978), pp. 6–7.

99. Fred Rogosch and Dante Cicchetti, "Child Maltreatment and Emergent Personality Organization: Perspectives from the Five-Factor Model," *Journal of Abnormal Child Psychology* 32:123–145 (2004).

100. Wendy Fisk, "Childhood Trauma and Dissociative Identity Disorder," *Child and Adolescent Psychiatric Clinics of North America* 5:431–447 (1996).

101. Centers for Disease Control and Prevention, "Heads Up: Prevent Shaken Baby Syndrome."

102. National Center for Shaken Baby Syndrome, www.dontshake.org (accessed July 31, 2012).

103. Mary Haskett and Janet Kistner, "Social Interactions and Peer Perceptions of Young Physically Abused Children," *Child Development* 62:679–690 (1991).

104. Kara Marie Brawn and Dominique Roe-Sepowitz, "Female Juvenile Prostitutes: Exploring the Relationship to Substance Use," *Children and Youth Services Review* 30:1395–1402 (2008).

105. Joe Drape, "Sandusky Guilty of Sexual Abuse of 10 Young Boys," *New York Times*, June 22, 2012, www.nytimes.com/2012/06/23/sports/ncaafootball/jerry-sandusky-convicted-of-sexually-abusing-boys.html (accessed August 14, 2012).

106. Catherine Grus, "Child Abuse: Correlations with Hostile Attributions," *Journal of Developmental and Behavioral Pediatrics* 24:296–298 (2006).

107. Kim Logio, "Gender, Race, Childhood Abuse, and Body Image Among Adolescents," *Violence Against Women* 9:931–955 (2003).

108. Jeanne Kaufman and Cathy Spatz Widom, "Childhood Victimization, Running Away, and Delinquency," *Journal of Research in Crime and Delinquency* 36:347–370 (1999).

109. N. N. Sarkar and Rina Sarkar, "Sexual Assault on Woman: Its Impact on Her Life and Living in Society," *Sexual and Relationship Therapy* 20: 407–419 (2005).

110. Michael Wiederman, Randy Sansone, and Lori Sansone, "History of Trauma and Attempted Suicide Among Women in a Primary Care Setting," *Violence and Victims* 13:3–11 (1998); Susan Leslie Bryant and Lillian Range, "Suicidality in College Women Who Were Sexually and Physically Abused and Physically Punished by Parents," *Violence and Victims* 10: 195–215 (1995); Downs and Miller, "Relationships Between Experiences of Parental Violence During Childhood and Women's Self-Esteem"; Sally Davies-Netley, Michael Hurlburt, and Richard Hough, "Childhood Abuse

as a Precursor to Homelessness for Homeless Women with Severe Mental Illness," *Violence and Victims* 11:129–142 (1996).

111. Jane Siegel and Linda Williams, "Risk Factors for Sexual Victimization of Women," *Violence Against Women* 9:902–930 (2003).

112. Michael Miner, Jill Klotz Flitter, and Beatrice Robinson, "Association of Sexual Revictimization with Sexuality and Psychological Function," *Journal of Interpersonal Violence* 21:503–524 (2006).

113. Lana Stermac and Emily Paradis, "Homeless Women and Victimization: Abuse and Mental Health History Among Homeless Rape Survivors," *Resources for Feminist Research* 28:65–81 (2001).

114. Murray Straus, Richard Gelles, and Suzanne Steinmentz, *Behind Closed Doors: Violence in the American Family* (Garden City, NY: Anchor Books, 1980); Richard Gelles and Murray Straus, "Violence in the American Family," *Journal of Social Issues* 35:15–39 (1979), at 24.

115. Richard Gelles and Murray Straus, *The Causes and Consequences of Abuse in the American Family* (New York: Simon & Schuster, 1988).

116. Julie Crandall, "Support for Spanking: Most Americans Think Corporal Punishment Is OK," http://a.abcnews.com/sections/us/DailyNews/spanking_poll021108.html (accessed July 31, 2012); Murray A. Straus and Anita K. Mathur, "Social Change and Trends in Approval of Corporal Punishment by Parents from 1968 to 1994," in *Violence Against Children*, ed. D. Frehsee, W. Horn, and K. Bussman (New York: Aldine de Gruyter, 1996), pp. 91–105.

117. Data in this and the following sections come from Department of Health and Human Services, *Child Maltreatment, 2010*, www.acf.hhs.gov/programs/cb/stats_research/index.htm#can (accessed July 31, 2012).

118. Richard Estes and Neil Alan Weiner, *The Commercial Sexual Exploitation of Children in the U.S., Canada and Mexico* (Philadelphia: University of Pennsylvania, 2001).

119. Carolyn Webster-Stratton, "Comparison of Abusive and Nonabusive Families with Conduct-Disordered Children," *American Journal of Orthopsychiatry* 55:59–69 (1985); Brandt F. Steele and Carl B. Pollock, "A Psychiatric Study of Parents Who Abuse Infants and Small Children," in *The Battered Child*, ed. Ray Helfer and C. Henry Kempe (Chicago: University of Chicago Press, 1968), pp. 103–145.

120. Douglas Ruben, *Treating Adult Children of Alcoholics: A Behavioral Approach* (New York: Academic Press, 2000).

121. Martin Daly and Margo Wilson, "Violence Against Stepchildren," *Current Directions in Psychological Science* 5:77–81 (1996).

122. Ibid.

123. Margo Wilson, Martin Daly, and Antonietta Daniele, "Familicide: The Killing of Spouse and Children," *Aggressive Behavior* 21:275–291 (1995).

124. Richard Gelles, "Child Abuse and Violence in Single-Parent Families: Parent Absence and Economic Deprivation," *American Journal of Orthopsychiatry* 59:492–501 (1989).

125. Susan Napier and Mitchell Silverman, "Family Violence as a Function of Occupation Status, Socioeconomic Class, and Other Variables," paper presented at the annual meeting of the American Society of Criminology, Boston, November 1995.

126. Robert Burgess and Patricia Draper, "The Explanation of Family Violence," in *Family Violence*, ed. Lloyd Ohlin and Michael Tonry (Chicago: University of Chicago Press, 1989), pp. 59–117.

127. Ibid., pp. 103–104.

128. *Troxel et vir. v. Granville* No. 99–138 (June 5, 2000).

129. 452 U.S. 18, 101 S.Ct. 2153 (1981); 455 U.S. 745, 102 S.Ct. 1388 (1982).

130. For a survey of each state's reporting requirements, abuse and neglect legislation, and available programs and agencies, see Costa and Nelson, *Child Abuse and Neglect*.

131. Linda Gordon, "Incest and Resistance: Patterns of Father–Daughter Incest, 1880–1930," *Social Problems* 33:253–267 (1986).

132. P.L. 93B247 (1974); P.L. 104B235 (1996).

133. Barbara Ryan, "Do You Suspect Child Abuse? The Story of 2-Year-Old Dominic James Made Headlines Not Only Because of His Tragic Death, but Because Criminal Charges Were Lodged Against a Nurse for Failing to Report His Suspicious Injuries. A Cautionary Tale," *RN* 66:73–76 (2003).

134. Robin Fretwell Wilson, "Children at Risk: The Sexual Exploitation of Female Children After Divorce," *Cornell Law Review* 86:251–327 (2001).

135. Sue Badeau and Sarah Gesiriech, *A Child's Journey Through the Child Welfare System* (Washington, DC: The Pew Commission on Children in Foster Care, 2003); Shirley Dobbin, Sophia Gatowski, and Margaret Springate, "Child Abuse and Neglect," *Juvenile and Family Court Journal* 48:43–54 (1997).

136. PBS Frontline, "Innocence Lost the Plea," www.pbs.org/wgbh/pages/frontline/shows/innocence/etc/other.html (accessed July 31, 2012); for an analysis of the accuracy of children's recollections of abuse, see Candace Kruttschnitt and Maude Dornfeld, "Will They Tell? Assessing

Preadolescents' Reports of Family Violence," *Journal of Research in Crime and Delinquency* 29:136–147 (1992).

137. Ibid.

138. Debra Whitcomb, *When the Victim Is a Child* (Washington, DC: National Institute of Justice, 1992), p. 33.

139. *White v. Illinois*, 502 U.S. 346; 112 S.Ct. 736 (1992).

140. Myrna Raeder, "*White*'s Effect on the Right to Confront One's Accuser," *Criminal Justice*, Winter 2–7 (1993).

141. *Coy v. Iowa*, 487 U.S. 1012 (1988).

142. *Maryland v. Craig*, 110 S.Ct. 3157 (1990).

143. Joshua Mersky, James Topitzes, and Arthur J. Reynolds, "Unsafe at Any Age: Linking Childhood and Adolescent Maltreatment to Delinquency and Crime" *Journal of Research in Crime and Delinquency*, first published on August 1, 2011; Cesar Rebellon and Karen Van Gundy, "Can Control Theory Explain the Link Between Parental Physical Abuse and Delinquency? A Longitudinal Analysis," *Journal of Research in Crime and Delinquency* 42:247–274 (2005).

144. Jennifer Lansford, Laura Wager, John Bates, Gregory Pettit, and Kenneth Dodge, Kenneth, "Forms of Spanking and Children's Externalizing Behaviors," *Family Relations* 6:224–236 (2012).

145. Sara Culhane and Heather Taussig, "The Structure of Problem Behavior in a Sample of Maltreated Youths," *Social Work Research* 33:70–78 (2009).

146. Egbert Zavala, "Testing the Link Between Child Maltreatment and Family Violence Among Police Officers," *Crime and Delinquency*, first published online November 22, 2010.

147. Cathy Widom and Michael Maxfield, "An Update on the 'Cycle of Violence'," National Institute of Justice, 2001, www.ncjrs.gov/pdffiles1/nij/184894.pdf (accessed July 31, 2012).

148. Min Kim Jung, Emiko Tajima, Todd Herrenkohl, and Bu Huang, "Early Child Maltreatment, Runaway Youths, and Risk of Delinquency and Victimization in Adolescence: A Mediational Model," *Social Work Research* 33: 19–28 (2009).

149. Timothy Ireland, Carolyn Smith, and Terence Thornberry, "Developmental Issues in the Impact of Child Maltreatment on Later Delinquency and Drug Use," *Criminology* 40:359–401 (2002).

150. Kristi Holsinger and Alexander Holsinger, "Differential Pathways to Violence and Self-Injurious Behavior: African American and White Girls in the Juvenile Justice System," *Journal of Research in Crime and Delinquency* 42:211–242 (2005).

151. Margaret Stevenson, "Perceptions of Juvenile Offenders Who Were Abused as Children," *Journal of Aggression, Maltreatment and Trauma* 18:331–349 (2009).

Chapter 8. Peers and Delinquency: Juvenile Gangs and Groups

1. For a general review, see Scott Cummings and Daniel Monti, *Gangs: The Origin and Impact of Contemporary Youth Gangs in the United States* (Albany: SUNY Press, 1993).

2. Paul Perrone and Meda Chesney-Lind, "Representations of Gangs and Delinquency: Wild in the Streets?" *Social Justice* 24:96–117 (1997).

3. John Hagedorn, "The Global Impact of Gangs," *Journal of Contemporary Criminal Justice* 21:153–169 (2005).

4. John Coie and Shari Miller-Johnson, "Peer Factors in Early Offending Behavior," in *Child Delinquents*, ed. Rolf Loeber and David Farrington (Thousand Oaks, CA: Sage, 2001), pp. 191–210.

5. Ibid.

6. Judith Rich Harris, *The Nurture Assumption: Why Children Turn Out the Way They Do* (New York: Free Press, 1998).

7. Ibid., p. 463.

8. J. C. Barnes and Robert Morris, "Young Mothers, Delinquent Children: Assessing Mediating Factors Among American Youth," *Youth Violence and Juvenile Justice* 10:172–189 (2012).

9. Peggy Giordano, "The Wider Circle of Friends in Adolescence," *American Journal of Sociology* 101:661–697 (1995).

10. Thomas Berndt and T. B. Perry, "Children's Perceptions of Friendships as Supportive Relationships," *Developmental Psychology* 22:640–648 (1986).

11. Annette La Greca and Hannah Moore Harrison, "Adolescent Peer Relations, Friendships, and Romantic Relationships: Do They Predict Social Anxiety and Depression?" *Journal of Clinical Child and Adolescent Psychology* 34:49–61 (2005).

12. Brett Laursen, Christopher Hafen, Margaret Kerr, and Hakin Stattin, "Friend Influence over Adolescent Problem Behaviors as a Function of Relative Peer Acceptance: To Be Liked Is to Be Emulated," *Journal of Abnormal Psychology* 121:88–94 (2012).

13. Shari Miller-Johnson, Philip Costanzo, John Coie, Mary Rose, Dorothy Browne, and Courtney Johnson, "Peer Social Structure and Risk-Taking Behaviors Among African-American Early Adolescents," *Journal of Youth and Adolescence* 32:375–384 (2003).

14. Caterina Gouvis Roman, Meagan Cahill, Pamela Lachman, Samantha Lowry, Carlena Orosco, and Christopher McCarty, with Megan Denver and Juan Pedroza, *Social Networks, Delinquency, and Gang Membership: Using a Neighborhood Framework to Examine the Influence of Network Composition and Structure in a Latino Community* (Washington, DC: Urban Institute, 2012), www.urban.org/UploadedPDF/412519-Social-Networks-Delinquency-and-Gang-Membership.pdf (accessed August 13, 2012).

15. Carter Rees and Greg Pogarsky, "One Bad Apple May Not Spoil the Whole Bunch: Best Friends and Adolescent Delinquency," *Journal of Quantitative Criminology* 27:197–223 (2011).

16. Albert Reiss, "Co-Offending and Criminal Careers," in *Crime and Justice*, vol. 10, ed. Michael Tonry and Norval Morris (Chicago: University of Chicago Press, 1988).

17. Maury Nation and Craig Anne Heflinger, "Risk Factors for Serious Alcohol and Drug Use: The Role of Psychosocial Variables in Predicting the Frequency of Substance Use Among Adolescents," *American Journal of Drug and Alcohol Abuse* 32:415–433 (2006).

18. Kevin Beaver and John Paul Wright, "Biosocial Development and Delinquent Involvement," *Youth Violence and Juvenile Justice* 3:168–192 (2005).

19. Richard Felson and Dana Haynie, "Pubertal Development, Social Factors, and Delinquency Among Adolescent Boys," *Criminology* 40:967–989 (2002).

20. Brett Johnson Solomon, "Other-Sex Friendship Involvement Among Delinquent Adolescent Females," *Youth Violence and Juvenile Justice* 4:75–96 (2006).

21. See Travis Hirschi, *Causes of Delinquency* (Berkeley: University of California Press, 1969).

22. James Short and Fred Strodtbeck, *Group Process and Gang Delinquency* (Chicago: Aldine de Gruyter, 1965).

23. Terence Thornberry and Marvin Krohn, "Peers, Drug Use, and Delinquency," in *Handbook of Antisocial Behavior*, ed. David Stoff, James Breiling, and Jack Maser (New York: Wiley, 1997), pp. 218–233.

24. Mark Warr, "Age, Peers, and Delinquency," *Criminology* 31:17–40 (1993).

25. Stephen W. Baron, "Self-Control, Social Consequences, and Criminal Behavior: Street Youth and the General Theory of Crime," *Journal of Research in Crime and Delinquency* 40:403–425 (2003).

26. Daneen Deptula and Robert Cohen, "Aggressive, Rejected, and Delinquent Children and Adolescents: A Comparison of Their Friendships," *Aggression and Violent Behavior* 9:75–104 (2004).

27. Kate Keenan, Rolf Loeber, Quanwu Zhang, Magda Stouthamer-Loeber, and Welmoet Van Kammen, "The Influence of Deviant Peers on the Development of Boys' Disruptive and Delinquent Behavior: A Temporal Analysis," *Development and Psychopathology* 7:715–726 (1995).

28. Kim C. I. M. Megens and Frank M. Weerman, "The Social Transmission of Delinquency: Effects of Peer Attitudes and Behavior Revisited," *Journal of Research in Crime and Delinquency*, first published August 22, 2011.

29. David Maimon and Christopher R. Browning, "Unstructured Socializing, Collective Efficacy, and Violent Behavior Among Urban Youth," *Criminology* 48:443–474 (2010).

30. Jacob Young, J. C. Barnes, Ryan Meldrum, and Frank Weerman, "Assessing and Explaining Misperceptions of Peer Delinquency," *Criminology* 49:599–630 (2011).

31. Derek Kreager, Kelly Rulison, and James Moody, "Delinquency and the Structure of Adolescent Peer Groups," *Criminology* 49:95–127 (2011).

32. Peggy Giordano, Stephen Cernkovich, and M. D. Pugh, "Friendships and Delinquency," *American Journal of Sociology* 91:1170–1202 (1986).

33. Jean Marie McGloin and Wendy Povitsky Stickle, "Influence or Convenience? Disentangling Peer Influence and Co-offending for Chronic Offenders," *Journal of Research in Crime and Delinquency* 48:419–447 (2011).

34. Gregory Zimmerman and Bob Edward Vásquez, "Decomposing the Peer Effect on Adolescent Substance Use: Mediation, Nonlinearity, and Differential Nonlinearity," *Criminology* 49:1235–1272 (2011).

35. Frank Weerman, "Delinquent Peers in Context: A Longitudinal Network Analysis of Selection and Influence Effects," *Criminology* 49:253–286 (2011).

36. Jean Marie McGloin, "Delinquency Balance and Time Use: A Research Note," *Journal of Research in Crime and Delinquency* 49:109–121 (2012).

37. David Farrington and Rolf Loeber, "Epidemiology of Juvenile Violence," *Child and Adolescent Psychiatric Clinics of North America* 9:733–748 (2000).

38. Well-known movie representations of gangs include *The Wild Ones* and *Hell's Angels on Wheels*, which depict motorcycle gangs, and *Saturday Night Fever*, which focused on neighborhood street toughs; see also David Dawley, *A Nation of Lords* (Garden City, NY: Anchor, 1973).

39. For a recent example of gang research, see Aleljandro del Carmen, John J. Rodriguez, Rhonda Dobbs, Richard Smith, Randall R. Butler, and Robert Sarver III, "In Their Own Words: A Study of Gang Members Through Their Own Perspective," *Journal of Gang Research* 16:57–76 (2009).

40. Walter Miller, *Violence by Youth Gangs and Youth Groups as a Crime Problem in Major American Cities* (Washington, DC: U.S. Government Printing Office, 1975).

41. Malcolm Klein, *The American Street Gang: Its Nature, Prevalence, and Control* (New York: Oxford University Press, 1995), p. 30.

42. National Gang Center, www.nationalgangcenter.gov/About/FAQ#q10 (accessed August 14, 2012).

43. Irving Spergel, *The Youth Gang Problem: A Community Approach* (New York: Oxford University Press, 1995).

44. Ibid., p. 3.

45. Christopher Adamson, "Defensive Localism in White and Black: A Comparative History of European-American and African-American Youth Gangs," *Ethnic and Racial Studies* 23:272–298 (2000).

46. Frederick Thrasher, *The Gang* (Chicago: University of Chicago Press, 1927).

47. Irving Spergel, *Street Gang Work: Theory and Practice* (Reading, MA: Addison-Wesley, 1966).

48. Miller, *Violence by Youth Gangs*, p. 2.

49. Ibid.

50. Felix Padilla, *The Gang as an American Enterprise* (New Brunswick, NJ: Rutgers University Press, 1992), p. 3.

51. Pamela Irving Jackson, "Crime, Youth Gangs, and Urban Transition: The Social Dislocations of Postindustrial Economic Development," *Justice Quarterly* 8:379–897 (1991); Joan Moore, *Going Down to the Barrio: Homeboys and Homegirls in Change*, (Philadelphia: Temple University Press, 1991), pp. 89–101.

52. Moore, *Going Down to the Barrio.*

53. Data in this and the following sections come from Arlen Egley, Jr., and James C. Howell, *Highlights of the 2009 National Youth Gang Survey* (Washington, DC: Office of Juvenile Justice and Delinquency Prevention, 2011), www.ncjrs.gov/pdffiles1/ojjdp/233581.pdf (accessed August 13, 2012).

54. Ibid.

55. William Julius Wilson, *The Truly Disadvantaged* (Chicago: University of Chicago Press, 1987).

56. David C. Pyrooz, "Structural Covariates of Gang Homicide in Large U.S. Cities," *Journal of Research in Crime and Delinquency*, first published on August 17, 2011.

57. Joan Moore, James Diego Vigil, and Robert Garcia, "Residence and Territoriality in Chicano Gangs," *Social Problems* 31:182–194 (1983).

58. Mark Warr, "Organization and Instigation in Delinquent Groups," *Criminology* 34:11–37 (1996).

59. Malcolm Klein, "Impressions of Juvenile Gang Members," *Adolescence* 3:59 (1968).

60. Scott Decker, Tim Bynum, and Deborah Weisel, "A Tale of Two Cities: Gangs and Organized Crime Groups," *Justice Quarterly* 15:395–425 (1998).

61. Information in this section comes from the National Gang Intelligence Center, *National Gang Threat Assessment, 2011*, www.fbi.gov/stats-services/publications/2011-national-gang-threat-assessment/2011-national-gang-threat-assessment#CurrentGang (accessed August 13, 2012).

62. Ibid.

63. Ibid.

64. Jeffrey Fagan, "The Social Organization of Drug Use and Drug Dealing Among Urban Gangs," *Criminology* 27:633–669 (1996).

65. Ibid.

66. Avelardo Valdez and Stephen J. Sifaneck, "Getting High and Getting By: Dimensions of Drug Selling Behaviors Among U.S. Mexican Gang Members in South Texas," *Journal of Research in Crime and Delinquency* 41:82–105 (2004).

67. National Gang Center, "Are Today's Youth Gangs Different from Gangs in the Past?" www.nationalgangcenter.gov/About/FAQ#q9 (accessed August 14, 2012).

68. Lewis Yablonsky, *The Violent Gang* (Baltimore: Penguin, 1966), p. 109.

69. James Diego Vigil, *Barrio Gangs* (Austin: Texas University Press, 1988), pp. 11–19.

70. David C. Pyrooz, Gary Sweeten, and Alex R. Piquero, "Continuity and Change in Gang Membership and Gang Embeddedness," *Journal of Research in Crime and Delinquency*, online publication February 7, 2012.

71. Jean Marie McGloin, "The Organizational Structure of Street Gangs in Newark, New Jersey: A Network Analysis Methodology" *Journal of Gang Research* 15:1–34 (2007).

72. Mark Warr, "Organization and Instigation in Delinquent Groups," *Criminology* 34:11–37 (1996).

73. Wilson, *The Truly Disadvantaged*.

74. Ibid.

75. John Hagedorn, "The Global Impact of Gangs," *Journal of Contemporary Criminal Justice* 21:153–169 (2005).

76. National Gang Center, 2012.

77. Finn-Aage Esbensen, Bradley Brick, Chris Melde, Karin Tusinski, and Terrance Taylor, "The Role of Race and Ethnicity of Gang Membership," in *Youth Gangs, Migration, and Ethnicity*, ed. Frank van Gemert, Dana Peterson, and Inger-Lise Lien (Uffculme, Devon, UK: Willan Publishing Company, 2008), pp. 117–139.

78. Mars Eghigian and Katherine Kirby, "Girls in Gangs: On the Rise in America," *Corrections Today* 68:48–50 (2006).

79. Ibid.

80. Mark Fleisher and Jessie Krienert, "Life-Course Events, Social Networks, and the Emergence of Violence Among Female Gang Members" *Journal of Community Psychology* 32:607–622 (2004).

81. Karen Joe-Laidler and Geoffrey Hunt, "Violence and Social Organization in Female Gangs," *Social Justice* 24:148–187 (1997); Moore, *Going Down to the Barrio*; Anne Campbell, *The Girls in the Gang* (Cambridge, MA: Basil Blackwell, 1984).

82. Karen Joe-Laidler and Meda Chesney-Lind, "'Just Every Mother's Angel': An Analysis of Gender and Ethnic Variations in Youth Gang Membership," *Gender and Society* 9:408–430 (1995).

83. Jody Miller, *One of the Guys: Girls, Gangs, and Gender* (New York: Oxford University Press, 2001).

84. Ibid.

85. Fleisher and Krienert, "Life-Course Events, Social Networks, and the Emergence of Violence Among Female Gang Members."

86. The following description of ethnic gangs leans heavily on the material developed in National School Safety Center, *Gangs in Schools*, pp. 11–23.

87. National Gang Intelligence Center, *National Gang Threat Assessment, 2009*.

88. Abigail Goldman, "What's in a Name? Police Guard Trove of Gangster Monikers, Often the Only Names by Which Suspects Are Known," *Las Vegas Sun*, April 7, 2008, www.lasvegassun.com/news/2008/apr/07/whats-name/ (accessed August 13, 2012).

89. Thomas Winfree, Jr., Frances Bernat, and Finn-Aage Esbensen, "Hispanic and Anglo Gang Membership in Two Southwestern Cities," *Social Science Journal* 38:105–118 (2001).

90. Douglas Yearwood and Alison Rhyne, "Hispanic/Latino Gangs: A Comparative Analysis of Nationally Affiliated and Local Gangs," *Journal of Gang Research* 14:1–18 (2007).

91. James Howell, *The Impact of Gangs on Communities* (Washington, DC: Office of Juvenile Justice and Delinquency Prevention, 2006).

92. Arian Campo-Flores, "The Most Dangerous Gang in the United States," *Newsweek*, March 28, 2006; Ricardo Pollack, "Gang Life Tempts Salvador Teens," BBC News, http://news.bbc.co.uk/2/hi/americas/4201183.stm (accessed August 13, 2012).

93. National Gang Intelligence Center, *National Gang Threat Assessment, 2009*.

94. James Diego Vigil and Steve Chong Yun, "Vietnamese Youth Gangs in Southern California," in *Gangs in America*, ed. C. Ronald Huff (Newbury Park, CA: Sage Publications, 1990), pp. 146–163.

95. Anthony Braga, Jack McDevitt, and Glenn Pierce, "Understanding and Preventing Gang Violence: Problem Analysis and Response Development in Lowell, Massachusetts," *Police Quarterly* 9:20–46 (2006).

96. For a review, see Lawrence Trostle, *The Stoners: Drugs, Demons and Delinquency* (New York: Garland, 1992).

97. Janice Joseph, "Gangs and Gang Violence in School," *Journal of Gang Research* 16:33–50 (2008); Darlene Wright and Kevin Fitzpatrick, "Violence and Minority Youth: The Effects of Risk and Asset Factors on Fighting Among African American Children and Adolescents," *Adolescence* 41:251–262 (2006).

98. G. David Curry, Scott Decker, and Arlen Egley, Jr., "Gang Involvement and Delinquency in a Middle School Population," *Justice Quarterly* 19:275–292 (2002).

99. Chris Melde and Finn-Aage Esbensen, "Gangs and Violence: Disentangling the Impact of Gang Membership on the Level and Nature of Offending," *Journal of Quantitative Criminology*, first published online January 24, 2012.

100. Uberto Gatti, Richard Tremblay, Frank Vitaro, and Pierre McDuff, "Youth Gangs, Delinquency and Drug Use: A Test of the Selection, Facilitation, and Enhancement Hypotheses," *Journal of Child Psychology and Psychiatry* 46:1178–1190 (2005).

101. Malcolm Klein, Cheryl Maxson, and Lea Cunningham, "Crack, Street Gangs, and Violence," *Criminology* 4:623–650 (1991); Mel Wallace, "The Gang-Drug Debate Revisited," paper presented at the annual meeting of the American Society of Criminology, New Orleans, November 1992.

102. Beth Bjerregaard, "Gang Membership and Drug Involvement: Untangling the Complex Relationship," *Crime and Delinquency* 56:3–34 (2010).

103. Kevin Thompson, David Brownfield, and Ann Marie Sorenson, "Specialization Patterns of Gang and Nongang Offending: A Latent Structure Analysis," *Journal of Gang Research* 3:25–35 (1996).

104. Sara Battin, Karl Hill, Robert Abbott, Richard Catalano, and J. David Hawkins, "The Contribution of Gang Membership to Delinquency Beyond Delinquent Friends," *Criminology* 36:93–116 (1998).

105. Geoffrey Hunt, Karen Joe-Laidler, and Kristy Evans, "The Meaning and Gendered Culture of Getting High: Gang Girls and Drug Use Issues," *Contemporary Drug Problems* 29:375 (2002).

106. Terence Thornberry, Marvin Krohn, Alan Lizotte, Carolyn Smith, and Kimberly Tobin, *Gangs and Delinquency in Developmental Perspective* (New York: Cambridge University Press, 2003).

107. Michael Vaughn, Matthew Howard, and Lisa Harper-Chang, "Do Prior Trauma and Victimization Predict Weapon Carrying Among Delinquent Youth?" *Youth Violence and Juvenile Justice* 4:314–327 (2006).

108. Thornberry et al., *Gangs and Delinquency in Developmental Perspective*.

109. Richard Spano and John Bolland, "Is the Nexus of Gang Membership, Exposure to Violence, and Violent Behavior a Key Determinant of First Time Gun Carrying for Urban Minority Youth?" *Justice Quarterly* 28: 838–862 (2011).

110. Howell, *The Impact of Gangs on Communities*, p. 3.

111. Ibid.

112. James C. Howell, "Youth Gang Drug Trafficking and Homicide: Policy and Program Implications," *Juvenile Justice Journal* 4:3–5 (1997).

113. Beth Bjerregaard and Alan Lizotte, "Gun Ownership and Gang Membership," *Journal of Criminal Law and Criminology* 86:37–53 (1995).

114. Ibid.

115. Pamela Lattimore, Richard Linster, and John MacDonald, "Risk of Death Among Serious Young Offenders," *Journal of Research in Crime and Delinquency* 34:187–209 (1997).

116. Scott Decker, "Collective and Normative Features of Gang Violence," *Justice Quarterly* 13:243–266 (1996).

117. Gini Sykes, *8 Ball Chicks: A Year in the Violent World of Girl Gangsters* (New York: Doubleday, 1998), pp. 2–11.

118. H. Range Hutson, Deirdre Anglin, and Michael Pratts, Jr., "Adolescents and Children Injured or Killed in Drive-By Shootings in Los Angeles," *New England Journal of Medicine* 330:324–327 (1994); Miller, *Violence by Youth Gangs*, pp. 2–26.

119. Herbert Block and Arthur Niederhoffer, *The Gang: A Study in Adolescent Behavior* (New York: Philosophical Library, 1958).

120. Ibid., p. 113.

121. James Diego Vigil, "Group Processes and Street Identity: Adolescent Chicano Gang Members," *Ethos* 16:421–445 (1988).

122. James Diego Vigil and John Long, "Emic and Etic Perspectives on Gang Culture: The Chicano Case," in *Gangs in America*, ed. C. Ronald Huff (Newbury Park, CA: Sage, 1990), p. 66.

123. Albert Cohen, *Delinquent Boys* (New York: Free Press, 1955), pp. 1–19.

124. Irving Spergel, *Racketville, Slumtown, and Haulburg: An Exploratory Study of Delinquent Subcultures* (Chicago: University of Chicago Press, 1964).

125. Malcolm Klein, *Street Gangs and Street Workers* (Englewood Cliffs, NJ: Prentice Hall, 1971), pp. 12–15.

126. Richard Cloward and Lloyd Ohlin, *Delinquency and Opportunity: A Theory of Delinquent Gangs* (New York: Free Press, 1960).

127. Charles M. Katz and Stephen M. Schnebly, "Neighborhood Variation in Gang Member Concentrations," *Crime and Delinquency* 57:377–407 (2011).

128. Spergel, *The Youth Gang Problem*, pp. 4–5.

129. Ibid.

130. John Hagedorn, Jose Torres, and Greg Giglio, "Cocaine, Kicks, and Strain: Patterns of Substance Use in Milwaukee Gangs," *Contemporary Drug Problems* 25:113–145 (1998).

131. Jon Gunnar Bernburg, Marvin Krohn, and Craig Rivera, "Official Labeling, Criminal Embeddedness, and Subsequent Delinquency: A Longitudinal Test of Labeling Theory," *Journal of Research in Crime and Delinquency* 43:67–88 (2006).

132. Chris Melde and Finn-Aage Esbensen, "Gang Membership as a Turning Point in the Life Course," *Criminology* 49:513–552 (2011).

133. Veronique Dupere, Eric Lacourse, J. Douglas Willms, Frank Vitaro, and Richard E. Tremblay, "Affiliation to Youth Gangs During Adolescence: The Interaction Between Childhood Psychopathic Tendencies and Neighborhood Disadvantage," *Journal of Abnormal Child Psychology* 35: 1035–1045 (2007).

134. Yablonsky, *The Violent Gang*, p. 237.

135. Klein, *The American Street Gang*.

136. Mercer Sullivan, *Getting Paid: Youth Crime and Work in the Inner City* (Ithaca, NY: Cornell University Press, 1989), pp. 244–245.

137. Finn-Aage Esbensen and David Huizinga, "Gangs, Drugs, and Delinquency in a Survey of Urban Youth, *Criminology* 31:565–587 (1993).

138. Padilla, *The Gang as an American Enterprise*, p. 103.

139. Kathleen MacKenzie, Geoffrey Hunt, and Karen Joe-Laidler, "Youth Gangs and Drugs: The Case of Marijuana," *Journal of Ethnicity in Substance Abuse* 4:99–134 (2005).

140. Terence Thornberry, Marvin Krohn, Alan Lizotte, and Deborah Chard-Wierschem, "The Role of Juvenile Gangs in Facilitating Delinquent Behavior," *Journal of Research in Crime and Delinquency* 30:55–87 (1993).

141. Spergel, *The Youth Gang Problem*, pp. 93–94.

142. Miller, *One of the Guys.*

143. Ibid., p. 93.

144. L. Thomas Winfree, Jr., Teresa Vigil Backstrom, and G. Larry Mays, "Social Learning Theory, Self-Reported Delinquency, and Youth Gangs: A New Twist on a General Theory of Crime and Delinquency," *Youth and Society* 26:147–177 (1994).

145. Karen Joe-Laidler and Geoffrey Hunt, "Violence and Social Organization in Female Gangs," *Social Justice* 24:148–187 (1997).

146. Chanequa Walker-Barnes and Craig A. Mason, "Delinquency and Substance Use Among Gang-Involved Youth: The Moderating Role of Parenting Practices," *American Journal of Community Psychology* 34:235–250 (2004).

147. Jerome Needle and W. Vaughan Stapleton, *Reports of the National Juvenile Justice Assessment Centers, Police Handling of Youth Gangs* (Washington, DC: Office of Juvenile Justice and Delinquency Prevention, 1983).

148. National Gang Center, *National Youth Gang Survey Analysis*.

149. Scott Armstrong, "Los Angeles Seeks New Ways to Handle Gangs," *Christian Science Monitor*, April 23, 1988, p. 3.

150. Barry Krisberg, "Preventing and Controlling Violent Youth Crime: The State of the Art," in *Violent Juvenile Crime*, ed. Ira Schwartz (Minneapolis: University of Minnesota, Hubert Humphrey Institute of Public Affairs, n.d.).

151. City of Stockton, California, "Operation Peacekeepers," www.stocktongov.com/government/departments/manager/peacekeepers.html (accessed August 13, 2012).

152. Quint Thurman, Andrew Giacomazzi, Michael Reisig, and David Mueller, "Community-Based Gang Prevention and Intervention: An Evaluation of the Neutral Zone," *Crime and Delinquency* 42:279–296 (1996).

153. Finn-Aage Esbensen, Dana Peterson, Terrance J. Taylor, and D. Wayne Osgood, "Results from a Multi-Site Evaluation of the G.R.E.A.T. Program," *Justice Quarterly* 29:125–151 (2012).

154. Curry and Spergel, "Gang Involvement and Delinquency Among Hispanic and African-American Adolescent Males."

155. Hagedorn, "Gangs, Neighborhoods, and Public Policy."

Chapter 9. Schools and Delinquency

1. Alexander Vazsonyi and Lloyd Pickering, "The Importance of Family and School Domains in Adolescent Deviance: African American and Caucasian Youth," *Journal of Youth and Adolescence* 32:115–129 (2003).

2. See, generally, Richard Lawrence, *School Crime and Juveniles* (New York: Oxford University Press, 1998).

3. U.S. Office of Education, *Digest of Educational Statistics* (Washington, DC: U.S. Government Printing Office, 1969), p. 25.

4. Kenneth Polk and Walter E. Schafer, eds., *Schools and Delinquency* (Englewood Cliffs, NJ: Prentice Hall, 1972), p. 13.

5. Gary LaFree and Richard Arum, "The Impact of Racially Inclusive Schooling on Adult Incarceration Rates Among U.S. Cohorts of African Americans and Whites Since 1930," *Criminology* 44:73–103 (2006).

6. National Center for Educational Statistics, "Status and Trends in the Education of Racial and Ethnic Minorities," http://nces.ed.gov/pubs2010/2010015/ (accessed August 15, 2012).

7. United States Department of Education, "Trends in International Mathematics and Science Study (TIMSS)," http://nces.ed.gov/timss/table07_1.asp (accessed August 15, 2012).

8. Lynn Karoly, M. Rebecca Kilburn, and Jill Cannon, *Early Childhood Interventions: Proven Results, Future Promise* (Santa Monica, CA: Rand Corporation, 2005).

9. Ibid.

10. Jay Teachman, Kathleen Paasch, and Karen Carver, "Social Capital and the Generation of Human Capital," *Social Forces* 75:1343–1360 (1997).

11. Secretary Arne Duncan's Remarks at the Release of America's Promise Alliance Report, "Building a Grad Nation," November 30, 2010, www.ed.gov/news/speeches/secretary-arne-duncans-remarks-release-america%E2%80%99s-promise-alliance-report-%E2%80%9Cbuilding-gra (accessed August 15, 2012).

12. Chris Chapman, Jennifer Laird, and Angelina Kewal Ramani, *Trends in High School Dropout and Completion Rates in the United States: 1972–2008, Compendium Report*, National Center for Education Statistics, December 2010, http://nces.ed.gov/pubs2011/2011012.pdf (accessed August 15, 2012).

13. G. Roger Jarjoura, "Does Dropping Out of School Enhance Delinquent Involvement? Results from a Large-Scale National Probability Sample," *Criminology* 31:149–172 (1993); Terence Thornberry, Melanie Moore, and R. L. Christenson, "The Effect of Dropping Out of High School on Subsequent Criminal Behavior," *Criminology* 23:3–18 (1985).

14. Gary Sweeten, Shawn D. Bushway, and Raymond Paternoster, "Does Dropping Out of School Mean Dropping into Delinquency?" *Criminology* 47:47–92 (2009).

15. Kimberly Henry, Kelly Knight, and Terence Thornberry, "School Disengagement as a Predictor of Dropout, Delinquency, and Problem Substance Use During Adolescence and Early Adulthood," *Journal of Youth and Adolescence* 41:156–166 (2012).

16. The following is from Jessica B. Heppen and Susan Bowles Therriault, "Developing Early Warning Systems to Identify Potential High School Dropouts," National High School Center, www.betterhighschools.org/pubs/ews_guide.asp (accessed August 15, 2012).

17. Spencer Rathus, *Voyages in Childhood* (Belmont, CA: Wadsworth, 2004).

18. Sherman Dorn, *Creating the Dropout* (New York: Praeger, 1996).

19. Michael Rocques and Raymond Paternoster, "Understanding the Antecedents of the 'School-to-Jail' Link: The Relationship Between Race and School Discipline," *Journal of Criminal Law and Criminology* 101:633–665 (2011).

20. Allison Ann Payne and Kelly Welch, "Modeling the Effects of Racial Threat on Punitive and Restorative School Discipline Practices," *Criminology* 48:1019–1062 (2010).

21. For reviews, see Bruce Wolford and LaDonna Koebel, "Kentucky Model for Youths at Risk," *Criminal Justice* 9:5–55 (1995); J. David Hawkins, Richard Catalano, Diane Morrison, Julie O'Donnell, Robert Abbott, and L. Edward Day, "The Seattle Social Development Project," in *The Prevention of Antisocial Behavior in Children*, ed. Joan McCord and Richard Tremblay (New York: Guilford Press, 1992), pp. 139–160.

22. Eugene Maguin and Rolf Loeber, "Academic Performance and Delinquency," in *Crime and Justice: A Review of Research*, vol. 20, ed. Michael Tonry (Chicago: University of Chicago Press, 1995), pp. 145–264.

23. Terence Thornberry, Alan Lizotte, Marvin Krohn, Margaret Farnworth, and Sung Joon Jang, "Testing Interactional Theory: An Examination of Reciprocal Causal Relationships Among Family, School, and Delinquency," *Journal of Criminal Law and Criminology* 82:3–35 (1991).

24. Carolyn Smith, Alan Lizotte, Terence Thornberry, and Marvin Krohn, "Resilience to Delinquency," *Prevention Researcher* 4:4–7 (1997); Matthew Zingraff, Jeffrey Leiter, Matthew Johnsen, and Kristen Myers, "The Mediating Effect of Good School Performance on the Maltreatment–Delinquency Relationship," *Journal of Research in Crime and Delinquency* 31:62–91 (1994).

25. Lyle Shannon, *Assessing the Relationship of Adult Criminal Careers to Juvenile Careers: A Summary* (Washington, DC: U.S. Government Printing Office, 1982).

26. Marvin Wolfgang, Robert Figlio, and Thorsten Sellin, *Delinquency in a Birth Cohort* (Chicago: University of Chicago Press, 1972).

27. Ibid., p. 94.

28. U.S. Department of Education, *Literacy Behind Bars, 2003*, http://nces.ed.gov/pubs2007/2007473_3.pdf (accessed August 15, 2012).

29. M. Brent Donnellan, Kali H. Trzesniewski, Richard W. Robins, Terrie E. Moffitt, and Avshalom Caspi, "Low Self-Esteem Is Related to Aggression, Antisocial Behavior, and Delinquency" *Psychological Science* 16:328–335 (2005).

30. Paul Bellair and Thomas McNulty, "Beyond the Bell Curve: Community Disadvantage and the Explanation of Black-White Differences in Adolescent Violence," *Criminology* 43:1135–1168 (2005).

31. Michael Gottfredson and Travis Hirschi, *A General Theory of Crime* (Stanford, CA: Stanford University Press, 1990); J. D. McKinney, "Longitudinal Research on the Behavioral Characteristics of Children with Learning Disabilities," *Journal of Learning Disabilities* 22:141–150 (1990).

32. Richard Felson and Jeremy Staff, "Explaining the Academic Performance–Delinquency Relationship," *Criminology* 44:299–320 (2006).

33. Albert K. Cohen, *Delinquent Boys* (New York: Free Press, 1955); see also Kenneth Polk, Dean Frease, and F. Lynn Richmond, "Social Class, School Experience, and Delinquency," *Criminology* 12:84–95 (1974).

34. Jackson Toby, "Orientation to Education as a Factor in the School Maladjustment of Lower-Class Children," *Social Forces* 35:259–266 (1957).

35. John Paul Wright, Francis Cullen, and Nicolas Williams, "Working While in School and Delinquent Involvement: Implications for Social Policy," *Crime and Delinquency* 43:203–221 (1997).

36. Polk, Frease, and Richmond, "Social Class, School Experience, and Delinquency," p. 92.

37. Delos Kelly and Robert Balch, "Social Origins and School Failure," *Pacific Sociological Review* 14:413–430 (1971).

38. Lance Hannon, "Poverty, Delinquency, and Educational Attainment: Cumulative Disadvantage or Disadvantage Saturation?" *Sociological Inquiry* 73:575–595 (2003).

39. Jeannie Oakes, *Keeping Track: How Schools Structure Inequality* (New Haven, CT: Yale University Press, 1985), p. 48.

40. Delos Kelly, *Creating School Failure, Youth Crime, and Deviance* (Los Angeles: Trident Shop, 1982), p. 11.

41. Travis Hirschi, *Causes of Delinquency* (Berkeley: University of California Press, 1969), pp. 113–124, 132.

42. *Learning into the 21st Century, Report of Forum* 5 (Washington, DC: White House Conference on Children, 1970).

43. Jane Sprott, Jennifer Jenkins, and Anthony Doob, "The Importance of School: Protecting At-Risk Youth from Early Offending" *Youth Violence and Juvenile Justice* 3:59–77 (2005); Patricia Jenkins, "School Delinquency and the School Social Bond," *Journal of Research in Crime and Delinquency* 34:337–367 (1997).

44. Richard Lawrence, "Parents, Peers, School and Delinquency," paper presented at the annual meeting of the American Society of Criminology, Boston, November 1995.

45. Gary Gottfredson, Denise Gottfredson, Allison Payne, and Nisha Gottfredson, "School Climate Predictors of School Disorder: Results from a National Study of Delinquency Prevention in Schools," *Journal of Research in Crime and Delinquency* 42:412–444 (2005).

46. National Institute of Education, U.S. Department of Health, Education and Welfare, *Violent Schools–Safe Schools: The Safe Schools Study Report to the Congress*, vol. 1 (Washington, DC: U.S. Government Printing Office, 1977).

47. National Center for Educational Statistics, *Indicators of School Crime and Safety: 2011*, http://nces.ed.gov/programs/crimeindicators/crimeindicators2011/ (accessed August 15, 2012).

48. Ibid.

49. Kate Gross, "Homophobic Bullying and Schools—Responding to the Challenge," *Youth Studies Australia* 25:60 (2006).

50. Jane Ireland and Rachel Monaghan, "Behaviors Indicative of Bullying Among Young and Juvenile Male Offenders: A Study of Perpetrator and Victim Characteristics," *Aggressive Behavior* 32:172–180 (2006).

51. T. Joscelyne and S. Holttum, "Children's Explanations of Aggressive Incidents at School Within an Attribution Framework," *Child and Adolescent Mental Health* 11:104–110 (2006).

52. Young Shin Kim and Bennett Leventhal, "Bullying and Suicide: A Review," *International Journal of Adolescent Medical Health* 20:133–154 (2008).

53. Jessie Klein, *School Shootings and the Crisis of Bullying in America's Schools* (New York: New York University Press, 2012).

54. Norman A. White and Rolf Loeber, "Bullying and Special Education as Predictors of Serious Delinquency," *Journal of Research in Crime and Delinquency* 45:380–397 (2008).

55. Ben Brown and William Reed Benedict, "Bullets, Blades, and Being Afraid in Hispanic High Schools: An Exploratory Study of the Presence of Weapons and Fear of Weapon-Associated Victimization among High School Students in a Border Town," *Crime and Delinquency* 50:372–395 (2004).

56. Jessie Klein, *School Shootings and the Crisis of Bullying in America's Schools*.

57. Christine Kerres Malecki and Michelle Kilpatrick Demaray, "Carrying a Weapon to School and Perceptions of Social Support in an Urban Middle School," *Journal of Emotional and Behavioral Disorders* 11:169–178 (2003).

58. Pamela Wilcox and Richard Clayton, "A Multilevel Analysis of School-Based Weapon Possession," *Justice Quarterly* 18:509–542 (2001).

59. Mark Anderson, Joanne Kaufman, Thomas Simon, Lisa Barrios, Len Paulozzi, George Ryan, Rodney Hammond, William Modzeleski, Thomas Feucht, Lloyd Potter, and the School-Associated Violent Deaths Study Group, "School-Associated Violent Deaths in the United States, 1994–1999," *Journal of the American Medical Association* 286:2695–2702 (2001).

60. Bryan Vossekuil, Marisa Reddy, Robert Fein, Randy Borum, and William Modzeleski, *Safe School Initiative: An Interim Report on the Prevention of Targeted Violence in Schools* (Washington, DC: United States Secret Service, 2000).

61. Gary Gottfredson and Denise Gottfredson, *Victimization in Schools* (New York: Plenum Press, 1985), p. 18.

62. Joan McDermott, "Crime in the School and in the Community: Offenders, Victims, and Fearful Youth," *Crime and Delinquency* 29:270–283 (1983).

63. Ibid.

64. Celia C. Lo, Young S. Kim, Thomas M. Allen, Andrea N. Allen, P. Allison Minugh, and Nicoletta Lomuto, "The Impact of School Environment and Grade Level on Student Delinquency: A Multilevel Modeling Approach," *Crime and Delinquency* 57:622–657 (2011).

65. Lisa Hutchinson Wallace and David C. May, "The Impact of Parental Attachment and Feelings of Isolation on Adolescent Fear of Crime at School," *Adolescence* 40:457–474 (2005).

66. Robert Brewer and Monica Swahn, "Binge Drinking and Violence," *JAMA: Journal of the American Medical Association* 294:16–20 (2005).

67. Tomika Stevens, Kenneth Ruggiero, Dean Kilpatrick, Heidi Resnick, and Benjamin Saunders, "Variables Differentiating Singly and Multiply Victimized Youth: Results from the National Survey of Adolescents and Implications for Secondary Prevention," *Child Maltreatment* 10:211–223 (2005); James Collins and Pamela Messerschmidt, "Epidemiology of Alcohol-Related Violence," *Alcohol Health and Research World* 17:93–100 (1993).

68. Nancy Weishew and Samuel Peng, "Variables Predicting Students' Problem Behaviors," *Journal of Educational Research* 87:5–17 (1993).

69. Ibid.

70. Rod Brunson and Jody Miller, "Schools, Neighborhoods, and Adolescent Conflicts: A Situational Examination of Reciprocal Dynamics," *Justice Quarterly* 26:1–27 (2009).

71. Marie Skubak Tillyer, Bonnie S. Fisher, and Pamela Wilcox, "The Effects of School Crime Prevention on Students' Violent Victimization, Risk Perception, and Fear of Crime: A Multilevel Opportunity Perspective," *Justice Quarterly* 28:249–277 (2011).

72. Sheila Heaviside, Cassandra Rowand, Catrina Williams, Elizabeth Burns, Shelley Burns, and Edith McArthur, *Violence and Discipline Problems in U.S. Public Schools: 1996–97* (Washington, DC: United States Government Printing Office, 1998).

73. Mike Kennedy, "Fighting Crime by Design," *American School and University* 73:46–47 (2001).

74. Bruce Jacobs, "Anticipatory Undercover Targeting in High Schools," *Journal of Criminal Justice* 22:445–357 (1994).

75. New York City Police Department, www.nyc.gov/html/nypd/ (accessed August 15, 2012).

76. Darcia Harris Bowman, "Curbing Crime," *Education Week*, April 4, 2004.

77. Stuart Tremlow, "Preventing Violence in Schools," *Psychiatric Times* 21:61–65 (2004).

78. Allison Ann Payne, Denise Gottfredson, and Gary Gottfredson, "Schools as Communities: The Relationships Among Communal School Organization, Student Bonding, and School Disorder," *Criminology* 41:749–777 (2003).

79. Susan L. Wynne and Hee-Jong Joo, "Predictors of School Victimization: Individual, Familial, and School Factors," *Crime and Delinquency* 57: 458–488 (2011).

80. Glenn Cook, "Education Debates Return to the Headlines as Midterms Near," *American School Board Journal* 193:6–7 (2006).

81. Stuart Yeh, "Reforming Federal Testing Policy to Support Teaching and Learning," *Educational Policy* 20:495–524 (2006).

82. U.S. Senate Subcommittee on Delinquency, *Challenge for the Third Century*, p. 95.

83. Douglas Breunlin, Rocco Cimmarusti, Joshua Hetherington, and Jayne Kinsman, "Making the Smart Choice: A Systemic Response to School-Based Violence," *Journal of Family Therapy* 28:246–266 (2006).

84. "When School Is Out," *The Future of Children*, vol. 9 (Los Altos, CA: David and Lucile Packard Foundation, Fall 1999).

85. *New Jersey v. T.L.O.*, 469 U.S. 325 (1985).

86. *Vernonia School District 47J v. Acton*, 515 U.S. 646 (1995); Bernard James and Jonathan Pyatt, "Supreme Court Extends School's Authority to Search," *National School Safety Center News Journal* 26:29 (1995).

87. *Board of Education of Independent School District No. 92 of Pottawatomie County et al. v. Earls et al.*, 536 U.S. 822 (2002).

88. *Safford United School District No. 1 v. Redding*, 557 U. S. ___ (2009).

89. Ibid.

90. Michael Medaris, *A Guide to the Family Educational Rights and Privacy Act* (Washington, DC: Office of Juvenile Justice and Delinquency Prevention, 1998).

91. Ibid.

92. *Tinker v. Des Moines School District*, 393 U.S. 503 (1969).
93. Ibid.
94. *Bethel School District No. 403 v. Fraser*, 478 U.S. 675, 106 S.Ct. 3159, 92 L.Ed.2d 549 (1986).
95. *Hazelwood School District v. Kuhlmeier*, 484 U.S. 260 (1988).
96. *Morse et al. v. Frederick*, 551 U.S. 393 (2007).
97. *Layshock v. Hermitage School District*, No. 07-4465 (2008).
98. *Santa Fe Independent School District, Petitioner v. Jane Doe*, individually and as next friend for her minor children, Jane and John Doe et al., No. 99–62 (June 19, 2000).
99. *Good News Club et al. v. Milford Central School*, 533 U.S. 98 (2001).
100. *Elk Grove Unified School District v. Newdow*, 542 U.S. 1 (2004).
101. Ibid.
102. *Ingraham v. Wright*, 430 U.S. 651 (1977).
103. ACLU and Human Rights Watch press release, "U.S.: Students with Disabilities Face Corporal Punishment at Higher Rates," August 10, 2009, www.hrw.org/en/news/2009/08/07/us-students-disabilities-face-corporal-punishment-higher-rates (accessed August 15, 2012).
104. *Goss v. Lopez*, 419 U.S. 565 (1976).

Chapter 10. Drug Use and Delinquency

1. Lloyd D. Johnston, Patrick M. O'Malley, Jerald G. Bachman, and John E. Schulenberg, *Monitoring the Future: National Results on Adolescent Drug Use: Overview of Key Findings, 2011* (Ann Arbor, MI: Institute for Social Research, University of Michigan, 2012), Table 5.
2. Peter W. Greenwood, "Substance Abuse Problems Among High-Risk Youth and Potential Interventions," *Crime and Delinquency* 38:444–458 (1992).
3. Office of Applied Studies, Substance Abuse and Mental Health Services Administration, "Youth Violence and Illicit Drug Use," *The NSDUH Report* 5 (Washington, DC: Author, 2006).
4. Gary M. McClelland, Linda A. Teplin, and Karen M. Abram, *Detection and Prevalence of Substance Use Among Juvenile Detainees* (Washington, DC: Office of Juvenile Justice and Delinquency Prevention, 2006), pp. 4, 6.
5. Jonathan G. Tubman, Andrés G. Gil, and Eric F. Wagner, "Co-occurring Substance Use and Delinquent Behavior During Early Adolescence: Emerging Relations and Implications for Intervention Strategies," *Criminal Justice and Behavior* 31:463–488 (2004).
6. Dennis Coon, *Introduction to Psychology* (St. Paul, MN: West, 1992), p. 178.
7. Alan Neaigus, Aylin Atillasoy, Samuel Friedman, Xavier Andrade, Maureen Miller, Gilbert Ildefonso, and Don Des Jarlais, "Trends in the Noninjected Use of Heroin and Factors Associated with the Transition to Injecting," in *Heroin in the Age of Crack-Cocaine*, ed. James Inciardi and Lana Harrison (Thousand Oaks, CA: Sage, 1998), pp. 108–130.
8. Johnston, O'Malley, Bachman, and Schulenberg, *Monitoring the Future: National Results on Adolescent Drug Use: Overview of Key Findings, 2011*, Tables 5 and 6.
9. "Drugs—The American Family in Crisis," *Juvenile and Family Court* 39:45–46 (special issue, 1988).
10. Federal Bureau of Investigation, *Crime in the United States, 2010* (Washington, DC: U.S. Government Printing Office, 2011), Tables 29, 38.
11. Henrick J. Harwood, *Updating Estimates of the Economic Costs of Alcohol Abuse in the United States: Estimates, Update Methods, and Data*, report prepared by the Lewin Group for the National Institute of Alcohol Abuse and Alcoholism (Rockville, MD: U.S. Department of Health and Human Services, 2000), Table 3.
12. D. J. Rohsenow, "Drinking Habits and Expectancies About Alcohol's Effects for Self versus Others," *Journal of Consulting and Clinical Psychology* 51:75–76 (1983).
13. Spencer Rathus, *Psychology*, 4th ed. (New York: Holt, Rinehart & Winston, 1990), p. 161.
14. National Drug Intelligence Center, *Methamphetamine Drug Threat Assessment* (Johnstown, PA: Author, 2005), p. 10.
15. Mary Tabor, "'Ice' in an Island Paradise," *Boston Globe*, December 8, 1989, p. 3.
16. Johnston, O'Malley, Bachman, and Schulenberg, *Monitoring the Future: National Results on Adolescent Drug Use: Overview of Key Findings, 2011*, Table 5.
17. National Drug Intelligence Center, *National Drug Threat Assessment, 2011* (Johnstown, PA: Author, 2011), Table 6, p. 34.
18. Dana Hunt, Sarah Kuck, and Linda Truitt, *Methamphetamine Use: Lessons Learned* (Cambridge, MA: Abt Associates Inc., 2005), pp. iv, v.
19. Fox Butterfield, "Fighting an Illegal Drug Through Its Legal Source," *New York Times*, January 30, 2005, p. A18; Kate Zernike, "Potent Mexican Meth Floods in as States Curb Domestic Variety," *New York Times*, January 23, 2006.
20. Nancy Nicosia, Rosalie Liccardo Pacula, Beau Kilmer, Russell Lundberg, and James Chiesa, *The Economic Cost of Methamphetamine Use in the United States, 2005* (Santa Monica, CA: RAND Corporation, 2009).
21. Paul Goldstein, "Anabolic Steroids: An Ethnographic Approach," unpublished paper (Narcotics and Drug Research, Inc., March 1989).
22. Centers for Disease Control and Prevention, "Use of Cigarettes and Other Tobacco Products Among Students Aged 13–15 Years—Worldwide, 1999–2005," *Morbidity and Mortality Weekly Report* 55:553–556 (2006).
23. Joe Nocera, "If It's Good for Philip Morris, Can It Also Be Good for Public Health?" *New York Times Magazine*, June 18, 2006, pp. 46–53, 70, 76–78.
24. Clete Snell and Laura Bailey, "Operation Storefront: Observations of Tobacco Retailer Advertising Compliance with Tobacco Laws," *Youth Violence and Juvenile Justice* 3:78–90 (2005).
25. Johnston, O'Malley, Bachman, and Schulenberg, *Monitoring the Future: National Results on Adolescent Drug Use: Overview of Key Findings, 2011*, Table 5.
26. Ibid., Table 6.
27. Office of National Drug Control Policy, *Prescription for Danger: A Report on the Troubling Trend of Prescription and Over-the-Counter Drug Abuse Among the Nation's Teens* (Washington, DC: Office of National Drug Control Policy, Executive Office of the President, 2008); Steven P. Kurtz, James A. Inciardi, Hilary L. Surratt, and Linda Cottler, "Prescription Drug Abuse Among Ecstasy Users in Miami," *Journal of Addictive Diseases* 24:1–16 (2005).
28. Johnston, O'Malley, Bachman, and Schulenberg, *Monitoring the Future: National Results on Adolescent Drug Use: Overview of Key Findings, 2011*, Tables 2, 6.
29. *PRIDE Questionnaire Report for Grades 6 to 12: National Summary Statistics for 2009–10* (Bowling Green, KY: PRIDE Surveys, September 27, 2010).
30. Substance Abuse and Mental Health Services Administration, *Results from the 2010 National Survey on Drug Use and Health: Summary of National Findings* (Rockville, MD: Department of Health and Human Services, Substance Abuse and Mental Health Services Administration, 2011).
31. Ibid., Fig. 2.6.
32. Ibid., Fig. 3.1.
33. Ibid., Fig. 2.9.
34. Office of National Drug Control Policy, *Girls and Drugs: A New Analysis: Recent Trends, Risk Factors, and Consequences* (Washington, DC: Office of National Drug Control Policy, Executive Office of the President, 2006), Fig. 3.
35. Substance Abuse and Mental Health Services, *Results from the 2010 National Survey on Drug Use and Health: Summary of National Findings*, Figs. 2.8, 2.9.
36. Diana C. Noone, "Drug Use Among Juvenile Detainees," in *Arrestee Drug Abuse Monitoring: 2000 Annual Report* (Washington, DC: National Institute of Justice, 2003), p. 135.
37. McClelland, Teplin, and Abram, *Detection and Prevalence of Substance Use Among Juvenile Detainees*.
38. Julia Yun Soo Kim, Michael Fendrich, and Joseph Wislar, "The Validity of Juvenile Arrestees' Drug Use Reporting: A Gender Comparison," *Journal of Research in Crime and Delinquency* 37:419–432 (2000).
39. G. E. Vallant, "Parent–Child Disparity and Drug Addiction," *Journal of Nervous and Mental Disease* 142:534–539 (1966).
40. Charles Winick, "Epidemiology of Narcotics Use," in *Narcotics*, ed. D. Wilner and G. Kassenbaum (New York: McGraw-Hill, 1965), pp. 3–18.
41. Justin Hayes-Smith and Rachel Bridges Whaley, "Community Characteristics and Methamphetamine Use: A Social Disorganization Perspective," *Journal of Drug Issues* 39:547–576 (2009).
42. Delbert Elliott, David Huizinga, and Scott Menard, *Multiple Problem Youth: Delinquency, Substance Abuse, and Mental Health Problems* (New York: Springer-Verlag, 1989).
43. Peter Reuter, Robert MacCoun, and Patrick Murphy, *Money from Crime: A Study of the Economics of Drug Dealing in Washington, D.C.* (Santa Monica, CA: Rand, 1990).
44. Thomas Dishion, Deborah Capaldi, Kathleen Spracklen, and Fuzhong Li, "Peer Ecology of Male Adolescent Drug Use," *Development and Psychopathology* 7:803–824 (1995).
45. C. Bowden, "Determinants of Initial Use of Opioids," *Comprehensive Psychiatry* 12:136–140 (1971).
46. Terence Thornberry and Marvin Krohn, "Peers, Drug Use, and Delinquency," in *Handbook of Antisocial Behavior*, ed. David Stoff, James Breiling, and Jack Maser (New York: Wiley, 1997), pp. 218–233.

47. Gregory M. Zimmerman and Bob Edward Vásquez, "Decomposing the Peer Effect on Adolescent Substance Use: Mediation, Nonlinearity, and Differential Nonlinearity." *Criminology* 49:1235–1274 (2011).

48. Richard Cloward and Lloyd Ohlin, *Delinquency and Opportunity: A Theory of Delinquent Gangs* (New York: Free Press, 1960).

49. Denise Kandel and Mark Davies, "Friendship Networks, Intimacy, and Illicit Drug Use in Young Adulthood: A Comparison of Two Competing Theories," *Criminology* 29:441–471 (1991).

50. James Inciardi, Ruth Horowitz, and Anne Pottieger, *Street Kids, Street Drugs, Street Crime: An Examination of Drug Use and Serious Delinquency in Miami* (Belmont, CA: Wadsworth, 1993), p. 43.

51. D. Baer and J. Corrado, "Heroin Addict Relationships with Parents During Childhood and Early Adolescent Years," *Journal of Genetic Psychology* 124:99–103 (1974).

52. Timothy Ireland and Cathy Spatz Widom, *Childhood Victimization and Risk for Alcohol and Drug Arrests* (Washington, DC: National Institute of Justice, 1995).

53. See S. F. Bucky, "The Relationship Between Background and Extent of Heroin Use," *American Journal of Psychiatry* 130:709–710 (1973); I. Chien, D. L. Gerard, R. Lee, and E. Rosenfield, *The Road to H: Narcotics Delinquency and Social Policy* (New York: Basic Books, 1964).

54. J. S. Mio, G. Nanjundappa, D. E. Verlur, and M. D. DeRios, "Drug Abuse and the Adolescent Sex Offender: A Preliminary Analysis," *Journal of Psychoactive Drugs* 18:65–72 (1986).

55. G. T. Wilson, "Cognitive Studies in Alcoholism," *Journal of Consulting and Clinical Psychology* 55:325–331 (1987).

56. John Hagedorn, Jose Torres, and Greg Giglio, "Cocaine, Kicks, and Strain: Patterns of Substance Use in Milwaukee Gangs," *Contemporary Drug Problems* 25:113–145 (1998).

57. For a thorough review, see Karol Kumpfer, "Impact of Maternal Characteristics and Parenting Processes on Children of Drug Abusers," paper presented at the annual meeting of the American Society of Criminology, Boston, November 1995.

58. For a comprehensive review of genetics and delinquency in general, see Melissa Peskin, Andrea L. Glenn, Yu Gao, Jianghong Liu, Robert A. Schug, Yaling Yang, and Adrian Raine, "Personal Characteristics of Delinquents: Neurobiology, Genetic Predispositions, Individual Psychosocial Attributes," in *The Oxford Handbook of Juvenile Crime and Juvenile Justice*, eds. Barry C. Feld and Donna M. Bishop (New York: Oxford University Press, 2012), pp. 73–106.

59. D. W. Goodwin, "Alcoholism and Genetics," *Archives of General Psychiatry* 42:171–174 (1985).

60. Ibid.

61. Patricia Dobkin, Richard Tremblay, Louise Masse, and Frank Vitaro, "Individual and Peer Characteristics in Predicting Boys' Early Onset of Substance Abuse: A Seven-Year Longitudinal Study," *Child Development* 66:1198–1214 (1995).

62. Ric Steele, Rex Forehand, Lisa Armistead, and Gene Brody, "Predicting Alcohol and Drug Use in Early Adulthood: The Role of Internalizing and Externalizing Behavior Problems in Early Adolescence," *American Journal of Orthopsychiatry* 65:380–387 (1995).

63. Ibid., pp. 380–381.

64. Jerome Platt and Christina Platt, *Heroin Addiction* (New York: Wiley, 1976), p. 127.

65. Rathus, *Psychology*, p. 158.

66. Eric Strain, "Antisocial Personality Disorder, Misbehavior, and Drug Abuse," *Journal of Nervous and Mental Disease* 163:162–165 (1995).

67. Dobkin, Tremblay, Masse, and Vitaro, "Individual and Peer Characteristics in Predicting Boys' Early Onset of Substance Abuse."

68. J. Shedler and J. Block, "Adolescent Drug Use and Psychological Health: A Longitudinal Inquiry," *American Psychologist* 45:612–630 (1990).

69. Greenwood, "Substance Abuse Problems Among High-Risk Youth and Potential Interventions," p. 448.

70. John Wallace and Jerald Bachman, "Explaining Racial/Ethnic Differences in Adolescent Drug Use: The Impact of Background and Lifestyle," *Social Problems* 38:333–357 (1991).

71. Marvin Krohn, Terence Thornberry, Lori Collins-Hall, and Alan Lizotte, "School Dropout, Delinquent Behavior, and Drug Use," in *Drugs, Crime, and Other Deviant Adaptations: Longitudinal Studies*, ed. Howard Kaplan (New York: Plenum Press, 1995), pp. 163–183.

72. B. A. Christiansen, G. T. Smith, P. V. Roehling, and M. S. Goldman, "Using Alcohol Expectancies to Predict Adolescent Drinking Behavior After One Year," *Journal of Counseling and Clinical Psychology* 57:93–99 (1989).

73. Inciardi, Horowitz, and Pottieger, *Street Kids, Street Drugs, Street Crime*, p. 135.

74. Ibid., p. 136.

75. Mary Ellen Mackesy-Amiti, Michael Fendrich, and Paul Goldstein, "Sequence of Drug Use Among Serious Drug Users: Typical vs. Atypical Progression," *Drug and Alcohol Dependence* 45:185–196 (1997).

76. The following sections lean heavily on Marcia Chaiken and Bruce Johnson, *Characteristics of Different Types of Drug-Involved Youth* (Washington, DC: National Institute of Justice, 1988).

77. Ibid., p. 100.

78. Inciardi, Horowitz, and Pottieger, *Street Kids, Street Drugs, Street Crime*.

79. Robert MacCoun and Peter Reuter, "Are the Wages of Sin $30 an Hour? Economic Aspects of Street-Level Drug Dealing," *Crime and Delinquency* 38:477–491 (1992).

80. Steven D. Levitt and Sudhir A. Venkatesh, "An Economic Analysis of a Drug-Selling Gang's Finances," *Quarterly Journal of Economics* 115: 755–789 (2000), Table III.

81. Ibid., Table II.

82. Chaiken and Johnson, *Characteristics of Different Types of Drug-Involved Youth*, p. 12.

83. John Hagedorn, "Neighborhoods, Markets, and Gang Drug Organization," *Journal of Research in Crime and Delinquency* 31:264–294 (1994).

84. Chaiken and Johnson, *Characteristics of Different Types of Drug-Involved Youth*, p. 14.

85. For an excellent overview of the drugs–crime relationship, see David A. Boyum, Jonathan P. Caulkins, and Mark A. R. Kleiman, "Drugs, Crime, and Public Policy," in *Crime and Public Policy*, eds. James Q. Wilson and Joan Petersilia (New York: Oxford University Press, 2011), pp. 370–373.

86. Eric Baumer, Janet Lauritsen, Richard Rosenfeld, and Richard Wright, "The Influence of Crack Cocaine on Robbery, Burglary, and Homicide Rates: A Cross-City, Longitudinal Analysis," *Journal of Research in Crime and Delinquency* 35:316–340 (1998).

87. Ibid.

88. James Inciardi, "Heroin Use and Street Crime," *Crime and Delinquency* 25:335–346 (1979); Inciardi, *The War on Drugs* (Palo Alto, CA: Mayfield, 1986); see also W. McGlothlin, M. Anglin, and B. Wilson, "Narcotic Addiction and Crime," *Criminology* 16:293–311 (1978); George Speckart and M. Douglas Anglin, "Narcotics Use and Crime: An Overview of Recent Research Advances," *Contemporary Drug Problems* 13:741–769 (1986); Charles Faupel and Carl Klockars, "Drugs-Crime Connections: Elaborations from the Life Histories of Hard-Core Heroin Addicts," *Social Problems* 34:54–68 (1987).

89. Eric Baumer, "Poverty, Crack, and Crime: A Cross-City Analysis," *Journal of Research in Crime and Delinquency* 31:311–327 (1994).

90. Mildred M. Maldonado-Molina, Jennifer M. Reingle, and Wesley G. Jennings, "Does Alcohol Use Predict Violent Behaviors? The Relationship Between Alcohol Use and Violence in a Nationally Representative Longitudinal Sample," *Youth Violence and Juvenile Justice* 9:99–111 (2011); Kelli A. Komro, Amy L. Tobler, Mildred M. Maldonado-Molina, and Cheryl L. Perry, "Effects of Alcohol Use Initiation Patterns on High-Risk Behaviors Among Urban, Low-Income, Young Adolescents," *Prevention Science* 11:14–23 (2010); Marvin Dawkins, "Drug Use and Violent Crime Among Adolescents," *Adolescence* 32:395–406 (1997); Helene Raskin White and Stephen Hansell, "The Moderating Effects of Gender and Hostility on the Alcohol–Aggression Relationship," *Journal of Research in Crime and Delinquency* 33:450–470 (1996).

91. Fox Butterfield, "Justice Department Ends Testing of Criminals for Drug Use," *New York Times*, January 28, 2004.

92. *Preliminary Data on Drug Use and Related Matters Among Adult Arrestees and Juvenile Detainees, 2002* (Washington, DC: Arrestee Drug Abuse Monitoring Program, National Institute of Justice, 2003), Tables 2, 3.

93. Carl McCurley and Howard Snyder, *Co-occurrence of Substance Use Behaviors in Youth* (Washington, DC: Office of Juvenile Justice and Delinquency Prevention, U.S. Department of Justice, 2008).

94. Boyum, Caulkins, and Kleiman, "Drugs, Crime, and Public Policy," p. 372.

95. B. D. Johnson, E. Wish, J. Schmeidler, and D. Huizinga, "Concentration of Delinquent Offending: Serious Drug Involvement and High Delinquency Rates," *Journal of Drug Issues* 21:205–229 (1991); see also Tubman, Gil, and Wagner, "Co-occurring Substance Use and Delinquent Behavior During Early Adolescence."

96. W. David Watts and Lloyd Wright, "The Relationship of Alcohol, Tobacco, Marijuana, and Other Illegal Drug Use to Delinquency Among Mexican-American, Black, and White Adolescent Males," *Adolescence* 25:38–54 (1990).

97. For a general review of this issue, see Helene Raskin White, "The Drug Use–Delinquency Connection in Adolescence," in *Drugs, Crime and Criminal Justice*, ed. Ralph Weisheit (Cincinnati: Anderson, 1990), pp. 215–256; Speckart and Anglin, "Narcotics Use and Crime"; Faupel and Klockars, "Drugs-Crime Connections."

98. Delbert Elliott, David Huizinga, and Susan Ageton, *Explaining Delinquency and Drug Abuse* (Beverly Hills, CA: Sage, 1985).

99. David Huizinga, Scott Menard, and Delbert Elliott, "Delinquency and Drug Use: Temporal and Developmental Patterns," *Justice Quarterly* 6:419–455 (1989).

100. See Evelyn H. Wei, Rolf Loeber, and Helene Raskin White, "Teasing Apart the Developmental Associations Between Alcohol and Marijuana Use and Violence," *Journal of Contemporary Criminal Justice* 20:116–183 (2004).

101. Jason A. Ford, "The Connection Between Heavy Drinking and Juvenile Delinquency During Adolescence," *Sociological Spectrum* 25:629–650 (2005).

102. Graham Farrell, "Drugs and Drug Control," in *Global Report on Crime and Justice*, ed. Graeme Newman (New York: Oxford University Press, 1999), p. 177.

103. *1998 International Narcotics Control Strategy Report* (Washington, DC: U.S. Department of State, February 1999).

104. Clifford Krauss, "Neighbors Worry About Colombian Aid," *New York Times*, August 25, 2000, pp. A3, A13; see also Juan Forero, "Columbia's Coca Survives U.S. Plan to Uproot It," *New York Times*, August 19, 2006.

105. Juan Forero with Tim Weiner, "Latin America Poppy Fields Undermine U.S. Drug Battle," *New York Times*, August 8, 2003, p. A1.

106. United Nations, *2007 World Drug Report* (Vienna, Austria: Office on Drugs and Crime, United Nations, 2007).

107. Carlotta Gall, "Another Year of Drug War, and the Poppy Crop Flourishes," *New York Times*, February 17, 2006.

108. United Nations Office on Drugs and Crime, *Afghanistan Opium Survey 2010: Summary of Findings* (Vienna: Author, September 2010), p. 1.

109. National Drug Intelligence Center, *National Drug Threat Assessment, 2011,* Table B3, p. 50.

110. United Nations, *2007 World Drug Report*, p. 8.

111. "Operation Webslinger Targets Illegal Internet Trafficking of Date-Rape Drug," *U.S. Customs Today* 38 (2002).

112. Gardiner Harris, "Two Agencies to Fight Online Narcotics Sales," *New York Times*, October 18, 2003.

113. National Drug Intelligence Center, *National Drug Threat Assessment 2011*.

114. Fox Butterfield, "Home Drug-Making Laboratories Expose Children to Toxic Fallout," *New York Times Magazine*, February 23, 2004.

115. International Centre for Science in Drug Policy, *Effect of Drug Law Enforcement on Drug-Related Violence: Evidence from a Scientific Review* (Vancouver, Canada: Author, 2010).

116. Mark Moore, *Drug Trafficking* (Washington, DC: National Institute of Justice, 1988).

117. Christopher L. Ringwalt, Susan Ennett, Amy Vincus, Judy Thorne, Louise Ann Rohrbach, and Ashley Simons-Rudolph, "The Prevalence of Effective Substance Use Prevention in U.S. Middle Schools," *Prevention Science* 3:257–265 (2002).

118. Jane Carlisle Maxwell, Melissa Tackett-Gibson, and James Dyer, "Substance Use in Urban and Rural Texas School Districts," *Drugs: Education, Prevention and Policy* 13:327–339 (2006).

119. Denise C. Gottfredson, David B. Wilson, and Stacy S. Najaka, "School-Based Crime Prevention," in *Evidence-Based Crime Prevention*, ed. Lawrence W. Sherman, David P. Farrington, Brandon C. Welsh, and Doris Layton MacKenzie (New York: Routledge, 2006, rev. ed.), Table 4.9; see also Phyllis L. Ellickson, Daniel F. McCaffrey, Bonnie Ghosh-Dastidar, and Douglas L. Longshore, "New Inroads in Preventing Adolescent Drug Use: Results from a Large-Scale Trial of Project ALERT in Middle Schools," *American Journal of Public Health* 93:1830–1836 (2003).

120. Christopher Ringwalt, Amy A. Vincus, Sean Hanley, Susan T. Ennett, J. Michael Bowling, and Susan Haws, "The Prevalence of Evidence-Based Drug Use Prevention Curricula in U.S. Middle Schools in 2008," *Prevention Science* 12:63–69 (2011).

121. *Partnership Attitude Tracking Study: Teens, 2004* (Washington, DC: Office of National Drug Control Policy, 2005), pp. 12, 24.

122. Substance Abuse and Mental Health Services Administration, *Results from the 2010 National Survey on Drug Use and Health: Summary of National Findings*, Figure 6.6.

123. Lori K. Holleran, Margaret A. Taylor-Seehafer, Elizabeth C. Pomeroy, and James Alan Neff, "Substance Abuse Prevention for High-Risk Youth: Exploring Culture and Alcohol and Drug Use," *Alcoholism Treatment Quarterly* 23:165–184 (2005).

124. Brandon C. Welsh and Akemi Hoshi, "Communities and Crime Prevention," in *Evidence-Based Crime Prevention*, ed. Lawrence W. Sherman, David P. Farrington, Brandon C. Welsh, and Doris Layton MacKenzie (New York: Routledge, 2006, rev. ed.), pp. 184–186.

125. Steven P. Schinke, Mario A. Orlandi, and Kristen C. Cole, "Boys and Girls Clubs in Public Housing Developments: Prevention Services for Youth at Risk," *Journal of Community Psychology*, Office of Substance Abuse Prevention, Special Issue (1992), p. 120.

126. Ibid., pp. 125–127.

127. Substance Abuse and Mental Health Services Administration, Office of Applied Studies, *Treatment Episode Data Sets (TEDS). Highlights—2007. National Admissions to Substance Abuse Treatment Services* (Rockville, MD: DASIS Series: S-45, DHHS Publication No. (SMA) 09-4360, 2009), Table 2b.

128. Scott W. Henggeler, Sonja K. Schoenwald, Charles M. Borduin, Melisa D. Rowland, and Phillippe B. Cunningham, *Multisystemic Treatment of Antisocial Behavior in Children and Adolescents* (New York: Guilford Press, 1998).

129. Eli Ginzberg, Howard Berliner, and Miriam Ostrow, *Young People at Risk: Is Prevention Possible?* (Boulder, CO: Westview Press, 1988), p. 99.

130. Laurie Chassin, "Juvenile Justice and Substance Abuse," *The Future of Children* 18(2):165–183 (2008); James C. Howell, *Preventing and Reducing Juvenile Delinquency: A Comprehensive Framework* (Thousand Oaks, CA: Sage, 2009, second edition), p. 272.

131. Ginzberg, Berliner, and Ostrow, *Young People at Risk: Is Prevention Possible?*

132. Donnie W. Watson, Lorrie Bisesi, Susie Tanamly, and Noemi Mai, "Comprehensive Residential Education, Arts, and Substance Abuse Treatment (CREASAT): A Model Treatment Program for Juvenile Offenders," *Youth Violence and Juvenile Justice* 1:388–401 (2003).

133. Steven R. Donziger, ed., *The Real War on Crime: The Report of the National Criminal Justice Commission* (New York: HarperPerennial, 1996), pp. 201, 202.

134. Charlotte Allan and Nat Wright, "Harm Reduction: The Least Worst Treatment of All: Tackling Drug Addiction Has Few Easy Solutions," *Student British Medical Journal* 12:92–93 (2004), p. 92.

135. Ibid.

136. Ibid; see also Erik K. Laursen and Paul Brasler, "Is Harm Reduction a Viable Choice for Kids Enchanted with Drugs?" *Reclaiming Children and Youth* 11:181–183 (2002).

137. Donziger, *The Real War on Crime*, p. 201.

138. Charles Puzzanchera, Benjamin Adams, and Melissa Sickmund, *Juvenile Court Statistics 2008* (Pittsburgh, PA: National Center for Juvenile Justice, 2011), p. 19.

139. Eric L. Jensen, Jurg Gerber, and Clayton Mosher, "Social Consequences of the War on Drugs: The Legacy of Failed Policy," *Criminal Justice Policy Review* 15:100–121 (2004).

140. Associated Press, "AP Impact: US Drug War Has Met None of Its Goals," *New York Times*, May 14, 2010.

141. Peter Reuter, ed., *Understanding the Demand for Illegal Drugs* (Washington, DC: National Research Council, National Academies Press, 2010), p. 103.

142. Kathryn Ann Farr, "Revitalizing the Drug Decriminalization Debate," *Crime and Delinquency* 36:223–237 (1990).

143. Reuter, MacCoun, and Murphy, *Money from Crime*, pp. 165–168.

Chapter 11. Delinquency Prevention and Juvenile Justice Today

1. Brandon C. Welsh and David P. Farrington, "Crime Prevention and Public Policy," in *The Oxford Handbook of Crime Prevention*, ed. Brandon C. Welsh and David P. Farrington (New York: Oxford University Press, 2012); Trevor Bennett, "Crime Prevention," in *The Handbook of Crime and Punishment*, ed. Michael Tonry (New York: Oxford University Press, 1998).

2. Paul J. Brantingham and Frederick L. Faust, "A Conceptual Model of Crime Prevention," *Crime and Delinquency* 22:284–296 (1976).

3. See Brandon C. Welsh, "Public Health and the Prevention of Juvenile Criminal Violence," *Youth Violence and Juvenile Justice* 3:23–40 (2005).

4. David P. Farrington, "Early Developmental Prevention of Juvenile Delinquency," *Criminal Behavior and Mental Health* 4:209–227 (1994).

5. David P. Farrington, "The Development of Offending and Antisocial Behavior from Childhood: Key Findings from the Cambridge Study in Delinquent Development," *Journal of Child Psychology and Psychiatry* 36:929–964 (1995).

6. Richard E. Tremblay and Wendy M. Craig, "Developmental Crime Prevention," in *Building a Safer Society: Strategic Approaches to Crime Prevention. Crime and Justice: A Review of Research*, vol. 19, ed. Michael Tonry and David P. Farrington (Chicago: University of Chicago Press, 1995), p. 151.

7. See Brandon C. Welsh and David P. Farrington, eds., *The Oxford Handbook of Crime Prevention* (New York: Oxford University Press, 2012); Tremblay and Craig, "Developmental Crime Prevention"; Gail A. Wasserman and

Laurie S. Miller, "The Prevention of Serious and Violent Juvenile Offending," in *Serious and Violent Juvenile Offenders: Risk Factors and Successful Interventions*, ed. Rolf Loeber and David P. Farrington (Thousand Oaks, CA: Sage Publications, 1998); Joan McCord, Cathy Spatz Widom, and Nancy A. Crowell, eds., *Juvenile Crime, Juvenile Justice*, panel on Juvenile Crime: Prevention, Treatment, and Control (Washington, DC: National Academy Press, 2001); Patrick Tolan, "Crime Prevention: Focus on Youth," in *Crime: Public Policies for Crime Control*, James Q. Wilson and Joan Petersilia (Oakland, CA: Institute for Contemporary Studies, 2002).

8. Deanna S. Gomby, Patti L. Culross, and Richard E. Behrman, "Home Visiting: Recent Program Evaluations—Analysis and Recommendations," *The Future of Children* 9(1):4–26 (1999).

9. David L. Olds, Charles R. Henderson, Robert Chamberlin, and Robert Tatelbaum, "Preventing Child Abuse and Neglect: A Randomized Trial of Nurse Home Visitation," *Pediatrics* 78:65–78 (1986).

10. David L. Olds, Charles R. Henderson, Charles Phelps, Harriet Kitzman, and Carole Hanks, "Effects of Prenatal and Infancy Nurse Home Visitation on Government Spending," *Medical Care* 31:155–174 (1993).

11. David L. Olds et al., "Long-Term Effects of Nurse Home Visitation on Children's Criminal and Antisocial Behavior: 15-Year Follow-Up of a Randomized Controlled Trial," *Journal of the American Medical Association* 280:1238–1244 (1998).

12. David L. Olds et al., "Long-Term Effects of Home Visitation on Maternal Life Course and Child Abuse and Neglect: Fifteen-Year Follow-Up of a Randomized Trial," *Journal of the American Medical Association* 278: 637–643 (1997).

13. Peter W. Greenwood, Lynn A. Karoly, Susan S. Everingham, Jill Houbè, M. Rebecca Kilburn, C. Peter Rydell, Matthew Sanders, and James Chiesa, "Estimating the Costs and Benefits of Early Childhood Interventions: Nurse Home Visits and the Perry Preschool," in *Costs and Benefits of Preventing Crime*, ed. Brandon C. Welsh, David P. Farrington, and Lawrence W. Sherman (Boulder, CO: Westview Press, 2001), p. 133.

14. John Eckenrode, Mary Campa, Dennis W. Luckey, Charles R. Henderson, Robert Cole, Harriet Kitzman, Elizabeth Anson, Kimberly Sidora-Arcoleo, Jane Powers, and David L. Olds, "Long-Term Effects of Prenatal and Infancy Nurse Home Visitation on the Life Course of Youths: 19-Year Follow-Up a Randomized Trial," *Archives of Pediatrics and Adolescent Medicine* 164:9–15 (2010).

15. Nurse-Family Partnership, *Nurse-Family Partnership Snapshot* (Denver, CO: Nurse-Family Partnership, September 2010).

16. Ned Calonge, "Community Interventions to Prevent Violence: Translation into Public Health Practice," *American Journal of Preventive Medicine* 28(2S1):4–5 (2005).

17. Helen Rumbelow and Alice Miles, "How to Save this Child from a Life of Poverty, Violence and Despair," *The Times*, June 9, 2007.

18. Anne K. Duggan et al., "Evaluation of Hawaii's Healthy Start Program," *The Future of Children* 9(1):66–90 (1999); Anne K. Duggan, Amy Windham, Elizabeth McFarlane, Loretta Fuddy, Charles Rohde, Sharon Buchbinder, and Calvin Sia, "Hawaii's Healthy Start Program of Home Visiting for At-Risk Families: Evaluation of Family Identification, Family Engagement, and Service Delivery," *Pediatrics* 105:250–259 (2000).

19. Matthew Manning, Ross Homel, and Christine Smith, "A Meta-Analysis of the Effects of Early Developmental Prevention Programs in At-Risk Populations on Non-Health Outcomes in Adolescence," *Children and Youth Services Review* 32:506–519 (2010).

20. Conduct Problems Prevention Research Group, "Fast Track Intervention Effects on Youth Arrests and Delinquency," *Journal of Experimental Criminology* 6:131–157 (2010); see also Richard E. Tremblay and Wendy M. Craig, "Developmental Crime Prevention," in *Building a Safer Society: Strategic Approaches to Crime Prevention*, ed. Michael Tonry and David P. Farrington (Chicago: University of Chicago Press, 1995).

21. Alex R. Piquero, David P. Farrington, Brandon C. Welsh, Richard E. Tremblay, and Wesley G. Jennings, "Effects of Early/Family Parent Training Programs on Antisocial Behavior and Delinquency," *Journal of Experimental Criminology* 5:83–120 (2009).

22. See Gerald R. Patterson, "Performance Models for Antisocial Boys," *American Psychologist* 41:432–444 (1986); Gerald R. Patterson, *Coercive Family Process* (Eugene, OR: Castalia, 1982).

23. Gerald R. Patterson, Patricia Chamberlain, and John B. Reid, "A Comparative Evaluation of a Parent-Training Program," *Behavior Therapy* 13:638–650 (1982); Gerald R. Patterson, John B. Reid, and Thomas J. Dishion, *Antisocial Boys* (Eugene, OR: Castalia, 1992).

24. Peter W. Greenwood, Karyn E. Model, C. Peter Rydell, and James Chiesa, *Diverting Children from a Life of Crime: Measuring Costs and Benefits* (Santa Monica, CA: Rand, 1998).

25. Farrington, "Early Developmental Prevention of Juvenile Delinquency," pp. 216–217.

26. Holly S. Schindler and Hirokazu Yoshikawa, "Preventing Crime Through Intervention in the Preschool Years," in *The Oxford Handbook of Crime Prevention*, ed. Welsh and Farrington; Greg J. Duncan and Katherine Magnuson, "Individual and Parent-Based Intervention Strategies for Promoting Human Capital and Positive Behavior," *Human Development Across Lives and Generations: The Potential for Change*, ed. P. Lindsay Chase-Lansdale, Kathleen Kiernan, and Ruth J. Friedman (New York: Cambridge University Press, 2004).

27. Lawrence J. Schweinhart, Helen V. Barnes, and David P. Weikart, *Significant Benefits: The High/Scope Perry Preschool Study through Age 27* (Ypsilanti, MI: High/Scope Press, 1993), p. 3.

28. Lawrence J. Schweinhart and David P. Weikart, *Young Children Grow Up: The Effects of the Perry Preschool Program through Age 15* (Ypsilanti, MI: High/Scope Press, 1980).

29. Schweinhart, Barnes, and Weikart, *Significant Benefits: The High/Scope Perry Preschool Study through Age 27*, p. xv.

30. W. Steven Barnett, *Lives in the Balance: Age 27 Benefit-Cost Analysis of the High/Scope Perry Preschool Program* (Ypsilanti, MI: High/Scope Press, 1996); W. Steven Barnett, "Cost-Benefit Analysis," in Schweinhart, Barnes, and Weikart, *Significant Benefits: The High/Scope Perry Preschool Study through Age 27* (Ypsilanti, MI: High/Scope Press, 1993).

31. Greenwood et al., "Estimating the Costs and Benefits of Early Childhood Interventions: Nurse Home Visits and the Perry Preschool."

32. Lawrence J. Schweinhart, "Crime Prevention by the High/Scope Perry Preschool Program," *Victims and Offenders* 2:141–160 (2007); Lawrence J. Schweinhart, Jeanne Montie, Xiang Zongping, W. Steven Barnett, Clive R. Belfield, and Milagros Nores, *Lifetime Effects: The High/Scope Perry Preschool Study through Age 40* (Ypsilanti, MI: High/Scope Press, 2005).

33. Arthur J. Reynolds, Judy A. Temple, Dylan L. Robertson, and Emily A. Mann, "Long-Term Effects of an Early Childhood Intervention on Educational Achievement and Juvenile Arrest: A 15-Year Follow-up of Low-Income Children in Public Schools," *Journal of the American Medical Association* 285:2339–2346 (2001).

34. Arthur J. Reynolds, Judy A. Temple, Suh-Ruu Ou, Dylan L. Robertson, Joshua P. Mersky, James W. Topitzes et al., "Effects of a School-Based, Early Childhood Intervention on Adult Health and Well-Being," *Archives of Pediatrics and Adolescent Medicine* 161:730–739 (2007).

35. Arthur J. Reynolds, Judy A. Temple, Suh-Ruu Ou, Irma A. Arteaga, and Barry White, "School-Based Early Childhood Education and Age-28 Well-Being: Effects by Timing Dosage and Subgroups," *Science* 333:360–364 (2011).

36. Arthur J. Reynolds, Judy A. Temple, and Suh-Ruu Ou, "School-Based Early Intervention and Child Well-Being in the Chicago Longitudinal Study," *Child Welfare* 82:633–656 (2003).

37. Schindler and Yoshikawa, "Preventing Crime Through Intervention in the Preschool Years"; Edward Zigler and Sally J. Styfco, "Extended Childhood Intervention Prepares Children for School and Beyond," *Journal of the American Medical Association* 285:2378–2380 (2001).

38. James C. Howell, ed., *Guide for Implementing the Comprehensive Strategy for Serious, Violent, and Chronic Juvenile Offenders* (Washington, DC: Office of Juvenile Justice and Delinquency Prevention, U.S. Department of Justice, 1995), p. 90.

39. MENTOR United States, *Mentoring in America, 2005* (Alexandria, VA: Author, 2006); McCord, Widom, and Crowell, eds., *Juvenile Crime, Juvenile Justice*, p. 147.

40. Edith Fairman Cooper, *Mentoring Programs Funded by the Federal Government Dedicated to Disadvantaged Youth: Issues and Activities. CRS Report for Congress* (Washington, DC: Congressional Research Service, The Library of Congress, March 20, 2006), p. 15.

41. Laurence C. Novotney, Elizabeth Mertinko, James Lange, and Tara Kelly Baker, *Juvenile Mentoring Program: A Progress Review* (Washington, DC: OJJDP Juvenile Justice Bulletin, 2000).

42. Thomas J. Dishion, Joan McCord, and François Poulin, "When Interventions Harm: Peer Groups and Problem Behavior," *American Psychologist* 54:755–764 (1999).

43. Information Technology International, *Jump Annual Report, 2003* (Alexandria, VA: Author, 2003).

44. Darrick Jolliffe and David P. Farrington, *The Influence of Mentoring on Reoffending* (Stockholm, Sweden: National Council for Crime Prevention, 2008).

45. Patrick Tolan, David Henry, Michael Schoeny, and Arin Bass, *Mentoring Interventions to Affect Juvenile Delinquency and Associated Problems* (Campbell Collaboration, 2008).

46. Renée Spencer, "Understanding the Mentoring Process Between Adolescents and Adults," *Youth and Society* 37:287–315 (2006), pp. 309–311.

47. Delbert S. Elliott, Beatrix Hamburg, and Kirk R. Williams, "Violence in American Schools: An Overview," in *Violence in American Schools: A New Perspective*, Delbert S. Elliott, Beatrix Hamburg, and Kirk R. Williams (New York: Cambridge University Press, 1998), p. 16.

48. Alexander T. Vazsonyi, Lara B. Belliston, and Daniel J. Flannery, "Evaluation of a School-Based, Universal Violence Prevention Program: Low-, Medium-, and High-Risk Children," *Youth Violence and Juvenile Justice* 2:185–206 (2004).

49. McCord, Widom, and Crowell, eds., *Juvenile Crime, Juvenile Justice*, pp. 150–151.

50. Rolf Loeber and David P. Farrington, eds., *From Juvenile Delinquency to Adult Crime: Criminal Careers, Justice Policy, and Prevention* (New York: Oxford University Press, 2012).

51. U.S. Department of Labor, "Job Corps: Success Lasts a Lifetime," August 24, 2010, www.jobcorps.gov/centers.aspx (accessed August 17, 2012).

52. Peter Z. Schochet, John Burghardt, and Sheena McConnell, "Does Job Corps Work? Impact Findings from the National Job Corps Study," *American Economic Review* 98:1864–1886 (2008).

53. David A. Long, Charles D. Mallar, and Craig V. D. Thornton, "Evaluating the Benefits and Costs of the Job Corps," *Journal of Policy Analysis and Management* 1:55–76 (1981).

54. Sheena McConnell and Steven Glazerman, *National Job Corps Study: The Benefits and Costs of Job Corps* (Washington, DC: Employment and Training Administration, U.S. Department of Labor, 2001).

55. YouthBuild U.S.A., "About YouthBuild," www.youthbuild.org/youthbuild-programs (accessed August 17, 2012); Tim Cross and Daryl Wright, "What Works with At-Risk Youths," *Corrections Today* 66:64–68 (2004), p. 64.

56. Ibid., p. 65.

57. Mark A. Cohen and Alex R. Piquero, "An Outcome Evaluation of the YouthBuild USA Offender Project," *Youth Violence and Juvenile Justice* 8:373–385 (2009).

58. For a comprehensive view of juvenile law, see, generally, Joseph J. Senna and Larry J. Siegel, *Juvenile Law: Cases and Comments*, 2nd ed. (St. Paul, MN: West, 1992).

59. For an excellent review of the juvenile process, see Jeffrey Butts and Gregory Halemba, *Waiting for Justice—Moving Young Offenders Through the Juvenile Court Process* (Pittsburgh: National Center for Juvenile Justice, 1996).

60. Federal Bureau of Investigation, *Crime in the United States 2010* (Washington, DC: U.S. Government Printing Office, 2011), Table 68.

61. Melissa Sickmund, T. J. Sladky, W. Kang, and Charles Puzzanchera, "Easy Access to the Census of Juveniles in Residential Placement," 2011, www.ojjdp.gov/ojstatbb/ezacjrp/ (accessed May 28, 2012).

62. Fox Butterfield, "Justice Besieged," *New York Times*, July 21, 1997, p. A16.

63. National Conference on State Legislatures, *A Legislator's Guide to Comprehensive Juvenile Justice, Juvenile Detention, and Corrections* (Denver: National Conference on State Legislators, 1996).

64. James C. Howell, *Preventing and Reducing Juvenile Delinquency: A Comprehensive Framework* (Thousand Oaks, CA: Sage, 2009, second edition), p. 218.

65. James C. Howell, Marion R. Kelly, James Palmer, and Ronald L. Mangum, "Integrating Child Welfare, Juvenile Justice, and Other Agencies in a Continuum of Services," *Child Welfare* 83:143–156 (2004).

66. David P. Farrington and Brandon C. Welsh, *Saving Children from a Life of Crime: Early Risk Factors and Effective Interventions* (New York: Oxford University Press, 2007).

67. Ibid.

68. Ibid.; see also Elizabeth K. Drake, Steve Aos, and Marna G. Miller, "Evidence-Based Public Policy Options to Reduce Crime and Criminal Justice Costs: Implications in Washington State," *Victims and Offenders* 4:170–196 (2009); Peter W. Greenwood, *Changing Lives: Delinquency Prevention as Crime-Control Policy* (Chicago: University of Chicago Press, 2006).

69. Eliana Garces, Duncan Thomas, and Janet Currie, "Longer-Term Effects of Head Start," *American Economic Review* 92:999–1012 (2002).

70. Anne K. Duggan, Amy Windham, Elizabeth McFarlane, Loretta Fuddy, Charles Rohde, Sharon Buchbinder, and Calvin Sia, "Hawaii's Healthy Start Program of Home Visitation for At-Risk Families: Evaluation of Family Identification, Family Engagement, and Service Delivery," *Pediatrics* 105:250–259 (2000); Ned Calonge, "Community Interventions to Prevent Violence: Translation into Public Health Practice," *American Journal of Preventive Medicine* 28:4–5 (2005).

71. *Youth Violence: A Report of the Surgeon General* (Rockville, MD: U.S. Department of Health and Human Services, 2001).

72. Jean Baldwin Grossman and Joseph P. Tierney, "Does Mentoring Work? An Impact Study of the Big Brothers Big Sisters Program," *Evaluation Review* 22:403–426 (1998), p. 405.

73. Lawrence F. Murray and Steven Belenko, "CASASTART: A Community-Based, School-Centered Intervention for High-Risk Youth," *Substance Use and Misuse* 40:913–933 (2005); National Center on Addiction and Substance Abuse, *CASASTART* (New York: Columbia University, 2007).

74. Adele V. Harrell, Shannon E. Cavanagh, and Sanjeev Sridharan, *Evaluation of the Children At Risk Program: Results 1 Year after the End of the Program* (Washington, DC: NIJ Research in Brief, 1999).

75. James C. Howell, *Preventing and Reducing Juvenile Delinquency: A Comprehensive Framework* (Thousand Oaks, CA: Sage, 2009, 2nd ed.), p. 220; see also Shelley Zavlek, *Planning Community-Based Facilities for Violent Juvenile Offenders as Part of a System of Graduated Sanctions* (Washington, DC: OJJDP Juvenile Justice Bulletin, 2005).

76. Peter W. Greenwood and Susan Turner, "Juvenile Crime and Juvenile Justice," in *Crime and Public Policy*, ed. James Q. Wilson and Joan Petersilia (New York: Oxford University Press, 2011).

77. "Summary of Drug Court Activity by State and County: Juvenile/Family Drug Courts" (Washington, DC: Bureau of Justice Assistance Drug Court Clearinghouse at American University, July 2010).

78. Office of Juvenile Justice and Delinquency Prevention, *How OJJDP is Serving Children, Families, and Communities: 2008 Annual Report* (Washington, DC: U.S. Department of Justice, OJJDP, 2009).

79. Ojmarrh Mitchell, David B. Wilson, Amy Eggers, and Doris Layton MacKenzie, "Assessing the Effectiveness of Drug Courts on Recidivism: A Meta-Analytic Review of Traditional and Non-Traditional Drug Courts," *Journal of Criminal Justice* 40:60–71 (2012).

80. Laurie Chassin, "Juvenile Justice and Substance Abuse," *The Future of Children* 18(2):165–183 (2008), at 170.

81. Mitchell, Wilson, Eggers, and MacKenzie, "Assessing the Effectiveness of Drug Courts on Recidivism: A Meta-Analytic Review of Traditional and Non-Traditional Drug Courts," Table 3, p. 64.

82. W. Craig Carter and R. Donald Barker, "Does Completion of Juvenile Drug Court Deter Adult Criminality?" *Journal of Social Work Practice in the Addictions* 11:181–193 (2011).

83. Joan McCord, Cathy Spatz Widom, and Nancy A. Crowell, eds., *Juvenile Crime, Juvenile Justice* (Washington, DC: National Academy Press, Panel on Juvenile Crime: Prevention, Treatment, and Control, 2001), p. 224.

84. See also Melissa M. Moon, Francis T. Cullen, and John Paul Wright, "It Takes a Village: Public Willingness to Help Wayward Youths," *Youth Violence and Juvenile Justice* 1:32–45 (2003).

85. Daniel P. Mears, Carter Hay, Marc Gertz, and Christina Mancini, "Public Opinion and the Foundation of the Juvenile Court," *Criminology* 45:223–258 (2007), p. 246.

86. McCord, Widom, and Crowell, *Juvenile Crime, Juvenile Justice*, p. 152.

87. Greenwood, *Changing Lives*.

88. Patrick Griffin, *Different from Adults: An Updated Analysis of Juvenile Transfer and Blended Sentencing Laws, with Recommendations for Reform* (Pittsburgh: National Center for Juvenile Justice, 2008).

89. Drake, Aos, and Miller, "Evidence-Based Public Policy Options to Reduce Crime and Criminal Justice Costs: Implications in Washington State"; see also Simon M. Fass and Chung-Ron Pi, "Getting Tough on Juvenile Crime: An Analysis of Costs and Benefits," *Journal of Research in Crime and Delinquency* 39:363–399 (2002).

Chapter 12. Police Work with Juveniles

1. This section relies on sources including Malcolm Sparrow, Mark H. Moore, and David Kennedy, *Beyond 911: A New Era for Policing* (New York: Basic Books, 1990); Daniel Devlin, *Police Procedure, Administration, and Organization* (London: Butterworth, 1966); Robert Fogelson, *Big City Police* (Cambridge, MA: Harvard University Press, 1977); Roger Lane, *Policing the City, Boston 1822–1885* (Cambridge, MA: Harvard University Press, 1967); Lane, "Urban Police and Crime in Nineteenth-Century America," in *Crime and Justice*, Vol. 2, ed. Norval Morris and Michael Tonry (Chicago: University of Chicago Press, 1980), pp. 1–45; J. J. Tobias, *Crime and Industrial Society in the Nineteenth Century* (New York: Schocken Books, 1967); Samuel Walker, *A Critical History of Police Reform: The Emergence of Professionalism* (Lexington, MA: Lexington Books, 1977); Walker, *Popular Justice* (New York: Oxford University Press, 1980); President's Commission on Law Enforcement and the Administration of Justice, *Task Force Report: The Police* (Washington, DC: U.S. Government Printing Office, 1967), pp. 1–9.

2. See, generally, Walker, *Popular Justice*, p. 61.

3. Law Enforcement Assistance Administration, *Two Hundred Years of American Criminal Justice* (Washington, DC: U.S. Government Printing Office, 1976).

4. August Vollmer, *The Police and Modern Society* (Berkeley: University of California Press, 1936).

5. O. W. Wilson, *Police Administration*, 2nd ed. (New York: McGraw-Hill, 1963).

6. Wesley G. Skogan, *Police and Community in Chicago: A Tale of Three Cities* (New York: Oxford University Press, 2006); Wesley G. Skogan, ed., *Community Policing: Can It Work?* (Belmont, CA: Wadsworth, 2004).

7. See Anthony A. Braga and David Weisburd, *Policing Problem Places: Crime Hot Spots and Effective Prevention* (New York: Oxford University Press, 2010); Wesley G. Skogan and Kathleen Frydl, eds., *Fairness and Effectiveness in Policing: The Evidence* (Washington, DC: The National Academies Press, 2004); David Weisburd and Anthony A. Braga, eds., *Police Innovation: Contrasting Perspectives* (New York: Cambridge University Press, 2006).

8. Franklin E. Zimring, *The City that Became Safe: New York's Lessons for Urban Crime and Its Control* (New York: Oxford University Press, 2011); Skogan and Frydl, *Fairness and Effectiveness in Policing*; Joel Wallman and Alfred Blumstein, "After the Crime Drop," in *The Crime Drop in America*, ed. Alfred Blumstein and Joel Wallman (New York: Cambridge University Press, 2006, rev. ed.); Lawrence W. Sherman, "Fair and Effective Policing," in *Crime: Public Policies for Crime Control*, ed. James Q. Wilson and Joan Petersilia (Oakland, CA: Institute for Contemporary Studies, 2002); Steven D. Levitt, "Understanding Why Crime Fell in the 1990s: Four Factors that Explain the Decline and Six that Do Not," *Journal of Economic Perspectives* 18:163–190 (2004).

9. Claudio G. Vera Sanchez and Ericka B. Adams, "Sacrificed On the Altar of Public Safety: The Policing of Latino and African American Youth," *Journal of Contemporary Criminal Justice* 27:322–341 (2011); Jamie L. Flexon, Arthur J. Lurigio, and Richard G. Greenleaf, "Exploring the Dimensions of Trust in the Police Among Chicago Juveniles," *Journal of Criminal Justice* 37:180–189 (2009); see also Yolander Hurst, James Frank, and Sandra Lee Browning, "The Attitudes of Juveniles Toward the Police: A Comparison of Black and White Youth," *Policing* 23:37–53 (2000).

10. Denise C. Herz, "Improving Police Encounters with Juveniles: Does Training Make a Difference?," *Justice Research and Policy* 3:57–77 (2001).

11. Donald Black and Albert J. Reiss, Jr., "Police Control of Juveniles," *American Sociological Review* 35:63 (1970); Richard Lundman, Richard Sykes, and John Clark, "Police Control of Juveniles: A Replication," *Journal of Research on Crime and Delinquency* 15:74 (1978).

12. American Bar Association, *Standards Relating to Police Handling of Juvenile Problems* (Cambridge, MA: Ballinger, 1977), p. 1.

13. Samuel Walker, *The Police of America* (New York: McGraw-Hill, 1983), p. 133.

14. Karen A. Joe, "The Dynamics of Running Away: Deinstitutionalization Policies and the Police," *Juvenile Family Court Journal* 46:43–45 (1995).

15. Mary Dodge, "Juvenile Police Informants: Friendship, Persuasion, and Pretense," *Youth Violence and Juvenile Justice* 4:234–246 (2006), p. 234.

16. Ibid., p. 244.

17. Richard J. Lundman, *Prevention and Control of Juvenile Delinquency*, 3rd ed. (New York: Oxford University Press, 2001), p. 23.

18. FBI, *Crime in the United States, 2010* (Washington, DC: U.S. Government Printing Office, 2011), Table 32.

19. See Franklin E. Zimring, *American Juvenile Justice* (New York: Oxford University Press, 2005), Ch. 8.

20. Braga and Weisburd, *Policing Problem Places: Crime Hot Spots and Effective Prevention*; David Weisburd, Cody W. Telep, Joshua C. Hinkle, and John E. Eck, "Is Problem-Oriented Policing Effective in Reducing Crime and Disorder? Findings from a Campbell Systematic Review," *Criminology and Public Policy* 9:139–172 (2010); Lawrence W. Sherman and John E. Eck, "Policing for Crime Prevention," in *Evidence-Based Crime Prevention*, ed. Lawrence W. Sherman, David P. Farrington, Brandon C. Welsh, and Doris Layton MacKenzie (New York: Routledge, 2006, rev. ed.), p. 321; for "hot spots" policing, see also Skogan and Frydl, *Fairness and Effectiveness in Policing*; Anthony A. Braga, "The Effects of Hot Spots Policing on Crime," *Annals of the American Academy of Political and Social Science* 578:104–125 (2001).

21. Christopher S. Koper and Evan Mayo-Wilson, "Police Crackdowns on Illegal Gun Carrying: A Systematic Review of Their Impact on Gun Crime," *Journal of Experimental Criminology* 2:227–261 (2006).

22. Linda Szymanski, *Summary of Juvenile Code Purpose Clauses* (Pittsburgh: National Center for Juvenile Justice, 1988); see also, for example, GA Code Ann. 15; Iowa Code Ann. 232.2; Mass. Gen. Laws, Ch. 119, 56.

23. Samuel M. Davis, *Rights of Juveniles—The Juvenile Justice System*, rev. (New York: Clark-Boardmen, June 1989), Sec. 3.3.

24. National Council of Juvenile and Family Court Judges, *Juvenile and Family Law Digest* 29:1–2 (1997).

25. See Fourth Amendment, U.S. Constitution.

26. *Arizona v. Gant*, 556 U.S. ___ (2009).

27. *Chimel v. Cal.*, 395 U.S. 752, 89 S.Ct. 2034 (1969).

28. *United States v. Ross*, 456 U.S. 798, 102 S.Ct. 2157 (1982).

29. *Terry v. Ohio*, 392 U.S.1, 88 S.Ct. 1868 (1968).

30. *Bumper v. North Carolina*, 391 U.S. 543, 88 S.Ct. 1788 (1968).

31. *Miranda v. Arizona*, 384 U.S. 436, 86 S.Ct. 1602 (1966).

32. 564 U.S.__(2011).

33. *Commonwealth v. Gaskins*, 471 Pa. 238, 369 A.2d 1285 (1977); *In re E.T.C.*, 141 Vt. 375, 449 A.2d 937 (1982).

34. *People v. Lara*, 67 Cal.2d 365, 62 Cal.Rptr. 586, 432 P.2d 202 (1967).

35. *West v. United States*, 399 F.2d 467 (5th Cir. 1968).

36. Barry C. Feld, "Police Interrogation of Juveniles: An Empirical Study of Policy and Practice," *Journal of Criminal Law and Criminology* 97: 219–316 (2006); Barry C. Feld, "Juveniles' Competence to Exercise *Miranda* Rights: An Empirical Study of Policy and Practice," *Minnesota Law Review* 91:26–100 (2006).

37. *Fare v. Michael C.*, 442 U.S. 707, 99 S.Ct. 2560 (1979).

38. *California v. Prysock*, 453 U.S. 355, 101 S.Ct. 2806 (1981).

39. See, for example, Larry Holtz, "*Miranda* in a Juvenile Setting—A Child's Right to Silence," *Journal of Criminal Law and Criminology* 79:534–556 (1987).

40. Kenneth C. Davis, *Discretionary Justice: A Preliminary Inquiry* (Baton Rouge: Louisiana State University Press, 1969); H. Ted Rubin, *Juvenile Justice: Police, Practice, and Law* (Santa Monica, CA: Goodyear, 1979).

41. Joseph Goldstein, "Police Discretion Not to Invoke the Criminal Process: Low-Visibility Decisions in the Administration of Justice," *Yale Law Journal* 69:544 (1960).

42. Victor Streib, *Juvenile Justice in America* (Port Washington, NY: Kennikat, 1978).

43. Herbert Packer, *The Limits of the Criminal Sanction* (Palo Alto, CA: Stanford University Press, 1968).

44. Black and Reiss, "Police Control of Juveniles"; Richard J. Lundman, "Routine Police Arrest Practices," *Social Problems* 22:127–141 (1974); Robert E. Worden and Stephanie M. Myers, *Police Encounters with Juvenile Suspects* (Albany: Hindelang Criminal Justice Research Center and School of Criminal Justice, State University of New York, 2001).

45. Nathan Goldman, *The Differential Selection of Juvenile Offenders for Court Appearance* (Washington, DC: National Council on Crime and Delinquency, 1963).

46. Irving Piliavin and Scott Briar, "Police Encounters with Juveniles," *American Journal of Sociology* 70:206–214 (1964); Theodore Ferdinand and Elmer Luchterhand, "Inner-City Youth, the Police, Juvenile Court, and Justice," *Social Problems* 8:510–526 (1970).

47. Paul Strasburg, *Violent Delinquents: Report to Ford Foundation from Vera Institute of Justice* (New York: Monarch, 1978), p. 11; Robert Terry, "The Screening of Juvenile Offenders," *Journal of Criminal Law, Criminology, and Police Science* 58:173–181 (1967).

48. Joan McCord, Cathy Spatz Widom, and Nancy A. Crowell, eds., *Juvenile Crime, Juvenile Justice* (Washington, DC: National Academy Press, Panel on Juvenile Crime: Prevention, Treatment, and Control, 2001), p. 163.

49. Worden and Myers, *Police Encounters with Juvenile Suspects*.

50. FBI, *Crime in the United States, 2010*, Table 68.

51. Douglas Smith and Christy Visher, "Street-Level Justice: Situational Determinants of Police Arrest Decisions," *Social Problems* 29:167–178 (1981).

52. Douglas Smith and Jody Klein, "Police Control of Interpersonal Disputes," *Social Problems* 31:468–481 (1984).

53. Goldman, *The Differential Selection of Juvenile Offenders for Court Appearance*, p. 25; Norman Werner and Charles Willie, "Decisions of Juvenile Officers," *American Journal of Sociology* 77:199–214 (1971).

54. Skogan and Frydl, *Fairness and Effectiveness in Policing*, pp. 301–303; Sherman, "Fair and Effective Policing," pp. 404–405.

55. Raymond Paternoster, Ronet Bachman, Robert Brame, and Lawrence W. Sherman, "Do Fair Procedures Matter? The Effect of Procedural Justice on Spouse Assault," *Law and Society Review* 31:163–204 (1997).

56. Jacinta M. Gau and Rod K. Brunson, "Procedural Justice and Order Maintenance Policing: A Study of Inner-City Young Men's Perceptions of Police Legitimacy," *Justice Quarterly* 27:255–279 (2010).

57. Ibid., p. 273.

58. Lyn Hinds, "Youth, Police Legitimacy and Informal Contact," *Journal of Police and Criminal Psychology* 24:10–21 (2009).

59. Skogan and Frydl, *Fairness and Effectiveness in Policing*, p. 7.

60. Aaron Cicourel, *The Social Organization of Juvenile Justice* (New York: Wiley, 1968).

61. Piliavin and Briar, "Police Encounters with Juveniles," p. 214.

62. David Klinger, "Demeanor or Crime? Why 'Hostile' Citizens Are More Likely to Be Arrested," *Criminology* 32:475–493 (1994).

63. Richard Lundman, "Demeanor or Crime? The Midwest City Police–Citizen Encounters Study," *Criminology* 32:631–653 (1994); Robert Worden and Robin Shepard, "On the Meaning, Measurement, and Estimated Effects of Suspects' Demeanor Toward the Police," paper presented at the annual meeting of the American Society of Criminology, Miami, November 1994.

64. Robert A. Brown, Kenneth J. Novak, and James Frank, "Identifying Variation in Police Officer Behavior Between Juveniles and Adults," *Journal of Criminal Justice* 37:200–208 (2009), p. 206.

65. James Fyfe, David Klinger, and Jeanne Flaving, "Differential Police Treatment of Male-on-Female Spousal Violence," *Criminology* 35:455–473 (1997).

66. Dale Dannefer and Russel Schutt, "Race and Juvenile Justice Processing in Police and Court Agencies," *American Journal of Sociology* 87:1113–1132 (1982); Smith and Visher, "Street-Level Justice: Situational Determinants of Police Arrest Decisions"; see also Ronald Weitzer, "Racial Discrimination in the Criminal Justice System: Findings and Problems in the Literature," *Journal of Criminal Justice* 24:309–322 (1996); Ronald Weitzer and Steven A. Tuch, "Perceptions of Racial Profiling: Race, Class, and Personal Experience," *Criminology* 40:435–456 (2002).

67. Patricia Warren, Donald Tomaskovic-Devey, William Smith, Matthew Zingraff, and Marcinda Mason, "Driving While Black: Bias Processes and Racial Disparity in Police Stops," *Criminology* 44:709–738 (2006); Richard J. Lundman and Robert L. Kaufman, "Driving While Black: Effects of Race, Ethnicity, and Gender on Citizen Self-Reports of Traffic Stops and Police Actions," *Criminology* 41:195–220 (2003).

68. Dan M. Kahan and Tracey L. Meares, "The Coming Crisis of Criminal Procedure," *Georgetown Law Journal* 86:1153–1184 (2000).

69. Randall Kennedy, *Race, Crime and the Law* (New York: Vintage, 1998).

70. Terence Thornberry, "Race, Socioeconomic Status, and Sentencing in the Juvenile Justice System," *Journal of Criminal Law and Criminology* 70:164–171 (1979); Dannefer and Schutt, "Race and Juvenile Justice Processing in Police and Court Agencies"; Jeffrey Fagan, Ellen Slaughter, and Eliot Hartstone, "Blind Justice? The Impact of Race on the Juvenile Justice Process," *Crime and Delinquency* 33:224–258 (1987).

71. Donna M. Bishop and Charles E. Frazier, "The Influence of Race in Juvenile Justice Processing," *Journal of Research in Crime and Delinquency* 25:242–261 (1988).

72. Ibid., p. 258; see also Howard N. Snyder and Melissa Sickmund, *Juvenile Offenders and Victims: 2006 National Report* (Pittsburgh: National Center for Juvenile Justice, 2006), p. 163.

73. Merry Morash, "Establishment of a Juvenile Record: The Influence of Individual and Peer Group Characteristics," *Criminology* 22:97–112 (1984).

74. Meda Chesney-Lind, "Judicial Enforcement of the Female Sex Role: The Family Court and Female Delinquency Issues," *Criminology* 8:51–71 (1973); Chesney-Lind, "Young Women in the Arms of Law," in *Women, Crime, and the Criminal Justice System*, 2nd ed., ed. L. Bowker (Lexington, MA: Lexington Books, 1978).

75. Donna Bishop and Charles Frazier, "Gender Bias in Juvenile Justice Processing: Implications of the JJDP Act," *Journal of Criminal Law and Criminology* 82:1162–1186 (1992).

76. Meda Chesney-Lind and Randall G. Shelden, *Girls, Delinquency, and Juvenile Justice*, 3rd ed. (Belmont, CA: Wadsworth, 2004), p. 35.

77. Douglas Smith, "The Organizational Context of Legal Control," *Criminology* 22:19–138 (1984); see also Stephen Mastrofski and Richard Ritti, "Police Training and the Effects of Organization on Drunk Driving Enforcement," *Justice Quarterly* 13:291–320 (1996).

78. John Irwin, *The Jail: Managing the Underclass in American Society* (Berkeley: University of California Press, 1985).

79. Darlene Conley, "Adding Color to a Black and White Picture: Using Qualitative Data to Explain Racial Disproportionality in the Juvenile Justice System," *Journal of Research in Crime and Delinquency* 31:135–148 (1994).

80. Robert Sampson, "Effects of Socioeconomic Context of Official Reaction to Juvenile Delinquency," *American Sociological Review* 51:876–885 (1986).

81. Judith Greene and Kevin Pranis, *Gang Wars: The Failure of Enforcement Tactics and the Need for Effective Public Safety Strategies* (Washington, DC: Justice Policy Institute, 2007).

82. Ibid., p. 5.

83. Brian A. Reaves, *Local Police Departments, 2007* (Washington, DC: Bureau of Justice Statistics, 2010), p. 28.

84. Finn-Aage Esbensen, Dana Peterson, Terrance J. Taylor, and D. Wayne Osgood, "Results from a Multi-Site Evaluation of the G.R.E.A.T. Program," *Justice Quarterly* 29:125–151 (2012).

85. Finn-Aage Esbensen and D. Wayne Osgood, "Gang Resistance Education and Training (G.R.E.A.T.): Results from the National Evaluation," *Journal of Research in Crime and Delinquency* 36:194–225 (1999).

86. Finn-Aage Esbensen, D. Wayne Osgood, Terrence J. Taylor, Dana Peterson, and Adrienne Freng, "How Great Is G.R.E.A.T.? Results from a Longitudinal Quasi-Experimental Design," *Criminology and Public Policy* 1:87–118 (2001).

87. Esbensen, Petersen, Taylor, and Osgood, "Results from a Multi-Site Evaluation of the G.R.E.A.T. Program."

88. Yale University Child Study Center, *Community Outreach Through Police in Schools* (Washington, DC: Office for Victims of Crime Bulletin, 2003), p. 2.

89. Ibid., p. 3.

90. For an analysis of this position, see George Kelling and James Q. Wilson, "Broken Windows: The Police and Neighborhood Safety," *Atlantic Monthly* 249:29–38 (1982).

91. Robert Trojanowicz and Hazel Harden, *The Status of Contemporary Community Policing Programs* (East Lansing: Michigan State University Neighborhood Foot Patrol Center, 1985).

92. Reaves, *Local Police Departments, 2007*, p. 27.

93. Ibid., p. 28.

94. See Anthony A. Braga, *Gun Violence Among Serious Young Offenders* (Washington, DC: Office of Community Oriented Policing Services, U.S. Department of Justice, 2004).

95. See Edward F. McGarrell, Nicholas Corsaro, Natalie Hipple, and Tim Bynum, "Project Safe Neighborhoods and Violent Crime Trends in U.S. Cities: Assessing Violent Crime Impact," *Journal of Quantitative Criminology* 26:165–190 (2010); Andrew V. Papachristos, Tracey Meares, and Jeffrey Fagan, "Attention Felons: Evaluating Project Safe Neighborhoods in Chicago," *Journal of Empirical Legal Studies* 4:223–272 (2007).

96. Susan Guarino-Ghezzi, "Reintegrative Police Surveillance of Juvenile Offenders: Forging an Urban Model," *Crime and Delinquency* 40:131–153 (1994).

97. See David Weisburd and John E. Eck, "What Can Police Do to Reduce Crime, Disorder, and Fear?" *Annals of the American Academy of Political and Social Science* 593:42–65 (2004), p. 57, Table 1.

98. Michael D. Reisig and Roger B. Parks, "Community Policing and Quality of Life," in *Community Policing: Can It Work?* ed. Skogan.

99. Mark H. Moore, "Problem-Solving and Community Policing," in *Modern Policing. Crime and Justice: A Review of Research*, Vol. 15, Michael Tonry and Norval Morris (Chicago: University of Chicago Press, 1992), p. 99.

100. Anthony A. Braga, *Problem-Oriented Policing and Crime Prevention*, 2nd ed. (Monsey, NY: Criminal Justice Press, 2008).

101. Moore, "Problem-Solving and Community Policing," p. 120.

102. Debra Cohen, *Problem-Solving Partnerships: Including the Community for a Change* (Washington, DC: Office of Community Oriented Policing Services, 2001), p. 2.

103. See Leanne F. Alarid, Barbara A. Sims, and James Ruiz, "Juvenile Probation and Police Partnership as Loosely Coupled Systems: A Qualitative Analysis," *Youth Violence and Juvenile Justice* 9:79–95 (2011); John L. Worrall and Larry K. Gaines, "The Effect of Police-Probation Partnerships on Juvenile Arrests," *Journal of Criminal Justice* 34:579–589 (2006).

104. See Weisburd, Telep, Hinkle, and Eck, "Is Problem-Oriented Policing Effective in Reducing Crime and Disorder? Findings from a Campbell Systematic Review."

105. Cohen, *Problem-Solving Partnerships*, p. 2.

106. Ibid., pp. 5–7.

107. Kelly Dedel Johnson, *Underage Drinking. Problem-Specific Guides Series*, No. 27 (Washington, DC: Office of Community Oriented Policing Services, 2004).

108. Anthony A. Braga, *Gun Violence Among Serious Young Offenders. Problem-Specific Guides Series*, No. 23, revised edition (Washington, DC: Office of Community Oriented Policing Services, 2010).

109. Ibid., p. 16.

110. Anthony A. Braga, David M. Kennedy, Elin J. Waring, and Anne Morrison Piehl, "Problem-Oriented Policing Deterrence, and Youth Violence: An Evaluation of Boston's Operation Ceasefire," *Journal of Research in Crime and Delinquency* 38:195–225 (2001).

111. Christopher J. Harris, "Police and Soft Technology: How Information Technology Contributes to Police Decision Making," in *The New Technology of Crime, Law and Social Control*, ed. James M. Byrne and Donald J. Rebovich (Monsey, NY: Criminal Justice Press, 2007).

112. Don Hummer, "Policing and 'Hard' Technology," in *The New Technology of Crime, Law and Social Control*, ed. Byrne and Rebovich.

113. Brandon C. Welsh and David P. Farrington, *Making Public Places Safer: Surveillance and Crime Prevention* (New York: Oxford University Press, 2009).

114. David Weisburd and John E. Eck, "What Can Police Do to Reduce Crime, Disorder, and Fear?" *Annals of the American Academy of Political and Social Science* 593:42–65 (2004); Skogan and Frydl, *Fairness and Effectiveness in Policing*.

Chapter 13. Juvenile Court Process: Pretrial, Trial, and Sentencing

1. Kelly Dedel, "National Profile of the Organization of State Juvenile Corrections Systems," *Crime and Delinquency* 44:507–525 (1998).

2. Charles Puzzanchera, Benjamin Adams, and Melissa Sickmund, *Juvenile Court Statistics 2008* (Pittsburgh: National Center for Juvenile Justice, 2011), p. 6.

3. Ibid., pp. 13, 19; see also Lori Guevara, Lorenzo M. Boyd, Angela P. Taylor, and Robert A. Brown, "Racial Disparities in Juvenile Court Outcomes: A Test of the Liberation Hypothesis," *Journal of Ethnicity in Criminal Justice* 9:200–217 (2011).

4. *Powell v. Alabama*, 287 U.S. 45, 53 S.Ct. 55, 77, L.Ed.2d 158 (1932); *Gideon v. Wainwright*, 372 U.S. 335, 83 S.Ct. 792, 9 L.Ed.2d 799 (1963); *Argersinger v. Hamlin*, 407 U.S. 25, 92 S.Ct. 2006, 32 L.Ed.2d 530 (1972).

5. See Judith B. Jones, *Access to Counsel* (Washington, DC: Office of Juvenile Justice and Delinquency Prevention, 2004).

6. For a review of these studies, see T. Grisso, "The Competence of Adolescents as Trial Defendants," *Psychology, Public Policy, and Law* 3:3–32 (1997).

7. Christine Schnyder Pierce and Stanley L. Brodsky, "Trust and Understanding in the Attorney–Juvenile Relationship," *Behavioral Sciences and the Law* 20:89–107 (2002).

8. Ibid., p. 102.

9. Melinda G. Schmidt, N. Dickon Reppucci, and Jennifer L. Woolard, "Effectiveness of Participation as a Defendant: The Attorney–Juvenile Client Relationship," *Behavioral Sciences and the Law* 21:175–198 (2003).

10. Ibid., p. 193.

11. George W. Burruss, Jr., and Kimberly Kempf-Leonard, "The Questionable Advantage of Defense Counsel in Juvenile Court," *Justice Quarterly* 19:37–67 (2002).

12. Loris Guevara, Denise Herz, and Cassia Spohn, "Race, Gender, and Legal Counsel: Differential Outcomes in Two Juvenile Courts," *Youth Violence and Juvenile Justice* 6:83–104 (2008), at 98.

13. Lori Guevara, Cassia Spohn, and Denise Herz, "Race, Legal Representation, and Juvenile Justice: Issues and Concerns," *Crime and Delinquency* 50:344–371 (2004), at 362–364.

14. Barry C. Feld and Shelly Schaefer, "The Right to Counsel in Juvenile Court: The Conundrum of Attorneys as an Aggravating Factor at Disposition," *Justice Quarterly* 27:713–741 (2010); Barry C. Feld and Shelly Schaefer, "The Right to Counsel in Juvenile Court: Law Reform to Deliver Legal Services and Reduce Justice by Geography," *Criminology and Public Policy* 9:327–356 (2010).

15. Howard Davidson, "The Guardian *ad litem*: An Important Approach to the Protection of Children," *Children Today* 10:23 (1981); Daniel Golden, "Who Guards the Children?" *Boston Globe Magazine*, December 27, 1992, p. 12.

16. Chester Harhut, "An Expanded Role for the Guardian *ad litem*," *Juvenile and Family Court Journal* 51:31–35 (2000).

17. Steve Riddell, "CASA: Child's Voice in Court," *Juvenile and Family Justice Today* 7:13–14 (1998).

18. American Bar Association, *A Call for Justice: An Assessment of Access to Counsel and Quality of Representation in Delinquency Proceedings* (Washington, DC: ABA Juvenile Justice Center, 1995).

19. Douglas C. Dodge, *Due Process Advocacy* (Washington, DC: Office of Juvenile Justice and Delinquency Prevention, 1997); see also Jones, *Access to Counsel*.

20. "ABA President Says New Report Shows 'Conveyor Belt Justice' Hurting Children and Undermining Public Safety," press release (Washington, DC: American Bar Association, October 21, 2003).

21. James Shine and Dwight Price, "Prosecutor and Juvenile Justice: New Roles and Perspectives," in *Juvenile Justice and Public Policy: Toward a National Agenda*, ed. Ira Schwartz (New York: Lexington Books, 1992), pp. 101–133.

22. James Backstrom and Gary Walker, "A Balanced Approach to Juvenile Justice: The Work of the Juvenile Justice Advisory Committee," *The Prosecutor* 32:37–39 (1988); see also *Prosecutors' Policy Recommendations on Serious, Violent, and Habitual Youthful Offenders* (Alexandria, VA: American Prosecutors' Institute, 1997).

23. Leonard P. Edwards, "The Juvenile Court and the Role of the Juvenile Court Judge," *Juvenile and Family Court Journal* 43:3–45 (1992); Lois Haight, "Why I Choose to Be a Juvenile Court Judge," *Juvenile and Family Justice Today* 7:7 (1998).

24. National Council of Juvenile and Family Court Judges, *Juvenile Delinquency Guidelines: Improving Court Practice in Juvenile Delinquency Cases* (Reno, NV: Author, 2005), p. 24.

25. Madeline Wordes and Sharon Jones, "Trends in Juvenile Detention and Steps Toward Reform," *Crime and Delinquency* 44:544–560 (1998).

26. Robert Shepard, *Juvenile Justice Standards Annotated: A Balanced Approach* (Chicago: American Bar Association, 1997).

27. Leslie Kaufman, "Child Detention Centers Criticized in New Jersey," *New York Times*, November 23, 2004.

28. Dylan Conger and Timothy Ross, "Project Confirm: An Outcome Evaluation of a Program for Children in the Child Welfare and Juvenile Justice Systems," *Youth Violence and Juvenile Justice* 4:97–115 (2006).

29. Puzzanchera, Adams, and Sickmund, *Juvenile Court Statistics 2008*, p. 32.

30. Ibid., pp. 33, 34.

31. Donna Bishop, Michael Leiber, and Joseph Johnson, "Contexts of Decision Making in the Juvenile Justice System: An Organizational Approach to Understanding Minority Overrepresentation," *Youth Violence and Juvenile Justice* 8:213–233 (2010); Nancy Rodriguez, "The Cumulative Effect of Race and Ethnicity in Juvenile Court Outcomes and Why Preadjudication Detention Matters," *Journal of Research in Crime and Delinquency* 47:391–413 (2010).

32. Katherine E. Brown and Leanne Fiftal Alarid, "Examining Racial Disparity of Male Property Offenders in the Missouri Juvenile Justice System," *Youth Violence and Juvenile Justice* 2:107–128 (2004), at 116.

33. Ibid., p. 119; see also Nancy Rodriguez, "Juvenile Court Context and Detention Decisions: Reconsidering the Role of Race, Ethnicity, and Community Characteristics in Juvenile Court Processes," *Justice Quarterly* 24:629–656 (2007), at 649.

34. Christopher A. Mallett, Patricia Stoddard-Dare, and Mamadou M. Seck, "Explicating Correlates of Juvenile Offender Detention Length: The Impact of Race, Mental Health Difficulties, Maltreatment, Offense Type, and Court Dispositions," *Youth Justice* 11:134–149 (2011).

35. James Maupin and Lis Bond-Maupin, "Detention Decision Making in a Predominantly Hispanic Region: Rural and Non-rural Differences," *Juvenile and Family Court Journal* 50:11–21 (1999).

36. Edward P. Mulvey and Anne-Marie R. Iselin, "Improving Professional Judgments of Risk and Amenability in Juvenile Justice," *The Future of Children* 18(2):35–57 (2008), at 47–48.

37. Earl Dunlap and David Roush, "Juvenile Detention as Process and Place," *Juvenile and Family Court Journal* 46:1–16 (1995).

38. "OJJDP Helps States Remove Juveniles from Jails," *Juvenile Justice Bulletin* (Washington, DC: U.S. Department of Justice, 1990).

39. Mark Soler, James Bell, Elizabeth Jameson, Carole Shauffer, Alice Shotton, and Loren Warboys, *Representing the Child Client* (New York: Matthew Bender, 1989), sec. 5.03b.

40. *Schall v. Martin*, 467 U.S. 253 (1984).

41. Jeffrey Fagan and Martin Guggenheim, "Preventive Detention for Juveniles: A Natural Experiment," *Journal of Criminal Law and Criminology*, 86:415–428 (1996).

42. Puzzanchera, Adams, and Sickmund, *Juvenile Court Statistics 2008*, p. 58.

43. Michael J. Leiber and Joseph D. Johnson, "Being Young and Black: What Are Their Effects on Juvenile Justice Decision Making?" *Crime and Delinquency* 54:560–581 (2008).

44. Alex R. Piquero, "Disproportionate Minority Contact," *The Future of Children* 18(2):59–79 (2008); Kimberly Kempf-Leonard, "Minority Youths and Juvenile Justice: Disproportionate Minority Contact After Nearly 20 Years of Reform Efforts," *Youth Violence and Juvenile Justice* 5:71–87 (2007).

45. Deborah A. Chapin and Patricia A. Griffin, "Juvenile Diversion," in *Juvenile Delinquency: Prevention, Assessment, and Intervention*, ed. Kirk Heilbrun, Naomi E. Sevin Goldstein, and Richard E. Redding (New York: Oxford University Press, 2005); see also Edwin E. Lemert, "Diversion in Juvenile Justice: What Hath Been Wrought?" *Journal of Research in Crime and Delinquency* 18:34–46 (1981).

46. Don C. Gibbons and Gerald F. Blake, "Evaluating the Impact of Juvenile Diversion Programs," *Crime and Delinquency Journal* 22:411–419 (1976); Richard J. Lundman, "Will Diversion Reduce Recidivism?" *Crime and Delinquency Journal* 22:428–437 (1976); B. Bullington, J. Sprowls, D. Katkin, and M. Phillips, "A Critique of Diversionary Juvenile Justice," *Crime and Delinquency* 24:59–71 (1978); Thomas Blomberg, "Diversion and Accelerated Social Control," *Journal of Criminal Law and Criminology* 68:274–282 (1977); Sharla Rausch and Charles Logan, "Diversion from Juvenile Court: Panacea or Pandora's Box?" in *Evaluating Juvenile Justice*, ed. J. Klugel (Beverly Hills, CA: Sage, 1983), pp. 19–30.

47. Arnold Binder and Gilbert Geis, "Ad Populum Argumentation in Criminology: Juvenile Diversion as Rhetoric," *Criminology* 30:309–333 (1984).

48. Christopher J. Sullivan and Edward Latessa, "The Coproduction of Outcomes: An Integrated Assessment of Youth and Program Effects on Recidivism," *Youth Violence and Juvenile Justice* 9:191–206 (2011).

49. Alison Evans Cuellar, Larkin S. McReynolds, and Gail A. Wasserman, "A Cure for Crime: Can Mental Health Treatment Diversion Reduce Crime Among Youth?" *Journal of Policy Analysis and Management* 25:197–214 (2006).

50. Peter W. Greenwood, *Changing Lives: Delinquency Prevention as Crime-Control Policy* (Chicago: University of Chicago Press, 2006), Ch. 8; Franklin E. Zimring, *American Juvenile Justice* (New York: Oxford University Press, 2005), Ch. 4.

51. Zimring, *American Juvenile Justice*, p. 47.

52. Albert W. Alschuler, "The Prosecutor's Role in Plea Bargaining," *University of Chicago Law Review* 36:50–112 (1968); Joyce Dougherty, "A Comparison of Adult Plea Bargaining and Juvenile Intake," *Federal Probation* 52:72–79 (1998).

53. Sanford Fox, *Juvenile Courts in a Nutshell* (St. Paul, MN: West, 1985), pp. 154–156.

54. See Darlene Ewing, "Juvenile Plea Bargaining: A Case Study," *American Journal of Criminal Law* 6:167 (1978); Adrienne Volenik, *Checklists for Use in Juvenile Delinquency Proceedings* (Chicago: American Bar Association, 1985); Bruce Green, "Package Plea Bargaining and the Prosecutor's Duty of Good Faith," *Criminal Law Bulletin* 25:507–550 (1989).

55. Joseph Sanborn, "Philosophical, Legal, and Systematic Aspects of Juvenile Court Plea Bargaining," *Crime and Delinquency* 39:509–527 (1993).

56. Puzzanchera, Adams, and Sickmund, *Juvenile Court Statistics 2008*, p. 58.

57. Patrick Griffin, Sean Addie, Benjamin Adams, and Kathy Firestine, *Trying Juveniles as Adults: An Analysis of State Transfer Laws and Reporting* (Washington, DC: Office of Juvenile Justice and Delinquency Prevention, 2011), p. 3.

58. Ibid.

59. Ibid.

60. *Kent v. United States*, 383 U.S. 541, 86 S.Ct. 1045, 16 L.Ed.2d 84 (1966); *Breed v. Jones*, 421 U.S. 519, 95 S.Ct. 1179, 44 L.Ed.2d 346 (1975).

61. Barry Feld, "The Juvenile Court Meets the Principle of the Offense: Legislative Changes in Juvenile Waiver Statutes," *Journal of Criminal Law and Criminology* 78:471–534 (1987); Paul Marcotte, "Criminal Kids," *American Bar Association Journal* 76:60–66 (1990); Dale Parent et al., *Transferring Serious Juvenile Offenders to Adult Courts* (Washington DC: U.S. Department of Justice, National Institute of Justice, 1997).

62. See Kareem L. Jordan and David L. Myers, "Juvenile Transfer and Deterrence: Reexamining the Effectiveness of a 'Get-Tough' Policy," *Crime and Delinquency* 57:247–270 (2011); Richard E. Redding, *Juvenile Transfer Laws: An Effective Deterrent to Delinquency?* (Washington, DC: Office of Juvenile Justice and Delinquency Prevention, 2010); Craig A. Mason, Derek A. Chapman, Chang Shau, and Julie Simons, "Impacting Re-Arrest Rates among Youth Sentenced in Adult Court: An Epidemiology Examination of the Juvenile Sentencing Advocacy Project," *Journal of Clinical Child and Adolescent Psychology* 32:205–214 (2003); David L. Myers, "The Recidivism of Violent Youths in Juvenile and Adult Court: A Consideration of Selection Bias," *Youth Violence and Juvenile Justice* 1:79–101 (2003).

63. Thomas Grisso, Laurence Steinberg, Jennifer Woolard, Elizabeth Cauffman, Elizabeth Scott, Sandra Graham, Fran Lexcon, N. Dickon Reppucci, and Robert Schwartz, "Juveniles' Competence to Stand Trial: A Comparison of Adolescents' and Adults' Capacities as Trial Defendants," *Law and Human Behavior* 27:333–363 (2003); Darla M. Burnett, Charles D. Noblin, and Vicki Prosser, "Adjudicative Competency in a Juvenile Population," *Criminal Justice and Behavior* 31:438–462 (2004).

64. Megan C. Kurlychek and Brian D. Johnson, "Juvenility and Punishment: Sentencing Juveniles in Adult Criminal Court," *Criminology* 48:725–758 (2010).

65. Aaron Kupchik, "The Decision to Incarcerate in Juvenile and Criminal Courts," *Criminal Justice Review* 31:309–336 (2006), at 321–322.

66. Megan C. Kurlycheck and Brian D. Johnson, "The Juvenile Penalty: A Comparison of Juvenile and Young Adult Sentencing Outcomes in Criminal Court," *Criminology* 42:485–517 (2004), at 498.

67. Richard E. Redding, "The Effects of Adjudicating and Sentencing Juveniles as Adults: Research and Policy Implications," *Youth Violence and Juvenile Justice* 1:128–155 (2003); see also Richard Redding, "Juvenile Offenders in Criminal Court and Adult Prison: Legal, Psychological, and Behavioral Outcomes," *Juvenile and Family Court Journal* 50:1–15 (1999).

68. Emily Gaarder and Joanne Belknap, "Tenuous Borders: Girls Transferred to Adult Court," *Criminology* 40:481–517 (2002).

69. Redding, "Juvenile Offenders in Criminal Court and Adult Prison."

70. Benjamin Adams and Sean Addie, *Delinquency Cases Waived to Criminal Court, 2005* (Washington, DC: U.S. Department of Justice, Office of Juvenile Justice and Delinquency Prevention, OJJDP Fact Sheet, 2009), p. 2.

71. Jeffrey Fagan, "Juvenile Crime and Criminal Justice: Resolving Border Disputes," *The Future of Children* 18(2):81–118 (2008).

72. Puzzanchera, Adams, and Sickmund, *Juvenile Court Statistics 2008*, p. 64.

73. Gerard Rainville and Steven K. Smith, *Juvenile Felony Defendants in Criminal Courts: Survey of 40 Counties, 1998* (Washington, DC: U.S. Department of Justice, Office of Juvenile Justice and Delinquency Prevention, 2003).

74. Puzzanchera, Adams, and Sickmund, *Juvenile Court Statistics 2008*, p. 44.

75. Barry Feld, "Delinquent Careers and Criminal Policy," *Criminology* 21:195–212 (1983).

76. Howard N. Snyder, Melissa Sickmund, and Eileen Poe-Yamagata, *Juvenile Transfers to Criminal Court in the 1990s: Lessons Learned from Four Studies* (Washington, DC: U.S. Department of Justice, Office of Juvenile Justice and Delinquency Prevention, 2000).

77. Rainville and Smith, *Juvenile Felony Defendants in Criminal Courts.*

78. Sanjeev Sridharan, Lynette Greenfield, and Baron Blakley, "A Study of Prosecutorial Certification Practice in Virginia," *Criminology and Public Policy* 3:605–632 (2004).

79. Franklin E. Zimring, "Treatment of Hard Cases in American Juvenile Justice: In Defense of the Discretionary Waiver," *Notre Dame Journal of Law, Ethics, and Policy* 5:267–280 (1991); Lawrence Winner, Lonn Kaduce, Donna Bishop, and Charles Frazier, "The Transfer of Juveniles to Criminal Courts: Reexamining Recidivism over the Long Term," *Crime and Delinquency* 43:548–564 (1997).

80. Rainville and Smith, *Juvenile Felony Defendants in Criminal Courts.*

81. Institute of Judicial Administration, American Bar Association Joint Commission on Juvenile Justice Standards, *Standards Relating to Adjudication* (Cambridge, MA: Ballinger, 1980).

82. Joseph B. Sanborn, Jr., "The Right to a Public Jury Trial—A Need for Today's Juvenile Court," *Judicature* 76:230–238 (1993). In the context of delinquency convictions to enhance criminal sentences, see Barry C. Feld, "The Constitutional Tension Between *Apprendi* and *McKeiver*: Sentence Enhancement Based on Delinquency Convictions and the Quality of Justice in Juvenile Courts," *Wake Forest Law Review* 38:1111–1224 (2003).

83. Linda Szymanski, *Juvenile Delinquents' Right to Counsel* (Pittsburgh: National Center for Juvenile Justice, 1988).

84. *In re Winship*, 397 U.S. 358, 90 S.Ct. 1068 (1970).

85. *McKeiver v. Pennsylvania*, 403 U.S. 528, 91 S.Ct. 1976 (1971).

86. See, generally, R. T. Powell, "Disposition Concepts," *Juvenile and Family Court Journal* 34:7–18 (1983).

87. Fox, *Juvenile Courts in a Nutshell*, p. 221.

88. This section is adapted from Jack Haynes and Eugene Moore, "Particular Dispositions," *Juvenile and Family Court Journal* 34:41–48 (1983); see also Grant Grissom, "Dispositional Authority and the Future of the Juvenile Justice System," *Juvenile and Family Court Journal* 42:25–34 (1991).

89. Barry Krisberg, Elliot Currie, and David Onek, "What Works with Juvenile Offenders," *American Bar Association Journal on Criminal Justice* 10:20–24 (1995).

90. Puzzanchera, Adams, and Sickmund, *Juvenile Court Statistics 2008*, p. 58.

91. Ibid., p. 55.

92. Ibid., pp. 50, 55.

93. Anthony Platt, *The Child Savers: The Invention of Delinquency* (Chicago: University of Chicago Press, 1969); David Rothman, *Conscience and Convenience: The Asylum and the Alternative in Progressive America* (Boston: Little, Brown, 1980).

94. Joseph Goldstein, Anna Freud, and Albert Solnit, *Beyond the Best Interests of the Child* (New York: Free Press, 1973).

95. See, for example, *in Interest on M.P.*, 697 N.E. 2d 1153 (Il. App. 1998); *Matter of Welfare of CAW*, 579 N.W. 2d 494 (MN. App. 1998).

96. See, for example, *Matter of Willis Alvin M.*, 479 S.E. 2d. 871 (WV 1996).

97. *Roper v. Simmons*, 125 S.Ct. 1183 (2005).

98. Erica Goode, "Young Killer: Bad Seed or Work in Progress?" *New York Times*, November 25, 2003.

99. Adam Liptak, "Court Takes Another Step in Reshaping Capital Punishment," *New York Times*, March 2, 2005.

100. *Roper v. Simmons*, 125 S.Ct. 1183 (2005).

101. Victor L. Streib, *The Juvenile Death Penalty Today: Death Sentences and Executions for Juvenile Crimes, January 1, 1973–September 30, 2003* (Ada, OH: Claude W. Pettit College of Law, Ohio Northern University, October 6, 2003), p. 3.

102. Ibid.

103. Steven Gerstein, "The Constitutionality of Executing Juvenile Offenders, *Thompson v. Oklahoma*," *Criminal Law Bulletin* 24:91–98 (1988); *Thompson v. Oklahoma*, 108 S.Ct. 2687 (1988).

104. 109 S.Ct. 2969 (1989); for a recent analysis of the *Wilkins* and *Stanford* cases, see the note in "*Stanford v. Kentucky* and *Wilkins v. Missouri*: Juveniles, Capital Crime, and Death Penalty," *Criminal Justice Journal* 11:240–266 (1989).

105. Victor Streib, "Excluding Juveniles from New York's Impendent Death Penalty," *Albany Law Review* 54:625–679 (1990).

106. Goode, "Young Killer: Bad Seed or Work in Progress?"

107. Peter J. Benekos and Alida V. Merlo, "Juvenile Offenders and the Death Penalty: How Far Have Standards of Decency Evolved?" *Youth Violence and Juvenile Justice* 3:316–333 (2006), p. 324.

108. Barry C. Feld, "A Slower Form of Death: Implications of *Roper v. Simmons* for Juveniles Sentenced to Life Without Parole," *Notre Dame Journal of Law, Ethics and Public Policy* 22:9–65 (2008).

109. See Simon I. Singer, "Sentencing Juveniles to Life in Prison: The Reproduction of Juvenile Justice for Young Adolescents Charged with Murder," *Crime and Delinquency* 57:969–986 (2011); Peter J. Benekos and Alida V. Merlo, "Juvenile Justice: The Legacy of Punitive Policy," *Youth Violence and Juvenile Justice* 6:28–46 (2008); Laurence Steinberg and Ron Haskins, "Keeping Adolescents Out of Prison," *The Future of Children* 18(2):1–7 (2008).

110. Feld, "A Slower Form of Death," p. 10.

111. Amnesty International and Human Rights Watch, *The Rest of Their Lives: Life Without Parole for Child Offenders in the United States* (New York: Human Rights Watch, 2005), p. 1.

112. Ashley Nellis, *The Lives of Juvenile Lifers: Findings from a National Survey* (Washington, DC: The Sentencing Project, 2012).

113. See Elizabeth S. Scott and Laurence Steinberg, "The Young and the Reckless," *New York Times*, November 14, 2009.

114. Scott and Steinberg, "The Young and the Reckless."

115. *Graham v. Florida*, 130 S. Ct. 2011 (2010).

116. Adam Liptak, "Supreme Court Revisits Issue of Harsh Sentences for Juveniles," *New York Times*, March 21, 2012, A15.

117. 567 U.S. __ (2012).

118. Paul Piersma, Jeanette Ganousis, Adrienne E. Volenik, Harry F. Swanger, and Patricia Connell, *Law and Tactics in Juvenile Cases* (Philadelphia: American Law Institute, American Bar Association, Committee on Continuing Education, 1977), p. 397.

119. J. Addison Bowman, "Appeals from Juvenile Courts," *Crime and Delinquency Journal* 11:63–77 (1965).

120. *In re Gault*, 387 U.S. 1 87 S.Ct. 1428 (1967).

121. *Davis v. Alaska*, 415 U.S. 308 (1974); 94 S.Ct. 1105.

122. *Oklahoma Publishing Co. v. District Court*, 430 U.S. 97 (1977); 97 S.Ct. 1045.

123. *Smith v. Daily Mail Publishing Co.*, 443 U.S. 97, 99 S.Ct. 2667, 61 L.Ed.2d 399 (1979).

124. Linda Szymanski, *Confidentiality of Juvenile Court Records* (Pittsburgh: National Center for Juvenile Justice, 1989).

125. Ira M. Schwartz, *Justice for Juveniles: Rethinking the Best Interests of the Child* (Lexington, MA: D. C. Heath, 1989), p. 172.

126. Richard E. Redding, "Use of Juvenile Records in Criminal Court," *Juvenile Justice Fact Sheet* (Charlottesville, VA: Institute of Law, Psychiatry, and Public Policy, University of Virginia, 2000).

127. Barry Feld, "Criminology and the Juvenile Court: A Research Agenda for the 1990s," in *Juvenile Justice and Public Policy*, ed. Schwartz, p. 59.

128. Barry C. Feld, "Juvenile and Criminal Justice Systems' Responses to Youth Violence," in *Youth Violence: Crime and Justice: A Review of Research*, Vol. 24, ed. Michael Tonry and Mark H. Moore (Chicago: University of Chicago Press, 1998), p. 222.

129. Robert O. Dawson, "The Future of Juvenile Justice: Is It Time to Abolish the System?" *Journal of Criminal Law and Criminology* 81:136–155 (1990); see also Leonard P. Edwards, "The Future of the Juvenile Court: Promising New Directions," *The Future of Children: The Juvenile Court* (Los Altos, CA: David and Lucille Packard Foundation, 1996).

130. Greenwood, *Changing Lives: Delinquency Prevention as Crime-Control Policy*; see also Daniel P. Mears, Joshua C. Cochran, Sarah J. Greenman, Avinash S. Bhati, and Mark A. Greenwald, "Evidence on the Effectiveness of Juvenile Court Sanctions," *Journal of Criminal Justice* 39:509–520 (2011).

131. Ibid., pp. 193–194.

132. Peter J. Benekos and Alida V. Merlo, "Juvenile Justice: The Legacy of Punitive Policy," *Youth Violence and Juvenile Justice* 6:28–46 (2008).

133. Daniel P. Mears, Carter Hay, Marc Gertz, and Christina Mancini, "Public Opinion and the Foundation of the Juvenile Court," *Criminology* 45:223–258 (2007), p. 250.

134. Ibid., p. 246; see also Brandon K. Applegate, Robin King Davis, and Francis T. Cullen, "Reconsidering Child Saving: The Extent and Correlates of Public Support for Excluding Youths from Juvenile Courts," *Crime and Delinquency* 55:51–77 (2009).

Chapter 14. Juvenile Corrections: Probation, Community Treatment, and Institutionalization

1. See Christina Stahlkopf, Mike Males, and Daniel Macallair, "Testing Incapacitation Theory: Youth Crime and Incarceration in California," *Crime and Delinquency* 56:253–268 (2010).

2. See Matt DeLisi, Alan J. Drury, Anna E. Kosloski, Jonathan W. Caudill, Peter J. Conis, Craig A. Anderson, Michael G. Vaughn, and Kevin M.

Beaver, "The Cycle of Violence Behind Bars: Traumatization and Institutional Misconduct Among Juvenile Delinquents in Confinement," *Youth Violence and Juvenile Justice* 8:107–121 (2010).

3. Charles Murray and Louis B. Cox, *Beyond Probation* (Beverly Hills, CA: Sage, 1979).

4. Robert Shepard, Jr., ed., *Juvenile Justice Standards, A Balanced Approach* (Chicago: American Bar Association, 1996).

5. George Killinger, Hazel Kerper, and Paul F. Cromwell, Jr., *Probation and Parole in the Criminal Justice System* (St. Paul, MN: West, 1976), p. 45; National Advisory Commission on Criminal Justice Standards and Goals, *Corrections* (Washington, DC: U.S. Government Printing Office, 1983), p. 75.

6. Ibid.

7. Jerome Miller, *Last One Over the Wall: The Massachusetts Experiment in Closing Reform Schools* (Columbus: Ohio State University Press, 1998).

8. Bureau of Justice Statistics, *Report to the Nation on Crime and Justice* (Washington, DC: U.S. Government Printing Office, 1988), pp. 44–45; Peter Greenwood, "What Works with Juvenile Offenders: A Synthesis of the Literature and Experience," *Federal Probation* 58:63–67 (1994).

9. Charles Puzzanchera, Benjamin Adams, and Melissa Sickmund, *Juvenile Court Statistics 2008* (Pittsburgh: National Center for Juvenile Justice, 2011), pp. 54–55.

10. Emily Gaarder, Nancy Rodriguez, and Marjorie S. Zatz, "Criers, Liars, and Manipulators: Probation Officers' Views of Girls," *Justice Quarterly* 21:547–578 (2004).

11. Puzzanchera, Adams, and Sickmund, *Juvenile Court Statistics 2008*, p. 55.

12. *In re J.G.*, 692 N.E. 2d 1226 (IL App. 1998).

13. *In re Michael D.*, 264 CA Rptr 476 (CA App. 1989).

14. *Morrissey v. Brewer*, 408 U.S. 471, 92 S.Ct. 2593, 33 L.Ed.2d 484 (1972); *Gagnon v. Scarpelli*, 411 U.S. 778, 93 S.Ct. 1756, 36 L.Ed.2d 655 (1973).

15. See Geoff Ward and Aaron Kupchik, "What Drives Juvenile Probation Officers? Relating Organizational Contexts, Status Characteristics, and Personal Convictions to Treatment and Punishment Orientations," *Crime and Delinquency* 56:35–69 (2010).

16. See Gina M. Vincent, Melissa L. Paiva-Salisbury, Nathan E. Cook, Laura S. Guy, and Rachael T. Perrault, "Impact of Risk/Needs Assessment on Juvenile Probation Officers' Decision Making: Importance of Implementation," *Psychology, Public Policy, and Law*, published online March 5, 2012.

17. Richard Lawrence, "Reexamining Community Corrections Models," *Crime and Delinquency* 37:449–464 (1991).

18. See Matthew J. Giblin, "Using Police Officers to Enhance the Supervision of Juvenile Probationers: An Evaluation of the Anchorage CAN Program," *Crime and Delinquency* 48:116–137 (2002).

19. See Richard G. Wiebush, "Juvenile Intensive Supervision: The Impact on Felony Offenders Diverted from Institutional Placement," *Crime and Delinquency* 39:68–89 (1993).

20. For a review of these programs, see James Austin, Kelly Dedel Johnson, and Ronald Weitzer, *Alternatives to the Secure Detention and Confinement of Juvenile Offenders* (Washington, DC: OJJDP Bulletin, 2005), pp. 18–19.

21. James Ryan, "Who Gets Revoked? A Comparison of Intensive Supervision Successes and Failures in Vermont," *Crime and Delinquency* 43:104–118 (1997).

22. Sheldon X. Zhang and Lening Zhang, "An Experimental Study of the Los Angeles County Repeat Offender Prevention Program: Its Implementation and Evaluation," *Criminology and Public Policy* 4:205–236 (2005).

23. Jodi Lane, Susan Turner, Terry Fain, and Amber Sehgal, "Evaluating an Experimental Intensive Juvenile Probation Program: Supervision and Official Outcomes," *Crime and Delinquency* 51:26–52 (2005).

24. Eve Brank, Jodi Lane, Susan Turner, Terry Fain, and Amber Sehgal, "An Experimental Juvenile Probation Program: Effects on Parent and Peer Relationships," *Crime and Delinquency* 54:193–224 (2008).

25. Angela A. Robertson, Paul W. Grimes, and Kevin E. Rogers, "A Short-Run Cost-Benefit Analysis of Community-Based Interventions for Juvenile Offenders," *Crime and Delinquency* 47:265–284 (2001).

26. Richard Ball and J. Robert Lilly, "A Theoretical Examination of Home Incarceration," *Federal Probation* 50:17–25 (1986); Joan Petersilia, "Exploring the Option of House Arrest," *Federal Probation* 50:50–56 (1986); Annesley Schmidt, "Electronic Monitors," *Federal Probation* 50:56–60 (1986); Michael Charles, "The Development of a Juvenile Electronic Monitoring Program," *Federal Probation* 53:3–12 (1989).

27. Sudipto Roy, "Five Years of Electronic Monitoring of Adults and Juveniles in Lake County, Indiana: A Comparative Study on Factors Related to Failure," *Journal of Crime and Justice* 20:141–160 (1997).

28. Marc Renzema and Evan Mayo-Wilson, "Can Electronic Monitoring Reduce Crime for Moderate- to High-Risk Offenders?" *Journal of Experimental Criminology* 1:215–237 (2005).

29. Anne Seymour and Trudy Gregorie, "Restorative Justice for Young Offenders and Their Victims," *Corrections Today* 64:90–92 (2002), at 90.

30. Lawrence W. Sherman and Heather Strang, *Restorative Justice: The Evidence* (London: The Smith Institute, 2007); Heather Strang and Lawrence W. Sherman, "Restorative Justice to Reduce Victimization," in *Preventing Crime: What Works for Children, Offenders, Victims, and Places*, ed. Brandon C. Welsh and David P. Farrington (New York: Springer, 2006), p. 148; see also Lawrence W. Sherman, Heather Strang, Caroline Angel, Daniel Woods, Geoffrey C. Barnes, Sarah Bennett, and Nova Inkpen, "Effects of Face-to-Face Restorative Justice on Victims of Crime in Four Randomized, Controlled Trials," *Journal of Experimental Criminology* 1:367–395 (2005).

31. Sherman and Strang, *Restorative Justice: The Evidence*, pp. 152–156.

32. Edmund F. McGarrell and Natalie Kroovand Hipple, "Family Group Conferencing and Re-Offending Among First-Time Juvenile Offenders: The Indianapolis Experiment," *Justice Quarterly* 24:221–246 (2007); Nancy Rodriguez, "Restorative Justice, Communities, and Delinquency: Whom Do We Reintegrate?" *Criminology and Public Policy* 4:103–130 (2005); see also Kathleen J. Bergseth and Jeffrey A. Bouffard, "The Long-Term Impact of Restorative Justice Programming for Juvenile Offenders," *Journal of Criminal Justice* 35:433–451 (2007).

33. Andrew J. DeAngelo, "Evolution of Juvenile Justice: Community-Based Partnerships Through Balanced and Restorative Justice," *Corrections Today* 67:105–106 (2005); Dennis Mahoney, Dennis Romig, and Troy Armstrong, "Juvenile Probation: The Balanced Approach," *Juvenile and Family Court Journal* 39:1–59 (1988).

34. Gordon Bazemore, "On Mission Statements and Reform in Juvenile Justice: The Case of the Balanced Approach," *Federal Probation* 61:64–70 (1992); Gordon Bazemore and Mark Umbreit, *Balanced and Restorative Justice* (Washington, DC: Office of Juvenile Justice and Delinquency Prevention, 1994).

35. Office of Juvenile Justice and Delinquency Prevention, *The 8% Solution*, fact sheet (Washington, DC: U.S. Department of Justice, Office of Juvenile Justice and Delinquency Prevention, 2001).

36. Ibid., pp. 1–2.

37. Peter R. Schneider and Matthew C. Finkelstein, eds., *RESTTA National Directory of Restitution and Community Service Programs* (Washington, DC: Office of Juvenile Justice and Delinquency Prevention, U.S. Department of Justice, 1998).

38. Gordon Bazemore, "New Concepts and Alternative Practice in Community Supervision of Juvenile Offenders: Rediscovering Work Experience and Competency Development," *Journal of Crime and Justice* 14:27–45 (1991).

39. Anne Schneider, "Restitution and Recidivism Rates of Juvenile Offenders: Results from Four Experimental Studies," *Criminology* 24:533–552 (1986).

40. Shay Bilchik, *A Juvenile Justice System for the 21st Century* (Washington, DC: Office of Juvenile Justice and Delinquency Prevention, 1998).

41. Schneider and Finkelstein, *RESTTA National Directory of Restitution and Community Service Programs*, Tables 12, 15.

42. Anne Schneider, "Restitution and Recidivism Rates of Juvenile Offenders," *Directory of Restitution Programs* (Washington, DC: OJJDP Juvenile Justice Clearinghouse, 1996). This directory contains information on more than 500 restitution programs across the country.

43. See Peter W. Greenwood and Susan Turner, "Juvenile Crime and Juvenile Justice," in *Crime and Public Policy*, ed. James Q. Wilson and Joan Petersilia (New York: Oxford University Press, 2011); Shelley Zavlek, *Planning Community-Based Facilities for Violent Juvenile Offenders as Part of a System of Graduated Sanctions* (Washington, DC: OJJDP Bulletin, 2005), p. 5.

44. Sharon F. Mihalic, Abigail Fagan, Katherine Irwin, Diane Ballard, and Delbert Elliott, *Blueprints for Violence Prevention* (Washington, DC: OJJDP Report, 2004).

45. Patricia Chamberlain and John B. Reid, "Comparison of Two Community Alternatives to Incarceration," *Journal of Consulting and Clinical Psychology* 66:624–633 (1998).

46. Patricia Chamberlain, L. D. Leve, and D. S. DeGarmo, "Multidimensional Treatment Foster Care for Girls in the Juvenile Justice System: 2-Year Follow-Up of a Randomized Clinical Trial," *Journal of Consulting and Clinical Psychology* 75:187–193 (2007).

47. *Children in Custody 1975–1985: Census of Public and Private Juvenile Detention, Correctional, and Shelter Facilities* (Washington, DC: U.S. Department of Justice, 1989), p. 4.

48. For a detailed description of juvenile delinquency in the 1800s, see J. Hawes, *Children in Urban Society: Juvenile Delinquency in Nineteenth-Century America* (New York: Oxford University Press, 1971).

49. D. Jarvis, *Institutional Treatment of the Offender* (New York: McGraw-Hill, 1978), p. 101.

50. Margaret Werner Cahalan, *Historical Corrections Statistics in the United States, 1850–1984* (Washington, DC: U.S. Department of Justice, 1986), pp. 104–105.

51. Clemens Bartollas, Stuart J. Miller, and Simon Dinitz, *Juvenile Victimization: The Institutional Paradox* (New York: Wiley, 1976), p. 6.

52. LaMar T. Empey, *American Delinquency—Its Meaning and Construction* (Homewood, IL: Dorsey, 1978), p. 515.

53. Edward Eldefonso and Walter Hartinger, *Control, Treatment, and Rehabilitation of Juvenile Offenders* (Beverly Hills, CA: Glencoe, 1976), p. 151.

54. Ibid., p. 152.

55. M. Rosenthal, "Reforming the Justice Correctional Institution: Efforts of U.S. Children's Bureau in the 1930s," *Journal of Sociology and Social Welfare* 14:47–73 (1987).

56. Peter W. Greenwood, *Changing Lives: Delinquency Prevention as Crime-Control Policy* (Chicago: University of Chicago Press, 2006), Ch. 8; Franklin E. Zimring, *American Juvenile Justice* (New York: Oxford University Press), Ch. 4.

57. National Conference on State Legislatures, *A Legislator's Guide to Comprehensive Juvenile Justice, Juvenile Detention, and Corrections* (Denver: National Conference on State Legislatures, 1996).

58. Ibid.

59. Sara Hockenberry, Melissa Sickmund, and Anthony Sladky, *Juvenile Residential Facility Census, 2008: Selected Findings* (Washington, DC: Office of Juvenile Justice and Delinquency Prevention, U.S. Department of Justice, 2011).

60. Melissa Sickmund, T. J. Sladky, Wei Kang, and Charles Puzzanchera, "Easy Access to the Census of Juveniles in Residential Placement" (2011), www.ojjdp.gov/ojstatbb/ezacjrp/ (accessed August 20, 2012).

61. Ibid.

62. Daniel P. Mears, "Exploring State-Level Variation in Juvenile Incarceration Rates: Symbolic Threats and Competing Explanations," *Prison Journal* 86:470–490 (2006).

63. Ira Schwartz, Marilyn Jackson-Beck, and Roger Anderson, "The 'Hidden' System of Juvenile Control," *Crime and Delinquency* 30:371–385 (1984).

64. Rebecca Craig and Andrea Paterson, "State Involuntary Commitment Laws: Beyond Deinstitutionalization," *National Conference of State Legislative Reports* 13:1–10 (1988).

65. Robert Pear, "Many Youths Reported Held Awaiting Mental Help," *New York Times*, July 8, 2004.

66. Richard Lezin Jones and Leslie Kaufman, "New Jersey Youths Out of Foster Homes End Up in Detention," *New York Times*, May 31, 2003.

67. Hockenberry, Sickmund, and Sladky, *Juvenile Residential Facility Census, 2008: Selected Findings*, p. 6.

68. John M. Broder, "Dismal California Prisons Hold Juvenile Offenders: Report Documents Long List of Mistreatment," *New York Times*, February 15, 2004, p. A12.

69. Shawn C. Marsh and William P. Evans, "Youth Perspectives on Their Relationships with Staff in Juvenile Correction Settings and Perceived Likelihood of Success on Release," *Youth Violence and Juvenile Justice* 7:46–67 (2009); Attapol Kuanliang, Jon R. Sorensen, and Mark D. Cunningham, "Juvenile Inmates in an Adult Prison System: Rates of Disciplinary Misconduct and Violence," *Criminal Justice and Behavior* 35:1186–1201 (2008).

70. Howard N. Snyder and Melissa Sickmund, *Juvenile Offenders and Victims: 2006 National Report* (Pittsburgh: National Center for Juvenile Justice, 2006), pp. 209, 215.

71. Sickmund, Sladky, Kang, and Puzzanchera, "Easy Access to the Census of Juveniles in Residential Placement."

72. Alex R. Piquero, "Disproportionate Minority Contact," *The Future of Children* 18(2):59–79 (2008); Michael J. Leiber and Kristan C. Fox, "Race and the Impact of Detention on Juvenile Justice Decision Making," *Crime and Delinquency* 51:470–497 (2005).

73. Snyder and Sickmund, *Juvenile Offenders and Victims*, p. 212.

74. Rodney L. Engen, Sara Steen, and George S. Bridges, "Racial Disparities in the Punishment of Youth: A Theoretical and Empirical Assessment of the Literature," *Social Problems* 49:194–220 (2002).

75. See Tina L. Freiburger and Alison S. Burke, "Status Offenders in the Juvenile Court: The Effects of Gender, Race, and Ethnicity on the Adjudication Decision," *Youth Violence and Juvenile Justice* 9:352–365 (2011).

76. Sickmund, Sladky, Kang, and Puzzanchera, "Easy Access to the Census of Juveniles in Residential Placement."

77. John F. Chapman, Rani A. Desai, Paul R. Falzer, and Randy Borum, "Violence Risk and Race in a Sample of Youth in Juvenile Detention: The Potential to Reduce Disproportionate Minority Confinement," *Youth Violence and Juvenile Justice* 4:170–184 (2006).

78. Heidi M. Hsia, George S. Bridges, and Rosalie McHale, *Disproportionate Minority Confinement: 2002 Update: Summary* (Washington, DC: Office of Juvenile Justice and Delinquency Prevention, 2004).

79. Ibid., pp. 16–17.

80. Ashley Nellis and Brad Richardson, "Getting Beyond Failure: Promising Approaches for Reducing DMC," *Youth Violence and Juvenile Justice* 8:266–276 (2010); Emily R. Cabaniss, James M. Frabutt, Mary H. Kendrick, and Margaret B. Arbuckle, "Reducing Disproportionate Minority Contact in the Juvenile Justice System: Promising Practices," *Aggression and Violent Behavior* 12:393–401 (2007).

81. Helene R. White, Jing Shi, Paul Hirschfield, Eun Young Mun, and Rolf Loeber, "Effects of Institutional Confinement for Delinquency on Levels of Depression and Anxiety Among Male Adolescents," *Youth Violence and Juvenile Justice* 8:295–313 (2010).

82. See David M. Halbfinger, "Care of Juvenile Offenders in Mississippi Is Faulted," *New York Times*, September 1, 2003.

83. Sickmund, Sladky, Kang, and Puzzanchera, "Easy Access to the Census of Juveniles in Residential Placement."

84. Bartollas, Miller, and Dinitz, *Juvenile Victimization*, Sec. C.

85. Christopher Sieverdes and Clemens Bartollas, "Security Level and Adjustment Patterns in Juvenile Institutions," *Journal of Criminal Justice* 14:145 (1986).

86. Many authors have written about this sexual double standard. See Meda Chesney-Lind and Randall G. Shelden, *Girls, Delinquency, and the Juvenile Justice System*, 3rd ed. (Belmont, CA: Wadsworth, 2004); E. A. Anderson, "The Chivalrous Treatment of the Female Offender in the Arms of the Criminal Justice System: A Review of the Literature," *Social Problems* 23:350–357 (1976); G. Armstrong, "Females Under the Law: Protected but Unequal," *Crime and Delinquency* 23:109–120 (1977); Meda Chesney-Lind, "Judicial Enforcement of the Female Sex Role: The Family Court and the Female Delinquent," *Issues in Criminology* 8:51–59 (1973); Chesney-Lind, "Juvenile Delinquency: The Sexualization of Female Crime," *Psychology Today* 19:43–46 (1974); Allan Conway and Carol Bogdan, "Sexual Delinquency: The Persistence of a Double Standard," *Crime and Delinquency* 23:131–135 (1977).

87. Sickmund, Sladky, Kang, and Puzzanchera, "Easy Access to the Census of Juveniles in Residential Placement."

88. Kristi Holsinger and Alexander M. Holsinger, "Differential Pathways to Violence and Self-Injurious Behavior: African American and White Girls in the Juvenile Justice System," *Journal of Research in Crime and Delinquency* 42:211–242 (2005).

89. Paul E. Tracy, Kimberly Kempf-Leonard, and Stephanie Abramoske-James, "Gender Differences in Delinquency and Juvenile Justice Processing: Evidence from National Data," *Crime and Delinquency* 55:171–215 (2009).

90. Sara Goodkind, Irene Ng, and Rosemary C. Sarri, "The Impact of Sexual Abuse in the Lives of Young Women Involved or at Risk of Involvement with the Juvenile Justice System," *Violence Against Women* 12:465–477 (2006); see also Emily Gaarder and Joanne Belknap, "Tenuous Borders: Girls Transferred to Adult Court," *Criminology* 40:481–518 (2002).

91. Elizabeth Cauffman, "Understanding the Female Offender," *The Future of Children* 18(2):119–142 (2008), at 124.

92. Leslie Acoca, "Outside/Inside: The Violation of American Girls at Home, on the Streets, and in the Juvenile Justice System," *Crime and Delinquency* 44:561–589 (1998).

93. Barbara Bloom, Barbara Owen, Elizabeth Piper Deschenes, and Jill Rosenbaum, "Improving Juvenile Justice for Females: A Statewide Assessment in California," *Crime and Delinquency* 48:526–552 (2002), at 548.

94. For a historical analysis of a girls' reformatory, see Barbara Brenzel, *Daughters of the State* (Cambridge, MA: MIT Press, 1983).

95. Ilene R. Bergsmann, "The Forgotten Few Juvenile Female Offenders," *Federal Probation* 53:73–79 (1989).

96. *Justice by Gender: The Lack of Appropriate Prevention, Diversion, and Treatment Alternatives for Girls in the Justice System: A Report* (Chicago: American Bar Association and National Bar Association, 2001), pp. 27–29.

97. Angela M. Wolf, Juliette Graziano, and Christopher Hartney, "The Provision and Completion of Gender-Specific Services for Girls on Probation: Variation by Race and Ethnicity," *Crime and Delinquency* 55:294–312 (2009); Margaret A. Zahn, Jacob C. Day, Sharon F. Mihalic, and Lisa Tichavsky, "Determing What Works for Girls in the Juvenile Justice System: A Summary of Evaluation Evidence," *Crime and Delinquency* 55:266–293 (2009).

98. Doris Layton MacKenzie, "Reducing the Criminal Activities of Known Offenders and Delinquents: Crime Prevention in the Courts and Corrections," in *Evidence-Based Crime Prevention*, ed. Lawrence W. Sherman, David P. Farrington, Brandon C. Welsh, and Doris Layton MacKenzie (New York: Routledge, 2006, rev. ed.), p. 352.

99. Patrick A. Langan and David J. Levin, *Recidivism of Prisoners Released in 1994* (Washington, DC: Bureau of Justice Statistics, 2002).

100. David Farabee, *Rethinking Rehabilitation: Why Can't We Reform Our Criminals?* (Washington, DC: American Enterprise Institute, 2005); for

a rebuttal of this view, see James M. Byrne and Faye S. Taxman, "Crime (Control) Is a Choice: Divergent Perspectives on the Role of Treatment in the Adult Corrections System," *Criminology and Public Policy* 4: 291–310 (2005).

101. Mark W. Lipsey and David B. Wilson, "Effective Intervention for Serious Juvenile Offenders: A Synthesis of Research," in *Serious and Violent Juvenile Offenders: Risk Factors and Successful Interventions*, ed. Rolf Loeber and David P. Farrington (Thousand Oaks, CA: Sage, 1998).

102. Shawn C. Marsh, William P. Evans, and Michael J. Williams, "Social Support and Sense of Program Belonging Discriminate Between Youth-Staff Relationship Types in Juvenile Correction Settings," *Child Youth Care Forum* 39:481–494 (2010).

103. Elizabeth Drake, Steve Aos, and Marna G. Miller, "Evidence-Based Public Policy Options to Reduce Crime and Criminal Justice Costs: Implications in Washington State," *Victims and Offenders* 4:170–196 (2009).

104. Michael F. Caldwell, Michael Vitacco, and Gregory J. Van Rybroek, "Are Violent Delinquents Worth Treating? A Cost-Benefit Analysis," *Journal of Research in Crime and Delinquency* 43:148–168 (2006).

105. Thomas Grisso, "Adolescent Offenders with Mental Disorders," *The Future of Children* 18(2):143–164 (2008).

106. See, generally, William Glasser, "Reality Therapy: A Realistic Approach to the Young Offender," in *Readings in Delinquency and Treatment*, ed. Robert Schaste and Jo Wallach (Los Angeles: Delinquency Prevention Training Project, Youth Studies Center, University of Southern California, 1965); see also Richard Rachin, "Reality Therapy: Helping People Help Themselves," *Crime and Delinquency* 16:143 (1974).

107. Helen A. Klein, "Toward More Effective Behavior Programs for Juvenile Offenders," *Federal Probation* 41:45–50 (1977); Albert Bandura, *Principles of Behavior Modification* (New York: Holt, Rinehart & Winston, 1969); H. A. Klein, "Behavior Modification as Therapeutic Paradox," *American Journal of Orthopsychiatry* 44:353 (1974).

108. Joan McCord, "Cures that Harm: Unanticipated Outcomes of Crime Prevention Programs," *Annals of the American Academy of Political and Social Science* 587:16–30 (2003); Thomas J. Dishion, Joan McCord, and François Poulin, "When Interventions Harm: Peer Groups and Problem Behavior," *American Psychologist* 54:755–764 (1999).

109. Larry Brendtero and Arlin Ness, "Perspectives on Peer Group Treatment: The Use and Abuses of Guided Group Interaction/Positive Peer Culture," *Child and Youth Services Review* 4:307–324 (1982).

110. Elaine Traynelis-Yurek and George A. Giacobbe, "Communication Rehabilitation Regime for Incarcerated Youth: Positive Peer Culture," *Journal of Offender Rehabilitation* 26:157–167 (1998).

111. Bruno Bettelheim, *The Empty Fortress* (New York: Free Press, 1967).

112. Sarah Livsey, Melissa Sickmund, and Anthony Sladky, *Juvenile Residential Facility Census, 2004: Selected Findings* (Washington, DC: Office of Juvenile Justice and Delinquency Prevention, U.S. Department of Justice, 2009), p. 10.

113. MacKenzie, "Reducing the Criminal Activities of Known Offenders and Delinquents: Crime Prevention in the Courts and Corrections," p. 355; Doris Layton MacKenzie, "Evidence-Based Corrections: Identifying What Works," *Crime and Delinquency* 46:457–471 (2000).

114. Thomas Castellano and Irina Soderstrom, "Therapeutic Wilderness Programs and Juvenile Recidivism: A Program Evaluation," *Journal of Offender Rehabilitation* 17:19–46 (1992).

115. MacKenzie, "Reducing the Criminal Activities of Known Offenders and Delinquents," p. 355.

116. Sandra Jo Wilson and Mark W. Lipsey, "Wilderness Challenge Programs for Delinquent Youth: A Meta-Analysis of Outcome Evaluations," *Evaluation and Program Planning* 23:1–12 (2003).

117. Jerald Burns and Gennaro Vito, "An Impact Analysis of the Alabama Boot Camp Program," *Federal Probation* 59:63–67 (1995).

118. Ronald Corbett and Joan Petersilia, eds., "The Results of a Multi-Site Study of Boot Camps," *Federal Probation* 58:60–66 (1995).

119. David B. Wilson and Doris Layton MacKenzie, "Boot Camps," in *Preventing Crime: What Works for Children, Offenders, Victims, and Places*, ed. Welsh and Farrington, p. 80, Table 2.

120. Ibid., p. 80.

121. Ibid., p. 80; Doris Layton MacKenzie, *What Works in Corrections: Reducing the Criminal Activities of Offenders and Delinquents* (New York: Cambridge University Press, 2006), p. 294.

122. Megan Kurlychek and Cynthia Kempinen, "Beyond Boot Camp: The Impact of Aftercare on Offender Reentry," *Criminology and Public Policy* 5:363–388 (2006).

123. MacKenzie, "Reducing the Criminal Activities of Known Offenders and Delinquents," p. 348.

124. Dale G. Parent, *Correctional Boot Camps: Lessons Learned from a Decade of Research* (Washington, DC: National Institute of Justice, 2003); see also

Livsey, Sickmund, and Sladky, *Juvenile Residential Facility Census, 2004*, p. 4.

125. Anthony Salerno, "Boot Camps—A Critique and Proposed Alternative," *Journal of Offender Rehabilitation* 20:147–158 (1994).

126. Joanne Ardovini-Brooker and Lewis Walker, "Juvenile Boot Camps and the Reclamation of Our Youth: Some Food for Thought," *Juvenile and Family Court Journal* 51:12–28 (2000).

127. Morton Birnbaum, "The Right to Treatment," *American Bar Association Journal* 46:499 (1960).

128. See, for example, *Matter of Welfare of CAW*, 579 N.W. 2d 494 (MN App. 1998).

129. *Inmates of the Boys' Training School v. Affleck*, 346 F. Supp. 1354 (D.R.I. 1972).

130. Ibid., p. 1343.

131. *Nelson v. Heyne*, 491. F. 2d 353 (1974).

132. *Morales v. Turman*, 383 F. Supp. 53 (E.D. Texas 1974).

133. *Pena v. New York State Division for Youth*, 419 F. Supp. 203 (S.D.N.Y. 1976).

134. *Ralston v. Robinson*, 102 S.Ct. 233 (1981).

135. Patricia Puritz and Mary Ann Scali, *Beyond the Walls: Improving Conditions of Confinement for Youth in Custody* (Washington, DC: Office of Juvenile Justice and Delinquency Prevention, 1998).

136. Joan McCord, Cathy Spatz Widom, and Nancy A. Crowell, eds., *Juvenile Crime, Juvenile Justice* (Washington, DC: National Academy Press, Panel on Juvenile Crime: Prevention, Treatment, and Control, 2001), p. 194.

137. David M. Altschuler and Rachel Brash, "Adolescent and Teenage Offenders Confronting the Challenges and Opportunities of Reentry," *Youth Violence and Juvenile Justice* 2:72–87 (2004), at 72.

138. Daniel P. Mears and Jeremy Travis, "Youth Development and Reentry," *Youth Violence and Juvenile Justice* 2:3–20 (2004), at 3.

139. Edward J. Latessa, "Homelessness and Reincarceration: Editorial Introduction," *Criminology and Public Policy* 3:137–138 (2004).

140. Joan Petersilia, *When Offenders Come Home: Parole and Prisoner Reentry* (New York: Oxford University Press, 2009, revised edition).

141. Margaret Beale Spencer and Cheryl Jones-Walker, "Intervention and Services Offered to Former Juvenile Offenders Reentering Their Communities: An Analysis of Program Effectiveness," *Youth Violence and Juvenile Justice* 2:88–97 (2004), at 91.

142. Pamela K. Lattimore, "Reentry, Reintegration, Rehabilitation, Recidivism, and Redemption," *The Criminologist* 31:1, 3–6 (2006), at 1; see also Laura Winterfield, Christine Lindquist, and Susan Brumbaugh, *Sustaining Juvenile Reentry Programming After SVORI* (Washington, DC: Urban Institute, 2007).

143. Jeffrey A. Bouffard and Kathleen J. Bergseth, "The Impact of Reentry Services on Juvenile Offenders' Recidivism," *Youth Violence and Juvenile Justice* 6:295–318 (2008); He Len Chung, Carol A. Schubert, and Edward P. Mulvey, "An Empirical Portrait of Community Reentry Among Serious Juvenile Offenders in Two Metropolitan Cities," *Criminal Justice and Behavior* 34:1402–1426 (2007).

144. David M. Altschuler and Troy L. Armstrong, "Juvenile Corrections and Continuity of Care in a Community Context: The Evidence and Promising Directions," *Federal Probation* 66:72–77 (2002).

145. David M. Altschuler and Troy L. Armstrong, "Intensive Aftercare for High-Risk Juveniles: A Community Care Model" (Washington, DC: Office of Juvenile Justice and Delinquency Prevention, 1994).

146. David M. Altschuler, "Juvenile Reentry and Aftercare," *Georgetown Journal on Poverty Law and Policy* 16:655–667 (2009).

147. See *Morrissey v. Brewer*, 408 U.S. 471, 92 S.Ct. 2593, 33 L.Ed.2d 484 (1972).

148. Thomas A. Loughran, Edward P. Mulvey, Carol A. Schubert, Jeffrey Fagan, Alex R. Piquero, and Sandra H. Losoya, "Estimating a Dose-Response Relationship Between Length of Stay and Future Recidivism in Serious Juvenile Offenders," *Criminology* 47:699–740 (2009); Kristin Parsons Winokur, Alisa Smith, Stephanie R. Bontrager, and Julia L. Blankenship, "Juvenile Recidivism and Length of Stay," *Journal of Criminal Justice* 36:126–137 (2008).

149. Greenwood and Turner, "Juvenile Crime and Juvenile Justice."

150. Alex R. Piquero, Francis T. Cullen, James D. Unnever, Nicole L. Piquero, and Jill A. Gordan, "Never Too Late: Public Optimism About Juvenile Rehabilitation," *Punishment and Society* 12:187–207 (2010); Alex R. Piquero and Laurence Steinberg, "Public Preferences for Rehabilitation versus Incarceration of Juvenile Offenders," *Journal of Criminal Justice* 38:1–6 (2010).

151. Rolf Loeber and David P. Farrington, "Never Too Early, Never Too Late: Risk Factors and Successful Interventions for Serious and Violent Juvenile Offenders," *Studies on Crime and Crime Prevention* 7:7–30 (1998).

152. See Piquero, Cullen, Unnever, Piquero, and Gordan, "Never Too Late"; Piquero and Steinberg, "Public Preferences for Rehabilitation versus Incarceration of Juvenile Offenders."

153. Stephanie Hartwell, Robert McMackin, Robert Tansi, and Nozomi Bartlett, "'I Grew Up Too Fast for My Age': Postdischarge Issues and Experiences of Male Juvenile Offenders," *Journal of Offender Rehabilitation* 49:495–515 (2010).

GLOSSARY

abandonment: Parents physically leave their children with the intention of completely severing the parent–child relationship.

abstainers: Kids who are never involved in typical adolescent misbehaviors such as drinking, smoking, sex, or petty crimes.

academic achievement: Being successful in a school environment.

active speech: Expressing an opinion by speaking or writing; freedom of speech is a protected right under the First Amendment to the U.S. Constitution.

addict: A person with an overpowering physical or psychological need to continue taking a particular substance or drug.

addiction-prone personality: The view that the cause of substance abuse can be traced to a personality that has a compulsion for mood-altering drugs.

adjudicatory hearing: The fact-finding process wherein the juvenile court determines whether there is sufficient evidence to sustain the allegations in a petition.

adolescent-limited offenders: Kids who get into minor scrapes as youth but whose misbehavior ends when they enter adulthood.

advisement hearing: A preliminary protective or temporary custody hearing in which the court will review the facts and determine whether removal of the child is justified and notify parents of the charges against them.

aftercare: Transitional assistance to juveniles equivalent to adult parole to help youths adjust to community life.

age of onset: Age at which youths begin their delinquent careers. Early onset is believed to be linked with chronic offending patterns.

aging-out process (also known as desistance from crime or spontaneous remission): The tendency for youths to reduce the frequency of their offending behavior as they age. Aging out is thought to occur among all groups of offenders.

alcohol: Fermented or distilled liquids containing ethanol, an intoxicating substance.

anabolic steroids: Drugs used by athletes and bodybuilders to gain muscle bulk and strength.

anesthetic drugs: Nervous system depressants.

anomie: Normlessness produced by rapidly shifting moral values; according to Merton, anomie occurs when personal goals cannot be achieved using available means.

appellate process: Allows the juvenile an opportunity to have the case brought before a reviewing court after it has been heard in juvenile or family court.

arrest: Taking a person into the custody of the law to restrain the accused until he or she can be held accountable for the offense in court proceedings.

at-risk youths: Young people who are extremely vulnerable to the negative consequences of school failure, substance abuse, and early sexuality.

attachment theory: Bowlby's view that the ability to have an emotional bond to another person has important lasting psychological implications for normal development from childhood into adulthood.

authority conflict pathway: Pathway to delinquent deviance that begins at an early age with stubborn behavior and leads to defiance and then to authority avoidance.

bail: Amount of money that must be paid as a condition of pretrial release to ensure that the accused will return for subsequent proceedings. Bail is normally set by the judge at the initial appearance, and if unable to make bail the accused is detained in jail.

balanced probation: A program that integrates community protection, accountability of the juvenile offender, competency, and individualized attention to the juvenile offender, based on the principle that juvenile offenders must accept responsibility for their behavior.

balancing-of-the-interests approach: Efforts of the courts to balance the parents' natural right to raise a child with the child's right to grow into adulthood free from physical abuse or emotional harm.

barrio: A Spanish word meaning "district."

battered child syndrome: Nonaccidental physical injury of children by their parents or guardians.

behaviorism: Branch of psychology concerned with the study of observable behavior rather than unconscious processes; focuses on particular stimuli and responses to them.

behavior modification: A technique for shaping desired behaviors through a system of rewards and punishments.

best interests of the child: A philosophical viewpoint that encourages the state to take control of wayward children and provide care, custody, and treatment to remedy delinquent behavior.

bifurcated process: The procedure of separating adjudicatory and dispositionary hearings so different levels of evidence can be heard at each.

biosocial theory: The view that both thought and behavior have biological and social bases.

bipolar disorder: A psychological condition producing mood swings between wild elation and deep depression.

blended families: Nuclear families that are the product of divorce and remarriage, blending one parent from each of two families and their combined children into one family unit.

boot camps: Programs that combine get-tough elements with education, substance abuse treatment, and social skills training.

broken home: Home in which one or both parents are absent due to divorce or separation. Children in such an environment may be prone to antisocial behavior.

bullying: Repeated, negative acts committed by one or more children against another, which may be physical or verbal.

chancery courts: Court proceedings created in fifteenth-century England to oversee the lives of highborn minors who were orphaned or otherwise could not care for themselves.

child abuse: Any physical, emotional, or sexual trauma to a child, including neglecting to give proper care and attention, for which no reasonable explanation can be found.

child savers: Nineteenth-century reformers who developed programs for troubled youth and influenced legislation creating the juvenile justice system; today some critics view them as being more concerned with control of the poor than with their welfare.

chivalry hypothesis: The view that low female crime and delinquency rates are a reflection of the leniency with which police treat female offenders.

choice theory: Holds that youths will engage in delinquent and criminal behavior after weighing the consequences and benefits of their actions. Delinquent behavior is a rational choice made by a motivated offender who perceives that the chances of gain outweigh any possible punishment or loss.

chronic juvenile offenders: Youths who have been arrested four or more times during their minority and perpetuate a striking majority of serious criminal acts. This small group, known as the "chronic 6 percent," is believed to engage in a significant portion of all delinquent behavior; these youths do not age out of crime but continue their criminal behavior into adulthood.

chronic recidivist: Someone who has been arrested five times or more before age 18.

classical criminology: Holds that decisions to violate the law are weighed against possible punishments and to deter crime the pain of punishment must outweigh the benefit of illegal gain. Led to graduated punishments based on seriousness of the crime (let the punishment fit the crime).

cliques: Small groups of friends who share intimate knowledge and confidences.

cocaine: A powerful natural stimulant derived from the coca plant.

cognitive theory: The branch of psychology that studies the perception of reality and the mental processes required to understand the world we live in.

collective efficacy: A process in which mutual trust and a willingness to intervene in the supervision of children and help maintain public order create a sense of well-being in a neighborhood and help control antisocial activities.

community policing: Police strategy that emphasizes fear reduction, community organization, and order maintenance rather than crime fighting.

community service restitution: Offenders assist some worthwhile community organization for a period of time.

community treatment: Using nonsecure and noninstitutional residences, counseling services, victim restitution programs, and other community services to treat juveniles in their own communities.

complaint: Report made by the police or some other agency to the court that initiates the intake process.

conditions of probation: Rules and regulations mandating that a juvenile on probation behave in a particular way.

confidentiality: Restricting information in juvenile court proceedings in the interest of protecting the privacy of the juvenile.

continuity of crime: The idea that chronic juvenile offenders are likely to continue violating the law as adults.

controversial status youth: Aggressive kids who are either highly liked or intensely disliked by their peers and who are the ones most likely to become engaged in antisocial behavior.

co-offending: Committing criminal acts in groups.

cottage system: Housing in a compound of small cottages, each of which can accommodate 20 to 40 children.

covert pathway: Pathway to a delinquent career that begins with minor underhanded behavior, leads to property damage, and eventually escalates to more serious forms of theft and fraud.

crack: A highly addictive crystalline form of cocaine containing remnants of hydrochloride and sodium bicarbonate; it makes a crackling sound when smoked.

crackdown: A law enforcement operation that is designed to reduce or eliminate a particular criminal activity through the application of aggressive police tactics, usually involving a larger than usual contingent of police officers.

criminal atavism: The idea that delinquents manifest physical anomalies that make them biologically and physiologically similar to our primitive ancestors, savage throwbacks to an earlier stage of human evolution.

critical feminism: Holds that gender inequality stems from the unequal power of men and women and the subsequent exploitation of women by men; the cause of female delinquency originates with the onset of male supremacy and the efforts of males to control females' sexuality.

critical theory: The view that intergroup conflict, born out of the unequal distribution of wealth and power, is the root cause of delinquency.

crowds: Loosely organized groups who share interests and activities.

cultural deviance theory: Links delinquent acts to the formation of independent subcultures with a unique set of values that clash with the mainstream culture.

cultural transmission: The process of passing on deviant traditions and delinquent values from one generation to the next.

culture conflict: When the values of a subculture clash with those of the dominant culture.

culture of poverty: The view that lower-class people form a separate culture with their own values and norms, which are sometimes in conflict with conventional society.

custodial interrogation: Questions posed by the police to a suspect held in custody in the prejudicial stage of the juvenile justice process. Juveniles have the same rights as adults against self-incrimination when being questioned.

cycle of violence: The process by which abused kids become abusers themselves.

dark figures of crime: Incidents of crime and delinquency that go undetected by police.

deinstitutionalization: Removing juveniles from adult jails and placing them in community-based programs to avoid the stigma attached to these facilities.

delinquency control or delinquency repression: Involves any justice program or policy designed to prevent the occurrence of a future delinquent act.

delinquency prevention: Involves any nonjustice program or policy designed to prevent the occurrence of a future delinquent act.

delinquent: Juvenile who has been adjudicated by a judicial officer of a juvenile court as having committed a delinquent act.

designer drugs: Lab-made drugs designed to avoid existing drug laws.

detached street workers: Social workers who went out into the community and established close relationships with juvenile gangs with the goal of modifying gang behavior to conform to conventional behaviors and helping gang members get jobs and educational opportunities.

detention hearing: A hearing by a judicial officer of a juvenile court to determine whether a juvenile is to be detained or released while proceedings are pending in the case.

determinate sentence: Specifies a fixed term of detention that must be served.

developmental theory: The view that criminality is a dynamic process, influenced by social experiences as well as individual characteristics.

differential association theory: Asserts that criminal behavior is learned primarily in interpersonal groups and that youths will become delinquent if definitions they learn in those groups that are favorable to violating the law exceed definitions favorable to obeying the law.

disaggregated: Analyzing the relationship between two or more independent variables (such as murder convictions and death sentence) while controlling for the influence of a dependent variable (such as race).

discretion: Use of personal decision making and choice in carrying out operations in the criminal justice system, such as deciding whether to make an arrest or accept a plea bargain.

disposition: For juvenile offenders, the equivalent of sentencing for adult offenders; juvenile dispositions should be more rehabilitative than retributive.

disposition hearing: The social service agency presents its case plan and recommendations for care of the child and treatment of the parents, including incarceration and counseling or other treatment.

diversion: Officially halting or suspending a formal criminal or juvenile justice proceeding at any legally prescribed processing point after a recorded justice system entry, and referral of that person to a treatment or care program, or a recommendation that the person be released.

drop out: To leave school before completing the required program of education.

dropout factories: Schools in which the graduation rate is 40 percent or less.

drug courts: Courts whose focus is providing treatment for youths accused of drug-related acts.

due process: Basic constitutional principle based on the concept of the primacy of the individual and the complementary concept of limitation on governmental power; safeguards the individual from unfair state procedures in judicial or administrative proceedings; due process rights have been extended to juvenile trials.

early onset: The view that kids who begin engaging in antisocial behaviors at a very early age are the ones most at risk for a delinquency career.

egalitarian families: Husband and wife share power at home; daughters gain a kind of freedom similar to that of sons, and their law-violating behaviors mirror those of their brothers.

ego identity: According to Erik Erikson, ego identity is formed when persons develop a firm sense of who they are and what they stand for.

electronic monitoring: Active monitoring systems consist of a radio transmitter worn by the offender that sends a continuous signal to the probation department computer; passive systems employ computer-generated random phone calls that must be answered in a certain period of time from a particular phone.

extraversion: Impulsive behavior without the ability to examine motives and behavior.

familicide: Mass murders in which a spouse and one or more children are slain.

family group homes: A combination of foster care and group home; they are run by a single family rather than by professional staff.

Federal Bureau of Investigation (FBI): Arm of the U.S. Department of Justice that investigates violations of federal law, gathers crime statistics, runs a comprehensive crime laboratory, and helps train local law enforcement officers.

final order: Order that ends litigation between two parties by determining all their rights and disposing of all the issues.

foster care programs: Placement of juveniles with families who provide attention, guidance, and care.

free will: The view that youths are in charge of their own destinies and are free to make personal behavior choices unencumbered by environmental factors.

gang: Group of youths who collectively engage in delinquent behaviors.

gateway drug: A substance that leads to use of more serious drugs; alcohol use has long been thought to lead to more serious drug abuse.

gender policing: Pressure to conform to gender expectations.

gender-schema theory: A theory of development that holds that children internalize gender scripts that reflect the gender-related social practices of the culture. Once internalized, these gender scripts predispose the kids to construct a self-identity that is consistent with them.

general deterrence: Crime control policies that depend on the fear of criminal penalties, such as long prison sentences for violent crimes. The aim is to convince law violators that the pain outweighs the benefit of criminal activity.

general strain theory: Links delinquency to the strain of being locked out of the economic mainstream, which creates the anger and frustration that lead to delinquent acts.

general theory of crime (GTC): A developmental theory that modifies social control theory by integrating concepts from biosocial, psychological, routine activities, and rational choice theories.

gentrified: The process of transforming a lower-class area into a middle-class enclave through property rehabilitation.

graffiti: Inscriptions or drawings made on a wall or structure and used by delinquents for gang messages and turf definition.

group homes: Nonsecured structured residences that provide counseling, education, job training, and family living.

group therapy: Counseling several individuals together in a group session.

guardian *ad litem*: A lawyer appointed by the court to look after the interests of those who do not have the capacity to assert their own rights.

guided group interaction (GGI): Through group interactions, a delinquent can acknowledge and solve personal problems with support from other group members.

hallucinogens: Natural or synthetic substances that produce vivid distortions of the senses without greatly disturbing consciousness.

harm reduction: Efforts to minimize the harmful effects caused by drug use.

hashish: A concentrated form of cannabis made from unadulterated resin from the female cannabis plant.

hearsay: Out-of-court statements made by one person and recounted in court by another. Such statements are generally not allowed as evidence except in child abuse cases wherein a child's statements to social workers, teachers, or police may be admissible.

heroin: A narcotic made from opium and then cut with sugar or some other neutral substance until it is only 1 to 4 percent pure.

hot spot: A particular location or address that is the site of repeated and frequent criminal activity.

house arrest: Offender is required to stay home during specific periods of time; monitoring is done by random phone calls and visits or by electronic devices.

House of Refuge: A care facility developed by the child savers to protect potential criminal youths by taking them off the street and providing a family-like environment.

identity crisis: Psychological state, identified by Erikson, in which youths face inner turmoil and uncertainty about life roles.

impulsive: Lacking in thought or deliberation in decision making. An impulsive person lacks close attention to details, has organizational problems, is distracted and forgetful.

indeterminate sentence: Does not specify the length of time the juvenile must be held; rather, correctional authorities decide when the juvenile is ready to return to society.

individual counseling: Counselors help juveniles understand and solve their current adjustment problems.

informant: A person who has access to criminal networks and shares information with authorities in exchange for money or special treatment under conditions of anonymity.

inhalants: Volatile liquids that give off a vapor, which is inhaled, producing short-term excitement and euphoria followed by a period of disorientation.

in loco parentis: In the place of the parent; rights given to schools that allow them to assume parental duties in disciplining students.

intake: Process during which a juvenile referral is received and a decision made to file a petition in juvenile court to release the juvenile, to place the juvenile under supervision, or to refer the juvenile elsewhere.

Intensive Aftercare Program (IAP): A balanced, highly structured, comprehensive continuum of intervention for serious and violent juvenile offenders returning to the community.

interstitial area: An area of the city that forms when there is a crack in the social fabric and in which deviant groups, cliques and gangs form.

intrafamily violence: An environment of discord and conflict within the family. Children who grow up in dysfunctional homes often exhibit delinquent behaviors, having learned at a young age that aggression pays off.

juvenile court judge: A judge elected or appointed to preside over juvenile cases whose decisions can only be reviewed by a judge of a higher court.

juvenile defense attorney: Represents children in juvenile court and plays an active role at all stages of the proceedings.

juvenile delinquency: Participation in illegal behavior by a minor who falls under a statutory age limit.

juvenile intensive probation supervision (JIPS): A true alternative to incarceration that involves almost daily supervision of the juvenile by the probation officer assigned to the case.

juvenile justice process: Under the parens patriae philosophy, juvenile justice procedures are informal and nonadversarial, invoked for juvenile offenders rather than against them. A petition instead of a complaint is filed, courts make findings of involvement or adjudication of delinquency instead of convictions, and juvenile offenders receive dispositions instead of sentences.

juvenile justice system: The segment of the justice system, including law enforcement officers, the courts, and correctional agencies, that is designed to treat youthful offenders.

juvenile officers: Police officers who specialize in dealing with juvenile offenders; they may operate alone or as part of a juvenile police unit in the department.

juvenile probation officer: Officer of the court involved in all four stages of the court process—intake, predisposition, postadjudication, and postdisposition—who assists the court and supervises juveniles placed on probation.

juvenile prosecutor: Government attorney responsible for representing the interests of the state and bringing the case against the accused juvenile.

klikas: Subgroups of same-aged youths in Latino gangs that remain together and have separate names and a unique identity in the gang.

labeling theory: Posits that society creates deviance through a system of social control agencies that designate (or label) certain individuals as delinquent, thereby stigmatizing them and encouraging them to accept this negative personal identity.

latent trait theory: The view that delinquent behavior is controlled by a "master trait," present at birth or soon after, that remains stable and unchanging throughout a person's lifetime.

learning disabilities (LD): Neurological dysfunctions that prevent an individual from learning to his or her potential.

least detrimental alternative: Choosing a program that will best foster a child's growth and development.

least restrictive alternative: A program with the least restrictive or secure setting that will benefit the child.

legalization of drugs: Decriminalizing drug use to reduce the association between drug use and crime.

liberal feminism: Asserts that females are less delinquent than males, because their social roles provide them with fewer opportunities to commit crimes; as the roles of girls and women become more similar to those of boys and men, so too will their crime patterns.

life course persisters: Delinquents who begin their offending career at a very early age and continue to offend well into adulthood.

life course theory: A developmental theory that focuses on changes in behavior as people travel along the path of life and how these changes affect crime and delinquency.

mandatory sentences: Sentences are defined by a statutory requirement that states the penalty to be set for all cases of a specific offense.

Mara Salvatrucha (MS-13): A violent, international gang begun in southern California by immigrants from El Salvador. Engages in such crimes as burglaries, narcotic sales, weapons smuggling, murder, rape, and witness intimidation.

marijuana: The dried leaves of the cannabis plant.

masculinity hypothesis: View that women who commit crimes have biological and psychological traits similar to those of men.

meta-analysis: A statistical technique that synthesizes results from prior evaluation studies.

milieu therapy: All aspects of the environment are part of the treatment, and meaningful change, increased growth, and satisfactory adjustment are encouraged.

minimal brain dysfunction (MBD): Damage to the brain itself that causes antisocial behavior injurious to the individual's lifestyle and social adjustment.

Miranda warning: Supreme Court decisions require police officers to inform individuals under arrest of their constitutional rights. Warnings must also be given when suspicion begins to focus on an individual in the accusatory stage.

monetary restitution: Offenders compensate crime victims for out-of-pocket losses caused by the crime, including property damage, lost wages, and medical expenses.

multisystemic therapy (MST): Addresses a variety of family, peer, and psychological problems by focusing on problem-solving and communication skills training.

nature theory: The view that intelligence is inherited and is a function of genetic makeup.

near-groups: Clusters of youth who outwardly seem unified, but actually have limited cohesion, impermanence, minimal consensus of norms, shifting membership, disturbed leadership, and limited definitions of membership expectations.

need for treatment: The criteria on which juvenile sentencing is based. Ideally, juveniles are treated according to their need for treatment and not for the seriousness of the delinquent act they committed.

negative affective states: Anger, depression, disappointment, fear, and other adverse emotions that derive from strain.

neglect: Passive neglect by a parent or guardian, depriving children of food, shelter, health care, or love.

neuroticism: A personality trait marked by unfounded anxiety, tension, and emotional instability.

nuclear family: A family unit composed of parents and their children. This smaller family structure is subject to great stress due to the intense, close contact between parents and children.

nurture theory: The view that intelligence is determined by environmental stimulation and socialization.

Office of Juvenile Justice and Delinquency Prevention (OJJDP): Branch of the U.S. Justice Department charged with shaping national juvenile justice policy through disbursement of federal aid and research funds.

orphan trains: A practice of the Children's Aid Society in which urban youths were sent west for adoption with local farm couples.

overt pathway: Pathway to a delinquent career that begins with minor aggression, leads to physical fighting, and eventually escalates to violent delinquency.

parens patriae: The power of the state to act on behalf of the child and provide care and protection equivalent to that of a parent.

parental efficacy: Families in which parents are able to integrate their children into the household unit while at the same time helping them assert their individuality and regulate their own behavior.

parental efficacy: Parents are said to have parental efficacy when they are supportive and effectively control their children in a noncoercive fashion.

Part I offenses: Offenses including homicide and non-negligent manslaughter, forcible rape, robbery, aggravated assault, burglary, larceny, arson, and motor vehicle theft. Recorded by local law enforcement officers, these crimes are tallied quarterly and sent to the FBI for inclusion in the UCR.

Part II offenses: All crimes other than Part I offenses. Recorded by local law enforcement officers, arrests for these crimes are tallied quarterly and sent to the FBI for inclusion in the UCR.

passive speech: A form of expression protected by the First Amendment, but not associated with actually speaking words; examples include wearing symbols or protest messages on buttons or signs.

paternalistic family: A family style wherein the father is the final authority on all family matters and exercises complete control over his wife and children.

petition: Document filed in juvenile court alleging that a juvenile is a delinquent, a status offender, or a dependent and asking that the court assume jurisdiction over the juvenile.

plea bargaining: The exchange of prosecutorial and judicial concessions for a guilty plea by the accused; plea bargaining usually results in a reduced charge or a more lenient sentence.

pledge system: Early English system in which neighbors protected each other from thieves and warring groups.

Poor Laws: English statutes that allowed the courts to appoint overseers for destitute and neglected children, allowing placement of these children as servants in the homes of the affluent.

population: All people who share a particular characteristic, such as all high school students or all police officers.

positive peer culture (PPC): Counseling program in which peer leaders encourage other group members to modify their behavior and peers help reinforce acceptable behaviors.

power-control theory: Holds that gender differences in the delinquency rate are a function of class differences and economic conditions that influence the structure of family life.

precocious sexuality: Sexual experimentation in early adolescence.

predatory crimes: Violent crimes against persons and crimes in which an offender attempts to steal an object directly from its holder.

prestige crimes: Stealing or assaulting someone to gain prestige in the neighborhood; often part of gang initiation rites.

pretrial conference: The attorney for the social services agency presents an overview of the case, and a plea bargain or negotiated settlement can be agreed to in a consent decree.

preventive detention: Keeping the accused in custody prior to trial, because the accused is suspected of being a danger to the community.

probable cause: Reasonable grounds to believe the existence of facts that an offense was committed and that the accused committed that offense.

probation: Nonpunitive, legal disposition of juveniles emphasizing community treatment in which the juvenile is closely supervised by an officer of the court and must adhere to a strict set of rules to avoid incarceration.

problem behavior syndrome (PBS): A cluster of antisocial behaviors that may include family dysfunction, substance abuse, smoking, precocious sexuality and early pregnancy, educational underachievement, suicide attempts, sensation seeking, and unemployment, as well as delinquency.

problem-oriented policing: Law enforcement that focuses on addressing the problems underlying incidents of juvenile delinquency rather than the incidents alone.

procedural justice: An evaluation of the fairness of the manner in which an offender's or another group's problem or dispute was handled by police.

propensity: A natural inclination or personal trait that exists at birth or soon after and remains constant over the life course.

protective factor: A positive prior factor in an individual's life that decreases the risk of occurrence of a future delinquent act.

psychodynamic theory: Branch of psychology that holds that the human personality is controlled by unconscious mental processes developed early in childhood.

psychopathic personality (also known as sociopathic or antisocial personality): A person lacking in warmth, exhibiting inappropriate behavior responses, and unable to learn from experience. The condition is defined by persistent violations of social norms, including lying, stealing, truancy, inconsistent work behavior, and traffic arrests.

psychotherapy: Highly structured counseling in which a therapist helps a juvenile solve conflicts and make a more positive adjustment to society.

public defender: An attorney who works in a public agency or under private contractual agreement as defense counsel to indigent defendants.

pulling levers policing: A focused deterrence strategy that involves applying all available measures or "levers" to police as well as communicating with offenders to reduce a targeted delinquent problem.

racial threat theory: As the size of the African American population increases, the amount of social control imposed against African Americans by police grows proportionately.

randomized controlled experiment: Considered the "gold standard" of evaluation designs to measure the effect of a program on delinquency or other outcomes. Involves randomly assigning subjects either to receive the program (the experimental group) or not receive it (the control group).

reality therapy: A form of counseling that emphasizes current behavior and requires the individual to accept responsibility for all of his or her actions.

reentry: The process and experience of returning to society upon release from a custody facility post-adjudication.

reform schools: Institutions in which educational and psychological services are used in an effort to improve the conduct of juveniles who are forcibly detained.

relative deprivation: Condition that exists when people of wealth and poverty live in close proximity to one another. The relatively deprived are apt to have feelings of anger and hostility, which may produce criminal behavior.

representing: Tossing or flashing gang signs in the presence of rivals, often escalating into a verbal or physical confrontation.

residential programs: Residential nonsecure facilities, such as a group home, foster home, family group home, or rural home, where the juvenile can be closely monitored and develop close relationships with staff members.

resource dilution: A condition that occurs when parents have such large families that their resources, such as time and money, are spread too thin, causing lack of familial support and control.

restorative justice: Nonpunitive strategies for dealing with juvenile offenders that make the justice system a healing process rather than a punishment process.

review hearings: Periodic meetings to determine whether the conditions of the case plan for an abused child are being met by the parents or guardians of the child.

right to treatment: Philosophy espoused by many courts that juvenile offenders have a statutory right to treatment while under the jurisdiction of the courts.

risk factor: A negative prior factor in an individual's life that increases the risk of occurrence of a future delinquent act.

role conflicts: Conflicts police officers face that revolve around the requirement to perform their primary duty of law enforcement and a desire to aid in rehabilitating youthful offenders.

role diffusion: According to Erik Erikson, role diffusion occurs when youths spread themselves too thin, experience personal uncertainty, and place themselves at the mercy of leaders who promise to give them a sense of identity they cannot develop for themselves.

routine activities theory: The view that crime is a normal function of the routine activities of modern living. Offenses can be expected if there is a motivated offender and a suitable target that is not protected by capable guardians.

rural programs: Specific recreational and work opportunities provided for juveniles in a rural setting, such as a forestry camp, a farm, or a ranch.

sampling: Selecting a limited number of people for study as representative of a larger group.

search and seizure: The U.S. Constitution protects citizens from any search and seizure by police without a lawfully obtained search warrant; such warrants are issued when there is probable cause to believe that an offense has been committed.

sedatives: Drugs of the barbiturate family that depress the central nervous system into a sleeplike condition.

self-control: Refers to a person's ability to exercise restraint and control over his or her feelings, emotions, reactions, and behaviors.

self-fulfilling prophecy: Deviant behavior patterns that are a response to an earlier labeling experience; youths act out these social roles even if they were falsely bestowed.

self-labeling: The process by which a person who has been negatively labeled accepts the label as a personal role or identity.

self-report survey: A research approach that requires subjects to reveal their own participation in delinquent or criminal acts.

sex trafficking: The recruitment and transportation of people for commercial sex through the use of force, fraud, or coercion.

shelter care: A place for temporary care of children in physically unrestricting facilities.

situational crime prevention: A crime prevention method that relies on reducing the opportunity to commit criminal acts by making them more difficult to perform, reducing their reward, and increasing their risks.

skinhead: Member of a European American supremacist gang, identified by a shaved skull and Nazi or Ku Klux Klan markings.

social bond: Ties a person to the institutions and processes of society; elements of the bond include attachment, commitment, involvement, and belief.

social capital: Positive relations with individuals and institutions, as in a successful marriage or a successful career, that support conventional behavior and inhibit deviant behavior.

social control: Ability of social institutions to influence human behavior. The justice system is the primary agency of formal social control.

social control theories: Posit that delinquency results from a weakened commitment to the major social institutions (family, peers, and school); lack of such commitment allows youths to exercise antisocial behavioral choices.

social disorganization: Neighborhood or area marked by culture conflict, lack of cohesiveness, a transient population, and insufficient social organizations. These problems are reflected in the problems at schools in these areas.

social investigation report: Developed by the juvenile probation officer, this report includes clinical diagnosis of the juvenile and the need for court assistance, relevant environmental and personality factors, and other information to assist the court in developing a treatment plan.

social learning theory: The view that behavior is modeled through observation, either directly through intimate contact with others or indirectly through media. Interactions that are rewarded are copied, whereas those that are punished are avoided.

social structure theories: Those theories that suggest that social and economic forces operating in deteriorated lower-class areas, including disorganization, stress, and cultural deviance, push residents into criminal behavior patterns.

socialization: The process of learning the values and norms of the society or the subculture to which the individual belongs.

specific deterrence: Sending convicted offenders to secure incarceration facilities so that punishment is severe enough to convince them not to repeat their criminal activity.

status offender: A child who is subject to state authority by reason of having committed an act forbidden to youth and illegal solely because the child is underage.

stigmatized: People who have been negatively labeled as a result of their participation, or alleged participation, in deviant or outlawed behaviors.

stimulants: Synthetic substances that produce an intense physical reaction by stimulating the central nervous system.

strain: A condition caused by the failure to achieve one's social goals.

substance abuse: Using drugs or alcohol in such a way as to cause physical harm to oneself.

suppression effect: A reduction of the number of arrests per year for youths who have been incarcerated or otherwise punished.

systematic review: A type of review that uses rigorous methods for locating, appraising, and synthesizing evidence from prior evaluation studies.

teen courts: Courts that make use of peer juries to decide nonserious delinquency cases.

tracking: Dividing students into groups according to their ability and achievement levels.

trait theory: Holds that youths engage in delinquent or criminal behavior due to aberrant physical or psychological traits that govern behavioral choices. Delinquent actions are impulsive or instinctual rather than rational choices.

trajectories: Differing paths, progressions, or lines of development.

trajectory theory: The view that there are multiple independent paths to a delinquent career and that there are different types and classes of offenders.

tranquilizers: Drugs that reduce anxiety and promote relaxation.

transfer process: Transferring a juvenile offender from the jurisdiction of juvenile court to adult criminal court.

transitional neighborhood: Area undergoing a shift in population and structure, usually from middle-class residential to lower-class mixed use.

truly disadvantaged: According to William Julius Wilson, those people who are left out of the economic mainstream and reduced to living in the most deteriorated inner-city areas.

turning points: Critical life events, such as career and marriage, which may enable adult offenders to desist from delinquency.

underachievers: Those who fail to meet expected levels of school achievement.

underclass: Group of urban poor whose members have little chance of upward mobility or improvement.

Uniform Crime Report (UCR): Compiled by the FBI, the UCR is the most widely used source of national crime and delinquency statistics.

victimization: The number of people who are victims of criminal acts.

victim service restitution: Offenders provide some service directly to the crime victim.

waiver (also known as bindover or removal): Transferring legal jurisdiction over the most serious and experienced juvenile offenders to the adult court for criminal prosecution.

watch system: Replaced the pledge system in England; watchmen patrolled urban areas at night to provide protection from harm.

widening the net: Phenomenon that occurs when programs created to divert youths from the justice system actually involve them more deeply in the official process.

wilderness probation: Programs involving outdoor expeditions that provide opportunities for juveniles to confront the difficulties of their lives while achieving positive personal satisfaction.

writ of *habeas corpus*: Judicial order requesting that a person detaining another produce the body of the prisoner and give reasons for his or her capture and detention.

zero tolerance policy: Mandating specific consequences or punishments for delinquent acts and not allowing anyone to avoid these consequences.

NAME INDEX

SUBJECT INDEX